The Cambridge Handbook of Sociology

Whether you are a student, an instructor, a researcher, or just someone interested in understanding the roots of sociology and our social world, *The Cambridge Handbook of Sociology*, Volume 2, is for you. This second volume of the *Handbook* covers specialties within sociology and interdisciplinary studies that relate to sociology. It includes perspectives on race, class, feminist theories, special topics (e.g. the sociology of nonhuman animals, quality of life / social indicators research, the sociology of risk, the sociology of disaster, the sociology of mental health, sociobiology, the sociology of science and technology, the sociology of violence, environmental justice, and the sociology of food), the sociology of the self, the sociology of the life course, culture and behavior, sociology's impact on society, and related fields (e.g. criminology, criminal justice studies, social work, social psychology, sociology of translation and translation studies, and women and gender studies). Each chapter includes a discussion of how the respective subfield contributes to the overall discipline and to society. Written by some of the most respected scholars, teachers, and public sociologists in the world, the essays are highly readable and authoritative.

Kathleen Odell Korgen is a professor of sociology at William Paterson University in Wayne, New Jersey. She has co-authored or co-edited numerous books that teach students to use the sociological tools they gain in their classes and to find inspiration from professional sociologists and fellow sociology students. Korgen has received William Paterson University's Award for Excellence in Scholarship / Creative Expression and the university's Award for Excellence in Teaching.

The Cambridge Handbook of Sociology

Volume 2

Specialty and Interdisciplinary Studies

Edited by
Kathleen Odell Korgen
William Paterson University

CAMBRIDGE
UNIVERSITY PRESS

University Printing House, Cambridge CB2 8BS, United Kingdom

One Liberty Plaza, 20th Floor, New York, NY 10006, USA

477 Williamstown Road, Port Melbourne, VIC 3207, Australia

314-321, 3rd Floor, Plot 3, Splendor Forum, Jasola District Centre, New Delhi - 110025, India

79 Anson Road, #06-04/06, Singapore 079906

Cambridge University Press is part of the University of Cambridge.

It furthers the University's mission by disseminating knowledge in the pursuit of education, learning and research at the highest international levels of excellence.

www.cambridge.org
Information on this title: www.cambridge.org/9781107564923

© Cambridge University Press 2017

This publication is in copyright. Subject to statutory exception and to the provisions of relevant collective licensing agreements, no reproduction of any part may take place without the written permission of Cambridge University Press.

First published 2017
First paperback edition 2021

A catalogue record for this publication is available from the British Library

Library of Congress Cataloging in Publication data
Names: Korgen, Kathleen Odell, 1967– editor.
Title: The Cambridge handbook of sociology / Kathleen Odell Korgen, William Paterson University.
Description: New York, NY : Cambridge University Press, 2017. | Includes index.
Identifiers: LCCN 2016052805| ISBN 9781107125896 (volume I : hbk) | ISBN 9781107125858 (volume II : hbk)
Subjects: LCSH: Sociology – History. | Sociology.
Classification: LCC HM435 .C36 2017 | DDC 301–dc23
LC record available at https://lccn.loc.gov/2016052805

ISBN 2 Volume Set 978-1-107-09974-6 Hardback
ISBN Volume 1 978-1-107-12589-6 Hardback
ISBN Volume 2 978-1-107-12585-8 Hardback
ISBN 978-1-107-56492-3 Paperback

Cambridge University Press has no responsibility for the persistence or accuracy of URLs for external or third-party internet websites referred to in this publication, and does not guarantee that any content on such websites is, or will remain, accurate or appropriate.

Contents

List of Figures	*page* viii
List of Tables	ix
List of Contributors	x
Introduction	1

PART I
PERSPECTIVES ON RACE

1. Racial Formation — 5
   Eileen O'Brien
2. Systemic Racism — 12
   Kimberley Ducey and Joe R. Feagin
3. Color-Blind Racism — 21
   Meghan A. Burke
4. Critical Race Theory — 30
   Mary Romero and Jeremiah Chin

PART II
PERSPECTIVES ON SOCIAL CLASS

5. Marxism and Class — 41
   Vishwas Satgar and Michelle Williams
6. Pluralism — 51
   Richard A. Zdan
7. The Class-Dominance Theory of Power in the United States — 60
   G. William Domhoff

PART III
FEMINIST PERSPECTIVES

8. Feminist Theories — 73
   Seung-Kyung Kim and Carole R. McCann
9. Feminist Methodologies — 82
   Shulamit Reinharz and Nicholas Monroe

PART IV
SPECIALTY AREAS

10. The Sociology of Non-human Animals and Society — 95
    Elizabeth Cherry
11. Quality-of-Life/Social Indicators Research — 105
    Kenneth C. Land

12. Visual Sociology 119
    Vincent O'Brien

13. The Sociology of Risk 129
    Jens O. Zinn

14. Sociology of Disaster 139
    Thomas E. Drabek

15. The Sociology of Mental Health 148
    Teresa L. Scheid

16. Sociobiology 156
    Rosemary L. Hopcroft

17. The Sociology of Science and Technology 166
    Miwao Matsumoto

18. The Sociology of Violence 178
    Larry Ray

19. Environmental Justice 188
    David N. Pellow

20. The Sociology of Food 199
    Anne Murcott

PART V
THE SOCIOLOGY OF THE SELF

21. Sociology of the Body and Embodiment 209
    Carla A. Pfeffer

22. The Sociology of Emotion 218
    Kathryn J. Lively

23. The Sociology of Friendship 229
    James Vela-McConnell

PART VI
THE SOCIOLOGY OF THE LIFE COURSE

24. The Sociology of Children 239
    Gertrud Lenzer

25. Sociology of Aging 246
    Elizabeth W. Markson and Peter J. Stein

26. The Sociology of Death and Dying 256
    Ruth McManus

PART VII
CULTURE AND BEHAVIOR

27. The Sociology of Consumption 265
    Stanley Blue

28. The Sociology of Leisure and Recreation 275
    Robert A. Stebbins

29. Popular Culture 284
    Dustin Kidd, Jennifer Kim, and Amanda Turner

30. The Sociology of Art 293
    Alain Quemin

31. The Sociology of Music 304
    Pamela M. Hunt

PART VIII
SOCIOLOGY'S IMPACT ON SOCIETY

32. Public Sociology 313
    Laura Nichols

33. Humanist Sociology 322
    Woody Doane

34. Applied Sociology and Sociotechnics 330
    Harry Perlstadt

35. Clinical Sociology 339
    Jan Marie Fritz

36. Teaching Sociology: Creating a Citizenry with a Sociological Imagination 348
    Kathleen S. Lowney

PART IX
RELATED FIELDS

37. Criminology 359
    Kaitlyn Clarke, Philip D. McCormack, and Larry J. Siegel

38. Criminal Justice Studies 367
    Gennifer Furst

39. Social Work 377
    Kathleen McInnis-Dittrich

40. Social Psychology 387
    Laurie T. O'Brien, Stefanie Simon, and Caroline Tipler

41. Sociology of Translation 399
    Rafael Schögler

42. Women and Gender Studies: Its Origins and Intersections with Sociology 408
    Angela Hattery and Earl Smith

Index 417

Figures

11.1.	Child and Youth Well-Being Index, 1975–2013	*page* 115
13.1.	Diagram Grid-Group Typology	131
17.1.	The Thematic Development of the Sociology of Science and Technology	168
17.2.	The Under-determination of Scientific Knowledge (Type 1) and That of Policy (Type 2)	174

Tables

11.1. Human Development Indices   *page* 109

Contributors

Stanley Blue is a lecturer in sociology at Lancaster University. His research examines the patterning of the social routines and practices that make up everyday life. His contribution was produced while teaching the sociology of consumption at the University of Manchester.

Meghan A. Burke is associate professor of sociology at Illinois Wesleyan University and the author of two books about contemporary racial discourse. Her current projects are advancing new ways to study color-blind racism.

Elizabeth Cherry is Associate Professor of Sociology at Manhattanville College in Purchase, NY. Her areas of teaching and research include human-animal studies, environmental sociology, social movements, and culture.

Jeremiah Chin is a J.D. Candidate and Ph.D. student in Justice Studies at Arizona State University. His dissertation research focuses on race, law, and scientific evidence.

Kaitlyn Clarke is an assistant professor of criminal justice at Saint Anselm College. Her areas of expertise are criminological theory, criminal justice systems, and wrongful convictions.

Ashley ("Woody") Doane is professor of sociology at the University of Hartford and past President of the Association for Humanist Sociology. He has written extensively on racism in the United States and co-edited (with Eduardo Bonilla-Silva) *White Out: The Continuing Significance of Racism* (2003).

G. William Domhoff is Distinguished Professor Emeritus and Research Professor at the University of California, Santa Cruz. His many books include *Who Rules America?* (1967, 2014), *The Power Elite and the State* (1990), *Class and Power in the New Deal* (2011), and *The Myth of Liberal Ascendancy* (2013).

Thomas E. Drabek is a John Evans Professor and Professor Emeritus at the University of Denver. He has completed extensive research and publications on group and organizational response to disaster. His most recent book is *The Human Side of Disaster* (2013).

Kimberley Ducey is associate professor at the University of Winnipeg in Manitoba, Canada, and recipient of Quebec's Forces AVENIR. She studies the entanglement of the oppression of humans and other animals. Her latest book is *Systemic Racism Theory: Making Liberty, Justice, and Democracy Real*.

Joe Feagin is Ella C. McFadden Professor and University Distinguished Professor at Texas A&M University and past president of the American Sociological Association. He has published sixty-seven books and hundreds of articles on racism, sexism, and classism, including *Systemic Racism: A Theory of Oppression* (2006), *Liberation Sociology* (with Hernan Vera and Kimberley Ducey, 3rd edn., 2015), and *How Blacks Built America* (2015).

Jan Marie Fritz is a professor at the University of Cincinnati, distinguished visiting professor at the University of Johannesburg, and a special education mediator for the state of Kentucky. She is the editor of the award-winning *International Clinical Sociology* (2008).

Gennifer Furst is an associate professor at William Paterson University. She has published research about the experiences of incarcerated people who are multi-racial and prison-based animal programs.

Angela J. Hattery is professor and Director of the Women and Gender Studies Program at George Mason University. She has authored ten books and dozens of peer reviewed articles and book chapters on gender, violence, race, family, and prisons.

Rosemary L. Hopcroft is professor of sociology at the University of North Carolina at Charlotte. She has published widely in the areas of evolutionary sociology and comparative and historical sociology and is the author of *Evolution and Gender: Why it matters for contemporary life* (2016).

Pamela M. Hunt is associate professor of sociology at the University of West Georgia. She has published in *Social Psychology Quarterly* and *Deviant Behavior* and is the author of *Where the Music Takes You: The Social Psychology of Music Subcultures* (2014).

Dustin Kidd is associate professor of sociology at Temple University in Philadelphia. He is the author of *Legislating Creativity: The Intersections of Art and Politics* (2010) and *Pop Culture Freaks: Identity, Mass Media, and Society* (2014).

Jennifer Kim is an adjunct professor in the Department of Sociology and Anthropology at Linfield College. Her current work focuses on the burgeoning culture of resistance humor in South Africa.

Seung-Kyung Kim is Korea Foundation Professor of East Asian Languages and Cultures; Director of the Institute for Korean Studies; and an affiliate faculty member of Gender Studies at Indiana University-Bloomington.

Kenneth C. Land is research professor in the Social Science Research Institute, and the John Franklin Crowell Professor of Sociology and Demography Emeritus at Duke University.

Gertrud Lenzer is professor of sociology and children's studies emerita at Brooklyn College and the Graduate Center of the City University of New York. She founded the interdisciplinary field of Children's Studies and the Sociology of Children Section of the American Sociological Association in 1991.

Kathryn J. Lively is professor of sociology at Dartmouth College. She has written extensively on issues relating to gender, emotion, and identity, including *Symbols, Selves, and Social Reality: A Symbolic Interactionist Approach to Social Psychology and Society* (2013).

Kathleen S. Lowney is a professor of sociology at Valdosta State University. Her research focuses on how the press constructs accused serial killer nurses, and good pedagogy for large classes. She is the Director of her university's Teaching and Learning Center.

Elizabeth W. Markson was a Resident Scholar at the Women's Studies Research Center, Brandeis University. She published extensively in the area of social gerontology, including *Older Women: Issues and Prospects* (1984), which received the Book of the Year Award from the *American Journal of Nursing*.

Miwao Matsumoto is professor and Chair of the Department of Sociology, the University of Tokyo. He has authored *Technology Gatekeepers for War and Peace* (2006) and papers published in *Social Studies of Science, Technology and Culture*.

Carole McCann is professor and Chair of Gender and Women's Studies and an affiliate faculty member of the Language, Literacy, and Culture Graduate Program at the University of Maryland, Baltimore County.

Philip D. McCormack is an assistant professor of Criminal Justice at Fitchburg State University. His areas of expertise are criminological theory, race/ethnicity, and quantitative methods.

Kathleen McInnis-Dittrich is associate professor and Chair of the Older Adults and Families Concentration and Teaching Support Services at the Boston College School of Social Work. Her research interests include the health and mental health concerns of older adults and theory and methods in social work education.

Ruth McManus is senior lecturer of sociology at the University of Canterbury, Christchurch,

New Zealand, past president of the Sociological Association of Aotearoa New Zealand (SAANZ), and inaugural executive member of the Society for Death Studies (New Zealand). She links the sociology of death and dying with social issues.

Nicholas Monroe is a Ph.D. student at Brandeis University. His research interests include race, gender, and class as well as cultural and historical sociology. His current project focuses on racial micro-aggressions and the ways in which different groups interpret them.

Anne Murcott is Honorary Professorial Research Associate, SOAS, London. She has researched the sociology of food for more than thirty years, in recognition of which she was awarded an honorary doctorate by the University of Uppsala in 2009.

Laura Nichols is associate professor of sociology at Santa Clara University in California. She works with undergraduates and conducts research with local communities using participatory action research techniques.

Eileen O'Brien is associate professor of sociology and Assistant Chair of Social Sciences at Saint Leo University's Virginia campus. She is author of *The Racial Middle* (2008) and many other race-related publications.

Laurie O'Brien is a social psychologist and associate professor in the Department of Psychology at Tulane University. Her research examines stigma and prejudice.

Vincent O'Brien is a musician and visual ethnographer based in Manchester, England. He is founder of Visible Voice, former professor of International Health and Visual Ethnography at the University of Cumbria, and has served on the Executive Board of the International Visual Sociology Association.

David N. Pellow is the Dehlsen Chair and Professor of Environmental Studies and Director of the Global Environmental Justice Project at the University of California, Santa Barbara.

Harry Perlstadt is Professor Emeritus of Sociology at Michigan State University. He conducted evaluation research for the Kellogg Foundation, the US Department of Health and Social Services (USDHSS) Health Resources and Services Administration, and the World Health Organization. He chaired the American Sociological Association section on Sociological Practice and Public Sociology.

Carla A. Pfeffer is assistant professor of sociology and women's and gender studies at the University of South Carolina. Her research engages with processes of identity and social marginalization and has focused on contemporary families, sex and gender, sexualities, and the body.

Alain Quemin is professor of sociology at Université Paris-8. His writings focus on sociology of culture and the arts, especially art markets and institutions, globalization, reputation, gender and the arts, visitors' studies, and the sociology of works of art. His works include *Les stars de l'art contemporain: Notoriété et consécration artistiques dans les arts visuels* (2013)

Larry Ray is professor of sociology at the University of Kent and a Fellow of the Academy of Social Sciences. His areas of research and publications include sociological theory, globalization, postcommunism, and collective and interpersonal violence.

Shulamit Reinharz is the Jacob Potofsky Professor of Sociology at Brandeis University. In 1997 she created the Hadassah-Brandeis Institute, and in 2001 she founded the Brandeis Women's Studies Research Center. Among twelve other books, she has published *Feminist Methods in Social Research* (1992).

Mary Romero is professor of justice studies and social inquiry at Arizona State University. She has written extensively on domestic work and immigration law enforcement, including *The Maid's Daughter: Living Inside and Outside of the American Dream* (2011) and *Maid in the U.S.A.* (2002).

Vishwas Satgar is associate professor in the Department of International Relations at Wits University and Chair of the Cooperative and Policy Alternative Center board. He edits the Democratic Marxism series and writes on systemic alternatives, Africa's political economy, South African politics, and Marxism.

Teresa L. Scheid is professor of sociology at the University of North Carolina at Charlotte, with joint appointments in Public Policy Psychology and Health Services Research. She has published extensively on mental health care services, mental health policy, and the impact of mental health reform.

Rafael Schögler is assistant professor at the Department of Translation Studies at the University of Graz, Austria. His research interests comprise sociology of translation, translation in the social sciences and humanities, history of translation studies, and empirical social research.

Larry J. Siegel has taught at Northeastern University, University of Nebraska-Omaha, Saint Anselm College, and the University of Massachusetts-Lowell. He is the author of eighteen books on law, justice, and theory.

Stefanie Simon is a social psychologist who received her Ph.D. from Tulane University in 2015 and is now a Postdoctoral Fellow at Carleton College. Her research examines prejudice, diversity, and leadership.

Earl Smith is Professor Emeritus, Wake Forest University and past President of the North American Society for the Sociology of Sport (NASSS). He has authored ten books and dozens of peer reviewed articles and book chapters on gender, violence, race, family, and prison.

Robert Stebbins is Professor Emeritus, Department of Sociology, University of Calgary; Fellow of the Royal Society of Canada; and author of *Serious Leisure: A Perspective for Our Time* (2007, 2015).

Peter J. Stein is Professor Emeritus at William Paterson University where he served as Director of Graduate Studies and Co-Director of the Genocide and Holocaust Studies Center. He has published widely in the areas of family, the single life, and aging.

Caroline Tipler received her Ph.D. from the Department of Psychology at Tulane University in 2016. Her work examines the interrelations between dehumanization, language, and attitude change.

Amanda Turner, MA, is in the Ph.D. program in Sociology at Temple University. Her primary research interests are in the sociology of culture/popular culture, gender, qualitative and mixed methods.

James Vela-McConnell is professor of sociology at Augsburg College in Minneapolis. As a social psychologist, he has particular interest in issues of inequality, stigma, mental illness, social cohesion, violence, and social problems.

Michelle Williams is associate professor in sociology at Wits University and is the Chairperson of the Global Labour University Programme at Wits. Her books include *The Roots of Participatory Democracy: Democratic Communists in South Africa and Kerala* (2008) and she co-edited *Marxisms in the 21st Century: Crisis, Critique and Struggle* (2013) with Vishwas Satgar.

Richard A. Zdan is a member of the sociology faculty at Rider University. His current teaching and research interests are in the areas of political and urban sociology and civic engagement.

Jens O. Zinn is associate professor in sociology at the University of Melbourne. He is an Awardee of the Alexander von Humboldt Foundation. He is particularly interested in people's management of risk and uncertainty.

Introduction

Whether you are a student learning about sociology, an instructor teaching a topic for the first time, a sociologist delving into a new area of research, or just a person interested in finding out more about the roots of sociology and what it contributes to our social world, *The Cambridge Handbook of Sociology* is for you. It provides a survey of the field of sociology, covering the most prevalent topics in research and teaching. A two-volume work, *The Cambridge Handbook of Sociology* gives an overview of the field that is both comprehensive and up-to-date. The chapters, produced by some of the most respected scholars, teachers, and public sociologists from all over the world, are highly readable and written with a lay, as well as a scholarly, audience in mind.

Sociology is a branch of learning well known for its fragmentation. This handbook, however, provides a unified perspective, showing how each subfield contributes to the overall discipline and to society. In addition to covering key areas in sociology, it offers a history of the field, showing how and why it developed, and entries on related areas of study. In doing so, it works to define the field of sociology and serves as an invaluable resource for all those working and teaching in sociology and related areas.

The first volume of the handbook focuses on core areas of sociology, such as theory, methods, culture, socialization, social structure, inequality, diversity, social institutions, social problems, deviant behavior, locality, geography, the environment, and social change. It also explains how sociology developed in different parts of the world, providing readers with a perspective on how sociology became the global discipline it is today.

The second volume covers specialties within sociology and interdisciplinary studies that relate to sociology. It includes perspectives on race, class, feminist theories, special topics (e.g., the sociology of nonhuman animals, quality-of-life/social indicators research, the sociology of risk, the sociology of disaster, the sociology of mental health, sociobiology, the sociology of science and technology, the sociology of violence, environmental justice, and the sociology of food), the sociology of the self, the sociology of the life course, culture and behavior, sociology's impact on society, and related fields (e.g., criminology, criminal justice studies, social work, social psychology, sociology of translation and translation studies, and women and gender studies).

Whatever your interest in sociology, you will find it in these two volumes. We hope that *The Cambridge Handbook of Sociology* increases your understanding and appreciation of both the overall field of sociology and closely related fields of study. As this handbook makes clear, all of society benefits from a sociological perspective.

Part I

PERSPECTIVES ON RACE

CHAPTER 1
Racial Formation

Eileen O'Brien

Racial formation is a theoretical framework, first published by sociologists Michael Omi and Howard Winant in 1986, that has influenced the fields of sociology, political science, law, ethnic studies, and other related disciplines steadily since its inception. One of racial formation theory's central premises is that "race" is a social and political reality that remains unfixed, due to the role of institutions and groups in shaping its meaning (Winant 2000). Many race relations scholars, both theoretical and empirical, have found racial formation to be a useful tool in analyzing the historical and contemporary dynamics of how racial boundaries form and reform. Others, though, have determined the racial formation perspective to be short-sighted, using such critiques as a springboard for their own frameworks about the relationship between race, individuals, and society. Racial formation theory's impact on the field of race relations is thus sizeable. It has assisted social scientists in understanding the extent to which the state and society define and control race, and in fueling debate and critique, it continues to influence future developments.

Breaking with Prior Paradigms

Many analysts agree that the publication of *Racial Formation in the United States: From the 1960s to the 1980s* – first in 1986, and again in 1994 – ushered in a much-needed, and perhaps long overdue, shift in sociological thinking on race. Even though ethnic studies had been highlighting how integral race had been in shaping social life since the late 1960s and early 1970s, the more established disciplines in the academy, such as sociology, had been slow to acknowledge this reality or incorporate it into the mainstream (Espiritu 1999; Jung and Kwon 2013). All too often, Omi and Winant (1986) argued, race was subsumed or explained away into other analytical categories in most social theory.

The racial formation perspective was an attempt to break with three major reductionist strains of sociological thought that did not do justice to the centrality of race in social life. The first group of theories, which Omi and Winant call ethnicity-based theories, basically view the role of the state as democratizing by creating laws making discrimination illegal. So the extent to which various racial-ethnic groups are able to assimilate culturally and politically to the dominant culture determines the degree to which they experience racial conflict and discord (Winant 2000). The second group of theories, class-based, Omi and Winant group together as blaming the capitalist marketplace for racial divisions – whether segmented, dual, or split labor market theories. These perspectives share the tendency to reduce race to a bargaining chip through which the capitalists exploit and divide the working class (Omi and Winant 1986). The third problematic category of theories is nation-based – positing that racial exploitation is exacerbated by a colonial power's decimation of groups' ties to the greater Diaspora, but such perspectives are deemed "retro" in the postcolonial era (Winant 2000).

As a corrective to these three paradigms, Omi and Winant offered their racial formation theory, positing race in itself as an "organizing principle of social relations" (1986: 68) – not reducible to ethnicity, class, or nation. The impact of this shift in sociological theorizing about race was "groundbreaking" (Espiritu 1999: 512), so much so that some of the initial negative reviews to the first edition (e.g., Nagel 1988) have been attributed to the initial resistance to such a major break with prior tradition (Jung and Kwon 2013). By the time Omi and Winant released a second edition in 1994, *Racial Formation*'s assertion that "race is present in every institution, every relationship, every individual" (1994: 158) was heralded as a "welcome" addition to the sociological tradition (Feagin and Elias 2012: 3). Indeed, it went on to become one of the most influential sociological perspectives on race and ethnicity of the late twentieth and early twenty-first century. Omi and Winant's work *Racial Formation* "has been cited in about 6% of all articles about race in sociology since its publication, making it one of the five most cited publications in this core sociological subfield" (Saperstein et al. 2013: 361). Having to break with major traditions made the initial climb steep, but their work eventually made great inroads into the field of the sociology of race and ethnicity.

Enduring Contributions of Racial Formation Theory

Omi and Winant's insistence that race is a "socio-historical concept" (1986: 60) in a constant state of flux, its meanings "unstable and politically contested" (Winant 2000: 182), is an enduring contribution to the field. As reflected in most race and ethnicity textbooks of the contemporary era, race is commonly now understood as a social construction in this way, in stark contrast to the two pitfalls of defining race that Omi and Winant most wanted to challenge with their work: that race is either a fixed essence, or a complete fictional illusion (Feagin and Elias 2012; Omi and Winant 1986). Racial formation theory clearly defines race as a phenomenon that is constantly in motion.

What we know as race is in perpetual movement because it is "an unstable and 'decentered' complex of social meanings constantly being transformed by political struggle" (Omi and Winant 1986: 68). To elucidate this focus on race as changeable, racial formation theory presented the concept of a "racial project" (Omi and Winant 1986: 64–65). One of many historical examples the authors offer of racial projects in the development of their theory is the formation of racial categories of "black" and "white" that simply did not exist prior to the late seventeenth century in the United States, but were formulated to provide an ideological underpinning to slavery. Africans who identified as Ibo or Yoruba, for instance, and spoke different languages, suddenly were grouped together in a category called "black," while immigrants of many different ethnic heritages, again with diverse linguistic backgrounds, got lumped together and called "white." Omi and Winant propose the concept of "racialization" to describe this "extension of racial meaning to a previously racially unclassified relationship, social practice or group" (1986: 64).

When a collective of individuals becomes racialized for the first time, this amounts to a racial project, but there can also be other types of racial projects that attempt to redefine and reshape the meanings of groups that have already been racialized. One such project that occurred during Omi and Winant's major era of focus in their *Racial Formation* text – the 1960s to the 1980s – was the rearticulation of African Americans as "the new racists" through the 1980s backlash against affirmative action. Blacks were framed as preferring to rely upon the notion of "group rights" rather than individualism, and the term "reverse discrimination" was created with the purpose of casting African Americans as preferring an unfair advantage for themselves in contrast to fair-minded whites (Omi and Winant 1986: 134). Such racial projects are thus both political and ideological.

Analysis of race relations can often view the state as neutral and basically well intentioned, positing racism as the result of bigoted actors corrupting the process. Therefore, Omi and Winant's attention to government processes as the agents of the creation and maintenance of race is a major development in sociological race theory (Feagin 2006; Feagin and Elias 2012). Omi and Winant's reference to government as the "racial state" illustrates their intent to cast political institutions as explicitly and nearly always racial. In their analysis of the racial state, Omi and Winant demonstrate how public policy and laws have consistently defined race in ways that ensure unequal distribution of resources. Yet, in order to maintain control over this racial formation process, the racial state must not become static. Even as the state enforces the racial order, it exists at an "unstable equilibrium" (Omi and Winant 1986: 80). That is, institutions within the racial state – such as legislature and the courts – must be constantly in flux, using tactics like including those who were once formally excluded, so that the racial state can keep from coming under attack as racist and thus maintain ultimate control over defining the structure of race (Jung and Kwon 2013). This conception of the state as racial as opposed to a neutral structure corrupted by racist individuals is a major development in race theory.

Racial formation theory asserts that "racial change is the product of the interaction of racially based social movements and the racial state" (Omi and Winant 1986: 83). For example, the creation of "Asian American" in the 1960s – as a political label that united diverse ethnic groups like Chinese Americans, Japanese Americans, and Korean Americans – came about as an interaction between social movements and the racial state. The racial state was already treating members of these divergent groups similarly, whether it was the census, the courts, the legislature, or the educational system, and this impacted how other Americans reacted to them. As with the aforementioned example, whereby blacks were rearticulated as "new racists," in the case of Asian Americans, the racial state collaborated with the media to wrap racial ideology around its racial formation.

When the United States economy was seen as being threatened by the rapid technological advancements and success of Japan in the 1980s, Americans who were not even Japanese Americans became targets of hate crimes, perpetrated by members of the downsized working class. The brutal killing of Vincent Chin in 1982 is one such example. Although Chin was Chinese American, his attackers' rage was directed at an individual from a group that had undergone the process of racialization to become Asian. The killers Ronald Ebens and Michael Nitz, were angry at having lost their jobs due to Chrysler downsizing because of competition with Japanese car manufacturers. Their association of Japan with all those who appeared to be of Asian descent could be seen as the result of a racial project that created a scapegoat of this relatively newly formed pan-ethnic racial group (Hwang 2007). As is often the case with social movement ignition, this single incident stimulated the Asian American civil rights movement and further unification across various Asian American ethnic lines. By 1990, the racial state collaborated in this racial project by adding a US census racial category called "Asian American." This process exemplifies the role of the racial state in a flexible interplay between the micro and the macro aspects of a racial project.

In specifying that race is a social construction as opposed to a fixed essence, racial formation theory made a contribution that solidified in sociology what came to be the accepted conceptual definition of "race," replacing prior formulations that focused on phenotypical characteristics and de-emphasized social, dynamic processes. As noted earlier, racial formation theory also insists that the racial state is a key agent in the creation and perpetuation of racism, in conjunction with micro- and macro-level forces.

A Race Theory to Bridge Macro and Micro

In addition to challenging ethnicity, class, and nationality-based perspectives that tended to dominate the race subfield of sociology at the time of their initial writings, Omi and Winant wanted to more effectively bridge micro and macro theorizing about race. Because a "notable and intriguing feature of race is its ubiquity, its presence in both the smallest and the largest features of social relationships, institutions, and identities" (Winant 2000: 181), Winant argued that sociologists have an "obligation" to address race relations in this multilevel way. Therefore, Winant describes racial formation theory in the following way:

> (a) It views the meaning of race and the content of racial identities as unstable and politically contested; (b) It understands racial formation as the intersection/conflict of racial "projects" that combine representational/discursive elements with structural/institutional ones; (c) It sees these intersections as iterative sequences of interpretations (articulations) of the meaning of race that are open to many types of agency, from the individual to the organizational, from the local to the global (Winant 2000: 182).

Thus, the designers of racial formation theory intended it to be applicable to both macro and micro levels of social life. For example, when deindustrialization resulted in high urban unemployment, results of such macro forces became inscribed into racial ideology in a way that targeted the most intimate space of personal relationships and families. A racial project rearticulated black urban unemployment as a "result of defective black cultural norms, of familial disorganization, etc." (Omi and Winant 1986: 66). The racial state with its welfare policy thus affects the lives of individual families by casting suspicion and stigma on African American parents and children, playing out in individual welfare offices around the country, and even in grocery lines, affecting Americans' racialized perceptions of each other.

Despite Omi and Winant's stated efforts to apply racial formation in a multilevel way, most of the historical evidence that Omi and Winant draw upon focuses on how race is defined by "battle between the state and social movements" (Saperstein et al. 2013: 363) and thus remains predominantly macro in its orientation. However, much social science research on the social construction of race at the micro-level that has proliferated since the initial publication of Omi and Winant's work – particularly studies of how people decide to categorize themselves racially and the socio-political influences on those individual variations – can owe an intellectual debt to the racial formation perspective with its emphasis on the fluidity of race and the way it is contested in everyday life. For instance, Rockquemore and Brunsma's study of biracial identities make use of Omi and Winant's "momentary crisis of racial meaning" (Rockquemore and Brunsma 2008: 24) in analyzing respondents' reactions to questions like "what are you?" that ask them to account for themselves in ways that others do not. Likewise, Clara Rodriguez's (2000) study of Latino Americans' changing racial identities draws upon racial formation theory by examining how changes in the US census racial categorization system affect how individuals identify.

Indeed, many of her respondents vary in how they answer the race question depending on who is asking, and for what purpose. Often they check "other" and write in how they prefer to be identified. Although Omi and Winant themselves did not rely upon ethnographic data like this to build their framework, Saperstein et al. (2013) maintain that much of such work builds upon the groundwork that racial formation theory set.

Critiques of Racial Formation

Even critics agree that racial formation theory broke new ground by frontlining the centrality of race in all institutions and emphasizing the role of the racial state. Likewise, few would deny that the racial formation perspective advanced the conversation about what race is, by positing race as fluid rather than static and enduringly relevant rather than mere fiction. Yet, in the twenty-first century, as the work in the subfield of sociology of race and ethnicity has proliferated, some have assessed racial formation theory as having certain blind spots.

One such blind spot concerns the everyday racism among citizenry that is woven into the culture. Eduardo Bonilla-Silva advanced a structural theory of racism in a 1997 article in the *American Sociological Review* that first acknowledged racial formation's important contributions but ultimately found fault with its overemphasis on "ideological and juridicopolitical" (Bonilla-Silva 1997: 466) racial projects. While racial formation perspective's development of the concept of the racial state was indeed notable, scholars like Bonilla-Silva rightly point out that it is not only explicitly political actors like "neoconservatives, members of the far right, liberals" (Bonilla-Silva 1997: 466) who infuse racial ideology throughout culture and society. Bonilla-Silva went on to employ empirical survey and in-depth interview work to emphasize how everyday actors (e.g., college students, members of the Detroit working class, etc.) maintain the ideological structure of racism through their discursive representations (Bonilla-Silva 2009). Many members of society use nearly identical racial frames in their everyday conversations about racial inequality, regardless of individual variations among them. One relevant question might be: If the formation of race is the product of struggles between social movements and the racial state, what is the process by which so many others fall in step?

Another aspect of structural racism that racial formation theory may not address fully is the foundation of material racial advantage. Racial privilege has an intergenerationally transmitted shelf-life that lingers, even long after policies of the racial state shift and rearticulate race in new ways. Although Omi and Winant do analyze the role of the racial state in defining a black race within slavery, Joe Feagin argues that "their historical analyses do not go far enough in analyzing how … European nation-state actors collaborated with elite economic actors to generate the imperialism, genocide, and slavery that created the racial underpinning of Western countries like the United States" (Feagin 2010: 24). To suggest, as Omi and Winant do, that the institutionalized racism that founded the US "lingers like a hangover or a sleepless night that has left us badly out of sorts" (Omi and Winant 1994: 157) may serve to minimize that history as an echo or an aftershock rather than to analyze how those arrangements directly affect the material distribution of resources in the present day (Feagin and Elias 2012: 5). To cast the formation of race as constantly in motion may inadvertently serve to gloss over the rigidity of structural racism.

More to the point, the concept of racism itself is not a central component of racial formation theory, nor is white racism in particular. To theorize racial formation as the outcome of struggles between social movements and the racial state is to leave open the assumption that such struggles occur between similarly socially situated actors. Yet, such a supposition would obscure "what racial group wins these (often fixed) contests over concrete resources most of the time, and what racial group, fundamentally and usually, has the power to impose most central racial meanings and structures of oppression on less-powerful racial groups" (Feagin and Elias 2012: 14). These critics argue that, by actually naming white racism and white privilege, and using concepts like systemic and structural racism, racial formation theory could go further in explaining how race is formed, reformed, and continues its pervasive influence in the fabric of social life.

Notably, none of racial formation theory's critics evaluate it as incorrect or inapplicable. It remains a useful framework that critics engage because they acknowledge its major contribution to the field. Indeed, the very contributions of racial formation theory that have made it so enduringly influential – that race is fluid and contested, and that race is formed through struggles between social movements and the racial state – are the same areas that some scholars argue are in need of further development. Critics caution that over-emphasis on race's fluidity can obscure the deeply entrenched foundation of systemic racism and white privilege. Yet none would deny that race is indeed a social construction, that the racial state has manipulated it in different ways over time, and that it cannot be reducible to nationality, ethnicity, or class. And although the focus of Omi and Winant's groundbreaking work was predominantly at the macro-level of state institutions and political actors, their theory has inspired other scholars working at both the micro and meso levels (Saperstein et al. 2013). Thus, racial formation theory continues to influence the field of race-and-ethnic relations within sociology, and even other disciplines, such as political science, history and critical race/legal theory (Jung and Kwon 2013). As the changing demographics of the United States and other immigration-friendly societies continue to shift in this age of increasingly global politics and economy, one can only expect that racial formation theory will continue to be relevant and helpful, whether in its current form or extended by the next generation of scholars seeking to add to its explanatory potential.

References

Bonilla-Silva, Eduardo. 1997. Rethinking Racism: Toward a Structural Interpretation. *American Sociological Review* 62: 465–480.

Bonilla-Silva, Eduardo. 2009. *Racism without Racists: Color-Blind Racism and the Persistence of Racial Inequality*. Lanham, MD: Rowman and Littlefield.

Espiritu, Yen Le. 1999. Disciplines Unbound: Notes on Sociology and Ethnic Studies. *Contemporary Sociology* 28: 510–514.

Feagin, Joe R. 2006. *Systemic Racism: A Theory of Oppression*. New York, NY: Routledge.

Feagin, Joe R. 2010. *The White Racial Frame: Centuries of Racial Framing and Counter-Framing*. New York, NY: Routledge.

Feagin, Joe R. and Sean Elias. 2012. Rethinking Racial Formation Theory: A Systemic Racism Critique. *Ethnic and Racial Studies* 36: 1–30.

Hwang, Victor M. 2007. The Interrelationship between Anti-Asian Violence and Asian America. In *Race, Ethnicity and Gender: Selected Readings*. 2nd edn. Thousand Oaks, CA: Sage. 309–321.

Jung, Moon-Kie and Yaejoon Kwon. 2013. Theorizing the US Racial State: Sociology since *Racial Formation*. *Sociology Compass* 7: 927–940.

Omi, Michael and Howard Winant. 1986. *Racial Formation in the United States: From the 1960s to the 1980s*. New York, NY: Routledge.

Omi, Michael and Howard Winant. 1994. *Racial Formation in the United States: From the 1960s to the 1980s*. 2nd edn. New York, NY: Routledge.

Nagel, Joane. 1988. Book Review. Racial Formation in the United States from the 1960s to the 1980s by Michael Omi and Howard Winant. *Political Science Quarterly* 103(1): 158–159.

Rockquemore, Kerry Ann and David L. Brunsma. 2008. *Beyond Black: Biracial Identity in America*. Lanham, MD: Rowman and Littlefield.

Rodriguez, Clara E. 2000. *Changing Race: Latinos, the Census, and the History of Ethnicity in the United States.* New York, NY: New York University Press.

Saperstein, Aliya, Andrew M. Penner, and Ryan Light. 2013. Racial Formation in Perspective: Connecting Individuals, Institutions, and Power Relations. *Annual Review of Sociology* 39: 359–378.

Winant, Howard. 2000. Race and Race Theory. *Annual Review of Sociology* 26: 169–185.

Systemic Racism

Kimberley Ducey and Joe R. Feagin

Systemic racism is the racial exploitation and institutionalized subordination of people of color by whites of European descent. It encompasses the racial stereotyping, prejudices, and emotions of whites, as well as the discriminatory practices and racialized institutions generated for the continuing domination of people of color. At the core of systemic racism are discriminatory practices that fundamentally deny people of color the dignity, opportunities, and privileges available to whites individually and collectively.

Take the globally important case of systemic racism in the United States. Recognition of racism's systemic character is even occasionally seen at the highest levels of US leadership. As an illustration, Justice John Marshall Harlan, dissenting in the 1883 *Civil Rights Cases*, explained why anti-black oppression persisted after US slavery:

> *That there are burdens and disabilities which constitute badges of slavery and servitude, and that the express power delegated to Congress to enforce, by appropriate legislation, the thirteenth amendment, may be exerted by legislation of a direct and primary character, for the eradication, not simply of the institution, but of its badges and incidents, are propositions which ought to be deemed indisputable (FindLaw).*

These burdens and disabilities, Harlan's term for racial discrimination, persist in substantial ways into the present day. White discrimination against Americans of color is a central part of the larger reality, of the normality, of systemic racism in the United States. Generally white Americans, and especially white elite men, have never actually supported freedom, liberty, and equality for all – not in racial, class, or gender terms – even as they regularly promoted the ideological framing that the United States is egalitarian, meritocratic, and democratic. In truth, the United States was and is *none* of these things. For example, racial segregation in public schools has long been a significant part of systemic racism. Attempts at genuine desegregation of public schools mostly

---

We are indebted to Joanna Tegnerowicz for useful comments and references on contemporary European racism.

occurred between the 1950s and 1970s; since then public schools have become more, rather than less, racially segregated (Feagin and Barnett 2004).

Another current example of systemic racism is the US Supreme Court's 2013 decision to nullify strategic parts of the 1965 Voting Rights Act, the landmark law intended to ensure all Americans can vote. The 5-to-4 Supreme Court vote freed nine mainly southern states to change election laws without advance federal approval. A well-known critic of the 1965 Act, white Chief Justice John G. Roberts, Jr. (the leader of the Court since 2005) insisted in his majority opinion that "things have changed dramatically" in the South in the nearly fifty years since the Voting Rights Act was signed. This was in spite of the fact that almost all US civil rights leaders disagreed with that opinion of the racial climate in the South (Liptak 2013). Symptoms of systemic racism are also apparent in the Supreme Court's incorrect depiction of the United States as having moved beyond the need for remedies for society's racial ills with respect to schools and numerous other institutions (Feagin 2014).

Systemic-Racism Theory: Core Features

Systemic-racism theory describes and explains the foundational, pervasive, and persisting structures, mechanisms, and operations of racial oppression that shape white-dominated societies. Central to the theory are the grounding of historical and contemporary white-dominated societies in the constant provision of large-scale wealth-generating resources for elite whites and the intergenerational transmission of these essential materials and related social resources. Systemic-racism theory views racial structures as being primarily about long-standing relationships of racialized groups with markedly dissimilar material and political-economic interests, group interests that are rooted in hugely different historical experiences with economic exploitation and associated oppression.

At systemic racism's core are inequitable practices that fundamentally deny people of color the privileges, dignity, and opportunities collectively and individually available to whites. For example, throughout US history, systemic racism has been a foundational and intricate reality and includes: (1) the countless exploitative and discriminatory practices of whites; (2) the unjustly gained resources and power for whites institutionalized in the still-dominant racial hierarchy; (3) the preservation of key material and other resource inequalities by white-controlled and well-institutionalized societal reproduction mechanisms; and (4) the countless racial prejudices, stereotypes, images, narratives, emotions, interpretations, and narratives of the dominant "white racial frame" (see below) designed to rationalize and effect persisting racial oppression (Feagin and Feagin 1978; Feagin and Vera 1995; Feagin 2010; 2014).

Resistance is a key feature of systemic racism. Systemic racism has never been impassively accepted by those who endure it. It is always accompanied by acts of resistance (e.g., demonstrations, boycotts, legal battles). Mumia Abu-Jamal and Angela Y. Davis (2014) describe US anti-oppression movements as such: "We are less exemplars of legendary 'founding fathers' than we are of 'founding freedom fighters' – inheritors of those who fought for their freedom, not from a British aristocracy, but from American slavocracy." Whites, however, are generally defiant in the face of resistance, and thus effective progress against racial discrimination persistently faces the risk of backtracking (e.g., the 2013 Supreme Court Voting Rights Act decision). Continuous organization for change has been crucial. In an attempt to preserve power, society's racial rulers – elite white men – work hard to maintain the racial hierarchy and encourage the continuation and legitimization of the exploitation and oppression of subordinated racial groups.

The White Racial Frame

Hostile white responses to resistance regularly produce heightened and renewed opposition, a dialectical and demanding process. The white racial frame is a concept useful in making sense of how systemic racism actually works. For instance, African American political commentator Chauncey DeVega (2015) has written movingly regarding aggressive white racial framing, something he experienced first-hand after daring to associate vicious white lynchings and torture of blacks between 1877 and 1950 with the disturbing 2015 murder by burning of a Jordanian pilot by the self-styled Islamic State of Iraq and Syria (ISIS). Even liberal whites responded with hostility out of a white racial framing of society. The following are lessons DeVega reports learning about contemporary whites' racism in the process of sorting through white-framed responses to his analysis:

> *White folks en masse are very sensitive. Many of them get very upset and angry when you tell the truth about racism, white supremacy, or white privilege. ... The white speaker effect [antiracism is elevated in the minds of whites by the inclusion of a white speaker or writer] is very real in America's racial discourse. See for example, the divergent responses to [white liberal] Bill Moyer's excellent piece on ISIS and America's lynching culture and my essay on the same topic ... White supremacists and liberal racists ... are invested in Whiteness as a type of racial innocence (DeVega 2015).*

Since its development in the seventeenth century by elite white men, this racial frame has been dominant, a governing worldview that provides a standard meaning system for the racialized society in the United States and other societies across the globe. The white racial frame makes available the vantage point from which white oppressors have long viewed the world. In this racial framing, whites combine racial stereotypes (the verbal-cognitive aspect), metaphors and interpretive concepts (the deeper cognitive aspect), images (the strong visual aspect), emotions (feelings), narratives (historical myths), and repetitive inclinations to discriminatory action. The frame reinforces and grows out of the material reality of racial oppression. The racial hierarchy, material oppression, and the rationalizing white racial frame are key dimensions of the systemic racism created, at the top decision-making level, by elite white men.

The white racial frame and associated white discriminatory actions are, both purposefully and inadvertently, perpetuated through the routine operation of society's racist institutions. Blatant and subtle racist attitudes, as in the past, are demonstrably widespread among present-day whites, frequently emerging in open frontstage actions and, even more often, in more secluded backstage performances of ordinary and elite whites (Picca and Feagin 2007; Feagin and O'Brien 2004). For example, whites bond over racist jokes sent to one another via email – a private backstage space. As sociologist Jesse Daniels (2008) explains: "What was once only said in private can now, through forwarded email, move beyond the private whites-only space for which such communication was intended." An illustration is the 2008 racist email about Barak Obama – "What black man holds a steady job for four years?" – only meant for the backstage. It was discovered and brought into the frontstage during a US federal civil rights investigation into the police department of Ferguson, Missouri (McCarthy 2015).

The white racial frame contains not only negative stereotypes, images, metaphors, narratives, and emotions concerning people of color, but also strongly positive stereotypes, images, metaphors, narratives, and emotions in regard to whites and white institutions. There are important differences in the operative white racial frame for individuals, and within countries and globally; yet the commonplace white frame encompasses thousands of cohesive racialized fragments that group and cohere into pro-white and anti-others subframes (Feagin 2006).

Competing Theories

Systemic-racism theory differs considerably from the conventional race-and-ethnic relations perspective, which is mainly concerned with racial bias or prejudice and individual discrimination. In the US case, generally absent from the mainstream framework of both scholars and popular commentators is the recognition that the United States was founded on and securely grounded in racial oppression targeting Native Americans, African Americans, and other Americans of color. Equally significant to the conventional race-and-ethnic relations perspective is the propensity among mainstream scholarly and media analysts to passively remove the dominant white agents of discrimination from the racial narrative (e.g., by using the passive tense), or to use abstract language so that some vaguely specified "institution" or "country" is said to somehow discriminate against people of color (Feagin and Feagin 2011; Feagin 2006; 2014).

An accurate theory of well-institutionalized white racism is impossible without a frank discussion of and research on the elite whites at the very top of the racial hierarchy. In spite of their domination in the United States and globally, elite white men have seldom been called out and systemically analyzed. They have received little to no explicit analytical attention with regard to systemic-racism issues, as well as associated classism and sexism issues. Almost all public and scholarly discussions of racism fail to explicitly highlight elite white men or to focus specifically on how their interlocking racial, class, and gender statuses affect their globally powerful decision-making. Vague nouns – at best simply "elites" – are a crucial part of the standard tip-toeing around these systemic dominance issues. Even critical race, neo-Marxist, and feminist theories tend to move between vague abstract nouns and passive tenses when dealing with this powerful white male elite. When progressive scholars address economics, politics, and culture, elite white men are rarely explicitly mentioned and analyzed as such. Indeed, most scholarship on US racial matters provides substantially more consideration of non-elite whites than of the white elite.

This tendency in present social science and humanities analysis of history means that ordinary whites are depicted as racially bigoted and biased but elite white actors (e.g., capitalists, politicians and military, religious, and intellectual leaders) who have greatly shaped structures of racial oppression over centuries are rarely called out conceptually or discussed systematically (Feagin and Vera 1995; Feagin and O'Brien 2004; Feagin 2014). In this way, the inequality-generating societal reproduction processes of unjust enrichment and improvement, and the institutionalized hierarchies that benefit all whites, are ignored or passively discussed so that white agents are removed from any thoughtful consideration.

We do not have space here to address intersectionality issues. Nonetheless, it should be noted that systemic-racism theorists acknowledge and study the importance of the intersectionalities of racial, class, gender, sexuality, and other societal hierarchies. An intersectionalist approach is indispensable in attempts to understand how whites of different backgrounds possess different types of racialized power. It is also needed when exploring the intersecting social inequalities, contexts, identities, and varied responses of those beset by racial and other forms of societal oppression.

Systemic-racism theory has also long exchanged ideas and analytical approaches with critical race theory (CRT) (e.g., "property interest in whiteness" and "racial realism"). Both of these "sibling" analytical traditions are rooted in and heavily shaped by the centuries-old tradition of black critical analysis of racism-based Western societies (see next section). CRT founder Derrick Bells' racial realism analysis has been a major influence on systemic-racism theory, for he early on, during and after the 1960s Civil Rights Movement, critically examined the US government's failures to advance race-based human rights and rejected with sustained argument the white mythology of meaningful advances toward racial equality (Bell 1980; 2005; 2008; Feagin and Elias 2013) (see Chapter 4 in this volume for more information about CRT).

Anti-Oppression Counter Frames

While most whites rarely acknowledge white racism's systemic character and regularly perpetuate the white racial frame, the anti-oppression counter-frames of Americans of color are also prevalent throughout US history. For example, in his famous 1829 pamphlet, *Appeal to the Coloured Citizens of the World*, the outspoken African American anti-slavery activist, David Walker refuted Jefferson's white-racist framing of black Americans in the latter's *Notes on the State of Virginia* (1787). Walker maintains that Jefferson's contention that enslaved blacks are naturally inferior to whites is as logical as arguing that a deer in an iron cage can "run as fast as the one at liberty" (Walker 1965: 7, 16, and 56).

Building on critical perspectives and counter-framing of African American analysts, and other analysts of color, including W. E. B. Du Bois, Oliver C. Cox, Kwame Ture, Charles Hamilton, Mary Francis Berry, Derrick Bell, Patricia Williams, Robert Staples, Ronald Takaki, Cheikh Diop, Joyce Ladner, Nell Painter, Molefi Asante, Rodolfo Acuña, and Michelle Alexander – to name but a few – and drawing on the considerable field research data on white racism by scholars working on institutionalized racism issues for decades (see Du Bois 2003[1920]; Ture and Hamilton 1967; Feagin and Feagin 1978; Feagin 2014), systemic-racism theory maintains that whites – as a racial group – have played the primary role in creating and shaping the still radically inegalitarian, hierarchical, and unjust relationships among North American racial groups. Additionally, these racially oppressive conditions have regularly generated African American and other counter-framing that assertively resists the dominant white racial frame and associated systemic racism with an insistence on authentic "liberty and justice for all."

Some European Examples of Systemic Racism

From a systemic-racism perspective, white-dominated societies across the world are structured as racist wholes with intricate and interdependent social systems, organizations, and institutions that consistently imbed racial group exploitation and white group dominance. Likewise, racialized framing by whites is frequently similar for whites of various class and national backgrounds the world over because they are usually socialized in media and other sociocultural environments engraining much white racial framing. Numerous white European commentators and scholars have recently written anti-immigrant and anti-Muslim screeds, all with an aggressive white racial frame. In Germany, economist Thilo Sarrazin's book *Deutschland Schafft Sich Ab* (2012) vigorously attacks Turkish and Kurdish immigrants in Germany, including presenting them as genetically inferior. Similarly, French philosopher Alain Finkielkraut's book, *L'identité malheureuse* (2013) attacks non-white immigrants in France. In his book *Le grand remplacement, suivi de discours d'orange* (2011), French writer Renaud Camus argues that blacks and Arab immigrants will eventually dominate white France. Moreover, the year 2014 was the first time that openly neo-Nazi parties sat in the European Parliament as representatives of their countries – marking that assembly's most Eurosceptic, far-right, anti-immigrant makeup since it began in 1952. Meanwhile, another well-known European elite white male, Jean Marie Le Pen – founder of France's extreme right-wing Front National Party – suggested that the spread of the Ebola virus in Africa could fix Europe's non-white immigration issue.

Two other contemporary examples of systemic racism show how white racial frames help support the idea of black inferiority. A series of posters from UNICEF Germany's 2007 "Schools for Africa" featured individual fair-haired white German boys and girls, but made up with mud on their faces to look like black children.

The posters reduced a continent to a village of muddy uneducated and uncivilized black people, with white Germans as saviors. Slogans such as "I'm waiting for my last day in school, the children in Africa still for their first one"; "In Africa, many kids would be glad to worry about school"; and "In Africa, kids don't come to school late, but not at all," accompanied the individual shots of the white girls and boys. Here we observe the persistence of negative stereotypes, images, and metaphors concerning black Africans, alongside assertively positive views of whites and white institutions. Nevertheless, following widespread criticism, a white male Press officer speaking for the German Committee for UNICEF explained: "Before publishing the ad, we had carefully discussed possible misinterpretations and the agency had also tested public reaction in a survey in Germany, without receiving negative comments...We apologize if you feel irritated by the make up of the children" (UNICEF Germany 2014). In other words, UNICEF Germany refused to recognize the "Schools for Africa" initiative as racist or offensive. Yet, similar to "blackface" performances for decades in the United States, the campaign judges black Africans through the lens of white German cultural ideals. One might further ponder, given Germany's own growing cultural diversity, why the campaign features only white children.

In the Netherlands Santa Claus is known as Sinterklaas. His black servant – typically a white person in blackface wearing an Afro wig – is called Black Pete (Zwarte Piet). Annually, beginning in November, Nederlanders will see Zwarte Pieten everywhere, from television to the streets. Children learn songs with these lyrics: "even if I'm black as coal I mean well" and "Saint Nicolas, enter with your black servant." Other songs portray Zwarte Piet as stupid, clumsy, and childlike. The imagery and performances of Zwarte Piet reveal again enduring white stereotypes, descriptions, and sentiments about black people seen across numerous Western countries. In 2013, the United Nations High Commission for Human Rights ruled that Black Pete propagated an image of people of African descent as second-class citizens, a "living trace of past slavery." Yet the white Prime Minister of the Netherlands proclaimed there would be no change: "Black Pete is black. There's not much I can do to change that." Most Nederlanders, at least 80 percent of whom are white, agree and argue that Black Pete is a harmless fun figure, and suggest that those who object to him should be ignored (Associated Press 2004). Witness again the role of elite and non-elite whites as originators and enforcers of systemic racism, as well as hostile resisters to black counter-framing.

Systemic-Racism Theory and Racial Formation Theory: Key Differences

As Joe R. Feagin and Sean Elias (2013) explain, on important socio-historical dimensions and theoretical points, systemic-racism theory differs substantially from Michael Omi and Howard Winant's (1994) racial formation theory, an influential perspective that was developed to counter mainstream assimilation and ethnicity theories. Like other current analysts in the United States and Europe (e.g., Miles 1989; Gilroy 1993), Omi and Winant focus heavily on the ideological construction of "race" and on the creation of racial identities and connotations (Bonilla-Silva 2001: 31, 514). They are mainly interested in how concepts of "race" shift over time and place, and in the ways that the concepts of race "shape both identities and institutions" (Omi and Winant 1994: vii). Yet in considering what they label "racial projects," they regularly call attention to struggles over racial meanings more than struggles over racially ordered institutional structures, material inequality of resources, and power networks (Omi and Winant 1994: 56) (see Chapter 1 in this volume to learn more about that perspective). In contrast, systemic-racism theory centers on a clear empirical acknowledgment of which racial group usually wins these societal contests over tangible resources and which racial group typically has the power to create and enforce dominant racial structures. Most systemic-racism theorists unequivocally emphasize the actual social structures, material conditions, knowledge, and everyday practices and experiences of racial oppression generated by white actors and agents. They also focus on the hierarchical organization of racial groups and the white racial frame rationalizing these oppressive structures put into place by elite white men (Feagin and Vera 1995; Feagin 2006).

Racial formation theorists like Omi and Winant neglect to fully consider how racial meanings and racial structures mutually interconnect in a society with deep and lasting racist structures. Their concept of "racial projects," while seeming to connect racial structure and meaning, fails to shed light on the truths of systemic racism because Omi and Winant do not examine centuries-old white-racist power and domination in significant detail. While systemic-racism theory also demonstrates how racial meanings influence structures, it deviates theoretically from formation theory in that it strongly emphasizes the numerous ways that white-dominated structures, white-controlled material conditions, and influential white actors within, continually create, replicate, and use pervasive racial meanings and understandings that have been and continue to be central to the prevailing white racial frame (Feagin and Elias 2013: 945).

A further problem with Omi and Winant's explanation of racial formation theory – as emphasized by Feagin and Elias (2013) – is that it provides only a vague analysis of white elites' dominant role in constructing and maintaining inegalitarian racial hierarchies, the material realities of racial domination, and white-framed analyses of racial issues. Nowhere in their influential 1994 book *Racial Formation* do they openly and critically discuss whites as a racial group responsible for the creation and maintenance of racial oppression in US society. Rarely do Omi and Winant present explicit and necessary descriptors like "whites" and "white Americans" in subject positions of their sentences – and most especially in regard to the critical determinative practices and actions creating and shaping the structures of centuries-old white racism. In contrast, systemic-racism theory defines and systematically analyzes both whites and elite whites as necessary units of empirical and theoretical analysis for systemic white racism (Feagin and O'Brien 2004; Picca and Feagin 2007).

As Feagin and Elias (2013) suggest, one gets the impression from Omi and Winant's *Racial Formation* that white racism is only an appendage to an otherwise vigorous American democracy. Moreover, Omi and Winant seem to suggest that contemporary whites are just one racial group among many other comparable groups competing on a progressively more equal playing field. They argue that there is nothing integrally white about racism (Omi and Winant 1994: 723). Discounting institutionalized power inequalities between whites, and people of color, Omi and Winant associate racism with bigoted discrimination, prejudice, or stereotyping. In their view, some black power advocates are racist (Omi and Winant 1994: 73).

Racial formation analysts like Omi and Winant do not seriously consider and analyze systemic white racism's "racially ordered social networks and macro-scale institutions and organizations as they are generated and maintained by white power elites, overseen by white supervisors or managers (middle-class whites) and maintained by white laborers (working-class whites), as well as by people of color who knowingly or unknowingly collude in the operation of systemic racism" (Feagin and Elias 2013: 943).

Conclusion

From daily racist affronts to discrimination in the labor market, housing, and education, the ubiquity of white racism in the United States should put to rest the idea that racial oppression is dying or an aberration from a US "democratic" norm.

Racism is systemic and reflected in all major US institutions. Americans who are not white generally face enormous disadvantages relative to whites (Feagin 2014). Since most white-privileged Americans are resistant to meaningful change, effective progress against racial discrimination constantly faces the danger of white backpedalling. In US society, perpetual organization for authentic racial change in the direction of liberty and justice for all is thus essential.

To make sense out of the experiences of people of color in the United States and globally, we must continuously accent the role of whites, particularly elite whites, as the originators, enforcers, and remodelers of systemic racism. Since the country's creation, whites have been the most socially, politically, and economically influential racial group in the United States, as well as the one with the most socioeconomic resources – those often unjust enrichments unfairly gained. Mainstream assimilation theories and the racial formation theory obscure the activities of the mostly white elite male decision-makers who control not only the patterns of systemic racism but also, more generally, the world's political economy. In this manner they help to disguise and maintain whites' great institutionalized power (see Frankenberg 1993; Royster 2003; Wingfield and Feagin 2010). In contrast, systemic-racism analysts delineate and examine exactly who the racial rulers (that is, whites, especially elite white men) and the racial ruled (most people of color) typically are.

Finally, moving beyond the United States, the deep roots of the racialized oppressions of immigrants of color in contemporary Europe can be understood with an application of systemic racism and its white racial frame. Indeed, as we see it, substantial attention needs to be paid to the reasons for the increase in nativistic white scholars, government anti-immigrant efforts, and far-right political groups. Systemic racism and the white racial frame offer deep insights for analysis of whites' racial actions worldwide.

References

Abu-Jamal, Mumia, and Angela Y. Davis. 2014. Alternatives to the Present System of Capitalist Injustice. *The Feminist Wire*. Available at http://thefeministwire.com/2014/01/alternatives-to-the-present-system-of-capitalist-injustice/, accessed February 28, 2015.

Associated Press. 2004. Dutch Santa Claus Sidekick 'Black Pete' is a Negative Stereotype, Court Rules. Available at http://mashable.com/2014/07/03/black-pete/, accessed February 28, 2015.

Bell, Derrick A. 1980. Brown v. Board of Education and the Interest-Convergence Dilemma. *Harvard Law Review* 93: 518–533.

Bell, Derrick. 2005. *Silent Covenants: Brown v. the Board of Education and the Unfulfilled Hopes for Racial Reform*. New York, NY: Oxford University Press.

Bell, Derrick. 2008. *Race, Racism, and American Law*. 6th edn. New York, NY: Aspen Publishers.

Bonilla-Silva, Eduardo. 2001. *White Supremacy and Racism in the Post-Civil Rights Era*. Boulder, CO: Lynne Rienner.

Camus, Renaud. 2011. *Le grand remplacement, suivi de discours d'orange*. Renaud Camus.

Daniels, Jesse. 2008. Two-Faced Racism at the Secret Service. RacismReview.com. Available at www.racismreview.com/blog/2008/05/12/two-faced-racism-at-the-secret-service/, accessed March 7, 2015.

DeVega, Chauncey. 2015. 20 things I Learned About Racism When I Dared to Talk About ISIS and the Lynchings of Black Americans. *We Are Respectable Negroes*. Available at www.chaunceydevega.com/2015/02/20-things-i-learned-about-racism-when-i.html, accessed February 28, 2015.

Du Bois, W. E. B. 2003[1920]. *Darkwater: Voices from Within the Veil*. New York, NY: Humanity Books.

Feagin, Joe R. 2006. *Systemic Racism: A Theory of Oppression*. New York, NY: Routledge.

Feagin, Joe R. 2010. *The White Racial Frame: Centuries of Racial Framing and Counter-framing*. New York, NY: Routledge.

Feagin, Joe R. 2014. *Racist America: Roots, Current Realities, and Future Reparations*. 3rd edn. New York, NY: Routledge.

Feagin, Joe R. and Bernice McNair Barnett. 2004. Success and Failure: How Systemic Racism

Trumped the Brown v. Board of Education Decision. *University of Illinois Law Review.* 1099–1130.

Feagin, Joe R. and Sean Elias. 2013. Rethinking Racial Formation Theory: A Systemic Racism Critique. *Ethnic and Racial Studies.* 136: 931–961.

Feagin, Joe R. and Clairece Booher Feagin. 1978. *Discrimination American style: Institutional Racism and Sexism.* Englewood Cliffs, NJ: Prentice Hall.

Feagin, Joe. R. and Clairece Booher Feagin. 2011. *Race and Ethnic Relations, Census Update.* 9th edn. New York, NY: Pearson.

Feagin, Joe R. and Eileen O'Brien. 2004. *White Men on Race: Power, Privilege, and the Shaping of Cultural Consciousness.* Boston, MA: Beacon Press.

Feagin, Joe R. and Hernan Vera. 1995. *White Racism: The Basics.* New York, NY: Routledge.

FindLaw. US Supreme Court Case. CIVIL RIGHTS CASES, 109 U.S. 3 (1883). Available at http://caselaw.lp.findlaw.com/scripts/getcase.pl?court=US&vol=109&invol=3, accessed November 24, 2016.

Finkielkraut, Alain. 2013. *L'identité malheureuse.* Paris: Editions Stock.

Frankenberg, Ruth. 1993. *White Women, Race Matters: The Social Construction of Whiteness.* Minneapolis, MN: University of Minnesota Press.

Gilroy, Paul. 1993. *The Black Atlantic: Modernity and Double Consciousness.* New York, NY: Verso.

Jefferson, Thomas. 1787. Notes on the State of Virginia. Available at http://avalon.law.yale.edu/18th_century/jeffvir.asp, accessed February 28, 2015.

Liptak, Adam. 2013. Supreme Court Invalidates Key Part of Voting Rights Act. *The New York Times.* Available at www.nytimes.com/2013/06/26/us/supreme-court-ruling.html?_r=0, accessed February 28, 2015.

McCarthy, Tom. 2015. Ferguson Report's Racist Obama Email: 'What black man holds a steady job for four years.' *The Guardian.* Available at www.theguardian.com/us-news/2015/mar/03/ferguson-report-obama-email-black-man-steady-job, accessed March 7, 2015.

Miles, Robert. 1989. *Racism.* London: Routledge.

Omi, Michael and Howard Winant. 1994. *Racial Formation in the United States: From the 1960s to the 1990s.* 2nd edn. New York, NY: Routledge.

Picca, Leslie H. and Joe R. Feagin. 2007. *Two-faced Racism: Whites in the Backstage and Frontstage.* New York, NY: Routledge.

Royster, Deirdre A. 2003. *Race and the Invisible Hand: How White Networks Exclude Black Men from Blue-collar Jobs.* Berkeley, CA: University of California Press.

Sarrazin, Thilo. 2012. *Deutschland schafft sich ab.* Verlagsgruppe Random House.

Ture, Kwame [Stokely Carmichael] and Charles Hamilton. 1967. *Black Power.* New York, NY: Random House Vintage.

UNICEF Germany. 2014. UNICEF: Werbung durch Herabwürdigung. Available at www.derbraunemob.info/unicef-werbung-durch-herabwurdigung/, accessed February 28, 2015.

Walker, David. 1965. *Appeal to the Coloured Citizens of the world*, with an introduction by Charles M. Wiltse. New York, NY: Hill and Wang.

Wingfield, Adia H. and Joe R. Feagin. 2010. *Yes we can?: White Racial Framing and the 2008 Presidential Campaign.* New York, NY: Routledge.

CHAPTER 3
Color-Blind Racism

Meghan A. Burke

In the decades since the Civil Rights Movement, scholars have sought to understand changing levels of racial inequality and the associated ideologies that surround them. While the Civil Rights Movement made many important gains, in particular the removal of overt, state-sanctioned forms of segregation and discrimination, it did nothing to address racialized wealth disparities. It also did not significantly unravel the notions about white supremacy or the fairness of the American system that surrounded it. The result is that racial inequality persists and seems to be growing, while most Americans believe that we live in a just society where any inequalities can be explained through individual efforts or cultural difference. Taken together, the persistence of this racial inequality, accompanied by an ideology that denies its significance, has come to be known as Color-Blind Racism.

Social psychologists appear to have been the first to name this phenomenon, sometimes calling it "symbolic racism" (Sears 1988) or "modern racism" (McConahay 1986). The first sociological treatments in this area were Smith's (1995) and Bobo et al.'s (1997) concept of "laissez faire racism" and Carr's *Color-Blind Racism* (1997). These projects situated ideologies in a broader socio-political structure that has maintained institutionalized racism and white privilege. Bonilla-Silva et al. (2004: 558) note: "Racial outcomes...are not the product of individual 'racists' but of the crystallization of racial domination into a racial structure."

Racial ideologies are a central feature of that racial structure (Omi and Winant 1994). Bonilla-Silva and Forman (2000: 52) described its "less overt expression of racial resentment about issues anchored in the Jim Crow era such as strict racial segregation in schools, neighborhoods, and social life in general, and...resentment on new issues such as affirmative action, government intervention, and welfare." They also emphasized the rhetorical strategies "that allow [whites] to safely voice racial views that might be otherwise interpreted as racist" (2000: 68–69). Although many sociological studies have followed since then (Gallagher 2003; Brown et al. 2003), all share an emphasis on this ideological framework and its associated material consequences.

Bonilla-Silva (2003) further developed this work in *Racism without Racists: Color-Blind Racism and the Persistence of Racial Inequality in America*. In that book, he also established four central frames, or "set paths for interpreting information" (26), common to this ideology. They are abstract liberalism, the belief that we have attained equal opportunity and the associated individualism that explains success on that basis; naturalization, the way that segregation is understood without the generational inequality or modern discrimination that creates it; cultural racism, the way that we have replaced biological notions of difference with an emphasis on perceived cultural differences; and the minimization of racism, which directly downplays the role of racism or favors other explanations such as the assumed centrality of social class. Perhaps due to the popularity of this text among both students and scholars, and because of Bonilla-Silva's paradigm-shifting piece "Rethinking Racism: Toward a Structural Interpretation" (1997) that also emphasized the social and ideological structure of white supremacy over racial attitudes, Bonilla-Silva's is now considered the central text.

Core Features

Many explorations of color-blind racism that have followed borrow on his early work and terminology, but all share features that tend to be shared across any treatment of color-blindness. The first is that the ideology is used to legitimate the status quo, which produces tremendous privileges for whites. This happens primarily in its denial of racism as an ongoing feature of contemporary life, and in the way that it minimizes the role of historical inequalities that continue to impact today's opportunities. This does not always mean that talk of race or segregation is always explicitly avoided. Instead, indirect, subtle, or coded language offers suggestions about group or individual preferences or traits that are, instead, mobilized to legitimate disparate outcomes. While at times this is a function of ignorance, as most are not taught about structural inequality in our education or media systems, it is also a defense of the racial order where many, mostly whites but also some people of color, believe that our racial hierarchies are the result of a fair system and are therefore earned.

Although closely related to the legitimation of the status quo, a second core feature of color-blind ideology is its complicity with neoliberal politics and ideologies. This aspect aligns neatly with Bonilla-Silva's (2003) frame of abstract liberalism, which uses reasoning and universalized scenarios, often hypothetical and without important context, to argue for the merits of individual competition – thus Bonilla-Silva's emphasis on its abstract nature. This aspect of the ideology assumes an equal playing field, and much like the first core feature, must also disavow a structural understanding of racism and deny any ongoing discrimination or bias. What makes it different is its direct use of free-market principles such as competition and a lack of regulation. Bonilla-Silva and Forman (2000) provide examples of this feature, such as the defense that: "Kids should be exposed to all kinds of cultures but it cannot be imposed on them through busing" (70). This reasoning insists that we do in fact live in a democratic, free, and equal society, where talent rises to the top and we have dispensed with our biases. It takes the social system that most believe we *should* have, and operates as though this system is already in place. As such, it affirms the neoliberal status quo and the inequalities that it produces.

Finally, the third core feature of color-blindness is, perhaps paradoxically, its ongoing use of racial stereotypes. However, what makes this color-blind rather than overtly or "traditionally" racist, is its reliance on subtle or coded inferences about racial groups, or the pervasive belief that culture is alone or primarily powerful in its ability to drive or explain inequalities. This is despite the fact that the culture of poverty thesis has been discredited for decades by both scholars and journalists (see Iversen and Farber 1996; Compton-Lilly 2003; Lareau and Horvat 1999; Birch and Heideman 2014). It claims that, for example, blacks lack the personal responsibility and work ethic to improve their situation or that Asians teach their children the values needed for success. Both assumptions ignore structural and institutional factors, such as a change in immigration policy in the 1960s that gave preference to Asians who were already skilled in high-paying professions or the deep, generational segregation that impacts black communities' access to home equity and quality public education. It is crucial to note that this feature of color-blindness upholds the notion of white supremacy *specifically*, whereas the others support the system of white advantage structurally.

To be clear, while the third and final feature of this framework is centered around the mobilization of racial stereotypes in indirect or coded fashion, or as some have called it, on this "new" form of racism, it is crucial to note that "traditional" or overt forms of racism have not disappeared. Journalists noted a rise in race-based hate groups after the election of Barack Obama, and social media has helped to document ongoing instances of racist language and imagery in both public and private life. Jane Hill (2008) has also documented the persistence of racism in the United States in quite overt forms, and Joe Feagin's recent work has outlined the persistence of a centuries-old white racial frame, which he defines as an "organized set of racialized ideas, stereotypes, emotions, and inclinations to discriminate" (2006, 27). Race talk, much of it quite obviously racist, was documented by Myers (2005) among college students, while Picca and Feagin (2007) and Hughey (2011) have noted how comfortably whites will express overt racism in the "backstage" – around trusted friends and family. In addition to this overt racism, Tyrone Forman (2004) has traced a rise in racial apathy, a concept which "captures the ways in which whites may publicly express indifference or lack of care about racial inequality while at the same time continuing to hold anti-minority views" (51). As such, it should be noted that color-blindness, it seems, is the core feature of "front stage" racial discourse, and does not necessarily constitute all contemporary race talk.

Methodology

It is worth noting that many studies, especially those in sociology, have empirically tested the use of color-blind ideologies with qualitative methods. Bonilla-Silva's formative book *Racism without Racists* (2003) used two samples – a random sample of interviews from participants in the Detroit Area Survey and a large number of interviews with college students from around the country in order to demonstrate the prevalence of color-blind ideology and to assert its core features and frames. In that book, he argues that qualitative methods are the most effective for the examination of these ideologies because "survey questions still restrict the free flow of ideas and unnecessarily constrain the range of possible answers for respondents" (11). Indeed, much of the recent work in the field has also used a variety of qualitative methodologies, most often interviews, to explore these ideologies in institutional settings.

That said, there have been effective strategies for studying color-blind ideologies using quantitative methods. Paul Croll's (2013) work on whiteness uses a survey measure specifically designed to understand nuances of racial ideologies and identities, and as such is able to demonstrate many of the same paradoxes and complexities as has qualitative research. Other disciplines, especially psychology, have consistently made use of statistical measures to study color-blindness, most often using the Color-blind Racial Attitude Scale, or CoBRAS, which Helen Neville et al. developed in 2000. This scale asks participants to answer a series of questions about racial and power evasion, and correlates with racial prejudice and a belief that society has already attained fairness and equal opportunity. It is worth noting that Bonilla-Silva and some other sociologists argue that the scale is not interchangeable with our framework of color-blind ideology. However, these signals seem to point to similar outcomes: "Although conceptually different, the CoBRAS measure of color-blind racism was positively correlated with many measures of racial prejudice. Other studies have found that the CoBRAS measure of color-blind racism was positively correlated with white fear of other races" (Bonilla-Silva and Dietrich 2011: 194).

Other studies have demonstrated a correlation between CoBRAS and racial prejudice, often mobilized, like color-blind ideology more broadly, as a defense of racial inequality (see Gushue 2004). Color-blind ideology has also been shown to interact with the contact hypothesis – the notion that increased interracial communication and interaction will decrease prejudice (Powers and Ellison 1995; Sigelman and Welch 1993). O'Brien and Korgen (2007) demonstrate that high degrees of color-blindness limit the impact of the contact hypothesis, noting that "[i]t is evident that even close interracial contacts can coexist with racist ideology in today's color-blind society" (375).

After all, an increasingly diverse society has coincided with the prevalence of color-blind ideology. This ideology is also flexible enough to incorporate "token" relationships that reinforce the "rule" of cultural racism specifically through the use of these imagined "exceptions."

Contexts

Perhaps the most pervasive trend in the color-blind racism literature has been to document the many contexts in which it is applied. This work expands beyond sociology and into law, psychology, education, criminal justice, medicine, and political science. This section provides an overview of these findings, with the hope of highlighting for readers just some of the ways the ideology has been studied. It cannot include the entirety of the literature on color-blindness in applied contexts, but it highlights some of the common themes associated with color-blindness's core features and what we now know about its impact.

The first setting where there is a preponderance of literature is in education. Color-blind ideologies have been explored in university settings, where their negative impact on students of color at predominately white institutions is documented (Lewis et al. 2000), and where others (see Zamudio and Roas 2006) have found them to be pervasive. Harper (2007) found that institutions themselves minimize racist institutional norms by adopting the framework to explain institution-specific racial inequalities, which K-12 settings also tend to adopt (see Stoll 2013), even around the explicit issue of multicultural education (Castagno 2013). It is perhaps then not surprising that Freeman (2005) has also demonstrated its impact on education policy at the national level. Perhaps troublingly, even scholars in fields like anthropology (Brodkin et al. 2011), and no doubt many others, tend to rely on color-blindness when explaining racial disparities within their discipline. Yet within the context of education, some studies suggest that these frames can be overcome by intentional training and a sociological perspective (Burke and Banks 2012; Goldsmith 2006; Haddad and Lieberman 2002).

Education is not the only area where color-blind ideologies have had an impact on policy. Anderson (2004) has demonstrated how color-blind principles have created a bar to intentional neighborhood integration, preserving de facto segregation. Lopez (2007), Berry and Bonilla-Silva (2008), and many others demonstrate its effect on affirmative action policy and its implementation. Welfare policy is deeply infused with color-blind rhetoric and beliefs, and Monnat (2010) demonstrates that a particular gendered form of color-blind racism emerges in this setting. This discourse was also prevalent in the response to Hurricane Katrina (Shelton and Coleman 2009;

Sweeney 2006). Further, it is not limited to the United States, as Rhodes (2009) demonstrates its influence in British politics.

These policy decisions also influence discourse and thinking within specific institutional sites. In other words, color-blind housing policy mirrors the urban debates about race and place (Burke 2012; Gottleib 2013). At the same time, Krysan et al. (2009) show that despite color-blind language and policy, whites prefer neighborhoods with few to no blacks in them. Color-blindness is pervasive among health care providers (Malat et al. 2010), and in public conversations among all-white focus-group participants when reflecting on racial profiling by the police (Alegria 2014). It is perhaps not surprising, then, that they are also connected to the racial sentencing disparities (Schlesinger 2011) that are well documented and have persisted for years.

In less formal, cultural settings, Perez (2013) has shown its influence on comedian training, even despite comedy's role in disrupting color-blindness. Rodriquez (2006) also shows it to be pervasive among youth who appropriate hip hop, which is often explicitly racial in its content and affinities. Those who hire domestic workers into their homes, particularly across the color line, use color-blindness to make sense of these inequalities and differences (Moras 2010); those who engage in transracial adoption tend to do the same (Goar 2014). In fact, Norton et al. (2006) demonstrate its pervasiveness even in experimental interracial interactions. In particular, they "propose that the incongruity between trying to appear color-blind while automatically noticing color complicates strategic efforts to appear unbiased, creating an inevitable tension between efforts to achieve color blindness and actual success at doing so" (949).

As these settings make clear, "the reproduction of social hierarchies through mystification and obfuscation is perhaps the most obvious and important function of the diversity discourse" (Bell and Hartmann 2007: 905). That discourse is dominated by color-blind ideology, which is not just a way of talking about race, but also a way of acting on that basis to implicitly or overtly sustain racial inequality and perpetuate racial stereotypes. As Bonilla-Silva and Dietrich (2011: 174) have emphasized, "coercion and violence are not the central practices responsible for the reproduction of racial domination in contemporary America." Rather, it is the much more insidious, even abstractly commendable, ethic of color-blindness that shapes so much racial inequality and indifference today.

Color-Blindness among Racial Groups

Yet while that is clear, it is also important to trace the expression of color-blindness among different racial groups. While color-blindness does the work of legitimating white privilege and the notion of white supremacy, this does not mean that whites are always intentionally using it as a tool of domination, nor that it is universally applied and enacted among whites. Lewis (2004), for example, has demonstrated that many whites are so impacted by color-blind and other racial logic that they do not even see their own race as salient in their lives, even when they are educated about racial inequality. Race remains something that "happens" to people of color, whose lives are, they imagine, the only ones impacted by the racialization process. This renders invisible the extent to which whites also have raced bodies, ones that grant them privileges in most social settings, often through the benefit of the doubt or the spoils of individualism. Bonilla-Silva's foundational work discussed above, and that of many others, makes it clear that many, probably most, whites adopt the ideology of color-blindness as their central framework on race.

That said, there are layers and other important findings buried underneath this important claim. For example, Ramsaran (2009) has shown that class dynamics mediate color-blindness for whites, shaping which frames resonate with them most deeply and those that they may choose to evade or deny. I have demonstrated that color-blind frames, most often considered a conservative framework, take on a distinctly liberal flair in progressive communities (Burke 2012), and Hughey (2012) has shown racist discourse that is also complicit with color-blindness even among explicitly anti-racist whites. Bonilla-Silva (2003) suggests that working-class women might be the least likely among whites to embrace the frames and larger ideology of color-blindness, a theory about which empirical evidence is still uneven. Either way, it is clear that color-blindness is not monolithic among whites, even while it is clear that whites most often, or are most likely to, apply the ideology as a byproduct of their lack of education around race or as a defense of their racial privilege.

Latino/as represent an ethnic rather than a racial group, as the population spans the racial spectrum from black to white. At the same time, they are often racialized by others as a distinct category in the United States, and many self-identify as such. But perhaps given that variance, some research suggests that they are as likely to support or adopt color-blind frameworks as whites (Bonilla-Silva and Dietrich 2011). McClain et al. (2006) suggest that this may be, in part, to distance themselves from blacks, who are most often seen as the abject racial category in the United States. Koreans in some studies also draw upon color-blind frames to explain their relative success (Nopper 2010: 81), ignoring or unaware of the changes in immigration law that facilitated social class mobility and middle-class performance among many Asians since 1965. Some research suggests a similar dynamic among biracial Americans in middle-class settings, who often embrace an "honorary white" status in their communities, which works to reify blackness as poor and undereducated (Korgen 2009).

That said, many blacks also show strong support for color-blind ideologies, though less so and in different ways than whites (Bonilla-Silva and Dietrich 2011). Bonilla-Silva (2003) suggests that some frames are more prevalent than others among blacks in the United States. That research is echoed by Welburn and Pittman (2012), who "find that while middle-class African Americans are united in their belief that members of their group face persistent racial inequality, they also attribute motivational factors to disadvantage for African Americans" (536). Among black youth, DeFreece (2014) found color-blindness articulated alongside a structural discourse, further suggesting that the frames are not used in a uniform or universal fashion among any racial group, regardless of its placement in racial or other hierarchies.

Conclusion

As the above sections indicate, sociologists and those working in other fields have convincingly demonstrated the prevalence of color-blindness as the dominant racial narrative of the post-Civil Rights era. This has been a crucially important project, for as Zamudio and Roas (2006: 484) note, "one aspect of the struggle against racial inequality must be to demystify this discourse, to look at how this seemingly benign discourse around race and the institutions that promote it, put their stamp on a continued racial project where whites benefit at the expense of the racialized Other." There remains little doubt that this racial project has been successful, and that we as scholars have held this discourse up for critique and as one of the tools of ongoing racial inequality. New research is beginning to trace its nuances and variations, but its impact on the racial status quo appears, for now, an entrenched feature of contemporary life.

References

Alegria, Sharla. 2014. Constructing Racial Difference through Group Talk: An Analysis of White Focus Groups' Discussion of Racial Profiling. *Ethnic and Racial Studies* 37: 241–260.

Anderson, Michelle Wilde. 2004. Colorblind Segregation: Equal Protection as a Bar to Neighborhood Integration. *California Law Review* 92: 841–844.

Bell, Joyce M. and Douglas Hartmann. 2007. Diversity in Everyday Discourse: The Cultural

Ambiguities and Consequences of "Happy Talk". *American Sociological Review* 72: 895–914.

Berry, Brent and Eduardo Bonilla-Silva. 2008. 'They Should Hire the one with the Best Score': White Sensitivity to Qualification Differences in Affirmative Action Hiring Decisions. *Ethnic and Racial Studies* 31: 215–242.

Birch, Jonah and Paul Heideman. 2014. The Poverty of Culture. *Jacobin* September 16: 16.

Bobo, Lawrence, James R. Kluegel, and Ryan A. Smith. 1997. Laissez-Faire Racism: The Crystallization of a Kinder, Gentler, Antiblack Ideology. *Racial Attitudes in the 1990s: Continuity and Change* 15: 23–25.

Bonilla-Silva, Eduardo. 1997. Rethinking Racism: Toward a Structural Interpretation. *American Sociological Review* 62: 465–480.

Bonilla-Silva, Eduardo. 2003. *Racism without Racists: Color-Blind Racism and the Persistence of Racial inequality in the United States*. Lanham MD: Rowman and Littlefield Publishers.

Bonilla-Silva, Eduardo and David Dietrich. 2011. The Sweet Enchantment of Color-Blind Racism in Obamerica. *Annals of the American Academy of Political and Social Science* 634: 190–206.

Bonilla-Silva, Eduardo and Tyrone A. Forman. 2000. "I Am Not a Racist But…": Mapping White College Students' Racial Ideology in the USA. *Discourse and Society* 11: 50–85.

Bonilla-Silva, Eduardo, Amanda Lewis, and David G. Embrick. 2004. "I Did Not Get That Job Because of a Black Man…": *The Story Lines and Testimonies of Color-Blind Racism. Sociological Forum* 19: 555–581.

Brodkin, Karen, Sandra Morgen, and Janis Hutchinson. 2011. Anthropology as White Public Space? *American Anthropologist* 113: 545–556.

Brown, Michael K., Martin Carnoy, Troy Duster, and David B. Oppenheimer. 2003. *Whitewashing Race: The Myth of a Color-Blind Society*. Berkeley, CA: University of California Press.

Burke, Meghan A. 2012. *Racial Ambivalence in Diverse Communities: Whiteness and the Power of Color-Blind Ideologies*. Lanham, MD: Lexington Books.

Burke, Meghan A. and Kira Hudson Banks. 2012. Sociology by Any Other Name: Teaching the Sociological Perspective in Campus Diversity Programs. *Teaching Sociology* 40: 21–33.

Carr, Leslie G. 1997. *Color-Blind Racism*. Thousand Oaks, CA: Sage.

Castagno, Angelina E. 2013. Multicultural Education and the Protection of Whiteness. *American Journal of Education* 120: 101–128.

Compton-Lilly, Catherine. 2003. *Reading Families: The Literate Lives of Urban Children*. New York, NY: Teachers College Press.

Croll, Paul R. 2013. Explanations for Racial Disadvantage and Racial Advantage: Beliefs about Both Sides of Inequality in America. *Ethnic and Racial Studies* 36: 47–74.

DeFreece, Alfred W. Jr. 2014. When the R Word Ain't Enough: Exploring Black Youths' Structural Explanations of Black Group Status. *Humanity and Society* 38: 25–48.

Feagin, Joe R. 2006. *Systemic Racism: A theory of Oppression*. New York, NY: Routledge.

Forman, Tyrone A. 2004. Color-Blind Racism and Racial Indifference: The Role of Racial Apathy in Facilitating Enduring inequalities. In *The Changing Terrain of Race and Ethnicity*. Edited by Maria Krysan and Amanda Lewis. New York, NY: Russell Sage Foundation.

Freeman, Eric. 2005. No Child Left Behind and the Denigration of Race. *Equity and Excellence in Education* 38: 190–199.

Gallagher, Charles A. 2003. Color-Blind Privilege: The Social and Political Functions of Erasing the Color Line in Post Race America. *Race, Gender and Class* 10: 22–37.

Goar, Carla. 2014. The Race Continuum: Colorblind and Race-Conscious Approaches among White Adoptive Parents at Culture Camps. In *Race in Transnational and Transracial Adoption*. Edited by Vilna Treitler. New York, NY: Palgrave Macmillan.

Goldsmith, Pat Antonio. 2006. Learning to Understand Inequality and Diversity: Getting Students Past Ideologies. *Teaching Sociology* 34: 263–277.

Gottlieb, Dylan. 2013. Sixth Avenue Heartache: Race, Commemoration, and the Colorblind Consensus in Zephyrhills, Florida, 2003–2004. *Journal of Urban History* 39: 1085–1105.

Gushue, George. 2004. Race, Colorblind Racial Attitudes, and Judgments about Mental Health: A Shifting Standards Perspective. *Journal of Counseling Psychology* 51: 398–407.

Haddad, Angela T. and Leonard Lieberman. 2002. From Student Resistance to Embracing the Sociological Imagination: Unmasking Privilege, Social Conventions, and Racism. *Teaching Sociology* 30: 328–341.

Harper, Shaun R. 2007. Race without Racism: How Higher Education Researchers Minimize Racist Institutional Norms. *The Review of Higher Education* 36: 9–29.

Hill, Jane H. 2009. *The Everyday Language of White Racism*. Oxford: John Wiley and Sons.

Hughey, Matthew W. 2011. Backstage Discourse and the Reproduction of White Masculinities. *The Sociological Quarterly* 52: 132–153.

Hughey, Matthew. 2012. *White Bound: Nationalists, Antiracists, and the Shared Meanings of Race*. Redwood City, CA: Stanford University Press.

Iversen, Roberta Rehner and Naomi B. Farber. 1996. Transmission of Family Values, Work, and Welfare among Poor Urban Black Women. *Work and Occupations* 23: 437–460.

Korgen, Kathleen Odell. 2009. Black/White Biracial Identity: The influence of Colorblindness and the Racialization of Poor Black Americans. *Theory in Action* 2: 23–39.

Krysan, Maria, Mick P. Couper, Reynolds Farley, and Tyrone A. Forman. 2009. Does Race Matter in Neighborhood Preferences? Results from a Video Experiment. *American Journal of Sociology* 115: 527–559.

Lareau, Annette and Erin McNamara Horvat. 1999. Moments of Social Inclusion and Exclusion: Race, Class, and Cultural Capital in Family-School Relationships. *Sociology of Education* 72: 37–53.

Lewis, Amanda E. 2004. "What Group?" Studying Whites and Whiteness in the Era of "Color-Blindness." *Sociological Theory* 22: 623–646.

Lewis, Amanda E., Mark Chesler, and Tyrone A. Forman. 2000. The Impact of "Colorblind" Ideologies on Students of Color: Intergroup Relations at a Predominantly White University. *The Journal of Negro Education* 69: 74–91.

Lopez, Ian F. Haney. 2007. "A Nation of Minorities": Race, Ethnicity, and Reactionary Colorblindness. *Stanford Law Review* 59: 985–1063.

Malat, Jennifer, Rose Clark-Hitt, Diana Jill Burgess, Greta Friedemann-Sanchez, and Michelle van Ryn. 2010. White Doctors and Nurses on Racial Inequality in Health Care in the USA: Whiteness and Colour-Blind Racial Ideology. *Ethnic and Racial Studies* 33: 1431–1450.

McClain, Paula D., Niambi M. Carter, Victoria M. Defrancesco Soto, Monique L. Lyle, Jeffrey D. Grynaviski, Shayla C. Nunnally, Thomas J. Scotto, J. Alan Kendrick, Gerald F. Lackey, and Kendra Davenport Cotton. 2006. Racial Distancing in a Southern City: Latino Immigrants' Views of Black Americans. *Journal of Politics* 68: 571–584.

McConahay, John B. 1986. Modern Racism, Ambivalence, and the Modern Racism Scale. In *Prejudice, Discrimination, and Racism*. Edited by John F. Davido. San Diego, CA: Academic Press.

Monnat, Shannon M. 2010. The Color of Welfare Sanctioning: Exploring the individual and Contextual Roles of Race on TANF Case Closures and Benefit Reductions. *The Sociological Quarterly* 51: 678–707.

Moras, Amanda. 2010. Colour-Blind Discourses in Paid Domestic Work: Foreignness and the Delineation of Alternative Racial Markers. *Ethnic and Racial Studies* 33: 233–252.

Myers, Kristen A. 2005. *Racetalk: Racism Hiding in Plain Sight*. Lanham, MD: Rowman and Littlefield Publishers.

Neville, Helen A., Roderick L. Lilly, Georgia Duran, Richard M. Lee, and Lavonne Browne. 2000. Construction and Initial Validation of the Color-Blind Racial Attitudes Scale (Cobras). *Journal of Counseling Psychology* 47: 59–70.

Nopper, Tamara K. 2010. Colorblind Racism and Institutional Actors' Explanations of Korean Immigrant Entrepreneurship. *Critical Sociology* 36: 65–85.

Norton, Michael I., Samuel R. Sommers, Evan P. Apfelbaum, Natassia Pura, and Dan Ariely. 2006. Color Blindness and Interracial Interaction: Playing the Political Correctness Game. *Psychological Science* 17: 949–953.

O'Brien, Eileen and Kathleen Odell Korgen. 2007. It's the Message, Not the Messenger: The Declining Significance of Black–White Contact in a "Colorblind" Society. *Sociological inquiry* 77: 356–382.

Omi, Michael and Howard Winant. 1994. *Racial Formation in the United States: From the 1960s to the 1990s*. New York, NY: Routledge.

Perez, Raul. 2013. Learning to Make Racism Funny in the "Color-Blind" Era: Stand-Up Comedy Students, Performance Strategies, and the (Re)Production of Racist Jokes in Public. *Discourse and Society* 24: 478–503.

Picca, Leslie Houts and Joe R. Feagin. 2007. *Two-Faced Racism: Whites in the Backstage and Frontstage*. New York, NY: Routledge.

Powers, Daniel A., and Christopher G. Ellison. 1995. Interracial Contact and Black Racial Attitudes: The Contact Hypothesis and Selectivity Bias. *Social Forces* 74: 205–226.

Ramsaran, Dave. 2009. Class and the Color-Line in a Changing America. *Race, Gender and Class* 16: 271–294.

Rhodes, James. 2009. Revisiting the 2001 Riots: New Labour and the Rise of "Colour Blind Racism." *Sociological Research Online* 14: 3.

Rodriquez, Jason. 2006. Color-Blind Ideology and the Cultural Appropriation of Hip-Hop. *Journal of Contemporary Ethnography* 35: 645–668.

Schlesinger, Traci. 2011. The Failure of Race Neutral Policies: How Mandatory Terms and Sentencing Enhancements Contribute to Mass Racialized Incarceration. *Crime and Delinquency* 57: 56–81.

Sears, David O. 1988. Symbolic Racism. In *Eliminating Racism: Perspectives in Social Psychology*. Edited by Phyllis A. Katz and Dalmas A. Taylor. New York, NY: Springer.

Shelton, Jason E., and M. Nicole Coleman. 2009. After the Storm: How Race, Class, and Immigration Concerns Influenced Beliefs about the Katrina Evacuees. *Social Science Quarterly* 90: 480–496.

Sigelman, Lee and Susan Welch. 1993. The Contact Hypothesis Revisited: Black-White Interaction and Positive Racial Attitudes. *Social Forces* 71: 781–795.

Smith, Robert Charles. 1995. *Racism in the Post-Civil Rights Era: Now You See It, Now You Don't*. New York, NY: SUNY Press.

Stoll, Laurie Cooper. 2013. *Race and Gender in the Classroom: Teachers, Privilege, and Enduring Social Inequalities*. Lanham, MD: Lexington Books.

Sweeney, Kathryn A. 2006. The Blame Game: Racialized Responses to Hurricane Katrina. *Du Bois Review* 3: 161–174.

Welburn, Jessica S., and Cassi L. Pittman. 2012. Stop "Blaming the Man": Perceptions of Inequality and Opportunities for Success in the Obama Era Among Middle-Class African Americans. *Ethnic and Racial Studies* 35: 523–540.

Zamudio, Margaret M. and Francisco Rios. 2006. From Traditional to Liberal Racism: Living Racism in the Everyday. *Sociological Perspectives* 49: 483–501.

CHAPTER 4
Critical Race Theory

Mary Romero and Jeremiah Chin

Numerous sociologists engaged in interdisciplinary critical studies on race have embraced the writings emerging from critical race theory (CRT). These race scholars reject the traditional emphasis on assimilation or separating communities as ethnic or racial but rather recognize race "as a mode of constructing political communities" (Jung 2009: 390) and challenge discourses on a "post-racial" era of "color-blindness" and meritocracy. Critical race scholars focus on power relations and domination central in maintaining boundaries of national belonging and critique scholarship on multiculturalism and diversity, which emphasizes integration and assimilation.

Legal scholar Derrick Bell forged the path for CRT in his powerful narratives, such as *And We Are Not Saved: The Elusive Quest for Racial Justice* (1987) and *Faces at the Bottom of the Well: The Permanence of Racism* (1992). Bell's use of personal narrative, critique of white supremacy, and commitment to an activist agenda, were ideal for teaching and researching the way that race is embedded in our social institutions and is reinforced and maintained through everyday practices. Weaving legal scholarship and the struggle for social justice, Bell's writings attracted race scholars in sociology who recognized that the study of race has never been neutral but has always involved issues of power, inequality, and oppression. CRT "rejects the prevailing orthodoxy that scholarship should be or could be 'neutral' and 'objective'" to pursue "engaged, even adversarial, scholarship" (Crenshaw 1995: xiii). In locating CRT in sociology today, we begin with a brief overview of CRT and its key themes. We then discuss the contributions of the founder of the sociology of race, W. E. B. Du Bois, to CRT, sociological perspectives that utilize CRT, and the works of some sociologists who have incorporated CRT into their research.

Origins of CRT

CRT did not emerge from a single person or moment, but rather grew from lawyers, law professors, and students actively working against racial inequity in legal systems, philosophies, and education. In the 1970s, the founders and proponents of CRT, calling themselves RaceCrits, took an active stance against the purported institutional color-blindness of the legal academy and legal institutions, particularly the Supreme Court. Drawing on Critical Legal Studies (CLS), which critiqued the economics and classism of legal institutional practice and philosophy, and the Civil Rights Movement, early RaceCrits looked to "move beyond the non-critical liberalism that often cabined civil rights discourses and a non-racial radicalism that was a line of debate within CLS" (Crenshaw 2012: 1264).

CRT was born by building on existing legal scholarship and creating a forum for new ways of thinking about the interactions between race, gender, law, society, economics, and a variety of other fields. While early CRT scholars did not always agree on the breadth or scale of the movement they had created, or even the tenets of the framework they had begun to establish, the spark generated by activist students and scholars spread to other fields. The interdisciplinary nature of CRT in the law began to feed back into other fields they had drawn so heavily from, like sociology.

Drawing on the initial activist scholarship of Bell (1980; 1987; 1992), Crenshaw (1989; 1995; 2012), Gotanda (1991) and many others, CRT grew from its roots as legal scholarship to a plethora of academic fields and to branch into its own subfields. For example, LatCrit emerged as a means of focusing the lens of CRT on Latina/o communities and particularized issues of colorism and immigration to disrupt black/white binaries of race. It evolved into a perspective of "rotating centers" and "shifting bottoms" to contemplate the varied effects of race, ethnicity, class, immigration status, and other issues affecting blacks, Latina/os, Asian Americans and other marginalized groups (Mutua 1999; Hernández-Truyol 1997). LatCrit, though nominally and intellectually grounded in Latina/o communities and experiences, has shown the power of intercultural/interracial coalitions in the search for justice, particularly in the histories of immigration, exclusion, and borders in the United States (Chang and Aoki 1997). Similarly, Critical Race Feminism broadens understanding of CRT by noting important contributions of feminist scholars of color in focusing on the links between law and the experiences of women from different social statuses, sexual orientations, geographies, and races (Wing 2003).

Key Themes of CRT

CRT has no definitive text, but grows organically from the activism and writing of key scholars, working to understand and change the "vexed bond" (Crenshaw 1995: xxi) between law, institutions, and racial power. However, several key themes ground CRT scholarship generally.

- First, racial inequality is enmeshed into social, political, and economic conditions of the United States (Carbado and Roithmayr 2014). Formal legal remedies, alone, are therefore ineffective in confronting racism in the everyday lived experiences of people of color, as "the elimination of intentional racism would not eliminate racial inequality" (Carbado and Roithmayr 2014: 152).
- Second, CRT contains the dual notions of intersectionality, originally theorized by Kimberlé Crenshaw (1989), and anti-essentialism. There is no single identity for any individual person; rather each person exists at the intersections of cultural, social, class, gendered, and many other identities which define who they are.
- Third, as Derrick Bell's interest convergence theory describes, court decisions or apparent advancement for people of color, and Blacks in particular, only occur when such a decision maintains the privilege and self-interests of whites (Bell 1980).
- Fourth, race is a social construction, fluid in meaning and contingent on social structures of power and historical periods (Lopez 1997).

- Fifth, CRT contains a critique of color-blindness/post-racialism. This applies not only in legal institutions and the supposed strategies of courts that obfuscate the ongoing role of race in the United States, but also prevailing attitudes in private and public sectors that would limit opportunities for people of color. Post-racialism and color-blindness impact everything – from immigration policy on who may legally enter the United States, to perceptions of peoples (e.g., the model minority myth among people of Chinese, Japanese, Korean, and Indian descent) (Chang 1993), and the (in)ability of professionals of color to advance in professional settings due to coded experience and interview expectations (Carbado and Gulati 2013).

Sociological Tradition of CRT Themes

CRT themes can be traced to W. E. B. Du Bois's famous quote in his book, *The Souls of Black Folk*: "[T]he problem of the Twentieth Century is the problem of the color line" (1903: v). By identifying the color line as the problem, the analysis shifted away from any perceived inferiority or superiority of individuals or groups of color and onto the "processes, practices, and institutions – of US society" (Treviño et al. 2008: 7). Du Bois began with the premise that racial inequality is not grounded in the inferiority of nonwhite people or their institutions, such as church and the family, as many sociologists have claimed. Rather Du Bois understood the sources of racial inequality were the social, political, and economic conditions blacks faced in the United States. He was the first sociologist to pursue major empirical studies investigating these conditions (e.g., *The Philadelphia Negro* 1899; *Black Reconstruction in America* 1935). Unlike his white contemporaries who "preached a scientific objectivity and detachment despite the fact that [their] work on race was based on the prescientific assumptions of the inferiority of blacks and the saving graces of assimilation" (Morris 2007: 505), Du Bois's scholarship focused on racial justice and practiced a connection between scholarship and activism.

Sociologists tracing the theoretical foundation of intersectionality in sociology have acknowledged Du Bois's contributions, particularly in explaining black political economy. The social hierarchies he identified were race, class, and nation (Collins 2000). While Du Bois's inclusion of gender is highly contested among black feminists, his writings do include a concern about the dangerous working conditions women workers faced – particularly sexual abuse in domestic service. More generally, he addressed the complexities of the black community, class, and family but did not specifically identify gender as a system of power (Collins 2000).

Critical race scholars in sociology, particularly those from the Du Boisian, anti-colonialism, or Marxist traditions were critical of civil rights reforms as "inadequate and tokenistic" (Winant 2007: 166) and pointed to the vast racial inequalities in education, income and wealth, housing, health care, and the criminal justice system. These scholars were galvanized by the Black Power Movement, the Chicano Movement and other social movements demanding the elimination of social inequality. As Robert Blauner (1972: viii) noted in the preface to *Racial Oppression in America*, he and other sociologists using a critical race perspective were developing a framework to understand racial inequality that "probably owes more to the social movements of the oppressed than to standard sociology..." His work identified four fallacies still entangled in mainstream sociology of race during the 1970s:

> First, the view that racial and ethnic groups are neither central nor persistent elements of modern societies. Second, the idea that race and racial oppression are not independent dynamic forces but are ultimately reducible to other casual determinates, usually economic or psychological. Third, the position that the most important aspects of racism are the attitudes and prejudices of white Americans.

And, ...there are no essential long-term differences – in relation to the larger society – between the Third World *or racial minorities and European ethnic groups (Blauner 1972: 2).*

Critical race scholars conceptualized the roots of racial oppression in slavery, conquest, and colonization, and, therefore, began their research with an examination of each and their relationship to the continued racialization of privilege and opportunities.

At the same time, the post-racial ideology gaining ground in US society rejected notions of internal colonialism and institutional racism and advanced an assimilationist position. In the 1970s and 1980s, widely publicized policy-oriented writings advocated for the elimination of affirmative action and welfare (Glazer 1975; Murray 1984). The neoconservative paradigm had taken the position that the "United States was entering a 'postracial' era of 'color blindness' and meritocracy" (Winant 2007: 166) and embraced cultural deficiency models to explain racial inequality. Stephen Steinberg (1995: 97) referred to these neoconservative writings as the "scholarship of backlash" and pointed to their impact in shaping decades of national policy. In opposition to the neoconservative paradigm, critical race scholars countered with research showing that the United States has always been and remains color-conscious.

Almost three decades ago, Michael Omi and Howard Winant introduced the concept of the social construction of race in their germinal book, *Racial Formation in the United States, from the 1960s to the 1980s*. They called attention to "[c]ivil rights struggles and ghetto revolts, as well as controversies over state policies of reform and repression, [that] highlighted a period of intense conflict where the very meaning of race was politically contested" (Omi and Winant 1986: 2). They argued that mainstream theories on race suffered from "an inability to grasp the uniqueness of race, its historical flexibility and immediacy in everyday experience and social conflict" (Omi and Winant 1986: 3). Racial formation and the social construction of race is now accepted in the sociology of race but has not yet fully replaced mainstream assimilation theories that turn attention to similarities and differences among groups rather than to the relations of power (Jung 2009).

Sociological Uses and Approaches to CRT

One of the most widely accepted themes of CRT in the sociology of race today is the recognition that racial inequality is systemic, and everyday practices that perpetuate inequality are integrated into the very fabric of social institutions. In his book, *Systemic Racism*, Joe Feagin (2006: xxi) focuses on "a broad range of racialized dimensions of this society: the racist framing, racist ideology, stereotyped attitudes, racist emotions, discriminatory habits and actions, and extensive racist institutions developed over centuries by whites." Feagin (2006: 16) argues that systemic racism in the United States "is an organized racist whole with complex, interconnected, and interdependent social networks, organizations, and institutions that routinely imbed racial oppression" (see Chapter 2 in this volume).

Recent debates between proponents of racial formation theory (RFT) and Joe Feagin and Sean Elias's systemic racism theory (SRT) illuminate the importance of Bell's theory of interest convergence, in naming the roles of the state, state actors, and communities of color in the persistence of racism in the United States (Bracey II, 2014: 13). Though Omi, Winant, Feagin, and Elias may all be considered a part of critical race scholarship in sociology, their perspectives illuminate the diversity of views on the current relationship between racism, the state, and peoples of color. While Omi and Winant's RFT considers "the present prospects for racial justice demoralizing at best," they argue that social and political victories for civil rights and racial justice cannot be overturned – particularly the "politicization of the social," making race and social identities political issues

(2012: 965–966). In this view, while the policies meant to benefit peoples of color may be rearticulated to benefit whites, specifically through color-blindness, the underlying benefits of these policies may not be eliminated. However, Feagin and Elias argue that this view fails to account for the overall system of white supremacy that produces racial justice only when doing so benefits whites and those in positions of power (Feagin and Elias 2012: 950). Omi and Winant's argument embraces key ideas shared by the themes of CRT – particularly the entrenchment of racial inequality, the social construction of race and the critique of color-blindness – while Feagin and Elias add in Bell's interest convergence theory to question whether the social gains of the civil rights movements are actually permanent, or merely temporary, formal accommodations by the state to diffuse racial tensions (but with an overall goal of keeping whites in power). Thus, while scholars in sociology and CRT similarly recognize how state institutions reify oppression (Bracey II, 2014; Feagin and Elias 2012; Jung et al. 2011; Omi and Winant, 2012), CRT adds skepticism on the permanence of progress, particularly in questioning why and how racial progress has been interpreted in legal institutions (Bell 1980).

Closely related to the study of systemic racism is the analysis of the social reproduction and transmission of race and privilege through schools. Given that several Supreme Court cases have been central to both maintaining (i.e. *Regents of the University of California v. Bakke*, 438 U.S. 265 1978; *Grutter v. Bollinger*, 539 U.S. 306 2003) and challenging (i.e., *Brown v. Broad of Education*, 347 U.S. 483 1954; *Plyer v. Doe*, 457 U.S. 202 1982) racial inequality in schools, many in the sociology of education have adopted CRT as a challenge to legal regimes that attempt to define standards for education. Among the key scholars in this area are Gloria Ladson-Billings and William Tate, who argue that race is "a significant factor in determining inequality in the United States" (1995: 47). Since US society is based on property rights, Ladson-Billings and Tate note that "the intersection of race and property creates an analytic tool though which we can understand social (and, consequently, school) inequity" (1995: 47).

In *Reproducing Racism: White Space, Elite Law Schools, and Racial Inequality*, Wendy Leo Moore (2007), a sociologist and lawyer, examines social reproduction and systemic racism occurring in elite law schools. Based on her ethnographic research at two elite law schools, Moore points to the cultural practices and racist ideology and discourse that maintain the law schools as white institutional spaces.

Daniel Solórzano (1998) and his former students (i.e., Solórzano and Villalpando 1998; Solórzano and Yosso 2001) have also extended the key themes of CRT to education, from laws to classroom environments and pedagogy. They examine racialized oppression in schools based on race, gender, class, immigration status, surname, phenotype, accent, and sexuality. These researchers have written extensively on micro-aggressions and used counter-storytelling to capture the permanency of racism in American schools.

Counter-storytelling has been used by other CRT scholars as well, to counter meta-narratives of whiteness by challenging dominant paradigms, as well as to analyze, subvert, and intervene in dominant conceptual frameworks that mask oppressive experiences. Adalberto Aguirre (2000) used counter-storytelling to study the institutional practices surrounding affirmative action programs that actually assure the marginalization of faculty of color. Likewise, Margaret Zamudio and her colleagues (2011) examined the disadvantages that university students of color face, through narratives, testimonies, and storytelling.

Researchers examining the everyday practices that maintain and reinforce racism frequently build on Peggy Davis's (1989) use of micro-aggressions, which she adopted from psychologist Chester Pierce. He defined micro-aggressions as "subtle, stunning, often automatic, and non-verbal exchanges which are 'put downs' of blacks by offenders" (Pierce et al. 1978: 66). Sociologists of education (i.e., Solórzano 1998; Solórzano and Yosso 2001), criminal justice (Russell 1998; Russell-Brown 2004; 2006; Milovanovic and Russell 2001; Glover 2009), and immigration (Romero 2006) have used micro- and macro-aggressions to capture how inequality is maintained in institutional practices and everyday social interactions. Dragan Milovanovic and Katheryn Russell (2001) applied micro- and macro-aggressions to covert-informal and overt-formal discriminatory practices in the criminal justice system. Mary Romero (2006) used the concepts to capture the use of racial profiling in immigration law enforcement.

Following Omi and Winant's (1986) initial theorizing of the social construction of race, scholars in sociology turned to CRT writings to further capture the fluidity and the contingency of racial construction on social structures. For example, Andrew Penner and Aliya Saperstein (2008; Saperstein and Penner (2012)) used data from the National Longitudinal Survey of Youth and found that whites who experienced sustained periods of incarceration, unemployment, or poverty, or other characteristics normally attributed to blacks, were less likely to be classified as white. Looking at the impact of identity and mental health, Mary Campbell and Lisa Troyer (2007) researched the discrepancies between the ways that American Indians constructed their racial identities and how others perceived them. They found the higher the discrepancy, the higher levels of psychological distress when faced with racism and discrimination.

Numerous family scholars have advocated CRT in examining race, ethnicity, and culture in family processes (Few 2007; DeReus et al. 2005; Burton et al. 2010). For example, April Few (2007) argues that a critical race feminist approach considers how racism shapes families' life chances, the power dynamics and politics of family decision-making, and creative culturally sensitive interventions. Linda M. Burton and her colleagues (2010) accessed CRT's contribution to research on families of color and found emerging interests in inequality and socio-economic mobility within and across families, interracial romantic pairings, and the racial socialization of children.

Sociologists focusing on the way that race shapes the immigrant experience, immigration policy, and law enforcement have incorporated CRT's perspective on the social construction of race and citizenship (Johnson 1996; Chang 1999). For example, in her study of immigration law enforcement, Romero (2006; 2008) and colleagues (Goldsmith et al. 2008; 2009) analyzed the social construction of racialized citizenship, particularly the use of racial profiling in immigration law enforcement and citizenship inspection. Attending to the intersectionality of race, class and citizenship in immigration raids and law enforcement practices, they point to five patterns that place low-income racialized immigrants and citizens at risk before the law: (1) discretionary stops based on ethnicity and class; (2) use of intimidation to demean and subordinate persons stopped; (3) restricting the freedom of movement of Mexicans but not others in the same vicinity; (4) reinforced stereotypes of Mexican as "alien," "foreign," inferior and criminal; and (5) limited access to fair and impartial treatment before the law (Romero 2006: 463).

Conclusion

CRT in sociology blends with the ongoing development of critical race studies that emerged from challenges to assimilation theories entrenched in studying inequality. Critical race sociologists understand that the roots of inequality are embedded in society's social structure, recognize intersectionality, and produce activist scholarship in opposition to color-blind ideologies and policies. Sociologists who use a critical race perspective engage in an ongoing exchange with CRT from other fields as they work together to understand and address racial inequality in society. Key themes of CRT – including the social construction of racism and its presence in everyday life, intersectionality and the complexities of identity that go unrecognized by the law, interest convergence, and critiques of post-racialism/color-blindness in liberal democracies – have become crucial to the sociological imagination. CRT not only contributes a critical lens to scholarship and research, but an activist paradigm that pushes for social change through legal and social reforms. Both sociologists and legal scholars have pushed CRT beyond its original critique of civil rights and retrenchment into various other areas, such as education, immigration, law enforcement, microaggressions, citizenship, families, and whiteness. Sociology and CRT have become intertwined in a larger activist-scholar effort for racial, gender, legal, and economic justice.

References

Aguirre, Adalberto. 2000. Academic Storytelling: A Critical Race Theory Story of Affirmative Action. *Sociological Perspectives* 43(2): 319–339.

Blauner, Robert. 1972. *Racial Oppression in America*. New York, NY: Harper and Row, Publishers.

Bell, Derrick A. 1980. Brown v. Board of Education and the Interest Convergence Dilemma. *Harvard Law Review* 93: 518–533.

Bell, Derrick A. 1987. *And We Are Not Saved: The Elusive Quest for Racial Justice*. New York, NY: Basic Books.

Bell, Derrick A. 1992. *Faces at the Bottom of the Well: The Permanence of Racism*. New York, NY: Basic Books.

Bracey II, Glenn E. 2014. Towards a Critical Race Theory of State. *Critical Sociology* (January): 1–21.

Burton, Linda M., Eduardo Bonilla-Silva, Victor Ray, Rose Buckelew, and Elizabeth Hordge Freeman. 2010. Critical Race Theories, Colorism, and the Decade's Research on Families of Color. *Journal of Marriage and Family* (June): 440–459.

Campbell, Mary E. and Lisa Troyer. 2007. The Implications of Racial Misclassification by Observers. *American Sociological Review* 72: 750–765.

Carbado, Devon W. and Mitu Gulati. 2013. *Acting White?: Rethinking Race in "Post-Racial" America*. New York, NY: Oxford University Press.

Carbado, Devon W. and Daria Roithmayr. 2014. Critical Race Theory Meets Social Science. *Annual Review of Law and Social Science* 10: 149–167.

Chang, Robert S. 1993. Toward an Asian American Legal Scholarship: Critical Race Theory, Post-Structuralism, and Narrative Space. *California Law Review* 81: 1241–1323.

Chang, Robert S. 1999. *Disoriented: Asian Americans, Law and the Nation-State*. New York, NY: New York University Press.

Chang, Robert S. and Kieth Aoki. 1997. Centering the Immigrant in the Inter/National Imagination. *California Law Review* 85(5): 1395–1447.

Collins, Patricia Hill. 2000. Gender, Black Feminism, and Black Political Economy. *Annals of the American Academy of Political and Social Science* 568: 41–53.

Crenshaw, Kimberlé. 1989. Demarginalizing the Intersection of Race and Sex: A Black Feminist Critique of Antidiscrimination Doctrine, Feminist Theory and Antiracist Politics. *University of Chicago Legal Forum* 139–167.

Crenshaw, Kimberlé. 1995. Introduction. In *Critical Race Theory: The Key Writings that Formed the Movement*. New York, NY: the New Press.

Crenshaw, Kimberlé. 2012. Twenty Years of Critical Race Theory: Looking Back to Move Forward. *Connecticut Law Review* 43(5): 1253–1352.

Davis, P. C. 1989. Law as Microaggressions. *Yale Law Journal* 98: 1559–1577.

DeReus, Lee Ann, April L. Few, and Libby Balter Blume. 2005. Multicultural and Critical Race Feminisms: Theorizing Families in the Third Wave. In *Sourcebook of Family Theory and Research*. Edited by Vern L. Bengtson, Alan C. Acock, Katherine R. Allen, Peggy Dilworth-Anderson, and David M. Klein. Thousand Oaks, CA: Sage, 447–469.

Du Bois, W. E. B. 1899. *The Philadelphia Negro: A Social Study*. New York, NY: Schocken Books.

Du Bois, W. E. B. 1903. *The Souls of Black Folk*. Chicago, IL: A. C. McClurg.

Du Bois, W. E. B. 1935. *Black Reconstruction in America*. New York, NY: Simon and Shuster.

Feagin, Joe R. 2006. *Systemic Racism: A Theory of Oppression*. New York, NY: Routledge.

Feagin, Joe R. and Sean Elias. 2012. Rethinking Racial Formation Theory: A Systemic Racism

Critique. *Ethnic and Racial Studies* 36(6): 931–960.
Few, April L. 2007. Integrating Black Consciousness and Critical Race Feminism into Family Studies Research. *Journal of Family Issues* 28: 452–473.
Glazer, Nathan. 1975. *Affirmative Discrimination: Ethnic Inequality and Public Policy.* New York, NY: Basic Books.
Glover, Karen S. 2009. *Racial Profiling, Research, Racism, and Resistance.* Lanham, MD: Rowman and Littlefield.
Goldsmith, Pat Rubio and Mary Romero. 2008. "Aliens", "Illegals" and Other Types of Mexicanness: Examination of Racial Profiling in Border Policing. In *Globalization and America: Race, Human Rights, and Inequality.* Edited by Angela Hattery, David Embrick and Earl Smith. Lanham, MD: Rowman and Littlefield.
Goldsmith, Pat Rubio, Mary Romero, Raquel Rubio Goldsmith, Manuel Escobedo, and Laura Khoury. 2009. Ethno-Racial Profiling and State Violence in a Southwest Barrio. *Aztlán: A Journal of Chicano Studies* 34(1): 93–123.
Gotanda, Neil. 1991. A Critique of "Our Constitution Is Color-Blind." *Stanford Law Review* 44: 1–68.
Hernández-Truyol, Berta Esperanza. 1997. Borders (En)Gendered: Normativities, Latinas, and a Latcrit Paradigm. *New York University Law Review* 72: 882–927.
Johnson, Kevin. 1996. "Aliens" and the U.S. Immigration Laws: The Social and Legal Construction of Nonpersons. *University of Miami International-American Law Review* 28: 263–287.
Jung, Moon-Kie. 2009. The Racial Unconscious of Assimilation Theory. *Du Bois Review* 6(2): 376–395.
Jung, Moon-Kie, João H. Costa Vargas, and Eduardo Bonilla-Silva. 2011. *State of White Supremacy: Racism, Governance, and the United States.* Stanford, CA: Stanford University Press.
Ladson-Billings, Gloria and William Tate. 1995. Toward a Critical Race Theory of Education. *Teachers College Record* 97(1): 47–65.
Lopez, Ian Haney. 1997. *White by Law: The Legal Construction of Race.* New York, NY: New York University Press.
Milovanovic, Dragan and Katheryn Russell. eds. 2001. *Petit Apartheid in the U.S. Criminal Justice System.* Durham, NC: Carolina Academic Press.
Moore, Wendy Leo. 2007. *Reproducing Racism: White Space, Elite Law School, and Racial Inequality.* Lanham, MD: Rowman and Littlefield.
Morris, Aldon. 2007. Sociology of Race and W. E. B. Du Bois: The Path Not Taken. In *Sociology in America: A History.* Edited by Craig Calhoun. Chicago, IL: University of Chicago Press.
Murray, Charles A. 1984. *Losing Ground: American Social Policy, 1950–1980.* New York, NY: Basic Books.
Mutua, Athena D. 1999. Shifting Bottoms and Rotating Centers: Reflections on Latcrit III and the Black/White Paradigm. *University of Miami Law Review* 53: 1177–1218.
Omi, Michael and Howard Winant. 1986. *Racial Formation in the United States from the 1960s to the 1980s.* New York, NY: Routledge.
Omi, Michael and Howard Winant. 2012. Resistance Is Futile?: A Response to Feagin and Elias. *Ethnic and Racial Studies* 36(6): 961–973.
Penner Andrew M. and Aliya Saperstein. 2008. How Social Status Shapes Race. *Proceedings of the National Academy of Sciences USA* 205: 19628–19630.
Pierce, Chester M., Jean V. Carew, Doama Pierce-Gonzalez, and Deborah Willis. 1978. An Experiment in Racism: TV Xommercials. In *Television and Education.* Edited by Chester Pierce. Beverly Hills, CA: Sage, 62–88.
Romero, Mary. 2006. Racial Profiling and Immigration Law Enforcement: Rounding Up of Usual Suspects in the Latino Community. *Critical Sociology* 32(2–3): 47–73.
Romero, Mary. 2008. Crossing the Immigration and Race Border: A Critical Race Theory Approach to Immigration Studies. *Contemporary Justice Review* 11(1): 23–37.
Russell, Katheryn K. 1998. *The Color of Crime: Racial Hoaxes, White Fear, Black Protectionism, Police Harassment and Other Macroaggressions.* New York, NY: New York University Press.
Russell-Brown, Katheryn. 2004. *Underground Codes: Race, Crime and Related Fires.* New York, NY: New York University Press.
Russell-Brown, Katheryn. 2006. *Protecting Our Own: Race, Crime, and African Americans.* Lanham, MD: Rowman and Littlefield.
Saperstein, Alia and Andrew Penner. 2012. Racial Fluidity and Inequality in the United

States. *American Journal of Sociology* 118(3): 676–727.

Solórzano, Daniel. 1998. Critical Race Theory, Racial and Gender Microaggressions, and the Experiences of Chicana and Chicano Scholars. *International Journal of Qualitative Studies in Education* 11(1): 121–136.

Solórzano, Daniel and Octavio Villalpando. 1998. Critical Race Theory, Marginality, and the Experiences of Students of Color in Higher Education. In *Sociology of Education: Comparative Perspectives*. Edited by C. Torres and T. Mitchell. New York, NY: State University of New York Press.

Solórzano, Daniel and Tara Yosso. 2001. Critical Race and Latcrit Theory and Method: Counter-Storytelling Chicana and Chicano Graduate School Experiences. *International Journal of Qualitative Studies in Education* 14(4): 471–495.

Steinberg, Stephen. 1995. *Turning Back, the Retreat from Racial Justice in American Thought and Policy*. Boston, MA: Beacon.

Treviño, A. Javier, Michelle A. Harris and Derron Wallace. 2008. What's So Critical about Critical Race Theory. *Contemporary Justice Review* 11(1): 7–10.

Winant, Howard. 2007. The Dark Side of the Force: One Hundred Years of the Sociology of Race. In *Sociology in America: A History*. Edited by Craig Calhoun. Chicago, IL: University of Chicago Press.

Wing, Adrien Katherine. 2003. *Critical Race Feminism: A Reader*. New York, NY: New York University Press.

Zumudio, Margaret M., Caskey Russell, Francisco A. Rios, and Jacquelyn L. Bridgeman. 2011. *Critical Race Theory Matters, Education and Ideology*. New York, NY: Routledge.

Part II
PERSPECTIVES ON SOCIAL CLASS

CHAPTER 5

Marxism and Class

Vishwas Satgar and Michelle Williams

Karl Marx (1818 to 1883) is considered one of the great modern thinkers. Marx's ideas about the emancipatory and oppressive dimensions of capitalism have inspired scholars, politicos, and activists across the globe for over 150 years and have led to an entire intellectual tradition known as Marxism. Marxism has simultaneously sought to *understand* and *explain* capitalism and also to *resist* it and *change* the world. In other words, Marxism's contribution derives from two sources: (1) as a set of analytical ideas about the changing dynamics of capitalism, and (2) as an ideology and guide to mass political practice. Marxism's influence is seen in the twentieth century proliferation of Marxist movements, groups, and states, covering vast areas of the world.

Marx's ideas also profoundly influenced modern social theory, especially in sociology, where he pioneered social enquiry about the nature of capitalist modernity. Today, Marx is included with Emile Durkheim and Max Weber in the classical canon of sociological theory. Marxism's influence is in part because it "continues to offer the most comprehensive critique of capitalism as well as a compelling guide to feasible alternatives" and its regeneration "depends on the incorporation of sociological ideas" (Burawoy 2003: 193, 196). His influence extends beyond sociology, however, as his ideas have inspired research across the social sciences, including politics, economics, philosophy, anthropology, and international relations as well as in the natural and hard sciences (e.g., geography, information technology) and humanities (e.g., the arts, literary studies, and education). In short, the intellectual and political influence of Marx and Marxism is immense and covers a vast range of issues, perspectives, and intellectual currents.

In order to bring some coherence to this vastness, we have chosen to focus on one of the most central themes within Marxism: class. We begin by setting out Marx's conception of class and its fragmentary legacy. We then map the different approaches in class analysis as it relates to class as a social relation, as structure, and as a formation process. In the second half of the chapter, we look at approaches to class from a contemporary neo-Marxist perspective – an

41

approach that adapts Marxist ideas to the contemporary world. We focus there on how Marxist social theory has grappled with various dimensions of contemporary capitalism and the extent to which class (re)articulates with race, gender, space, ecology, and global capitalism in the reconstruction and elaboration of historical materialism.

Marx and Class

To understand Marx, we must situate him within his historical context, as it had profound influence on his thought. This setting included the transition from feudalism to capitalism, the vicissitudes of nineteenth-century Victorian capitalism, Marx's disengagement from German philosophy, and his own political involvements (e.g., the League of Communists, revolution in Germany, reflections on the national question, the First International (1864–1876), and the first wave of workers parties such as the French and German Social Democratic Parties). Marx's major theoretical works include his method of social enquiry known as "historical materialism" (i.e., a historicized understanding of the successive modes of production and material determinants of historical change), the critique of classical political economy, a theory of capitalism (including alienation, fetishism of commodities, labor theory of value, surplus value, accumulation, and crisis), and his extensive political writings (including revolutionary struggles in France and the Paris Commune of 1871).[1]

Marx recognized that class was a key feature of capitalist society and a crucial category to explain the nature of capitalism, but he failed to fully develop these ideas. In particular, four conceptual issues relating to class require elaboration. First, Marx only gave superficial attention to the development of classes in pre-capitalist societies, a task taken up subsequently by Marxists (e.g., Wood 1998; Brenner 2003; De Ste. Croix 1981). Second, Marx recognized that class has both an objective and subjective element: objective conditions enabled class divisions in a capitalist society, but classes had to develop a conscious awareness of such divisions and their own class interests. Marx famously put this as developing from a "class-in-itself" to a "class-for-itself." While Marx recognized that class location was not a sufficient condition for classes to automatically emerge, he did not spell out the various determinants of this shift.

Third, Marx saw class as relational, referring to the relationship between capital and labor at the means of production. In short, capital owns the means of production and exploits labor, while labor sells its labor power to capital. In the *Communist Manifesto* Marx describes a two-class model at work within mid-nineteenth-century capitalism. Within this framework, all other classes would eventually end up in one of the two classes. Fierce competition would eventually drive the petty bourgeoisie into the ranks of the working class. While this two-class model captures the major classes of nineteenth-century capitalism, it is inadequate to map the complex class patterns in twentieth and twenty-first-century capitalist society. Finally, in *Capital* Marx theorizes a more structurally determined approach to the three great classes – workers, capitalists, and land owners – and how they relate to the allocation of surplus. He does not, however, theorize what constitutes the "three great classes" and only makes a brief reference to them at the end of Volume 3 of *Capital*.

Thus, while class is a key concept in many of Marx's ideas, it is inadequately developed and under-theorized throughout his work.

---

[1] Historical materialism is a complex and multifaceted concept. Marx's conception of historical materialism is set out in the preface to *A Contribution to the Critique of Political Economy* (1981[1859]), *The German Ideology* (1998[1845]), *Economic and Philosophical Manuscripts of 1844* (1981) and the *Theses on Feurbach* (1998). His critique of classical political economy and capitalism as well as his theory of capitalism is set out in the three volumes of *Capital* (1991). His critique of capitalism and his theory of capitalism also embraces his earlier work particularly through the link to historical materialism. For further readings see Cohen (2000), Callinicos (2004), and Harvey (2007[1982]).

He does, however, provide the basis for systematic theorizing around the concept of class for later generations.

Class After Marx

Class as Social Relation

Building on Marx's idea of class as a social relation, subsequent theorists have developed two crucial approaches. First, the distribution of ownership of productive assets is the basis of class (Corrigan et al. 1978). Property rights (vested in the means of production) delineate class as it provides a boundary between owners and non-owners. Various Marxist parties and movements have used this conception of class to address stratification in their societies and to juxtapose public ownership with private ownership of productive assets.

Second, and more recently, Marxist theorists have developed a surplus labor understanding of class, which argues that the central conflicts of society can be understood through the way in which surplus labor is organized and institutionalized (Resnick and Wolff 2008; Ruccio 2011). Scholars in this tradition argue that Marx recognized that labor is organized to produce not only what it needs, but also to produce surplus labor. The production, appropriation, and distribution of surplus labor is central to all capitalist societies and constitutes classes. In other words, class is defined by who produces, appropriates, and distributes surplus labor. Thus, to transform the class structure of society, a conception of class and a politics centered on transforming surplus labor has to drive change.

While some Marxists focus on class as a social relation, others emphasize the structural aspects of class. We now turn to a structural Marxist analysis of class.

Class Structure

For Marxists, class structure refers to the ensemble of property relations that make up the means of production as well as the relationship of social forces to these property relations. In the 1960s and 1970s, Marxists critically challenged functionalist sociology and its conception of social integration (Therborn 1983: 162–165) by introducing a crucial role for class structure and class conflict. Poulantzas's (1975) path-breaking work rejected Marx's notion of "class-in-itself" and "class-for-itself" as a Hegelian residue in Marx and instead focused on class structure to understand the complex class patterns of advanced capitalist societies. In addition, Poulantzas theorized the emergence of new middle-class strata and the place of American capital within the European political economy.

Erik Olin Wright (1978) and Harry Braverman (1998[1974]) took this line of inquiry further in American sociology. Wright produced a novel way of operationalizing class through cross-national surveys, mapping class structures, and providing an original approach to middle-class structures. From his perspective, the middle class occupies a "contradictory class location" such that the middle class simultaneously takes on characteristics of both the worker and capitalist (Wright 1978). Wright's analysis has engendered further studies on the characteristics of class structures as well as empirical studies testing the concepts of class in various locations across the world.

Another line of enquiry on class structure looks at the labor process, which refers to the way in which production is organized through a division of labor and the extraction of surplus labor. Harry Braverman's classic book on the American working class, *Labour and Monopoly Capital* (1998[1974]), provides an original study of the labor process but does not connect it to class formation. Rather Braverman interrogates aspects of class structure that relate to the labor process and shows how labor is actually deskilled in its experience of Fordist assembly production.

Class Formation

While class as a social relation and as a structure are vital to understanding the existence, characteristics, and features of class in capitalist society, they do not automatically help us understand class interests or class politics and hence class formation. To understand class formation, we must bring relational, structural, and process aspects of class into articulation with each other and with the political and ideological determinants of class.

By looking at class formation, we also enter the terrain of class struggle. This more historical understanding of class formation and the role of consciousness challenges the Poulantzian structural analysis of class formation by introducing political and ideological determinants. In this regard, E. P. Thompson's seminal *The Making of the English Working Class* (1966) stands out as it highlights class formation as a historically constituted process. Thompson brings culture and politics to the fore in the making of class and class consciousness. Thompson's work inspired a whole generation of social historians focusing on historically contingent processes of class formation (e.g., Kaye 1995[1984]; Kaye and McClelland 1990).

Michael Burawoy moves to a focus on labor and economic, political, and ideological determinants of class formation in his seminal works including *Manufacturing Consent* (1982) and *Politics of Production* (1985). Building on rich ethnographic fieldwork, Burawoy shows how the labor process is shaped through orchestrating consent for the rule of capital by providing workers with greater self-organization. More recent social historians and sociologists of class have broadened their gaze from working-class formation to look at capitalist class formation,[2] drawing interconnections between corporate finance and political systems as well as interlocking relations of corporate boards of directors and the socialization entailed in business communities.[3]

In the latter half of the twentieth century, a number of themes emerged challenging Marxism to look beyond its exclusive focus on class in order to address issues of race, gender, spatiality, and the global nature of capitalism. In the remaining part of the chapter, we look at the ways in which Marxism has engaged these different themes.

New Directions for Marxism

Race and Class

Marxism has not developed an adequate approach to race. Marxism's failure to address issues of race stems from the fact that early Marxists tended to view race as a social construction and a reflection of false consciousness. Because race is not integral to or situated within the social relations of production, it was deemed an epiphenomenon of the class system. In other words, race and racial oppression is not an essential structural contradiction within capitalism. The issue of race repeatedly arose throughout the twentieth century, however, in such contexts as the demise of the British Empire, the Russian revolution, decolonization, and the struggle against apartheid.

As Marxists began to take up the issue of race, they tended to focus on the relationship between race and class, often reducing race to class and racism to its functionality within capitalist accumulation. Marxists have argued that racism divides the working class and needs to be challenged through a politics of solidarity among the working class. Marxism sees the universality in working-*class* identity trumping the particularity of racism.

More sophisticated theoretical analyses examined the intersection between race and class by highlighting historical contingency as well as articulations between pre-capitalist and capitalist modes of production (Wolpe 1980 and 1988). In South Africa, the articulation between race and class took on a particular urgency with the apartheid state's systemic race-based political oppression that converged with capitalist exploitation. However, despite the end of apartheid, patterns of racial oppression have

---

[2] Some scholarship in social history reduces class to a social identity, undermining its capacity as a structuring principle.
[3] See Chibber (2009[2005]).

continued in contemporary South Africa through a capitalism that has both eroded and reproduced forms of racial oppression. To understand the continuation of racial oppression there and in many other places of the world within global capitalism requires a new Marxist analysis, which has thus far not emerged.

Feminism and Class

In the 1960s and 1970s, Western feminists creatively engaged Marxism to forge a productive theoretical body of work most commonly known as Marxist feminism. Today, however, much of feminism has converged with neoliberalism in reducing the women's question to representational issues in politics rather than the more systemic policy mechanisms to socialize social reproduction. The quieting of Marxist feminism occurred at the same time as trade unions lost ground and were systematically weakened by neoliberal forces in the 1980s and 1990s. However, with the rise of new transnational activists and left movements mobilizing against neoliberalization, a revisiting of Marxist feminism has begun. The renewal of Marxist feminism is both an ideological project and a political movement that seeks to achieve four important outcomes.

First, contemporary Marxist feminists are revisiting the history of feminism to ensure Marxist feminism is not distorted and misread in present anti-feminist conditions. In this regard, the engagement between Meg Luxton and Nancy Fraser is informative. Luxton (2014: 141) argues that Fraser conflates various currents of feminism when looking at the 1960s and 1970s and thus fails to appreciate the nuances and diversity of feminism's history. In particular, Luxton argues that Marxist feminism is left out of the narratives of the past including the mobilizing of working-class women, women of color, and indigenous women. In this narrative, we are left with a second wave Western feminism equal to liberal feminism. Thus, contemporary Marxist feminists focus on getting this history right by dispelling the caricatures and distortions in the liberal narrative and paying particular attention to language and contextual variation.

Second, contemporary Marxist feminists highlight the limits of classical Marxist understandings of gender and seek to update them. While Marx did not explicitly work on feminism, in *Capital* (1991) he recognized that capitalists and workers and ultimately social life had to be reproduced. This insight, together with Engels's work on the *Origin of the Family, Private Property and the State* (1972) – which revealed how family relations between men and women coincided with different labor relations and modes of production – provided the basics for Marxist feminism.

In the latter half of the twentieth century, three important conceptual approaches among Marxist feminists came to the fore:[4] (1) The dual systems theory elaborates the production/reproduction formulation by treating both these realms as equal and important (i.e., economic production coexists with a gendered division of labor). Here, patriarchy is seen either as a transhistorical and unchanging "patriarchal mode of production" or as an ideological structure coexisting with the capitalist mode of production. (2) The "expanded mode of production" views the reproduction of the working class and life as inherent to the capitalist mode of production as opposed to the duality of the dual systems theory. In other words, childbirth, child care, and care of elderly and sick (i.e., women take on the care responsibilities in the household) are integral to any mode of production. Class and gender cannot be separated; the daily and intergenerational propagation of the species is tied in with the mode of production. (3) Domestic labor is unpaid labor outside the market in the realm of the household. While largely unrecognized, it functions to support paid labor and is, therefore, central to the capitalist mode of production.

Third, the Marxist feminist concept of social reproduction draws attention to

---

[4] See Cock and Luxton (2013) for a nuanced overview.

how neoliberal capitalism undermines social reproduction, and explores ways to advance class struggles against transnational neoliberal restructuring. According to Bakker and Gill (2003), neoliberal restructuring is inducing a crisis of social reproduction through the increased precarious conditions created by flexible, casual labor. Moreover, they argue that as neoliberalism remakes the state to meet the needs of the market, social reproduction is undermined at the level of the conditions of species reproduction related to child birth and rearing; the reproduction of the labor force through household and education institutions; and finally the provisioning of social infrastructure to provide for care and the social needs of citizens.

Fourth, Marxist feminist scholars reaffirm the need for a Marxist feminism within contemporary struggles. They note the need for such a perspective in order to ensure that the liberation of women is linked to the liberation of everyone, to deepen democracy through the politics of solidarity, to connect politics to how we live our daily lives, to emphasize caregiving in anti-capitalist struggles, and to ensure that we keep working toward utopian alternatives for society (Luxton 2014: 149).

Spatiality and Class

Some early Marxists addressed spatial issues in creative ways. For example, Lenin (1977) developed his notion of space through the concept of the "law of uneven development" to characterize the development of capitalism in Russia and to understand imperialism. Similarly, Trotsky's notion of "combined and uneven development" evokes the spatial dimension in characterizing the dynamics of capitalism, the level of class struggle and strategy (Dunn and Radice 2006). For Gramsci, space is integral to his historical materialism, especially in relation to the "Southern question" (Ekers et al. 2013).

Since the 1970s, the fertile intersection of geography and Marxist theory has brought spatial issues to the fore. Henri Lefebvre (2009) played a pioneering role in recognizing how capital produces space and uses it to survive crisis. In his work, Lefebvre argues that space is political. He grappled with the vicissitudes of Fordist "regimes of accumulation" and how spatial planning in Europe featured in state strategies to create the conditions for redistribution and accumulation (Brenner and Elden 2009: 33). Through his conceptualization of the "state mode of production" he showed how capitalist spatiality was produced by the state through regulation, production, and reproduction to ensure capitalist accumulation and the making of a capitalist class (Brenner and Elden 2009: 20).

David Harvey systematically brings Marx into dialog with geography. He begins with urban spaces under capitalism and then takes this into a dialog with Marx's *Capital*. His reading of Marx is captured in the monumental *Limits to Capital* (2007 [1982]), in which he elaborates a spatial dimension to historical materialism and invents a historical geographical materialism, which he further elaborates in *The Condition of Postmodernity* (1990). Harvey develops various themes that help us understand class and historical geographical materialism, including "space-time compression," new forms of flexible capital accumulation, uneven geographical development of capitalism, and spatio-temporal fixes. The latter directly addresses the issue of how capital overcomes crisis and reproduces itself.

In his more recent work, Harvey (2003) elaborates the notion of "new imperialism" married to the idea of primitive accumulation, which he calls "accumulation through dispossession." Through this concept, Harvey shows that, while Marx thought primitive accumulation was a necessary condition for the development of capitalism (at least since the 1500s until the 1800s) resulting in the separation of the means of production from producers, this process continues to mark contemporary processes of accumulation. He shows how, while the commons are commodified, peasantries dispossessed, and workers live through further precariousness, capital reproduces itself and destroys spaces in order to ensure surplus accumulation. Through historical geographical materialism, our understandings of class and class struggle are recast to understand the importance of spatiality.

Ecology and Class

The contemporary ecological crisis – stemming from human-induced climate change, planetary overshoot of key ecological boundaries, and widespread pollution and environmental destruction – is also a challenge to Marxism. In dominant strands of twentieth-century Marxism, Marx was read as giving license for productivism and the conquest of nature through industrialization, which had disastrous ecological effects. This resulted in powerful ecological critiques of Marxism and the need for Marxists to explain the contemporary ecological crises of capitalism, which has led to ecological readings of Marxism.

There has been a concerted effort to (re)discover nature in Marx's historical materialism as well as to green Marxism more generally. John Bellamy Foster's *Marx's Ecology* (2000) is groundbreaking in rediscovering Marx's concern for nature within his materialism as it related to capitalist agriculture and soil ecology, philosophical naturalism, and evolutionary theory. Bellamy Foster argues that the ecological dimension has been ignored in Marx's work. He shows how Marx was not just concerned with the relational connection between humans but was also deeply concerned about our relationship to nature. Moreover, Michael Burawoy (2013) has extended the idea of commodification of labor power as essential to understanding class to the commodification of nature as a distinctive feature of contemporary third wave marketization.

The movement to green Marxism has also thrown up its own theoretical themes. First, there is the issue of ecological Marxism versus Marxist ecology, which turns on the two following issues:[5] (1) the question of whether Marx was a proto-ecologist and sufficiently brought nature into his materialism in order to break with the Promethean idea of unlimited material growth. Marxist ecologists suggest that Marx had integrated nature into his materialism, while ecological Marxists recognize that there is a dimension of nature in Marx's materialism but also acknowledge that Marx had not sufficiently broken with productivism. (2) The second issue is the marriage of the Marxist critique of capitalism with the ecological critique of productivism. Some Marxists prefer to draw on aspects of Marx's work like the notion of alienation, general and specific labor process, and the rationality of capitalist accumulation to highlight the limits of productivism and to situate society in nature. This enables an understanding of class dynamics and power relations which green politics has not been able to achieve.

The second theme relates to explaining environmental crises. Marxism has developed the idea of the second contradiction (O' Connor 1994; Kovel 2003; Burkett 2009) in capitalism, which sees capitalism as an enemy of nature. Capitalism's incessant need for limitless growth on a planet with finite resources, the pollution from capitalism including carbon emissions in the context of climate change, and its propensity to turn nature into market-based commodities translates into a destructive relationship with nature. For capitalism, nature is something to be exploited (both in resource extraction as well as dumping of waste) and from which profits can be made. Other Marxists focus on the disproportionate consequences on class structures, exploitation, and income inequality, highlighting the class bias of the capitalist-induced environmental crisis (Hughes 2000; Nixon 2011). The class bias can be seen at multiple levels. At the international level, climatologists argue that Africa will be the hardest hit by the anticipated increased temperatures from climate change. At the national level, megadam projects displace millions of poor people, usually rural, throughout the world, often bringing unintended environmental problems in their wake. At the local level,

---

[5] Harribey (2009) provides a useful overview of these divergences.

poor communities lose access to clean water through damming of rivers, privatization of water resources, and the unaffordability of basic services. This tradition of Marxism demonstrates that there is a class character to environmental issues, which is inherent to capitalist accumulation.

The third theme to arise out of the engagement between ecology and Marxism focuses on rethinking class struggle and socialism. By engaging ecological issues, class struggle has taken on various challenges including questioning versions of "green capitalism," rethinking unionism, red-green alliances, systemic alternatives, the just transition, and a post-productivist socialism, namely eco-socialism.

Global Political Economy and Transnational Class Formation

With the remaking of capitalism over the past few decades, national accumulation processes, state forms, class structures, and global economic relations have been remade. A national and internationalized capitalist economy has given way to a globalized economy. In response, Marxist political economy has also been globalized (Cox 1995).

The rise of a Marxist approach to global political economy locates class formation in the context of neoliberalized global restructuring, the internationalizing of the state, the emergence of a new imperialism and the contemporary nature of capitalist crisis. The adjustment of the global political economy to the requirements of transnational capital accumulation has serious implications for class formation and class theory. It poses critical questions (Carroll 2013): Does transnationalization produce a transnational capitalist class? How is such a class transformed from a class-in-itself to a class-for-itself? Does such a class displace national capitalist classes? How widespread is the emergence of the transnational capitalist class?

Within Marxist global political economy with its premise of globalized production, financial, and trade structures, there have been three moments of development of transnational class analysis. The first harks back to Poulantzas's (1979) work on the penetration of US multinationals into Europe. The second moment locates transnational class theory within global political economy. For instance, Van der Pijl (1984 and 1998) emphasizes how fractions of capital exist as abstract forms of money capital and productive capital, but are also expressed in more concrete forms such as merchant houses, financial firms, and industry. Van der Pijl (1984) demonstrates this empirically in his study on the formation of an Atlantic ruling class and how capital fractions formed and linked in particular circuits of accumulation. These fractions contest and constitute a ruling historical bloc through hegemonic concepts of control. The bargaining and negotiation around these concepts of control determine the direction of the historical bloc in terms of accumulation models, state forms, state-civil society relations, and international relations.

The third moment in the development of transnational class analysis is network analysis's empirical demonstration of how the transnational class structure exists and operates. By looking at the interlocks of corporate directorships, shared ownership, and financialization relationships, a transnational capitalist class structure has been mapped to show particular corporate power relations. William Carroll's (2013) work on power structure analysis on a global scale compares transnational interlocking over time (1976–1996), examines the world's 500 leading corporations and their interlocking directorates (between 1997 and 2007), and describes elite corporate-policy networks and financial-industrial intercorporate ownership relations.[6]

Conclusion

Marxism has gone through many variations and addresses a wide range of issues. Indeed, it might be more appropriate to refer to this

---

[6] See Carroll (2010) for an in-depth study.

vast tradition as "Marxisms." A large part of its durability and adaptability has to do with its variation and constant evolution. If read simply as sacred scriptures, Marx's writings would have died an ignominious death long ago. It is the continual renewal and rethinking of Marxisms that has led to its enduring relevance as a social theory, a means of understanding class issues, and an inspiration for social change.

References

Bakker, Isabella and Stephen Gill. eds. 2003. *Power, Production and Social Reproduction*. Hampshire and New York, NY: Palgrave Macmillan.

Bellamy Foster, John. 2000. *Marx's Ecology: Materialism and Nature*. New York, NY: Monthly Review Press.

Braverman, Harry. 1998[1974]. *Labour and Monopoly Capital: The degradation of work in the Twentieth Century*. London and New York, NY: Monthly Review Press.

Brenner, Neil and Stuart Elden. 2009. Introduction. In *State, Space, World: Selected Essays* by Henri LeFebvre. Minneapolis, MN, and London: University of Minnesota Press.

Brenner, Robert. 2003. *Merchants and Revolution: Commercial Change, Political Conflict, and London's Overseas Traders, 1550–1653*. London and New York, NY: Verso.

Burawoy, Michael. 1982. *Manufacturing Consent: Changes in the Labor Process under Monopoly Capitalism*. Chicago, IL: University of Chicago Press.

Burawoy, Michael. 1985. *The Politics of Production: Factory Regimes under Capitalism and Socialism*. London: Verso.

Burawoy, Michael. 2003. For a Sociological Marxism: The Complementary Convergence of Antonio Gramsci and Karl Polanyi. *Politics and Society* 31(2): 193–261.

Burawoy, Michael. 2013. Marxism after Polanyi. In *Marxisms in the Twenty First Century: Crisis, Critique and Struggle*. Edited by Michelle Williams and Vishwas Satgar. Johannesburg: Wits University Press, 34–52.

Burkett, Paul. 2009. *Marxism and Ecological Economics: Toward a Red and Green Political Economy*. Chicago, IL: Haymarket Books.

Callinicos, Alex. 2004. *Making History: Agency, Structure, and Change in Social Theory*. 2nd edn. Leiden and Boston, MA: Brill.

Carroll, William. 2010. *The Making of a Transnational Capitalist Class: Corporate Power in the Twenty-First Century*. London and New York, NY: Zed Books.

Carroll, William. 2013. Whither the Transnational Capitalist Class?. In *Socialist Register: Registering Class*. Edited by Leo Panitch, Greg Albo, and Vivek Chibber. London: The Merlin Press Ltd.

Chibber, Vivek. 2009[2005]. Developments in Marxist Class Analysis. In *Critical Companion to Contemporary Marxism*. Edited by Jacques Bidet and Stathis Kouvelakis. Chicago, IL: Haymarket Books.

Cock, Jacklyn and Meg Luxton. 2013. Marxism and Feminism: "Unhappy Marriage" or Creative Partnership?. In *Marxisms in the Twenty First Century: Crisis, Critique and Struggle*. Edited by Michelle Williams and Vishwas Satgar. Johannesburg: Wits University Press, 116–142.

Cohen, G. A. 2000. *Karl Marx's Theory of History*. Princeton, NJ: Princeton University Press.

Corrigan, Philip, Harvie Ramsay, and Derek Sayer. 1978. *Socialist Construction and Marxist Theory: Bolshevism and its Critique*. New York, NY, and London: Monthly Review Press.

Cox, Robert. 1995. Critical Political Economy. In *International Political Economy: Understanding Global Disorder*. Edited by Bjorn Hettne. London and New Jersey: Zed books.

Croix, G. E. M. De Ste. 1981. *The Class Struggle in the Ancient Greek World: From the Archaic Age to the Arab Conquests*. Ithaca, NY: Cornell University Press.

Dunn, Bill and Hugo Radice. 2006. *100 Years of Permanent Revolution: Results and Prospects*. London and Ann Arbor, MI: Pluto Press.

Ekers, Michael, Gillian Hart, Stefan Kipfer and Alex Loftus. eds. 2013. *Gramsci: Space, Nature, Politics*. Sussex: Wiley-Blackwell.

Engels, Friedrich. 1972. *The Origin of the Family, Private Property and the State*. New York, NY: International Publisher.

Harribey, Jean-Marie. 2009. Ecological Marxism or Marxian Political ecology?. In *Critical Companion to Contemporary Marxism*. Edited by Jacques Bidet and Stathis Kouvelakis. Chicago, IL: Haymarket Books.

Harvey, David. 1990. *The Condition of Postmodernity*. Malden, MA: Wiley and Blackwell.

Harvey, David. 2003. *The New Imperialism: Accumulation by Dispossession*. New York, NY: Oxford University Press.

Harvey, David. 2007[1982].*The Limits to Capital*. London: Verso.

Hughes, Jonathan. 2000. *Ecology and Historical Materialism*. Cambridge: Cambridge University Press.

Kaye, Harvey J. 1995[1984]. *The British Marxist Historians*. New York, NY: St. Martin's Press.

Kaye, Harvey J. and Keith McClelland. 1990. *E. P. Thompson Critical Perspectives*. Philadelphia, PA: Temple University Press.

Kovel, Joel. 2003[2002]. *The Enemy of Nature: the End of Capitalism or the End of the World?*. New Delhi: Tulika Books.

Lefebvre, Henri. 2009. *State, Space, World: Selected Essays*. Minneapolis, MN, and London: University of Minnesota press.

Lenin, V. I. 1977. *The Development of Capitalism in Russia*. Moscow: Progress Publishing.

Luxton, Meg. 2014. Marxist Feminism and Anticapitalism: Reclaiming Our History, Reanimating Our Politics. *Studies in Political Economy* 94: 137–160.

Marx, K. 1981. *Economic and Philosophic Manuscripts of 1844*. Moscow: Progress Publishers.

Marx, K. 1981[1859]. *A Contribution to the Critique of Political Economy*. Moscow: Progress Publishers.

Marx, K. 1991. *Capital*. Vol. 3. London: Penguin Classics.

Marx, K. 1998. *Theses on Feuerbach*. Amherst, NY: Prometheus Books.

Marx, Karl and Friedrich Engels. 1998[1845]. *The German Ideology*. Amherst, NY: Prometheus Books.

Marx, Karl and Friedrich Engels. 2002[1848]. *The Communist Manifesto*. London: Penguin Books.

Nixon, Robert. 2011. *Slow Violence and Environmentalism of the Poor*. Cambridge, MA: Harvard University Press.

O'Connor, Martin. 1994. Introduction: Liberate, Accumulate – and Bust?. In *Is Capitalism Sustainable: Political Economy and the Politics of Ecology*. Edited by Martin O'Connor. New York, NY, and London: The Guilford Press.

Poulantzas, Nicos. 1975. *Classes in Contemporary Capitalism*. New York, NY: New Left Books.

Poulantzas, Nicos. 1979. *Classes in Contemporary Capitalism*. London: Verso.

Resnick, Stephen A. and Richard D. Wolff. eds. 2008[2006]. *New Departures in Marxian Theory*. London and New York, NY: Routledge.

Ruccio, David F. 2011. *Development and Globalization: A Marxian Class Analysis*. New York, NY: Routledge.

Therborn, Goran. 1983. Problems of Class Analysis. In *Marx 100 Years On*. Edited by Betty Matthews. London: Lawrence and Wishart Ltd.

Thompson, E. P. 1966. *The Making of the English Working Class*. 1st edn. New York, NY: Vintage Books.

Van der Pijl, Kees. 1984. *The Making of an Atlantic Ruling Class*. London and New York, NY: Verso.

Van der Pijl, Kees. 1998. *Transnational Classes and International Relations*. New York, NY: Routledge.

Wolpe, Harold. 1980. *The Articulation of Modes of Production*. London: Routledge and Kegan Paul.

Wolpe, Harold. 1988. *Race, Class, and the Apartheid State*. London, Addis Ababa, and Paris: James Curry, OAU Inter-Africa Cultural Fund, and UNESCO Press.

Wood, Ellen Meiksins. 1998. The Agrarian Origins of Capitalism. *Monthly Review* 50(3). Available at http://monthlyreview.org/1998/07/01/the-agrarian-origins-of-capitalism/, accessed December 20, 2016.

Wright, Erik Olin. 1978. *Class, Crisis, and the State*. London and New York, NY: Verso.

CHAPTER 6
Pluralism

Richard A. Zdan

The origins of the democratic system of government in the United States of America can be traced all the way back to the city-state of Athens in the sixth century BCE. Ancient Athens saw itself as "a community in which all citizens could and indeed should participate in the creation and nurturing of a common life [and] citizens faced no obstacles to involvement in public affairs based on rank or wealth" (Held 1996: 17). All citizens of Athens – defined in a somewhat limited fashion as native-born, free, adult men who had served in the military – were voting members of a legislative assembly called the Ekklesia. The Ekklesia had responsibilities similar to those of the United States Congress, including passing laws, nominating and appointing state officials, and declaring war. There is, however, one important way in which the Ekklesia differed from the United States Congress; the Ekklesia was made up of *all* Athenian citizens.

Think about how difficult it has been in recent years for the United States Congress to come to an agreement about how to resolve the various issues with which it has been confronted. Now, imagine if every citizen of the United States who was eligible to vote was also a member of Congress. Based on the most recent United States census, that would be a legislative assembly with over 200 million members. If we limit the size of our fictive legislature to only registered voters instead of eligible voters, it would still have over 140 million members. Imagine the difficulty of accomplishing the day-to-day business of the government when 140 million people all have a right to speak up on every issue and propose changes and amendments before a vote is taken. The United States government would grind to a halt. Putting into practice this classical Athenian system of democracy, known today as *direct democracy*, where the assembled citizens directly controlled the entire political process and were actively responsible for making all the decisions of the state, would obviously be very difficult, if not impossible, in the modern world.

Consequently, most modern democratic states instead utilize a system where the sovereign power of the state remains in the hands of its citizens, but decision and policy-making authority is vested in the hands of a group of elected representatives. In this type of *representative democracy*, the citizens do not actively vote on every single issue the government must address but instead vote to elect a group of representatives who then make decisions on behalf of the voters who elected them. These representatives must periodically stand for re-election, which insures that they act in a manner consistent with the wishes of their constituents. Representatives who cannot secure the votes of a majority (or, at minimum, a plurality) of their constituent voters are replaced with a different representative who the voters think will better represent their interests. A representative who wishes to remain in office must, therefore, as United States Supreme Court Chief Justice John Roberts writes, "be cognizant of and responsive to [the] concerns" of their constituents. But, how do representatives decide what to do when some of the concerns of their constituents are mutually exclusive?

Let us consider the example of a representative who must vote "Yes" or "No" on a bill that will raise taxes in order to fund increased spending on public works programs. The local Chamber of Commerce sends the representative a letter stating that their members oppose the tax increase. However, if the representative votes "No" and supports a policy favored by one group of constituents who want lower taxes, it means that there will be less revenue and, consequently, less money available to spend on the program to maintain and repair local bridges and highways that is favored by a different group of his constituents. To encourage the representative to increase funding for the public works program, the "Fix the Roads" interest group circulates a petition to allow local citizens to go on the record about how dissatisfied they are with the state of the roads. Simultaneously, the "Lower the Taxes" interest group begins running advertisements on local television and radio stations to educate the citizens about the perceived benefits that lower taxes would create. Soon, the representative's office is flooded with letters, calls and emails, some of them demanding that the representative vote "Yes," while others demand that the representative vote "No."

One of the ways in which political sociologists seek to understand how representatives attempt to balance the competing demands presented in this example is through a theoretical perspective called *pluralism*. Pluralism sees the political system as a struggle between competing interest groups for power and control of the decision-making process where no single group is in control all the time. Arthur F. Bentley, one of the original exponents of the pluralist perspective, claimed that examining the activities of interest groups was the only valid way to study the political process, remarking:

> *Always and everywhere our study must be a study of the interests that work through government; otherwise we have not got down to the facts. Nor will it suffice to take a single interest group and base our interpretation upon it, not even for a special time and place. No interest group has meaning except with reference to other interest groups... (Bentley 1949[1908]: 271).*

In the pluralist perspective, the government itself, also known as the *state*, has no preference on any particular issue or policy, but instead exists as a kind of neutral forum where the preferences of different interest groups and individual citizens can be gathered and evaluated in an effort to provide the public with the sorts of policies and services that are most broadly desired. Individual representatives, on other hand, may have their own personal policy preferences on any number of issues or policies before them and may have their own ideas about what is 'best' for the public. Nonetheless, the numerous structural constraints on their ability to advance their preferences – ranging from the need to stand for re-election, to the threat of being removed from office, to being subjected to withering criticism in the Press – effectively reduce them to just one more voice in the chorus expressing a preference on any particular issue.

While it might seem that this diffusion of power among powerful competing interests would lead to division and instability, pluralists believe that the inverse is true. They argue that, by preventing any one group or branch of government from consolidating too much power over too long a period of time, a democratic state becomes, in fact, more stable because it is less likely to descend into tyranny. Robert A. Dahl, one of the foremost pluralist theorists, explained this idea with a simple syllogism: "Tyranny means the accumulation of all powers, etc. Tyranny is undesirable. Therefore, the accumulation of all powers, etc., is undesirable" (1956: 12).

Pluralism vs. Elite Theory

In many ways, the pluralist perspective stands in opposition to the *elite theory* perspective for understanding the political process. The elite theory perspective, as articulated by C. Wright Mills, postulates that power is not diffused throughout society, but rather consolidated in the hands of a small group of people, referred to by Mills as the *power elite*, who "can look down upon, so to speak, and by their decisions mightily affect, the everyday worlds of men and women" (1956: 3). Whereas the decisions made by most people – even personally important decisions such as who to marry, what to study in school or what career to pursue – do not have much impact beyond their own personal lives, the power elite "are in positions to make decisions having major consequences" and, in many cases, "their failure to make decisions, is itself an act that is often of greater consequence than the decisions they do make" (1956: 4). In contradistinction to the pluralist focus on the overall stability of the democratic state, the only stability that concerns the power elite is "for some sort of organization for enduring and stable prestige" (1956: 91).

Privileging Observed Outcomes over Categorical Assumptions about Power

Nelson Polsby (*Community Power and Political Theory*, 1963) identified four key features of the pluralist perspective that distinguish it from the elite theory perspective articulated by Mills and others. First, and perhaps most fundamentally, pluralists directly reject the fundamental assumption held by elite theorists that one particular group dominates the decision-making process in all states and communities. As a consequence, the first question a pluralist researcher asks upon starting to examine a state or community "is likely to not be 'Who runs this community?' but rather 'Does anyone at all run this community?'" (1963: 113). Since pluralists believe that power cannot be taken for granted, they must instead empirically "study specific outcomes in order to determine who actually prevails in community decision-making" (1963: 113). Most often, this entails simply observing who took which side on a series of issues and taking note of the ultimate winners and losers.

This empirical focus pervades every aspect of the pluralist perspective. Bentley stated that "[t]he way to find out how a thing works is to take it to pieces and examine the parts" (1949[1908]: 254) and, with regards to the political process, he argued that "[i]f we can get our social life stated in terms of activity, and of nothing else, we have not indeed succeeded in measuring it, but we have at least reached a foundation upon which a coherent system of measurements can be built up" (1949[1908]: 202). By abandoning preconceived assumptions, utilizing this process of disassembling a system to see how the pieces fit together to systematically examining a wide range of issues important to communities of interest, and looking for any patterns that emerge, pluralists are able to determine not only who, if anyone, is able to exercise power, but to also gain some insight into the scope and limits of that power.

The passage of time has only reinforced the importance of empiricism in evaluating political processes. For example, the very concept of "democracy" has become nearly ubiquitous in the modern world. Dahl observes that "[most] regimes stake out some sort of claim to the title of 'democracy'; and those that do not often insist that their particular instance of non-democratic rule is a necessary stage along the road to ultimate 'democracy'" (1989: 2). With democracy, however, just like anything else, "a term that means anything means nothing" (1989: 2). Since the multiplicity of self-styled democracies "vary enormously in the extent to which their governments meet the criteria of the democratic process" (1989: 233), empirical focused observations provide a mechanism for pluralist researchers to determine which are truly democratic in practice.

Transitory Power Structures

A second feature of pluralism that distinguishes it from the elite theory perspective is that, when a particular individual or group demonstrates the ability to exercise power, that power is neither permanent nor all-encompassing. In contrast to a more or less permanent dominant class composed of "the possessors of power and wealth and celebrity;...people of superior character and energy" (Mills 1956: 13), the pluralist conception of power, according to Polsby, is "tied to issues, and issues can be fleeting or persistent, provoking coalitions among interested groups ranging in their duration from momentary to semi-permanent" (1963: 113). The group that holds power over a particular issue at any particular point in time is the group that is best able to build and mobilize an effective coalition to achieve a policy victory over the other side.

There are, at any time, many issues about which a particular individual may be concerned and a range in the degree to which any individual may be committed to a particular issue. Consequently, membership in political coalitions is necessarily fluid. There are costs to every political action a person takes. These can range from making political enemies at one extreme, to the opportunity costs associated with investing time, money, and effort in the political effort at the other. Because of this, individuals will only participate in the political process when there is an issue that concerns them being discussed at a depth where the differences between potential outcomes are significant to them.

For example, it can be assumed that the majority of citizens favor having a safe and secure community and would, consequently, be willing to join a coalition supporting policies intended to enhance the security of their community. However, they would only be willing to do so if they perceived that impact of the policy was worth the cost of achieving it. Hiring a few additional police officers might increase security, but perhaps might not be seen as having a big enough impact to be worth the cost of taking action. Advocating a program to make necessary infrastructure safer from terrorists, however, might be viewed as worth the cost. Conversely, very few people are so concerned about security that they would be willing to join a coalition supporting policies intended to create an Orwellian police state. The difference between these policy preferences is not related to the issue – security – but rather to the depth of commitment any particular individual has to that issue. Some people are only committed to the issue of security to the extent that it does not impact their personal freedoms while others are sufficiently committed to be willing to sacrifice many of their freedoms to achieve it; any number of additional levels of commitment exist between these two extremes.

In this way, depth of commitment directly impacts the size of the coalition that can be mobilized around any particular issue at any particular point in time. The provisional nature of these coalitions also serves to contribute to maintaining the stability of a democratic society. The more extreme a policy position, the more difficult it is to mobilize a coalition to support it that is larger, and thus more influential, than the coalition mobilized in opposition.

Pluralists contend that there are several aspects of the democratic system that prevent these protean coalitions from calcifying into more enduring structures. First is the fact that, while pluralists acknowledge that social inequalities do exist, they argue that they tend to be dispersed rather than cumulative; if an individual has control of a particular resource (specialized knowledge and expertise, as an example) they tend not to have control over other resources (such as dissemination of information through the media). This dispersal of inequality throughout the society does not prevent the rise of a power elite, but nonetheless provides internal checks on the ability of any one individual or group to consolidate power. Second, pluralists argue that, while individual resources may be unequally distributed, one resource is not more intrinsically valuable than any other. A group that controls a disproportionately large amount of economic resources can always be checked by a second group with minimal economic resources, but a vast reserve of skilled and dedicated members willing to invest time and effort, or by a third group with control over the dissemination of information. Third and finally, even groups without control of any resources of significance, can combine their efforts into an aggregate that is sufficiently formidable to challenge more resource advantaged groups (Rose 1967: 286).

It is worth reiterating that, while this system of internal checks does not necessarily provide a path for resource-disadvantaged groups to seize power in a community, it does establish a sufficiently stable mechanism for the advancement of symmetrical challenges to power consolidation. Just because there are interest groups that have effectively consolidated power around some particular issue in some community, the existence of an overarching dominant class cannot be assumed.

Supremacy of Interest Groups over Social Classes

The role of these transitory, voluntary coalitions in the political process leads to the third distinguishing feature of pluralism. Pluralists believe that it is not social class, but rather "the 'interest groups' and the 'public' [that] are the social collectives most relevant to the analysis of political processes" (Polsby 1963: 117). In lieu of shared class interests driven by conscious awareness of a shared social position, pluralists argue that individual political action is instead motivated by affiliation with any number of the hundreds of small, self-selected interest groups with over-lapping memberships. By looking at the overlaps in membership among interest groups and the specific leadership roles that exist in individual groups, pluralists can even go so far as to analyze empirically the precise contours of any power structure that is found to exist. If, for example, there is significant overlap between the people who occupy decision-making positions in different groups interested in related issues, that information provides insight into exactly who holds power in a particular coalition and how the coalition is assembled and maintained.

Pluralists do not dispute the existence of social class; however, they see it as generally inefficient and unnecessary for accomplishing political mobilization. When the political process is broken down to the level of individual issues, not all members of a particular social class will necessarily have the same interests. Even if we assume that entire social classes can be mobilized in support of a particular issue, they are likely to have only a low level of commitment to a favored policy position, whereas the smaller, more intense minorities that comprise special-interest groups are much easier to mobilize and have a higher degree of commitment to the issues that they favor.

Moreover, pluralists argue that shared class interests are often superseded by shared group interests due to the fact that group memberships not only overlap but generally cut across class lines. Regardless of the issue embraced by a particular interest group – capital punishment, gay rights, gun control – it is unreasonable to assume that policy preferences about that issue break down exactly along class lines. Seymour Martin Lipset attributes this to the fact that "other characteristics and group affiliations such as religious belief are more salient in particular situations than high or low social and economic position" (1960: 229). Consequently, any particular interest group is likely to be composed of individuals from different social classes.

This cross-class sense of comradery around issues where individuals have equally deep levels of commitment creates cleavages that break down class solidarity. According to Lipset, "[w]hen faced with such conflicting social pressures, some men will respond more to one than to another, and therefore appear to deviate from the pattern of class voting" (1960: 229). Furthermore, these cleavages contribute to increased stability of the democratic process because "to the extent that groups and individuals have a number of crosscutting, politically relevant affiliations...[they] have an interest in reducing the intensity of political conflict" (1960: 88–89). Dahl advances this idea further and hypothesizes that lower class people are empowered to "make their feelings known to these members of the tentative majority who also, at some psychological level, identify themselves with [members of] the minority...[who] will shift their support away from the majority alternative and the majority will crumble" (1956: 105).

Focus on Active Power over Potential Power

The fourth and final distinguishing feature of the pluralist perspective relates to the way power itself is defined. Max Weber's classic definition understands power as "the chance of a man or number of men to realize their own will in a communal action even against the resistance of others who are participating in the action" (1946: 180). This is often interpreted by elite theorists to simply mean passive control over a pool of resources that would enable an individual or group to exercise power *if* they should choose to do so. Mills states that "[t]he power elite is composed of men whose positions enable them to transcend the ordinary environments of ordinary men" (1956: 3) and who "[have] access to the command of major institutions" (1956: 9). However, pluralists argue that occupying a position of importance and possessing a pool of useful resources does not necessarily translate into the ability to achieve a victory in a contested action; it merely confounds power with social status. Consequently, pluralists focus not on cataloging the potential to exercise power, but on observing the active exercise of power.

There are two primary reasons for this focus. First, possessing the potential to exercise power does not mean that power will be exercised, even if it would be advantageous. Polsby (1963: 120) invites us to imagine a multi-million dollar corporation with a vital interest in the outcome of a particular decision which, despite its massive pool of resources and potential to exercise power, is unable to use that power to leverage the outcome of the decision. Perhaps the corporation is prohibited from doing so by external regulation or internal policy. Perhaps most of the value of the corporation is tied up in investments and holdings and thus insufficiently liquid to be brought into play. Regardless of the reason, if political actors do not actively exercise their power to influence the outcome of a policy decision in which they have a vital interest, the fact that they have the potential power to do so is largely irrelevant.

The second reason for the pluralist focus on the active exercise of power is that resources can be deployed to greater or lesser effect. A multi-million dollar corporation that chooses to use its economic resources to influence a policy decision is not guaranteed to be successful just because it can outspend supporters of the opposing side; it must also target those expenditures wisely. For example, Comcast's spring 2015 attempt to merge with Time Warner Cable failed, despite the two corporations having combined to spend an average annual sum of $25.5 million dollars on lobbying over the previous four years. Despite this massive expenditure of resources, Comcast was unable to exercise active power to influence political decision-making, in large part, because it did not expend its resources in a precise and skillful manner to address concerns that Congressional Representatives had about the deal (Lipton 2015). It was not the amount of money spent on lobbying that determined the merger's chances of success, but rather the way in which those lobbying dollars were spent.

The Comcast example cited above is not anecdotal. A recent study by Amy McKay (McKay 2012) examined the relationship between the resources provided by clients to individual lobbying firms and the success rate of those firms in achieving their clients' preferred policy outcomes. When she controlled for lobbyist experience, connections, and intensity – all variables which did have a positive relationship to success rate – McKay confirmed that access to greater financial resources had no significant impact on lobbyist success rate. Just as pluralist theorists predict, power, in the classic Weberian sense, is not best measured by control of resources, but rather by the effect to which the resources one does control are deployed.

Criticism

Like any other theoretical perspective, the pluralist perspective is not without its critics. Not surprisingly, one of the most powerful critiques comes from the elite theory perspective to which pluralism can be directly contrasted. One of the most powerful critiques of the pluralist perspective comes from G. William Domhoff, a theorist in the class-domination perspective which is related to elite theory. Domhoff rebuts several key points of Dahl's 1957–1959 study of the political power structure of New Haven, CT detailed in *Who Governs?*, the seminal pluralist text that serves as the empirical foundation for much of pluralist theory.

In his critique, Domhoff revisits New Haven and re-examines the same structures, institutions and relationships studied by Dahl. Contrary to Dahls's claim that "an elite no longer rules New Haven" (Dahl 1961: 86), Domhoff concludes that, "the city of New Haven has a power structure which intervenes decisively in local affairs of concern to it and is part of the national ruling class" (Domhoff 1978: 174). To support his analysis, Domhoff argues that Dahl's work had several key methodological flaws – specifically, that he "had only a partial picture of membership in the social and economic notables, an incomplete decisional network that he did not follow to its institutional bases in corporations, banks, law firms and business associations and only a situational indicator of power – successful intervention in government decision-making" and that, in the end, he was led astray in his conclusions by "the incompleteness of his network analysis and his theoretical neglect of systemic and structural power" (Domhoff 1978: 1145–1146). If the research upon which much of pluralist theory is based is so flawed, the conclusions based on that research must be called into question as well.

A second critique focuses, not on the empirical foundation of the pluralist perspective, but rather on the validity of one of its fundamental assumptions. Pluralism is, at root, a *society-centered* perspective. As described earlier, pluralists see the state as having no autonomous agency of its own and being little more than a container for aggregating, weighing, and advancing the preferences of the populace. However, this assumption is challenged by advocates of a more *state-centered* perspective, such as Eric Nordlinger. Nordlinger argues that, contrary to the pluralist assumption:

> the preferences of the state are at least as important as those of civil society in accounting for what the democratic state does and does not do; the democratic state is not only frequently autonomous in so

far as it regularly acts upon its preferences, but also markedly autonomous in doing so even when its preferences diverge from the demands of the most powerful groups in civil society (Nordlinger 1981: 1).

In support of his critique, Nordlinger points out how the same cross-cutting group interests to which pluralists attribute a key role in maintaining the stability of the democratic system can be perverted by the state to fracture group cohesion and limit the extent and effectiveness with which groups can deploy their resources. Public officials, working as agents of the state, can actively influence the way in which issues are defined, link otherwise unrelated issues, and manipulate the order and speed with which issues are brought up for debate. If this is done skillfully it can "place [interest] group members in a conflicted and/or cross pressured situation, thereby reducing group cohesiveness, mobilization efforts, and perhaps the size of the group" (Nordlinger 1981: 154) in an effort to eliminate a society-centered challenge to the state's preferred policy outcome.

It may not even be necessary for the state to be that proactive in the pursuit of its own policy preferences. The state can take advantage of the natural state of equilibrium between interest groups that regularly oppose one another. In such cases, the state can simply "tip the scales in favor of its own preferences" or, alternatively, "choose which group's demands to satisfy on different issues – doing so according to [its own] preferences and without suffering an overall loss of support" (Nordlinger 1981: 154).

Conclusion

Despite the prominent role it played in mid-twentieth century political analysis, pluralism has seen more criticism than support over the last fifty years and has largely fallen out of favor among modern political sociologists. Nonetheless, it is indeed more than just an idealized view of how high school civics textbooks tell us that government should work. Pluralism has played a central role in the discourse over the nature of power in the United States that has taken place over the last century. Even if just for challenging their assumptions and thereby sharpening their arguments, the more popularly accepted perspectives in modern political sociology owe a debt to the early pluralist theorists.

References

Bentley, Arthur F. 1949[1908]. *The Process of Government: A Study of Social Pressures.* Evanston, IL: The Principia Press of Illinois Inc.

Dahl, Robert A. 1956. *A Preface to Democratic Theory.* Chicago, IL: University of Chicago Press.

Dahl, Robert A. 1961. *Who Governs? Democracy and Power in an American City.* New Haven, CT: Yale University Press.

Dahl, Robert A. 1989. *Democracy and its Critics.* New Haven, CT: Yale University Press.

Domhoff, G. William. 1978. *Who Really Rules? New Haven and Community Power Reexamined.* New Brunswick, NJ: Transaction Books.

Held, David. 1996. *Models of Democracy.* 2nd edn. Stanford, CA: Stanford University Press.

Lipset, Seymour Martin. 1960. *Political Man: The Social Bases of Politics.* Garden City, NY: Doubleday and Company Inc.

Lipton, Eric. 2015. Intense Lobbying Failed to Assure Comcast's Deal. *The New York Times*, April 24.

McKay, Amy. 2012. Buying Policy? The Effects of Lobbyists' Resources on their Policy Success. *Political Research Quarterly* 65(4): 908–923.

Mills, C. Wright. 1956. *The Power Elite.* New York, NY: Oxford University Press.

Nordlinger, Eric A. 1981. *On the Autonomy of the Democratic State.* Cambridge, MA: Harvard University Press.

Polsby, Nelson W. 1963. *Community Power and Political Theory.* New Haven, CT: Yale University Press.

Rose, Arnold M. 1967. *The Power Structure: Political Process in American Society.* New York, NY: Oxford University Press.

Summary of Annual Lobbying by Comcast Corp. Available at www.opensecrets.org/lobby/clientsum.php?id=D000000461&year=2014, accessed November 25, 2016.

Summary of Annual Lobbying by Time Warner Cable. Available at www.opensecrets.org/lobby/clientsum.php?id=D000000881&year=2015, accessed November 25, 2016.

Weber, Max. 1946. *From Max Weber: Essays in Sociology*. Translated by H. H. Gerth and C. Wright Mills. New York, NY: Oxford University Press.

The Class-Dominance Theory of Power in the United States

G. William Domhoff

A General Theoretical Overview

The class-dominance theory of power in the United States begins at the abstract level with the idea that power, defined as the ability to achieve desired social outcomes, has both collective and distributive dimensions. "Collective power," the capacity of a group, class, or nation to be effective and productive, concerns the degree to which a collectivity has the technological resources, organizational forms, and social morale to achieve its general goals. "Distributive power" is the ability of a group, class, or nation to be successful in conflicts with other groups, classes, or nations on issues of concern to it.

Collective and distributive power emerge from the same organizational bases. Although peoples' array of purposes have led to a large number of organizations, the historical record shows that economic, political, military, and ideological (usually religious) organizations weigh heavily in terms of generating societal power. These four organizational bases are conceptualized as over-lapping and intersecting socio-spatial networks of power that have widely varying extensions in physical space at different times in Western history.

The early outlines of the four networks of power can be seen in small hunting and gathering societies when hunting parties are organized (economic organization, with meat shared equally among all members of the society), when communal gatherings are called in an attempt to defuse interpersonal disputes that threaten to rip the group apart (political organization, which involves the regulation of human interactions within a specific territory), when the men band together to fight rival groups or clans (organized violence), and when rituals to deal with anxiety, guilt, and fear are performed (religious organization). Generally speaking, these nascent and temporary forms of power organization do not become the basis for distributive power in hunting and gathering or in tribal-level societies because the leaders are controlled by an "inverted power structure" in which people are able to maintain an egalitarian social structure through collective actions that range from gossip, chastisement, shunning, and if necessary, assassination (Boehm 1999). However, the secretive men's huts in which religion is practiced often exclude women on pain of gang rape or death, and men will band together to kill women who resist changes in the social order. This suggests that male dominance was the first power hierarchy to arise in human history (Gregor 1985; Sanday 1981).

According to this four-network theory, a permanent division of labor emerges within organizations in the four networks because of the advantages it provides in efficiency, ease of training, and greater overall effectiveness, all of which increase collective power. However, the division of labor also leads to a hierarchical distribution of power within the organization because "those who occupy supervisory and coordinating positions have an immense organizational superiority over the others" (Mann 1986: 6–7). Those who supervise and coordinate turn the organization into a power base for themselves. Inter-organizational alliances then generate a more general power structure that has the potential to greatly increase collective power. But the process of creating an overall power structure is fraught with tensions and dangers because the mobilization of greater collective power depends on the resolution of prior questions about distributive power arrangements within and between the four power networks. Who has power over whom has to be settled within organizations, classes, and nation-states before collective power can be exercised in any useful way, as the collapse of states, armies, and dominant economic classes over the centuries amply demonstrates.

No one network came first historically or is more basic than the others, so it is not possible to reduce power to one primary form. However, the fact that all four networks have always existed does not mean that they are of necessity equal in terms of their social power in any given time or place. For a variety of reasons, including logistical and organizational advances in one or another network, different networks have been ascendant in different times and places, as seen, for example, in the military empires that dominated Western civilization for several thousand years after the rise of the first city-states (Mann 1986: chs. 5–9).

The economic network in large-scale societies consists of a set of organizations concerned with satisfying material needs. This network gives rise to "classes," which can be defined as positions in a social structure that are shaped by their relationship to, and power over, the different parts of the economic process. These classes consist of "groups with differential power over the social organization of the extraction, transformation, distribution, and consumption of the objects of nature" (Mann 1986: 23). Because economic classes are also social relationships among the people in those classes, who often have different interests in terms of how the economic system is organized and how its output is distributed, the economic network often generates class conflicts. Since the rise of capitalism, class conflicts involve disagreements over such matters as wage rates, working conditions, unionization, and sometimes the fact of private ownership.

In most of the economic networks that have arisen in the course of Western history, and obviously in a capitalist system, there is an "ownership class" that holds legal possession of the entities that do the mining, producing, distributing, and retailing of the goods and services available in the society. However, this class can be defined as a "dominant" or "ruling" class only if it has been successful in subordinating the workers in the economic network and the leaders in the other three networks (Mann 1986: 25). Thus, it is not inevitable that owners will become a dominant class.

The Case of the United States

In the case of the United States, the four-network theory claims that the owners and top-level executives in corporations, agri-businesses, and commercial real estate, which are the three main segments of the country's ownership class, dominate the country. "Domination" is then more specifically defined as "the institutionalized outcome of great distributive power," which is in turn further specified as the ability "to establish the organizations, rules, and customs through which everyday life is conducted" (Domhoff 2014b: 192). Studies of alumni lists from prestigious private day schools and boarding schools, membership lists from exclusive social clubs, attendance at debutant balls and other high-status celebratory events, and involvement in other exclusionary social settings demonstrate that members of the ownership class have a very large overlap with the highest status group in the United States, which establishes that the dominant class is also a "social upper class" (Domhoff 1967: 4 and ch. 1; 2014b; Weber 1998).

Domination is maintained by the ownership-based social upper class through a leadership group called "the power elite," defined as those people who serve as directors or trustees in profit and non-profit institutions controlled by the "corporate community" (which includes all corporations that are linked by common ownership or interlocking directorates). This control is exercised through stock ownership, financial support, involvement on the governing board, or some combination of these factors (Domhoff 2014b: 104–105). The power elite has moderately conservative and ultra-conservative policy leanings within it, as indexed by the policy preferences expressed by specific organizations; however, some large corporations have directorships in both moderate and ultra-conservative policy-discussion organizations (e.g., Domhoff 1990: 35–37; 2014b: 17–18, 75–76).

Class-domination developed in the United States for reasons that are made more apparent by a very brief general historical comparison with major European countries, which at least until recently had much more complex power structures. First, the absence of a feudal economic class based in the exploitation of peasant agriculture meant that the newly forming American capitalist class had no economic rivals that it had to fend off or assimilate (e.g., Hamilton 1991). Second, the pre-revolutionary history of the United States as a set of separate colonial territories led to a federal form of government easily dominated by local and regional economic elites because many government functions were located at the state and local levels. Even when the Founding Fathers created a more centralized government in 1789, potentially powerful government leaders were circumscribed by the well-known system of checks and balances, and were further hampered by the fact that they could not play off one strong economic class against another in an attempt to gain autonomy from the early merchant, plantation, and manufacturing capitalists.

Third, the absence of any dangerous rival states on American borders, along with the protection against continental European states throughout most of the nineteenth century by the British navy, meant that the country did not have a large standing army until World War II and thereafter. Finally, the United States does not have one established church, which means that there is no large-scale ideology network that can rival corporate leaders for power. Protestant churches had a big role in shaping American morality and culture, but they continually splintered into new denominations, which limited them as a source of distributive social power.

Since the second or third decade of the twentieth century, class-domination has been exercised through four relatively distinct but over-lapping network-based processes. In terms of Max Weber's (1998) definition of a "party" as the means by which a class, status group, or coalition of groups tries to influence communal action in a conscious and planned manner, these four networks are the party of the dominant class.

The *special-interest process* deals with the narrow and short-run policy concerns of wealthy families, specific corporations, and the many different sectors of business. It operates primarily through lobbyists, company lawyers, and trade associations, with a focus on Congressional committees, departments of the executive branch, and regulatory agencies. Many of the lobbyists are former elected or appointed government officials who are in effect cashing in on their experience in the federal government and their connections within it. Those who focus on "interest-group politics" have studied this process through hundreds and maybe thousands of case studies, almost always showing that one or another business group usually wins, and that unions, liberals, and strong environmentalists (the main members of the liberal-labor alliance that opposes the corporate community on many issues) usually lose.

The *policy-planning process* formulates the general interests of the corporate community through a policy-planning network made up of foundations, think tanks, and policy-discussion groups, with a focus on the White House, relevant Congressional committees, and the high-status newspapers and opinion magazines published in New York and Washington. The policy-discussion groups within this network provide a setting in which corporate leaders can familiarize themselves with general policy issues by listening to and questioning experts, a forum in which conflicts between the moderate conservatives and ultra-conservatives in the corporate community can be discussed and compromised, and an informal training ground for the many corporate leaders who are appointed to high positions in the government. Case studies and historical analysis show that the moderate conservatives won several major policy battles in the twentieth century that permanently shaped the American institutional structure, including the key provisions in the Agricultural Adjustment Act of 1933, which has provided subsidies to larger-scale farms, plantations, and agri-businesses ever since, and the Social Security Act of 1935 (Domhoff 2014b: ch. 4; Domhoff and Webber 2011: chs. 2 and 4). Their proposals also shaped foreign policy after World War II (Domhoff 2014a).

The *opinion-shaping process* attempts to influence public opinion and keep some issues off the public agenda. It usually takes its direction from the major organizations within the policy-planning network. In addition to the large public relations firms and many small organizations within it, the opinion-shaping network includes a wide variety of patriotic, anti-tax, and other single-issue organizations funded by corporate foundations and individual members of the dominant class. There is no evidence that it can shape long-term public opinion, but it does have an impact on specific decisions when it can create doubt and hesitation or introduce plausible alternatives and delays.

The *candidate-selection process* is concerned with the election of politicians who are sympathetic to the agenda put forth in the special-interest and policy-planning processes. It operates through large campaign donations and hired political consultants; it is focused on the presidential campaigns of both major political parties and the Congressional campaigns of the Republican Party. Historically, the Republican Party was supported by Northern industrialists and bankers from Anglo-Saxon Protestant backgrounds and the Democrats were favored by Southern plantation owners and urban land, real estate, and department store owners from Catholic and Jewish backgrounds (Domhoff 1990: ch. 9; Webber 2000).

The shared concerns of the wealthy owners that are the primary financial backers of both political parties were expressed between 1937 and the mid-1990s by the conservative coalition in Congress, which consisted of a majority of Southern Democrats and a majority of Republicans voting against a majority of non-Southern Democrats. The conservative coalition formed on four general issues that were of great concern to employers North and South and which in essence defined the substance of class conflict – labor unions, social welfare, government regulation of business, and the continued subordination of African American workers in the South through the denial of their civil rights. This coalition was informally coordinated by the top Southern Democrats and Northern Republicans (Manley 1973). It rarely lost on any of these issues except during the 1965–1966 Congress (Shelley 1983: 34, 39), and it never lost on labor legislation (Brady and Bullock 1980; Katznelson et al. 1993). Since the late 1990s and the complete replacement of traditional white Southern Democrats by Republicans, the conservative coalition has disappeared into history, but it played a major role in establishing the laws and institutions that shape twenty-first-century America.

Although the dominant class has many shared interests, it was and is divided over the use of federal subsidies to benefit specific segments of the ownership class. Southern Democrats wanted subsidies for plantation owners and urban machine Democrats in large Northern cities wanted to subsidize urban development and housing for commercial land and real estate interests; their mutual support for each other's subsidies became the basis for a spending coalition. Subsidies for urban growth also had the support of the construction unions in the American Federal of Labor (Logan and Molotch 1987). The spending coalition was joined by the contingent of liberal Democrats in Congress because of its desire to expand domestic spending that would benefit middle- and low-income people (Clausen 1973; Domhoff 2013: 15–17; Sinclair 1982). In the post-World War II era, the spending coalition sometimes had the support of the corporate moderates in the Republican Party because they were for urban renewal and downtown growth, federal money for university science and engineering programs, and aid to schools in low-income inner cities and rural areas (Domhoff 2013: 80, 116–120, 258). However, the ultra-conservative corporate owners in the Republican Party oppose such subsidies, as demonstrated by the policy stances taken by the National Association of Manufacturers and the US Chamber of Commerce on most spending issues (Domhoff 2013: 15–17).

The Rise and Fall of Unions: A Useful Test Case

The National Labor Relations Act of 1935 presents the strongest challenge to the class-dominance theory of the American power structure because it passed against the well-organized and vehement opposition of the entire corporate community and led to a very large union movement over the next forty to fifty years. The story, however, of how the corporate moderates helped create the labor act, then turned against it shortly before it was proposed to Congress, and slowly weakened it over the first thirty-five years of the postwar era is the most revealing window possible into the nature of class-domination and conflict in the United States.

Archival findings reveal that corporate moderates within the Roosevelt Administration, serving as members of the Department of Commerce's Business Advisory Council and the National Recovery Administration's Industrial Advisory Board, suggested the creation of the original National Labor Board (NLB) to deal with the unanticipated union organizing drive that followed the passage of the National Industrial Recovery Act in 1933; they also introduced several of the original labor board's policies and procedures, and served on the NLB itself in an effort to bring about strike settlements (Domhoff and Webber 2011: ch. 3; McQuaid 1979). Thanks to the apparent success of the small handful of corporate-sponsored Employee Representation Plans they had initiated in the 1920s, which encouraged workers at individual work sites to meet and confer with management about working conditions and other issues of concern, the corporate moderates thought they had little to fear from unions. They also thought they could limit unions to the relatively small number of craft unions at the time if worse came to worse, leaving their growing number of unskilled industrial workers unorganized.

Still other archival findings reveal how they miscalculated and why they lost control of the legislative process on this issue. Due to problems in dealing with the many corporate employers that refused to accept the decisions of the NLB, especially in the automobile and steel industries, liberals in the Senate, led by Senator Robert F. Wagner of New York and the lawyers that worked for the NLB, fashioned stronger legislation that would make union organizing more possible. Among several pro-union amendments, it included a clause stating that a majority vote for a union would be sufficient for it to have the right to represent all workers in the bargaining unit.

The corporate moderates objected to this new legislative proposal for several reasons, including its threat to their Employee Representation Plans and its failure to ban coercion by union organizers as well as by corporations. From a corporate-dominance perspective, however, the corporate moderates most of all resisted on the issue of majority rule, which meant that Employee Representation Plans would have to be closed down if the majority of those voting favored a union. Corporate moderates therefore insisted upon an approach called "proportional representation," which would allow Employee Representation Plans to coexist with unions or make it possible to deal with craft workers separately from industrial workers (Domhoff and Webber 2011: 121–125; Gross 1974: 57–58, 89–103, 136–139). In private meetings with the top corporate leaders, Senator Wagner agreed to remove clauses that directly banned Employee Representation Plans, but Wagner and several American Federation of Labor (AFL) leaders were no longer willing to accept proportional representation, as the union leaders had as members of the temporary War Labor Board during World War I (Domhoff and Webber 2011: 125–126). This change in position by liberal Democrats and organized labor led to an unbridgeable gulf between them and the corporate moderates, as revealed by correspondence between the head of General Electric and his counterparts at Standard Oil of New Jersey and the DuPont Corporation (Domhoff and Webber 2011: 119–124).

Senator Wagner's new legislation was defeated in 1934, but it passed in 1935 despite the massive corporate campaign against it. This was first of all possible because the newly formed liberal-labor alliance had a large majority in both houses due in part to labor militancy in 1933 and 1934. In the final analysis, however, it passed because the Southern Democrats, who had the power to obstruct through their many reciprocal relationships with President Franklin D. Roosevelt, did not block it. They also had leverage through their control of a majority of key Congressional committees, which meant they could slow down or eliminate many of the recovery plans, and they resorted to filibusters whenever they thought the plantation capitalists' insistence on subordinating African American workers and keeping out unions was in any way at risk. Any tension for Southern Democrats over supporting the labor act was resolved quickly because the liberal-labor leaders in Congress continued to agree that any labor legislation would exclude agricultural workers and domestic servants (Farhang and Katznelson 2005).

Due to increased worker militancy, aided by the refusal of the president and Democratic governors to send troops to break strikes in two or three large industrial states, union membership nearly tripled from 3.1 million in 1934 to 8.8 million in 1939 despite vigorous opposition by both corporate moderates and ultra-conservatives (Mayer 2004: 23, Table A1). However, this burst of union organizing, which included sit-down strikes and attempts to organize biracial unions in the South, turned the Southern Democrats against the Act by late 1937, which united all segments of the dominant class as well as the conservative coalition against any further progress for unions. By 1938, the conservative coalition had launched a serious challenge to the new National Labor Relations Board (NLRB), which led to a reduced budget and the replacement of its most liberal member by 1940 (Gross 1981: 2 and chs. 6–8).

The effort to cripple or dismantle the NLRB was delayed by the preparations for World War II. Nevertheless, by that point the conservative coalition had crafted a set of amendments to the labor act; most of these amendments were enacted in 1947 as part of the Taft-Hartley Act, the first of several legislative setbacks for the fractured union movement in the postwar era (Gross 1981: 3 and chs. 5, 10, and 13). Furthermore, total union membership declined by 46,000 in 1940, and union density (defined as the percentage of non-agricultural workers in unions) declined from 28.6 percent in 1939 to 26.9 percent in 1940 (Mayer 2004: 23, Table A1).

With the election of a Republican Congress in 1946, at least in part in reaction to a strike wave shortly after World War II ended, the corporate community and the conservative coalition were able to pass the Taft-Hartley Act in 1947, which had serious consequences for the union movement (Gross 1981: ch. 1; 1995: ch. 1). For example, the Act included fundamental changes in labor policy that gave corporate executives more leeway to hamper organizing and appeal to the courts. One was a seemingly harmless addition to the "Findings and Policy" section, which asserts that "some practices engaged in by unions were obstructing commerce"; another addition asserted the employers' right of "free speech" (Gross 1995: 2). Other amendments banned mass picketing and secondary boycotts. The usefulness of picketing in the actual disruption of work was further limited by a Supreme Court ruling in 1951 stating that it was illegal for a union to shut down an entire construction project based on a dispute with only one contractor or subcontractor (sit-down strikes, perhaps the most powerful of organizing strategies, already had been lost to a Supreme Court ruling in 1939). Due to government support for already existing unions during World War II, union membership had grown from 8.7 million in 1940 to 14.3 million in 1945. But that year also turned out to be the high point for union density, 35.4 percent, a figure that had declined to 30.4 percent by 1950 (Mayer 2004: 23, Table A1).

During the 1950s the corporate lawyers appointed to the NLRB by President Dwight D. Eisenhower did everything they could to undermine unions, and the Landrum-Griffin Labor-Management law of 1959 further limited the ability of unions to picket (Gross 1995: chs. 7–8, and 142–143). Thanks to a big assist from the low employment rates, brought about by the Korean War and the rise in defense spending, union density had risen from 30.4 percent in 1950 to a near high point of 34.8 percent in 1954, but the figure had fallen to 30.9 percent by 1960 and to 28.2 percent by 1965 in the face of the corporate counterattack after that war ended (Mayer 2004: 22–23, Table 1A).

Union decline accelerated during the 1960s because white workers and their families resisted the integration of workplaces, unions, schools, and neighborhoods, leading increasing numbers of them to turn to the Republicans starting in 1966 (Boyle 1995; Quadagno 1994; Frymer 2008). As a result, the liberal-labor electoral alliance was severely weakened in large industrialized states and Southern whites of all classes switched to the Republican Party over the course of three or four elections (e.g., Boyle 1995; Carmines and Stimson 1989). At the same time, the most powerful of the corporate moderates were increasingly determined to defeat unions. They blamed the inflation of the late 1960s on wage increases won in successful strikes. These corporate moderates urged that the wage increases went beyond productivity gains and created a "cost-push" inflation, even though union members were responding to an inflationary spiral caused by the failure to raise taxes and reduce rising federal deficits in the face of inflationary spending.

The victory in the presidential elections in 1968 by Republican Richard M. Nixon, along with corporate pressures to thwart unions, led to successful attempts by the White House and the Department of Labor to undercut construction unions. Anti-union decisions by the Republican-controlled NLRB crippled all unions in several ways, including a ruling that made it easier for corporations to outsource work from unionized to non-unionized factories and to move production overseas (Domhoff 2013: ch. 9; Gross 1995: ch. 12). Then the resurgent conservative coalition blocked labor-law reforms during the Ford and Carter administrations that might have helped unions. Rulings by the Reagan Administration's appointees to the NLRB made it even easier to defeat unions, especially in the context of President Reagan's abrupt firing of striking members of the air traffic controllers union after behind-the-scenes negotiations with them failed despite the offer of an 11.4 percent raise (McCartin 2011). By 1988 union density had fallen to 16.2 percent, less than half of its all-time high in 1945 (Mayer 2004: Table A1). The dominant class triumphed again in 2009 in defeating a union-sponsored initiative, the Employee Free Choice Act, which might have revived union organizing. The percentage of employees in unions was down to 11.8 percent in 2011, and even lower in the private sector: 6.9 percent (BLS 2012).

The rise of unions within the context of the Great Depression reveals that the dominant class is not invincible, especially when it is divided and workers use the opportunity to organize unions and elect union-friendly officials. But the decline of unions shows that the dominant class can regain lost ground when it is united and able to enlarge the conservative coalition in Congress. Both the non-profit organizations it created to develop the Employee Representation Plan in the 1920s and those it financed to create plans to undercut the unions in the postwar era demonstrate how it fashions plans in the policy-planning network that can be brought to the attention of the corporate-friendly elected officials that it supported in the candidate-selection process. The vehemence with which the dominant class opposed the passage of the National Labor Relations Act and the lengths to which it went in order to weaken unions suggests corporate control of labor markets is one of their major concerns, perhaps second only to their desire to dominate aspects of government that are crucial to them.

A Contrast with Marxist Theory

Because the concept of "class" is so strongly identified with Marxism in the social sciences, it is useful to distinguish class-dominance theory from Marxism. At the most general level, Marxism is based on a theory of history in which there is an inevitable and growing clash between capitalists and workers due to the nature of the capitalist system and the constant drive for increased profits in the face of a falling rate of profits, which leads to more serious economic crises, heightened class struggle, the eventual triumph of the property-less proletariat, and the replacement of capitalism with a non-market planned economy called socialism. Class-dominance theory, on the other hand, claims that it is only barely possible to discern any patterns in history and does not forecast any inevitable outcomes (Mann 1986).

At a more sociological level, the technologies and social arrangements (the means and mode of production) within the economic system are the starting point for understanding social structure in general by Marxism. The other three networks, which are seen as independent ones by class-dominance theorists, are relegated by Marxists to a secondary role as contributors to shaping the overall mode of production; they are the "superstructure." For example, Marxism claims that the state arose to protect the institution of private property from the non-owning classes, but archaeological, anthropological, and historical findings do not support that conclusion (Mann 1986). Thus, aside from an emphasis on classes and class conflict in capitalist economies, and on class and corporate dominance of the American government, class-dominance theory shares nothing in common with Marxist theory.

Conclusion

As this chapter reveals, the theory of class-domination in the United States is rooted in three concepts that are basic in sociology: organizations, classes, and institutions. It takes organizational theory as its basic starting point, including its emphasis on the strong tendency for power to accumulate at the top in most organizations. The theory next builds on the fact that the institution of private property within the economic network leads to the dominant organizational form in the United States, the corporation, as well as an ownership class that has great economic resources and the potential for political power, but which at the same time generates ongoing conflict over wages, profits, works rules, taxes, unionization, and government regulation. It then explains how the economic resources generated by the corporations are used to institutionalize the exclusionary social settings of the social upper class (separate neighborhoods and suburban enclaves, private schools, exclusive social clubs, debutante balls, and elite cultural institutions), which create a unique life style and generates a sense of specialness and a right to rule.

Corporate resources are also used to create and finance a wide array of non-profit organizations. The non-profit organizations, and most importantly those that are part of the policy-planning network, provide wealthy owners and high-level executives in the corporations and the non-profit organizations (the power elite) with institutional bases from which they can deploy their class resources for what are ultimately political ends, making it possible for them to compromise many of their own differences within the policy-planning network and to contain class conflict through their domination of government.

It is therefore the interaction of organizational imperatives (e.g., the division of labor, leadership from the top down) and class imperatives (e.g., constantly rising profits, control of labor markets) that leads to class-domination by the power elite through the special-interest, policy-planning, opinion-shaping, and candidate-selection networks. According to this theory, it is the combination of insights from organizational, class, and institutionalist theories that explains the strength of the dominant class in America. Unlike pluralist theory, which builds on a narrative of gradual democratization, and Marxism, which forecasts an upheaval that presages a better future, the class-domination of power in the United States contains no political prescriptions and leads to no predictions about the future. It combines sociological concepts with an attention to historical detail, including cross-national historical comparisons, in an attempt to explain the present-day power structure in the United States.

References

BLS. 2012. Union Membership 2011 Usdl-12-0094: Bureau of Labor Statistics. Washington: Department of Labor.

Boehm, Christopher. 1999. *Hierarchy in the Forest: the Evolution of Egalitarian Behavior*. Cambridge: Harvard University Press.

Boyle, Kevin. 1995. *The UAW and the Heyday of American Liberalism*. Ithaca, NY: Cornell University Press.

Brady, David and Charles Bullock. 1980. Is there a Conservative Coalition in the House? *Journal of Politics* 42: 549–559.

Carmines, Edward G. and James A. Stimson. 1989. *Issue Evolution: Race and the Transformation of American Politics*. Princeton, NJ: Princeton University Press.

Clausen, Aage R. 1973. *How Congressmen Decide: A Policy Focus*. New York, NY: St. Martin's Press.

Domhoff, G. W. 1967. *Who Rules America?* Englewood Cliffs, NJ: Prentice-Hall.

Domhoff, G. W. 1990. *The Power Elite and the State: How Policy is Made in America*. Hawthorne, NY: Aldine De Gruyter.

Domhoff, G. W. 2013. *The Myth of Liberal Ascendancy: Corporate Dominance from the Great Depression to the Great Recession*. Boulder, CO: Paradigm Publishers.

Domhoff, G. W. 2014a. The Council on Foreign Relations and the Grand Area: Case Studies on the Origins of the IMF and the Vietnam War. *Class, Race and Corporate Power* 2. Available at http://digitalcommons.fiu.edu/classracecorporatepower/vol2/iss1/1, accessed November 25, 2016.

Domhoff, G. W. 2014b. *Who Rules America? The Triumph of the Corporate Rich*. 7th edn. New York, NY: McGraw-Hill.

Domhoff, G. W. and M. Webber. 2011. *Class and Power in the New Deal: Corporate Moderates, Southern Democrats, and the Liberal-Labor Coalition*. Palo Alto, CA: Stanford University Press.

Farhang, Sean and Ira Katznelson. 2005. The Southern Imposition: Congress and Labor in the New Deal and Fair Deal. *Studies in American Political Development* 19: 1–30.

Frymer, Paul. 2008. *Black and Blue: African Americans, the Labor Movement, and the Decline of the Democratic Party*. Princeton, NJ: Princeton University Press.

Gregor, Thomas. 1985. *Anxious Pleasures: The Sexual Lives of an Amazonian People*. Chicago, IL: University of Chicago Press.

Gross, James A. 1974. *The Making of the National Labor Relations Board*. Albany, NY: State University of New York Press.

Gross, James A. 1981. *The Reshaping of the National Labor Relations Board*. Albany, NY: State University of New York Press.

Gross, James A. 1995. *Broken Promise: The Subversion of U.S. Labor Relations Policy*. Philadelphia, PA: Temple University Press.

Hamilton, Richard. 1991. *The Bourgeois Epoch: Marx and Engels on Britain, France, and Germany*. Chapel Hill, NC: University of North Carolina Press.

Katznelson, Ira, Kim Geiger, and Daniel Kryder. 1993. Limiting Liberalism: The Southern Veto in Congress 1933–1950. *Political Science Quarterly* 108: 283–306.

Logan, John and Harvey Molotch. 1987. *Urban Fortunes: The Political Economy of Place*. Berkeley, CA: University of California Press.

Manley, John F. 1973. The Conservative Coalition in Congress. *American Behavioral Scientist* 17: 223–247.

Mann, Michael. 1986. *The Sources of Social Power: A History of Power from the Beginning to A.D. 1760*. Vol. 1. New York, NY: Cambridge University Press.

Mayer, Gerald. 2004. *Union Membership Trends in the United States*. Federal Publications. Paper 174 Congressional Research Service. Available at http://digitalcommons.ilr.cornell.edu/key_workplace/174, accessed November 25, 2016.

McCartin, Joseph. 2011. *Collision Course: Ronald Reagan, the Air Traffic Controllers, and the Strike that Changed America*. New York, NY: Oxford University Press.

McQuaid, Kim. 1979. The Frustration of Corporate Revival in the Early New Deal. *Historian* 41: 682–704.

Quadagno, Jill. 1994. *The Color of Welfare: How Racism Undermined the War on Poverty*. New York, NY: Oxford University Press.

Sanday, Peggy. 1981. *Female Power and Male Dominance: On the Origins of Sexual Inequality*. New York, NY: Cambridge University Press.

Shelley, Mack. 1983. *The Permanent Majority: The Conservative Coalition in the United States Congress*. Tuscaloosa, AL: University of Alabama Press.

Sinclair, Barbara. 1982. *Congressional Realignment, 1925–1978*. Austin, TX: University of Texas Press.

Webber, Michael. 2000. *New Deal Fat Cats: Business, Labor, and Campaign Finance in the 1936 Presidential Election*. New York, NY: Fordham University Press.

Weber, Max. 1998. Class, Status, and Party. In *Social Class and Stratification: Classic Statements and Theoretical Debates*. Edited by R. F. Levine. Lanham, MD: Rowman and Littlefield.

Part III
FEMINIST PERSPECTIVES

CHAPTER 8

Feminist Theories

Seung-Kyung Kim and Carole R. McCann

Feminist theories originated in the 1960s to explain gender oppression as a social phenomenon and by the 1980s had expanded to examine its intersections with racial, sexual, class, and geopolitical oppressions. In contrast to theories that claim apolitical objectivity, feminist theories historically emerged from and remain connected to global movements for social change and social justice. The term "feminist" reflects this internationalism. In the 1880s, the term, combining the French word for women "femme" with the suffix meaning political position "ism," came to refer to those who defended the cause of women. It did not become widely used in the United States, however, until the 1970s, when the term was taken up by the US women's movements to indicate opposition to women's subordinate social positions, spiritual authority, political rights, and economic opportunities (McCann and Kim 2013: 1).

The connection between theory and activism within feminist theory arose in part because mainstream social and political theory and the institutions which fostered them largely excluded women. Thus, efforts to secure positions for women as legitimate producers of knowledge in the academy and efforts to explain the sources of systemic gender oppression and its connection to other forms of oppression went hand-in-hand. Feminist theory has thus been constituted through continued engagement with and critique of both the everyday experiential world and canons of intellectual thought across the disciplines. It reflects the input of diverse and scattered communities of feminist scholars and draws from and contributes to the major intellectual trends of our times.

Despite a common concern with women's oppression, and general agreement that gender is central to understanding the world, the multiplicity and fluidity of feminist theories defy attempts to set out a standard taxonomy of "types." Indeed, a major characteristic of feminist theories is that they have been "brave enough to take [their] own history and presumptions as critical objects of inquiry" (Hemmings 2006: 14). Contestation over its foundational categories – "woman," "gender," "sex," "sexuality," "experience," "feminism," and "theory" – has and will continue to energize feminist theoretical debates. In light of the diversity of women's experiences and the multiplicity of feminist theories, in this chapter we lay out key themes and the leading epistemologies to present an overview of the ever-changing field. From our location in the United States, we provide a local perspective on these debates but place them in a global context, reflecting the increasing transnational circulation of feminist theories. Although feminist theory and activism have always crossed borders, new global social networks and technologies have accelerated those travels as feminists address the challenges and divisions of the twenty-first century. Lastly, we review the contributions of feminist theory to sociology.

Identity

Feminist theory has always been concerned with "identity;" indeed, it originated through attention to the identity category, "women." Early feminist theorizing took inspiration from the question famously posed by Simone de Beauvoir, "what is a woman?" and her answer that "one is not born, but rather becomes a woman" (de Beauvoir 1952: xv, 301). From many different disciplines, feminists investigated the social construction of gender in order to dislodge time-worn misconceptions about women's nature and capacities, to construct knowledge about women and the world from women's perspective, and to produce an account of how gender works alone and in concert with other oppressions. Proponents of the different approaches to feminist theorizing, however, have very different takes on the concept of identity.

Using the tools of conventional social science, early feminist empiricists gathered and interpreted observational data to disprove claims of women's inferiority to men, document socially created gender inequities, and illuminate issues that otherwise would remain hidden, such as domestic and sexual violence against women. By "adding women," feminist empiricists in many disciplines also exposed the androcentric bias in traditional research, which treated men as the exemplar of the human experience. Their work forced reconsideration of many prior conclusions, and expanded research models to focus attention on women's experiences.

In contrast to traditional empiricists who claim to construct "objective" theories with no political purpose, feminists have always tied theory construction to political aims of achieving gender equality. Some, such as Charlotte Bunch, argue that "no theory is totally 'objective' because it reflects the interests, values and assumptions of those who created it" (Bunch 2005: 13). Others believe it is possible to remain objective while constructing theories for political purposes. Either way, feminist empiricists believe in the potential of social research to improve women's lives and transform society in the interests of social justice. They believe scientific facts can be subversive in undermining androcentric conceptions of women, and can provide alternative visions of how to achieve a better, more egalitarian world.

Initially, many (white, Western) feminists also sought to construct comprehensive theories, or grand narratives, to explain the oppression of all women and the common obstacles faced by women throughout the world. These feminists believed that understanding the historical roots of women's subordination across societies was necessary to form effective political strategies to achieve women's liberation. Feminists such as Gayle Rubin (1975), Heidi Hartmann (1981), and Nancy Chodorow (1978) drew on the ideas of Claude Lévi-Strauss, Karl Marx, and Sigmund Freud to understand women's systematic oppression. Their work formulated the foundational concept of feminist theory, the sex/gender system, to describe the social/cultural system that turned female bodies into feminine women coupled and subordinated to men in the family, economy, and politics. With this concept, feminist theorists tied together the productive and reproductive, social consciousness and psyche, the public and private across human history.

Difference

Such universalizing theories drew criticisms from feminists inside and outside the United States for reproducing historical exclusions based on race, sexuality, and geopolitical location. Within feminist circles formed in the United States through women's movement organizations and the emerging field of women's studies, feminists such as the Combahee River Collective, bell hooks, Audre Lorde, Gloria Anzaldúa, and Cherrie Moraga expressed an "oppositional consciousness" that intervened in the flow of "hegemonic feminist theory" (Sandoval 1990). They drew on their own lives and situations as women of color to demonstrate that these universalizing generalizations about women were inaccurate because they ignored differences among women. Moreover, "false universals," they contended, could not effectively guide feminist activism because they privilege the priorities of socially dominant women at the expense of women of color, working-class women, and lesbians (McCann and Kim 2013: 18).

Outside the United States, United Nations conferences during the Decade for Women between 1975 and 1985 gave women from around the world the opportunity to meet and discuss their visions on how to improve women's lives. These discussions revealed stark differences between the experiences and priorities of women from the Global North and the Global South. Women from the South, who were focused on "poverty, equality and basic needs," were critical of the hegemony of Western feminism focused on individual rights (Basu 2000: 70). Western feminist theory, they contended, either did not take adequate account of the different cultural, socio-economic, and political contexts that shaped women's lives in other geographical locations or they used those differences for their own purposes, in acts of cultural appropriation. Moreover, Western efforts to universalize feminism focused on sexism as the primary oppression and overlooked processes of colonialism and imperialism through which Western women participate in the oppression of women in other parts of the world. Chandra Talpade Mohanty's 1986 article, "Under Western Eyes: Feminist Scholarship and Colonial Discourses," offered one of the best known of these critiques. She argued that the colonizing tendencies of Western feminist thought contributed to the divisions among predominantly white Western feminists and working-class and feminists of color around the world.

While difficult, even contentious, these dialogs across differences have been enormously productive for advancing feminist politics and knowledge. Recognizing and working through difference, in relation to both gender and other identity categories, remains a prevailing theme of feminist theory. Feminist scholars such as Amrita Basu, Manisha Desai, Valentine Moghadam, Chandra Talpade Mohanty, and Nancy Naples have demonstrated how difference can be a resource. In organizing for the rights of women and other subordinated groups, drawing upon differences among group members can in fact enrich and strengthen organizing efforts. In her 2003 article, "'Under Western Eyes' Revisited: Feminist Solidarity through Anticapitalist Struggles," Mohanty provides guidance on how to weigh differences and commonalities across historically specific locations to effectively practice solidarity against capitalist globalization (McCann and Kim 2013: 483).

Intersectionality

In light of criticisms of grand theory as exclusionary and ethnocentric, feminist intellectuals also sought new ways to construct theory that were reflective of the many differences and complicated power relationships among women. In place of theories examining women in general, feminist scholarship began to privilege historical specificity – concrete analyses of women's experiences in particular times and places – along with exploring how gender oppression intersected with other forms of oppression.

In attending to difference, feminist theories began to analyze social identities such as gender, race, class, and sexuality not in isolation from one another but in how they intersect and overlap to shape individuals' experiences of oppression and/or privilege. Theorizing on intersectionality grew out of the explosion of writings by women of color and transnational feminist scholars in the 1980s (McCann and Kim 2013: 161). Initially formulated by Kimberlé Crenshaw in her 1989 article, "Mapping the Margins," intersectionality theory offered a "methodology that ultimately will disrupt the tendencies to see race and gender as exclusive or separable" (Crenshaw 1993: 1244). More recent feminist analyses build upon Crenshaw's work by directing attention to the "relationships and interactions between multiple axes of identity and multiple dimensions of social organization – at the same time" (Dill and Zambrana 2009: 4).

Intersectionality theorists devote particular attention to the contradictory and overlapping nature of social identities. In their view, identity is not only relational, ever-changing, and fluid, but also contradictory, layered, and conflicting (McCann and Kim 2013: 172). They help us to understand how multiple domains of power operate in and through social structures, interpersonal relationships, discourse, and representation, in order to construct effective knowledge and strategies for securing social justice. For this reason, the study of identity, including how individuals form their identities, the social meaning of identities, and how to utilize identities in research studies, remains an important theme in feminist scholarship. Identity now, however, is configured through intersecting systems of difference and domination.

Standpoint Epistemologies

The feminist epistemological approaches to analysis of the complex intersectional interplay of identity and difference fall into two major trends. In the 1980s and 1990s, drawing on the tools of historical materialism, and with varying degrees of commitment to empiricism and universalism, standpoint theories extended insights of Marxist theory to theorize gender systems (McCann and Kim 2013: 343). Feminist standpoint theorists, such as Sandra Harding, Nancy Hartsock, Patricia Hill Collins, and Dorothy Smith, started from the perspective of women's experiences to build more accurate and complex understanding of gender in all realms of social life. They reject the idea that scientific knowledge can be neutral, and view all knowledge as informed by individuals' social locations, including their gender, race, class, and sexuality. As Harding argues, standpoint theory begins by acknowledging that in societies stratified by gender, race, class, and sexuality, "one's social situation enables and sets limits on what one can know" (Harding 1993: 54–55). Further, Hartsock contends, the privileged knowledge of dominant groups distorts the real relationship among groups. But such a distorted view of social life "cannot be dismissed as simply false," because it organizes the social system in which all must participate (Hartsock 1983: 232).

A central goal of standpoint epistemologies is to make apparent the power relations in conventional knowledge production, arguing that such socially situated research will produce a clearer understanding of the "relations of ruling" (Smith 1990: 14–15). Yet, as sociologist Collins argues, subordinated groups can provide a unique insight into the societal structures that subordinate them. Grounded in the subjugated knowledge of African American women, she points to the position of "outsider within," who participates in, yet remains invisible in, and excluded from, white society.

Standpoint theory has been a central theme of feminist of color theorizing because it enables analysis of oppression as a complex "matrix of domination," an interlocking web of forces that operate simultaneously in social structures and ideologies (Collins 2013[1990]: 222–225). In this view, oppressions may intersect or not, and intersecting oppressions shift over time. Thus, experiences of oppression differ depending on one's social location within historically contingent webs of dominations. As a result, Collins argues, everyone has only a partial view from which to produce valuable, if incomplete, knowledge. Given that power relations shape all knowledge and that all views are partial, standpoint theorists encourage a reflexive approach to knowledge-building through which researchers reveal their roles in theory construction and the ways in which their social locations may impact their findings (Mann 2012: 23).

Postmodern Epistemologies

The ready acceptance of experience as a basis for feminist knowledge-building received criticism from postmodern and queer theorists, however. They argue that to the extent that such theories attribute specific qualities as characteristic of all its members, they fall back into the essentialism they intended to criticize. Drawing upon the work of French post-structuralist scholars such as Jacques Derrida (1976), Jacques Lacan (2007[1977]), Roland Barthes (1978), and especially Julia Kristeva and Michel Foucault (1978) in the late 1970s and 1980s, postmodern feminisms articulated an alternative theory of sex difference and gender identity. In so doing, they re-problematized the category of "woman" and the concept of "experience" as reliable bases of knowledge.

Postmodern feminist theorists such as Judith Butler, Jane Flax (1990), Inderpal Grewal, Caren Kaplan, and Joan Scott share post-structuralism's commitment to revealing the constructedness of naturalized objects/concepts such as "experience," "the self," and "the body." In their view, social reality and human subjectivity are mutually constituted through systems of language and discourse. Therefore, human knowledge cannot make sense of a "real" world outside of discourse. It can, however, analyze how order and coherence are imposed on the world through discourses and practices. Postmodern feminists particularly focus on the ways in which cultural discourses and social practices normalize and regulate gendered and sexualized forms of subjectivity (McCann and Kim 2013: 348). As Scott's classic 1986 article, "Gender: A Useful Category of Historical Analysis," argued, effective analysis of gender required attention to power in gender's multiple and intertwining "elements": "cultural available symbols," "social organizations and institutions," "normative concepts," and "subjective identity" (Scott 1986: 1067–1068).

Post-structuralism particularly critiques the liberal humanist concept of subjectivity as an essential aspect of humanity that exists prior to and outside of the social/symbolic order. Picking up on this claim, postmodern feminists have produced a richer understanding of how gender power operates to regulate and normalize persons at the level of the body and subjectivity. In particular, Butler problematized the sexed body, which initial conceptualizations of gender uncritically accepted as a natural category. In her view, the "gender binary," a regulatory frame that mutually configures masculine and feminine bodies, consists of stylized repetitions of acts, gender performances, which create the fiction of an abiding gendered self within a stable sexed body. In this sense, sex as well as gender is socially constructed. For Butler, the gender binary is predicated on the "heterosexual contract," which necessitates sex difference to justify the heterosexual couple as the basic unit of society (Butler 1990: xxx, 36). Her theories have been an important point of connection between feminist theory, queer theory, and the emerging field of transgender studies. In addition, because postmodernism throws all categories into question, it has been taken up by feminist and queer theorists of color worldwide to challenge the normative Western feminist subject, as well as the Orientalist view of gender in the Global South (McCann and Kim 2013: 349).

Emerging Epistemologies

The contentions between standpoint and postmodernist feminisms related to questions of identity and power have been focused on the question of women's agency. Postmodern epistemologies emphasize how discourses can both empower and silence and how the positions of both the privileged and the subjugated are mutually constituted. They argue that historically specific discourses determine and constrain what can be said. As a result, giving voice to women's experiences will not disrupt regulatory regimes of power as oppositional strategies should do. Standpoint theorists contend that postmodern feminist theories conceptualize such a contingent sense of subjectivity that they diminish the potential of feminist agency too greatly. If individual's identity and voice are simply effects of discourse, what is the ground of resistant agency (McCann and Kim 2013: 351–352)?

In response, feminists have re-devoted attention to questions of identity, with the aim of developing theories that provide productive, non-essentialist, ways to speak about the injustices of women's situations. Nancy Fraser, for instance, proposes "a conception of discourse that lets us examine identities, groups, and hegemony" by locating subjects as socially situated agents, acknowledging the plurality of discourses in society, and recognizing that social identities are not monolithic (Fraser 1997: 380–381). Linda Alcoff addresses the dilemma regarding identity by proposing a concept of "positionality" that defines "woman" "not by a particular set of attributes but by a particular position" so that "the internal characteristics of the person thus identified are not denoted so much as the external context within which that person is situated" (Alcoff 1997: 349). For Alcoff, women's identity is fluid and based in historical context, but also a concrete identity that women can utilize as a political tool.

In response to the "affective turn" in many disciplines in the late 1990s, feminist theory has also returned again to questions of bodies and emotions. Alison Jaggar's 1989 essay, "Love and Knowledge: Emotion in Feminist Epistemology," critiqued the empiricist view that emotions act as "an impediment to knowledge," instead arguing that they are fundamental because they shape the values by which research questions, methods, and findings are deemed significant (McCann and Kim 2013: 479–480). Sara Ahmed argues that attention to the affective components of life – visceral responses, emotional states, and the mood of the room – offers a productive means of connecting the discursive and the material by theorizing how the "discursive" affects bodies and identities. In her view, affective economies, the circulation of affects in discourse and practice, regulate and structure feeling, bringing subjects into alignment with regimes of gender, race, class, sexuality, etc. (Ahmed 2004).

Contributions of Feminist Theory to Sociology

Feminist theory has had a strong influence on the discipline of sociology through challenges to its traditional epistemology, methodology, concepts, research topics, and the organization of its subfields. Feminist thought has critiqued the exclusion of women and other marginalized groups from sociological theories and drawn attention to issues of gender, race, class, sexuality, power, and domination.

In challenging sociological epistemology, feminists have pointed out that what sociologists have traditionally considered "objectivity" is in actuality an elitist standpoint, one that historically has been white and male. Smith and Collins have argued that the assumptions, conceptual tools, and language of sociology are male-created. They challenge this hegemony by arguing for an emphasis on women's experiences in everyday life. Smith and Collins, along with other standpoint theorists, contributed the insight that all knowledge emerges from the social position of the knower and can, at best, reflect only a partial understanding of the world. Today, it is widely accepted in sociology that "different standpoints lead to differences in what scholars think about" (Chafetz 1997: 100).

Feminists have been particularly influential in encouraging a shift from discussion of "sex roles" to a more critical application through the concept of "gender." The term "sex roles," a product of the structural-functional approach of Talcott Parsons that predominated in the mid-twentieth century, described how individuals acquired and carried out socially prescribed roles in the public and private spheres. For structural-functionalists, the expressive (emotional, care-taking) roles taken on by women complemented the instrumental (rational, task-oriented) roles played by men, and, grounded in the nuclear family, were necessary for the smooth functioning of social life (Carrigan et al. 1985: 553–557). Given the limiting role ascriptions assigned to men and women and the greater value assigned to men, feminists developed scathing critiques of sex role theory.

Through their critique, feminist theorists have successfully added "gender" as a major focus of sociology. Prior to feminist interventions, sociologists concentrated on the public sphere, understood to be the world of men, and research rarely took gender differences into account. Subfields looking at the private sphere of the family were considered secondary concerns and, although gender differences were noted in this area, women were defined primarily by their relationship to men. Feminist theorists challenged this framework in three important ways. They put women at the center of analysis, even in those areas usually dominated by men, such as work and politics. They challenged constructs drawn exclusively from male experience, such as stratification and workplace competition. They devoted more focused attention to the private sphere, traditionally understood to be women's domain, and explored issues such as housework and the socialization of children (Feltey and Rushing 1998: 214–215).

Sociologists have also significantly influenced the development of more productive ways to talk about gender. In 1987, Candace West and Don Zimmerman published their well-known article "Doing Gender," which was one of the first to present gender as an accomplishment of ongoing performances. They view gender not as an individual character trait but as an emergent feature of social structure, resulting from and legitimating existing societal institutions. They argue that doing gender is unavoidable, as one's gender is tied to allocations of power in all societal spheres and interpersonal relations (West and Zimmerman 1987). Judith Lorber continued this line of thought in her 1994 book *Paradoxes of Gender*, which argues that gender itself is a social institution. It "establishes patterns of expectations for individuals, orders the social processes of everyday life, is built into the major social organizations of society...and is also an entity in and of itself" (Lorber 1994: 1). She maintains that only by consciously restructuring the institution of gender can more egalitarian gender relations be established (Lorber 1994: 10). More recently, the 2008 book *Gendering Bodies* by Sara Crawley, Lara Foley, and Constance Shehan re-examines "doing gender," demonstrating how gender constructs the body through performance.

Conclusion

Feminist theory has made many important contributions to sociology's efforts to understand and improve the world, and indeed has redirected these efforts in numerous ways. Feminists have pushed women's issues and the concept of gender to the center of sociological analysis and have demanded that these issues be addressed from the standpoint of women. Additionally, feminists have highlighted the importance of issues of power, oppression, and domination, and the intersection of various forms of domination based on gender, race, class, and sexuality in sociological theory.

As noted in this chapter, feminists approach their research through a variety of insightful epistemologies and perspectives. Despite this variety, a central concern of feminist theory remains informing social change toward greater gender equality. For feminists, theory is necessarily tied to politics and, as globalization processes continue to accelerate, politics on the transnational level.

Informed by feminist theorizing more sharply attuned to difference, transnational feminist networks have emerged as major players organizing on issues such as violence against women, poverty, job security, land rights, the distribution of domestic work, and reproductive rights. They seek to influence international norms and conventions and thereby "reinvent globalization and reorient it from a project of markets to a project of peoples" (Moghadam 2005: 195, 199). Thus, while feminists have drawn upon and adapted sociological theories in efforts to reach their political objectives, they also aim to transform the field of sociology to be more responsive to women. Thus far, the relationship between feminism and sociology has proved to be mutually enlightening, as both work toward the shared goal of engendering a more egalitarian society.

References

Ahmed, Sara. 2004. Affective Economies. *Social Text* 22(2): 117–139.

Alcoff, Linda. 1997. Cultural Feminism versus Post-Structuralism: The Identity Crisis in Feminist Theory. In *The Second Wave: A Reader in Feminist Theory*. Edited by Linda Nicholson. New York, NY: Routledge.

Barthes, Roland. 1978. The Death of the Author. In *Image, Music, Text*. Selected and translated by Stephen Heath. New York, NY: Hill and Wang.

Basu, Amrita. 2000. Globalization of the Local/Localization of the Global: Mapping Transnational Women's Movements. *Meridians* 1(1): 68–109.

Beauvoir, Simone de. 1952. *The Second Sex*. New York, NY: Knopf.

Bunch, Charlotte. 2005[1979]. Not by Degrees: Feminist Theory and Education. In *Feminist Theory: A Reader*. Edited by Wendy K. Kolmar and Frances Bartkowski. 2nd edn. Boston, MA: McGraw-Hill.

Butler, Judith. 1990. *Gender Trouble: Feminism and the Subversion of Identity*. New York, NY: Routledge.

Carrigan, Tim, Bob Connell, and John Lee. 1985. Towards a New Sociology of Masculinity. *Theory and Society* 14(5): 551–604.

Chafetz, Janet Saltzman. 1997. Feminist Theory and Sociology: Underutilized Contributions for Mainstream Theory. *Annual Review of Sociology* 23(1997): 97–120.

Collins, Patricia Hill. 2013[1990]. *Defining Black Feminist Thought*. In *Feminist Theory Reader: Local and Global Perspectives*. Edited by Carole R. McCann and Seung-kyung Kim. New York, NY: Routledge.

Crawley, Sara, Lara Foley, and Constance Shehan. 2008. *Gendering Bodies*. Lanham, MD: Rowman and Littlefield.

Chodorow, Nancy. 1978. *The Reproduction of Mothering: Psychoanalysis and the Sociology of Gender*. Berkeley, CA: University of California Press.

Crenshaw, Kimberlé. 1993. Mapping the Margins. *Stanford Law Review* 43: 1241–1299.

Derrida, Jacques. 1976. *Of Grammatology*. Baltimore, MD: The Johns Hopkins University Press.

Dill, Bonnie Thornton and Ruth Enid Zambrana. 2009. *Emerging Intersections: Race, Class, and Gender in Theory, Policy and Practice*. New Brunswick, NJ: Rutgers University Press.

Feltey, Kathryn M. and Beth Rushing. 1998. Women and Power in Sociology: SWS as an Arena of Change. *Sociological Spectrum* 18(3): 211–219.

Flax, Jane. 1990. *Thinking Fragments: Psychoanalysis, Feminism, and Postmodernism in the Contemporary West*. Berkeley, CA: University of California Press.

Foucault, Michel. 1978. *A History of Sexuality. Vol. 1: An Introduction*. New York, NY: Vintage.

Fraser, Nancy. 1997. Structuralism or Pragmatics? On Discourse Theory and Feminist Politics. In *The Second Wave: A Reader in Feminist Theory*.

Edited by Linda Nicholson. New York, NY: Routledge.

Harding, Sandra. 1993. Rethinking Standpoint Epistemology: "What is Strong Objectivity?" In *Feminist Epistemologies*. Edited by Linda Alcoff and Elizabeth Potter. New York, NY: Routledge.

Hartmann, Heidi. 1981. The Unhappy Marriage of Marxism and Feminism. In *Women and Revolution*. Edited by Lydia Sargent. London: Pluto Press, 40–53.

Hartsock, Nancy. 1983. *Money, Sex and Power*. New York, NY: Longman.

Hemmings, Clare. 2006. The Life and Times of Academic Feminism. In *Handbook of Gender and Women's Studies*. Edited by Kathy Davis, Mary Evans, and Judith Lorber. Thousand Oaks, CA: Sage.

Jaggar, Alison M. 2013[1989]. Love and Knowledge: Emotion in Feminist Epistemology. In *Feminist Theory Reader: Local and Global Perspectives*. Edited by Carole R. McCann and Seung-Kyung Kim. New York, NY: Routledge.

Lacan, Jacques. 2007[1977]. *Ecrits: The First Complete English Edition*. New York, NY: W. W. Norton and Company.

Lorber, Judith. 1994. *Paradoxes of Gender*. New Haven, CT: Yale University Press.

Mann, Susan Archer. 2012. *Doing Feminist Theory: From Modernity to Postmodernity*. New York, NY: Oxford University Press.

McCann, Carole R., and Seung-Kyung Kim. eds. 2013. *Feminist Theory Reader: Local and Global Perspectives*. New York, NY: Routledge.

Moghadam, Valentine M. 2005. *Globalizing Women: Transnational Feminist Networks*. Baltimore, MD: John Hopkins University Press.

Mohanty, Chandra Talpade. 1991[1986]. Under Western Eyes: Feminist Scholarship and Colonial Discourses. In *Third World Women and the Politics of Feminism*. Edited by Chandra Talpade Mohanty, Ann Russo, and Lourdes Torres. Bloomington, IN: Indiana University Press.

Mohanty, Chandra Talpade. 2003. "Under Western Eyes" Revisited: Feminist Solidarity through Anticapitalist Struggles. In *Feminism Without Borders: Decolonizing Theory, Practicing Solidarity*. Durham, NC: Duke University Press.

Rubin, Gayle. 1975. The Traffic in Women. In *Toward an Anthropology of Women*. Edited by Rayna Reiter. New York, NY: Monthly Review Press, 157–210.

Sandoval, Chela. 1990. Feminism and Racism. In *Making Face, Making Soul/Hacienda Caras*. Edited by Gloria Anzaldúa. San Francisco, CA: Aunt Lute.

Scott, Joan. 1986. Gender: A Useful Category of Historical Analysis. *The American Historical Review* 91(5): 1053–1075.

Smith, Dorothy. 1990. *The Conceptual Practices of Power*. Boston, MA: Northeastern Press.

West, Candace and Don H. Zimmerman. 1987. Doing Gender. *Gender and Society* 1(2): 125–151.

Feminist Methodologies

Shulamit Reinharz and Nicholas Monroe

Contemporary historians generally agree that sociologist/journalist Betty Friedan's stirring 1963 book, *The Feminine Mystique* (TFM), sparked the second wave of the US Women's Movement. American women's parallel experiences in Civil Rights, free speech, and anti-war activities also helped lay the groundwork for the "aha moment" women experienced when reading Friedan's book. TFM unleashed a desire for social liberation while also spurring immediate changes in academia. At the women's educational institution, Barnard College, for example, all incoming first-year students in 1963 received a free copy of TFM with a request to read it over the summer and be prepared to discuss it during the fall orientation period. Future historians may be able to imbed the story of minority women's formulations of womanism and of non-Western feminists' struggles into a broader understanding of the origins of the Second Wave, but most agree that 1963 was a formative year.

Six years after the appearance of TFM, in 1969, Roberta Salper (2014) at San Diego State University established the first Women's Studies Program (WSP) in the nation, offering students a wide array of courses and support for political activism on- and off-campus. Since then, WSPs have proliferated in the United States and around the world. In the early years, WSP founders embraced three goals: to *add* courses and material about women into the curriculum in every academic field; to *delete* sexist courses and or modify sexist material about women that existed in the curriculum; and to *review* the research methods of every discipline in order to understand how those methods contributed to the dominance of sexist and misogynist "knowledge" (Reinharz 1989). Heretofore, the academy had believed that research methods were objective and without bias. How was it, then, that standard methods could produce "tainted" studies? In the early 1970s, faculty in the departments of history, sociology, anthropology and more – in addition to WSPs – began to study the impact of feminist ideas on research methods.

Because these methodological studies were not always welcome in traditional academic journals, feminist scholars recognized the need for alternative publication outlets. Beginning with *Feminist Studies* established in 1972, many new academic journals were launched. In the 2015 annual review of existing journals and reports, The Women and Gender Studies Section of the Association of College and Research Libraries identified at least thirty-seven contemporary examples. The best known are *Feminist Studies; Gender and Society; Journal of Feminist Studies in Religion; Signs: Journal of Women in Culture and Society; Psychology of Women Quarterly; Journal of Women's History;* and *Women's Studies International Forum.* Feminist scholars also produced countless book-length investigations, feminist monographs, edited collections, articles, chapters, and essays (Reinharz 1983). Published reviews in academic journals and in *The Women's Review of Books* (est. 1983) provided easy access to this literature.

As mentioned above, the question of research methods arose early in the development of feminist (or women's) studies. At first, many scholars asserted that a distinctive feminist research method existed. Its defining characteristic eschewed quantitative techniques in favor of qualitative, narrative approaches that gave voice to individuals or groups with limited social power. The rationale for this argument was that quantification of women's experience distorted and minimized it while trying to measure it or determine how widespread it was. Much of women's experience, such as sexual harassment, a term coined in 1991, was not yet even named! Others argued vigorously that to abandon quantitative techniques was to *dis*-empower women and to buy into the derogatory stereotype of female essentialist math-phobia. In addition, discarding quantitative research meant that certain questions could not be asked because qualitative techniques could not serve as substitutes.

If the quantitative/qualitative divide was not the way to differentiate feminist from non-feminist research, what was? In response to this question, numerous thinkers proposed new theoretical and epistemological stances. These began with standpoint theory, which asserts that people situated in different places in a social hierarchy understand the world differently from those in other places and thus have different types of knowledge. Moreover, it behooves researchers to construct effective knowledge from the insights of women's experience. Major standpoint theorists include sociologists Dorothy Smith (1987) and Patricia Hill Collins, philosophers Sandra Harding (1987; 2006) and Nancy Hartsock (1998), and theorist of science Donna Haraway (1991). Each of these scholars has published extensively about the theory she believes should underpin feminist research. Standpoint theory challenges the objectivist or positivist view that there is one reality "out there" that can be grasped intellectually if proper methods are used.

Standpoint theory gave birth to other methodological concepts including intersectionality, multiculturalism, and transnational feminisms. Intersectionality is a methodological position that requires the study of intersections between systems of oppression, domination, or discrimination (see the work of Patricia Hill Collins, Susan Mann, and Kimberlé Crenshaw (1989; 1991; 2014). Typically, an intersectional study integrates an examination of class, race, gender, and more. Multiculturalism concerns the reality of multiple groups, each with its own culture or cultures existing within one society (see the work of political theorist Susan Okin (1999)). The methodological implication of multiculturalism is the need for awareness of ethnocentrism and overgeneralization in research. The concept of transnational feminisms refers to the idea that feminism means different things in different societies and that, ironically, some forms of feminism are rooted in colonialism (see Chandra Mohanty 2013). Epistemological positions from critical theory, post-structuralism and queer theory further expanded the search for "feminist research methods."

As early as 1992, sufficient research and epistemological writing had been accomplished to warrant an overview that would address the question: is there a single (or several or no) feminist method(s)? In the book, *Feminist Methods in Social Research*, Shulamit Reinharz (with then graduate student Lynn Davidman) addressed that question empirically by reviewing a broad array of studies that authors stated were conducted from a feminist perspective. This book reached ten conclusions, including the following ideas: (1) feminism is a perspective, not a research method; (2) feminists use a multiplicity of research methods; (3) feminist research involves an ongoing critique of non-feminist scholarship; and (4) feminist research is guided by feminist theory.

From the late 1980s until today, there has been a continuous and intensive exploration of feminist research methods. Some of the important contributors to these debates include Sandra Harding, Caroline Ramazanoglu and Janet Holland (2002), Marjorie DeVault (1999), Nancy Naples (2003), Joey Sprague (2005), and Sharlene Hesse-Biber (Hesse-Biber and Leavy 2007). A major conclusion that arises from their work is that feminist researchers are highly attuned to epistemology and that the debate about the existence and nature of feminist research methods is ongoing.

The last two decades (1995–present) ushered in other significant developments in feminist academic studies. Women's studies expanded into gender studies (including the study of men and masculinity) and sexuality studies (including queer and transgender studies). While some feminist scholars believe that this transformation comes at the expense of the study of women, methodological discussions within gender and sexuality studies are now part of the discourse on feminist research methods.

Although not every social scientist is interested in feminism or gender, the work of feminist researchers has had a salutary impact on research in general. For example, it has shown the weakness of male-only or whites-only studies of social phenomena. Researchers have come to understand that women and men differ and are alike in various ways and that studies cannot make assumptions from one gender about another. Research topics of feminist researchers are likely to include those of concern to women in particular or to examine phenomena or people whose "voices" have not been heard (Reinharz 1994). In general, therefore, although strictly objectivist sociologists may consider the concept of "feminist research" to be an oxymoron because it links a social movement with scientific investigation, sociological research has benefited from the new epistemologies and questions raised by applying a feminist lens to research activity. To the extent that the concept of feminist research introduces new topics, new groups of people, and new explorations of bias, it has improved social research.

Intersectionality and Black Feminist Thought

Intersectionality has arguably been the most important recent theoretical and analytical contribution of feminist thinkers (MacKinnon 2013). Though Kimberlé Crenshaw actually coined the term "intersectionality," it represents the work of a long line of black feminists and activists (Nash 2011: 452). Building upon Crenshaw and others, Patricia Hill Collins's influential book *Black Feminist Thought* (2009) solidified intersectionality's place as a central theoretical and analytic tool for contemporary scholars. While its meaning and potential uses are debated, its contribution to research practices remains irrefutable.

Intersectionality emerged from a critique of Second Wave feminists' theoretical exclusion of black women's unique social location. In other words, "central to intersectionality is the idea that all of us have multiple identities – race, gender, class, sexual orientation, etc. – and these multiple social identities intersect in ways that shape the form and extent of the discrimination we experience." Intersectionality helped reveal that "Black women and White women are not equally vulnerable to the same specific forms of gender discrimination" (Carbado and Gulati 2013: 529). This focus on black women does not exhaust the ways in which intersectionality is useful. In fact, nowhere does Kimberlé Crenshaw "state that intersectionality is linked only with black women or that the theory is just about race and gender." Rather she "focused on race and gender and black women specifically because of [intersectionality's] intellectual tradition" (Carbado and Gulati 2013: 530). Researchers should not conflate intersectionality's origins with its functions as an analytical tool.

Intersectionality has been criticized for simply adding variables of human identity. This critique fails to recognize the ways in which identities are dynamically constructed and evolve. Patrick Grzanka notes that intersectionality is "primarily concerned with how social inequalities are formed and maintained; accordingly, identities and the politics thereof are the *products* of historically entrenched, institutional systems of domination and violence" and "intersectional analyses direct their critical attention to categories, structure, and systems that produce and support multiple *dimensions of difference*" (Grzanka 2014: xv). Intersectional analysis recognizes the dynamic realities that constitute human experience and their locations within various structures of domination.

Chief among the many themes intersectional scholars address are the notions of normativity and exclusion. Intersectional researchers acknowledge "differences among women...[and touch on] the most pressing problem facing contemporary feminism – the long and painful legacy of exclusions" (Davis 2008: 70). Davis's reflection on intersectionality identifies the ways it corrects scholarship that fails to acknowledge the multiplicity of human experiences and the ways in which a person's unique social location impacts her/his life experiences and outcomes. However, intersectionality is not simply about moving particular groups from "margin to center." It also examines the processes by which "margins" and "centers" are created and the ways groups are marginalized or privileged within society.

In addition, intersectional scholars contest researchers' exclusionary practices (Davis 2008). Intersectional scholars imagine alternative ways of knowing in response to the historically biased and privileged standpoints of many white scholars (Collins 2009[2000]; Davis 2008; Grzanka 2014). Frost and Elichaoff note that "Collins's work (*Black Feminist Thought*) identified a standpoint that allowed for an identification and examination of how social location makes for a perspective connected to lived experience. This approach allowed critical questions about knowledge and the role of power in constructing knowledge to be asked...the invisible history of black women started to be uncovered through the adoption of the intersectionality approach" (2014: 58). Thus, intersectionality requires researchers to explore both the various ways knowledge is constructed and to critique privileged knowledge.

Intersectional scholars examine their relationships with the individuals and groups they study and how those relationships impact the production of knowledge. Reflexivity is particularly important to intersectional scholars who wish to locate themselves within the multiple and over-lapping categories of human organization (Reinharz 2011). Intersectional scholars are "constantly engaged in critique of their own work and refinement of their ideas and practices" in order to consider their own social location and examine the ways in which they have omitted vital components or interpretations of the lives of those they research (Grzanka 2014: xix–xx). Isolating single variables of human identity does not offer the sociologist the most effective, nuanced, or comprehensive manner in which to examine social life. No matter the research question, it is incumbent upon sociologists to consider the ways in which the various components of a person are made relevant through social processes and circumstances.

Intersectionality strives to perform social justice oriented scholarship (Jaggar 2008). Created by women who recognized that individuals could not be reduced to a single category, scholars who use an intersectional perspective explore how categories are constructed and how a person's location within a matrix of categories, in turn, defines her/his life. Intersectional legal scholars argued that a black woman could be discriminated against for being a *black woman* even if she was not discriminated against for being *either* black *or* a woman. While "intersectionality" was initially developed within a legal context, the idea is relevant across the social sciences.

Black "feminist ideology...declares the visibility of black women. It acknowledges the fact that two innate and inerasable traits, being both black and female, constitute our special status in American society...[and that] black feminism asserts self-determination as essential" (King 1988: 72). This declaration of visibility originates from the distinct location of black women as African Americans *and* as women and emerges from the historical exclusion of black women's concerns from white feminist agendas. Unlike many other intellectual traditions, Black Feminist Thought includes the ideas of academics, non-academics, and women not perceived as intellectuals (Collins 2009; Christian 2007).

Third World/Non-Western Feminism

Although there is no agreed upon definition of Third World, in Western parlance it generally refers to countries that formerly were colonies of Western powers (e.g., Netherlands, Belgium, Great Britain, Portugal, France, Germany, and Italy) or to countries whose economies are under-developed, frequently because of Western intervention (Lopman, forthcoming). Third World feminist research explores the experiences of non-Western and indigenous women throughout the world and then treats their experiences as central to feminist research. This definition does not resolve the conflicts among non-Western feminists. One example is the mixed response to Somali-born, Dutch-American feminist writer, Ayaan Hirsi Ali's (2010) condemnation of Islamic practices, such as genital mutilation (some view her as promoting Islamophobia and as, therefore, disrespectful of Muslim feminists). Geraldine Heng notes:

> *Third-World feminism, by virtue of its vexed historical origins and complicated negotiations with contemporary state apparatuses, is necessarily a chimerical, hydra-headed creature, surviving in a plethora of lives and guises. In some countries, it may manifest itself as an organized national movement, complete with networks and regional chapters. In other countries, it may exist only as a kind of hit-and-run guerila feminism: a feminism, perhaps, that arises spontaneously around issue-centered activity, that organizes itself in small, temporary neighborhood groupings which may eschew or refuse the name of feminism...the difficulty of discussing Third-World feminism arises in the first instance as a difficulty of identifying the concretions and forms of effectivity in the Third-World that can be grasped as feminist (1997: 30).*

In their interaction with Western thought, Third World feminists typically reject essentialist interpretations of people who represent a wide variety of racial, ethnic, national, and class backgrounds. These feminist scholars seek precision in defining Third World feminism, asking who enacts it, exploring who/what are its foci, and then examining how it is practiced. Third World feminist research faces many challenges in reconciling Western feminist ideas, a prime example of which is how to study the widespread practice of female genital mutilation – as a valued cultural practice or a harmful bodily practice?

Third World feminists reject the idea that Western, white, middle-class perspectives represent all women, and simultaneously challenge stereotypes about Third World women. They maintain that researchers must be very specific in describing which women they study and which conclusions they can draw based on their sample. They also point out the uniqueness of the Third World feminist perspective. For example, Alexander and Mohanty resist Western feminism's status as the originator and leader of feminist thought and dismiss notions that Third World feminism is merely a response to or copy of Western feminism (1997: xx). Instead, they point out that Third World feminism is always connected to its Third World roots. While individual Third World feminists undertake varied types of research, all Third World feminist research remains tied to the diverse circumstances of Third World women. Mohanty notes that many feminist writings "discursively colonize the material and historical heterogeneities of the lives of women in the Third World, thereby producing/representing a composite, singular 'Third World women' – an image that appears arbitrarily constructed but nevertheless carries with it the authorizing signature of Western humanist discourse" (2003:19). This singular portrayal of Third World women fails to capture the diversity of the Third World, thus crippling opportunities for effective activism and research.

Third World feminists also resist depictions of the Third World as "traditional." Mohanty notes that referring to Third World women "as a stable category of analysis...assumes an ahistorical, universal unity between women based on a generalized notion of their subordination...this analytical move limits the definition of the female subject to gender identity, completely bypassing social class and ethnic identities" (2003: 31). These portrayals of Third World women marginalize their views by locating their perspectives outside contemporary feminist discourse (Spivak 1988).

Furthermore, Third World Feminism recognizes the agency and subjectivity of Third World women and rejects attempts to "other" them. Mohanty notes that, "universal images of the Third World woman (the veiled woman, chaste virgin, etc.)...are predicated upon (and hence obviously bring into sharper focus) assumptions about Western women as secular, liberated, and having control of their own lives" (2003: 42). Narayan adds that "problems that affect particular groups of Third-World women are more often assumed to be primarily, if not entirely, results of an imagined unitary complex called 'their Traditions/Religions/Cultures' – where these terms are represented as virtually synonymous with each other...completely misrepresenting the real nature of these problems" (Narayan 1997: 50). Third World feminism contributes to social research by refocusing discourse and analysis on the margins, thus building more comprehensive and representative research findings. As is true of all feminist research, Third World feminist studies compel scholars to think reflexively about their orientation to their research and to consider how their biases affect the types of questions, analysis, and conclusions they create (Wilson et al. 2005).

Non-Print Media

Recent technological advances have impacted the capabilities and content of feminist research. As mentioned above, feminist research initially relied on qualitative methods involving face-to-face interactions. But just as new technologies – particularly the internet, available at home, work, and via the cell phone everywhere and at all times – have shaped contemporary life worldwide, so too they have shaped methodological possibilities and practices. In turn, these new opportunities have enlarged the scope of research opportunities.

One of the most significant developments is the ubiquity of social media whose platforms (e.g., Facebook, Twitter, and YouTube) offer resources to conduct research and to consider the impact technology has on feminist research. Brown and Thomas (2014) ask how online forums can be used as tools of violence and oppression, while also considering the impact social media have on the construction of identity and agency of teenage girls. They complicate recent findings that focus on the ways in which girls and queer youth articulate and develop identities through online "safe spaces." While Brown and Thomas acknowledge the relevance of these findings, they also note "self-representation ultimately does not enable girls to redefine the ways that girlhood is coded through normative meanings of gender, race, class, and sexuality" (Brown and Thomas 2014: 952). Pro-ana (pro-anorexia) sites, for example, with information that girls use to starve themselves, are prime examples of the fact that sites that define themselves as safe spaces may actually endanger girls and women (Schall 2004). While the internet offers some space for identity formation and expression, it remains important to consider how these identities exist within and in relation to hegemonic patriarchal power structures.

Abbasgholizadeh (2014) notes that women can use the internet to gather, participate in social movements, sign petitions, organize, and expand existing social networks. This is important to feminist research in at least two ways. First, the contemporary person's online presence provides vast sources of data never before available (although the existence of avatars and other online personalities must be taken into consideration). The internet also offers feminist researchers opportunities to access the perspectives of more people than ever before. For example, interviews can take place over Skype, which provides free access to people all over the world. Simple emails can elicit large groups of research participants and online surveys can access immediately the opinions of large numbers of people. Of course, this information can lead to concerns with validity. Also, ethical considerations in this burgeoning research field are in their infancy. Feminist researchers are considering how technology influences the gathering, processing, and analyzing of data as well as the kinds of research questions asked (Turkle 1984).

Sexuality and Queer Studies

Adrienne Rich's 1980 article on "Compulsory Heterosexuality," alerting feminist researchers that they assumed the ubiquity of heterosexuality, contributed to the emergence of Sexuality and Queer Studies. One foundational thought in the studies that followed is that sex, gender, and sexuality are relevant to every aspect of human existence, and that sexualities occupy a central place in our understanding of the social construction of reality, experiences, and oppression.

Sexuality Studies responded to the historically narrow focus on white middle-class heterosexual sexuality as normative. Sexuality and Queer Studies challenge this normativity and recognize the multitude of human experiences. Moreover, this relatively new field emphasizes the historically situated nature of sexuality, pointing out that contemporary paradigms of sex and gender are relatively new phenomena (Donnan and Magowan 2010). Sexuality should thus be understood as a historically situated, socially constructed phenomenon.

Sexuality scholars tend to focus on context: spatial location, temporality, cultural attitudes, and norms. The interaction between public and private realms in relation to sex, gender, and sexuality are crucial for sexuality and queer scholars. As Richardson point out, sex "is not just a private matter, or one of individuality." He challenges "the fiction that there is a public/private divide when it comes to sexual practices" (Richardson et al. 2013: 7–8). This perspective has obvious implications for research design and coincides with feminist researchers who contest binary systems as they illuminate the social construction of systems and institutions. Queer theory, according to Richardson, "contends that fixed ideas about gender and sexuality are never 'normal', they are 'normative.'" Furthermore, "queer, both as theory and method, refuses to categorize people or things according to binary oppositions" (Richardson et al. 2013: 45). The "*analytical* purpose of queer theory [...] is to denaturalize the discursive constructs that inform debates and identities associated with 'deviant' practices..." (Richardson et al. 2013: 52).

Queer Studies and transgender awareness are having a profound impact on feminist research. Building on the works of Foucault and Judith Butler (1993; 1999; 2004), feminist and sexuality scholars are developing specific orientations to research and activism. The efforts of scholars of sexuality shift the focus of marginalized sexual communities to the center. Sexuality researchers challenge the construction of normativity and help develop a more complete and representative understanding of sex, gender, and sexuality. Clearly, Sexuality and Queer Studies recognize that social experiences and identities continuously evolve and exist in specific spatial and temporal contexts.

Concluding Remarks

Feminist research methods and methodology are not fixed entities. While originally formed in the early 1960s in the United States, by the 1970s and 1980s, heated conversations were taking place among feminist, as well as mainstream, researchers, about how to go about studying the world, given new feminist insights. Intersectionality broadened the discussion to challenge researchers to understand dimensions of existence in their intersection with the status of girl/woman. Third World approaches broadened the field even further to include a worldwide scope that does not define women exclusively in Western terms. New technologies challenged feminist research to harness and make use of new tools. Finally, Sexuality/Queer Studies further challenged feminist research not to assume heterosexual norms among women and girls.

Feminist methodologies have benefited the discipline of sociology and society and continue to challenge normative thinking. For example, feminist emphasis of seeing the other as subject, not only as object, changes the status of the individual in research. Other assumptions about binary sexualities and sexual orientations are also challenged. As researchers apply feminist perspectives, their research is increasingly understood as a social act in which meaning is created through multiple parties. The role of the researcher is part of this equation rather than standing outside the research space. Finally, feminist research has aided numerous disciplines by making the invisible visible, by seeking to understand voices, not only "research responses," by uncovering Western world bias, and by including factors of oppression in the understanding of phenomena.

References

Abbasgholizadeh, Mahboubeh. 2014. To do Something We are Unable to do in Iran: Cyberspace, the Public Sphere, and the Iranian Women's Movement. *Signs* 39(4): 831–840.

Alexander, M. Jacqui and Chandra Talpade Mohanty. eds. 1997. Introduction: Genealogies, Legacies, Movements. In *Feminist Genealogies, Colonial Legacies, Democratic Futures*. New York, NY, and London: Routledge.

Ali, Ayaan Hirsi. 2010. *Nomad. A Personal Journey from Islam to America through a Clash of Civilizations*. New York, NY: Simon and Schuster.

Brown, Adriane and Mary E. Thomas. 2014. I Just like Knowing They Can Look at It and Realize Who I Really Am: Recognition and the Limits of Girlhood Agency on MySpace. *Signs* 39(4): 949–972.

Butler, Judith. 1993. *Bodies That Matter: On the Discursive Limits of Sex*. New York, NY: Routledge.

Butler, Judith. 1999. *Gender Trouble: Feminism and the Subversion of Identity*. New York, NY: Routledge.

Butler, Judith. 2004. *Undoing Gender*. New York, NY: Routledge.

Carbado, Devon W. and Mitu Gulati. 2013. The Intersectional Fifth Black Woman. *Du Bois Review* 10(2): 527–540.

Christian, Barbara. 2007. In *New Black Feminist Criticism, 1985–2000*. Edited by Gloria Bowles, M. Giulia Fabi, and Arlene R. Keizer. Urbana and Chicago, IL: University of Illinois Press.

Collins, Patricia Hill. 2009[2000]. *Black Feminist Thought: Knowledge, Consciousness, and the Politics of Empowerment*. 2nd edn. New York, NY, and London: Routledge Classics.

Crenshaw, Kimberlé. 1989. Demarginalizing the Intersection of Race and Sex: A Black Feminist Critique of Antidiscrimination Doctrine, Feminist Theory and Antiracist Politics. *University of Chicago Legal Forum*, 139–167.

Crenshaw, Kimberlé. 1991. Mapping the Margins: Intersectionality, Identity Politics, and Violence Against Women of Color. *Stanford Law Review* 43(6): 1241–1299.

Crenshaw, Kimberlé Williams. 2014. The Structural and Political Dimensions of Intersectional Oppression. In *Intersectionality: A Foundations and Frontiers Reader*. Edited by Patrick R. Grzanka. Boulder, CO: Westview Press.

Davis, Kathy. 2008. Intersectionality as Buzzword: A Sociology of Science Perspective on What Makes a Feminist Theory Successful. *Feminist Theory* 9(67): 67–85.

DeVault, Marjorie L. 1999. *Liberating Method: Feminism and Social Research*. Philadelphia, PA: Temple University Press.

Donnan, Hastings and Fiona Magowan. 2010. *The Anthropology of Sex*. New York, NY: Berg.

Friedan, Betty. 1963. *The Feminine Mystique*. New York, NY: Norton.

Frost, Nollaig and Frauke Elichaoff. 2014. Feminist Research Practice: A Primer. In *Feminist Research Practice: A Primer*. Edited by Sharlene Nagy Hesse-Biber. 2nd edn. Los Angeles, CA: Sage.

Grzanka, Patrick R. 2014. Introduction: Intersectional Objectivity. In *Intersectionality: A Foundations and Frontiers Reader*. Edited by Patrick R. Grzanka. Boulder, CO: Westview Press.

Haraway, Donna. 1991. *Simians, Cyborgs, and Women: The Reinvention of Nature*. New York, NY: Routledge.

Harding, Sandra G. 1987. *Feminism and Methodology: Social Science Issues*. Bloomington, IN: Indiana University Press.

Harding, Sandra. 2006. *Science and Social Inequality: Feminist and Postcolonial Issues*. Urbana, IL: University of Illinois Press.

Hartsock, Nancy. 1998. *The Feminist Standpoint Revisited and Other Essays*. Boulder, CO: Westview Press.

Heng, Geraldine. 1997. "A Great Way to Fly": Nationalism, the State, and the Varieties of Third-World Feminism. In *Feminist Genealogies, Colonial Legacies, Democratic Futures*. Edited by M. Jacqui Alexander and Chandra Talpade Mohanty. New York, NY and London: Routledge.

Hesse-Biber, Sharlene Nagy, and Patricia Leavy. eds. 2007. *Feminist Research Practice: A Primer*. Thousand Oaks, CA: Sage.

Jaggar, Alison M. 2008. *Just Methods: An Interdisciplinary Feminist Reader*. Boulder, CO, and London: Paradigm Publishers.

King, Deborah K. 1988. Multiple Jeopardy, Multiple Consciousness: The Context of a Black Feminist Ideology. *Signs* 14(1): 42–72.

Lopman, Louise. *El Salvador NOT For Sale! Postwar Struggles for Dignity, Human Rights, and Social Justice* (forthcoming).

MacKinnon, Catherine A. 2013. Intersectionality as Method: A Note. *Signs* 38(4): 1019–1030.

Mohanty, Chandra Talpade. 2003. *Feminism without Borders: Decolonizing Theory, Practicing Solidarity*. Durham, NC: Duke University Press.

Mohanty, Chandra Talpade. 2013. Transnational Feminist Crossings: On Neoliberalism and Radical Critique. *Signs* 38(4): 967–991.

Naples, Nancy A. 2003. *Feminism and Method: Ethnography, Discourse Analysis, and Activist Research*. London and New York, NY: Routledge.

Narayan, Uma. 1997. *Dislocating Cultures: Identities, Traditions, and Third-World Feminism*. New York, NY, and London: Routledge.

Nash, Jennifer C. 2011. "Home Truths" on Intersectionality. *Yale Journal of Law and Feminism* 23(2): 445–470.

Okin, Susan. 1999. *Is Multiculturalism Bad for Women?* Princeton, NJ: Princeton University Press.

Ramazanoglu, Caroline and Janet Holland. 2002. *Feminist Methodology: Challenges and Choices*. London and Thousand Oaks, CA: Sage Publications.

Reinharz, Shulamit. 1989. Teaching the History of Women's Contributions to Sociology: Or, D. S. Thomas, Wasn't She the One Who Was Married to W.I? *The American Sociologist* 20(1): 87–94.

Reinharz, Shulamit. 1994. Toward an Ethnography of "Voice" and "Silence." In *Human Diversity: Perspectives on People in Context*. Edited by Edison Trickett, Roderick Watts and Dina Birman. San Francisco, CA: Jossey-Bass, 178–200.

Reinharz, Shulamit. 2011. *Observing the Observer: Understanding Our Selves in Field Research*. New York, NY: Oxford University Press.

Reinharz, Shulamit, with Lynn Davidman. 1992. *Feminist Methods in Social Research*. New York, NY: Oxford University Press.

Reinharz, Shulamit with Marti Bombyk and Jan Wright. 1983. Methodological Issues in Feminist Research: A Bibliography of Literature in Women's Studies, Sociology and Psychology. *Women's Studies International Forum* 6(4): 437–454.

Rich, Adrienne. 1980. Compulsory Heterosexuality and Lesbian Existence. *Signs* 5(4): 631–660.

Richardson, Niall, Clarissa Smith, and Angela Werndly. eds. 2013. *Studying Sexualities: Theories, Representations, Cultures*. Houndmills, Basingstoke, Hampshire and New York, NY: Palgrave Macmillan.

Salper, Roberta. 2014. *Domestic Subversive: A Feminist's Take on the Left 1960–1976*. Tucson, AZ: Anaphora Literary Press.

Schall, Lindsay B. 2004. The Irony of Pro-Anorexia Websites: The Two Faces of Support. Honors Thesis, Sociology, Brandeis University.

Smith, Dorothy. 1987. *The Everyday World as Problematic: A Feminist Sociology* (Northeastern Series on Feminist Theory). Boston, MA: Northeastern University Press.

Spivak, Gayatri Chakravorty. 1988. Can the Subaltern Speak? In *Marxism and the Interpretation of Culture*. Edited by Cary Nelson and Lawrence Grossberg. Urbana, IL: University of Illinois Press, 271–313.

Sprague, Joey. 2005. *Feminist Methodologies for Critical Researchers: Bridging Differences*. New York, NY: AltaMira/Rowman and Littlefield.

Turkle, Sheryl. 1984. *The Second Self: Computers and the Human Spirit* New York, NY: Simon and Schuster.

Wilson, Shamillah, Anasuya Sengupta, and Kristy Evans. eds. 2005. *Defending Our Dreams: Global Feminist Voices for a New Generation*. London and New York, NY: Zed Books.

Part IV
SPECIALTY AREAS

CHAPTER 10

The Sociology of Non-human Animals and Society

Elizabeth Cherry

Introduction

The sociological study of non-human animals in society is relatively new within the broader field of sociology, though it has its roots in early sociology. Foundational sociological theorists frequently used animals as a comparative group when explaining human behavior and some even called for the study of animals in society. The contemporary sociology of non-human animals in society emerged in the 1970s, when sociologists began to pay more attention to the interrelationship between the social world and the natural world. Since then, sociologists have studied animal issues in nearly every major field of sociological research, and they have developed a subfield specifically on the study of non-human animals in society. While the broader fields of human-animal studies and critical animal studies are truly interdisciplinary, this chapter focuses on the development of and variations within sociology. This chapter looks at classical sociological theorists' conceptions of animals and how contemporary sociologists study social problems related to companion animals, farm animals, wildlife, animal testing, animals in entertainment, and animal rights and vegetarian issues.

Classical Sociology and Animals

Since one of the major goals of early sociologists was to develop sociology as a social science, two of their main strategies were to demonstrate the unique qualities of human interaction and to establish human society as an object of study. One of the tactics classical sociologists used to achieve these goals was to distinguish human and animal behavior. Animals merely follow instincts, they argued, but humans have agency, and therefore we need sociology to study why and how human society functions as it does. Many foundational sociological theorists, including Karl Marx, Emile Durkheim, Max Weber, and George Herbert Mead, employed these tactics in their writings, and this foundational perspective remained largely in place until the 1970s.

In his early descriptions of "species being" in *Capital*, Karl Marx (1976: 283–284) compared human workers to animals merely following their instincts:

> We presuppose labor in a form in which it is an exclusively human characteristic. A spider conducts operations which resemble those of the weaver, and a bee would put many a human architect to shame by the construction of its honeycomb cells. But what distinguishes the worst architect from the best of bees is that the architect builds the cell in his mind before he constructs it in wax.

To Marx, humans' ability to envision a plan ideally (i.e., in thought), and then carry it out, differentiated humans from nonhuman animals. Moreover, Marx argued that humans are driven to fulfill their "species being" by working with these higher-order levels of engagement and thought. Even if a beaver could build a better dam than a human, Marx viewed humans as superior because we are able to envision our poorly constructed dam in our heads before carrying it out in wood.

Emile Durkheim did not use animals as comparisons for human behavior, but he discussed animals as representations of society through the totemic principle (1995). Totems are publicly available, collective symbols that are shared by most members of a society and that represent society to its members. A key aspect of totems is that they are not based on powerful, "cosmic" images, such as the moon, the sun, or the stars. Instead, totems are based on relatively insignificant animals or plants, which represent the sacred. Therefore religions do not worship the animals or plants themselves, but rather the sacred things they represent.

In the introduction to their reader on animals and society, Arluke and Sanders (2009) cite Max Weber's writing on animals:

> In so far [as the behavior of animals is subjectively understandable] it would be theoretically possible to formulate a sociology of the relations of men to animals, both domestic and wild. Thus, many animals "understand" commands, anger, love, hostility, and react to them in ways which are evidently often by no means purely instinctive and mechanical and in some sense both consciously meaningful and affected by experience (Weber 1947: 104).

Although this quote indicates that Weber appeared to be interested in including animals in sociological research, they never became a central aspect of his work.

The most famous example of a classical sociologist engaging animal issues is George Herbert Mead, in his writing on the development of the self. Mead used animals as a foil for human interaction, claiming that animals were social beings but that their interactions did not involve the use of shared symbols. He noted that, "[w]e do not assume that the dog says to himself, 'If the animal comes from this direction he is going to spring at my throat and I will turn in such a way'" (1934: 42). In contrast, humans use "significant symbols" (1934: 47) or a (typically vocal) gesture that elicits the same meaning from the sender and the receiver. Since animals do not use significant symbols, Mead claimed, they cannot negotiate meaning or take the role of the other.

This exclusion of animals from sociological study continued throughout the better part of the twentieth century. In the 1970s, as society focused increased attention on environmental issues, sociologists also began to pay more attention to the interconnectedness of the natural and the social worlds. William Catton and Riley Dunlap (1978) called this the move from the HEP to the NEP. The HEP, or the Human Exemptionalist Paradigm, is the idea that humans are fundamentally different from other animals, and that humans are exempt from the laws of nature. Dunlap and Catton said sociology had been functioning under this Human Exemptionalist Paradigm and called for a move to the NEP, or New Ecological Paradigm, under which we would view humans as one part of a larger ecosystem and society as interconnected with the natural world and the laws of nature. Around the same time, Clifton Bryant (1979) wrote an article calling on sociologists to focus on the "zoological connection" or relationships between humans and animals. In the years that followed, many sociologists heeded this call, and the study of animals and society emerged.

Animal Studies in Symbolic Interaction

The first major works in human-animal studies came from symbolic interactionists. These sociologists focused on the interactions between humans and animals, as well as that among humans related to animal behavior. Building upon the works of Mead, Cooley, and James, among others, they explored animal selfhood and the use of language beyond spoken human language.

Arnold Arluke and Clinton Sanders (1996) explored the interactions among humans with regard to animal behavior, as well as interactions between humans and animals. For example, they studied the interactions between dogs and their owners at a dog training group. Going further, they looked at how animals factored into human interaction. They showed how dog owners "speak for" their dogs at the veterinarian's office, sometimes putting on a special voice for their dog. They also explored the emotion management of animal shelter employees as they work with irresponsible owners surrendering their dogs. Looking at the social construction of animals, they asked: How do we as a society differentiate between wild and domesticated animals? How do we distinguish between companion animals and lab animals, especially when they are the same breed? Their interviews with technicians in animal laboratories help us understand the symbolic and social boundaries constructed between these types of animals.

Continuing the tradition of symbolic interaction, Leslie Irvine's (2004) *If You Tame Me* focused more on animal selfhood and subjectivity. Irvine critiqued George Herbert Mead for his over-emphasis on spoken human language, giving examples of chimpanzees and gorillas who learned American Sign Language. Using William James's definition of the "I," she showed how we might understand selfhood among animals. Animals have a sense of agency, of coherence, of affectivity, and of self-history (or continuity), she argued, and therefore animals have a sense of self and of their own subjectivity. Animals understand humans' emotions and moods, and by interacting with humans in different ways according to those different moods, animals and humans share intersubjectivity.

Companion animals can also help humans develop a social self. Animals help us define ourselves and others (Sanders 1999), and we use animals to define ourselves with regards to gender (Ramirez 2006). In his study of dog owners, Michael Ramirez showed how people use animals as props to display their own gender identities. Women emphasized the loving relationships they had with their dogs, whereas men emphasized participating in outdoor activities with their dogs, thus exemplifying traditional gender behaviors.

Companion Animals and Social Problems

Sociologists studying companion animal issues in relation to social problems tend to focus on two main aspects: one, companion animals as comfort for people experiencing social problems, and two, companion animals experiencing social problems themselves. Early research in this area centered on the animal companions of women experiencing intimate partner violence. In Clifton Flynn's (2000) interviews with battered women, 50 percent of women said their partners threatened and/or harmed their companion animals. Twenty percent of all women with companion animals, and 40 percent of women whose companion animals had been harmed, said they delayed seeking shelter out of concern for their pet. The abusers used their female partners' companion animals as a way of showing power and maintaining control in the relationship. To the women, their pets helped to comfort them, and sometimes even protect them from their abusers. These companion animals, however, also experienced emotional responses to witnessing women's abuse.

Companion animals also comfort prisoners, and they play a role in prison-based animal training programs. Gennifer Furst (2011) studied animal interventions in prison programs, and she found that working with the animals positively changed the prisoners. Prisoners received positive social feedback from the prison staff and from family members, who saw the prisoners' animal training as making a positive contribution to society. Participants in these programs also grew emotionally, becoming better in touch with their emotions, exhibiting better social interactions with others, and even experiencing positive physical changes, such as weight loss from taking their dogs on walks.

In her study of companion animals in natural disasters, Leslie Irvine (2009) also found that companion animals provided comfort to their human guardians. However, these companion animals, like those in Clifton Flynn's (2000) research, experienced negative stress as a result of these ties. In the aftermath of Hurricane Katrina, Irvine found that rescuers told families they could not be rescued with their pets and that rescuers would only save humans. Some families stayed behind to care for their companion animals and others were forced to make the difficult decision between saving human family and non-human animal family members. Some of the companion animals who were left behind were killed by police, and others were saved by the Humane Society of the United States, who set up shelters to help reconnect people with their companion animals.

Perhaps the most common form of social problem related to companion animals is that of animal abuse. Arnold Arluke and his colleagues (1999) tested the violence graduation hypothesis against the deviance generalization hypothesis to try to find whether animal abuse precedes, predicts, follows, or otherwise accompanies other forms of abuse and crime. They found that animal abusers were significantly more likely than those who did not abuse animals to commit other types of abuse and anti-social acts, but, contrary to popular conceptions, found that animal abuse tended to follow, rather than precede, non-violent crimes.

Farm Animals and Social Problems

More than 9 billion farm animals were slaughtered in the United States in 2013 (Humane Society of the United States 2016). Issues related to farmed animals are a primary area of concern for sociologists interested in human-animal relations. Researchers in this area study farm and slaughterhouse communities, as well as how farm animals are raised, treated, and slaughtered.

With 28,752,000 cattle slaughtered for meat production in the United States in 2015 (Humane Society of the United States 2016), many people might think that all ranchers would treat their cattle simply as commodities. However, sociological research has shown that ranchers develop emotional ties to their cattle. Ranchers have to navigate both emotional and business relationships with their animals – they develop emotional relationships with their cattle, while treating them as economic commodities (Ellis 2014). The ranchers Colter Ellis interviewed said they could not help but develop emotional bonds with their cattle, and they had to perform emotional labor to remind themselves to view the cattle as economic entities.

There is a difference, though, between raising cattle and working in a slaughterhouse. British sociologist Rhoda Wilkie (2005) found that farmers working with raising cattle developed emotional attachments to cattle, whereas workers who deal with cattle at the end of the cattle's life cycle (finishers and slaughterhouse workers) developed methods of detaching emotionally from the animals by de-individualizing the animals. This process of de-individualization is just one of the factors that other sociologists have studied when investigating the relationship between crime and slaughterhouse communities.

In her study of the historical development of slaughterhouses, Amy Fitzgerald (2010) noted the first step in the shift from an agrarian to an industrial society was the move from local, backyard cattle slaughter, to centralized, industrial slaughterhouses. These contemporary slaughterhouses have been found to be associated with various types of crimes. Communities with slaughterhouses have higher rates of arrests for violent crimes, rapes, and other sex offenses than do comparable communities that rely on other forms of industrial work, such as manufacturing, which led researchers to suggest a "spillover" or "Sinclair effect" from the violent workplace into the larger community (Fitzgerald et al. 2009). These cases demonstrate the issues with industrialized animal agriculture, but similar human-animal boundary issues exist with wildlife, as well.

Wildlife and Social Problems

Scholars of human-animal studies also research wildlife issues as social problems. Such research often includes a treatment of the symbolic boundaries between human culture and "the wild," including humans invading animal spaces and vice versa.

Perhaps the most common form of human-animal engagement in the wild is hunting. Sociologists studying this practice typically focus on the relationship between hunters and their prey. Linda Kalof and Amy Fitzgerald (2003) researched the display of dead animals in photos in hunting magazines and found that hunters marginalized and objectified animal bodies, rather than demonstrating a reverence for the majesty of these wild animals or a love or respect for nature. Stephen Eliason (2008) conducted a qualitative survey of hunters, comparing resident and non-resident (or tourist) hunters, to try to understand the motivations for trophy hunting. Non-resident hunters were more likely to seek trophy-class animals than resident hunters, who more often hunted for food.

More than simply helping us to understand the relationship between hunters and the animals they kill, sociologists studying wildlife help us to understand our social constructions of nature and wildlife themselves. Paul Colomy and Robert Granfield (2010) studied a case in Estes Park, Colorado, where a bull elk named Samson freely roamed around the town and was known by residents and tourists, who frequently took photos with him. Hunters frequently visited Estes Park to hunt elk, and in 1995, Samson was killed by poachers. Samson was well known to both residents and tourists, and his death sparked such moral outrage that the state of Colorado passed Samson's Law against trophy poaching. In passing this law, Colorado helped create a boundary marker between trophy-class animals and normal-sized ones, between "good" and "bad" animals (i.e., non-predators and predators), and between legitimate hunters and poachers.

Sociologists also study the relationships between humans and wildlife in urban spaces. In response to the colony collapse disorder, urban beekeepers called for increased attention to the plight of bees, and encouraged more city dwellers to start their own hives. Lisa Jean Moore and Mary Kosut (2013: 217) studied these urban beekeepers, and found that beekeepers encourage an "ethical entanglement" with bees – rather than leaving bees alone to die at the hands of colony collapse disorder, which is caused by human intervention with the environment, these beekeepers argue that people should create "more deliberate and thoughtful working conditions for bees."

Similarly, Colin Jerolmack (2008) studied the relationship between city dwellers and urban birds. He found that in the nineteenth century, Americans viewed sparrows and starlings as "nuisance birds." In the twentieth century, people in New York, Philadelphia, and London began to view pigeons as a nuisance and a pest for a variety of reasons, including noise and excrement from feeding pigeons, as well as (largely uncorroborated) public health arguments. The argument that pigeons carried disease led to their sullied reputation as "rats with wings." While many urban dwellers complained of wild animals in urban spaces, they also were among the first to protest using animals for testing purposes.

Animal Testing

Activism against animal testing has comprised a large part of the animal protection movement since early anti-vivisectionist (anti-animal-testing) groups began militating in the nineteenth century. Early anti-vivisectionists were largely urban, upper-class women, who viewed protection to animals as an important part of the civilizing process (Elias 1978). However, relatively little attention has been paid to animals in science from a sociological perspective. Early research in this area focused on laboratory workers and their interactions with animals. Mary Phillips (1993: 77) conducted an ethnography of laboratories in research institutions, and she found that even though the laboratory researchers understood that non-human animals felt pain, this understanding remained at an abstract, theoretical level: "Laboratory animals are categorized and perceived as distinctive creatures whose purpose and meaning is constituted by their role as bearers of scientific data." This finding is supported by Arnold Arluke and Clinton Sanders's (1996) research on systems of meaning in primate labs. Whereas some researchers saw primates as "morally elevated" animals because they were physiologically so close to humans, many workers saw the lab animals as solely utilitarian, drawing symbolic boundaries between human and non-human primates, as well as between their own companion animals and laboratory animals.

A newer area of research linking farmed animals to science is that of biotechnology and genetic engineering. Richard Twine (2010) studied animal biotechnology, including marker-assisted selection, genomic selection, transgenics (or genetic modification), and cloning, as they were used in breeding farmed animals. Farmed animals can now be bred for specific traits, such as hardiness or muscle mass. Instead of viewing biotechnology as a way to move toward sustainability, Twine argues that we need to transform this form of human-animal relationship by moving toward sustainable eating practices. Justifications for animal testing persist, however, and are also found in the use of animals in entertainment.

Animals in Entertainment

While animal rights and welfare organizations critique a wide variety of uses of animals as entertainment (e.g., circuses, aquariums, aquatic theme parks, zoos, etc.), sociologists studying this phenomenon have primarily focused on zoos, and to a much lesser extent, dogfighting. Dogfighting is understudied because of the illegality of the activity and the secrecy of those who participate in it. Craig Forsyth and Rhonda Evans (1998) studied dogfighters through interviews and participant observation, and found that dogfighters engaged in a variety of techniques of neutralization in order to legitimize their behavior and to counter stigma and criminal identities. One way dogfighters neutralized responses was to say dogfighting is akin to boxing – a similar form of entertainment. Activists hope that dogfighting will dissipate since a new federal law went into effect in the United States in 2007, making dogfighting a felony offense in all fifty states. This will also make it even more difficult to study dogfighters from an in-depth, qualitative perspective.

Much more sociological research has been devoted to studying the use of animals as entertainment in zoos. Zoos and menageries date back to the earliest forms of agriculture-based societies, where animals were kept for religious purposes, for public entertainment, or for private, royal menageries. In late modernity, zoos began to attempt to redefine themselves as educational and as part of a larger conservation effort rather than as a form of entertainment. Sociologists who study zoos critique these efforts as inadequate, insincere, and largely ineffective.

The "Disneyization" of zoos, a process akin to McDonaldization, involves applying "Disney theme park principles on a range of organizations and institutional settings" (Beardsworth and Bryman 2001: 90), and includes four different processes: (1) theming – collecting animals to present together, such as in the "monkey house"; (2) the dedifferentiation of consumption – the process of blurring the boundaries between different arenas of consumption, such as placing a zoo in the middle of Walt Disney World or putting theme parks inside other zoos; (3) merchandizing – when zoos commodify wild animals, using "iconic" animals to attract people to zoos; and (4) emotional labor – the requirement that zoo employees serve as ever-helpful, always-smiling entertainers, rather than as experts in a particular field of zoology.

With the passing of the Species Survival Plan in 1981 and the CITES treaty (Convention on International Trade in Endangered Species of Wild Fauna and Flora), zoos' practices of captive breeding came under legal attack. In this context, Todd Bayma (2012) studied zoos' attempts at moving from entertainment to education and conservation. He found that CITES constrained zoos' ability to engage in captive breeding, unless they could convince the conservation community that captive breeding was an important contribution to saving endangered species. In this way, captive breeding in order to help ensure the survival of endangered species became a "rational myth" or a way for zoos to attempt to provide a social legitimacy to their organizational identity and practices.

David Grazian (2012) studied the behind-the-scenes makings of modern American zoos. He explored the tension between providing an environment that was appropriate to the animals, and one that was expected by the human visitors. In doing so, he investigated the production of nature and culture. He pointed out that "representations of nature always rely on the materials of culture, and, in zoo exhibits, they include man-made synthetics, animal management practices, and live interpretive performances by zoo staff and volunteers" (Grazian 2012: 548). Through a process of "nature making," or impression management, zoos attempt to create "naturalistic" zoo exhibits. All of these animal issues – testing, wildlife, entertainment, and the like – are taken up by animal rights advocates.

Vegetarianism and Animal Rights

With the growing interest in animal issues at the beginning of the 1990s, scholars began investigating the animal rights movement as a new form of social movement. The first major work in this area was James Jasper and Dorothy Nelkin's *The Animal Rights Crusade* (1992), which outlined the origins of the contemporary animal rights movement. This contemporary movement focused on a wide variety of animal issues, including the use of animals for testing, fur, entertainment, and food.

Moving from descriptions of the origins of the movement or the makeup of activists working in it, newer research investigated the motivations behind animal rights activists' work. Studies of these contemporary animal rights activists showed them to be primarily motivated by moral concerns, such as becoming vegetarian as a way to show compassion for animals (Lowe and Ginsberg 2002). Those who become activists often experienced a "moral shock" (Jasper and Poulsen 1995) or a "fateful moment" (Munro 2005), when they understood speciesism as a social problem. Speciesism is a term created by animal rights scholar-activists to describe humans' bias for their own species and their discrimination and prejudice against other species.

Since women comprise the vast majority of animal rights activists, a significant portion of scholarship on the movement focuses on gender issues. Rachel Einwohner

(1999) studied the effect of gender on tactical effectiveness. When female protesters encountered male hunters, for example, the hunters were likely to dismiss their critiques as merely women's emotional reactions. Emily Gaarder (2011) studied the preponderance of men as movement leaders in a movement comprised primarily of women, and she and other researchers critique the use of women in advertising for animal rights and vegetarian organizations, highlighting the use of women's nude bodies as a sexualized advertisement for animal rights and vegetarianism.

A significant portion of research on animals and society focuses on vegetarianism and veganism. Vegetarians avoid all meat products, but vegans avoid all animal products, including dairy and eggs. Ethical vegans, spurred by a belief in animal rights, also avoid animal products and animal testing in their clothing, toiletries, and other household products. Given the cultural constraints of these lifestyles, researchers have focused on how vegans learn about, become, and stay vegan (Cherry 2006). Vegans successfully maintain their lifestyle by cultivating supportive social networks that help them to maintain a vegan perspective on their consumption choices.

Conclusion

Understanding the relationships between humans and animals has helped us to better understand human society, and, having moved beyond viewing animals as mere foils for understanding human society, it has also helped us to better understand and value non-human animals' lives. For a field that primarily developed in the 1990s, the sociological study of non-human animals and society has covered a significant amount of ground. However, it still has a long way to go and many areas to cover. Most of the current research focuses on companion animals. It is likely that future research will continue to speak to companion animal issues, as that is the primary relationship that most people have with animals.

For the field of non-human animals and society to grow, however, we will also need more studies of farm animals, wildlife, animals in laboratories, and animals in entertainment or captivity, as well as studies of animal rights and vegetarian issues. Many scholars integrate their studies of animal issues with studies of the environment, such as David Pellow's (2014) book *Total Liberation*, which investigated animal rights and environmental activists, and Anthony Ladd and Bob Edwards's (2002) research, which showed how pollution from industrial hog farms affected the environment in North Carolina. A more wide-reaching strategy would be for scholars to integrate the study of animals and society into all of the major areas of sociology, such as culture, social movements, inequality, criminology, and the like.

References

Arluke, Arnold and Clinton Sanders. 1996. *Regarding Animals*. Philadelphia, PA Temple University Press.

Arluke, Arnold and Clinton Sanders. 2009. *Between the Species: Readings in Human-Animal Relations*. New York, NY: Pearson.

Arluke, Arnold, Jack Levin, Carter Luke, and Frank Ascione. 1999. The Relationship of Animal Abuse to Violence and Other Forms of Antisocial Behavior. *Journal of Interpersonal Violence* 14: 963–975.

Bayma, Todd. 2012. Rational Myth Making and Environment Shaping: The Transformation of the Zoo. *The Sociological Quarterly* 53: 116–141.

Beardsworth, Alan and Alan E. Bryman. 2001. The Wild Animal in Late Modernity: The Case of the Disneyization of Zoos. *Tourist Studies* 1(1): 83–104.

Bryant, Clifton. 1979. The Zoological Connection: Animal Related Human Behavior. *Social Forces* 58(2): 399–421.

Catton, William R. and Riley E. Dunlap. 1978. Environmental Sociology: A New Paradigm. *The American Sociologist*. 13: 41–49.

Cherry, Elizabeth. 2006. Veganism as a Cultural Movement: A Relational Approach. *Social Movement Studies* 5(2): 155–170.

Colomy, Paul and Robert Granfield. 2010. Losing Samson: Nature, Crime and Boundaries. *The Sociological Quarterly* 51(3): 355–383.

Durkheim, Emile. 1995. *The Elementary Forms of Religious Life*. New York, NY: The Free Press.

Einwohner, Rachel. 1999. Gender, Class, and Social Movement Outcomes: Identity and Effectiveness in Two Animal Rights Campaigns. *Gender and Society* 13(1): 56–76.

Elias, Norbert. 1978. *The Civilizing Process*. New York, NY: Urizen Books.

Eliason, Stephen. 2008. A Statewide Examination of Hunting and Trophy Nonhuman Animals: Perspectives of Montana Hunters. *Society and Animals* 16: 256–278.

Ellis, Colter. 2014. Boundary Labor and the Production of Emotionless Commodities: The Case of Beef Production in the United States. *The Sociological Quarterly* 55(1): 92–118.

Fitzgerald, Amy. 2010. A Social History of the Slaughterhouse: From Inception to Contemporary Implications. *Research in Human Ecology* 17(1): 58–69.

Fitzgerald, Amy, Linda Kalof, and Thomas Dietz 2009. Slaughterhouses and Increased Crime Rates: An Empirical Analysis of the Spillover from "the Jungle" into the Surrounding Community. *Organization and Environment* 22(2): 1–27.

Flynn, Clifton. 2000. Woman's Best Friend: Pet Abuse and the Role of Companion Animals in the Lives of Battered Women. *Violence Against Women* 6: 162–177.

Forsyth, Craig J. and Rhonda D. Evans. 1998. Dogmen: The Rationalization of Deviance. *Society and Animals* 6(3): 203–218.

Furst, Gennifer. 2011. *Animal Programs in Prison: A Comprehensive Assessment*. Boulder, CO: Firstforum Press.

Gaarder, Emily 2011. *Women and the Animal Rights Movement*. New Brunswick, NJ: Rutgers University Press.

Grazian, David. 2012. Where the Wild Things Aren't: Exhibiting Nature in American Zoos. *The Sociological Quarterly* 53(4): 547–566.

Humane Society of the United States. 2016. Farm Animal Statistics: Slaughter Totals. 2016. Available at www.humanesociety.org/news/resources/research/stats_slaughter_totals.html, accessed December 1, 2016.

Irvine, Leslie. 2004. *If You Tame Me: Understanding Our Connection with Animals*. Philadelphia, PA: Temple University Press.

Irvine, Leslie. 2009. *Filling the Ark: Animal Welfare in Disasters*. Philadelphia, PA: Temple University Press.

Jasper, James and Dorothy Nelkin. 1992. *The Animal Rights Crusade: The Growth of a Moral Protest*. New York, NY: the Free Press.

Jasper, James and Jane Poulsen. 1995. Recruiting Strangers and Friends: Moral Shocks and Social Networks in Animal Rights and Anti-Nuclear Protests. *Social Problems* 42(4): 493–512.

Jerolmack, Colin. 2008. How Pigeons Became Rats: The Cultural-Spatial Logic of Problem Animals. *Social Problems* 55: 72–94.

Kalof, Linda and Amy Fitzgerald. 2003. Reading the Trophy: Exploring the Display of Dead Animals in Hunting Magazines. *Visual Studies* 18(2): 112–122.

Ladd, Anthony and Bob Edwards. 2002. Corporate Swine and Capitalist Pigs: A Decade of Environmental Injustice and Protest in North Carolina. *Social Justice* 29(3): 26–46.

Lowe, Brian and Caryn Ginsberg. 2002. Animal Rights as a Post-Citizenship Movement. *Society and Animals* 10(2): 203–215.

Marx, Karl. 1976. *Capital: A Critique of Political Economy*. Vol. 1. London: Penguin Books.

Mead, George Herbert. 1934. *George Herbert Mead on Social Psychology*. Chicago, IL: University of Chicago Press.

Moore, Lisa Jean and Mary Kosut. 2013. *Buzz: Urban Beekeeping and the Power of the Bee*. New York, NY: NYU Press.

Munro, Lyle. 2005. *Confronting Cruelty: Moral Orthodoxy and the Challenge of the Animal Rights Movement*. Leiden, the Netherlands: Brill.

Pellow, David Naguib. 2014. *Total Liberation: The Power and Promise of Animal Rights and the Radical Earth Movement*. Minneapolis, MN: University of Minnesota Press.

Phillips, Mary. 1993. Savages, Drunks, and Lab Animals: The Researcher's Perception of Pain. *Society and Animals* 1: 61–82.

Ramirez, Michael. 2006. "My Dog's Just Like Me": Dog Ownership as a Gender Display. *Symbolic Interaction* 29(3): 373–391.

Sanders, Clinton. 1999. *Understanding Dogs: Living and Working with Canine Companions*. Philadelphia, PA: Temple University Press.

Twine, Richard. 2010. *Animals as Biotechnology*. Abingdon: Earthscan.

Weber, Max. 1947. *The Theory of Social and Economic Organization.* New York, NY: Free Press. Quoted in Arnold Arluke and Clinton Sanders. 2009. *Between the Species: Readings in Human-Animal Relations.* New York, NY: Pearson.

Wilkie, Rhoda. 2005. Sentient Commodities and Productive Paradoxes: The Ambiguous Nature of Human-Livestock Relations in Northeast Scotland. *Journal of Rural Studies* 21: 213–230.

CHAPTER 11
Quality-of-Life/Social Indicators Research

Kenneth C. Land

How are we doing with respect not only to our economic level-of-living but more generally the quality of our lives, our well-being? Improving, staying about the same, or deteriorating? Compared to our past? Compared to other countries/societies? And, if improving, are the improvements shared throughout the society or only among some of us? These are the kinds of questions that have motivated social indicators and quality-of-life research over the past fifty years. This research has resulted in a substantial number of conceptual and empirical contributions to the measurement of quality-of-life/well-being and to the development of a number of new indicators thereof. In what follows, I first review two traditions of research, one based on objective statistical indicators of the conditions of life and the second based on how people subjectively assess those conditions in terms of their overall life satisfaction and happiness. I then describe two major contemporary research programs on indicators of well-being and the empirical findings associated therewith. A final section describes some recent research findings and topics for future research.

The Objective and Subjective Social Indicators Traditions

The term *social indicators* was born and given its initial meaning in an attempt, undertaken in the early 1960s by the American Academy of Arts and Sciences for the National Aeronautics and Space Administration, to detect and anticipate the nature and magnitude of the second-order consequences of the space program for American society (Land 1983: 2; Noll and Zapf 1994: 1). Frustrated by the lack of sufficient data to detect such effects and the absence of a systematic conceptual framework and methodology for analysis, some of those involved in the Academy project attempted to develop a system of social indicators with which to detect and anticipate social change as well as to evaluate specific programs and determine their impact. The results of this part of the Academy project were published in a volume (Bauer 1966) bearing the name *Social Indicators* and the following definition:

> social indicators – statistics, statistical series, and all other forms of evidence – that enable us to assess where we stand and are going with respect to our values and goals (Bauer 1966: 1)

Thus, efforts to develop *objective social indicators* began with the initial wave of identity and interest in the topic in the 1960s and extend to the present.

The emphasis in this tradition is on the development of statistics that reflect important social conditions and the monitoring of trends in a range of areas of social concern over time. The key undefined terms here require the identification of:

- the "social conditions" to be measured, and
- the "areas of social concern" for which trends are to be monitored.

The Objective Tradition

Since the 1970s, the primary approach to the identification and definition processes has been through the creation of "expert, or objective" panels of social scientists, statisticians, and citizens. These panels have applied a variety of approaches to their work, such as:

- the "indicators of social change" approach (Sheldon and Moore 1968);
- the Swedish "level-of-living" approach (Erickson 1974); and
- the "goals commissions" approach (e.g., the *U.S. Healthy People 2010* Goals; see US Department of Health and Human Services 2000).

A key element of the objective approach (Noll 2002: 175) is that the experts must achieve consensus on:

- the conditions and areas of concern to be measured;
- good and bad conditions; and
- the directions in which society should move.

These, of course, are strong requirements. And, in its reliance on "expert" panels, the objective social indicators tradition is always open to the criticism that the conditions identified have not been corroborated as relevant to how people actually experience happiness, life satisfaction, and subjective well-being. This criticism motivates the other major tradition of work on the measurement of the quality of life, the subjective well-being approach.

The Subjective Well-Being Tradition

The subjective well-being indicators tradition commenced with the work of Campbell et al. (1976) and Andrews and Withey (1976). These studies examined domains of social life ranging from the highly specific (house, family, etc.) to the global (life-as-a-whole) and used various social science research techniques, including in-depth interviews, focus-group discussions, clinical studies, and sample surveys to study how people define their happiness and satisfaction with life and the social conditions of life that they experience on a day-to-day basis. A large number of other studies and applications of these concepts and techniques have appeared over the past four decades (for reviews, see Diener 1994; Diener et al. 1999; Sirgy 2011; Veenhoven 1984: 1996) and continue to appear – one or more studies of *subjective well-being indicators* (happiness and/or life satisfaction) can be found in almost any issue of the journal *Social Indicators Research* (which began publication in 1974) and in the *Journal of Happiness Studies* (which began publication in 2000).

In the past four decades, research in the subjective well-being indicators tradition has articulated *global life satisfaction* as a cognitive evaluation of one's life-as-a-whole (Shin and Johnson 1978). Although affect/emotion can influence life satisfaction reports, life satisfaction is distinguished from transitory affective states. Emotions refer to specific momentary reactions to specific events that occur in people's lives, such as anger, joy, anxiety, and so forth. Life satisfaction reports typically refer to more general, enduring background appraisals encompassing one's overall life or major facets of one's life (Diener et al. 1999; Lazarus 1991). Although experiences of frequent positive emotions, infrequent negative emotions, and life satisfaction tend to intercorrelate, suggesting a higher-order subjective well-being factor, affective and life satisfaction reports can diverge over time and demonstrate different determinants (see Diener 1994).

As a result of the many subjective well-being studies conducted since the 1970s, we know a lot more about what makes people happy and satisfied with life today. In particular, Cummins (1996: 1997) reached the following conclusions about the quality of life based on comparisons of findings across numerous subjective well-being studies:

- there is *a potential for tremendous variety of assessments of satisfaction with life experiences*, with individuals often differing in their ratings of importance of the key elements associated with their life satisfactions and happiness;
- but, at the same time, the accumulation of findings across many studies shows that *certain domains of well-being/areas of social life occur over and over again*;
- there is also *a fairly high degree of similarity among individuals on the relative weightings given to these domains in determining overall life satisfaction;*
- and, perhaps most interestingly, there is *much similarity between the domains of well-being identified in subjective well-being studies and the areas of concern identified by expert panels in objective social indicators studies.*

Two Contemporary Composite Well-being Indices

In brief, the dominant conception of social indicators among scholars and public policy officials is that they are statistical measures with some significance for the quality of life (broadly construed) that are useful for evidence-based public policy-making. *Subjective social indicators* are statistics that have some significance for measuring the quality of life from the point of view of some particular subject(s) (e.g., self-reported health) and *objective social indicators* are statistics that have some significance for measuring the quality of life from the point of view of any independent observer (e.g., official mortality and morbidity rates). Social indicators pertaining to specific aspects of life or domains of well-being are often combined into *composite social indictors* that seek to give a sense of overall quality of life or well-being in specific countries, populations, or other social units. A number of composite or summary well-being indices have been developed in recent decades, including the Human Development Index and the child and youth well-being index.

The Human Development Index

The Human Development Index (HDI) is a composite social indicator/well-being index that has been calculated and published in Human Development Reports (HDRs) since 1990 by the United Nations Development Programme (UNDP). The objective of the HDI is to rank countries of the world on a scale of human development conceptualized in terms of capabilities of humans within the countries to function. The concept of *capabilities* refers to what human beings can do and be, instead of what they have, and is broadly conceived of as the abilities or power of individuals to do certain things in order to obtain what they desire and to utilize the resources they have in the way they desire in order to be who they want to be (Nussbaum and Sen 1992; Sen 1987).

Because it seeks to be as inclusive as possible of the countries of the world, the HDI is based on only four statistics measuring three dimensions: *health* (measured by *life expectancy at birth*, that is, the number of years a newborn infant could expect to live if prevailing patterns of age-specific mortality rates at the time of birth stay the same throughout the infant's life); *education* (measured by *mean years of schooling*, that is, the average number of years of education received by people ages twenty-five and older, converted from educational attainment levels using official durations of each level, and *expected years of schooling*, that is, the number of years of schooling that a child of school entrance age can expect to receive if prevailing patterns of age-specific enrolment rates persist throughout the child's life); and *living standards* (measured by *gross national income per capita*; that is, aggregate income of an economy generated by its production and its ownership of factors of production, minus the incomes paid for the use of factors of production owned by the rest of the world, converted to international dollars using purchasing power parity rates, divided by midyear population). These statistics then are combined into the composite HDI which can vary from 0 to 1, with higher numerical values representing higher levels of human development (for a more comprehensive review of the HDI, its statistical methodology, and empirical findings therefrom, see Land 2015).

In recent years, the HDI has been supplemented with three other indices. The Inequality-Adjusted HDI (IHDI) reflects inequality in each dimension of the HDI. Under perfect equality the IHDI is equal to the HDI, but falls below the HDI when inequality rises. The objective of the IHDI is to measure the actual level of human development (taking into account inequality) of a country, with the HDI viewed as an index of the potential human development that could be achieved if there is no inequality.

Similarly, the Gender Inequality Index (GII) addresses disadvantages facing women and girls, which are a major source of inequality. Findings from the GII indicate that gender inequality varies tremendously across countries – the losses in achievement due to gender inequality (not directly comparable to total inequality losses because different variables are used) range from 4.9 percent to 76.9 percent. It has also been found that countries with unequal distribution of human development also experience high inequality between women and men, and countries with high gender inequality also experience unequal distribution of human development.

The Multidimensional Poverty Index (MPI) is the third supplementary index to the HDI. The objective of this poverty measure is to give a "multidimensional" picture of people living in poverty that could help target development resources more effectively. The MPI identifies deprivations across the same three dimensions as the HDI and shows the number of people who are multidimensionally poor (suffering deprivations in at least 33 percent of weighted indicators) and the number of deprivations with which poor households typically contend. It can be deconstructed by region, ethnicity, and other groupings as well as by dimension, making it an apt tool for policy-makers.

As a specific example, the 2011 HDR gives rankings for a total of 187 countries. These are grouped into quartiles labeled from high to low as: Very High Human Development, High Human Development, Medium Human Development, and Low Human Development. The full table for all 187 countries for three of the indices described above, the HDI, the IHDI, and the GII, from pp. 17–20 of the Summary of the 2011 HDR Report is reproduced in Table 11.1. Due to differential data availability across the countries, the indices use data from different years. In addition, due to the lack of availability of the data necessary for their computation, the IHDI and GII indices are reported for 134 and 142 countries, respectively.

The numerical values of the indices, the rankings of the countries, and the quartiles have a good amount of face validity with what one might expect, given the composition of the indices. Developed countries with relatively small, homogeneous populations tend to be ranked in the first quartile. Larger, more geographically and racially/ethnically diverse populations and less developed countries tend to rank lower.

Table 11.1. Human Development Indices

	Human Development Indices				
	Human Development Index (HDI)	Inequality-adjusted HDI		Gender Inequality Index	
HDI rank	Value	Value	Rank	Value	Rank
VERY HIGH HUMAN DEVELOPMENT					
1 Norway	0.943	0.890	1	0.075	6
2 Australia	0.929	0.856	2	0.136	18
3 Netherlands	0.910	0.846	4	0.052	2
4 United States	0.910	0.771	23	0.299	47
5 New Zealand	0.908	..	..	0.195	32
6 Canada	0.908	0.829	12	0.140	20
7 Ireland	0.908	0.843	6	0.203	33
8 Liechtenstein	0.905	..	..	..	..
9 Germany	0.905	0.842	7	0.085	7
10 Sweden	0.904	0.851	3	0.049	1
11 Switzerland	0.903	0.840	9	0.067	4
12 Japan	0.901	..	..	0.123	14
13 Hong Kong, China (SAR)	0.898	..	..	..	..
14 Iceland	0.898	0.845	5	0.099	9
15 Korea, Republic of	0.897	0.749	28	0.111	11
16 Denmark	0.895	0.842	8	0.060	3
17 Israel	0.888	0.779	21	0.145	22
18 Belgium	0.886	0.819	15	0.114	12
19 Austria	0.885	0.820	14	0.131	16
20 France	0.884	0.804	16	0.106	10
21 Slovenia	0.884	0.837	10	0.175	28
22 Finland	0.882	0.833	11	0.075	5
23 Spain	0.878	0.799	17	0.117	13
24 Italy	0.874	0.779	22	0.124	15
25 Luxembourg	0.867	0.799	18	0.169	26
26 Singapore	0.866	..	..	0.086	8
27 Czech Republic	0.865	0.821	13	0.136	17
28 United Kingdom	0.863	0.791	19	0.209	34
29 Greece	0.861	0.756	26	0.162	24
30 United Arab Emirates	0.846	..	..	0.234	38
31 Cyprus	0.840	0.755	27	0.141	21
32 Andorra	0.838	..	..	..	..
33 Brunei Darussalam	0.838	..	..	..	..
34 Estonia	0.835	0.769	24	0.194	30
35 Slovakia	0.834	0.787	20	0.194	31
36 Malta	0.832	..	..	0.272	42
37 Qatar	0.831	..	..	0.549	111
38 Hungary	0.816	0.759	25	0.237	39
39 Poland	0.813	0.734	29	0.164	25
40 Lithuania	0.810	0.730	30	0.192	29
41 Portugal	0.809	0.726	31	0.140	19
42 Bahrain	0.806	..	..	0.288	44
43 Latvia	0.805	0.717	33	0.216	36
44 Chile	0.805	0.652	44	0.374	68

(cont.)

Table 11.1 (cont.)

	Human Development Indices				
	Human Development Index (HDI)	Inequality-adjusted HDI		Gender Inequality Index	
HDI rank	Value	Value	Rank	Value	Rank
45 Argentina	0.797	0.641	47	0.372	67
46 Croatia	0.796	0.675	38	0.170	27
47 Barbados	0.793	..	..	0.364	65
HIGH HUMAN DEVELOPMENT					
48 Uruguay	0.783	0.654	43	0.352	62
49 Palau	0.782	..	..	..	..
50 Romania	0.781	0.683	36	0.333	55
51 Cuba	0.776	..	..	0.337	58
52 Seychelles	0.773	..	..	..	..
53 Bahamas	0.771	0.658	41	0.332	54
54 Montenegro	0.771	0.718	32	..	..
55 Bulgaria	0.771	0.683	37	0.245	40
56 Saudi Arabia	0.770	..	..	0.646	135
57 Mexico	0.770	0.589	56	0.448	79
58 Panama	0.768	0.579	57	0.492	95
59 Serbia	0.766	0.694	34	..	..
60 Antigua and Barbuda	0.764	..	..	..	..
61 Malaysia	0.761	..	..	0.286	43
62 Trinidad and Tobago	0.760	0.644	46	0.331	53
63 Kuwait	0.760	..	..	0.229	37
64 Libya	0.760	..	..	0.314	51
65 Belarus	0.756	0.693	35	..	..
66 Russian Federation	0.755	0.670	39	0.338	59
67 Grenada	0.748	..	..	..	..
68 Kazakhstan	0.745	0.656	42	0.334	56
69 Costa Rica	0.744	0.591	55	0.361	64
70 Albania	0.739	0.637	49	0.271	41
71 Lebanon	0.739	0.570	59	0.440	76
72 Saint Kitts and Nevis	0.735	..	..	..	..
73 Venezuela, Bolivarian Republic of	0.735	0.540	67	0.447	78
74 Bosnia and Herzegovina	0.733	0.649	45	..	..
75 Georgia	0.733	0.630	51	0.418	73
76 Ukraine	0.729	0.662	40	0.335	57
77 Mauritius	0.728	0.631	50	0.353	63
78 Former Yugoslav Republic of Macedonia	0.728	0.609	54	0.151	23
79 Jamaica	0.727	0.610	53	0.450	81
80 Peru	0.725	0.557	63	0.415	72
81 Dominica	0.724	..	..	..	..
82 Saint Lucia	0.723	..	..	..	..
83 Ecuador	0.720	0.535	69	0.469	85
84 Brazil	0.718	0.519	73	0.449	80
85 Saint Vincent and the Grenadines	0.717	..	..	..	..
86 Armenia	0.716	0.639	48	0.343	60
87 Colombia	0.710	0.479	86	0.482	91

Table 11.1 (cont.)

| | Human Development Indices ||||||
| HDI rank | Human Development Index (HDI) Value | Inequality-adjusted HDI ||Gender Inequality Index ||
		Value	Rank	Value	Rank
88 Iran, Islamic Republic of	0.707	..	..	0.485	92
89 Oman	0.705	..	..	0.309	49
90 Tonga	0.704	..	..	..	..
91 Azerbaijan	0.700	0.620	52	0.314	50
92 Turkey	0.699	0.542	66	0.443	77
93 Belize	0.699	..	..	0.493	97
94 Tunisia	0.698	0.523	72	0.293	45
MEDIUM HUMAN DEVELOPMENT						
95 Jordan	0.698	0.565	61	0.456	83
96 Algeria	0.698	..	..	0.412	71
97 Sri Lanka	0.691	0.579	58	0.419	74
98 Dominican Republic	0.689	0.510	77	0.480	90
99 Samoa	0.688	..	..	..	..
100 Fiji	0.688	..	..	..	..
101 China	0.687	0.534	70	0.209	35
102 Turkmenistan	0.686	..	..	..	..
103 Thailand	0.682	0.537	68	0.382	69
104 Suriname	0.680	0.518	74	..	..
105 El Salvador	0.674	0.495	83	0.487	93
106 Gabon	0.674	0.543	65	0.509	103
107 Paraguay	0.665	0.505	78	0.476	87
108 Bolivia, Plurinational State of	0.663	0.437	87	0.476	88
109 Maldives	0.661	0.495	82	0.320	52
110 Mongolia	0.653	0.563	62	0.410	70
111 Moldova, Republic of	0.649	0.569	60	0.298	46
112 Philippines	0.644	0.516	75	0.427	75
113 Egypt	0.644	0.489	85	..	..
114 Occupied Palestinian Territory	0.641	..	..	..	..
115 Uzbekistan	0.641	0.544	64	..	..
116 Micronesia, Federation States of	0.636	0.390	94	..	..
117 Guyana	0.633	0.492	84	0.511	106
118 Botswana	0.633	..	..	0.507	102
119 Syrian Arab Republic	0.632	0.503	80	0.474	86
120 Namibia	0.625	0.353	99	0.466	84
121 Honduras	0.625	0.427	89	0.511	105
122 Kiribati	0.624	..	..	..	..
123 South Africa	0.619	..	..	0.490	94
124 Indonesia	0.617	0.504	79	0.505	100
125 Vanuatu	0.617	..	..	..	..
126 Kyrgyzstan	0.615	0.526	71	0.370	66
127 Tajikistan	0.607	0.500	81	0.374	61
128 Viet Nam	0.593	0.510	76	0.305	48
129 Nicaragua	0.589	0.427	88	0.506	101
130 Morocco	0.582	0.409	90	0.510	104

(cont.)

Table 11.1 (cont.)

	Human Development Indices					
	Human Development Index (HDI)	Inequality-adjusted HDI		Gender Inequality Index		
HDI rank	Value	Value	Rank	Value	Rank	
131 Guatemala	0.574	0.393	92	0.542	109
132 Iraq	0.573	..	..	0.579	117
133 Cape Verde	0.568	..	..	..	..
134 India	0.547	0.392	93	0.617	129
135 Ghana	0.541	0.367	96	0.598	122
136 Equatorial Guinea	0.537	..	..	..	..
137 Congo	0.533	0.367	97	0.628	132
138 Lao People's Democratic Republic	0.524	0.405	91	0.513	107
139 Cambodia	0.523	0.380	95	0.500	99
140 Swaziland	0.522	0.338	103	0.546	110
141 Bhutan	0.522	..	..	0.495	98
LOW HUMAN DEVELOPMENT						
142 Solomon Islands	0.510	..	..	..	..
143 Kenya	0.509	0.338	102	0.627	130
144 São Tomé and Principe	0.509	0.348	100	..	..
145 Pakistan	0.504	0.346	101	0.573	115
146 Bangladesh	0.500	0.363	98	0.550	112
147 Timor-Leste	0.495	0.332	105	..	..
148 Angola	0.486	..	..	..	..
149 Myanmar	0.483	..	..	0.492	96
150 Cameroon	0.482	0.321	107	0.639	134
151 Madagascar	0.480	0.332	104	..	..
152 Tanzania, United Republic of	0.466	0.332	106	0.590	119
153 Papua New Guinea	0.466	..	..	0.674	140
154 Yemen	0.462	0.312	108	0.769	146
155 Senegal	0.459	0.304	109	0.566	114
156 Nigeria	0.459	0.278	116	..	..
157 Nepal	0.458	0.301	111	0.558	113
158 Haiti	0.454	0.271	121	0.599	123
159 Mauritania	0.453	0.298	112	0.605	126
160 Lesotho	0.450	0.288	115	0.532	108
161 Uganda	0.446	0.296	113	0.577	116
162 Togo	0.435	0.289	114	0.602	124
163 Comoros	0.433	..	..	..	..
164 Zambia	0.430	0.303	110	0.627	131
165 Djibouti	0.430	0.275	118	..	..
166 Rwanda	0.429	0.276	117	0.453	82
167 Benin	0.427	0.274	119	0.634	133
168 Gambia	0.420	..	..	0.610	127
169 Sudan	0.408	..	..	0.611	128
170 Côte d'Ivoire	0.400	0.246	124	0.655	136
171 Malawi	0.400	0.272	120	0.594	120
172 Afghanistan	0.398	..	..	0.707	141
173 Zimbabwe	0.376	0.268	122	0.583	118
174 Ethiopia	0.363	0.247	123	..	..

Table 11.1 (cont.)

	Human Development Indices				
	Human Development Index (HDI)	Inequality-adjusted HDI		Gender Inequality Index	
HDI rank	Value	Value	Rank	Value	Rank
175 Mali	0.359	..	..	0.712	143
176 Guinea-Bissau	0.353	0.207	129	..	..
177 Eritrea	0.349	..	..	..	..
178 Guinea	0.344	0.211	128	..	..
179 Central African Republic	0.343	0.204	130	0.669	138
180 Sierra Leone	0.336	0.196	131	0.662	137
181 Burkina Faso	0.331	0.215	126	0.596	121
182 Liberia	0.329	0.213	127	0.671	139
183 Chad	0.328	0.196	132	0.735	145
184 Mozambique	0.322	0.229	125	0.602	125
185 Burundi	0.316	..	..	0.478	89
186 Niger	0.295	0.195	133	0.724	144
187 Congo, Democratic Republic of the	0.286	0.172	134	0.710	142
OTHER COUNTRIES OR TERRITORIES					
Korea, Democratic People's Rep. of	..	..	..	..	..
Marshall Islands	..	..	..	..	..
Monaco	..	..	..	..	..
Nauru	..	..	..	..	..
San Marino	..	..	..	..	..
Somalia	..	..	..	..	..
Tuvalu	..	..	..	..	..
Human Development Index groups					
Very High Human Development	0.889	0.787	–	0.244	–
High Human Development	0.741	0.590	–	0.409	–
Medium human development	0.630	0.480	–	0.475	–
Low human development	0.456	0.304	–	0.606	–
Regions					
Arab States	0.641	0.472	–	0.563	–
East Asia and the Pacific	0.671	0.528	–	..	–
Europe and Central Asia	0.751	0.655	–	0.311	–
Latin America and the Caribbean	0.731	0.540	–	0.445	–
South Asia	0.548	0.393	–	0.601	–
Sub-Saharan Africa	0.463	0.303	–	0.610	–
Least developed countries	0.439	0.296	–	0.594	–
Small island developing states	0.640	0.458	–	..	–
World	0.682	0.525	–	0.492	–

A high ranking on the HDI scale does not ensure a comparable ranking on the IHDI and GII scales. The United States, which ranks 4th on the HDI, 23rd on the IHDI, and 47th on the GII, and Canada, which ranks 6th on the HDI, 12th on the IHDI, and 20th on the GII, are illustrative. By comparison, the Netherlands with 3rd, 4th, and 2nd ranks on the respective three indices is relatively more consistent.

The HDI and the HDRs have contributed to the development of composite social indicators and reporting thereof, thus making knowledge of human conditions around the world more accessible and, in this way, contributing to human enlightenment. At least at the level of UNDP discourse, the HDI, its supplemental indices, and the HDRs have broadened the conception of developmental economics beyond income alone to include measures of health and knowledge. Perhaps just as important from a social indicators/social reporting perspective, the HDI reports have received substantial public distribution and media attention and have helped to inform publics around the world. And, as the saying goes, imitation is the subtlest form of flattery – the development and production of the HDI has stimulated the development of many other composite social indicators at the international level (e.g., the Democracy Index, the Gender Parity Index), the national level (e.g., the Australian Unity Wellbeing Index), and the sub-national level (e.g., the American HDI at the state and regional levels). By this measure, the HDI is an exemplary composite social indicator.

The Child and Youth Well-Being Index

The development of the objective social indicators and subjective well-being traditions over the past fifty years described above leads to the question: Can we bring these two social indicators/quality-of-life research traditions into intersection so that we may construct composite social indicators based on objective social indicators (demographic, social, and economic statistics) of specific aspects of social life that are more firmly grounded in what we have learned about subjective well-being over the past three decades? The response to this and related rhetorical questions of Land et al. (2001; 2007; 2012a; 2015) is "yes" with respect to the development of a composite Child and Youth Well-Being Index (CWI).

As compared to the HDI, the main objective of which is a cross-sectional ranking of countries and regions of the world with respect to its composite measure of human capabilities, the main objective of the CWI is to measure trends over time in the overall/composite well-being of children and youth in the United States relative to their well-being levels at a base time period (year), analogously to the way in which consumer price indices measure changes in the market prices of the goods and services from a base year. The CWI is designed to address questions such as the following:

- Overall, on average, how did child and youth well-being in the United States change in the last quarter of the twentieth century and beyond?
- Did it improve or deteriorate?
- By approximately how much?
- In which domains of social life?
- For specific age groups?
- For particular race/ethnic groups?
- For each of the sexes?
- And did race/ethnic group and sex disparities increase or decrease?

The approach to the assessment of child and youth well-being taken in the construction of the CWI, thus, is that of the development of an evidence-based social indicator that can be used to address these and related questions. The CWI is evidence-based in two senses (Land et al. 2012a). First, the Index is based on demographic, social, and economic statistical time series of empirical data on the Key Indicators. Second, the seven CWI Domains of Well-Being (Family Economic Well-Being, Safe/Risky Behavior, Social Relationships, Emotional/Spiritual Well-Being, Community Engagement, Educational Attainment, and Health) and the choices of the Key Indicators within each Domain are based on decades of studies of subjective well-being, including both quantitative and qualitative research on the well-being of children, adolescents, teenagers, and young adults.

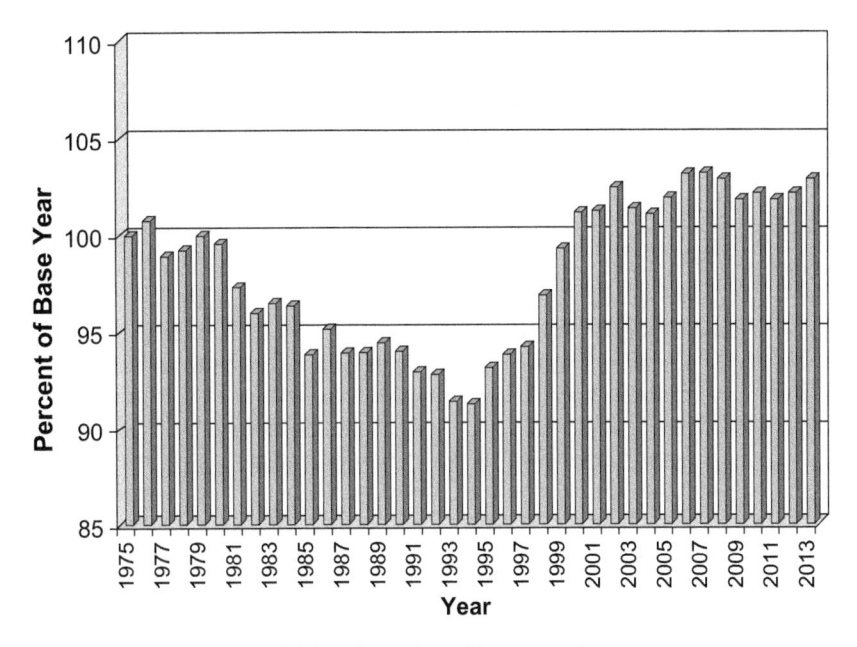

Figure 11.1 Child and Youth Well-Being Index, 1975–2013

The Index is calculated and updated annually from the time series data in order to track changes in the well-being of children compared to 1975 base-year values. As a composite index of changes over time, the most important information to be found in the CWI is in the direction of change in Indicators and Well-Being Domains: Are the indices up and thus indicative of overall improvements? Down and thus indicative of deterioration? Flat and thus indicative of little or no change?

As an example of CWI numerical results, Figure 11.1 charts annual percentage changes from 1975 to 2013 in the overall composite CWI, with the value of the CWI in the base year 1975 set equal to 100 (Land 2014). Observed data on all twenty-eight of the twenty-eight Key Indicators currently (December 2014) are available for the year 2011; observations are available on twenty-two of the 28 Key Indicators for 2012, and on thirteen of the 28 Key Indicators for 2013. In order to calculate values of the CWI through 2013, the remaining Indicators were projected for 2012 and 2013 by use of statistical time series models. Trends in the overall, composite CWI give a sense of changes in child and youth well-being both in the short-term (the last few years) and the long-term (since the base year 1975). The latter time frame yields a historical perspective, as values of the Index for the late 1970s and early 1980s now pertain to individuals who were children at that time but are part of today's parental cohorts.

Over the *long-term* of thirty-eight years (1975–2013), the CWI shows periods of both deterioration and improvement. Through the late 1970s, the CWI oscillated at levels near the base-year value of 100; then shows a decline beginning in 1980 and ending in 1994 with a value of 91.37. The roots of this decline (Land et al. 2012b) were in the economic recession of the early 1980s (which negatively affected the Family Economic Well-Being Domain); changing family structures (toward more single-parenting); an upturn in risky behavior (especially increases in teenage childbearing, illicit drug-use, and violent crime victimization and offending); and the beginnings of the trend toward an increasing prevalence of obese children (which negatively impacted the Health Domain).

In the *medium-term* of the past twenty years from 1994 to 2013, the CWI increased through the late 1990s, reaching a peak of 102.49 in 2002. This period of increase was associated with the rapidly expanding economy of the late-1990s, the stabilization of family structures, and downturns in risky behavior (Land et al. 2012b). Since 2002, the Index has oscillated at or near this peak, with values of 101.85 in 2011, 102.19 in 2012, and an initial estimate of 102.90 for 2013. The CWI since 2002 exhibits the imprint of the economic expansions and contractions of the first decade of the twenty-first century, especially the Great Recession of 2008–2009.

Focusing on *short-term changes* in the CWI, the past six years 2008–2013 were a turbulent time for the United States, with the impacts of the Great Recession in 2008–2009 and the slow recovery in 2010–2013. For these most recent years, Figure 11.1 shows that:

- The CWI decreased by 1.34 percent, from 103.22 in 2007 to 101.84 in 2009, the years of impact of the Great Recession.
- The CWI then is 102.23 for 2010, the last year for which data are available on all twenty-eight Key Indicators.
- In the following years, the CWI shows partially projected values of 101.85 in 2011, 102.19 in 2012 and 102.90 in 2013.

In sum, these recent annual numerical changes in the CWI indicate that the declines of 2008–2009 did not continue in the four most recent years. However, the annual changes for 2010 through 2013 are indicative of just small short-term improvements in overall child and youth well-being.

Conclusion

The past half century has seen substantial progress toward the development of social indicators that help individuals and policy-makers to achieve the original objective stated by Bauer in 1966 as cited above, that is, "to assess where we stand and are going with respect to our values and goals." These developments are based on a large body of new data sources and time series, statistical analyses thereof, and associated conceptual developments. Sociologists along with other social and behavioral scientists have contributed to this work.

As summarized above, research on social indicators has proceeded along both the objective and subjective indicators pathways. This then leads to questions concerning the extent to which empirical findings from objective and subjective well-being indicators are consistent and corroborative. Consider the HDI. If the HDI is, broadly speaking, functioning as a well-being/quality-of-life index, then the expectation is that it should have a positive association with more direct measures of subjective well-being, at least in cross-sectional analyses. And, since average levels of happiness and overall life satisfaction tend to be positively associated cross-nationally with GDP per capita (Easterlin 2010: 66; Eckersley 2005: 32–35), albeit at a decreasing rate at higher income levels, it likely is the case that the national HDI scores have a positive cross-sectional association with average happiness levels.

In a recent study of these expectations, Hall (2013) describes analyses of the relationships between the HDI and its components to country-specific subjective overall life evaluations measured using average national responses (averaged for the three years 2010 to 2012) to the Gallup World Poll Question. Please imagine a ladder, with steps numbered from zero at the bottom to ten at the top. Suppose we say that the top of the ladder represents the best possible life for you, and the bottom of the ladder represents the worst possible life for you. On which step of the ladder would you say you personally feel you stand at this time, assuming that the higher the step the better you feel about your life, and the lower the step the worse you feel about it? Which step comes closest to the way you feel? The results (based on data from 124 to 152 countries depending on the variables used) are as follows:

- Higher life expectancy at birth is strongly correlated with average national life evaluations, with a correlation coefficient of 0.70.

- Expected years and mean years of schooling are correlated 0.69 and 0.63, respectively, with average national life evaluations.
- The logarithm of Gross National Income per capita is correlated 0.78 with average life evaluations.
- The correlation between the HDI and average national life evaluations is 0.77.
- After adjusting/controlling for the effect of gross national income per capita, there remains a strong correlation (0.67) between average national life evaluations and non-income HDI, that is, the life expectancy and education components.

These findings by Hall (2013) corroborate that, for cross-sectional, cross-national comparisons, the HDI is, broadly speaking, a surrogate subjective well-being/quality-of-life index.

Recent research by sociologists Ono and Lee (2013) on the determinants of individuals' happiness in a comparative perspective is relevant to the analysis of the interrelationships of objective and subjective well-being indicators. In this study, using data from the 2002 International Social Survey Programme with roughly 42,000 individuals nested within twenty-nine countries, aggregate (national average) happiness was not greater in the social democratic welfare states, but happiness was found to be redistributed from low-risk to high-risk individuals, e.g., women with small children are significantly happier, but single persons are significantly less happy in the welfare states. In addition, the happiness gap between high-and-low-income earners was considerably smaller in the social democratic welfare states, suggesting that, just as social democratic welfare states redistribute income, they also redistribute happiness from the privileged to the less privileged.

Additional studies of the relationship of objective social indicators, such as the HDI and the CWI and their components, to measures of subjective well-being are needed, especially for over-time relationships. For instance, the evidence to date indicates that economic growth alone (as measured by annual growth rates in GDP per capita) is not sufficient to produce over-time increases in average subjective well-being levels at the country level; rather, full employment and a generous and comprehensive safety net are necessary (Easterlin 2013). Sociologists, with their focus on social structure and social dynamics, can contribute to this research. For instance, Land et al. (2007: 2012b) found that changes over time in the CWI show a positive correlation with survey data on percentages of "quite or completely satisfied" responses to a life satisfaction question in annual survey data of US high school seniors, thus validating the ability of the CWI, which is based on objective statistical time series data, to serve as a well-being index. Similarly, as over-time cross-national survey data become available, replication of the Ono and Lee (2013) study described in the previous paragraph and its extension to an over-time analysis can specifically address questions concerning the relationship of changes over time in economic growth, unemployment, and safety nets to subjective well-being. Moreover, it can do so in the context of the sorts of changes over time in population and social structures that are core subject matters in sociology. Again, however, these are only illustrative of the many research questions regarding quality-of-life/well-being indicators – both as explanatory and as outcome variables – that remain to be explored and to which sociologists can contribute.

References

Andrews, Frank M. and Stephen B. Withey. 1976. *Social Indicators of Well-being: Americans' Perceptions of Life Quality*. New York, NY: Plenum.

Bauer, Raymond A. ed. 1966. *Social Indicators*. Cambridge, MA: The M.I.T. Press.

Campbell, Angus, Phillip E. Converse, and Willard L. Rodgers. 1976. *The Quality of American Life: Perceptions, Evaluations, and Satisfactions*. New York, NY: Russell Sage Foundation.

Cummins, Robert A. 1996. The Domains of Life Satisfaction: An Attempt to Order Chaos. *Social Indicators Research* 38: 303–328.

Cummins, Robert A. 1997. Assessing Quality of Life. In *Quality of Life for Handicapped People*. Edited by R. I. Brown. London: Chapman and Hall.

Diener, Ed. 1994. Assessing Subjective Well-being: Progress and Opportunities. *Social Indicators Research* 31: 103–157.

Diener, Ed, E. M. Suh, R. E. Lucas, and H. L. Smith. 1999. Subjective Well-being: Three Decades of Progress. *Psychological Bulletin* 125: 276–302.

Easterlin, Richard A. 2010. *Happiness, Growth, and the Life Cycle*. New York, NY: Oxford University Press.

Easterlin, Richard A. 2013. Happiness, Growth, and Public Policy. *Economic Inquiry* 51: 1–15.

Eckersley, Richard. 2005. *Well and Good: Morality, Meaning and Happiness*. 2nd edn. Melbourne: Text Publishing.

Erikson, R. 1974. Welfare as a Planning Goal. *Acta Sociologica* 17: 273–288.

Hall, Jon. 2013. From Capabilities to Contentment: Testing the Links Between Human Development and Life Satisfaction. In *World Happiness Report 2013*. Edited by J. F. Helliwell, R. Layard, and J. Sachs. New York, NY: UN Sustainable Development Solutions Network.

Land, Kenneth C. 1983. Social Indicators. *Annual Review of Sociology* 9: 1–26.

Land, Kenneth C. 2014. *Child and Youth Well-being Index Report: 2014*. Durham, NC: Duke University Center for Child and Family Policy.

Land, Kenneth C. 2015. The Human Development Index. In *Global Handbook of Well-being and Quality of Life*. Edited by Wolfgang Glatzer. New York, NY: Springer.

Land, Kenneth C., Vicki L. Lamb, and Sarah K. Mustillo. 2001. Child and Youth Well-being in the United States, 1975–1998: Some Findings from a New Index. *Social Indicators Research* 56: 241–320.

Land, Kenneth C., Vicki L. Lamb, Sarah O. Meadows, and Ashley Taylor. 2007. Measuring Trends in Child Well-being: An Evidence-Based Approach. *Social Indicators Research* 80: 105–132.

Land, Kenneth C., Vicki L. Lamb, and Sarah O. Meadows. 2012a. Conceptual and Methodological Foundations of the Child and Youth Well-being Index. In *The Well-being of America's Children: Developing and Improving the Child and Youth Well-being Index*. Edited by K. C. Land. New York, NY: Springer.

Land, Kenneth C., Vicki L. Lamb, Sarah Meadows, Hui Zheng, and Qiang Fu. 2012b. The CWI and Its Components: Empirical Studies and Findings. In *The Well-being of America's Children: Developing and Improving the Child and Youth Well-being Index*. Edited by K. C. Land. New York, NY: Springer.

Land, Kenneth C., Vicki L. Lamb, and Qiang Fu. 2015. Measuring Trends in Child Well-being and Child Suffering in the United States, 1975–2013. In *A Life Devoted to Quality of Life: Festschrift In Honor of Alex C. Michalos*. Edited by Filomena Maggino. New York, NY: Springer.

Lazarus, R. S. 1991. *Emotion and Adaptation*. New York, NY: Oxford University Press.

Noll, Heinz-Herbert. 2002. Social Indicators and Quality of Life Research: Background, Achievements and Current Trends. In *Advances in Sociological Knowledge over Half a Century*. Edited by N. Genov. Paris: ISSC.

Noll, Heinz-Herbert and Wolfgang Zapf. 1994. Social Indicators Research: Societal Monitoring and Social Reporting. In *Trends and Perspectives in Empirical Social Research*. Edited by I. Borg and P. P. Mohler. New York, NY: Walter De Gruyter.

Nussbaum, Martha and Amartya Sen. eds. 1992. *The Quality of Life*. Oxford: Clarendon Press.

Ono, Hiroshi and Kristen S. Lee. 2013. Welfare States and the Redistribution of Happiness. *Social Forces* 92: 789–814.

Sen, Amartya. 1987. *The Standard of Living*. Cambridge: Cambridge University Press.

Sheldon, Eleanor B. and Wilbert E. Moore. eds. 1968. *Indicators of Social Change: Concepts and Measurements*. New York, NY: Russell Sage Foundation.

Shin, D. and D. M. Johnson. 1978. Avowed Happiness as an Overall Assessment of the Quality of Life. *Social Indicators Research* 5: 475–492.

Sirgy, M. Joseph. 2011. Theoretical Perspectives Guiding QOL Indicator Projects. *Social Indicators Research* 103: 1–22.

US Department of Health and Human Services. 2000. *Healthy People 2010*. Washington, DC: US Government Printing Office.

Veenhoven, Ruut. 1984. *Conditions of Happiness*. Boston, MA: D. Reidel.

Veenhoven, R. 1996. Developments in Satisfaction Research. *Social Indicators Research* 37: 1–46.

CHAPTER 12

Visual Sociology

Vincent O'Brien

The International Visual Sociology Association (www.visualsociology.org), founded in 1981 (Harper 1998), describes Visual Sociology as a broad-ranging sociological field that includes, but is not limited to: documentary studies of everyday life, interpretive analysis of art and popular visual representation, the commercial use of images and visual media, analysis of archival images, and the study of the purpose and meaning in everyday image-making. In this chapter, I outline the development of Visual Sociology and, using examples from my own practice as a visual ethnographer, introduce some of the basic research methods employed by visual sociologists during field work studies.

The narrative performances and messages captured in visual materials are integral to everyday life and reveal how we make sense of our lives and convey understandings of social reality. Narrative performances may be formal, self-consciously constructed versions of reality designed to convey particular social messages. They may also be informal 'snapshot' retellings of remembered events or indicators of underlying values or future expectations. The social significance of visual images lies not only in the content of the images themselves, but also in the author's intent, the framing of and composition of subjects, and reception by audiences. The meaning and significance of images is always socially contingent. For example, family photo albums may start out as simple records of births, weddings, social events, and other gatherings. At a later date, they may take on a greater historical significance, providing viewers with a visual insight into family relationships, clothing, environments, and personal histories. Visual materials help to convey rich and complex narrative messages that extend beyond the visual artefacts themselves. They function as dialogic triggers, initiators of reflection, interpretation, and debate.

Narratives are naturally occurring behavioral performances informed by an array of explicit and implicit personal and social values. They emerge as essential expressions of engagement in the social world and are at the heart of how we organize, construct, navigate and explain our lived experiences to others. This public enactment of social life draws on the dynamic inner ecologies of values, beliefs, and understandings that make us who we are. For a sociologist, observation, analysis, and interpretation of social narratives can provide an insight into how people make sense of their lives. Sociologists studying the social world of others enter into a reflexive and dynamic encounter in which we attempt to view the social world through a critical lens – a considered and transparent analytical frame that, like everything else, arises from our own lived experiences. Acknowledging the social contingency of knowledge creation, we are called upon to reflect upon our own understandings and those of others; mirroring the everyday of our lives in which dialogic encounters with others enables us to construct, make sense of, and express particular versions of social reality.

The 'Visual Turn' in sociology has emerged in part because of a growing sense of the importance of visual communications and also because of technological developments in photography and videography that have widened access to image creation and video recording in the last few decades. Visual narratives take many forms, and are used to convey social messages and meanings through the creation and display of drawings, maps, diagrams, still images, and image sequences. The ubiquity of these visual materials reflects our underlying desire to record and share our lives. They give voice to personal and social identities – the values, expectations, roles, and affiliations that are composite parts of our dynamic social world. It is not simply the visual materials themselves that are of interest to visual sociologists. The process of making and sharing of visual materials also provides insights into social lives represented in visual narratives that extend from early cave paintings depicting hunting scenes, gods, and spirits, through to the family snapshots, wedding videos, and YouTube broadcasts of contemporary society.

In the early twentieth century, some anthropologists (Bateson and Mead 1942) began to use photography to illustrate cultural practices, stimulating an interest in visual methods within anthropology. Sociological interest was much slower to develop. It was not until the 1970s that some ethnographers began to use photography in field work studies (Becker 1974) as a means of documenting everyday life and drawing out the social and cultural conventions that informed community life. Early use of photography and film in social research was primarily documentary, with social researchers using visual recordings to survey and document observable environments, living conditions, social and cultural practices. Howard Becker, an early advocate for Visual Sociology, argued for a more critical analysis of the underlying meanings, motives and messages contained within and around visual images. Reflecting a more interpretive approach to social research, Becker argued that images are socially constructed (Becker 1995) and represent the ways in which we contextualize and give meaning to our lives from particular social perspectives.

While some sociologists have used visual methods to record, interpret, and explain social worlds, others have sought to understand social relationships through the analysis and interpretation of found visual materials. In the 1970s, Erving Goffman (1976) used extensive visual examples from advertising to explore the ways in which images convey gender expectations, conventions, and assumptions. At that time, photography and film making was largely limited to those with specialized technical knowledge and access to expensive, technically complex equipment and production facilities. More recently, the emergence of affordable and relatively simple-to-use digital media technologies has increased accessibility to the means and the volume of visual narratives outputs. Combined with emergence of social media platforms such as Facebook, YouTube, and Vimeo, we have witnessed an exponential growth in the public display of visual narratives documenting social life in all of its diversity.

The realization that we are witnessing a profound shift in social communication and the potential for a profound democratization of visual narrative production has informed a growing interest in Visual Sociology, especially among those who seek to explore and understand cultural experiences, perceived meanings, social behaviour, and the symbolic nature of human interaction. While some visual sociologists focus attention on found visual materials, others have recognized the potential of using visual methods to engage with people and communities in ethnographic studies of social life in naturalistic settings. The use of multiple and emergent research methods has become relatively commonplace in qualitative fieldwork as sociologists have come to realize that meaningful insights into social life depend on finding creative ways to capture the rich diversity of data that occurs naturally in an uncontrolled, naturalistic environment. Visual methods such as Photo Elicitation (Harper 2002), Photo Voice (Wang and Burris 1997), and Participatory Video (White 2003) have extended the means and scope of fieldwork studies that at one time relied largely on participant observation, interviews, and detailed researcher produced field notes and diaries.

Using visual methods, such as participatory video and photography, provides opportunities for dialogic engagement between researchers and participants that are less dependent on language and shared cultural understandings. Collaborative Visual Ethnography is an iterative process in which researchers and participants work together to identify, explore, and collaboratively analyze social issues and lived experiences. The process of making images, producing videos, and presenting visual narratives in public exhibitions opens up a rich array of dialogical exchanges, internal and interpersonal dialogs that emerge as individuals reflect upon what they want to say and how they can represent their ideas and experiences in their visual work. Wider situational dialogs are also enacted as visual materials are collaboratively produced, reviewed, edited, and displayed in public exhibitions. A collaborative ethos and an iterative dialogic process run through the whole research process, contributing to the formation of more fluid researcher/participant relationships than would normally arise in traditional social research settings. Collaborative visual ethnography challenges the traditional balance of power that privileges researcher viewpoints over those of participants. That power relationship is gradually displaced as the participants themselves become co-researchers, initiators of inquiries, and the authors of their own ethnographies.

Visual Methods

Visual recordings have the advantage of producing a relatively permanent source of complex data that includes both verbal and non-verbal information. They capture the fine details of human social interactions – the talk, non-verbal interactions, and visual records of place, bodily adornment, and material objects. Both still and moving image sequences provide an observational permanence that offers advantages over live field observation, allowing for repeated cycles of review, analysis, and interpretation over time. Visual recordings provide us with more than a simple copy of the subject and objects contained in the images; they also provide visible fragments of particular engagements, indicators of relationships, and memory prompts that enable researchers, study participants, and audiences to dialogically engage with the materials. This facilitates an ongoing interpretative analysis of the materials and the social world that informed their production.

Visual exhibits (completed photographs and video sequences) have a meaning for the author that may not be identical to that of the viewer. Meanings and messages are not always stable. They are subject to change over time according to the social and cultural contexts in which the images are produced and viewed. The ongoing iterative processes of production and public exhibition subtly alter the way in which we make sense of and give meaning to images and image sequences. The recognition of these dialogic qualities and the iterative process of image production, display, and reception have prompted some visual researchers to develop participatory visual methods for use in different field work studies. Participatory visual methods enable researchers to engage with participants and their communities, observing the complex ways in which people draw on prior knowledge, personal experiences, and socio-cultural values to shape and reconfigure understandings and actions in the social world.

Participatory Methods and Collaborative Research

Participatory research methods (Cornwall and Jewkes 1995; Odutola 2003) emerged from within a phenomenological paradigm which accepts that knowledge is created through interaction between people. In participatory studies, the researcher is considered to be part of the knowledge construction process and not independent of it. Participatory research explicitly aims to undermine the traditional power relationships between the researcher and object/subject of the research, with the intention of making visible the critical relationships that shape the focus, analysis and interpretation of social reality.

An increased interest in participatory methods in recent years has subsequently opened up further opportunities for collaborative research (Lassiter 2005), in which the participants and researchers' work together throughout all phases of the research and dissemination process. In collaborative research, participant voices and knowledge are defined as credible interpretations of social reality situated alongside, although different from, the academically formulated interpretations of the researcher. The knowledge produced through collaborative research is constructed for, by, and with the participants, challenging dominant "expert" representations that draw on research traditions favoring hierarchical researcher/researched relationships.

Within Visual Sociology, there is a growing interest in the development of participatory methods and collaborative research practices, often within the framework of collaborative visual ethnography (O'Brien et al. 2007). While participatory methods place the participant within the framework of data collection, collaborative research extends this participation across and beyond the normal boundaries of academic research. Participatory visual methods are often used as a means of engaging participants and communities in the wider collaborative process in which other research methods, such as interviews, field observation, documentary, and archive research, may also play a part. Some examples of participatory visual methods are outlined below.

Visual Tours

Visual tours (Pink 2007) can be a useful way to capture and gain insights into the social and physical environments in which people live. At its most basic, the visual tour is a simple process in which the researcher walks around a specific area making video or still image recordings of social environments. The materials created during the tour provide a rich source of visual data that can be thematically organized, subjected to content and semiotic analysis by the researcher, and used to support photo elicitation interviews or to document observable changes in the social environment over time.

In visual tours, the image creation process is carried out collaboratively and includes documentation of the encounters between the researcher and participants. Participants normally accompany the researcher during walks, suggesting subjects, places of interest, and providing local knowledge about specific locations. Collaborative visual tours can focus on aspects of the physical and multisensorial environment, with collaborative production and analysis providing ways of exploring material and sensorial practices along with indicators of meanings and the significance of space and place in participants lives (Pink 2008b).

Photo Elicitation

Photography is an excellent way for social researchers to capture data about locations, people, and their environments. Images taken in the field provide a visual record upon which the researcher can reflect and expand when compiling field work notes. Photography can also be used during interviews, and to illustrate and make arguments for social change. Photo elicitation (Harper 2002) is essentially an interview technique in which the interviewer invites the interviewee to talk about the content, meaning, or significance of images.

Photo elicitation interviews based on photographs that people have made themselves provide a direct entry into the point of view of the participant rather than starting from the initial assumptions of the researcher. Using the respondent's own images facilitates collaborative interviewing, not just as a means of producing a description of the photograph and its contents, but also as an aid for reviewing and revising misconceptions or omissions that the researcher might have inadvertently introduced in the initial working hypothesis. Photo elicitation enables the researcher to become aware of new insights or unexpected thematic issues arising in the respondent's narrative explanation of the meaning and significance of the image and its contents.

Photo Voice

Photo Voice (Wang and Burris 1997) is an explicitly reflexive, participatory technique designed to engage people in a process through which they can identify, represent, and enhance everyday life in their community (Wang and Redwood-Jones 2001). It involves using still images captured by participants, as a means of constructing visual narratives that represent key concerns. In my Visible Voice projects (O'Brien et al. 2008) (www.visiblevoice.info), participants are given cameras and invited to photograph scenes, objects, people or places illustrating, or figuratively representing, their perception of life in their own community. Some time is spent in the initial workshops introducing participants to very basic photographic skills: basic composition, framing, lighting, and the placement of narrative elements with an image. Participants then work individually and in groups taking photographs and selecting those they wish to submit for public exhibition. The process of choosing subjects, topics, and themes is done collectively by each group. The process of selecting and editing images (normally just simple cropping, sharpening, etc.) engages the group in dialog about the issues and the best way to represent their ideas as visual exhibits that tell a story about life in the community.

Researchers act as participant observers, providing technical support as appropriate. Researcher field notes and reflexive journals are developed using ad hoc documentary photography, interview notes, and audio visual recordings made with participants during the production and exhibition process. The images produced by researchers and participants feed into an ongoing collaborative review of the process, analysis, and interpretive outputs.

Participatory Video

A similar approach is used in the participatory video workshops. Participatory video has its origins in Don Snowden's (Snowden 1998) early work on the remote Newfoundland island of Fogo. In 1967, Snowden went to Fogo, a community threatened with forced relocation by the Canadian government, and led a film making process in which community members articulated problems, ideas, and aspirations during the filming of a series of documentaries. The practice of involving participants in the construction of visual narratives that emerged from Snowden's work became more widely known as the Fogo Process (MacLeod 2004).

In the late 1960s, filmmaking was a complex and expensive procedure that required the involvement of professional filmmakers with high levels of technical expertise. The emergence of new digital media technologies over the last decade has greatly simplified video production, reduced the cost of equipment, and placed the means of design, production, and dissemination more directly in the hands of ordinary people.

Participatory video production is a collaborative process in which all of the participants get to play a role and make a contribution according to their interest and abilities. Roles and responsibilities can be shared among group members, and, in practice, many participants will move from one group to another during the production process. Sometimes this is the result of group dynamics and relationships shifting and changing during the production process, but often movement between groups comes about as technically skilled individuals are asked to help out with filming and editing by other groups. The variability in personal circumstances across the groups means that some people have less time available to engage in long and intensive video editing workshops.

An important feature of participatory video production is that simply taking part and contributing to the construction of the narrative is what is important. As participants work through story ideas, narrative themes, representations, edits, and distribution discussions, the process begins to reveal the extent of consensus, dissension, diversity, and relational factors that emerge as participants explore and share their thoughts and experiences. Participation in the technical process of production, while not evenly spread among each group's members, is variable and flexible enough to enable all participants to contribute to the production and the dialog that it prompts. Some participants are keen to perform narratives by appearing in front of the camera; others want to frame and compose the narrative by operating the cameras. Others take on a coordinating role, and some like to be more involved in the technical aspects of production through editing the materials, working on scripts, titles, music etc. Movement in and out of the production groups is often fluid, with members of the crew entering and leaving according to their availability, abilities, and interest in a particular phase of the production process.

Collaborative Visual Ethnography

Collaborative Visual Ethnography refers to field work based research practices that make use of co-production and public exhibition of visual narratives as a means of engagement and focus for ethnographic research. The process of visual production and public exhibition facilitates a fluid, yet rich collaborative environment in which there are multiple opportunities for participants and researchers to engage in reflection and critical thinking about socio-cultural forces that shape everyday lives and social conditions in different communities.

Throughout the field work process, researchers and participants use visual and other collaborative methods to identify, explore, and share lived experiences and social and cultural perspectives in an attempt to bridge the perceptual gaps that exist between communities, service providers, and policy-makers. Participants are both the focus of these ethnographic research encounters and the creators of their own ethnographic narratives. They engage in a self-determined visual production process deciding how and what to record, making editing decisions, and developing narrative styles. Sharing and debating viewpoints is an integral part of a long-term dialogic process of production and public exhibition, leading to researcher-participant co-analysis of completed visual narratives and audience responses. Researchers and participants produce their own ethnographic accounts (often in the form of videos and photographic exhibitions) to reach out to their respective audiences. Visible Voice provides a practical example of collaborative visual ethnography practice research in action across different communities and cultural groups.

Public Exhibition

Public exhibition is an essential part of the Visible Voice process, situating it within an emerging practice of public ethnography (Lassiter 2008; Gans 2010). Public ethnography developed from a desire to make research socially useful and to use it as a means of changing, for the better, the conditions encountered through research. Public ethnography is informed by a commitment to activism, but at the same time it must also stand up as research rather than just political rhetoric. It must engage with and be treated seriously by both academic and non-academic audiences. As a collaborative study, the Visible Voice process needs to be carefully and continuously reviewed to ensure that the methods and findings to be presented in both public and academic spheres provide an authentic interpretation of the experiences and ideas shared by the participants.

Public Exhibition embeds the research process firmly within a participatory activist performance tradition, a research tradition that aims to give back to the community by creating a legacy of inquiry, stimulating a process of transformational change in the lives and social practices of participants and their communities. Photographs produced during the collaboration are edited and printed for public exhibition, often with the addition of participant contributed captions. These Photo Voice exhibits provide a relatively simple but effective means of drawing public attention to the narrative messages that participants wish to share. Participants are usually present at exhibitions as their work is viewed and interpreted by the wider community. Exhibitions are co-curated with the contributors and often include video narratives, cultural artefacts and live performances (music and dance) provided by the participants to enhance the intercultural communicative potential of the events. For example, since we began in 2006, Visible Voice has regularly held exhibitions and video screenings in local communities in different locations around the world in which our collaborating research and community partners operate. Some of the materials have also been displayed as part of an annual Visible Voice traveling exhibition which has been shown to numerous audiences in Brazil, Canada, Kyrgyzstan, Kazakhstan, and at various events taking place in Argentina, Armenia, Austria, Belgium, Sweden, Romania, and the United States. Images and video materials are frequently shared online and international groups meet via Skype from time to time to share experiences and ideas.

Public exhibition often prompts a group desire for a more formal collaborative review. Groups, acting on their own initiative, call review and planning meetings in which they share their experiences of seeing their work displayed for a wider public and develop new narrative ideas to improve the scope and quality of future exhibitions. Engaging in collaborative review is an essential iterative component of project development. It represents a reflexive way of working that identifies the socially and rhetorically constructed boundaries that constrain our view of the social field. It also prompts us to transgress those limits and provides a basis for creative, ethical alternatives to hierarchical knowledge creation practices inherent in traditional "expert" led social research.

Visual Ethics

Research involving visual methods, such as participatory video and photography, entails a special requirement for ethical integrity, largely because of the power of video and photography. Text-based field notes containing information about participants, interviews, and observed interactions are relatively easy to anonymize, but capturing visual data often means that participants and others visible in the recordings may remain identifiable to others. Special care is needed to take into consideration issues such as anonymity, consent, privacy, and dignity. Visual displays of materials raise questions of responsibility regarding dissemination of visual research. For example, in our Visible Voice work, each person interviewed during field recordings is asked to state their name and give oral confirmation of their consent to the recording. Field recordings are made in full view and never involve discreet recording of social interactions. We review all images and audio visual recordings to identify potentially problematic ethical, and sometimes legally, sensitive materials. Not all visual materials gathered during the study are released for public viewing.

Visual researchers, even those who use primarily participatory methods, need to be constantly aware of potential ethical implications of audio visual recording when they or the participants take photographs or make video recordings. A three-stage consent process can be helpful. At stage one, participants give their consent to take part in the project, including consent to appear in generic photography and video recordings made during workshops and other project events. For audio and video recordings, participants give second level consent to enable us to work with selected extracts during the production of public exhibits. Final stage consent may be required before the public release of completed exhibits. During production workshops participants can veto the public use of images of themselves or images they have created.

In our Visible Voice work, before photography and video sessions we discuss the ethical implications of visual recording and talk about how and whether non-participants might be included in images and recordings. Not surprisingly, as many participants have families, they sometimes want to interview or photograph members of their own family and others not directly involved in the project. We discuss and define the acceptable boundaries, taking into account legal, cultural, and individual versions of "good practice" as we prepare for, and make decisions about, the nature and content of public exhibits. In general, all identifiable persons in a video recording or image need be fully aware that a recording is being made and its potential use in public exhibitions. As we work on production and editing, we look collaboratively at the materials with a view to identifying potential harm or dignity issues that may arise through capture and future publication. Different cultures have different views on this, and we always need to try to accommodate these cultural viewpoints while recognizing the legal and ethical principles that govern research ethics in the United Kingdom and other countries in which we work.

Summarizing Visual Sociology

Visual Sociology is a broad and varied methodological approach to social inquiry that draws attention to the importance of visual images in shaping life and communicating personal, cultural, and societal values. Visual sociologists' interests may focus, solely or simultaneously, on found images – those that are already present in the everyday of social life – or on new images created as part of a research process. Research methods employed by visual sociologists include photo elicitation (Harper 2002), Photo Voice (Wang and Burris 1997), video diaries (Pini 2001), video and photographic field tours (Pink 2008) and participatory video (White 2003). Visual images and artefacts may be the primary source of data (Margolis 1999), or, alternately, their content or creation may be the means through which researchers engage with participants and communities as part of more broadly framed multi-method studies. For some researchers it is the emancipatory (Wang and Burris 1997) and collaborative potential (O'Brien et al. 2007) that motivates and informs research practice.

The rapid development of digital media technologies and social media platforms during the last decade has helped to stimulate sociological interest in the visual world and more transparent and collaborative approaches in social research and promote calls for the development of a Public Sociology in which the goal is, at least in part, to produce research outputs that engage people and their communities in the act of creating knowledge. The relative ease with which researchers and participants can capture and create visual representations of the social world through digital media has stimulated interest in the application of photography and video as a primary means of gathering and analyzing examples of rich and complex sources of social data in naturalistic settings. In most studies, visual methods are used alongside other methods. In field work based studies, participant observation of image creation processes can be combined with co-analysis and interpretation of visual data produced by researchers and participants. Using participatory and collaborative research practices participants and researchers can produce insider and outsider versions of the social world. Working visually prompts researchers (and participant communities) to engage in ongoing reflexive dialog around the content, composition, meaning, and significance of the explicit and implicit symbols, messages, and values that may be present in the constructed images and visual sequences. In short, Visual Sociology enables us to engage in more transparent, reflexive research practices and outputs. It is a form of public sociology that offers new insights into the visual materiality of our social world while simultaneously stimulating an open dialogic engagement with the nature, purpose, and social value of sociological inquiry.

References

Bateson, Gregory and Margaret Mead. 1942. *Balinese Character: A Photographic Analysis*. New York, NY: New York Academy of Sciences.

Becker, Howard. 1974. Photography and Sociology. *Studies in the Anthropology of Visual Communication* 1(1): 3–26.

Becker, Howard. 1995. Visual Sociology, Documentary Photography, and Journalism: It's (Almost) All a Matter of Context. *Visual Sociology* 10(2): 5–14.

Cornwall, Andrea and Rachel Jewkes. 1995. What is Participatory Research? *Social Science and Medicine* 41(12): 1667–1676.

Gans, Herbert. 2010. Public Ethnography; Ethnography as Public Sociology. *Qualitative Sociology* 33(1): 97–104.

Goffman, Erving. 1976. *Gender Advertisements*. New York, NY: Harper and Row.

Harper, Douglas. 1998. An Argument for Visual Sociology. In *Image-Based Research: A Sourcebook for Qualitative Researchers*. Edited by Jon Prosser. London: Falmer Press, 24–41.

Harper, Douglas. 2002. Talking about Pictures: A Case for Photo Elicitation. *Visual Studies* 17(1): 13–26.

Lassiter, Luke. 2005. *The Chicago Guide to Collaborative Ethnography*. Chicago, IL: University of Chicago Press.

Lassiter, Luke. 2008. Moving Past Public Anthropology and Doing Collaborative Research. *NAPA Bulletin* 29(1): 70–86.

MacLeod, Paul. 2004. Participatory Filmmaking and Video – Building on the Legacy of the Fogo Process. Symposium on Communication for Social and Environmental Change. University of Guelph.

Margolis, Eric. 1999. Class Pictures: Representations of Race, Gender and Ability in a Century of School Photography *Visual Studies* 14(1): 7–38.

O'Brien, Vincent, Kenesh Dzhusipov, and Flavio Wittlin. 2007. Visible Voices, Shared Worlds: Using Digital Video and Photography in Pursuit of a Better Life. Social Interaction and Mundane Technologies (SIMTECH) ACM SIG.

O'Brien, Vincent, Kenesh Dzhusipov, and Nazgul Esengulova. 2008. Embracing the Everyday: Reflections on Using Video and Photography in Health Research. *Social Interaction and Mundane Technologies (SIMTECH) ACM SIG*.

Odutola, Kole Ade. 2003. Participatory Use of Video: A Case Study of Community Involvement in Story Construction. *Global Media Journal* 2(2).

Pini, Maria. 2001. Video Diaries: Questions of Authenticity and Fabrication. In *Screening the Past* Issue 13. Available at http://tlweb.latrobe.edu.au/humanities/screeningthepast/, accessed December 1, 2001.

Pink, Sarah. 2007. Walking with Video. *Visual Studies* 22(3): 240–252.

Pink, S. 2008a. An Urban Tour: The Sensory Sociality of Ethnographic Place-Making. *Ethnography* 9(2): 175–196.

Pink, Sarah. 2008b. Mobilising Visual Ethnography: Making Routes, Making Place and Making Images. *Forum Qualitative Sozialforschung/Forum: Qualitative Social Research* 9(3).

Snowden, Don. 1998. Eyes See; Ears Hear. In *The First Mile of Connectivity – Advancing Telecommunications for Rural Development through a Participatory Approach*. Edited by Don Richardson, and Lynnita Paisley. New York, NY: Food and Agriculture Organisation UN.

Wang, Caroline and Mary Ann Burris. 1997. Photovoice: Concept, Methodology, and Use for Participatory Needs Assessment. *Health Education and Behavior* 24(3): 369–387.

Wang, Caroline C. and Yanique A. Redwood-Jones. 2001. Photovoice Ethics: Perspectives from Flint Photovoice. *Health Education and Behavior* 28(5): 560–572.

White, Shirley A. 2003. *Participatory Video: Images that Transform and Empower*. London: Sage.

CHAPTER 13

The Sociology of Risk

Jens O. Zinn

The Sociology of Risk

The study of risk is a relatively new enterprise within sociology. After World War II, science was increasingly perceived as dangerous, and suspicion crept into the public discourse that the use of some scientific discoveries had already started to change and destroy our natural environment. The bestselling book, *Silent Spring* (Carson 1962), warned about the harmful side-effects of the intensive use of pesticides on human health and signaled the erosion of the dominant positive view of commercial uses of scientific products. Social scientists tried to make sense out of the increasingly critical attitude toward new technologies that had previously been seen primarily as means for social advancement, increasing living standards, and reducing poverty.

Early studies focused on the organizational management of risk and employees' risk-taking behavior. *Man-Made Disasters* (Turner 1978) highlighted how dangerous practices establish in organizations over time. Little deviations become routines and build up and finally lead to major disasters. *The Other Price of Britain's Oil* (Carson 1982) showed how economic pressure might support unsafe practices through, for example, encouraging employees to take greater risks at work. In the 1980s, the early focus on organizational risk management was complemented by the development of theories on the broader socio-cultural and socio-structural dimensions and how these influenced societies' understanding of and responses to risk. During this period, the sociological subfield of risk was still trying to establish its place among those of more dominant disciplines such as the sciences, economics, and psychology, which had already framed the notion of risk as objective, calculable, and manageable. As noted above, however, this perspective had come under pressure since the 1960s, when it became clear that public perception of risk did not always follow experts' views. Moreover, even when provided with expert knowledge, the public often disagreed with it, had biased views of the world (Slovic 2000), or based their decisions on intuition rather than evidence (Tversky and Kahneman 1974).

Such observations supported a dominant distinction in interdisciplinary risk research between superior expert knowledge about risk and inferior lay knowledge (e.g., Pidgeon et al. 1992). Sociologists rejected this binary of the lay–expert distinction and focused, instead, on the dynamic processes through which risk knowledge becomes socially acknowledged or not (Wynne 1989). These conflicts not only challenged the authority of experts but also brought to light issues of trust during public risk conflicts. For example, the imbalance of power between experts employed by corporations and lay people had for decades prevented pesticides (e.g., with a base of Agent Orange or DDT) with harmful side-effects from being taken off the market. The public's discovery of these side-effects led to further distrust of experts hired by powerful business interests.

At the time, however, it was puzzling for many technical experts and decision-makers that even when the available knowledge seemed clear, social groups were often unable to agree on how risks should be managed or what risks should be taken. Mary Douglas (1992; 1990) emphasized the socio-structural dimension related to risks. She pointed out that controversies about how to manage risk result from fundamentally different worldviews rooted in deep cultural beliefs about how a good society should function, rather than a lack of or biased knowledge.

With Ulrich Beck's seminal book *The Risk Society*, published in German in 1986 (*Risikogesellschaft*) and in English in 1992, risk moved from being one sociological concept among others to a central social category that describes how societies reproduce and change. Beck challenged fundamental sociological assumptions, sometimes triggering fierce debates. Central to his thinking were the new social dynamics driven by global risks that would fundamentally transform our world toward a *World Risk Society* (Beck 2009). His work is responsible for the sociology of risk becoming broadly recognized in academia and society more generally.

In addition to Douglas's and Beck's work, there are a number of other influential approaches which represent what could be called the *sociology of risk and uncertainty*, which have become sociologically influential beyond the original focus on environmental and technological risks. Besides the *risk and culture* and the *risk society* approaches, other key methods of theorizing risk include the *governmentality* perspective developed by scholars on the basis of Michel Foucault's work, Niklas Luhmann's modern *systems theory*, and Stephen Lyng's *edgework* perspective on voluntary risk-taking.

One of the characteristics of the sociology of risk is that the key concept itself – risk – is contested. Sometimes it is used interchangeably with the notion of danger or threat, and at other times it is used as a more technical concept linked to statistics and probability theory. While it can be understood as an ontological entity that exists independently of human beings, it is also seen as a semantic or a particular cognitive/social construction. Most approaches accept that all these different notions of risk are entangled and relevant to the understanding of risk phenomena, even though every approach has a particular understanding of its key concept.

In the proceeding text I will highlight how different approaches have contributed to the *sociology of risk and uncertainty*. I will conclude with a number of key areas where further research is needed.

Risk and Culture

Mary Douglas's (1921–2007) *cultural symbolic* approach to risk challenged the dominant technical, psychological, and economics approaches of the time. Her work with Aaron Wildavsky, *Risk and Culture: An Essay on the Selection of Technical and Environmental Dangers* (1982), was a milestone in social science risk theorizing. As noted above, their central argument was that the perceptions of and responses to risk are fundamentally culturally structured. They argued that technical, economic, and psychological approaches fail to understand risk conflicts since these are often not caused by a lack of comprehension of the facts, as suggested by technicians and cognitive psychologists, but deeply rooted value differences.

Trained as an anthropologist in the 1940s and 1950s, when the *structural-functionalist* thinking of Radcliffe-Brown and Durkheim was very influential, Douglas aimed to develop a universal theory which would enable an understanding of the different ways in which social entities (such as small groups, organizations, or whole societies) perceive and respond to risk.

Douglas's early anthropological work (1963; 1966) prepared the basis for her later analysis on risk. She argued that social concerns regarding dirt and pollution are less about bacteria, viruses, or pollutants and more about socio-symbolic disorder and the lack of control of a group's boundaries. The control of the body and its margins serves as a symbol for controlling the rules that define a social group. The reality of *danger* becomes important for a social group as a threat to its boundaries, orders, and values. Similarly, the modern notion of *risk* in secularized societies serves to protect the boundaries of social groups in modern societies and is therefore *functionally equivalent* to the earlier notions of danger and sin.

On this basis, Douglas argued that risks are fundamentally socially constructed. While dangers are real, how a social community experiences and responds to them is, in her view, a social activity, determined by how a community is organized and the social values it holds (Douglas 1990: 8). In order to characterize the different ways in which social groups perceive and respond to risk, Douglas introduced the so-called "grid-group" typology (see Figure 13.1). The typology characterized social groups, first by the extent to which individual identities and cultural outlooks are fixed and predetermined and the amount of control members accept (grid-dimension), and second by the degree of commitment or

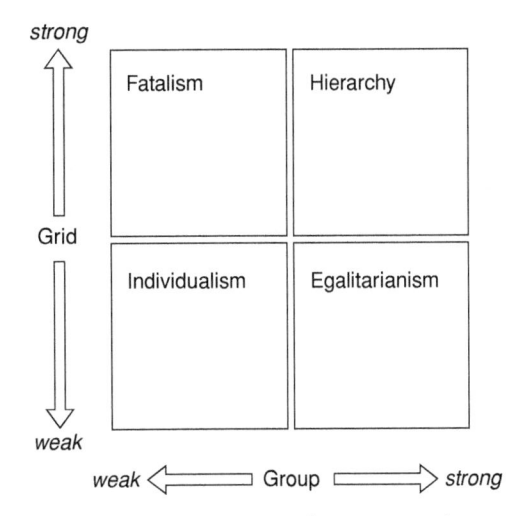

Figure 13.1 Diagram Grid-Group Typology

solidarity individuals exhibit or feel toward a social group (group-dimension). The combination of these two dimensions resulted in four ideal types to be used to characterize empirical, observable worldviews. They reveal that fierce debates about risk can continue even when the scientific knowledge is relatively uncontested, because they are rooted in fundamentally different worldviews.

The first ideal-type, *hierarchy*, is characterized by a high predetermination of identities and control and a high degree of commitment to the group, which is typical for organizations such as the military, the Catholic Church, and traditional bureaucracies. Conversely, in markets we find low predetermination and control and relatively little commitment to the group. This second ideal-type is termed *individualism*. Low predetermination and control of individual identity but high degree of commitment and solidarity characterizes the third ideal-type, *egalitarianism*, which is typical for grassroots movements and communal groups. The fourth type, *fatalism*, occurs when predetermination of identity and control is high but solidarity and commitment are low, and when people are rather isolated and lack influence and commitment to a social group.

On this basis, Douglas (1990: 15ff) argued that in an *individualist* culture, social concerns focus on the risks associated with the competitive culture of markets where the weak and the losers have to carry the blame for their failure. In a *hierarchical* culture, the focus is on social risks and those who deviate from the dominant social norms tend to be blamed for risks. In an *egalitarian* culture there is the tendency to focus on natural risks and to blame the system and faction leaders. In the *fatalist* perspective only fate, itself, is blamed. The cultural approach has been used in a variety of studies to explain, for example, the different responses of social groups to AIDS (Douglas 1992), the financial crisis (Hindmoor 2010), and climate change (Verweij et al. 2006).

The cultural approach contributed to an improved understanding of why risk conflicts are difficult to solve when they are based on fundamental differences in worldviews or how a society should be organized. It also helps explain why sometimes particular groups are singled out as being responsible for a particular risk even though there is no evidence to support such a view. For example, when the swine flu threatened nations worldwide, the Muslim-led Egyptian government ordered the slaughter of all swine as a precautionary measure, even though there were no reported cases of the swine flu in Egypt. This order makes sense in light of the Muslim belief that swine are unclean and that the swine breeders were mainly poor members of the Christian minority that lived at the boundaries of society.

Cultural theorists such as Thompson (2008) have argued that good and sustainable social decision-making requires integrating different social worldviews rather than excluding some from the process. From this perspective, conflict should be seen as a valuable part of the social process that will, eventually, improve outcomes and efficiency. Cultural theory, however, has been critiqued for its inability to satisfactorily explain how social changes come about. Since it frames risk as a threat to a particular set of social values, the characteristic of a particular risk itself has no (direct) influence on the ways people perceive and respond to it. Changes are seen as resulting from cultural shifts and social movements, giving little scope to explain changes through the types of risk, themselves (Douglas and Wildavsky 1982). While the cultural perspective conceptualizes risk as a danger to the boundaries and valued institutions of a social group, another perspective, as we will see in the next section, views risk as a driver of social change.

Risk Society

Ulrich Beck's (1944–2015) distinguished work was in many respects central for risk becoming a key, defining dimension of modern societies. Beck's theories differ from most other socio-cultural approaches to risk in that he claims that the occurrence of new risks will propel us into a *risk society* characterized by *reflexive modernization*. These new risks will occur not as a result of failure but as a side-effect of successful modernization (1992).

Beck distinguishes new risks, which occur as a result of our successes of modernization and are, thereby, human-made, from the older risks, which had been managed by science, industry, and insurance during *first modernization*. For example, advances in scientific methods for dealing with many infectious diseases such as polio, plague, and tetanus and the development of social insurance to moderate the negative social effects of early industrialization (Ewald 1986) characterize successful risk management during first modernization. In contrast, *new risks* might be hidden or hit us unexpectedly. They result as unexpected consequences of social and scientific advancement and the fragmentation and complexity of the production of expert knowledge.

Beck focused on the global new mega risks which have driven us into a world risk society. These mega risks, such as "nuclear, chemical, ecological and genetic engineering risks (a) can be limited in terms of neither time nor place, (b) are not accountable according to the established rules of causality, blame and liability, and (c) cannot be compensated for or insured against" (Beck 1992a: 2). New global mega risks might even challenge whole social systems (e.g., financial crisis) or humanity itself (e.g., climate change).

There are at least two reasons for the difficulties experienced in managing the new risks with science and insurance. Mega risks are catastrophes that cannot be easily covered by insurance (instead the state has to jump in as last insurer or the public has to bear the effects) and the scientific knowledge is limited or uncertain regarding the risks; the degree of ignorance is high and scientific expertise is often contradictory. This is typically the case when new technologies are introduced, such as genetic engineering. As a result the *risk society* is dominated by social conflicts about the production and allocation of risk rather than class conflicts and the allocation of wealth that characterized *first modernity* and the *class society* (Beck 1992b).

Beck's approach also differs from the cultural theory of Douglas, who positioned concerns about nuclear power in social movements at the boundaries of society that reject large technologies and big business in general. Instead, Beck saw concerns about nuclear power as an expression of a fundamental social change that confronts society with new risks to be addressed by society as a whole. In his view, the resistance to new risks comes not just from the boundaries of society or from the irrational thinking of social movements, as implied by Douglas and Wildavsky (1982), but forms across different social groups and constitutes a new political subject, a *coalition of anxiety* (Beck 1992b: 49ff).

The coalition of anxiety consists of people affected by or worried about particular risks. Even though class differences do not disappear they are not the most important factor in this coalition. Some risks, such as climate change, can impact all social classes (to varying degrees). The *coalition of anxiety* engages in *subpolitics* (Beck 1999: 39, 91), which characterizes a new form of political engagement when stakeholders across common political camps and constituencies come together to support political change (Beck 1999). Beck also uses the notion of a *political consumer* to characterize how basic decisions, such as which food to buy, can become politicized. We not only have to make a decision about a lifestyle (e.g., organic food) but also about the production process (e.g., fair trade).

There is a second important development that characterizes the *risk society* and is responsible for risk and uncertainty becoming a normal experience of our times. Beck claimed that, since World War II, complex patterns of social change have led to another thrust of individualization that has started to fundamentally transform the social realm. Increasingly, social institutions address citizens as individuals rather than as part of social units such as the family (Beck and Beck-Gernsheim 2002). Beck stressed that with the institutional support systems of the traditional family and social class weakened, individuals have to rely more on the opportunities of the labor market and the fluidity of social policy to guide their behavior. Institutions increasingly frame social inequalities as individual inequalities to be managed individually. As a result, where resources are lacking, individualized inequalities soar as institutional support structures decrease (Beck 1992b: 87).

Another important contribution of risk society theories is the assumption that new mega risks would *support the development* of a *cosmopolitan* worldview and *cosmopolitical* arrangements (Beck 2004). Risks such as international terrorism, the global financial crisis, genetic engineering, and climate change require transnational arrangements, such as international and transnational organizations like the Intergovernmental Panel on Climate Change (IPCC) to manage them.

Furthermore, globalization has generated new global dynamics such as transnational families. For example, family members can live and work in different parts of the world as so-called *care chains* are formed, with women from poorer countries caring for the children and elderly in richer countries while experiencing new risks and uncertainties. Beck maintains that we must have a global perspective in a world risk society where dynamics of environmental, technological, and social risks are increasingly transnational and require a transnational and cosmopolitan perspective to be dealt with successfully.

As the above indicates, risk society theorizing originally focused on technical and environmental risks and then began to emphasize the transformative power of new mega risks, including genetic engineering, climate change, terrorism, and the global financial crisis (Beck 2009). However, not all scholars agree that risk is about the prevention and management of "real" dangers. Instead, a stream of research analyzes how risk technologies and discourses about risk have become a means to govern populations in modern societies.

Governmentality

Scholars referring to Michel Foucault's (1926–1984) work emphasize that *risk* stands less for possible harm or a threat to social institutions than as part of a strategy to govern people (Foucault 1991). They observe that different techniques such as actuarial risk and formal methods such as statistics and probability theories have been used in an increasing number of areas from psychiatry, social work, and crime prevention to social insurance and public policy to manage people (e.g., Castel 1991; Dean 1999; Kelly 2001; O'Malley 2004). From this perspective, *risk* has become a dominant discourse and technology that is used to govern populations in the context of neoliberalism.

These scholars build on the seminal work of Foucault, who observed that forms of governing that rely on the threat and use of punishment and surveillance have recently been complemented by more indirect forms of governing using calculative technologies and general norms of individual self-improvement to manage populations. Foucault introduced the phrase *governmentality* that combines the notions of *govern* and *mentality* to express this new form of indirect governing through knowledge discourses and social practices. It also reflects his view that power would no longer be mainly enforced top down but dispersed throughout social relations in society. This power is not only restrictive but productive. Political, scientific, and public stakeholders all have some power that circulates and is negotiated within society. In modern societies, power is increasingly exercised through risk knowledge and technology carried by normative discourses about appropriate behavior.

A good example of such power is the governing of pregnancy (Lupton 1999). Most societies hold strong social norms to protect and nourish not only babies and children but also the unborn life. Today, there is a continuous stream of articles in the news and literature advising how pregnant women can ensure that their baby will have the best possible start to life. In most wealthy countries, health services give extensive advice and supervise women during pregnancy and conduct certain tests to monitor the development of the foetus. Scholars who have researched the social regulation of pregnancy in the perspective of governmentality have argued that the regulation of pregnancy has undergone a significant shift, which is characterized by the conflation of two dimensions (e.g., Weir 1996; Ruhl 1999). First, a moral discourse conceives the pregnant woman as being responsible for the well-being of the foetus and for securing its healthy development. Second, the development of medical knowledge and technologies provide (probabilistic) knowledge about good and bad behavior during pregnancy (e.g., eating healthy foods and not drinking and smoking). Pregnancy is now increasingly managed through pressure on women to follow the probabilistic knowledge defining risk factors to ensure the health of their foetus.

From this perspective, governing takes place from a distance. Instead of direct enforcement of behavior, responsibility is handed over to the individual to make the right decisions. However, as O'Malley (2008) has noted, governmentality does not fully replace other forms of regulation. Direct enforcement and surveillance work together in today's forms of governing, and pregnant women observed behaving in ways perceived to negatively impact the health of a foetus risk government intervention.

The combination of normative expectations and calculative technologies used to govern populations has been examined in a growing number of studies, from historical analysis of the introduction of life insurance in the United States (Zelizer 1979), social insurance in France (Ewald 1986), or insurance more generally (O'Malley 2004; Baker and Simon 2002) to the governing of youth (Kelly 2006), offenders (O'Malley 1992; Garland 1997), health services, and other social services (Kemshall 2002).

Organizations' tendencies toward risk aversion have become obvious with the introduction of risk technologies. For example, in social work, changes in risk management have led to a stronger emphasis on working to avoiding risk and establishing formal routines and measures for service quality. The emphasis has shifted from protecting the well-being of the service user to the protection of services providers (against being blamed when things go wrong) (Hood and Rothstein 2000). Critics of this shift note that risk-taking, as well as risk aversion, is a crucial part of good service delivery for the service-users' well-being (e.g., Titterton 2011). Finding the right balance is crucial. Taking risks, in many cases, can lead to positive results.

Edgework

In interdisciplinary risk research and in many social science approaches, risk is mainly understood as something negative to be reduced or prevented. Stephen Lyng challenged this orthodoxy. With his *edgework* (Lyng 1990; 2005; 2008) approach to high risk-taking, he claims that people expose themselves voluntarily to risk because of the excitement they feel when doing so. Lyng's edgework approach is the most well-established attempt to link voluntary risk-taking on the micro-level to general societal changes at the macro-level. Many studies in criminology and sociology have applied the idea of *edgework*, which was originally developed through studies of white male, high-risk activities (Miller 1991; Lyng 1991), and eventually included a variety of risk-taking activities of other social groups and milieus (e.g., Roth 2015; Lois 2001).

Edgework emphasizes the exploration of human boundaries when people engage in risk-taking activities. Originally the emphasis was on life and death boundaries, but others, such as sanity and insanity and consciousness and unconsciousness have also been explored. At the core of understanding the edgework experiences are the "skilful practices and powerful sensations that risk takers value so highly" (Lyng 2005: 4). People engaging in edgework are not reckless. They are usually experts in what they are doing and are keen to prove their ability to perform well under difficult conditions. A central motive for edgework is to provide people with a feeling of self-worth and self-confidence through mastering personal challenges.

The focus of Lyng's work is less the application of edgework in different social contexts than the core experience which people share when exploring the edge. He emphasizes that when "people separated by division of age, gender, class, race, occupation, and intellectual temperament come together and discover deep-seated commonalities of personal experience, they often feel a sense of connection rooted in something basic to their souls" (Lyng 2005: 4).

In 'Edgework: A Social Psychological Analysis of Voluntary Risk-taking' (1990), Lyng sees people's growing engagement in edgework as a response to the *alienating* (Karl Marx) and *oversocializing* (George Herbert Mead) reality of modern societies. Edgework contrasts with experiences of disenchantment with the modern world (Max Weber) and provides a way to "escape from, to resist the imperatives of emotional control, rational calculation, routinization, and reason in modern society" (O'Malley and Mugford 1994: 198). People develop honed skills to manage risks and uncertainties while they experience intense sensations of self-determination and control when engaging in edgework.

In later work, Lyng complemented the argument of edgework as escape and resistance with the idea that *edgework* is a "pure expression of the central institutional and cultural imperatives of the emerging social order" (Lyng 2005: 5). The insecurity of the risk society is reflected in almost every aspect of our increasingly individualistic lives, from the dangers we confront in work and consumption to the uncertainties involved in leisure activities and the maintenance of our bodies and health. This shift of responsibility from institutions and collectives toward the individual increasingly requires edgework skills. As a result, edgework is increasingly required by people to manage their lives.

Other Contributions to the Sociology of Risk

Each sociological approach to risk highlights a particular social dimension that helps make sense of social dynamics related to risk. They respectively highlight particular dimensions of risk. However, they do not provide a coherent framework, nor are they exhaustive. The sociology of risk and uncertainty is a vibrant domain of research with a wide range of theories contributing to the debate.

One such theory is modern systems theory, which explains increased communication of social risks by functional differentiation of modern societies. Functionally differentiated societies increasingly produce decision-making situations where social systems try to prevent themselves from being blamed for negative outcomes (Japp and Kusche 2008). For example, during the last financial crisis the economic system tended to blame faulty government regulations while the political system blamed the uncontrolled market forces and prescribed more government regulations. Both tried to shift the blame to the other system.

Another theory, actor network theory, reconstructs the complex dynamics of materialities and socialities in actor networks and focuses on overcoming the artificial division between nature and culture in the modern worldview (Van Loon 2002). This approach is important since it emphasizes that risks themselves can be seen as actors which trigger social dynamics. It brings back into debate the ontological dimension of risk.

Many approaches view the media as having a significant impact on risk debates. Media studies and risk studies, however, have remained relatively separate spheres until recently (Tulloch and Zinn 2011). Further research is still needed to better understand the dynamics of risk reporting in the media.

Finally, Ortwin Renn has summarized insights from a number of different disciplines to develop a comprehensive framework for good *Risk Governance* (2008). He positioned common practices in risk assessment, management and communication in their social contexts to develop an argument for a comprehensive risk governance approach. He assumes that different risks require different approaches and that complex and contested risks require participative approaches.

Conclusion

Social science risk studies have provided comprehensive knowledge about the social processes framing the perception and responses to risk on societal, organizational, and individual levels. Challenging the rationalist orthodoxy in the sciences and economics of risk, sociology has shown how social processes play a major part in risk conflicts and are key components of good societal decision-making. In highlighting these social dimensions, as well as power, values, complexity, and emotions in conflicts and decisions, sociology has contributed to a better understanding and management of risk. Ignoring insights from social science risk research can lead to inefficient, undesirable, and sometimes harmful outcomes. Successful social risk management requires sociological knowledge.

References

Baker, Tom and Jonathan Simon. 2002. *Embracing Risk: The Changing Culture of Insurance and Responsibility*. Chicago, IL: The University of Chicago Press.

Beck, Ulrich. 1992a. From Industrial Society to the Risk Society: Questions of Survival, Social Structure and Ecological Enlightenment. *Theory, Culture and Society* 9(2): 101.

Beck, Ulrich. 1992b. *Risk Society: Towards a New Modernity*. London and Newbury Park, CA: Sage.

Beck, Ulrich. 1999. *World Risk Society*. Cambridge: Polity Press.

Beck, Ulrich. 2004. Cosmopolitical Realism: On the Distinction between Cosmopolitanism in Philosophy and the Social Sciences. *Global Networks. A Journal of Transnational Affairs* 4(2): 131–156.

Beck, Ulrich. 2009. *World at Risk*. Cambridge: Polity.

Beck, Ulrich and Elisabeth Beck-Gernsheim. 2002. *Individualization: Institutionalized Individualism and Its Social and Political Consequences*. London and Thousand Oaks, CA: Sage.

Carson, Rachel. 1962. *Silent Spring*. Cambridge, MA: Houghton Mifflin.

Carson, Wesley G. 1982. *The Other Price of Britain's Oil: Safety and Control in the North Sea*. New Brunswick, NJ: Rutgers University Press.

Castel, Robert. 1991. From Dangerousness to Risk. In *The Foucault Effect. Studies in Governmentality*. Edited by Graham Burchell, Colin Gordon, and Peter Miller. London: Harvester/Wheatsheaf, 281–298.

Dean, Mary. 1999. *Governmentality: Power and Rule in Modern Society*. London:Sage.

Douglas, Mary. 1963. *The Lele of the Kasai*. Published for the International African Institute by Oxford University Press.

Douglas, Mary. 1966. *Purity and Danger: An Analysis of Concepts of Pollution and Taboo*. New York, NY: Praeger.

Douglas, Mary. 1990. Risk as a Forensic Resource. *DAEDALUS* 119(4): 1–16.

Douglas, Mary. 1992. *Risk and Blame: Essays in Cultural Theory*. London and New York, NY: Routledge.

Douglas, Mary and Aaron B. Wildavsky. 1982. *Risk and Culture: An Essay on the Selection of Technical and Environmental Dangers*. Berkeley, CA: University of California Press.

Ewald, François. 1986. *L'état providence*. Paris: Grasset.

Foucault, Michel. 1991. Governmentality. In *The Foucault Effect*. Edited by G. Burchell, C. Gordon, and P. Miller. Chicago, IL: University of Chicago Press, 87–104.

Garland, David. 1997. "Governmentality" and the Problem of Crime: Foucault, Criminology, Sociology. *Theoretical Criminology* 1(2): 173–214.

Hindmoor, Andrew. 2010. The Banking Crisis: Grid, Group and the State of the Debate. *The Australian Journal of Public Administration* 69(4): 442–456.

Hood, Christopher and Henry Rothstein. 2000. Business Risk Management in Government: Pitfalls and Possibilities. *CARR Discussion Paper No. 0* (Launch Paper), London: LSE.

Japp, Klaus-Peter and Isabel Kusche. 2008. Risk and Systems Theory. In *Social Theories of Risk and Uncertainty: An Introduction*. Edited by Jens O. Zinn. Malden, MA: Blackwell.

Kelly, Peter. 2001. Youth at Risk: Processes of Individualisation and Responsibilisation in the Risk Society. *Discourse: Studies in the Cultural Politics of Education* 22(1): 23–33.

Kelly, Peter. 2006. The Entrepreneurial Self and "Youth At-Risk": Exploring the Horizons of Identity in the Twenty-first Century. *Journal of Youth Studies* 9(1): 17–32.

Kemshall, Hazel. 2002. *Risk, Social Policy, and Welfare*. Buckingham: Open University Press.

Lois, Jennifer. 2001. Peaks and Valleys: The Gendered Emotional Culture of Edgework. *Gender and Society* 15: 381–406.

Lupton, Deborah. 1999. Risk and the Ontology of Pregnant Embodiment. In *Risk and Sociocultural Theory: New Directions and Perspectives*. Edited by D. Lupton. Cambridge: Cambridge University Press, 34–58.

Lyng, Stephen. 1990. Edgework: A Social Psychological Analysis of Voluntary Risk Taking. *The American Journal of Sociology* 95(4): 851–886.

Lyng, Stephen. 1991. Edgework Revisited: Reply to Miller. *American Journal of Sociology* 96(6): 1534–1539.

Lyng, Stephen. 2005. *Edgework: The Sociology of Risk-Taking*. New York, NY and London: Routledge.

Lyng, Stephen. 2008. Edgework, Risk, and Uncertainty. In *Social Theories of Risk and Uncertainty*. Edited by J. Zinn. Malden, MA and Oxford: Blackwell, 106–137.

Miller, Eleanor M. 1991. Assessing the Inattention to Class, Race/Ethnicity and Gender: Comment on Lyng. *American Journal of Sociology* 96: 1530–1534.

O'Malley, Pat. 1992. Risk, Power and Crime Prevention. *Economy and Society* 21(3): 252–275.

O'Malley, Pat. 2004. *Risk, Uncertainty and Government*. London: Routledge.

O'Malley, Pat. 2008. Governmentality and Risk. In *Social Theories of Risk and Uncertainty*. Edited by J. O. Zinn. Oxford: Blackwell Publishers, 52–75.

O'Malley, Pat and Stephen Mugford. 1994. Crime, Excitement, and Modernity. In *Varieties of Criminology. Readings from a Dynamic Discipline*. Edited by Gregg Barak. Westport, CT and London: Praeger, 189–211.

Pidgeon, Nick, Christopher Hood, David Jones, Barry Turner, and Rose Gibson. 1992. *Risk Perception*. In *Risk: Analysis, Perception and Management: Report of a Royal Society Study Group*. Edited by The Royal Society. London: The Royal Society, 89–134.

Renn, Ortwin. 2008. *Risk Governance. Coping with Uncertainty in a Complex World*. Sterling, VA: Earthscan.

Roth, Silke. 2015. Aid Work as Edgework – Voluntary Risk-Taking and Security in Humanitarian Assistance, Development and Human Rights Work. *Journal of Risk Research* 18(2): 139–155.

Ruhl, Lealle. 1999. Liberal Governance and Prenatal Care: Risk and Regulation in Pregnancy. *Economy and Society* 28: 91–117.

Slovic, Paul. 2000. *The Perception of Risk*. London: Earthscan.

Thompson, Michael. 2008. *Organising and Disorganising: A Dynamic and Non-Linear Theory of Institutional Emergence and its Implications*. Axminster: Triarchy Press.

Titterton, Mike. 2011. Positive Risk Taking with People at Risk of Harm. In *Good Practice in Assessing Risk: Current Knowledge, Issues and Approaches*. Edited by Hazel Kemshall and Bernadette Wilkinson. London and Philadelphia, PA: Jessica Kingsley Publishers, 30–47.

Tulloch, John and Jens O. Zinn. 2011. Risk, Health and the Media. *Health, Risk and Society* 13(1): 1–16.

Turner, Brian A. 1978. *Man-Made Disasters*. London: Wykeham Publications.

Tversky, Amos and Daniel Kahneman. 1974. Judgement under Uncertainty: Heuristics and Biases. *Science* 185: 1127–1131.

Van Loon, Joost. 2002. *Risk and Technological Culture: Towards a Sociology of Virulence*. London and New York, NY: Routledge.

Verweij, Marco, Mary Douglas, Richard Ellis, Christoph Engel, Frank Hendriks, Susanne Lohmann, Steven Ney, Steve Rayner, and Michael Thompson. 2006. Clumsy Solutions for a Complex World: The Case of Climate Change. *Public Administration* 84(4): 817–843.

Weir, Lorna. 1996. Recent Developments in the Government of Pregnancy. *Economy and Society* 25: 372–392.

Wynne, Brian. 1989. Frameworks of Rationality in Risk Management: Towards the Testing of Naive Sociology. In *Environmental Threats: Perception, Analysis and Management*. Edited by Jennifer Brown. London and New York, NY: Belhaven Press, 33–47.

Zelizer, Vivian. 1979. *Morals and Markets: The Development of Life Insurance in the United States*. New York, NY: Columbia University Press.

CHAPTER 14

Sociology of Disaster

Thomas E. Drabek

Disasters have impacted human societies throughout history. While volcanic eruptions, floods, hurricanes, and other such events have been described over the centuries, it was not until Voltaire discussed the impacts of the Lisbon earthquake (November 1, 1755; 70,000 killed) that a social scientific perspective rooted within social and cultural contexts framed an analysis. This paradigm reflected a new cultural context wherein "the bonds of traditional religious authority were being challenged by a growing enthusiasm for intellectual freedom and for reason" (Dynes 2000: 97–98).

Most sociological research on disaster has been framed within commonly used definitions that include the following key ideas, that is, disasters are accidental or uncontrollable events, actual or threatened, that cause a society or a subsystem such as a community to incur human and/or physical losses or significant disruption of some essential functions like shelter, food or public safety (Perry and Quarantelli 2005). While explicitly recognizing that such events vary across a wide variety of characteristics, e.g., scope, agent, predictability, duration, suddenness, and the like, most researchers differentiate three "types" of disasters: (1) natural, (2) technological, and (3) conflict-based.

Early Studies and Emergent Research Centers

On December 6, 1917, at 9:06 in the morning, a French munitioner ship rammed a Belgian ship near the docks of Halifax, Nova Scotia. The munitioner was loaded with trinitrotoluene (TNT). A massive explosion occurred that killed nearly 2,000 people and injured 9,000 others (Drabek 2013: 58). As he had done following the Titanic ship disaster (1912), Samuel Henry Prince, a young Episcopal priest, assisted in the recovery effort. Shortly thereafter he enrolled in a doctoral

I wish to thank Ruth Ann Drabek for her work on this article. Partial support was provided by the University of Denver through the John Evans Professorship Program. Any opinions, findings, conclusions or recommendations expressed in this article are those of the author and do not necessarily reflect the views of the University of Denver.

program at Columbia University. His dissertation (1920) was the first truly sociological study of disaster.

Following World War II, under the direction of Charles E. Fritz, the first continuing set of field studies were initiated through the National Opinion Research Center (NORC) housed at the University of Chicago. One NORC graduate student, Enrico Quarantelli, focused on the social dimensions of panic behavior (1954) and studied a series of public myths about disaster response (1960). Other students picked different topics, such as the processes whereby the public assigned blame to people who they thought caused or worsened the disaster (Bucher 1957). Later, Fritz (1961) summarized the results of this multiyear project in a chapter that appeared in a widely used social problems text edited by Robert Merton and Robert Nisbet. Making use, for the first time, of empirical research conducted after numerous disasters with different "causes," e.g., airplane crash, tornadoes, floods, etc., he described several important aspects of disasters. Fritz emphasized the commonality of convergence behavior, or the movement of people toward sites of disasters immediately after they occur, and the development of emergent norms that initiate an "altruistic mood" immediately after disasters. These interpretations were in direct contrast to alternative expectation sets that continued to guide many emergency planners for decades, i.e., images of mass hysteria and the need for immediate governmental actions focused on command and control, looting prevention and other public security measures.

Shifts in areas of public policy occurred following Fritz's relocation to the National Academy of Sciences, where he recruited a series of expert panels whose publications had some impact, especially in hurricane warning and evacuation planning, e.g., Moore et al. 1963. Policy applications were expanded greatly in 1963 when the Disaster Research Center was established at the Ohio State University by Russell Dynes, Enrico Quarantelli and J. Eugene Haas. In 1985 the Center was relocated to the University of Delaware, where both Dynes and Quarantelli continue to provide limited direction despite their retirements. Haas left OSU in the mid-1970s and teamed briefly with Gilbert F. White, a social geographer, who had relocated from the University of Chicago to the University of Colorado. They initiated the Natural Hazards Research and Applications Information Center, which also continues today as an important driving force in hazards research and policy formulation. White influenced public policies related to usage of flood-prone and other high-risk locations and was instrumental in the creation of the National Flood Insurance Program. Graduates of both of these centers initiated sustained research programs (e.g., Mileti 1999; Drabek 2013) and formal institutional units at other universities and organizations, e.g., Hazard Management Group within Oak Ridge National Laboratory; Hazard Reduction and Recovery Center, Texas A&M University. Similar centers have been developed in Italy, Japan, Australia, Germany, and elsewhere.

Research findings and conclusions from scholars working within these centers and independently at other locations have been synthesized and/or summarized in several works. Most important among these are the following: Barton 1969; Dynes 1970; Drabek 1986; Dynes et al. 1987; Rodríguez et al. 2006. In contrast to these more technical syntheses, others have published materials designed to assist emergency management professionals. Examples include Drabek and Hoetmer (1991), and Waugh and Tierney (2007).

In 1995, the Federal Emergency Management Agency (FEMA) initiated the FEMA Higher Education Project to facilitate the development of courses and degree programs within colleges and universities, whereby students could become introduced to disaster and hazard research and the emerging profession of emergency management (Drabek 1996). By 2014, over 200 such programs were operational. Seeing a new market, publishing companies began to recruit textbook authors, e.g., Haddow et al.

2009; McEntire 2007; Phillips and Morrow 2008; Lindell et al. 2007.

As the number of empirical studies of disaster increased, new professional journal opportunities became sustainable. While researchers continue to publish in standard sociology journals, their work frequently appears in these more specialized outlets, e.g., *International Journal of Mass Emergencies and Disasters; Disasters: The Journal of Disaster Studies, Policy and Management; Australian Journal of Disaster Management; Journal of Emergency Management* and *Disaster Prevention and Management: An International Journal.*

Major Research Areas and Key Findings

In 1932, Lowell Carr provided an organizing framework for disaster research which other scholars used to frame and synthesize their work and that of others (Carr 1932). Disaster events reflected a series of sequential phases including warning, evacuation, impact, and recovery. Gradually, civil defense planners began to create a broader approach that ultimately became known as "comprehensive emergency management" (CEM). In 1979, the National Governors Association (NGA), whose members had become disappointed at fragmented federal agency responses, proposed that this framework be adopted nationally, so that key planning functions could be identified for local government officials (National Governors Association 1979). The CEM framework notes that, while every disaster has its unique qualities, four key comprehensive emergency management functions can be identified: (1) preparedness, including warning and evacuation; (2) response; (3) recovery; and (4) mitigation. These somewhat parallel the disaster "phases" identified by Carr.

Since the terrorist attacks of September 11, 2001, another CEM function has been added that often is referred to as "detection," "threat assessment," or "infrastructure security," e.g., airport screening. Few sociologists have conducted major research projects in this area, however. Rather, work in this area most often consists of critiques of federal experiments like the color-coded national alert system or fear-mongering activities designed to legitimate anti-terrorism programs (see Lustick 2008; Tierney 2006). Most sociological studies can be clustered into one of the four phases of disaster response.

Preparedness

Some families are more prepared to confront disaster than others. Their actions reflect the constraints of wealth, education, and history. Surveys have demonstrated that families in poverty will do little or nothing to prepare their households. Participation in various educational programs, however, increases the likelihood that families will have a reunification plan and take basic actions like securing hot water tanks or stocking food and water. These programs usually provide information about major community hazards, specific recommended actions including storage of emergency equipment such as flashlights and batteries, water and food, and family evacuation procedures. Typically, people living in communities that experience events or alerts more frequently will evidence greater levels of family preparedness (Mileti and Darlington 1995).

When disaster warnings are issued, numerous studies have documented that disbelief, not panic, is the initial response. If people do anything, they will seek to confirm the warning information. Often they will consult a media outlet or contact family or friends (Drabek 2013: 65–67, 97–101). The characteristics of the people or demographic groups receiving the warnings pattern responses in clearly defined ways. For example, males typically deny the threat far longer than females or primary-school aged-children. Racial minorities tend to distrust public officials more and hence are less likely to evacuate their residences, as are those over sixty-five years of age (Lindell and Perry 2004). The characteristics of warning messages also influence community response profiles. The core qualities that increase evacuation compliance are specificity, precision as to when the threat will arrive, the geographical boundaries at risk, and the nature of the threat. Finally, messages that contain specific instructions for what people should do have been found to be most effective (Mileti et al. 1981).

Most people evacuate their homes or work places and seek shelter with relatives or friends. Those fleeing to public shelters tend to be poor and/or of minority group status (Peacock et al. 1997). Family pets frequently complicate evacuation decisions, since most people do not wish to leave their animals. Announced provisions for pets at shelters will result in higher levels of evacuation compliance. Once families leave, there is great pressure on public officials to permit returns home as soon as possible, often before public safety requirements are met.

Response

In contrast to false images of hysteria, anti-social behavior, and non-rational inaction, the research evidence clearly portrays human responses after disaster impacts tending to be positive and active. People are quick to take actions they perceive as protective and will reach out to help others despite personal risk or injury. Every disaster studied has documented instances of heroic behavior by some of the survivors, and typically a few individuals engage in life-saving actions and become publically identified as heroes. Disaster scenes are thus filled with unofficial volunteers who engage in a wide range of actions intended to help survivors physically, financially, or emotionally. Widespread convergence occurs shortly after any disaster, and this convergence reflects personnel, information, and physical items ranging from emergency response equipment to media broadcast vans. Media outlets, despite urging people to stay away from impacted areas, actually increase interest in the event and stimulate others to go to the impacted areas to assist or satisfy their curiosity. Some of the curious discover that their assistance may be helpful and thereby alter their anticipated actions. With the popularization of mobile phones, the population routinely uses this technology and social media outlets like Facebook, Twitter, etc. These technologies and their consequences define an important new research agenda.

Communities tend to reveal an elaborate division of labor among government and non-governmental organizations. American society is comparatively decentralized, when compared to other nations. Disaster changes the task environment so that high levels of agency autonomy can result in fragmented responses, what some analysts have labeled "organized-disorganization" (Drabek 2013: 175–199). Despite years of documentation and extensive training in multi-organizational coordination, these patterns of decentralized responses continue to be documented, e.g., the 9/11 World Trade Center attacks (2001) (Kendra and Wachtendorf 2006) and the Aurora theater shooting (July 20, 2012) (Tri Data Division 2014). While progress has been made through implementation of emergency operations centers (EOCs), interoperable emergency radio systems, cell phones, and other technologies, human factors continue to produce fragmented responses. Research has documented the problem and pointed toward solutions, but implementation remains problematic in most communities. When disaster is less frequent, the implementation costs in both training and equipment may not be viewed as cost-effective. In a changing world of increased threats reflecting population increases, greater densities in high-risk areas, expanded terrorist activity, climate change, and other factors, increased funding for emergency management capabilities seems necessary.

Recovery

Depending on the scope, intensity, and other characteristics of a disaster event *and* the relative structural capabilities of the impacted community and external resource units, recovery times vary widely. Many families experience what some observers have labeled "the bitch phase" once the altruistic mood and informal help sources dissipate and they confront the realities of bureaucracy associated with insurance companies, city building permits, and the like. Complicated bureaucratic structures often slow down government assistance and impede recovery efforts (Lansford et al. 2010: 82–98).

Seeking closure in some form or another becomes paramount, including attending to the dead, construction of memorials, and assisting children, some of whom will have nightmares and others sleep disturbances. Divorce and marriage rates oscillate in the short term after disasters, as some will put off these life-changing acts until damaged homes are fixed and other home and work patterns re-established. Within a year, both patterns normalize once the "catch-up" is completed. The same is true for short-term increases in alcohol consumption, use of prescription drugs like tranquilizers, and other use patterns reflecting short-term coping behavior. These, like increased kin interactions – a vital source of short-term help – gradually return to prior patterns, although some evidence indicates that kin relationships are strengthened over the years after disaster.

Some studies (Erikson 1976) have documented extensive and long lasting trauma. These have been limited, however, to instances of extreme destruction and losses of community networks. But even in these cases, new interpretations have indicated that three decades later processes of healing and community resilience have mitigated the traumas (Schwartz-Barcott 2008). Resilience is the dominant theme in research on disaster recovery. The most profound change noted in many of the studies reflects altered life perspectives – decrease in materialistic ambitions and increased appreciation of family and personal ability to cope with future tragedy.

Mitigation

Long before disaster strikes, some community members will have advocated various approaches to risk reduction. These vary from repairing infrastructure (e.g., bridges and dams), curbing building in high-risk areas (e.g., flood, wildfire, or earthquake-prone areas), enhancing disease monitoring and control (e.g., Ebola outbreaks), and working to prevent potential terrorist attacks (e.g., airport security), to increasing regulation of technologies (e.g., nuclear power plants, off-shore oil drilling), and the like. All of these activities reflect the differential perceptions of risk for varying stakeholder and community groups. Like different responses to warnings, these perceptions are constrained by social factors. For example, females typically reveal higher fear levels, especially if potential impacts may affect children (Drabek 2013: 253). Similarly, older individuals may know more about the flood history of their community, but their level of acceptable risk expands over time as does their sense of skepticism about both so-called "experts" and government programs and regulations (Drabek 1986: 327–331). Poorer sectors of the community often reflect more fatalistic interpretations of risk. Hence, attitudes toward future disasters that may be defined as "Acts of God" dovetail with suspicion and distrust when local activists initiate new regulations such as those prohibiting mobile housing in designated flood-prone areas.

Meanwhile, centralized and computerized banking systems, air traffic control, and even basic utility networks for energy and water have increased societal vulnerability to both terrorist attack and various natural disasters (Perrow 2007). Drabek (2013: 273–298) proposed that emergency management professionals must redefine their vision so as to become community change agents with two clear goals: (1) implementing strategies designed to increase community resilience, including increased engagement, empowerment, cohesiveness, and social capital, and (2) actively seeking to decrease community vulnerabilities. Emergency management professionals reduce threats to communities by advocating policies and procedures designed to reduce the degrees of centralization in community systems and encroachment into high-risk locations, increase programs of threat detection and prevention, increase construction standards, and increase maintenance and infrastructure renewal programs. Community vulnerability must also be reduced through efforts to decrease economic inequalities, and reduce discrimination of all types including race, ethnicity, religion, gender, and sexual identity differences.

New Directions

While many have noted the gap between sociological theory and disaster studies, one exception is the work of Kreps and his associates (1994). They have identified specific linkages between disaster field data and themes introduced by Simmel, Giddens, Alexander, and others. Through analyses of microsystems that have emerged during actual disaster responses, they have provided insight into the processes of order and action that have been constrained by both preparedness programs and perception of need. While every disaster is unique, there are common patterns of response and recovery, but future conceptual precision is required so that the limits of generalization can be established with greater rigor across specific taxonomic niches of social systems (Erikson 1994). Future analysts must focus on popular culture as it reflects disaster (Webb et al. 2000) including emergent memorials, permanent monuments, folk tunes, and a host of other consequences that assist in community healing processes (Quarantelli and Davis 2011). During the next decade sociologists focused on disaster must address at least four additional core research areas: (1) Vulnerability Analyses; (2) Understanding Resilience; (3) Improving Warning Systems; and (4) Emergency Management Applications.

Vulnerability Analyses

Future research must also focus on structural dimensions of social vulnerability (Wisner et al. 2005), especially as reflected in children, minority groups, and women (Enarson et al. 2006; Phillips and Morrow 2008). Pioneering explorations have documented the subtle and not-so-subtle negative impacts of Hurricane Katrina, for example: family displacement, spouse abuse, and child adjustment to "permanent temporariness" (Weber and Peek 2012; Fothergill and Peek 2014; David and Enarson 2012). Dimensions of vulnerability require further study both for theory expansion and program insight for those seeking to help in the aftermath of future disasters.

Understanding Resilience

Through links to theories of social capital, Aldrich (2012) provided documentation that underscored the impact of social connections on community recovery. After extensive study of the recovery processes that occurred after Hurricane Katrina, Lansford and his colleagues concluded that "social capital instills in the community a foundational level of trust. This trust is the community's strength against hazards and is what enables it to become socially resilient" (Lansford et al. 2010: 56). As more research in this area is completed, it can inform efforts directed at enhancing community resilience. Further studies like those completed by Aldrich (2012), combined with the vulnerability analyses by Peek, Fothergill, Enarson, and others, can pave the way for a greatly enhanced understanding of the structural origins and consequences of disaster.

Improving Warning Systems

The National Weather Service has implemented tornado and hurricane warning systems that have saved thousands of lives during the past two decades. Sociological research on warning and evacuation responses has guided the design of these systems. But failures still happen and new research is required to document these and identify the gaps that resulted in death and injury (Committee on Disaster Research in the Social Sciences 2006). Equally important is the rapidly changing social landscape, especially reflective of the adoption of social media venues, use of internet-based mobile text message applications, and rapid photo and video exchanges (Renda-Tanalli 2014). Worldwide, Sultan (2014) reported survey data indicating that in 2012 there were more than 60 million Blackberry Messenger (BBM) users and another 300 million WhatsApp users. Within the United States, parallel results have been reported (Crosswhite et al. 2014). Documentation of these types of usage patterns during disaster responses and their consequences both for users and emergency officials form a research agenda.

Emergency Management Applications

Numerous application examples have been noted throughout this chapter. The first Instructor Guide (IG) completed within the FEMA Higher Education Program was titled "Sociology of Disaster" (Drabek 1996). Drabek expanded it greatly in 2004 and retitled it *Social Dimensions of Disaster*. These guides have aided numerous university and college professors who have initiated new programs in emergency management. Another IG (Waugh 2000), that focused on terrorism, helped professors and students to develop a historical and cross-national perspective on this conflict strategy.

The small cluster of individuals who used to wear hats with "Civil Defense" labels on them, have now been replaced by emerging professionals who are implementing programs that will decrease community risk and guide more effective response and recovery operations after disaster. These emergency managers must interface with executives in the private sector such as managers of media organizations and tourist businesses and other public sector units, ranging from public works and public health to planning and building inspection divisions (Laws et al. 2007). As the planet warms and conflicts increase because of food and water shortages and expansion of religious extremism, the profession of emergency management will become even more internationalized. Research completed by sociologists focused on the non-routine social problem of disaster will be at the forefront of this process.

References

Aldrich, Daniel P. 2012. *Building Resilience: Social Capital in Post-disaster Recovery*. Chicago, IL: University of Chicago Press.

Barton, Allen H. 1969. *Communities in Disaster: A Sociological Analysis of Collective Stress Situations*. Garden City, NY: Doubleday and Company Inc.

Bucher, Rue. 1957. Blame and Hostility in Disaster. *American Journal of Sociology* 62: 467–475.

Carr, Lowell. 1932. Disasters and the Sequence-Pattern Concept of Social Change. *American Journal of Sociology* 38: 207–218.

Committee on Disaster Research in the Social Sciences. 2006. *Facing Hazards and Disasters: Understanding Human Dimensions*. Washington, DC: The National Academies Press.

Crosswhite, Jennifer, Denise Rice, and Sylvia M. Asay. 2014. Texting among United States Adults: An Exploratory Study on Texting and Its Use within Families. *The Social Science Journal* 51: 20–78.

David, Emmanuel and Elaine Enarson. eds. 2012. *The Women of Katrina: How Gender, Race, and Class Matter in an American Disaster*. Nashville, TN: Vanderbilt University Press.

Drabek, Thomas E. 1986. *Human System Responses to Disaster: An Inventory of Sociological Findings*. New York, NY: Springer-Verlag.

Drabek, Thomas E. 1996. *Sociology of Disaster*. Emmitsburg, MD: Emergency Management Institute, Federal Emergency Management Agency.

Drabek, Thomas E. 2013. *The Human Side of Disaster*. 2nd edn. Boca Raton, FL: CRC Press.

Drabek, Thomas E. and Gerard J. Hoetmer. eds. 1991. *Emergency Management: Principles and Practice for Local Government*. Washington, DC: International City Management Association.

Dynes, Russell R. 1970. *Organized Behavior in Disaster*. Lexington, MD: Heath Lexington Books.

Dynes, Russell R. 2000. The Dialogue between Voltaire and Rousseau on the Lisbon Earthquake: The Emergence of a Social Science View. *International Journal of Mass Emergencies and Disasters* 18: 97–115.

Dynes, Russell R., Bruna De Marchi, and Carlo Pelanda. eds. 1987. *Sociology of Disasters: Contributions of Sociology to Disaster Research*. Milano: Franco Angeli.

Enarson, Elaine, Alice Fothergill, and Lori Peek. 2006. Gender and Disaster: Foundations and Directions. In *Handbook of Disaster Research*. Edited by Havidán Rodríguez, Enrico L. Quarantelli, and Russell R. Dynes. New York, NY: Springer, 130–146.

Erikson, Kai. 1976. *Everything in Its Path: Destruction of Community in the Buffalo Creek Flood*. New York, NY: Simon and Schuster.

Erikson, Kai. 1994. *A New Species of Trouble: Explorations in Disasters, Trauma, and Community*. New York, NY: W. W. Norton.

Fothergill, Alice and Lori Peek. 2014. Lessons from Katrina: Recommendations for Fostering More Effective Disaster Preparedness, Responses and Recovery Efforts for Children and Youth. *Haznet* 5(2)(Spring): 4–9.

Fritz, Charles E. 1961. Disasters. In *Contemporary Social Problems*. Edited by Robert K. Merton and Robert A. Nisbet. New York, NY: Harcourt, 651–694.

Haddow, George D., Jane A. Bullock, and Kim S. Haddow. 2009. *Global Warming, Natural Hazards, and Emergency Management*. Boca Raton, FL: CRC Press.

Kendra, James M. and Tricia Wachtendorf. 2006. Community Innovation and Disasters. In *Handbook of Disaster Research*. Edited by Havidán Rodríguez, Enrico L. Quarantelli, and Russell R. Dynes. New York, NY: Springer, 316–334.

Kreps, Gary A. and Susan Lovegren Bosworth with Jennifer A. Mooney, Stephen T. Russell, and Kristen A. Myers. 1994. *Organizing, Role Enactment, and Disaster: A Structural Theory*. Newark, DE: University of Delaware Press.

Lansford, Tom, Jack Covarrubias, Brian Carriere, and Justin Miller. 2010. *Fostering Community Resilience: Homeland Security and Hurricane Katrina*. Farnham, England: Ashgate Publishing Limited.

Laws, Eric, Bruce Prideaux, and Kaye Chon. 2007. *Crisis Management in Tourism*. Wallingford, UK and Cambridge, MA: CAB International.

Lindell, Michael K. and Ronald W. Perry. 2004. *Communicating Environmental Risk in Multiethnic Communities*. Thousand Oaks, CA: Sage.

Lindell, Michael K., Carla S. Prater, and Ronald W. Perry. 2007. *Introduction to Emergency Management*. Hoboken, NJ: John Wiley and Sons.

Lustick, Ian S. 2008. The War on Terror: When the Response Is the Catastrophe. In *Emergency Management in Higher Education: Current Practice and Conversation*. Edited by Jessica A. Hubbard. Fairfax, VA: Public Entity Risk Institute, 73–98.

McEntire, David A. 2007. *Disaster Response and Recovery*. Hoboken, NJ: John Wiley and Sons.

Mileti, Dennis S. 1999. *Disasters by Design: A Reassessment of Natural Hazards in the United States*. Washington, DC: Joseph Henry Press.

Mileti, Dennis S. and Joanne Derouen Darlington. 1995. Societal Response to Revised Earthquake Probabilities in the San Francisco Bay Area. *International Journal of Mass Emergencies and Disasters* 13: 119–145.

Mileti, Dennis S., Janice R. Hutton, and John H. Sorensen. 1981. *Earthquake Prediction Response and Options for Public Policy*. Boulder, CO: Institute of Behavioral Science, University of Colorado.

Moore, Harry Estill, Frederick L. Bates, Marvin V. Layman, and Vernon J. Parenton. 1963. *Before the Wind: A Study of Response to Hurricane Carla*. Washington, DC: National Research Council, National Academy of Sciences.

National Governors' Association. 1979. *Comprehensive Emergency Management: A Governor's Guide*. Washington, DC: US Government Printing Office.

Peacock, Walter Gillis, Betty Hearn Morrow, and Hugh Gladwin. eds. 1997. *Hurricane Andrew: Ethnicity, Gender and the Sociology of Disasters*. London: Routledge.

Perrow, Charles. 2007. *The Next Catastrophe: Reducing Our Vulnerabilities to Natural, Industrial and Terrorist Disasters*. Princeton, NJ: Princeton University Press.

Perry, Ronald W. and E. L. Quarantelli. eds. 2005. *What Is a Disaster? New Answers to Old Questions*. Philadelphia, PA: Xlibris Corporation.

Phillips, Brenda D. and Betty Hearn Morrow. 2008. *Women and Disasters: From Theory to Practice*. Philadelphia, PA: Xlibris Corporation.

Prince, Samuel Henry. 1920. Catastrophe and Social Change, Based upon a Sociological Study of the Halifax Disaster. Ph.D. Thesis. New York, NY: Department of Political Science, Columbia University.

Quarantelli, E. L. 1954. The Nature and Conditions of Panic. *American Journal of Sociology* 60: 267–275.

Quarantelli, E. L. 1960. Images of Withdrawal Behavior in Disasters: Some Basic Misconceptions. *Social Problems* 8(Summer): 68–79.

Quarantelli, E. L. and Ian Davis. 2011. *An Exploratory Research Agenda for Studying the Popular Culture of Disasters (PCD): Its Characteristics, Conditions, and Consequences*. Newark, DE: Disaster Research Center, University of Delaware.

Renda-Tanalli, Irmak. 2014. Use of Social Media in Response to Hurricane Sandy in Maryland's Emergency Management Organizations. *Haznet* 5(2)(Spring): 9–15.

Rodríguez, Havidán, Enrico L. Quarantelli, and Russell R. Dynes. eds. 2006. *Handbook of Disaster Research*. New York, NY: Springer.

Schwartz-Barcott, T. P. 2008. *After the Disaster: Re-Creating Community and Well-Being at Buffalo Creek since the Notorious Coal-Mining Disaster in 1972*. Amherst, MA: Cambria Press.

Sultan, Abdullah. 2014. Addiction to Mobile Text Messaging Applications Is Nothing to 'Lol' About. *The Social Science Journal* 51: 57–69.

Tierney, Kathleen J. 2006. Recent Developments in U.S. Homeland Security Policies and their Implications for the Management of Extreme Events. In *Handbook of Disaster Research*. Edited by Havidán Rodríguez, Enrico L. Quarantelli, and Russell R. Dynes. New York, NY: Springer, 405–412.

Tri Data Division. 2014. Aurora Century 16 Theater Shooting After Action Report for the City of Aurora, Arlington, VA: System Planning Corporation.

Waugh, William L., Jr. 2000. Terrorism and Emergency Management. Emmitsburg, MD: Emergency Management Institute, Federal Emergency Management Agency.

Waugh, William L., Jr. and Kathleen Tierney. 2007. *Emergency Management: Principles and Practice for Local Government*. 2nd edn. Washington, DC: International City Management Association.

Webb, Gary R., Tricia Wachtendorf, and Anne Eyre. 2000. Bringing Culture Back In: Exploring the Cultural Dimensions of Disaster. *International Journal of Mass Emergencies and Disasters* 18: 5–19.

Weber, Lynn and Lori Peek. eds. 2012. *Displaced: Life in the Katrina Diaspora*. Austin, TX: University of Texas Press.

Wisner, Ben, Piers Blaikie, Terry Cannon, and Ian Davis. 2005. *At Risk: Natural Hazards, People's Vulnerability and Disasters*. 2nd edn. New York, NY: Routledge.

The Sociology of Mental Health

Teresa L. Scheid

Introduction

One of the most fascinating disciplinary areas of research and theory in sociology is mental health and illness. Sociological scholarship on mental health and illness links macro-level structures to micro-level individual experiences. The exemplar is Emile Durkheim in his classic study *Suicide*, where he provided empirical evidence that the most private of acts, suicide, is actually a result of the level of group cohesion. Sociologists continue to focus on mental health and illness in its social context, with an emphasis on the relationship between social structure (or context) and mental health. There are three broad areas of research within the Sociology of Mental Health which I will use to organize this review. First is scholarship which examines those social factors which play an important role in understanding how some conditions or behaviors come to be viewed as "mental illnesses." Second is research that utilizes what has come to be referred to as the "stress process model," and which examines how stress and social support influence mental health outcomes. The third area of research focuses attention on the organization and delivery of mental health care and includes mental health policy.

Definitions of Mental Health and Illness

Most sociologists examine mental illness or disorders rather than mental health. David Mechanic, one of the most influential scholars in the Sociology of Mental Health, has argued that the term "mental health" has no clear meaning (Mechanic 2006), although it is defined broadly by the World Health Organization as a general state of well-being (World Health Organization 2004). Mental health is not merely the absence of disease; it involves mastery, or sense of social efficacy, and fulfilling social relationships. Keyes and Michalec (2010) conceptualize mental health as "flourishing"; in contrast, poor mental health is described as "languishing." However, most sociologists focus on the opposite of mental health or well-being, studying mental health problems or distress, although there is a great deal of diversity in approaches to defining and measuring mental health problems. A basic question is what causes mental health problems? Sociologists have challenged the dominance of biological models of mental illness and critique psychiatry for reducing mental health problems to discrete diagnoses that do not take into account the role of social context. Allan Horwitz's (2002) book, *Creating Mental Illness*, does an excellent job of reviewing the evidence for biological explanations for mental disorders. Horwitz (2002) argues that twin and adoption studies (which posit a genetic link for mental disorder) do not really examine the environment. Further, even where there is evidence for genetic causation, the environment explains variations between groups over space and time. For example, schizophrenia affects approximately 1 percent of the population. With a family history of schizophrenia one is at a higher risk for developing schizophrenia. However, the vast majority of the population with NO family history of schizophrenia will account for most cases of schizophrenia. Furthermore, living in an urban environment is more important (and predictive) for the development of schizophrenia than is genetics. Horwitz (2002) argues that the view that mental illnesses or disorders are brain diseases is a cultural belief and that social changes hold far more promise than biological changes for improving mental health. Rather than biology, researchers need to focus on the social causes of distress and mental disorder: those life events that are negative and uncontrollable – including poverty, instability, unemployment, and neighborhood disorganization.

A second question which a number of sociologists have addressed and is still not resolved is how to measure mental health problems, disorders, or illnesses. One way to measure mental health or illness is to use a continuum, such as the framework for assessing flourishing versus languishing, or commonly utilized scales for psychological well-being versus psychological distress. With a continuum, one assesses levels, or degrees, of mental health or distress. The idea is that over time all of us will move from relative mental health to some degree of mental distress and back again, generally tied to the social context which influences our levels of stress (see below). However, medical models use dichotomous categories to determine who is sick and who is not, so that physicians know who to treat. As described by Michael Foucault in *Madness and Civilization* (1988[1965]), psychiatry developed in the mental asylum as a result of the need to differentiate the madman from other suspect populations such as criminals.

The American Psychiatric Association (APA) develops the Diagnostic and Statistical Manual (currently DSM-5), which outlines the classification system used by clinicians to make a psychiatric diagnosis. The DSM is also used by researchers in order to provide estimates of the prevalence of mental disorder in a population (Wakefield and Schmitz 2010). In the United States, the National Comorbidity Survey is used by sociologists to collect data on the incidence, age of onset, prevalence, and treatment of mental disorders using DSM classifications (Kessler 2010). Horwitz (2002) argues that the DSM overstates the amount of mental disorder by not distinguishing normal reactions to social stressors from pathological behaviors. More recently, Whooley (2014) has critiqued the DSM-5 for its decontextualization of mental distress; that is the DSM-5 does not take into account the social context within which psychiatric symptoms occur and develop.

In examining the role of social structure and culture on social distress, sociologists emphasize the importance of social reactions to behavior. Sociologists ask two fundamental questions: who is labeled mentally ill, and what are the consequences of these labels (Link and Phelan 2010)? Labeling theory has been described as "radically sociological" because it views mental illness as "created and sustained by society itself" (Thoits 2010: 121). The label of "mentally ill" involves negative stereotypes and is highly stigmatized, often resulting in outright discrimination.

Pescosolido (2013) provides a concise summary of the empirical research on how people view mental illness and the stigma of mental illness. The first basic finding is that, in general, the public has become more open to the recognition and treatment of mental health problems. The second basic finding is that the stigma of mental illness has not changed much over time, and that the association of mental illness with dangerousness and violence has actually increased. Third, whether the focus is on the "label" of mentally ill or the behavior, social reactions involve stigma. Finally, while viewing mental illnesses as having a genetic basis had led to increased public support for treatment (especially medications), those who believe mental health problems have a biological basis also report higher levels of stigma. The most recent research on stigma involves cross-national research, and preliminary findings show an important link between cultural levels of stigma and individual stigma (Pescosolido 2013). Pescosolido (2013: 15) concludes that "stigma is fundamentally a social phenomenon rooted in social relationships and shaped by the culture and structure of society." In conclusion, whether mental health problems are understood as illnesses, psychiatric disorders, psychological distress, or the result of processes of social reaction and labeling, social context plays a vital role in how these problems are defined, experienced, and treated.

The Influence of Social Context on Mental Health and Illness

One of the most persistent findings in the field of Sociology of Mental Health is the inverse relationship between social class and mental health, with those in the lower classes suffering from higher rates of mental distress. There are three major explanations for this finding: social causation, social selection, and social reaction. Social causation refers to the reality that those in the lower classes are subject to higher levels of stress as a consequence of poverty and economic instability. This stress or instability results in higher levels of mental distress. Social selection (or drift) occurs when individuals with mental health problems are less able to complete education or sustain employment because of their mental illnesses and consequently fall into a lower social class position. Social reaction explanations argue that the restricted opportunities available to those in the lower classes lead to less mastery or a sense of personal efficacy and higher levels of fatalism, resulting in higher levels of depression (especially for women), psychological distress (particularly for racial and ethnic minorities), or substance abuse (principally for men). While there is some evidence for social selection, or drift, in that certainly some individuals with mental health problems do indeed "drift" down the socio-economic ladder, the prevailing evidence has been for social causation and social reaction. It is one's social class position that provides access to resources which then influence one's risk for mental health problems rather than the fact that mental health problems determine socio-economic status or class position. Sociologists have contributed a great deal to our understanding of how diverse socio-cultural and demographic groups experience and respond to mental health problems. There is extensive research on the role played by socio-demographic categories including gender, race, ethnicity, and age. Marriage, divorce, work, unemployment, and neighborhood are also important factors which influence mental health. The *Handbook for the Study of Mental Health* (Scheid and Brown 2010) provides a concise overview of these broad areas of research. More recent empirical evidence on the social factors associated with mental health and illness can be found in the two American Sociological Association journals: *The Journal of Health and Social Behavior* or *Society and Mental Health*. What unites much of this research is a focus on the role played by social stress and social support, which is increasingly referred to as the stress process model.

Sociologists developed the stress process model in the 1970s (Turner 2013). The model posits that social characteristics (gender, race/ethnicity, socio-economic position, neighborhood disadvantage, and segregation/integration) directly influence exposures to stress, the social resources to deal with stress, and the personal resources to cope with stress. The social resources include social supports and network ties, while the personal resources include mastery, self-esteem, emotional reliance, and mattering to others. Obviously one's personal resources for coping are influenced by social supports and network ties as well as one's social status.

The past forty years of research on the stress process have revealed that it is vital to include multiple measures of stress. In the 1970s life event scales were commonly used; researchers now include recent eventful stressors, chronic stress, lifetime trauma, and discrimination (Turner 2013). It is also important to include multiple outcomes, including mental health disorder, psychological distress, and substance abuse problems.

Stress, an important source of mental health distress, is "generated and conditioned by social factors" (Turner 2013: 182). Consequently, the treatment of mental health problems cannot be directed solely at the individual. Interventions must be aimed at reducing the health disparities which result in increased exposure to stress, less mastery and resiliency for disadvantaged and minority groups, or those with less power relative to the majority. Inequality, in terms of social positions and relative power, can increase vulnerability to stress and impact one's ability to cope with stress.

Sociologists also contribute to our understanding of social support, which we know mitigates the effects of stress and can improve mental health. Social ties and supports provide us with a sense of belonging as well as concrete resources (i.e., emotional and tangible supports). However, we do not really know how or why social supports work (Thoits 2011). Thoits (2011) makes an important distinction between everyday social supports which influence our overall levels of well-being, and stress-associated social supports which are triggered during times of adversity and mitigate the negative effects of stress by providing us with active coping mechanisms to deal with the current stressor. For example, most women have extensive networks of family with whom they remain in close contact who provide everyday social supports. Following a divorce, family is often not as supportive and friends may be used to provide more intensive social supports to compensate for either the loss of family ties or needing some distance from family who may be a reminder of one's loss through divorce.

Thoits (2011) also argues that those who have faced a similar stressor (be it work, family, etc.) are more important than significant others who are not familiar with the experience of a given stressor. Similar others can provide us with a source of comparison and can serve as role models, inspiring hope. For example, family and friends are often not very supportive in times of mental distress or in the face of severe mental illnesses, as they may not be familiar or comfortable with mental health problems, and they may even contribute to both internalized and externalized stigma. In contrast, peer supports may provide someone experiencing mental health problems with more empathy and emotional support, as well as concrete information and advice about treatment options.

While addressing the structural sources of stress is clearly necessary, improving access to social resources and social supports can also improve mental health outcomes. Meaningful social relationships are an indication of well-being (World Health Organization 2004), and far too many individuals with mental health problems are isolated due to the stigma of mental illness. Reducing stigma and increasing social supports are important components of "recovery" – a sought after outcome of mental health treatment.

Mental Health Service Delivery and Policy

In terms of questions about mental health treatment, there is a critical division between research that focuses on acute mental health problems and psychological distress and that which focuses on individuals with severe mental illnesses. In terms of public policy, the most critical group is those with severe, persistent mental illness. They are often poor and depend on Medicaid to finance their care. Individuals with severe mental illnesses are generally served in the public mental health sector, face significant functional limitations, and need a broad array of services. Public mental health care is funded by federal, state, and local monies and provides services to those with chronic mental health problems. The unique needs of those with severe and persistent illness have not been adequately recognized; these individuals require long-term care, and there is a notable lack of efficacious treatment technology. That is, we do not know how to "cure" such illness, and there is wide disagreement over what services can provide those with severe mental illnesses the best quality of life. As noted by Mechanic (2006), while most care for those with severe, persistent illness is provided in the community (rather than the hospital), there is tremendous diversity in treatment programs for this population. Too often, no care is available and many end up in jail or prison, which has become the de facto system of public care.

There are also, however, forces promoting community-based care, social integration, and recovery. *The 1999 Surgeon General's Report on Mental Health* devoted an entire chapter to recovery and the 2003 President's New Freedom Commission of Mental Health also placed attention on recovery. Recovery is described by Jacobson and Greenley (2001) as including internal conditions (hope, healing, empowerment, and connection) and external conditions (human rights, positive culture of health, services to link consumers to the community). Recovery moves beyond the management of symptoms to the idea of building a productive life (Jacobson 2004). However, recovery has multiple meanings and has been used as a slogan by diverse groups promoting different ideological positions (Jacobson 2004). Recovery can be used to promote an expanded service model, as once individuals are stabilized medically they have increased need for social support services and skills building to obtain independence from the service system. Recovery can also mean reduced reliance (and cost savings) on service systems when defined as meeting certain limited functional goals. As described more fully by Jacobson (2004) there have been a number of efforts to develop recovery based "best practices" and standards for care, and these standards are often tied to funding for service provision.

Whether mental health systems can truly promote recovery depends on whether resources are invested into the kinds of supportive services so necessary for community stability. Funding for public sector mental health (via Medicaid) has not kept up with demand nor has it allowed for recovery with an expanded service model. Community care in many localities is marginal at best, resulting in the criminal justice system becoming the de facto system of care. An important idea clearly articulated by Foucault (1988[1965]) and developed by sociologists is that mental health treatment often involves social control (Goffman 1961). The current "criminalization" of those with mental health problems is an obvious indication of a generalized societal preference for social control rather than therapeutic care. The stigma of mental illness also contributes to the isolation and control of those with more serious mental illnesses and a reluctance to fund community-based services.

At the other end of the spectrum are what used to be referred to as the "worried well" – the majority of us who suffer from acute mental health problems and distress. While those with severe mental illness often go without mental health care, the worried well are over-treated with psychiatric medications (Frances 2013). Today, the dominant form of medical treatment for mental distress involves medications, and this treatment is reinforced by managed care and its reliance on cost-effective, clinically efficacious treatment. The growing reliance on the use of primary care physicians to diagnose and treat mental health problems also reinforces the use of medications, as opposed to therapy with a specialty mental health provider. A major finding of the National Comorbidity Survey Replication (as described above) is that while more people are being treated for mental health problems by general medical providers, the adequacy of this treatment has declined (Kessler 2010).

The reliance on a medical model of mental distress is a reflection of the broader trend of medicalization, where behavior is defined as a medical problem or illness and treatment is delegated to medical professionals. Peter Conrad (2007) originated research on the medicalization of mental health problems with his path-breaking analysis of Attention Deficit Disorder and his subsequent analysis of the social forces propelling medicalization. Recent decades have seen tremendous expansion in the use of psychiatric medications for both adults and children, with a great deal of critical analysis aimed at the pharmaceutical industry and the role it has played in marketing drugs for mental health problems to the public. Pharmaceutical companies not only market drugs, they market diseases (referred to generally as disease branding), such as anxiety disorder and use public media to encourage individuals to seek treatment for what are fairly normal responses to life stressors.

Conrad (2007: 160) argues that "medicalization in our society is related to the way in which we finance human services." Reimbursement for treatment is tied to a clinical diagnosis, reinforcing the biomedical model and reliance upon DSM categories to differentiate those who require services from those who do not. Furthermore, treatments must be found to be clinically efficacious, a standard which can be easily met with clinical drug trials and not so easily met with therapy or counseling. The essential criticism of medicalizaton is that treatment is always focused on the individual rather than the social context in which mental health problems develop and are treated. There is a rich tradition in the Sociology of Mental Health which examines the ways in which various mental health problems have been and continue to be medicalized and the dominance of the medical model in mental health treatment. For example, Smith (2014) interviewed twenty psychiatrists and found that, despite intensive training in psychoanalysis, the majority adhered to a medical model of treatment and relied upon medications.

There is also a group of sociologists who focus on mental health policy (Mechanic et al. 2013). There is no clear-cut federal policy governing mental health care, and there is tremendous variation at both the state and local levels in the provision and management of mental health services. Gerald N. Grob and Howard H. Goldman, in *The Dilemma of Mental Health Policy: Radical Reform or Incremental Change?* (2006), describe changes in federal mental health policy from World War II to the turn of the century. During this time, there was a continued shift of care from state institutions to the community, and a contradictory shift in fiscal responsibility for this care from local communities and states to the federal government. At the same time, as we have already described, the numbers of people with psychiatric diagnoses has rapidly expanded. However, the mental health system has become more fragmented and those with the greatest needs, individuals with severe mental disorders, have experienced deterioration in care. Except for the passage of the Mental Health Parity and Addictions Act of 2008, which requires insurers who provide mental health benefits to provide comparable levels of mental and physical health benefits, there has not been any focused policy efforts at the federal level to improve mental health.

Mental health reform is more apparent at the state level, and Hernandez and Uggen

(2012) provide a good example of sociological research which examines those factors important to understanding the prospects for health reform with their analysis of state level parity legislation. While there is a great deal of variability, parity legislation was more likely to pass in states with low unemployment, a less conservative political ideology, and those with long-standing advocacy organizations such as the Mental Health Association or the National Alliance on Mental Illness. Sociological research will no doubt focus on the effects of the Affordable Care Act on the provision of mental health services, as well as on both state and federal initiatives, which will work to increase the availability of mental health care in the wake of recent mass shootings attributed to the mental illness of the shooter.

Future research on mental health services, delivery systems, and public policy will have to address system wide fragmentation. Mental health is fragmented with diverse funding streams and conflicting levels of accountability at the federal, state, and local levels. Mental health and primary health care systems are also poorly integrated. As noted earlier, primary care providers are increasingly providing mental health treatment (in the form of medications) but have little mental health training. For those with serious mental illnesses, issues of system fragmentation occur not only within the mental health system or in the interface between mental and physical health systems, but in the integration of the mental health system with other service systems, including the criminal justice system.

Conclusion

The Sociology of Mental Health has made important contributions to our understanding of how social context matters: first, in how we define and measure mental health; second, in how stress affects different groups, and third, in those treatment systems and policies which respond to mental health problems. In addition, the Sociology of Mental Health has made significant contributions to major substantive areas in sociology including sociological theory, social inequalities and health disparities, social psychology, life course research, and the sociology of organizations to name a few. I direct readers interested in how the Sociology of Mental Health has not only informed, but been informed by, sociology more generally to an edited volume *Mental Health: Social Mirror* (Avison et al. 2007). The introduction to this volume includes a very thorough review of the history of research in the Sociology of Mental Health and Illness and reviews the published research.

In terms of future research, the sociological study of mental health is a growing field as evidenced by the new journal, *Society and Mental Health*, and the excellent articles in the early volumes of this journal by leading sociologists. I anticipate more research on the effects of the stagnant and declining economy on mental health outcomes for various groups, including suicide. I also anticipate a growing tradition critical of the emerging dominance of research which focuses on the brain and ignores not only social context, but the role played by psychology and cognition. Sociologists will continue to articulate how social context, personality, and biology influence, and are influenced by one another.

References

Avison, William R., Jane D. McLeod, and Bernice A. Pescosolido. eds. 2007. *Mental Health: Social Mirror*. New York, NY: Springer Science and Business Media, LLC.

Conrad, Peter. 2007. *The Medicalization of Society: On the Transformation of Human Conditions into Treatable Disorders*. Baltimore, MD: John Hopkins University Press.

Foucault, Michel. 1988[1965]. *Madness and Civilization: A History of Insanity in the Age of Reason*. New York, NY: Vintage Books.

Frances, Allan. 2013. *Saving Normal: An Insider's Revolt against Out-of-Control Psychiatric Diagnosis, DSM-5, Big Pharma, and the Medicalization of Ordinary Life*. New York, NY: Harper Collins.

Goffman, Erving. 1961. *Asylum: Essays on the Social Situation of Mental Patients and Other Inmates*. Garden City, NY: Anchor Books.

Grob, Gerald N. and Howard H. Goldman. 2006. *The Dilemma of Federal Mental Health Policy: Radical Reform or Incremental Change?* New Brunswick, NJ: Rutgers University Press.

Hernandez, Elaine M. and Christopher Uggen. 2012. Institutions, Politics, and Mental Health Parity. *Society and Mental Health* 2(3): 154–171.

Horwitz, Allan. 2002. *Creating Mental Illness*. Chicago, IL: University of Chicago Press.

Jacobson, Nora S. 2004. *In Recovery: The Making of Mental Health Policy*. Nashville, TN: Vanderbilt University Press.

Jacobson, Nora S. and Diane Greenley. 2001. What Is Recovery? A Conceptual Model and Explication. *Psychiatric Services* 52: 482–485.

Kessler, Ronald C. 2010. The Prevalence of Mental Illness. In *Handbook for the Sociology of Mental Health*. Edited by Teresa L. Scheid and Tony N. Brown. New York, NY: Cambridge University Press, 46–63.

Keyes, Corey L. M. and Barret Michalec. 2010. Viewing Mental Health from the Complete State Paradigm. In *Handbook for the Sociology of Mental Health*. Edited by Teresa L. Scheid and Tony N. Brown. New York, NY: Cambridge University Press, 125–134.

Link, Bruce G. and Jo C. Phelan. 2010. Labeling and Stigma. In *Handbook for the Sociology of Mental Health*. Edited by Teresa L. Scheid and Tony N. Brown. New York, NY: Cambridge University Press, 571–587.

Mechanic, David. 2006. *The Truth About Health Care: Why Reform Is Not Working in the U.S.* New Brunswick, NJ: Rutgers University Press.

Mechanic, David, Donna D. McAlpine, and David A. Rochefort. 2013. *Mental Health and Social Policy: Beyond Managed Care*. 6th edn. New York, NY: Pearson Publishing.

Pescosolido, Bernice A. 2013. The Public Stigma of Mental Illness: What Do We Think; What Do We Know; What Can We Prove? *Journal of Health and Social Behavior* 54(1): 1–21.

Scheid, Teresa L. and Tony N. Brown. 2010. *A Handbook for the Study of Mental Health: Social Contexts, Theories, and Systems*. 2nd edn. New York, NY: Cambridge University Press.

Smith, Dena T. 2014. The Diminished Resistance to Medicalization in Psychiatry: Psychoanalysis Meets the Medical Model of Mental Illness. *Society and Mental Health* 4: 75–91.

Thoits, Peggy A. 2010. Sociological Approaches to Mental Illness. In *Handbook for the Sociology of Mental Health*. Edited by Teresa L. Scheid and Tony N. Brown. New York, NY: Cambridge University Press, 106–123.

Thoits, Peggy A. 2011. Mechanisms Linking Social Ties and Support to Physical and Mental Health. *Journal of Health and Social Behavior* 52(2): 145–161.

Turner, R. Jay. 2013. Understanding Health Disparities: The Relevance of the Stress Process Model. *Society and Mental Health* 3: 170–186.

Wakefield, Jerome C. and Mark F. Schmitz. 2010. The Measurement of Mental Disorder. In *Handbook for the Sociology of Mental Health*. Edited by Teresa L. Scheid and Tony N. Brown. New York, NY: Cambridge University Press, 20–45.

Whooley, Owen. 2014. Nosological Reflections: The Failure of DSM-5, The Emergence of RDOC, and the Decontextualization of Mental Distress. *Society and Mental Health* 4: 92–110.

World Health Organization. 2004. *Promoting Mental Health: Concepts, Emerging Evidence, Practice*. Geneva: World Health Organization.

CHAPTER 16
Sociobiology

Rosemary L. Hopcroft

Introduction

Sociobiology first rose to prominence with the publication in 1975 of the book of the same name by the biologist E. O. Wilson. Wilson (1980[1975]: 4) defines sociobiology as "the systematic study of the biological basis of all social behavior." As such, it would seem relevant to sociology, and Wilson explicitly stated that he thought sociology would eventually incorporate insights from sociobiology (Wilson 1980[1975]: 4, 300). Yet while sociobiology applied to non-human behavior was largely non-controversial, applied to human behavior it was highly controversial (see Segerstråle 2000 for details). Despite a few early proponents (e.g., Van den Berghe 1974; Lopreato 1984), sociobiology was resoundingly rejected by the majority of sociologists and by the 1990s had largely disappeared from the field (Machalek and Martin 2004).

Sociobiology found more acceptance in anthropology, where anthropologists such as Napoleon Chagnon, Sarah Hrdy, David Barash, Monique Borgerhoff Mulder, Laura Betzig, Richard Alexander, and William Irons (among others) became leading proponents. Sociobiology also found a home in psychology, in a slightly revised form called evolutionary psychology (Cosmides and Tooby 1987). Rather than examining the biological basis of social behavior directly, evolutionary psychologists focused on the evolved apparatus of human cognition, the evolved psychological mechanisms (also called cognitive modules) that influenced social behavior. Evolutionary psychology took off as a subfield within psychology in the 1990s and beyond.

More recently, various incarnations of sociobiology have found new adherents in sociology. Jonathan Turner and coauthors have examined the evolved basis of human emotions, and his work was cited by Douglas Massey in his presidential address to the American Sociological Association (Massey 2002). In 2004, the Evolution, Biology and Society Section of the American Sociological Association became a section-in-formation.

This chapter is an overview of the rise, fall, and rise again of sociobiology within sociology. It examines the central issues facing sociobiology in sociology, including the dislike of most sociologists for the area. I argue that the reasons given for this dislike are largely unfounded, and that sociobiology is of great use to sociology. I discuss current work in sociology that examines the biological basis of social behavior and suggest that sociology will increasingly incorporate biology in its examination of society and social life.

Criticisms of Sociobiology by Sociologists

Many early arguments against sociobiology, both within sociology and within other social sciences, were based on the idea that sociobiology simply did not apply to humans. Our sophisticated cultures, it was argued, overrode any role of biology in social behavior (Eckberg 1977; Quadagno 1979). One fundamental problem, according to these early arguments, was that there was no evidence that individuals maximized reproductive success in terms of number of offspring – a basis of sociobiology that has been shown to apply to non-humans. In a well-known article entitled "Social versus Reproductive Success: The Central Theoretical Problem of Human Sociobiology" the demographer Daniel Vining (1986) noted that in modern human societies, unlike in groups of non-human primates, socially successful individuals had fewer offspring than their less successful peers.

Evolutionary psychologists largely dealt with this issue by side-stepping it. For example, Pérusse (1993), in a well-cited article, argued that while high-status men in contemporary advanced industrial societies did not maximize reproductive success at the ultimate level (number of children), they did maximize reproductive success at the proximate level (copulation frequency). If not for modern birth control, high-status men would have more children than low-status men in modern societies. This conclusion aligned with the practice in evolutionary psychology of examining the proximate motivations for behavior, which evolved to maximize reproductive success, and not necessarily the results of that behavior (which may or may not serve to maximize reproductive success in the modern environment). As an illustration, evolutionary psychologists often note that a taste for sweets and fats in humans evolved because it was adaptive for individuals in the environments of evolution. In modern day environments, tastes for sweets and fats are maladaptive when they promote obesity and consequent health problems.

For anthropologists, the lack of apparent relationship between social status and number of offspring in modern societies was less of an issue, as abundant evidence from pre-industrial societies around the world did show that for men at least, social status was positively related to number of offspring (see Hopcroft 2006, table 1). However, for sociologists who study social behavior in modern industrialized societies the "central problem of sociobiology" seemed a major stumbling block to any further inroads by sociobiology into the discipline. For most of the 1980s, sociobiology had little if any presence in the major journals of the discipline.

The apparent lack of correlation between social status and reproductive success was not the only criticism sociologists had of sociobiology. Sociobiology was attacked as reductionist, and therefore "antisociological." According to this argument, it was the rejection of reductionism that shaped sociology as a distinctive social science (e.g., see Rose 2000a: 144; Schneiberg and Clemens 2006). Yet there is nothing in sociobiology that denies that societies and groups may have emergent properties that are hard to predict simply by knowledge of the individuals in the group. The recognition of emergent effects at the level of the group is in fact central to sociobiology (Wilson 1980[1975]: 7). Sociobiology merely suggests that individual responses to social and environmental realities are shaped by "the behavior constraints imposed by the genetic constitution of the species" (Wilson 1980[1975]: 5).

Sociobiology has also been mistaken for Social Darwinism. The mechanistic process by which particular genes and groups of genes are selected through the process of evolution and lead to species-typical traits and behaviors has been misunderstood as supporting the idea that socially dominant individuals and/or groups are "better" or "stronger" than others, and this therefore provides a justification for racism and such horrors as the Nazi eugenic program. Yet, this is a terrible abuse of biology. Sociobiology merely notes that species-typical traits were shaped in the evolutionary past. A trait exists because in the evolutionary past it helped its bearer survive and reproduce and did so repeatedly over evolutionary time. All members of a species share those traits, with some variation across individuals. This is true of all species and also humans – homo sapiens sapiens. Currently successful people are simply individuals who are doing well in the current environment, for whatever reason. Perhaps their particular variation on the human genotype is well suited to the current environment, or there may be any one of myriad social and political reasons. In a very different environment, or within a different social and political context, that individual would likely not do as well.

As for the idea that some groups are genetically "superior" to others, there is little evidence that groups differ dramatically from each other genetically. All humans share 100 percent of their genes. There is some variation in alleles (alternative forms of the same gene) that cluster by ancestry – more alleles for dark skin in people whose ancestors came from the tropics, for instance – but there is always more genetic variation within groups than between groups (Fujimura et. al. 2014). Further, there is little acceptance of group selection in evolutionary biology – the idea that there is selection of individual traits because they primarily help the group (rather than the individual) succeed (Abbot et al. 2011; Dawkins 2012). The existence of group selection would promote the genetic differentiation of groups, yet group selection, if it does exist, is much weaker than selection at the level of the individual organism. So there is no evidence of substantial genetic variation between groups, nor is there much evidence of a mechanism by which that outcome could be obtained; thus it makes little sense to say that any group is genetically superior to another group.

Sociobiology has also been accused of teleological functionalism (e.g., Quadagno 1979; Jackson and Rees 2007). This is true only in the sense that all of the theory of evolutionary biology can be labeled as "teleologically functionalist." Natural selection is based on the idea that if a genetic trait helps its bearer survive and reproduce over evolutionary time, that trait is likely to be found in subsequent generations. This is end-oriented (the trait helped the bearer survive and reproduce) and functionalist in that the trait was "functional" for the bearer (as it helped the bearer survive and reproduce). In the current environment, the same trait may no longer be functional. There is an overwhelming amount of evidence of this process of evolution by natural selection, and this theory lies at the heart of modern biology (Dawkins 2009). But this is all at the level of the individual organism, and is far removed from *socio-cultural* functionalism that posits that some trait or feature of a society exists because it is functional for that society. At the level of society, there is no equivalent to the mechanism of evolution by natural selection, as the society is not an organism in the sense a living thing is an organism. A society does not live or die in the sense that an organism lives and dies. When an organism dies, all its components die with it; when a society disappears, this does not mean all the components (individuals) in the society also die (although in rare cases it may). Many of the individuals have likely moved to another society. Societies do not live or die as organisms do, nor do they compete as organisms do. So although it may sometimes be convenient to use the analogy to a living organism when discussing a society, it is only an analogy, and an imprecise one at that.

Sociobiology posits that all humans share common traits that predispose all humans to certain social behaviors – such as a sex drive, tendency toward kin selection (favoring relatives), etc. This feeds into another criticism – the common sense nature of the evolved actor model means it is not necessary to make it explicit for successful sociology (Heuveline 2004). To some extent this is true, as long as our implicit assumptions about individuals are consistent with what is known about the species in biology. When our assumptions veer way off the mark, then this will influence the credibility of sociology. An example is the assertion that sex and gender and sex-typical behaviors are entirely social constructions, which is contradicted by much evidence in biology and elsewhere (e.g., Udry 2000). Sex has such an important role to play in reproduction and hence evolution that it would be strange if there were not evolved sex differences.

Another complaint against sociobiology is that it is biologically determinist (Rose 2000a). This criticism is unfounded. The development and behavior of any organism (humans included) is always contingent on circumstance, including the social as well as the material context. It is an interactional process, where environmental circumstance is critical to how the organism follows genetic instructions for development. Genes are best considered "if, then" packages similar to lines in computer code, telling the organism how to develop given the prevailing circumstances (Marcus 2003). Behavior is also similarly flexible and responsive to environment and context, within the limits posed by physiological design. Human behavior is no exception to this (Bateson 2000; Rose 2000b). Biologists refer to this interactional process as the "norm of reaction" (see Wilson 1980[1975]; Machalek and Martin 2004).

All these criticisms of sociobiology by sociologists meant that sociobiology essentially disappeared from sociology during the 1980s and 1990s. Yet, beginning in the new century, there were several movements that have helped to pave the way for a revival of sociobiology. First, there emerged a scholarly interest within sociology in the evolutionary basis of the emotions and brain functions that promote and enhance human sociality. Second, there was the fallout from the Human Genome Project and the new methods available that allow researchers to pinpoint individual genes and groups of genes that predispose their bearers to various traits, including diseases and social behaviors. Last, most recently a number of scholars have found evidence that male fertility (although not female fertility) is positively correlated with some measures of status (notably personal income) suggesting that the so-called "central problem of sociobiology" may not be such a problem after all. In what follows I deal with each of these developments in turn.

The Revival of Sociobiology within Sociology

Sociology of Emotions and Neurosociology

Jonathan Turner and coauthors (e.g., Turner 2007; Turner and Stets 2006; Turner and Maryanski 2008) have been responsible for bringing attention to the evolutionary basis of human emotions and the centrality of those evolved emotions for social behavior. Turner and Maryanski (2008) draw a picture of the evolved human that emerged some 150,000 years ago and has changed little since: an individualistic hominid, tied by emotional ties to group members, but resistant to domination by other hominids. They note that this is the human nature that cultures have built on but not eradicated. Turner and Maryanski argue that:

> We will never have a complete picture of human behavior and social processes, to say nothing of humans as a species, without greater knowledge from the biological sciences. This conclusion does not mean that sociology can be reduced to biology or some other extreme reductionist argument, but it does mean that we can have a more robust understanding of humans and their socio-cultural creations when we add biology to our arsenal of analytical tools and empirical database (Turner and Maryanski (2008): 24– 25).

Drawing on such insights, Massey (2005) suggests that humans evolved for small group life, and life in a large-scale, anonymous society poses challenges and dilemmas for individuals as a result.

In addition to those who do research on how individual emotions influence social relations, there are other scholars within this group who examine the reverse – how social relations and situations in turn influence emotions (Stets and Asencio 2008; Ten Houten 2005). Robinson et al. (2004) discuss how the experience in group interactions (e.g., of being high and low status) influences emotional and physiological states. Much of the research shows that occupying a low-status position is more stressful than occupying a high-status position. Similarly, Massey (2004) theorizes that exposure to stress leads to a variety of deleterious health and cognitive outcomes for African Americans (see also Davis and Werre 2008).

Similarly, David Franks has argued that social psychology must take into account the neural circuitry of the human brain, which underlies social processes including the formation of the self, role-taking, social learning, attachment, and aggression (Franks 2010; Franks and Turner 2013). Franks (2010) further argues that research on mirror neurons supports the work of the Chicago pragmatists. For example, mirror neurons are importantly involved in empathy and understanding the minds of others. They also likely comprise the mechanism for what Charles Horton Cooley referred to as the "looking glass self" – that is, our understanding of ourselves as we think others see us. Hammond (2004) argues that studies of human neural circuitry support the Durkheimian idea that religion promotes social solidarity.

Genes and Social Behavior

Sociobiology suggests that genes influence human behavior in conjunction with the environment. The specific genes involved in various social behaviors and how their effects are shaped by the environment of the individual are now being discovered by a variety of researchers, some in sociology. The Human Genome Project (1990–2003), which mapped the entire human genome and the International HapMap Project (International HapMap Consortium 2003; 2005) have enabled researchers to pinpoint genes and genetic clusters associated with a variety of different traits, including behaviors. For instance, the DAT1 Gene is associated with risky behaviors. Relative to the DAT1*10R/10R and DAT1*10R/9R genotypes, men with the DAT1*9R/9R genotype scored considerably lower on scales measuring propensity for serious and violent delinquency (Guo et al. 2008a; Guo and Adkins 2008; Vaughn et al. 2009) and reported fewer sexual partners (Guo et al. 2008b).

Associations with particular genotypes have been found for delinquent and criminal behavior (Beaver 2008; Beaver et al. 2008; Guo et al. 2008a; Vaughn et al. 2009); school continuation (Shanahan et al. 2008); and substance dependence including drinking behavior (Guo et al. 2009). There is also evidence of gene-environment interactions on number of sexual partners (Guo et al. 2008b) and age at first intercourse (Guo and Tong 2006). This research program pinpointing the role of specific genes in specific social behaviors continues apace both within and without the discipline of sociology.

Behavioral Genetics Research

Behavioral genetics research utilizes data on twins to estimate how much of the variance in a social behavior is due to genes, shared environment and non-shared environment. This technique has been used by a number of sociologists to study a variety of different issues. For example, Boardman et al. (2010) find that that 35 percent of the variance in regular smoking is due to genetic influences. Nielsen (2006) similarly uses behavioral genetics models to evaluate the relative contribution of genes, family environment, and individual-specific environments to the occupational attainment of individuals. Kohler et al. (1999) use data on Danish twins to examine genetic influences on fertility. They find that these exist, but their relative magnitude and pattern are contingent on the sex and socio-economic environment of the individual. Eaves et al. (2008) find relatively small genetic influences and much larger effects of the social environment on adolescent religious attitudes and practices.

One general finding that emerges from many of these behavioral genetic studies is that genetic influence on behavior is stronger during affluent time periods when individuals (presumably) have more choice, while environmental influences on behavior are stronger during less affluent time periods.

Status and Reproductive Success

In the last ten years a variety of scholars have published papers showing a positive relationship between status and number of offspring (for males, not females) in modern societies in Europe and the United States. Different studies have used different measures of individual social status, but common measures of status include personal income and education. In the United States and the United Kingdom, personal income is positively associated with number of offspring for men, while it is negatively associated with number of offspring for women (Hopcroft 2006; 2015; Weeden et al. 2006; Nettle and Pollet 2008; Huber et al. 2010). Also in the United States, Fieder and Huber (2012) show that holding a supervisory position within an organization is associated with more offspring for men but not women. In Sweden, both income and education are positively associated with number of offspring for men only (Fieder and Huber 2007; Goodman and Koupil 2009; 2010). In Norway, Lappegård and Rønsen (2013) find that both education and income increase the probability of additional children for men only. In Finland, Nisén et al. (2013) find more highly educated men have more children than less educated men. Fieder et al. (2011), using data from Brazil, Mexico, Panama, South Africa, United States, and Venezuela, find that the lowest income men and the highest income women are least likely to have one of their own children in the household.

Lappegård and Rønsen (2013) show evidence that part of the mechanism for the relationship between socio-economic status and number of offspring for men in Norway is multi-partner fertility by high-status men (see also Forsberg and Tullberg 1995 for Sweden; Bereczkei and Csanaky 1996 for Hungary; Jokela et al. 2010 for the United States). However, it appears that the primary driver of the relationship between socio-economic status and reproductive success for men in Europe is the greater likelihood of childlessness among low-status men (Fieder and Huber 2007; Fieder et al. 2011; Barthold et al. 2012; Goodman et al. 2012).

These findings of an association between status and number of offspring for men only are consistent with theory from both sociobiology and evolutionary psychology, which suggests that women are more likely than men to prefer good financial prospects in a mate (Buss 1989; Wiederman and Allgeier 1992; Buss et al. 2001; Henry et al. 2013). They suggest that the so-called "central theoretical problem of modern sociobiology" may not be such a problem after all.

This work and the other work described above on emotions and social behavior, neurosociology, genes and social behavior, and behavioral genetics, illustrate how examining the role of biology in social behavior can add to our understanding of topics long of concern to sociologists, including self-identity, social solidarity, deviance, stratification and fertility. This in turn has created an environment in sociology that is more conducive to incorporating biology and its theories, including sociobiology, than it was forty years ago when the sociobiology controversy first began. Indeed, special issues of two of the flagship journals of the field were devoted to biosociology (*Social Forces* in 2006 and the *American Journal of Sociology* in 2008). This is likely a harbinger of things to come. Indeed, E. O. Wilson (1980[1975]), suggested that sociology was in a phase similar to the natural history phase in biology – more concerned with description than theoretical explanation – and that it was just a matter of time before sociology incorporated sociobiology.

Conclusion

Sociobiology – the study of the biological basis of social behavior – continues to be controversial within sociology. However, recent developments within the discipline, including the growing evidence of links between genetic potentials and social behaviors, as well as evidence of the positive association that sociobiology predicts between social status and reproductive success among modern humans, have meant that sociobiology is not as resoundingly rejected by sociologists as it once was. Just as our neighboring social sciences (psychology, political science, economics, and anthropology) have all begun to include more theory and evidence from biology, including sociobiology, into their disciplines, so it is likely that in the future sociology will throw off its biophobia and begin to incorporate insights from sociobiology into the study of human social behavior and society. Such a development is to be welcomed rather than feared. As I have argued previously (Hopcroft 2009), incorporating sociobiology into sociology will only reinforce the discipline as it currently stands, and will help create the kind of scientific sociology that the founders of the discipline envisioned.

References

Abbot, Patrick et al. 2011. Inclusive Fitness Theory and Eusociality. *Nature* 471: E1–E4.

Barthold, J. A., M. Myrskylä, and O. R. Jones. 2012. Childlessness Drives the Sex Difference in the Association between Income and Reproductive Success of Modern Europeans. *Evolution and Human Behavior* 33(6): 628–638.

Bateson, P. 2000. Taking the Stink Out of Instinct. In *Alas, Poor Darwin: Arguments Against Evolutionary Psychology*. Edited by H. Rose and S. Rose. New York, NY: Harmony Books, 189–208.

Beaver, Kevin M. 2008. Nonshared Environmental Influences on Adolescent Delinquent Involvement and Adult Criminal Behavior. *Criminology* 46(2): 341–369.

Beaver, Kevin M, John Paul Wright, Matt Delisi, and Michael G. Vaughn. 2008. Desistance from Delinquency: The Marriage Effect Revisited and Extended. *Social Science Research* 37(3): 736–752.

Bereczkei, Tamas and Andras Csanaky. 1996. Mate Choice, Marital Success, and Reproduction in a Modern Society. *Ethology and Sociobiology* 17: 17–36.

Boardman, Jason D., Casely L. Blalock, and Fred C. Pampel. 2010. Trends in the Genetic Influences on Smoking. *Journal of Health and Social Behavior* 51(1): 108–123.

Buss, D. M. 1989. Sex Differences in Human Mate Preferences: Evolutionary Hypotheses Tested in 37 Cultures. *Behavioral and Brain Sciences* 12: 1–49.

Buss, D. M., T. K. Shackelford, L. A. Kirkpatrick, and R. J. Larsen. 2001. A Half Century of Mate Preferences: The Cultural Evolution of Values. *Journal of Marriage and Family* 63(2): 491–503.

Cosmides, Leda and John Tooby. 1987. From Evolution to Behavior: Evolutionary Psychology as the Missing Link. In *The Latest on the Best: Essays on Evolution and Optimality*. Edited by John Dupré. Cambridge, MA: The MIT Press, 276–306.

Davis, Jeff and Daniel Werre. 2008. A Longitudinal Study of the Effects of Uncertainty on Reproductive Behaviors. *Human Nature* 19(4): 426–452.

Dawkins, Richard. 2009. *The Greatest Show on Earth: The Evidence for Evolution*. New York, NY: Free Press.

Dawkins, Richard. 2012. The Descent of Edward Wilson: A New Book on Evolution by a Great Biologist Makes a Slew of Mistakes. *Prospect Magazine* June. Available at www.prospectmagazine.co.uk/magazine/edward-wilson-social-conquest-earth-evolutionary-errors-origin-species, accessed November 29, 2016.

Eaves, Lindon J., Peter K. Hatemi, Elizabeth C. Prom-Womley, and Lenn Murrelle. 2008. Social and Genetic Influences on Adolescent Religious Attitudes and Practices. *Social Forces* 86(4): 1621–1646.

Eckberg, Douglas Lee. 1977. Sociobiology and the Death of Sociology: An Analytic Reply to Ellis. *The American Sociologist* 2(4): 191–200.

Fieder, M. and S. Huber. 2007. The Associations of Sex and Childlessness on the Association between Status and Reproductive Output in Modern Society. *Evolution and Human Behavior* 28: 392–398.

Fieder, M. and S. Huber. 2012. An Evolutionary Account of Status, Power, and Career in Modern Societies. *Human Nature* 23: 191–207.

Fieder, M., S. Huber, and F. Bookstein. 2011. Socio-Economic Status, Marital Status and Childlessness in Men and Women: An Analysis of Census Data from Six Countries. *Journal of Biosocial Science* 43: 619–635.

Forsberg, Anna J. L. and Birgitta S. Tullberg. 1995. The Relationship between Cumulative Number of Cohabiting Partners and Number of Children for Men and Women in Modern Sweden. *Ethology and Sociobiology* 16: 221–232.

Franks, David. 2010. *Neurosociology: The Nexus between Neuroscience and Social Psychology.* New York, NY: Springer.

Franks, David D. and Jonathan H. Turner. eds. 2013. *Handbook of Neurosociology.* New York, NY: Springer.

Fujimura, Joan H., Deborah A. Bolnick, Ramya Rajagopalan, Jay S. Kaufman, Richard C. Lewontin, Troy Duster, Pilar Ossorio, and Jonathan Marks. 2014. Clines without Classes: How to Make Sense of Human Variation. *Sociological Theory* 32: 208.

Goodman, A. and I. Koupil. 2009. Social and Biological Determinants of Reproductive Success in Swedish Males and Females Born 1915–1929. *Evolution and Human Behavior* 30: 329–341.

Goodman, A. and I. Koupil. 2010. The Association of School Performance upon Marriage and Long-term Reproductive Success in 10,000 Swedish Males and Females Born 1915–1929. *Evolution and Human Behavior* 31(6): 425–435.

Goodman, A., I. Koupil, and D. W. Lawson. 2012. Low Fertility Increases Descendant Socioeconomic Position but Reduces Long-term Fitness in a Modern Post-Industrial Society. *Proceedings of the Royal Society B.* 279: 4342–4351. Doi: 10.1098/Rspb.2012.1415.

Guo, Guang and Daniel E. Adkins. 2008. How Is a Statistical Link Established between a Human Outcome and a Genetic Variant? *Sociological Methods and Research* 37(2): 201–226.

Guo, Guang and Yuying Tong. 2006. Age at First Sexual Intercourse, Genes, and Social and Demographic Context: Evidence from Twins and the Dopamine D4 Receptor Gene. *Demography* 43(4): 747–769.

Guo, Guang, Michael Roettger, and Tianji Cai. 2008a. The Integration of Genetic Propensities into Social Control Models of Delinquency and Violence among Male Youths. *American Sociological Review* 73(4): 543–568.

Guo, Guang, Yuying Tong, and Tianji Cai. 2008b. Gene by Social-Context Interactions for Number of Sexual Partners among White Male Youths: Genetics-Informed Sociology. In Special Issue: Genetics and Social Structure. Edited by Peter Bearman. *American Journal of Sociology* 114(3): 36–66.

Guo, Guang, Glen H. Elder, Tianji Cai, and Nathan Hamilton. 2009. Gene-Environment Interactions: Peers' Alcohol Use Moderates Genetic Contribution to Adolescent Drinking Behavior. *Social Science Research* 38(1): 213–224.

Hammond, Michael. 2004. The Enhancement Imperative and Group Dynamics in the Emergence of Religion and Ascriptive Inequality. *Advances in Group Processes* 21: 167–188.

Henry, J., H. W. Helm, and N. Cruz. 2013. Mate Selection: Gender and Generational Differences. *North American Journal of Psychology* 15(1): 63–70.

Heuveline, P. 2004. Reviews of Animal Traditions: Behavioural Inheritance in Evolution by Eytan Avital and Eva Jablonka. *American Journal of Sociology* 109: 1500–1506.

Hopcroft, Rosemary L. 2006. Sex, Status and Reproductive Success in the Contemporary U.S. *Evolution and Human Behavior* 27: 104–120.

Hopcroft, Rosemary L. 2009. The Evolved Actor in Sociology. *Sociological Theory* 27(4): 390–406.

Hopcroft, Rosemary L. 2015. Sex Differences in the Relationship between Status and Number of Offspring in the Contemporary U.S. *Evolution and Human Behavior* 36(2): 146–151.

Huber, S., F. Bookstein, and M. Fieder. 2010. Socio-Economic Status and Reproduction in Modern Women – an Evolutionary-Ecological Perspective. *American Journal of Human Biology* 22: 578–587.

International Hapmap Consortium. 2003. 'The International Hapmap Project.' *Nature* 426: 789–796.

International Hapmap Consortium. 2005. 'A Haplotype Map of the Human Genome.' *Nature* 437: 1299–1320.

Jackson, Stevi and Amanda Rees. 2007. The Appalling Appeal of Nature: The Popular Influence of Evolutionary Psychology as a Problem for Sociology. *Sociology* 41(5): 917–930.

Jokela, Markus, Anna Rotkirch, Ian J. Rickard, Jenni Pettay, and Virpi Lummaa. 2010. Serial Monogamy Increases Reproductive Success in Men but Not in Women. *Behavioral Ecology* 21: 906–912.

Kohler, Hans-Peter, J. L. Rodgers, and K. Christensen. 1999. Is Fertility Behavior in Our Genes? Findings from a Danish Twin Study. *Population and Development Review* 25(2): 253–288.

Lappegård, T. and M. Rønsen. 2013. Socioeconomic Differences in Multipartner Fertility among Norwegian Men. *Demography* 50: 1135–1153.

Lopreato, Joseph. 1984. *Human Nature and Biocultural Evolution*. Boston, MA: Allen and Unwin.

Machalek, Richard and Michael W. Martin. 2004. Sociology and the Second Darwinian Revolution: A Metatheoretical Analysis. *Sociological Theory* 22(3): 455–476.

Marcus, G. 2003. *The Birth of the Mind: How a Tiny Number of Genes Creates the Complexities of Human Thought*. New York, NY: Basic Books.

Massey, Douglas S. 2002. A Brief History of Human Society: The Origin and Role of Emotion in Social Life. *American Sociological Review* 67: 1–29.

Massey, Douglas S. 2004. Segregation and Stratification: A Biosocial Perspective. *Du Bois Review* 1(1): 7–25.

Massey, Douglas S. 2005. *Strangers in a Strange Land: Humans in an Urbanizing World*. New York, NY: Norton.

Nettle, D. and T. V. Pollet. 2008. Natural Selection on Male Wealth in Humans. *The American Naturalist* 172: 658–666.

Nisén, J., P. Martikainen, J. Kaprio, and K. Silventoinen. 2013. Educational Differences in Completed Fertility: A Behavioral Genetic Study of Finnish Male and Female Twins. *Demography* 50: 1399–1420.

Nielsen, François. 2006. Achievement and Ascription in Educational Attainment: Genetic and Environmental Influences on Adolescent Schooling. *Social Forces* 85(1): 193–216.

Pérusse, Daniel. 1993. Cultural and Reproductive Success in Industrial Societies: Testing the Relationship at the Proximate and Ultimate Levels. *Behavioral and Brain Sciences* 16: 267–322.

Quadagno, Jill S. 1979. Paradigms in Evolutionary Theory: The Sociobiological Model of Natural Selection. *American Sociological Review* 44(1): 100–109.

Robinson, Dawn T., Christabel L. Rogalin, and Lynn Smith-Lovin. 2004. Physiological Measures of Theoretical Concepts: Some Ideas for Linking Deflection and Emotion to Physical Responses during Interaction. *Advances in Group Processes* 21: 77–115.

Rose, H. 2000a. Colonizing the Social Sciences? In *Alas, Poor Darwin: Arguments Against Evolutionary Psychology*. Edited by H. Rose and S. Rose. New York, NY: Harmony Books.

Rose, H. 2000b. Escaping Evolutionary Psychology. In *Alas, Poor Darwin: Arguments Against Evolutionary Psychology*. Edited by H. Rose and S. Rose. New York, NY: Harmony Books, 299–320.

Segerstråle, Ullica Christina Olofsdotter. 2000. *Defenders of the Truth: The Battle for Science in the Sociobiology Debate and Beyond*. Oxford and New York, NY: Oxford University Press.

Shanahan, Michael J., Stephen Vaisey, Lance D. Erickson, and Andrew Smolen. 2008. Environmental Contingencies and Genetic Propensities: Social Capital, Educational Continuation, and Dopamine Receptor Gene DRD2. In Special Issue: Genetics and Social Structure Edited by Peter Bearman. *American Journal of Sociology* 114(3): S260–S286.

Schneiberg, M. and E. S. Clemens. 2006. The Typical Tools for the Job: Research Strategies in Institutional Analysis. *Sociological Theory* 24: 195–227.

Stets, Jan E. and Emily K. Asencio. 2008. Consistency and Enhancement Processes in Understanding Emotions. *Social Forces* 86(3): 1055–1078.

Ten Houten, Warren D. 2005. Primary Emotions and Social Relations: A First Report. *Free Inquiry in Creative Sociology* 33(2): 79–92.

Turner, Jonathan H. 2007. *Human Emotions: A Sociological Theory*. New York, NY: Routledge.

Turner, Jonathan H. and Alexandra Maryanski. 2008. *On the Origins of Societies by Natural Selection*. Boulder, CO: Paradigm Publishers.

Turner, Jonathan H. and Jan E. Stets. 2006. Sociological Theories of Human Emotions. *Annual Review of Sociology* 32: 25–52.

Udry, J. Richard. 2000. Biological Limits of Gender Construction. *American Sociological Review* 65(3): 443–457.

Van den Berghe, Pierre L. 1974. Bringing Beasts Back in: Toward a Biosocial Theory of Aggression. *American Sociological Review* 39(6): 777–788.

Vaughn, Michael G., Matt Delisi, Kevin M. Beaver, and John Paul Wright. 2009. DAT1 and 5HTT are Associated with Pathological Criminal Behavior in a Nationally Representative Sample of Youth.*Criminal Justice and Behavior* 36(11): 1103–1114.

Vining, D. R. 1986. Social versus Reproductive Success: The Central Theoretical Problem of Human Sociobiology. *Behavioral and Brain Sciences* 9(1): 167–187.

Weeden, Jason, Michael J. Abrams, Melancie C. Green, and John Sabini. 2006. Do High-Status People Really Have Fewer Children? *Human Nature* 17(4): 377–392.

Wiederman, M. W. and E. R. Allgeier. 1992. Gender Differences in Mate Selection Criteria: Sociobiological or Socioeconomic Explanation? *Ethology and Sociobiology* 13: 115–124.

Wilson, Edward O. 1980[1975]. *Sociobiology. The Abridged Edition*. Cambridge, MA: Harvard University Press.

CHAPTER 17
The Sociology of Science and Technology

Miwao Matsumoto

Introduction

Science and technology have been long neglected subjects in sociology. One might recall that Auguste Comte, who coined the term, *sociologie*, described the field with his law of three stages (*loi des trois états*), which was based on the progress of science and technology. However, his vision of sociology did not take up science and technology as objects for sociological exploration. Instead, they were assumed to be the model for such exploration. This peculiar attitude seems to have been retained in sociology since then and has resulted in most sociologists seeing science and technology as a given while viewing everything else as social phenomena.

The sociology of science and technology has emerged from endeavors to challenge this situation. This chapter analyzes the development trajectory of the sociology of science and technology by formulating three different universes of discourse in the field. Based on this conceptual mapping, the chapter reconstructs the development trajectory of frameworks, issues, and insights accumulated with particular reference to the sociology of scientific knowledge, the social construction of technology, actor network theory, and other bases of the field. It then describes the "third wave" arguments to reveal new complexities and participatory practices in the field. The chapter illustrates the double under-determination (the difficulty of one-to-one correspondence between scientific statements and policy options) to be expected from such a trajectory and suggests hitherto unnoticed but important tasks for the sociology of science and technology. Finally, the summary presents future prospects for the development of the sociology of science and technology.

Internal Structure, Institutionalization, Interaction

The subjects of the sociology of science and technology have proliferated, and range from dams (Espeland 1998) to DNA (Lynch et al. 2010). Yet, the increased variety in topics does not necessarily ensure a wider understanding because the variety makes it difficult to obtain an overview of the development trajectory of the field. What is needed is a conceptual mapping that enables the various topics to be systematically arranged and organized.

Given this focus, it makes sense to re-categorize previous research into three types by introducing the following concepts:

(1) the internal structure of the community of scientists and engineers (abbreviated to scientific community hereafter);
(2) the institutionalization of science and technology; and
(3) the interaction of science, technology, and society.

Discourse on the internal structure of the scientific community asks questions about the behaviors of individual scientists and engineers, their networks, the group structure of the community, including normative structures, reward systems, evaluation systems, and the relationships among them. Using a variety of methods, including quantitative analysis using SCI (Science Citation Index) and thick ethnographical description, the research questions in this discourse pertain to the internal state of the scientific community. Discourse on the institutionalization of science and technology treats the social processes through which the scientific community has developed as institutions that provide their members with professional career opportunities and relative autonomy. Discourse on the interaction of science, technology, and society addresses how science and technology, thus institutionalized, interact with different sectors of society through the exchange of information, money, goods, and human resources.

Looking back over the development trajectory of the sociology of science and technology, there is a chronology of research leading from (2), to (1), and on to (3). The thematic development in the sociology of science and technology depicted in Figure 17.1 on page 168 exemplifies this sequence.

Rather than engaging with the dynamics of the development of the subfield of sociology of science and technology in detail, this chapter focuses on (3) the interaction of science, technology, and society to delineate a sociologically important question and its implications: how to establish the foundations of the sociology of science and technology so that its insights become sociologically relevant. Given this focus, this chapter will elucidate the frameworks, issues, insights, and implications obtained in the field.

The Foundation of Theoretical Frameworks: Merton's Thesis and the Early Days

One of the most important and earliest frameworks of the sociology of science and technology can be traced to the thesis "Science, Technology, and Society in Seventeenth Century England" by a theoretical sociologist, Robert K. Merton (Merton 1938; 1970). This work developed Weber's argument about the unintended consequences of purposive social action arising from the relationship between Protestant ethics and the spirit of capitalism to those emerging from the relationship between Protestant ethics and the spirit of modern experimental science. The Merton thesis invited fairly heated controversy with historians of science over intricate relationships between evidence and interpretations (Cohen 1990); these might be regarded as a forerunner to the disputes over the relationship between narratives and concepts in describing the social dimensions of technological development (*Technology and Culture* 1991).

Controversy aside, Merton's thesis provided two pioneering ideas about methods and theoretical frameworks in the sociology of science and technology. First, it provided a prototype of what was later called prosopography for describing and analyzing social action and networks by quantitative aggregation of biographical information. Second, and more importantly, Merton's thesis

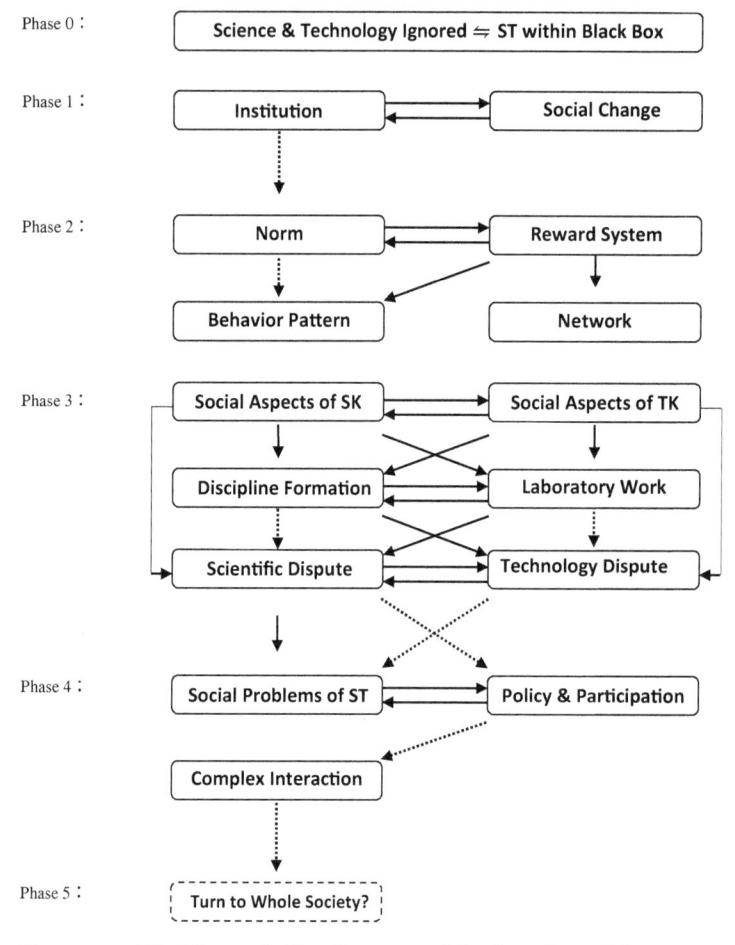

Figure 17.1. The Thematic Development of the Sociology of Science and Technology
Source: Matsumoto (2010).
Notes: Solid lines indicate direct influences, and dotted lines indicate indirect ones. Phase 1 roughly corresponds to the discourse on the institutionalization of science and technology, Phase 2 to that on the internal structure of the scientific community, phase 3 and, more probably, phase 4 to discourse on the interaction of science, technology, and society. Phase 5 is one of the possible phases expected in the near future by the present writer. SK: Scientific Knowledge; TK: Technological Knowledge.

embodied a theoretical framework for describing and analyzing the dynamic interaction between heterogeneous social institutions such as science, technology, and religion, and the unanticipated consequences of purposive social action (Merton 1936). In short, it depicted the theoretical foundations for coupling interdependent multiple social institutions with individual social actions.

The Mertonian School and the Autonomy of the Scientific Community

Studies by sociologists in the Mertonian school have focused on the workings of the reward and evaluation systems in the scientific community by using SCI indexes and quantitative analysis. They have contributed to clarification of the community's internal structure by measuring papers produced by scientists and their citations, scientists' social networks, and group formation of scientists (Cole and Cole 1973; Cole 1992; Mullins 1973; Zuckerman 1977). Empirical investigation of the degree of universalism (evaluating scientific results by scientific contribution alone regardless of sex, age, ethnicity, and other attributes of scientists), as a key element of the normative structure of the scientific community, provided a sociological frame of reference into the internal structure of the scientific community. This approach by the Mertonian school culminated in the mid-1970s when sociologists applied the same perspective to the development trajectory of the sociology of science and technology itself, and showed the preponderance of Merton's place in that development (Cole and Zuckerman 1975). However, the interpretation of such data is heavily reliant upon the autonomy the scientific community enjoys. For example, if there is little substantial room for autonomy, such as in the physics community in which Aryan scientists predominated in Nazi Germany or in the Lysenko-led genetics community in the Stalinist USSR, then universalism, in the literal sense of the word, cannot apply.

Assuming autonomy in the description and analysis of the scientific community's internal state obviously allows a high degree of interpretive flexibility regarding the nature of the internal state of the community, which could range from a "gentleman's drawing room" to a "Panopticon of Truth" (Shapin 1994: 413). To fix the meaning of this internal state, it is necessary to embark on an empirical investigation into the nature of the autonomy enjoyed by the community. Yet no sociological work on the social conditions that influence the scientific community's autonomy in relation to society has appeared from within the Mertonian school. It is true that the assumption of autonomy enables us to efficiently confine ourselves to the internal structure of the scientific community independent of the characteristics of the surrounding society because the assumption is almost tantamount to regarding the community as a closed system. However, without due efforts to empirically examine the assumption (see Gieryn 1999; Moore 2008), our attention could be diverted from the reality of the dynamic science-technology-society interface.

Neo-Kuhnian School

From the viewpoint of the interaction of science, technology, and society, the public acknowledgment of this drawback for the Mertonian school came from those who were called the "Neo-Kuhnian" sociologists of science in the 1970s (named after Kuhn 1962). They criticized the Mertonian sociology of science and technology as "black boxism," which had largely dismissed the cognitive contents of science. They argued that the result was the separation of the description and analysis of the internal state of the scientific community from the day-to-day reality of scientific activities (Whitley 1972). Sociologists of science after the "Neo-Kuhnians" school attempted to restore the reality of scientific activities through thick description of the social production processes of knowledge, including replication processes and crucial experiments (Pickering 1984; Collins 1985). This alternative way of investigation accompanied clarification of the social conditions of the autonomy of the scientific community from within.

The Strong Programme and the Sociology of Scientific Knowledge

One of the earliest endeavors to find how scientific knowledge is created within particular configurations of the social conditions stems from the "strong programme." According to Bloor (1976: 4–5), who initially formulated the program, any knowledge can be explained according to the following principles:

1) Causality. Any type of knowledge, including scientific knowledge, can be understood as a product of those agents

who have particular social interests in it whether the agents are aware of causality in this sense or not.

2) Impartiality. Any type of knowledge, whether true or false, rational or irrational, successful or not, requires impartial sociological explanation regarding its production processes.

3) Symmetry. In each instance of impartiality, a causal explanation (in the sense of principle 1) can be made for any type of knowledge.

4) Reflexivity. The first three principles can be applied not only to scientists but also to all those who attempt to explain the social production process of scientific knowledge.

An illustration of causality can be found in the widespread social interest in the use of steam power for drainage in mining, which prompted the use of diagrams in heat theory. Impartiality can be illustrated by the impartial sociological explanation of the formation processes of concepts such as correlation, regression, and eugenics, all of which were produced by a single person, Francis Galton (MacKenzie 1981). Symmetry and reflexivity have been variously expanded and broadly shared in the sociology of science and technology (Wynne 1996a).

As noted earlier, while the traditional sociology of knowledge had argued for a sociological explanation of knowledge that specified its social origins instead of assuming a "social vacuum" in the explanation, science and technology have escaped the coverage of sociological explanation in the traditional sociology of knowledge. The "strong programme," despite roughness in some details, first challenged this limited scope, and laid the theoretical foundations for a new sociology of scientific knowledge (abbreviated to SSK), which accumulated detailed case studies on mathematics (Bloor 1976), pseudo-science (Wallis 1979), mathematical statistics (MacKenzie 1981), particle physics (Pickering 1984), natural philosophy (Shapin and Shaffer 1985), and others.

The Social Construction of Technology

Around the mid-1980s, a new sociological approach to technology arose that viewed technology as artefacts to be described and analyzed on an equal footing with science. This repudiated from an SSK perspective a long-standing and simplistic assumption that technology could be understood as a mere application of science (Barnes 1982). In particular, the thick description of the process by which one type of technology is singled out from multiple types of almost equal performance proliferated under the name "social construction of technology" or SCOT. A variety of technologies such as the inertial guidance system of nuclear missiles (Mackenzie 1990), bicycles (Bijker 1995), synthesizers (Pinch and Trocco 2004), simulation models to estimate the degree and range of nuclear bombing (Eden 2004), and others were brought under scrutiny by the SCOT perspective. Against the background of SCOT arguments together with a critical examination of social constructionism (Woolgar and Pawluch 1985; Hacking 1999), a criterion for evaluating work in the sociology of science and technology gradually emerged, which required researchers to use thick descriptions of a specific case to substantiate their sociological arguments and implications.

Actor Network Theory as an Alternative Framework

Another stream of thought has provided the sociology of science and technology with a different theoretical framework since the 1980s, namely, actor network theory (ANT). Though one of the earliest forms of ANT's core ideas originated in a laboratory study based on participant observation (Latour and Woolgar 1979), a clear formulation of its theoretical foundations appeared in the mid-1980s with reference to scallop-raising technologies (Callon 1986). According to Callon (1986), the "strong programme" principle of reflexivity is not consistently applied to sociological explanations of SSK and a kind of sociological imperialism ensues. ANT called for a new theoretical framework, giving science, technology, and society equal weight.

The following three principles constitute this new theoretical framework (Callon 1986; Latour 1991).

1) The principle of generalized reflexivity: An agnostic or skeptical attitude is applied to the social sciences, including sociology, in explaining society; no particular framework is given a privileged position as a way of explaining society; and an equal distance from any framework should be retained in the explanation.
2) The principle of generalized symmetry: Terminologies employed for describing science and technology should be consistently employed for describing society and vice versa.
3) The principle of *"libre association"*: Any kind of a priori distinction between natural and social events should be abolished; equally, any kind of a priori connection should be abolished in associating actors in nature with those in society.

Society resides in everything. So, there is no need to detect society externally as in the case of SSK identifying relevant social groups. For example, Callon, as an observer, found a social association among scallops, government researchers, scientists, and fishermen, with government researchers dynamically negotiating heterogeneous problems of the different actors (Callon 1986). ANT enables us to translate a microscopic description of research sites, such as laboratories, to a macrosociological description of society as a whole by explicating the working of networks of actors. Of course, the working of networks accompanies the transformation of meanings (*déplacement*), through the dynamics of the incessant boundary setting and resetting between nature and society.

Difference and Similarity Between the Sociology of Scientific Knowledge and Actor Network Theory

ANT's way of thinking is unique and also convenient in the sense that we are able to find society in any object taken up for investigation. It has generated intensive case studies, including those on bacteriology (Latour 1984), electrical vehicles (Callon 1986), underground control systems (Latour 1996[1993]), and jet engines (Law 2002). In the process of applying ANT to various exemplars, the so-called "epistemological chicken" dispute arose between SSK and ANT (Pickering 1992: part 2). At issue was the explanatory power of SSK and ANT. Considering that metaphysical elements are important constituents of ANT (Latour 2005: 50–51), the relative advantages of SSK and ANT for empirical investigation could be seen as arguable. In any event, the loose coupling of SSK and SCOT on the one hand, and ANT on the other, have formed the two major axes of the theoretical development in the field. The substantiation of theoretical frameworks by thick description has been a requirement for both frameworks to vindicate their capability.

Participatory Practices and New Complexities

In the mid-1990s, the participation of lay people in the decision-making processes at the science-technology-society interface became increasingly popular and introduced different standards, including bilateral communication, deliberation, and engagement with the interface. Complex problems with high degrees of uncertainty in the science-technology-society interface had arisen, for which it was difficult to provide unique or optimum solutions. Bioethics-related issues springing from genomic medical treatment, high-level radioactive waste disposal, and the regulation standards for toxic materials exemplify these problems. Because of the difficulties in providing singular solutions for highly complex problems that are global and very long-term, the problems became public and lay people were invited to participate in the decision-making.

Of course, the participation of lay people does not necessarily reduce uncertainty. On the contrary, there is even the possibility of inviting different sorts of process-related uncertainties, such as how to nominate lay persons as opposed to experts and vice versa, how to guarantee the representativeness of those who participate, how to secure appropriate relationships with bureaucrats, and others. When appropriate measures are not taken to address these new uncertainties, there is the possibility that the problems will become still more complicated.

Owing to these new complexities, a reflexive feedback loop came to accompany participatory practices to check the side-effects of these practices and to continuously amend them (Lin 2006; Irwin 2006; Evans and Plows 2007; Kerr et al. 2007; Rothstein 2007). In addition to the standard scholarly practices reaffirmed by theoretical frameworks such as SSK, SCOT, and ANT, and realized in thick description, the participatory practices that became popular in the 1990s have resulted in dynamic borders among research, policy, and participatory practices. The situation has generated greater flexibility among the channels linking science, technology, and society, including the opportunity to embrace a wider perspective at the science-technology-society interface (Wynne 1996b; Hess 2007), but also created risks, such as that envisaged by the "third wave" argument (Collins and Evans 2002; 2007).

The "Third Wave" Argument

The "third wave" argument has attracted wide attention in the sociology of science and technology and beyond. According to Collins and Evans (2002), wave 1 is the wave of positivism starting around 1950, and wave 2 is the wave of constructivism that began around 1970. They argue that wave 2 showed that wave 1 was "intellectually bankrupt" based on the sociological extension of the concept of under-determination (an indeterminate state where empirical evidence available at a given time may be essentially insufficient to validate scientific statements). In contrast, they argue, wave 3 is the application of wave 2 to social issues in the public sphere (namely, the "policy turn"). Wave 2 corresponds to the standard scholarly practices embodied in SSK, SCOT, and ANT mentioned above. In this sense, the standard practices can be said to have invited the "policy turn." Similarly, the sociological account of scientific and technical controversy through social factors in wave 2 corresponds to the participation of lay people in wave 3 in public disputes over expertise-related issues. According to the "third wave" argument, if expertise-related issues could be defined in such a relative manner, then it could regress downstream and eventually lead to a state in which there are "lay experts'" everywhere. Collins and Evans (2002) called this possibility the "expert's regress."

Collins and Evans (2002) maintain that there are cases where the engagement of "lay experts" is desirable and cases where it is undesirable, such as safety assessments by "lay experts" about the transportation of spent fuels from nuclear power plants. If it is generally assumed that the more participation by lay people the better, then who will take responsibility for damages incurred as a result of "lay experts'" participation? This is one of the most acute questions posed to all of us by the sociology of science and technology in the current context. There are a couple of mutually associated corollaries that are derived from this question: One is the need for sociological examination of the social construction of participation; the other is to carefully examine the possibility of mobilizing such participatory practices as a smokescreen to prevent something uncertain and delicate from being disclosed in the public sphere.

Beyond the "Third Wave": The Social Construction of Participation

With regard to the sociological examination of how participation is socially constructed, it is necessary to examine the assumption that roughly equates participation with something democratic. Intuition certainly tells us participation and democracy are correlated. Yet there is no a priori reason to believe that participation always guarantees democracy; participation could go hand-in-hand with techno-mass democracy, in which a particular stakeholder acts with legitimate self-interest by skillfully using various procedures of participatory decision-making, the results of which could be represented as the results of "social" decision-making.

From this point of view, the outcomes of participatory decision-making strongly depend on the social contexts in which the decision-making process is designed, implemented, and evaluated. Who can participate? Who is, in actual terms, excluded? Who are regarded as experts and/or lay citizens and by whom, and with regard to what? Who evaluates success or failure and in what respect? Furthermore, who subsidizes whom for what? It hardly needs saying that well-devised participatory procedures could enhance the quality of democracy and promote the public interest, while seemingly similar procedures could be a kind of a co-opting device, depending on the actual social settings of participatory experiments. For example, Café Scientifique provides public discussions and debates about science and technology with expert speakers and lay audiences in various non-scientific settings (such as cafés). The elucidation of the social process of participation and the formulation of new frameworks for designing social decision-making processes will provide important theoretical tasks for the future sociology of science and technology.

Beyond Double Under-Determination

If there is a possibility of under-determination of scientific knowledge as wave 2 argues, people are all the more likely to see the under-determination of the entire process of policy-making, implementation, and evaluation in the science-technology-society interface. This is not only because indeterminate scientific knowledge is one of the key elements involved in the process, but also because the process includes a different kind of under-determination of its own owing to factors of a different nature. These may include the delicate relationships between experts and lay people, the changing limits of budgets and the necessity of executing them within strict timelines, the need for face-saving in the public sphere, the particularistic interests of a specific public body, and others, which are usually fixed by implicit assumptions. This chapter calls the under-determination of scientific knowledge "type 1 under-determination," and all other under-determination involved in the process of policy-making, implementation, and evaluation—"type 2 under-determination" (see Figure 17.2).

Until now, this double under-determination has escaped the scholarly attention it deserves. The complicated situation owing to the double under-determination has been "black boxed" by appealing to dichotomies such as technocratic vs. participatory decision-making. As a result, the dichotomy has blurred the delicate realities of relationships between experts and laypeople such as the use of participatory practices as a smokescreen to prevent something sensitive from being disclosed publicly. The suppression of negative information under the name of communication activities before the Fukushima nuclear accident in 2011 is a telling example. Various communication activities to facilitate links between science, technology, and society had been carried out with public funds through Café Scientifique. However, there had been only one Café Scientifique held on anything nuclear (July 24, 2010) out of 253 carried out in the Tohoku District, which includes the Fukushima prefecture (and the topic discussed at the one event had nothing to do with any kind of risk from nuclear power plants) (Matsumoto 2014: 211). Thus participatory practices, which thus contributed to the myth of safety, and were supposed to facilitate links among science, technology, and society, in reality played no early-warning role against the Fukushima nuclear accident.

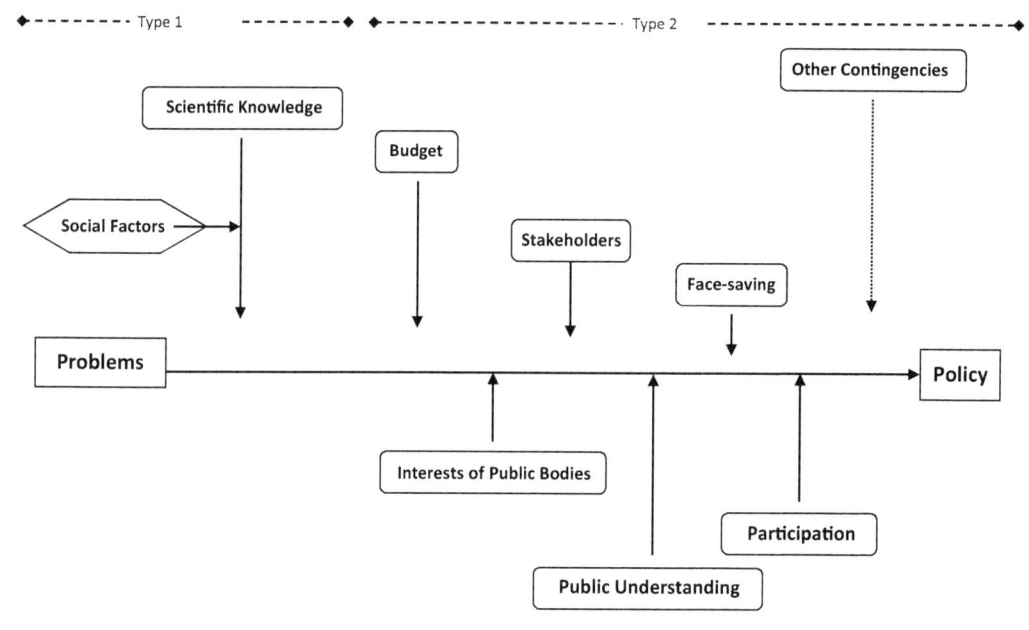

Figure 17.2. The Under-determination of Scientific Knowledge (Type 1) and That of Policy (Type 2)
Source: Matsumoto (2010)

To address this problem, in-depth elucidation of the hitherto unexplored realities of type 2 under-determination should be sought separately from those of type 1. How can this type of under-determination arise from the relationships between experts and lay people, the changing limits of budgets, the need for face-saving, and the particularistic interests of a public body? How are these issues handled in the social process of policy-making, implementation, and evaluation, and what kinds of assumptions and practices are involved? The sociology of science and technology should create frameworks that make it possible to investigate these questions.

Conclusion

This chapter makes four points regarding theoretical frameworks, issues, and insights of the sociology of science and technology, and their broader implications.

1) The sociology of science and technology covers three different units of investigation: the internal structure of the scientific and/or engineering community; the institutionalization process of science and technology; and the interaction of science, technology, and society. The interaction provides the theoretical foundation for examining internal structures and institutionalization because they determine the autonomy of science and technology on which the state of the internal structures and institutionalization depend.

2) The interaction of science, technology, and society has been described and analyzed by two theoretical frameworks: The first includes SSK and SCOT, which are broadly based on the principles of causality, impartiality, symmetry, and reflexivity; the second framework is ANT, which is based on the principle of generalized reflexivity, generalized symmetry, and *"libre association."* Because of their varying principles, a controversy between advocates for each of the two frameworks arose over their explanatory power, but the substantiation of theoretical frameworks by thick description became the common standard of scholars using either framework.

3) Participatory practices emerged during the 1990s. Whether participatory decision-making will lead us to democracy or techno-mass democracy remains an open-ended question, but elucidation of the social process of participation using standard scholarly practices and formulating new frameworks for designing social decision-making processes will be an important theoretical task for the future.

4) The realities of double underdetermination must be examined. If there is a possibility of the underdetermination of scientific knowledge, we are more likely to see the underdetermination of the entire process of policy-making, implementation, and evaluation at the science-technology-society interface. Formulation of the frameworks that make it possible to probe into such intricate realities provides another important analytic task for the future.

Based on these points, the delicate relationships between mutually incommensurable experiences and reason including science and technology have the foremost importance. For example, nationality, ethnicity, religion, gender, class, and heterogeneous sectors in a social system can generate invisible borders within which incommensurable experiences arise and breach the proper relationship to reason by making any of these experiences absolute and destroying common grounds for judgment and behavior in the public sphere. When coupled with hardships such as extreme events and/or wars, these invisible borders can break such proper relationships, which in turn can lead to the collapse of local or global social systems. The sociology of science and technology could play some role in the early detection of such a devastating possibility in the science-technology-society interface by demystifying both scientism and the absolutism of experiences. I hope people deploy their reason in this manner in the future.

References

Barnes, Barry. 1982. The Science-Technology Relationship: A Model and a Query. *Social Studies of Science* 12(2): 166–172.

Bijker, Wiebe E. 1995. *Of Bicycles, Bakelites, and Bulbs: Toward a Theory of Sociotechnical Change*. Cambridge MA: The MIT Press.

Bloor, David. 1976. *Knowledge and Social Imagery*. London: Routledge and Kegan Paul.

Callon, Michel. 1986. Éléments pour une sociologie de la traduction: la domestication des coquilles saint-jacques et des marins-pêcheurs dans la baie de saint-brieuc. *L'Année Sociologique* 36: 169–208.

Cohen, I. B. 1990. *Puritanism and the Rise of Modern Science: The Merton Thesis*. New Brunswick, NJ: Rutgers University Press.

Cole, J. and S. Cole. 1973. *Social Stratification in Science*. Chicago, IL: The University of Chicago Press.

Cole, J. and H. Zuckerman. 1975. The Emergence of a Scientific Specialty: The Self-Exemplifying Case of the Sociology of Science. In *The Idea of Social Structure: Papers in Honor of R. K. Merton*. Edited by L. Coser. New York, NY: Harcourt Brace Jovanovich, 139–174.

Cole, Stephen. 1992. *Making Science: Between Nature and Society*. Cambridge, MA: Harvard University Press.

Collins, Harry M. 1985. *Changing Order: Replication and Induction in Scientific Practice*. Chicago, IL: The University of Chicago Press.

Collins, Harry. M. and Rob Evans. 2002. The Third Wave of Science Studies: Studies of Expertise and Experience. *Social Studies of Science* 32(2): 235–296.

Collins, Harry. M. and Rob Evans. 2007. *Rethinking Expertise*. Chicago, IL: The University of Chicago Press.

Eden, Lynn. 2004. *Whole World on Fire: Organizations, Knowledge, and Nuclear Weapons Devastation*. Ithaca, NY: Cornell University Press.

Espeland, Wendy N. 1998. *The Struggle for Water: Politics, Rationality, and Identity in the American Southwest*. Chicago, IL: The University of Chicago Press.

Evans, Rob and A. Plows. 2007. Listening without Prejudice?: Re-Discovering the Value of the Disinterested Citizen. *Social Studies of Science* 37(6): 827–853.

Gieryn, Thomas H. 1999. *Cultural Boundaries of Science: Credibility on the Line*, Chicago, IL: The University of Chicago Press.

Hacking, Ian. 1999. *The Social Construction of What?*. Cambridge, MA: Harvard University Press.

Hess, David. 2007. *Alternative Pathways in Science and Industry: Activism, Innovation, and the Environment in an Era of Globalization*. Cambridge, MA: The MIT Press.

Irwin, A. 2006. The Politics of Talk: Coming to Terms with the "New" Scientific Governance. *Social Studies of Science* 36(2): 299–320.

Kerr, A., S. Cunningham-Burley, and R. Tutton. 2007. Shifting Subject Positions: Experts and Lay People in Public Dialogue. *Social Studies of Science* 37(3): 385–411.

Kuhn, Thomas S. 1962. *The Structure of Scientific Revolutions*. Chicago, IL: The University of Chicago Press.

Latour, Bruno. 1984. *Les Microbes: guerre et paix, suivi de Irreductions*. Paris: Editions A.-M. Metailie.

Latour, Bruno. 1991. *Nous n'avons jamais été modernes: essai d'anthropologie symétrique*. Paris: Editions La Découverte.

Latour, Bruno. 1996[1993]. *Aramis ou l'Amour des Techniques*. Paris. La Découverte. Translated by C. Porter, *Aramis or the Love of Technology*. Cambridge, MA. Harvard University Press.

Latour, Bruno. 2005. *Reassembling the Social: An Introduction to Actor-Network-Theory*. Oxford: Oxford University Press.

Latour, Bruno and Steve Woolgar. 1979. *Laboratory Life: The Construction of Scientific Facts*. Beverly Hills, CA: Sage.

Law, John. 2002. *Aircraft Stories: Decentering the Object in Technoscience*. Durham, NC: Duke University Press.

Lin, K. 2006. Inequalities, Knowledge and Public Deliberation: Three Consensus Conferences in Taiwan. Proceeding of EASTS Conference, 1–28.

Lynch, Michael, Simon A. Cole, Ruth McNally, and Kathleen Jordan. 2010. *Truth Machine: The Contentious History of DNA Fingerprinting*. Chicago, IL: The University of Chicago Press.

MacKenzie, Donald. 1981. *Statistics in Britain: 1865–1930*. Edinburgh: Edinburgh University Press.

MacKenzie, Donald. 1990. *Inventing Accuracy: A Historical Sociology of Nuclear Missile Guidance*. Cambridge, MA: The MIT Press.

Matsumoto, Miwao. 2010. Theoretical Challenges for the Current Sociology of Science and Technology: A Prospect for Its Future Development. *East Asian Science, Technology and Society: An International Journal* 4(1): 129–136.

Matsumoto, Miwao. 2014. The "Structural Disaster" of the Science-Technology-Society Interface. In *Reflections on the Fukushima Daiichi Nuclear Accident*. Edited by J. Ahn, C. Carson, M. Jensen, K. Juraku, S. Nagasaki, and S. Tanaka. Heidelberg: Springer, 189–215.

Merton, Robert K. 1936. The Unanticipated Consequences of Purposive Social Action. *American Sociological Review* 1: 894–904.

Merton, Robert K. 1938. Science, Technology and Society in Seventeenth Century England. *Osiris* IV(2): 360–632.

Merton, Robert K. 1970. *Science, Technology and Society in Seventeenth Century England*. New York, NY: Howard Fertig.

Moore, Kelly. 2008. *Disrupting Science: Social Movements, American Scientists, and the Politics of the Military, 1945–1975*. Princeton, NJ: Princeton University Press.

Mullins, Nicholas C. 1973. *Theories and Theory Groups in Contemporary American Sociology*. New York, NY: Harper and Row.

Pickering, Andrew. 1984. *Constructing Quarks: A Sociological History of Particle Physics*. Chicago, IL: The University of Chicago Press.

Pickering, Andrew. ed. 1992. *Science as Practice and Culture*. Chicago, IL: The University of Chicago Press.

Pinch, T. J. and F. Trocco. 2004. *Analog Days: The Invention and Impact of the Moog Synthesizer*. Cambridge, MA: Harvard University Press.

Rothstein, H. 2007. Talking Shops or Talking Turkey?: Institutionalizing Consumer Representation in Risk Regulation. *Science, Technology and Human Values* 32(5): 582–607.

Shapin, Steven. 1994. *A Social History of Truth: Civility and Science in Seventeenth-Century England*. Chicago, IL: The University of Chicago Press.

Shapin, Steven and Simon Schaffer. 1985. *Leviathan and the Air-Pump: Hobbes, Boyle and the Experimental Life*. Princeton, NJ: Princeton University Press.

Technology and Culture. 1991 Dialogue: Theory and Narrative in the History of Technology. *Technology and Culture* 32(2): 365–393.

Wallis, R. ed. 1979. *On the Margins of Science: The Social Construction of Rejected Knowledge*. London: Routledge and Kegan Paul.

Whitley, Richard D. 1972. Black Boxism and the Sociology of Science: A Discussion of the Major Development of the Field. In *The Sociological Review Monograph 18: The Sociology of Science*. Edited by P. Halmos and M. Albrow. Keele: University of Keele, 61–92.

Woolgar, Steve and D. Pawluch. 1985. Ontological Gerry-Mandering: The Anatomy of Social Problems Explanations. *Social Problems* 32(3): 214–227.

Wynne, Brian. 1996a. SSK's Identity Parade: Signing-Up and Off-and-on. *Social Studies of Science* 26(2): 357–391.

Wynne, Brian. 1996b. Misunderstood Misunderstandings: Social Identities and Public Uptake of Science. In *Misunderstanding Science?: The Public Reconstruction of Science and Technology*. Edited by A. Irwin and B. Wynne. Cambridge: Cambridge University Press, 19–46.

Zuckerman, H. 1977. *Scientific Elite: Nobel Laureates in the United States*. New York, NY: The Free Press.

The Sociology of Violence

Larry Ray

What is Violence?

The field of violence research is interdisciplinary, and theories range through the neurological, psychiatric, psychological, and criminological as well as sociological. This chapter discusses the contours of an emerging sociology of violence, although an interdisciplinary approach is unavoidable given the nature of this field. The sociology of violence is emerging (e.g., Ray 2011; Walby 2013; Kilby and Ray 2014) but the field is not integrated and there is debate about whether a "general theory of violence" is possible (Karstedt and Eisner 2009).

That the sociology of violence has developed somewhat late is curious in view of the persistence and significance of violence through known human history. This was perhaps because sociology, as Delanty (2001) points out, emerged in relatively peaceful times and was animated by a vision of social order within a world of internally pacified nation-states. Violence had been addressed by sociologists, of course, but mostly in relation to specific topics such as crime, domestic violence, war, conflict, and genocide (although the latter has not been of central concern to sociologists either, with a few exceptions, such as Zygmunt Bauman, Anthony Giddens, and Michael Mann).

Mary Jackman (2002: 387) commented that the sociological analysis of violence is divided into "disparate clusters of research on various forms of violence" that are "the object of urgent social concern" and that focus on violence that is "socially deviant and motivated by willful malice. The resulting literature is balkanized and disjointed, and yet narrowly focused." Looking toward a more comprehensive analysis, it is important to move away from this exclusive focus. Not only is most crime not violent but much violence is not criminal and is perpetrated by organizations such as states, armed forces, militias, and other authorities.

What, exactly, though, is violence? It is often described as "meaningless," although sociologists would generally say that it always has meaning to perpetrators, victims, and probably witnesses, too (Stanko 2003). While there are multiple definitions of violence, it seems clear in all of them that violence is normatively negative. To call something "violent," says Bäck (2004: 223), is "to give at least a prima facie reason why it is morally wrong." This in turn means that perpetrators of both "legitimate" and illegal violence will often appeal to normative justifications, which Ray et al. (2004) observed among racially motivated offenders. There are "minimalist conceptions" that limit the term to actual physical harm (e.g., Collins 2008) and more "comprehensive" conceptions that include aggression, threats and psychological harm (Jackman 2002). The former is criticized for ignoring the wider social and psychological effects of violence, while Collins argues that since most aggressive confrontations do not result in violence it is essential to maintain a distinction between the two. Then, there is Galtung's (1969) wider concept of "structural violence" as physical and psychological harm that results from exploitive and unjust social, political, and economic systems that prevent people from realizing their potential.

A further distinction is often made between instrumental and expressive violence (e.g., Wieviorka 2009: 35 and 88–89). Instrumental violence is generally limited to a specific goal, such as obtaining money by threats, while expressive violence is performed for intrinsic gratification, such as hate crime, where terrorization of the victim is the end in itself. McDevitt et al.'s (2002) famous typology of hate crime offenders distinguishes violence that is defensive (to "protect neighborhoods") and retaliatory (a response to an actual or rumored incident) from expressive violence motivated by a "mission" ("to rid the world of evil"). A similar picture emerges from Topalli's (2004) account of the "hardcore street offending" and Bourgois's (2003) ethnography of East Harlem crack cocaine dealers where violence is an ingrained way of life – albeit one in which many feel trapped.

Expressive violence performed for the enjoyment of domination and cruelty is potentially more unlimited than instrumental violence. However, the distinction has been criticized, since in practice the two are often combined. Violence might involve a heightened state of affective arousal, a "high" even if it is aimed at instrumental gain, such as a robbery (Levi and Maguire 2002: 811). Even so, the analytical distinction is useful in identifying different patterns of violence – even if both are likely to be present in many empirical instances.

Trends and Debates

The sociological understanding of violence addresses fundamental questions about the nature of humanity, evil, and civilization. While it is often claimed that we are living in an exceptionally violent age (e.g., Unger et al. 2002), there is the contrary view that, as Steven Pinker claims, there has been a historical "decline of violence" that is "visible at the scale of millennia, centuries, decades, and years." He argues that this decline applies over several orders of magnitude – from genocide to war to rioting and from homicide to the treatment of children and animals. Indeed, he says, "we may be living in the most peaceable era in our species' existence" Pinker (2012: xix). Although this thesis is not particularly new and draws heavily (if selectively) on Norbert Elias's theory of the "civilizing process," it has stimulated wide debate. Elias and Pinker evoke control theories that see aggressive and violent impulses as innate ("most of us – including you, dear reader – are wired for violence" Pinker 2012: 483) but gradually moderated by complex socio-psychological bonds.

Elias's work has been influential in the sociology of violence, and Pinker (2012: 82) regards his own work as providing empirical support.[1] Elias described the history of the growth of mannered social interactions (e.g., eating with cutlery, not spitting, defecating or having sex in public) and state formation from the medieval to modern periods.

---

[1] Although Pinker seems to think he has discovered Elias ("the most important thinker you've never heard of" (Pinker 2012: 72)) and since Elias accumulated considerable evidence himself this claim is rather condescending.

He aimed to "historicize Freud" and show that the conflict between civilization and instincts is not timeless but rather has evolved historically, especially through the extension of "figurations." These are long distance communications between people that involve increased inter-human empathy through which people are obliged to attune their actions to those of others. The consequential pacification of everyday life molded "affects and instincts" (Elias 1994: 201), resulting in more self-controlled behavior. This also required "functional democratization" through which the lower classes were included in the legal and political system while the upper classes became subject to it. So, for example, rioting and dueling, respectively, ceased to be frequent means of resolving conflicts (see also Cooney 2015).

With social pacification, there is an expansion of civilian society and decline in the role of the warrior/military caste. However, Elias emphasized the fragility of this process, which, as in Nazi Germany, could enter a "decivilizing downswing" (Elias 1996).[2] The latter possibility is rather understated in Pinker but both agree that this transition entailed complex social, cultural, and psychological changes along with new sensibilities, especially rising thresholds of repugnance toward interpersonal violence and public displays of cruelty, such as public torture and executions. Compassion was generalized beyond people's immediate circles and by the eighteenth century movements in Europe and the United States, such as anti-slavery campaigns, aimed to alleviate the suffering of others near and far (Wilson and Brown 2015). This decline in violence was for Pinker the consequence of what are essentially value shifts during this period known as the "Humanitarian Revolution," "Age of Reason and Enlightenment," and the "Rights Revolution."

The claim that the modern world is less violent than in the past might appear counter-factual. But evidence can be sought in falling numbers and mortality rates in wars and civil conflicts in the later twentieth century (Lacina and Gleditsch 2005) and in other multiple sources, including the transnational decline in homicide (see also Eisner 2001; Ray 2011: 126–134; and Spierenburg 1994) and generally falling crime rates in OECD countries since the 1990s (Levitt 2004).[3] However, the crucial and in many ways most problematic measure Pinker uses is battle death in proportion to the population. So he suggests that the "hemoclysm" or bloodbath of the twentieth century, when 0.7 per cent of the world's population (40 million) died in battles, would have risen to 6 billion had the death rate been comparable to warfare in say Papua, New Guinea (Pinker 2012: 57ff). Pinker gives considerable weight to this ratio which will always serve his argument since the global population rose exponentially in the twentieth century and by 2000 was six times that of 1800.

However, by contrast, Malešević (2013) argues that war is novel in human development, having emerged around 3,000 years ago in sedentary, stratified societies with social hierarchies. Further, the twentieth century was the bloodiest period in human history with 200 million deaths, including deaths in the Holocaust, Soviet Gulag, and Mao's "Great Leap Forward." While there was a sharp decline in inter-state war in the later twentieth century, contemporary war is decentralized, less focused on territory, often does not distinguish between civilians and combatants, and (with the rise of paramilitary states) has a looser monopoly over the means of violence. Further, while the need to finance war through the tax-revenue base can impose limits on state wars (for example the UK and US's decisions to withdraw from Iraq and Afghanistan) modern wars are often rentier wars in which the violence itself is a means of accumulation

---

[2] He also argues that in Germany the civilizing process was arrested because of the initial failure of state formation in the seventeenth century and subsequent unification under the warrior cast (Prussian aristocracy) in 1871, compounded by the consequences of defeat in 1918.

[3] Although these are fairly short-term, not epochal changes, and could be reversed even if Pinker thinks this unlikely (Pinker 2012: 366).

and will therefore become self-sustaining. Examples might be wars between drug cartels in South America or ISIS in Iraq and Syria, which "has zealously acquired and guarded the assets that generate money" (Tripp 2015).

The decline of violence thesis focuses on battle deaths although the processes whereby in 2015 around 60 million people have become stateless refugees from conflict, dispossession, and unsustainable environments, which Sasson (2014: 221) calls a "savage sorting," are also forms of global violence. Malešević (2015) further argues that Pinker's methodology is flawed – he is not comparing like with like (pre-modern and contemporary violence), and historical statistics are unreliable and often exaggerate death tolls. Moreover, recent social "pacification" in the United States and the United Kingdom has a "dark side" in the steep growth in the percentage of the population imprisoned, including non-criminal detainees, such as asylum-seekers (Hall 2015; HM Inspectorate of Prisons 2015).

Zones of Violence

These debates raise questions about the relationship between violence, social control, and social structures. Control theories (see also Gottfredson and Hirschi 1990) claim that violent proclivities are deeply embedded but ameliorated through socialization such that attachments to family, school, and peers keep people from committing crimes. While there is some validity in this, the implication that individuals are inherently asocial and therefore require restraint by external controls obscures the extent to which violence and society are entwined. Violence is not simply an eruption of animal passions but has symbolic and ritual meanings. Elias famously refers to Midsummer's Eve live cat burning festivals in sixteenth-century France, which he saw simply as amusements for the gratification of cruelty (2001: 171). However, as Keith Tester (2004: 68–69) argues, this violence had meanings that were complexly rooted in cultural difference and the social meaning of cats in early modern Europe. Further, Elias did not consider the possible sacrificial significance of summoning the social presence through violent public rituals (Ray 2013) and Foucault (1976) has shown how public spectacles of violence have social and political meanings and cannot therefore be reduced to unleashed displays of primal affects.

Other sociologists have drawn attention to the types of social configuration conducive to creating zones of violence and here, too, the influence of Elias often remains evident. Messner et al. (2008) attribute urban violence to the marketization of public goods, which generates social marginalization, loss of social bonds, egoistic individualism, loss of empathy, and high risk taking – all of which are conducive to higher levels of violence. Helmut Thome (2007) melds Elias and Durkheim with Habermas to account for rising homicide in the 1970s–1980s. He focuses on factors such as weakening of the state's monopoly of violence, neoliberal globalization that erodes the state's tax basis, rising inequality and social marginalization, a shift from "cooperative individualism" to "disintegrative individualism," and *Entgrenzung*, that is, dissolution of boundaries between public and private – all of which reduce sensitivity to vulnerability and capacities for self-control.

One advantage of these approaches is that they offer ways of understanding the highly differentiated patterns of violence on macro- and micro-levels, first analyzed by the ecological urban sociology of the Chicago School in the 1920s. Subsequently a "second wave" of ecological studies (Hayward 2004: 98) has involved identifying "hot spots," that is, areas that have a greater than average number of criminal events, or areas where people have a higher than average risk of victimization. In economically abandoned areas of UK cities, the rate of recorded violence quadrupled between 1960 and 2000 (Rosen 2003: 33), and Castells (1998: 138) argues that there is a systematic relationship between the structural transformations of capital, post-industrialism, the growing dereliction of the ghetto, and the emergence of a global, yet decentralized criminal economy. The resultant spatial patterning of this is complex since, according to Soja (2000: 265), the "older polarities have not disappeared, but a much more polymorphous and fractured social geometry has taken shape" (Soja 2000: 265). Similarly, Parker (2008) attributes the spatial patterns of recorded violent crime as linked to changing socio-economic stratification that had differential impacts on urban space and ethnicity.

With reference to Chicago, Loïc Wacquant (2004) similarly describes "hyperghettoization" following neoliberal restructuring in the later twentieth century, which created highly racialized patterns of spatial exclusion, a collapse of structures of political representation, isolation from extended networks, and a rise of drugs trade, sex work, itinerant hawkers, and low paid casual work. This "hyperghetto" became a "dumping ground for supernumerary" people for whom society had no economic or political use entailing de-pacification and the growth of a "culture of terror"(Wacquant 2004: 113).

Actors and Subjects

Explanations of spatial concentrations of violence should incorporate an understanding of agency and the emergence of affective responses to structural conditions. One cannot move directly from objective analysis of socio-economic conditions to a subjective understanding of practices (Wieviorka 2009: 103). It may not be the existence of inequality in itself that stimulates crime and violence in deprived areas, in which the majority of inhabitants are not violent. Collins (2008: 2–3) insists that whatever remote background factors may lie behind violent actions, it is patterns of "confrontation, tension and emotional flow" that define situations of violent confrontation. Further, Collins (2009) claims structural explanations are "useless in explaining violence on the other side of the law, such as police violence, military snipers, ace pilots, not to mention upper-class carousing."

Moreover, violence entails processes – of mirroring, spirals, and dissipation. Collins argues that humans are "hardwired" for social solidarity which means that violence is difficult, at an interpersonal level often incompetently done, and most conflict goes no further than blustering gestures and words. Actual violence involves overcoming inhibitions and what he calls the confrontation-tension fear (*ct/f*) barrier. Detailed analysis of the body language and facial expressions of people in violent situations, he claims, shows that fear rather than aggression is the dominant emotion and that confrontations are likely to tip into violence only through a process of mutual entrainment, that is, synchronizing to each other's emotional rhythm. Thus "successful violence" (on both sides of the law) requires expertise in a number of pathways that reduce *ct/f* and allow the attacker to gain dominance in attention space. These include:

- attacking the weak – e.g., bullies and many street robberies;
- audience-oriented – e.g., where a few individuals are prominent in riots and "play to the crowd";
- remote violence – e.g., much of modern warfare such as the use of drones;
- deception – concealing intent, as with "hit men" and army snipers;
- acquiring techniques to overcome *ct/f* such as "feeling comfortable" with being a habitual abuser.

What is clear though is that despite the *ct/f* barrier, violence can be enjoyable for those who perpetrate it, especially during a temporary relaxation of conventional constraints, which Collins calls a "moral holiday" of carousing and bravado. Weenink (2013) suggests that in these situations, typified by riots, there is a "decontrolled solidarity" where behavior is guided more by the group than by internal monitoring. The process of entrainment can spiral into "forward panic," which involves intense emotional arousal – rage, frenzy, elation, "roaring down a tunnel," and lack of control (Collins 2008: 91–94). As people enter into an antagonistic interactional situation, their fear/tension is heightened and these emotions at first block violence but heightened arousal can be suddenly released in a state that "resembles panic" but "instead of running away...the fighters rush forward, toward their enemy" (Collins 2008: 85). In this state of arousal people might commit extreme violence and atrocities, although these can also occur as a result of direct orders from authorities. "Forward panic" might be short-lived, as in troops entering the heat of battle or last for the remainder of the perpetrator's life – as when "rampage shooters" end their mass killing by committing suicide.

Although this might appear to be an overly psychological rather than sociological theory of violence, Collins insists that the crucial factor is the interaction sequences between participants rather than individual states of mind. One limitation, however, is the implication that violence arises only or largely from the situational dynamics of the act, which pays less attention to violent predispositions. Winlow (2015) has shown how violent men sustain "a form of subjectivity that understands itself principally in relation to violence." Based on ethnographic work in economically depressed urban areas in Northern England, he found that the experience of traumatic events and prolonged periods of insecurity during childhood, set against a cultural background which values violent responses to perceived humiliation, can act to create a deep commitment to physical violence. This approach resonates with Thomas Scheff's shame theory, which claims that while shame is part of the "social glue" that binds social relations, since most human actions involve the anticipation of potential shame, it is also painful for the self and can be repressed (unacknowledged). Relationships in which unacknowledged shame is embedded typically go through cycles of anger and alienation/withdrawal – and can erupt into violence. Those who experience unacknowledged shame are, they claim, more prone than those who do not to commit acts of violence (e.g., Scheff and Retzinger 2001).[4]

Intimacy, Gender, and Violence

Violence is embedded in gendered systems of power. Scheff identifies gendered pathways through shame in the forms of passive internalized violence/depression and active externalization. Thus "Hypermasculine men are silent about their feelings to the point of repressing them altogether" which leads to "silence or withdrawal" or acting out anger (Scheff 2006). The well-known association between masculinity and violence is often explained by sociologists in terms of gender socialization in which men may learn to affirm positive self-concepts through aggression, which reflect wider structures of patriarchal power. Reflecting the "performative turn" in social sciences and humanities, and rather than viewing gendered behavior as fixed, Connell and Messerschmidt's (2005) theory of "hegemonic masculinities" emphasizes the central role of performance and choice. In this context, violent behavior is *chosen* while actors call upon dominant discourses of masculinity for support and legitimation, which will manifest differently in social situations structured by race, class, and age. So, while middle-class boys might "achieve" masculinity through academic success, sports, and preparation for a career, less privileged boys develop an "opposition masculinity" that demonstrates to peers dominance, control, and aggressiveness. This approach restores agency to actors and avoids various types of determinism. It has been criticized, however, as inadequately explaining violence perpetrated by women or, for that matter, why most men are not violent (see Miller 2002; Ray 2011: 88–91).

Violence entails what Appadurai (1998) calls a "grotesque intimacy" in that it

---

[4] Readers might want to visit Scheff's website www.soc.ucsb.edu/faculty/scheff/ which posts a large number of papers.

involves intrusion in and opening of the body. It is, further, frequently perpetrated by and against intimates, as with violence against women and children within the family (Walby 2013). Reported domestic violence varies considerably worldwide and definitions vary considerably too, along with levels of culturally accepted violence (Krug et al. 2002: 87–122). Sociological explanations include gendered socialization, family conflict (Gelles 1997), family histories of abuse and violence (Gadd 2002), and gendered power relations. As with many other forms of violence, there is an association between the incidence of reported domestic violence and low socio-economic status (Finney 2006; Walby and Allen 2004). These accounts do not explain middle-class domestic violence (Pahl et al. 2004) and explanations need to account for ways in which structures of socio-economic and patriarchal power intersect.

In war, sexual violence is a common tool of torture as the body becomes a "necrographic map" of intimate brutality and enactment of ethno-patriarchal power (Appadurai 1998). The grotesque intimacy of violence is increasingly made public through communication technologies, one infamous example being the images of Abu Ghraib torture and prisoner abuse. This exposure represents a newly public violence. Mendible (2005: 60) points out that although the systematic use of women's bodies as tactical warfare is not new, "mediated images of rape and humiliation are now part of the arsenal of war" and are "used to transact power and control." Conquest and dominance over the enemy, she says, is enacted on women's bodies, not to achieve a direct military aim but to create spectacles of humiliation and violence for mass consumption.

War, Genocide, and the State

While the state's monopoly of the means of force might be part of the civilizing process, states are clearly agents of violence too and totalitarian states have enacted mass violence against their own citizens. Whereas Elias (and later Pinker) identify modernity with a decline of violence, Bauman's (1989) account of the Holocaust argued that mass extermination was precisely *made possible* by modern technologies and the bureaucratic separation between actions and moral reasoning. While this thesis has been very influential, it does not explain all aspects of the Holocaust (Ray 2011: 169–190) nor the particular circumstances in which genocide occurs. As Waller (2002) notes, since most societies do not commit genocide and most people do not become genocidal killers, there is a tendency to look for its source in particularities of those peoples who do perpetrate "extraordinary evil." But again more differentiated explanations are required.

The greatest catastrophes occur (as Elias might have said) with the dissolution of distinctions between military and criminal conduct, between civility and barbarity, and when political or ethnic groups embrace collective violence against a defenseless victim group as "warfare." Gerlach (2010) argues that extreme violence depends on broad and diverse support from the authorities but also a range of other factors. These include a loss of the state's monopoly of violence, a temporary state of crisis, a drastic drop in living standards, new groups having ascended to elites, a transformation of the countryside, forced decline of middlemen minorities who are accused of being linked to foreign interests, and violence both from "above," from state agents, and "below," from local militias. Further, foreign armies induce violence in societies that were often ridden with ethnic, religious, and class conflicts. Seen in these terms, mass violence is a social event of crisis and panic in which ethical norms and values are devalidated and social polarization offers perpetrators new solidarity through participation in atrocities. Public spectacles of violence serve to constitute and dramatize a new moral hegemony and power of the social order. From the point of view of these broader sociological and historical studies, mass violence can be a consequence of multiple factors that need to be understood in particular historical contexts but nonetheless permit comparisons among different instances.

Conclusions

The emerging sociology of violence attempts to explain the social, historical, and spatial differentiation of patterns of violence while engaging with the central sociological problem of reconciling analysis of agency and structures. While there is no general theory of violence, and there may never be one, it is clear that violence requires differential explanations. There is disagreement about dominant trends in violence and how these should be explained. What is clear, though, is that sociology situates violence within social systems of power and hierarchy that are always gendered. Moreover, while violence has a structural context, violence is always enacted, always done to someone, and is never passive. Explanations are incomplete, then, unless they also connect with actors engaged in social processes. The sociology of violence throws into relief some of the core problems of sociology and the meaning and fate of modernity and civilization.

References

Appadurai, Arjun. 1998. Dead Certainty: Ethnic Violence in the Era of Globalization. *Public Culture* 10 2: 225–247.

Bäck, Allan. 2004. Thinking Clearly About Violence. *Philosophical Studies* 117: 219–30.

Bauman, Zygmunt. 1989. *Modernity and the Holocaust*. Cambridge: Polity Press.

Bourgois, Phillipe. 2003. *In Search of Respect*. Cambridge: Cambridge University Press.

Castells, Manuel. 1998. *End of Millennium: The Information Age: Economy, Society and Culture*. Vol. 3. Oxford: Blackwell.

Collins, Randall. 2008. *Violence: A Micro-Sociological Theory*. Princeton, NJ: Princeton University Press.

Collins, Randall. 2009. Micro and Macro Causes of Violence. *International Journal of Conflict and Violence*. 3(1): 9–22.

Connell, Raewyn and James Messerschmidt. 2005. Hegemonic Masculinity – Rethinking the Concept. *Gender and Society*. 19(6): 829–59.

Cooney, Mark. 2015. Family Honour and Social Time. In *Violence and Society – Toward a New Sociology*. Edited by Jane Kilby and Larry Ray, New York, NY: Wiley-Blackwell, 87–106.

Delanty, Gerard. 2001. Cosmopolitanism and Violence: The Limits of Global Civil Society. *European Journal of Social Theory*. 4(1): 41–52.

Eisner, Manuel. 2001. Modernization, Self-Control and Lethal Violence: The Long-term Dynamics of European Homicide Rates in Theoretical Perspective. *British Journal of Criminology*. 41(4): 618–638.

Elias, Norbert. 1994. *The Civilizing Process*. Oxford: Blackwell.

Elias, Norbert. 1996. *The Germans*. New York, NY: University of Colombia Press.

Elias, Norbert. 2001. *Society of Individuals*. London: Continuum.

Finney, Andrea. 2006. Domestic Violence, Sexual Assault and Stalking: Findings from the 2004/05 British Crime Survey. Home Office Online Report 12/06. Available at http://webarchive.nationalarchives.gov.uk/20110218135832/http://rds.homeoffice.gov.uk/rds/pdfs06/rdsolr1206.pdf, accessed November 30, 2016.

Foucault, Michel. 1976. *Discipline and Punish*. London: Allen Lane.

Gadd, David. 2002. Masculinities and Violence against Female Partners. *Social and Legal Studies*. 11: 61–80.

Galtung, Johan. 1969. Violence, Peace and Peace Research, *Journal of Peace Research*. 6(3): 167–191.

Gelles, Richard. J. 1997. *Intimate Violence in Families*. London: Sage.

Gerlach, Christian. 2010. *Extremely Violent Societies: Mass Violence in the Twentieth Century World*. Cambridge: Cambridge University Press.

Gottfredson, Michael R. and Travis Hirschi. 1990. *A General Theory of Crime*. Stanford, CA: Stanford University Press.

Hall, Steve. 2015. The Socioeconomic Function of Evil. In *Violence and Society – Toward a New Sociology*. Edited by Jane Kilby and Larry Ray. New York, NY: Wiley-Blackwell, 13–31.

Hayward, Keith. 2004. *City Limits: Crime, Consumer Culture and the Urban Experience*. London: Glass House Press.

HM Inspectorate of Prisons. 2015. HM Chief Inspector of Prisons for England and Wales Annual Report 2014–2015. Available at www.justiceinspectorates.gov.uk/hmiprisons/wp-content/uploads/sites/4/2015/07/HMIP-AR_2014-15_TSO_Final1.pdf, accessed December 1, 2016.

Jackman, Mary. 2002. Violence in Social Life. *Annual Review of Sociology* 28(1): 387–415.

Karstedt, Susanne and Manuel Eisner. 2009. Is a General Theory of Violence Possible? *International Journal of Conflict and Violence* 3(1): 4–8.

Kilby, Jane and Larry Ray. 2014. Introduction. *Sociological Review* 62: 1–12.

Krug, Etienne G., Linda L. Dahlberg, James A. Mercy, Anthony B. Zwi, and Rafael Lozano. 2002. World Report on Violence and Health. WHO Report. Available at http://apps.who.int/iris/bitstream/10665/42495/1/9241545615_eng.pdf, accessed November 30, 2016.

Lacina, Bethany and Nils Petter Gledistch. 2005. Monitoring Trends in Global Combat: A New Dataset of Battle Deaths. *European Journal of Population* 21(2-3): 145–166.

Levi, Michael and Mike Maguire. 2002. Violent Crime. In *Oxford Handbook of Criminology*. Edited by M. Maguire, R. Morgan and R. Reiner. Oxford: Oxford University Press, 795–843.

Levitt, Steven D. 2004. Understanding Why Crime Fell in the 1990s: Four Factors that Explain the Decline and Six that Do Not. *Journal of Economic Perspectives* 18(1): 163–190.

Malešević, Sinisa. 2013. Forms of Brutality: Towards a Historical Sociology of Violence. *European Journal of Social Theory* 16(3): 273–291.

Malešević, Sinisa. 2015. Is War Becoming Obsolete? A Sociological Analysis. In *Violence and Society – Toward a New Sociology*. Edited by Jane Kilby and Larry Ray. New York, NY: Wiley-Blackwell, 65–86.

McDevitt, Jack, Jack Levin, and Susan Bennett. 2002. Hate Crime Offenders: An Expanded Typology, *Journal of Social Issues* 58: 303–317.

Mendible, Myra. 2005. Dominance and Submission in Postmodern War Imagery. *Peace Review: A Journal of Social Justice* 17: 55–63.

Messner, Steven F., Helmut Thome, and Richard Rosenfeld. 2008. Institutions, Anomie, and Violent Crime: Clarifying and Elaborating Institutional-Anomie Theory. *International Journal of Conflict and Violence* 2(2): 163–181.

Miller, Jody. 2002. The Strengths and Limits of "Doing Gender" for Understanding Street Crime. *Theoretical Criminology* 6(4): 433–460.

Pahl, Jan., Claudia Hasanbegovic, and Mei-Kuei Yu. 2004. Globalisation and Family Violence. In *Global Social Problems and Global Social Policy*. Edited by Vic George and R. Page. Cambridge: Polity Press, 142–159.

Parker, Karen F. 2008. *Unequal Crime Decline*. Albany, NY: New York University Press.

Pinker, Steven. 2012. *The Better Angels of Our Nature: A History of Violence and Humanity*. London: Penguin.

Ray, Larry J. 2011. *Violence and Society*. London: Sage.

Ray, Larry J. 2013. Mark of Cain – Shame, Desire and Violence. *European Journal of Social Theory* 16(3): 292–309.

Ray, Larry J., David Smith, and Elizabeth Wastell. 2004. Shame, Rage and Racist Violence. *British Journal of Criminology* 44: 350–368.

Rosen, Andrew. 2003. *The Transformation of British Life, 1950–2000: A Social History*. Manchester: Manchester University Press.

Sasson, Saskia. 2014. *Expulsions*. Cambridge: Polity.

Scheff, Thomas J. 2006. Hypermasculinity and Violence as a Social System. Available at http://uwf.edu/dearle/cold%20war/hypermasculine.pdf, accessed November 30, 2016.

Scheff, Thomas J. and Suzannem Retzinger. 2001. *Emotions and Violence: Shame and Rage in Destructive Conflicts*. Lexington, MD: Lexington Books.

Soja, Edward. 2000. *Postmetropolis: Critical Studies of Cities and Regions*. Oxford: Blackwell.

Spierenburg, Pieter. 1994. Faces of Violence: Homicide Trends and Cultural Meanings: Amsterdam, 1431–1816. *Journal of Social History* 27(4): 701–716.

Stanko, Elizabeth. ed. 2003. *The Meanings of Violence*. London: Routledge.

Tester, Keith. 2004. *Animals and Society*. London: Routledge.

Thome, Helmut. 2007. Explaining the Long-term Trend in Violent Crime: A Heuristic

Scheme and Some Methodological Considerations. *International Journal of Conflict and Violence* 1(2): 185–202.

Topalli, Volkan. 2004. The Seductive Nature of Autotelic Crime: How Neutralization Theory Serves as Boundary Condition for Understanding Hardcore Street Offending. *Sociological Inquiry* 76(4): 475–501.

Tripp, Charles. 2015. IS: The Rentier Caliphate with No New Ideas. Available at www.alaraby.co.uk/english/politics/2015/2/8/is-the-rentier-caliphate-with-no-new-ideas, accessed November 30, 2016.

Unger, Mark, Sally Avery Bermanzohn, and Kenton Worcester. 2002. Introduction. In *Violence and Politics: Globalization's Paradox*. Edited by K. Worcester, S. Bermanzohn and M. Ungar. London: Routledge, 1–12.

Wacquant, Loïc. 2004. Decivilizing and Demonizing: The Weakening of the Black American Ghetto. In *The Sociology of Norbert Elias*. Edited by S. Loyal and S. Quilley. Cambridge: Cambridge University Press, 95–121.

Walby, Sylvia. 2013. Violence and Society: Introduction to an Emerging Field of Sociology. *Current Sociology* 61(2): 95–111.

Walby, Sylvia and Jonathan Allen. 2004. Domestic Violence, Sexual Assault and Stalking: Findings from the British Crime Survey. Home Office Research Study 276. Available at http://womensaidorkney.org.uk/wp-content/uploads/2014/08/Home-office-research.pdf, accessed November 30, 2016.

Waller, James. 2002. *Becoming Evil: How Ordinary People Commit Genocide and Mass Murder*. Oxford: Oxford University Press.

Weenink, Don. 2013. Decontrolled by Solidarity: Understanding Recreational Violence in Moral Holidays. *Human Figurations* 2(3). Available at http://hdl.handle.net/2027/spo.11217607.0002.305/, accessed November 30, 2016.

Wieviorka, Michel. 2009. *Violence – A New Approach*. London: Sage.

Wilson, Richard A. and Richard D. Brown. eds. 2015. *Humanitarianism and Suffering: The Mobilization of Empathy*. Cambridge: Cambridge University Press.

Winlow, Simon. 2015. Trauma, Guilt and the Unconscious: Some Theoretical Notes on Violent Subjectivity. In *Violence and Society – Toward a New Sociology*. Edited by Jane Kilby and Larry Ray. New York, NY: Wiley-Blackwell, 32–49.

Environmental Justice

David N. Pellow

Environmental Justice is the "principle that all people and communities are entitled to equal protection of environmental and public health laws and regulations" (Bullard 1996: 495). Scholars generally agree that the movement for environmental justice (EJ) in the United States began in the early 1980s when communities of color began rising up in protest against locally unwanted land uses (LULUs) such as landfills, incinerators, waste treatment plants, mines, petrochemical plants, coal-fired power plants, and other polluting industrial facilities. These facilities were viewed as an eyesore, a threat to public health, and an example of what happens when institutional racism takes on an environmental manifestation, something activists termed environmental racism.

The EJ Movement

The EJ movement drew on the ideas, tactics, strategies, frames, and participants of numerous social movements that predated it, including the civil rights and human rights, public health and anti-toxics, labor, and indigenous sovereignty movements (Cole and Foster 2001). Thus, they signed petitions, led marches, held organizing conferences, filed lawsuits, and staged sit-ins with the aim of: (1) preventing the establishment of particularly hazardous industries in vulnerable communities; (2) reducing the volume of pollution emitted from various existing industries or negotiating other reforms (such as economic benefits and multilingual public warning systems during industrial accidents) through citizen-worker participation in management decision-making; (3) shutting down offending facilities; and (4) articulating a vision of change that fused environmental sustainability and social justice (i.e., EJ), a model of a society in which humans and other species could coexist in relationships of mutual respect and integrity (see e.g., Bullard 2000; Gottlieb 1994). Finally, EJ movement activists suspected that LULUs were being unfairly and disproportionately located in working class and people of color communities. Scholars later confirmed this suspicion when studying the spatial proximity of LULUs and community demographics (see below).

The EJ movement was soon recognized as a transnational and global social movement, as activists, organizations, and networks from Asia, Latin America, Africa, the Arctic, Australia, Europe, Canada, and the United States collaborated to share information and resources to confront environmental hazards that threatened domestic communities of color and indigenous peoples and those that crossed national borders and threatened humanity and the biosphere. By the 1990s and 2000s, transnational EJ movement networks were targeting myriad global EJ issues including mining, incineration and solid waste, agriculture, electronics, hydroelectric power, energy, free trade, climate change, and many others (Pellow 2007).

While the EJ movement is a relatively new phenomenon, the problems of environmental racism and injustice are not. The centuries-long process of European colonization and conquest of indigenous communities and lands in the global South can be understood as a form of environmental racism if we broaden the often restrictive definition of this concept (Du Bois 1977[1935]). For example, the theft of land and displacement of native peoples in "the New World" could be said to constitute an environmental injustice. Moreover, the recognition and resistance against environmental inequalities by ordinary people extends deep into human history (Mizelle 2014).

The Development and Growth of EJ Studies

Beginning in the 1980s and 1990s, EJ studies grew as an interdisciplinary field in the United States – and later globally – as scholars recognized and gathered evidence of the highly uneven impacts of industrialization and environmental policy-making across the social landscape. Specifically, scholars found that race, class, nationality, and geography seemed to play a powerful role in the location of environmental and industrial hazards and the level of enforcement of environmental laws. Since the beginning, many EJ studies have been undertaken as a response to requests, inquiries, and demands by non-academic community leaders who suspected discriminatory hazardous facility siting practices and uneven government enforcement against violators of environmental laws. So, while scholars have documented the broad trends of environmental racism and inequality, in many cases that research was a reaction to the grassroots EJ movement's calls for such studies.

Much of the work of EJ studies scholars centers on the documentation of disproportionate environmental and/or industrialized hazards facing various populations. Countless studies conclude that communities with high percentages of people of color, low-income residents, indigenous persons, and immigrants are disproportionately exposed to environmental risks through residential proximity, via the location of schools, and through other spatial organizational relationships (see e.g., Crowder and Downey 2010). More recently, research by scholars exploring the concept of food justice and food justice movements finds that many of the same populations confronting toxic and industrial hazards in the United States and globally are also frequently vulnerable to a lack of access to healthy, nutritious, affordable, culturally appropriate, and sustainably grown foods. Stemming from government policies that generally subsidize and legitimate the industrial agricultural system, working-class communities and communities of color in rural and urban areas are marked by high percentages of residents experiencing hunger, malnutrition, and obesity. They enjoy little to no control over food systems that are dominated by a small number of corporations whose primary charge is return on investment rather than ensuring that people have access to healthy food (Alkon and Agyeman 2011). Thus, the literature on food justice is an important dimension and extension of EJ studies. Since the 1980s, scholars have debated the causes, consequences, and degrees of environmental inequality across myriad communities. These debates generally reflect scholars' preferences for distinct methodological tools, scales of analysis, particular data sources, varying geographies, and the kind of environmental threat under consideration. The clear majority of studies find overwhelming support for the conclusion that the racial composition of a community is the best predictor for where we find environmental inequalities (Downey 2006; Mohai and Bryant 1992; Mohai et al. 2009), while some studies offer findings that age composition, poverty concentrations, and social class matter as much as or more than race (Mennis and Jordan 2005).

While EJ studies remain largely focused on the spatial relationship between environmental risks and race and class dynamics, emerging research considers the intersections between environmental quality and other social categories of difference. Recent scholarship, for example, finds that women are often concentrated in some of the most hazardous spaces in homes, corporations, and other sites – an environmental inequality issue that has yet to garner sufficient attention (Pellow and Park 2002). A number of other studies examine the many ways that women engage and confront discriminatory environmental policies on the job, in neighborhoods, and elsewhere (Buckingham and Kulcur 2010). Despite the fact that women form the overwhelming majority of the EJ movement's leadership, they tend to be less visible and prominent because they frequently work in under-resourced, smaller, community-based organizations that rarely garner media attention and subsist on the efforts of volunteers and small foundation grants (Brown and Ferguson 1995; Bell and Braun 2010). Furthermore, the physical and social terrain – the rivers, mountains, land, and neighborhoods – that many EJ struggles are fought to defend are marked by symbolism and cultural meanings that are deeply gendered and sexualized.

The editors and contributors to the book *New Perspectives on Environmental Justice* seek to widen and deepen the scholarship on EJ issues to explore the ways that gender and sexuality shape the realities of people confronting a diversity of social and ecological perils. For example, a contributor to this book, Greta Gaard, writes:

> *From a queer ecofeminist perspective...we can examine the ways queers are feminized, animalized, eroticized, and naturalized in a culture that devalues women, animals, nature, and sexuality...We can also examine how persons of color are feminized, animalized, eroticized, and naturalized. Finally, we can examine how nature is feminized, eroticized, even queered. The critical point to remember is that each of the oppressed identity groups, each characteristic of the other, is seen as "closer to nature" in the dualisms and ideology of Western culture (Gaard 2004: 26).*

This framework is generative and important not just because it expands EJ studies to consider the role of gender and sexuality (as well as species) in relation to spatial dynamics of race, class, and risk, but also because it stresses the significance of the social construction of "nature" and its links to the very social categories through which humans define ourselves and others (see also Mills 2001 and Pateman 1988).

Research in EJ studies reveals that citizenship, immigration, indigeneity, and nation are also strongly predictive of when and where we find environmental hazards (Cole and Foster 2001; Taylor 2009). Immigrants in the United States are more likely than non-immigrants to live in residential communities with high concentrations of pollution (Hunter 2000; Mohai and Saha 2007; Bullard et al. 2007). Ethnographic studies reveal similar dynamics and demonstrate how ideologies of exclusion, privilege, and nativism support the production and maintenance of such an unequal socioecological terrain, both inside and outside the workplace and in residential communities where immigrants are concentrated (Pellow and Park 2002; Park and Pellow 2011). Indigenous peoples in various nations around the globe are systematically excluded from participation in environmental decision-making, frequently evicted from their lands, disproportionately exposed to pollution, and restricted from using ecological materials within their territories while states and corporations unilaterally appropriate them (Smith 2005; Agyeman et al. 2010). This research on the links between environmental inequality and citizenship, immigration, indigeneity, and nation speaks to the significance, scale, and placing of EJ studies in a transnational and global framework.

A prime example of the global dimensions of environmental inequality is the international trade in hazardous industrial chemical wastes (Clapp 2001; Frey 2001). Even a brief perusal of the actors and sites involved in the legal and illegal trade of hazardous waste suggests quite clearly that, for the most part, those nations accepting these wastes exist on the global political and economic margins, have experienced the trauma of colonization, and often have populations that are majority people of color. In that regard, the global trade in hazardous wastes is also a case of global environmental inequality that reflects enduring historical divides between Global North and South, and a multinational/global matrix of social movement networks has arisen to draw attention to and combat these practices (Pellow 2007).

Theories of Justice

Recent work in EJ studies has begun to grapple with the foundational question of justice, drawing from political theory and philosophy to underscore the importance of defining EJ from within these traditions. EJ studies scholars like Jill Harrison (2011) and David Schlosberg (2007) have turned our attention to these crucial areas of inquiry in order to build a stronger theoretical basis for EJ studies and a more robust interdisciplinary foundation for the field. The work of philosopher John Rawls (2001) figures prominently in this framework. Rawls argues that to achieve justice in society we must reduce social inequalities and increase opportunities for all. This perspective is often called the *distributional* approach to justice, since it focuses on the goal of distribution of social goods and on how to attain that goal.

While distribution is of great importance in any consideration of justice, other theorists argue that material goods should be only one component of this discussion. Iris Marion Young (1990) and Nancy Fraser (1996) view the question of uneven power relations and the oppression of various groups as central to scholarly perspectives on justice. In their framework, scholars should concentrate on the social forces that give rise to and produce injustice in the first place, and solutions to this problem must involve the recognition and inclusion of excluded groups. Fraser (2013) defines *recognition* as a process of acknowledging and valorizing cultural and status differences and distinctions, including national, gender, sexual, racial, class, etc. In other words, as Jill Harrison writes – building on Rawls, Young, and Fraser – the achievement of EJ will not only require an effort to confront the unequal distribution of resources in society, but also an acknowledgment "of social structures that oppress certain social groups" (Harrison 2011: 15).

Achieving justice through recognition, inclusion, and distributional approaches also requires procedures for *participatory parity*, an arrangement that facilitates full access to decision-making bodies and procedures for all members of society (Fraser 1996; Schlosberg 2007). For economist and philosopher Amartya Sen (1993), justice is unattainable without the presence of *capabilities* – the resources, opportunities, freedoms, and institutions necessary for all of society's denizens to experience full membership and inclusion. According to Harrison, capabilities might include "jobs, living wages, clean air and water, and affordable and accessible public transit, health care, housing, and food" (Harrison 2011: 15).

In sum, distribution, recognition, participation, and capabilities are core aspects of justice in general and EJ in particular. Gaining access to material (distribution) social goods requires inclusion (recognition) via access to decision-making bodies (participation) and the basic institutions in any given society (capabilities) (see also Principles of Environmental Justice 1991). Banerjee (2014) extends this framework by articulating the concept of "cultural justice," which she defines as contestations over knowledge claims that arise during EJ struggles that center on efforts to combat the de-legitimization of local lay environmental knowledge in favor of expert scientific traditions.

Earlier EJ scholars actually went to great pains to point out that they were not simply advocating a more democratic and even distribution of industrial pollution and other hazards – they wanted to see the entire system that produced these hazards transformed (Faber 1998; Hamilton 1993; Schnaiberg 1980; Taylor 1997). Moreover, I contend that the dynamic nature of distributional politics and impacts has still yet to be fully explored. For example, environmental inequality has almost entirely been defined through the lens of environmental disadvantage, while *environmental privilege* goes largely unexamined (Norgaard 2011b; Park and Pellow 2011; Taylor 2009). Environmental privilege is characterized by exclusive access to coveted amenities like forests, parks, green space, healthy food, coastal properties, elite neighborhoods, and clean air. That is, environmental privilege is evident in the fact that some groups can access spaces and resources that are protected from the kinds of ecological harm that other groups are forced to contend with every day. These advantages include organic and pesticide-free foods, neighborhoods with healthier air quality, and energy and other products siphoned from the living environments of other peoples. In my view, environmental privilege is the flipside *and source* of environmental injustice/inequality. Thus, while I agree that earlier studies that only sought to document the distribution of environmental damage are limited, the deeper distributional questions around where power resides and how privilege drives environmental injustice are only beginning to be explored.

EJ, Religion, and Spirituality

A growing number of scholars are exploring the various ways that religion and spirituality play a role in shaping EJ struggles. From my review of various literatures in which religion and EJ (broadly defined) intersect, I find that there are three dynamics that are generally in evidence: (1) cases in which religious institutions, leaders, or doctrines are invoked (and therefore supported) to legitimate the existence and practice of environmental injustice; (2) cases in which religious or spiritual practices are harmed by environmental injustice; and (3) cases in which religion or spirituality becomes a source of resistance and resilience against environmental injustice, an example of what Roger Gottlieb (2009) might call "religious environmentalism." I explore these three dynamics below.

Religion – particularly in the form of institutions like churches – has all too often been used to justify or legitimate the perpetration of environmental injustices. The historical record is replete with instances of such practices, including, for example, the ways church leaders facilitated the conquest of Native American peoples and their lands (Kaalund 2004; LaDuke 2005; Smith 2005). In one case, the conflict over the construction of the Mount Graham International Observatory by the University of Arizona and the Vatican pit academia and the Catholic Church against the indigenous Apache nation, for whom Mount Graham is a sacred place. Despite opposition by the Apache and dozens of national and international environmental organizations, the US Congress approved the construction of three telescopes at the site, including one built by the Vatican. The construction of the telescopes on Mount Graham threatens the Apache's access to their sacred sites and destroys key elements of the mountain, while also putting at risk the endangered Mount Graham red squirrel (LaDuke 2005).

More common perhaps, are instances in which states and/or corporate actors commit acts of environmental injustice that curtail, restrict, or even make impossible the spiritual practices of affected communities. As Smith (2005) points out, this occurs frequently because colonial governments and their corporate partners often seize land and water ways sacred to indigenous peoples, and then disallow access and religious practices in those spaces. Smith writes, "[n]ative spiritualities are land based – they are tied to the land base from which they originate. When native peoples fight for cultural/spiritual preservation, they are ultimately fighting for the land base which grounds their spirituality and culture" (Smith 2005: 121). Unfortunately, the US court system has consistently disallowed many native peoples access to sacred sites and lands that are critical to their practice-centered spiritualities, despite the fact that spirituality and land are at the heart of the very survival of native peoples (see Norgaard 2011a).

Finally, the literature is rich with examples that reveal how religion and spirituality have been central components in the toolkit of activist movements building support for resisting environmental injustice (Binder 1999; Gedicks 2001; McCutcheon 2011). It is well known that a number of faith-based organizations and institutions have been at the center of much of the EJ movement since its beginnings. For example, among the 500 people arrested for protesting against a toxic waste landfill in Warren County, North Carolina in 1982, was the Director of the United Church of Christ's Commission for Racial Justice (Reverend Benjamin Chavis) and the co-founder of the Southern Christian Leadership Conference (Dr. Joseph Lowery). This was a protest that may have marked the first instance in US history that people were jailed for attempting to stop the siting and expansion of a toxic waste landfill (Washington 2005: 62). And in 1987, the United Church of Christ published the first national study of what came to be known as environmental racism in the United States.

"Natural Disasters" and Climate Change

Former UN Secretary General, Kofi Annan famously stated, "there is no such thing as a natural disaster." Scholars studying natural disasters have produced countless studies that support that statement. Many disasters are actually caused or triggered by human activities and the impacts, aftermath, recovery, and legacy of such events are shaped, if not determined, by social structures (Tierney 1999). The landmark publication on natural disasters in the United States (Mileti 1999), draws on all the major studies of natural disasters in the twentieth century and states clearly that "[i]n the United States the key characteristics that seem to influence disaster vulnerability most are socioeconomic status, gender, and race or ethnicity." Mileti notes that people of color and the poor are more likely to occupy old and more hazardous housing, less likely to receive disaster warnings, and more likely to have language barriers to the information they do receive. Also, women across the board are more vulnerable because they are disproportionately poor and often remain with family members in emergencies to assist them (see also Klinenberg 2002).

The location of commercial hazardous waste facilities around the United States is highly unequal and discriminatory, with African Americans constituting 20 percent of the population of such communities, as compared to 12 percent in non-host communities. The level of public health risk is elevated when we consider the potential impact of a hurricane or tropical storm on such a facility and community, as anyone living close by will be more likely to experience exposure to any toxins released. The historic concentration of African Americans in the US South places that population in greater jeopardy from climate-related "natural disasters." For example, the states at greatest risk from Atlantic hurricanes are located on the Gulf and Atlantic coasts and have the largest percentage of African Americans in the country. Disaster relief and recovery efforts in these communities are also notoriously unimpressive and under-funded (Mizelle 2014).

Climate Change and Climate Justice

Without a doubt, in the twenty-first century, global climate change has become the leading environmental policy challenge, from the UN to local governments. Accordingly, climate change has also inspired increased attention within EJ studies, as the production of greenhouse gases and carbon emissions imperils the stability of life on this planet and mirrors the vast geopolitical and economic hierarchies within and across nations and regions of the globe. For example, Global North nations are responsible for producing the majority of carbon emissions while the Global South experiences the harshest impacts of climate change. This stark divide across nations and regions with regard to our respective contributions to and suffering from climate change speaks to the persistent relevance of histories of colonialism during which a minority of wealthy states enjoyed dominance over the economies and lands of lower-income countries (Bond 2012). Consider the fact that the European Union, United States, Canada, Australia, and Russia are responsible for the lion's share of global carbon emissions, while sub-Saharan Africa is responsible for only 2 percent (Hoerner and Robinson 2008). More specifically, people of color, women, indigenous communities, and Global South nations contribute comparatively little to the problem of climate change, but bear the brunt of climate disruption in terms of ecological, economic, and health burdens – giving rise to the concept of *climate injustice* (Bullard and Wright 2012; Kasperson and Kasperson 2001; Roberts and Parks 2007). These populations and communities are on the front lines of climate change impacts, which may include "natural" disasters, increasing rates of respiratory illness and infectious disease, heat-related morbidity and mortality, and significant spikes in energy costs.

Phoenix, Arizona is one of many US cities where Latinos and African Americans reside in the urban core as a result of residential segregation, which places them at greater risk for health threats associated with climate change (Bolin et al. 2005). In a study of the micro-climate of Phoenix, Arizona, Harlan et al. (2006) find that neighborhoods with lower median incomes, lower educational attainment, higher poverty rates, and larger people of color populations lived in the city's most intensely heat-stressed neighborhoods (also known as the Urban Health Island) and had the fewest resources to cope with such environmental conditions. Those neighborhoods with higher educational attainment, higher incomes, and larger Anglo populations experience less heat stress because they are more likely to have air conditioned homes, roofing materials to reflect rather than absorb heat, more green space, parks, and vegetation that can provide cooling and heat mitigation properties (see also Harlan et al. 2013).

The majority of deaths during heat waves occur in urban areas. People of color experience greater heat-related stress and illness than whites and are twice as likely as whites to die in a heat wave (Kalkstein 1992). In the 1995 Chicago heat wave, residents in African American neighborhoods suffered the greatest death rates – 50 percent higher than whites (Klinenberg 2002). These challenges are expected to intensify in the future as the expansion of global cities continues unabated.

Gender and climate change also intersect in highly consequential ways across the globe. Due to cultural expectations and social hierarchies, women often work in and occupy spaces that increase their vulnerability to extreme weather events and climate change (Nagel 2012). In one example of how gender influences risk perception, behavior, and impact of disasters, Seager (2012[2005]) noted that during Hurricane Katrina, women were less likely to have a car or a driver's license, limiting their mobility and increasing their level of risk. Future population displacements associated with climate change (i.e., flooding, storms, drought, sea level rises, etc.) are predicted to disproportionately impact women due to their social roles as primary child care and elderly care providers, limited land ownership and land rights, dependency on subsistence agriculture, and lower social status and lower income status across numerous nations (Cannon 2002; United Nations WomenWatch 2009).

Conclusion

Where we find social inequalities by race, class, gender, and nation, we also tend to find environmental inequalities, which are harmful in their material and cultural impacts on human health and social structures, and ecosystems. This enduring – and in some cases increasing – unequal allocation of ecological advantage and privilege across and within societies is the primary focus of EJ studies. The institutional violence and discrimination of environmental inequality and injustice are met with a demand for EJ – a vision and practice of sustainability inseparable from social justice.

The field of EJ studies emerged in part as a result of scholarly curiosity about the association among pollution, demography, and place and also in large part as a response to calls for documentation and research by community advocates. From the vantage point of the social sciences, while there are clearly myriad technical phenomena that are critical to grasping the problem of environmental inequality, it is also clear that this is not, at base, an *environmental* challenge per se; rather, environmental inequality is first and foremost a *social* problem because it is rooted in and supported by social structures and discourses (Hurley 1995; Sze 2007). This makes EJ studies a particularly important focus for sociologists. Future research will expand the category of the *social* and further explore the ways that species and the non-human world reflect, inform, interact with and challenge the concept of the human.

The EJ movement in the United States and globally does have significant limitations, however, that make it challenging to enact the kind of transformative change some scholars conclude is necessary for the realization of EJ (Cole and Foster 2001). If, as many theorists conclude, states are inherently authoritarian and exclusionary social forces (Goldberg 2002; Smith 2011), then environmental and social justice movements should be cautious in their expectations that such institutions might be capable of securing a world in which justice prevails. Yet, this is exactly the view that EJ movements implicitly support as they work to introduce (or undo) legislation, state and corporate policies, and pursue claims through the courts. Future research will likely take up questions concerning this deeply resilient and hierarchical nature of states and how EJ movements should engage them.

The EJ movement has left an indelible mark on the field of sociology by: (1) fostering and deepening the links between the subfield of environmental sociology and broader areas of scholarship on social inequality; (2) urging scholars to produce research that draws from multiple and emerging methodological traditions (e.g., qualitative, quantitative, case studies, comparative-historical, and participatory action research); and (3) encouraging sociologists to be more engaged with non-governmental organizations and other civil society groups advocating EJ policy changes at all geographic scales. EJ movements have made significant impacts on the larger society by: (1) inspiring ordinary people and scholars to participate in a global social movement; (2) sparking the passage of new laws, policies, corporate practices, and executive orders supporting EJ; and (3) introducing a new cultural vocabulary that speaks to the many intersections between social inequality and environmental policy. The EJ movement and the discipline of sociology will continue to be intimately linked in the coming years.

References

Agyeman, J., P. Cole, R. Haluza-DeLay, and P. O'Riley. eds. 2010. *Speaking for Ourselves: Environmental Justice in Canada*. Seattle, WA: University of Washington Press.

Alkon, Alison Hope and Julian Agyeman. eds. 2011. *Cultivating Food Justice: Race, Class, and Sustainability*. Cambridge, MA: The MIT Press.

Banerjee, Damayanti. 2014. Toward an Integrative Framework for Environmental Justice Research: A Synthesis and Extension of the Literature. *Society and Natural Resources* 27: 805–819.

Bell, S. E., and Y. Braun. 2010. Coal, Identity and the Gendering of Environmental Justice Activism in Central Appalachia. *Gender and Society* 24(6): 794–813.

Binder, Lisa. 1999. Religion, Race, and Rights: A Rhetorical Overview of Environmental Justice Disputes. *Wisconsin Environmental Law Journal* 6(1): 1–63.

Bolin, Bob, Sara Grineski, and Timothy Collins. 2005. The Geography of Despair: Environmental Racism and the Making of South Phoenix, Arizona, USA. *Human Ecology Review* 12(2): 156–168.

Bond, Patrick. 2012. *Politics of Climate Justice: Paralysis Above, Movement Below*. Scottsville, South Africa: University of KwaZulu-Natal Press.

Brown, P. and F. Ferguson. 1995. "Making a Big Stink": Women's Work, Women's Relationships, and Toxic Waste Activism. *Gender and Society* 9: 145–172.

Buckingham, S. and R. Kulcur. 2010. Gendered Geographies of Environmental Justice. In *Spaces of Environmental Justice*. Edited by R. Holifield, M. Porter, and G. Walker. Hoboken, NJ: Wiley-Blackwell.

Bullard, Robert D. 1996. Symposium: The Legacy of American Apartheid and Environmental Racism. *St. John's Journal of Legal Commentary* 9: 445–474.

Bullard, Robert D. 2000. *Dumping In Dixie: Race, Class, and Environmental Quality*. Boulder, CO: Westview Press.

Bullard, R. D. and B. Wright. 2012. *The Wrong Complexion for Protection: How the Government Response to Disaster Endangers African American Communities*. New York, NY: New York University Press.

Bullard, R. D., P. Mohai, R. Saha, and B. Wright. 2007. *Toxic Wastes and Race at Twenty, 1987–2007*. New York, NY: United Church of Christ.

Cannon, Terry. 2002. Gender and Climate Hazards in Bangladesh. *Gender and Development* 10: 45–50.

Clapp, Jennifer. 2001. *Toxic Exports: The Transfer of Hazardous Wastes from Rich to Poor Countries*. Ithaca, NY: Cornell University Press.

Cole, Luke and Sheila Foster. 2001. *From the Ground Up: Environmental Racism and the Rise of the Environmental Justice Movement*. New York, NY: New York University Press.

Crowder, Kyle and Liam Downey. 2010. Inter-Neighborhood Migration, Race, and Environmental Hazards: Modeling Microlevel Processes of Environmental Inequality. *The American Journal of Sociology* 115(4): 1110–1149.

Downey, Liam. 2006. Environmental Racial Inequality in Detroit. *Social Forces* 85(2): 771–796.

Du Bois, W. E. B. 1977[1935]. *Black Reconstruction: An Essay toward a History of the Part which Black Folk Played in the Attempt to Reconstruct Democracy in America, 1860–1880*. New York, NY: Atheneum.

Faber, D. 1998. *The Struggle for Ecological Democracy: Environmental Justice Movements in the United States*. New York, NY: The Guilford Press.

Fraser, Nancy. 1996. *Justice Interruptus: Critical Reflections on the "Post Socialist" Condition*. New York, NY: Routledge.

Fraser, Nancy, 2013. *Fortunes of Feminism: From State-Managed Capitalism to Neoliberal Crisis*. London: Verso.

Frey, R. Scott. 2001. The Hazardous Waste Stream in the World-System. In *The Environment and Society Reader*. Edited by R. Scott Frey. Boston, MA: Allyn and Bacon, ch. 6.

Gaard, Greta. 2004. Toward a Queer Ecofeminism. In *New Perspectives on Environmental Justice: Gender, Sexuality, and Activism*. Edited by Rachel Stein. New Brunswick, NJ: Rutgers University Press, 21–44.

Gedicks, Al. 2001. *Resource Rebels: Native Challenges to Mining and Oil Corporations*. Cambridge, MA: South End Press.

Goldberg, David Theo. 2002. *The Racial State*. Malden, MA: Blackwell Publishers.

Gottlieb, Robert. 1994. *Forcing the Spring: The Transformation of the American Environmental Movement*. Washington, DC: Island Press.

Gottlieb, Roger S. 2009. *A Greener Faith: Religious Environmentalism and Our Planet's Future*. Oxford: Oxford University Press.

Hamilton, C. 1993. Coping with Industrial Exploitation. In *Confronting Environmental Racism: Voices from the Grassroots*. Edited by R. D. Bullard. Boston, MA: South End Press.

Harlan, Sharon L., Anthony Brazel, Lela Prashad, William L. Stefanov, and Larissa Larsen. 2006. Neighborhood Microclimates and Vulnerability to Heat Stress. *Social Science and Medicine* 63: 2847–2863.

Harlan, Sharon L., Juan Declet-Barreto, William L. Stefanov, and Diana Petitti. 2013. Neighborhood Effects on Heat Deaths: Social and Environmental Predictors of Vulnerability in Maricopa County, Arizona. *Environmental Health Perspectives* 121(2): 197–204.

Harrison, J. L. 2011. *Pesticide Drift and the Pursuit of Environmental Justice*. Cambridge, MA: The MIT Press.

Hoerner, J., Andrew and Nia Robinson. 2008. A Climate of Change: African Americans, Global Warming, and a Just Climate Policy in the U.S. Environmental Justice Climate Change Initiative (EJCC). Available at http://rprogress.org/publications/2008/climateofchange.pdf, accessed December 2, 2016.

Hunter, L. 2000. The Spatial Association between U.S. Immigrant Residential Concentration and Environmental Hazards. *International Migration Review* 34(2): 460–488.

Hurley, Andrew. 1995. *Environmental Inequalities: Class, Race, and Industrial Pollution in Gary, Indiana, 1945–1980*. Chapel Hill, NC: University of North Carolina Press.

Kaalund, Valerie Ann. 2004. Witness to Truth: Black Women Heeding the Call for Environmental Justice. In *New Perspectives on Environmental Justice: Gender, Sexuality, and Activism*. Edited by Rachel Stein. New Brunswick, NJ: Rutgers University Press, 78–92.

Kalkstein, L. S. 1992. Impacts of Global Warming on Human Health: Heat Stress-Related Mortality. In *Global Climate Change: Implications, Challenges and Mitigating Measures*. Edited by S. K. Majumdar, L. S. Kalkstein, B. Yarnal, E. W. Miller and L. M. Rosenfield. Pennsylvania Academy of Science.

Kasperson, R. E. and J. X. Kasperson. 2001. Climate Change, Vulnerability and Social Justice. Stockholm Environment Institute, Risk and Vulnerability Programme. Stockholm, Sweden. Available at http://stc.umsl.edu/essj/unit4/climate%20change%20risk.pdf, accessed October 28, 2013.

Klinenberg, Eric. 2002. *Heat Wave: A Social Autopsy of Disaster in Chicago*. Chicago, IL: University of Chicago Press.

LaDuke, Winona. 2005. *Recovering the Sacred: The Power of Naming and Claiming*. Cambridge, MA: South End Press.

McCutcheon, Priscilla. 2011. Community Food Security "For Us, By Us". In *Cultivating Food Justice: Race, Class, and Sustainability*. Edited by Alison Hope Alkon and Julian Agyeman. Cambridge, MA: The MIT Press, 177–196.

Mennis, J. and L. Jordan. 2005. The Distribution of Environmental Equity: Exploring Spatial Nonstationarity in Multivariate Models of Air Toxic Releases. *Annals of the Association of American Geographers* 95: 249–268.

Mileti, D. 1999. *Disasters by Design: A Reassessment of Natural Hazards in the United States*. Washington, DC: Joseph Henry Press.

Mills, Charles W. 2001. *The Racial Contract*. Ithaca, NY: Cornell University Press.

Mizelle, Richard M. Jr. 2014. *Backwater Blues: The Mississippi Flood of 1927 in the African American Imagination*. Minneapolis. MN: University of Minnesota Press.

Mohai, P. and B. Bryant. 1992. Environmental Racism: Reviewing the Evidence. In *Race and the Incidence of Environmental Hazards: A Time for Discourse*. Edited by B. Bryant and P. Mohai. Boulder, CO: Westview Press, 163–176.

Mohai, P. and R. Saha. 2007. Racial Inequality in the Distribution of Hazardous Waste: A National-Level Reassessment. *Social Problems* 54(3): 343–370.

Mohai, Paul, David N. Pellow, and J. Timmons Roberts. 2009. Environmental Justice. *Annual Review of Environment and Resources* 34: 405–430.

Nagel, Joane. 2012. Intersecting Identities and Global Climate Change. *Identities: Global Studies in Culture and Power* 19(4): 467–476.

Norgaard, Kari. 2011a. A Continuing Legacy: Institutional Racism, Hunger and Nutritional Justice on the Klamath. In *Cultivating Food Justice: Race, Class, and Sustainability*. Edited by Alison Hope Alkon and Julian Agyeman. Cambridge, MA: The MIT Press, 23–46.

Norgaard, Kari. 2011b. *Living in Denial: Climate Change, Emotions, and Everyday Life*. Cambridge, MA: The MIT Press.

Park, Lisa Sun-Hee and David Naguib Pellow. 2011. *The Slums of Aspen: The War on Immigrants in America's Eden*. New York, NY: New York University Press.

Pateman, Carol. 1988. *The Sexual Contract*. Palo Alto, CA: Stanford University Press.

Pellow, David N. 2007. *Resisting Global Toxics: Transnational Movements for Environmental Justice*. Cambridge, MA: The MIT Press.

Pellow, David N. and Lisa Sun-Hee Park. 2002. *The Silicon Valley of Dreams: Environmental Injustice, Immigrant Workers, and the High-Tech Global Economy*. New York, NY: New York University Press.

Principles of Environmental Justice. 1991. Environmental Justice Resource Center at Clark Atlanta University. Available at www.ejnet.org/ej/principles.html, accessed June 4, 2014.

Rawls, John. 2001. *Justice as Fairness: A Restatement*. Edited by E. Kelly. Cambridge, MA: Harvard University Press.

Roberts, J. Timmons and Bradley Parks. 2007. *A Climate of Injustice: Global Inequality, North-South Politics, and Climate Policy*. Cambridge, MA: The MIT Press.

Schlosberg, David. 2007. *Defining Environmental Justice: Theories, Movements, and Nature*. Oxford: Oxford University Press.

Schnaiberg, A. 1980. *The Environment: From Surplus to Scarcity*. New York, NY: Oxford University Press.

Seager, J. 2012[2005]. Noticing Gender (Or Not) in Disasters. In *The Women of Katrina: How Gender, Race, and Class Matter in an American Disaster*. Edited by E. David and E. Enarson. Nashville, TN: Vanderbilt University Press, 7–9.

Sen, Amartya. 1993. Capability and Well-being. In *The Quality of Life*. Edited by Amartya Sen and Martha Nussbaum. Oxford: Clarendon Press, 30–53.

Smith, Andrea. 2005. *Conquest: Sexual Violence and American Indian Genocide*. Cambridge, MA: South End Press.

Smith, M. 2011. *Against Ecological Sovereignty: Ethics, Biopolitics, and Saving the Natural World*. Minneapolis, MN: University of Minnesota Press.

Sze, J. 2007. *Noxious New York, NY: The Racial Politics of Urban Health and Environmental Justice*. Cambridge, MA: The MIT Press.

Taylor, Dorcetta E. 1997. Women of Color, Environmental Justice, and Ecofeminism. In *Ecofeminism: Women, Culture, Nature*. Edited by Karen Warren. Bloomington, IN: Indiana University Press, 38–81.

Taylor, D. 2009. *The Environment and the People in American Cities, 1600s-1900s: Disorder, Inequality, and Social Change*. Durham, NC: Duke University Press.

Tierney, K. 1999. Toward a Critical Sociology of Risk. *Sociological Forum* 14(2): 215–242.

United Nations WomenWatch. 2009. Women, Gender Equality and Climate Change. Available at www.un.org/womenwatch/feature/climate_change/downloads/Women_and_Climate_Change_Factsheet.pdf, accessed June 25, 2011.

Washington, Sylvia Hood. 2005. *Packing Them in: An Archaeology of Environmental Racism in Chicago, 1865–1954*. Lanham, MD: Lexington Books.

Young, Iris M. 1990. *Justice and the Politics of Difference*. Princeton, NJ: Princeton University Press.

CHAPTER 20
The Sociology of Food

Anne Murcott

Although the subfield of the sociology of food is now firmly established, this chapter paradoxically begins with a much-needed search for it. Thereafter, it provides an introduction and guide to the emergence of a nameable sociology of food, identifying key contributions, noting intellectual inheritances, and indicating central themes and topics. It is impossible to cover the range and dramatic growth in the field over the last thirty years comprehensively and even though examples can only be illustrative, references have been chosen to enable the interested reader to find their own way into the literature. What follows is principally confined to the English language literature emanating primarily from Australasia, Europe, and North America, where most of the work to date has been developed.

Adopted here is a potentially controversial depiction of the sociology of food – one which runs counter to current trends in its parsimonious, even restricted, characterization. It assumes that the researcher is in some fashion trained in sociology. It also assumes that the researcher is posing research questions inspired by accepted social theories and/or modes of research concerning food's relation to social structures, social relationships, social organization, and the place of the material in socio-cultural worlds. Applied research is included, on the assumption that a sociologically trained researcher proceeds by bringing those theories, modes of research, and methods, etc. to bear when seeking to illuminate some food-related social or policy problem.

Searching for the "Sociology of Food"

Locating the field requires several careful discriminations, for it occupies a compressed niche between other, often longer established, scholarly areas, activities, and practices also closely involved with food. Thus, close by within the academy, yet distinctively different, are approaches to the study of food in other social sciences as well as the humanities and business schools (especially marketing) while further away are those in the biological- life- and earth-sciences and especially agricultural studies.

Straddling the boundary between the academy and professional practice are nutrition and dietetics, clinical medicine, epidemiology and public health, along with health promotion and public nutrition education. Elsewhere beyond the academy, are professions such as journalism, cookery book- and food-writing, which may or may not be associated with forms of (political) engagement, sometimes known as "food activism," as well as advocacy for disadvantaged social groups or campaigns by individuals and/or non-governmental organizations (NGOs), for changes in social-food- or nutrition-policies.

To complicate matters still further, there are significant distinctions within sociology's boundaries. Notable is the division between the so-called sociology of food – concentrating on consumption – and agrifood (agro-food) studies – focusing on production (with the latter, to confuse matters even more, not always counted as sociology, but shading into human geography or political economy) (Marsden 2000; McMichael 1993; Rosin and Campbell 2009). All this has to be understood in the general context of the widespread promotion of interdisciplinarity that is coupled with the specific and strong efforts in the United States and Canada (far more so than in Europe) to establish "food studies" as a multidisciplinary field in which a virtue is made of disregarding boundaries between the disciplines across the humanities and social sciences.

Several persistent features of all sociological work, however, are just as evident in the sociology of food as in other subspecialties of sociology. One is what Everett Hughes described as the chronically perilous condition of the discipline poised between science and profession (Hughes 1971). Sociologists remain ambivalent as to whether study is to be only for its own sake, as science, dispassionately standing apart no matter what the social circumstances, or is it to be a profession, framed by political, practical, and moral concern geared to social and material amelioration. Then there is the way that everyone may be said to be some sort of sociologist. To get by in life, people develop an analysis of the social world and the nature of social relationships that may endow them with a sense that they are experts to rival academic sociologists. When it comes to the sociological study of food, there is the added dimension that the subject matter – especially the consumption side, shopping, meals, eating etc. – is, self-evidently, familiar. While this may affect the reception of research results, it also affects the position of researchers, arguably contributing to difficulties in devising distinctively sociological research questions or developing scholarly, as opposed to lay, interpretations of results (Cherry et al. 2011). Sociologists have occasionally fallen into the trap of recommending cookery books, praising recipes, or extolling particular cuisines as part of their work, without noticing that the equivalent in other subfields would be deemed obviously inappropriate; a sociologist researching illegal drug-use would very likely take care neither to endorse a pamphlet on how to grow marijuana nor to praise a judge known to take a hard line on dealing in heroin.

Early Beginnings and the Establishment of Key Substantive Themes

The existence of a sociology of food is not readily apparent if approaching sociology via textbooks, university curricula, the range of work represented in sociological associations' activities, publishers' lists, or the contents of most sociological journals. Nor is it revealed in an examination of the sociological "classics" except in passing (Mennell et al. 1992) – not even in Thorsten Veblen's analyses of conspicuous consumption (1994[1899]), Norbert Elias's (1978[1939]) inclusion of table manners in his expositions of the civilizing process in Europe, or Herbert Blumer's (1969) use of responses to feeling hungry to illustrate what symbolic interactionists mean by self-indication, that it represents a fundamental element of the formation of meaning in social life whereby a person has to indicate to themselves whatever or whoever (including their own bodily experience) it is toward which they are acting. Georg Simmel's 1910 discussion of "the meal" is possibly one of the exceptions in that he takes it as a substantive focus, examining its role in the emergence of sociality and temporal regularity (Symons 1994). Certainly mention of food can be found in the literature. Cooking and the kitchen are present in studies of housework (Lopata 1971; Oakley 1974). Peter Townsend (1979) uses the inability to afford roast meat on Sundays as an indicator of relative poverty. But until comparatively recently, if sociologists included food, it was primarily as part of studying something else – with rare exceptions, such as the wartime study of Illinois food and culture geared to providing a basis for education to improve diet and cooking skills (Bennett et al. 1942).

Eventually, a distinct sociology of food subfield emerged (exhibiting a sustained influence of the longer established social anthropological study of food, cuisine, and culture, notably the work of Mary Douglas; for exposition see Murcott 1988). Its origin can be cautiously dated to the early 1980s (Murcott 1983a; Whit 1995). Sociological work in that decade includes important landmarks which established themes and substantive interests still pursued in the second decade of the twenty-first century. One such is Stephen Mennell's (1985) Eliasian analysis of the social development of taste in French and English cuisines since the late Middle Ages. On the one hand, it remains a lone, pioneering example of the potential of Elias's hypotheses for the sociological study of centuries' long historical changes in food habits that no one has attempted to emulate. But on the other, its importance lies in establishing that, with Durkheimian echoes, taste both metaphorically and literally is not simply innate or only a matter of individual psychology, but is shared, socially transmitted, and collective (consider the *socially* distributed variation in the physiological experience of disgust/enthusiasm for eating oysters, dog, witchetty grubs, or sweetbreads).

Approaching from a different direction, Claude Fischler makes the same point, arguing for culture's independence from biology in shaping human food habits (Fischler 1980; 1988). He also focuses on the symbolic significance of food and eating, not just on feast days but also in the mundane and routine. Fischler presents the following additional themes, as well. He notes that, in industrial society, people have become "*mere* consumers" in that they eat foods "they have not helped produce, or even *seen* being produced" (Fischler 1980: 945; Beardsworth and Keil 1997). Borrowing from the US psychologist, Paul Rozin, Fischler also points out the "omnivore's paradox," the existential double bind of the human omnivore who enjoys the liberty born of the need for a varied diet to seek new foods, but, by the same token, has to mistrust any unknown foods lest they are poisonous. Fischler hypothesizes that modern society "tends to increase the anxiety of the paradox instead of regulating it" (Fischler 1980: 945). He claims a further feature of modern society is the emergence of two basic modes of eating – meals vs. snacks and "junk food" – in which eating "is becoming less of a social, and more of a strictly individual, practice" (Fischler 1980: 947). Fischler can also be credited with an early discussion of food and identity – a theme widely taken up in the early part of the twenty-first century.

A further preoccupation of sociologists in the subfield of the sociology of food in the 1980s was the social organization of the home and the gendered production and consumption of domestic eating (Charles and Kerr 1988; Murcott 1983b). This period also included works concerned with nutrition (Sobal et al. 1993). Most of these themes were taken up by the end of the decade with work in the Nordic countries, culminating in an edited collection (Fürst et al. 1991) including works presaging developments to come – notably, attention to "trust in food." Later work on trust developed a sociological approach that rejects the assumption that trust is a psychological attribute and instead analyzes it as a feature of social relationships (Kjaernes et al. 2007).

It is important to note that sociologists of the 1980s did not neglect the study of food production – quite the reverse. But the study of food from the supply side developed from rural sociology and more recently environmental sociology (Murcott 2013), separately from the consumption side. It is for the latter that the title "sociology of food" tends to be reserved, and there is scant cross reference between the two bodies of work.

Subsequent Expansion

The advent of textbooks (Beardsworth and Keil 1997; McIntosh 1996; Whit 1995), edited collections (Maurer and Sobal 1995; Zubaida and Tapper 1994), and journals are reasonable markers of the establishment of a field. Journals established in the 1980s such as *Food and Foodways* (emphasizing history and anthropology) and *Appetite* (primarily psychology) and thereafter, notably, *Food, Culture and Society* (interdisciplinary with cultural studies well represented) carry sociological, mostly consumption-focused, contributions to the study of food. Studies of food production – including those by sociologists – are typically carried in *Sociologia Ruralis*, *Agriculture and Human Values*, and *Journal of Rural Sociology*, underlining the division already noted.

Against this background of expansion, themes already noted continued to be pursued. Hereafter, these are selectively illustrated, starting with noting extra-sociological concerns sociologists address. I then consider two key contributions to the study of the social organization of domestic eating and end by considering the impact of the rise in the sociology of consumption and the theoretical inheritance of Pierre Bourdieu, as they come together in an exposition of the practice of eating.

Extra-Sociological Topics Addressed by Sociologists of Food

The close link between sociologists studying aspects of food consumption and interest in nutrition is, from time to time, institutionalized in the employment of sociologists in departments of nutrition, health sciences, or public health. Correspondingly, this cross-disciplinary work is reflected in collaborations with scholars and practitioners in related disciplines, the adoption of applied sociological approaches, and the study of practical, dietary topics such as vitamin use, obesity, or the relation between food intake and teenage body image (Nissen and Holm 2015; Sobal and Daly 1990; Wills et al. 2006). Research investigating the consequences of changes in working conditions for public health generally and "healthy eating" in particular (Dixon et al. 2013) offers a more structural stance.

A different starting point is researchers' own eating habits and personal/political attitudes. This was the case for Maurer's (2002) decision to study vegetarianism. The same topic, however, was selected by Beardsworth and Keil (1992) on the grounds that adherents had already become reflexive about their eating, thus enabling smoother sociological investigation of the topic.

Still other topics reflect current policy and/or mass media concerns. Notable over the last two decades is the emergence of risk as a dominant frame for policy discussion. Associated is a rise in investigations which link Beck's (1999) risk society and a succession of "food scares" such as alar in apples, salmonella in eggs, or genetically modified foodstuffs (Levidow 2001; MacIntyre et al. 1998; Rodgers 1996). From a different quarter come public and media concerns that illustrate a different type of fear. One such concern is a supposed decline in "family meals" and the worrying changes in family life and organization it might presage. In response, sociologists have noted the need for trend data, pointing out the relative historical novelty of this form of social organization of domestic eating, adding, most particularly, the need to avoid confusing conviviality with the dispassionate study of shared eating (Grignon 2001). It is all too easy to mistake the enjoyable experience of eating with others as signaling something enduring and universal about family meals, instead of realizing that this style of eating is only about a century old and specific to certain social groups in "Western" societies.

The Social Organization of Domestic Eating

Two landmark books on the social organization of domestic eating are De Vault's 1991 *Feeding the Family* and Julier's 2013 *Eating Together* (though neither author explicitly describes her work as "sociology of food" research). Both authors are from the United States, are primarily ethnographic, and pursue the study of commensality. Some sociologists of food use the strong version of the term commensality, as anthropologists do, and define it as revolving around the social rules and conventions governing who may eat with whom. Others, using what is referred to as the weak version, define commensality simply as "eating together." Both De Vault's and Julier's books use the strong version.

Feeding the Family is a fine-grained, subtle study that picks up two preoccupations of feminist scholarship of the late 1980s: the significance of household labor for women's lives and the (un)paid work of caring for other people. *Eating Together* also focuses on the household but ventures beyond to include potlucks etc. In some ways, De Vault's task of studying food and eating serves as a lens via which to study other features of social life. Crucial is her refusal to take for granted well-known concepts of social life used in everyday discourse as well as, all too commonly, uncritically adopted by sociologists. Instead of assuming the notion of family in which conventional roles of breadwinning are assigned to men and homemaking assigned to women, she seeks to bring to light and explain the ideas and discourse which sustain such assumptions as normal and "natural." Concentrating on the activities and the social interaction among those involved, she shows how the work of feeding others reproduces family and how those who do such work "do" family and its associated gendered roles.

At the same time, De Vault insists that, though seemingly primarily a biological affair, eating is fundamentally social. What people eat, how food is prepared, and who does the preparing (and when, where, and with whom), depends on, and simultaneously reflects, social arrangements. She argues that the work "of feeding others is also shaped by, and in turn expresses, beliefs and customs of the society at a particular time. More than just the provision of edibles, feeding work means staging the rather complex social events that we label meals" (1991: 35). So, De Vault shows that while women "do" family, they create patterns of eating and feeding that are distinctive in their own right.

Critical is the invisibility of the work involved in feeding. Indeed, it is only semi-visible even to those busily engaged in it. De Vault records how this work proceeds as a continuous background to women's lives (e.g., planning what to put in a husband's lunch box in the few moments between the alarm clock ringing in the morning and actually climbing out of bed), part of a set of assumptions of family life and their place in it. Despite historical trends in the United States for household members to eat together less and less frequently, De Vault points out that her interviewees are very concerned about bringing the family together for meals – an act which now requires a new type of effort and continued "strategizing" to accomplish. Meals are used as a means of orchestrating family life, both reflecting and (re-)creating households' ideas and understanding of what such life ought to be like.

Two features lies at the core of De Vault's analysis. One is the way that the work of feeding the family involves coordinating the often disparate range of activities in which household members are engaged – either by choice or by necessity – which tend to pull them away from such shared acts that constitute "family" in the image they value. Enmeshed with it is the other, the fact that such coordinating efforts – made visible by the ethnographer's methods – are usually invisible to most family members. The result is that those very efforts "simultaneously produce the illusion that this form of life is a 'natural one'" (1991: 91).

Julier's book acknowledges a debt to De Vault's, but in a quiet, thorough, and detailed fashion breaks new ground by extending research beyond the walls of the home and outside the kin group to enquire about circumstances under which non-kin are included. Degrees of formality are unearthed: more when the guests for dinner are the boss and his wife, less when visitors are a couple of the same social status. De Vault deals with class in terms of the constraints of poverty, the opportunities of affluence, and status characterized as style. Julier pursues the latter still further, not just to identify status groupings in respect to who eats with whom, but to note the drawing of boundaries which exclude as well as include. As she observes, "class based distinctions are inscribed in the material and interactional work of social events that subscribe to the cultural template of a dinner party" (Julier 2013: 103). Furthermore, she notes that even when staging dinner parties, both men's and women's actions in producing home-based hospitality do so in ways that do not disrupt any participants' expectations for "doing gender" – continuing to reproduce feeding as "naturally" women's work.

Theories of Practice and Eating

A spur to the further development of studies in the sociology of food is the rise since the late 1990s of the sociology of consumption, taking study beyond purchasing to include the way goods and services are valued socially and used to convey identity. In this neighboring subfield, the influence of Pierre Bourdieu's work is particularly prominent, notably his theories about the way in which different social strata are distinguished from each other in terms of taste and attitudes to high/popular culture. These come together in Alan Warde's *The Practice of Eating* (2015), possibly the first, book-length attempt at theorizing eating sociologically.

Warde regards the sociology of food to date as deficient, with an undue reliance on cultural communication. He proposes that theories of practice hold greater promise for analyzing eating in sociological terms. Eating is commonly habitual, part of an everyday routine – at least for those well enough off to be able to eat three times a day – that ordinarily lies below consciousness. So identifying what constitutes eating is not straightforward, for it is multifaceted and includes: bodily incorporation (habits), social occasions (routines) and menu selection (conventions). Eating requires the orchestration and performance of alternative combinations of bodily technique, manners, and food selection, all in a context of many other kinds of associated practices dealing with social pressure (e.g., eating with others, the management of income and other relevant resources, etc.).

In his criticism of previous work, Warde is persuasive. Too much fails to *theoretically* address the combination of that trio of central topics – routines, meals, and commensality – without losing sight of embodiment, simultaenously analyzing the manner in which social environments and infrastructure constrain behavior. Theories focused on the practice of eating allow effective moves toward the analytic exposition of eating as collectively sanctioned or approved in (explicit) evaluations of performances, cued by environment and situation.

Concluding Observations

Partly because Bourdieu's work is dense and unfamiliar to many and practice theories demand an investment of time that may not be available to all in the field, it is probably still too early to say what influence theories focused on practice will have on the subdiscipline. All the same, the sociology of food continues to expand rapidly. Locating it continues to require care, for, overall, scholarly interest in food across the social sciences and humanities is even more intense than it is in sociology, in particular. In many ways the whole is just as fragmented as a decade ago, but now boundaries between disciplines are less and less easy to identify – with fewer thinking it worth the effort of trying to distinguish one from the other. Perversely, despite claims to the contrary (e.g., Carolan 2012), the division between sociologies of the consumption and production of food remains surprisingly conspicuous, evidenced by each "side's" persisting unfamiliarity with, and even complete neglect of, the other's literatures.

If fields can be said to have phases of development, the sociology of food remains at a stage of rapid expansion, covering a growing variety of topics, yet with relatively little intellectual cohesion sociologically and continuing to be comparatively under-theorized – despite the promise of practice theory approaches. What remains to be further developed is a sense of intellectual debate within the field and of explicit discussion of what would count as sociologically secure and adequate apprehensions of topics under study. In the meantime, the sociology of food represents an important contribution to sociology more generally in increasingly and prominently bringing the material into analytic focus with the social. It is moving beyond understanding that eating is symbolically significant or may be used as a means of displaying social distinction. This subfield enables us to recognize that to ignore food's materiality, questions of embodiment, and uneven distributions of access to food and to (literal) taste, itself, is to omit a significant element of social reality.

References

Beardsworth, A. and T. Keil. 1992. The Vegetarian Option: Varieties, Conversions, Motives and Careers. *The Sociological Review* 40: 253–293.

Beardsworth, A. and T. Keil. 1997 *Sociology on the Menu: An Invitation to the Study of Food and Society*. London: Routledge.

Beck, U. 1992. *Risk Society: Towards a New Modernity*. London: Sage.

Bennett, J. W., H. L. Smith, and H. Passin. 1942. Food and Culture in Southern Illinois – A Preliminary Report. *American Sociological Review* 7: 645–660.

Blumer, Herbert. 1969. *Symbolic Interactionism: Perspective and Method*. Englewood Cliffs, NJ: Prentice-Hall.

Carolan, Michael. 2012. *The Sociology of Food and Agriculture*. New York, NY: Routledge.

Charles, N. and M. Kerr. 1988. *Women, Food and Families*. Manchester: Manchester University Press.

Cherry, E., C. Ellis, and M. Desoucey. 2011. Food for Thought, Thought for Food: Consumption, Identity, and Ethnography. *Journal of Contemporary Ethnography* 40(2): 231–258.

De Vault, M. L. 1991. *Feeding the Family: The Social Organization of Caring as Gendered Work*. Chicago, IL: University of Chicago Press.

Dixon, J., D. Woodman, L. Strazdins, C. Banwell, D. Broom, and J. Burgess. 2013. Flexible Employment, Flexible Eating and Health Risks. *Critical Public Health* 24(4): 461–475.

Elias, N. 1978[1939]. *The Civilising Process*. Oxford: Blackwell.

Hughes, E. C. 1971. *The Sociological Eye: Selected Papers*. Chicago, IL: Aldine-Atherton.

Fischler, C. 1980. Food Habits, Social Change and the Nature/Culture Dilemma. *Social Science Information* 19(6): 937–953.

Fischler, C. 1988. Food, Self and Identity. *Social Science Information* 27: 275–293.

Fürst, E. L., R. Prättälä, M. Ekström, L. Holm, and U. Kjaernes. eds. 1991. *Palatable Worlds: Sociocultural Food Studies*. Oslo: Solum Forlag.

Grignon, C. 2001. Commensality and Social Morphology: An Essay of Typology. In *Food, Drink and Identity: Cooking, Eating and Drinking in Europe since the Middle Ages*. Edited by P. Scholliers. Oxford: Berg.

Julier, Alice P. 2013. *Eating Together: Food, Friendship, and Inequality*. Chicago, IL: University of Illinois Press.

Kjaernes, U., M. Harvey, and A. Warde. 2007. *Trust in Food: A Comparative and Institutional Analysis*. London: Palgrave Macmillan.

Levidow, L. 2001. Precautionary Uncertainty: Regulating GM Crops in Europe. *Social Studies of Science* 31(6): 842–874.

Lopata, H. Z. 1971. *Occupation: Housewife*. Oxford: Oxford University Press.

Macintyre, S., J. Reilly, D. Miller, and J. Eldridge. 1998. Food Choice, Food Scares, and Health: The Role of the Media. In *"The Nation's Diet": The Social Science of Food Choice*. Edited by Anne Murcott. London: Longman.

Marsden, T. 2000. Food Matters and the Matter of Food: Towards a New Food Governance? *Sociologia Ruralis* 40(1): 20–29.

Maurer, D. 2002. *Vegetarianism: Movement or Moment?* Philadelphia, PA: Temple University Press.

Maurer, D. and J. Sobal. eds. 1995. *Eating Agendas: Food and Nutrition as Social Problems*. New York, NY: Aldine.

Mennell, S. 1985. *All Manners of Food: Eating and Taste in England and France from the Middle Ages to the Present*. Oxford: Blackwell.

Mennell, S., A. Murcott, and A. van Otterloo. 1992. *The Sociology of Food: Diet, Eating and Culture*. London: Sage.

McIntosh, W. A. 1996. *Sociologies of Food and Nutrition*. New York, NY: Plenum.

McMichael, P. 1993. World Food System Restructuring Under a GATT Regime. *Political Geography* 12(3): 198–214.

Murcott, A. ed. 1983a. *The Sociology of Food and Eating* Aldershot: Gower.

Murcott, A. 1983b. "It's a Pleasure to Cook for Him...": Food, Mealtimes and Gender in Some South Wales Households. In *The Public and the Private*. Edited by E. Gamarnikow, D. Morgan, J. Purvis, and D. Taylorson. London: Heinemann.

Murcott, A. 1988. Sociological and Social Anthropological Approaches to Food and Eating. *World Review of Nutrition and Dietetics* 55: 1–40.

Murcott, A. 2013. A Burgeoning Field: Introduction to the Handbook of Food Research. In *Handbook of Food Research*. Edited by Anne Murcott, Warren Belasco and Peter Jackson. London: Bloomsbury.

Nissen, N. K. and L. Holm. 2015. Literature Review: Perceptions and Management of Body Size among Normal Weight and Moderately Overweight People. *Obesity Reviews* 16(2): 150–160.

Oakley, A. 1974. *The Sociology of Housework*. London: Martin Robertson.

Rodgers, K. E. 1996. Multiple Meanings of Alar after the Scare: Implications for Closure. *Science, Technology and Human Values* 21(2): 177–197.

Rosin, C. and H. Campbell. 2009. Beyond Bifurcation: Examining the Conventions of Organic Agriculture in New Zealand. *Journal of Rural Studies* 25: 35–47.

Sobal, J. and M. P. Daly. 1990. Vitamin/Mineral Supplement Use among General Practice Patients in the United Kingdom. *Family Practice* 7: 181–183.

Sobal, J., W. A. McIntosh, and W. Whit. 1993. Teaching the Sociology of Food, Eating, and Nutrition. *Teaching Sociology* 21(1): 50–59.

Symons, M. 1994. Simmel's Gastronomic Sociology: An Overlooked Essay. *Food and Foodways* 5(4): 333–351.

Townsend, P. 1979. *Poverty in the United Kingdom*. London: Allen Lane.

Veblen, T. 1994[1899]. *The Theory of the Leisure Class*. New York, NY: Penguin.

Warde, A. 2015. *The Practice of Eating*. Cambridge: Polity.

Whit, W. C. 1995. *Food and Society: A Sociological Approach*. New York, NY: General Hall.

Wills, W. K. Backett-Milburn, S. Gregory, and J. Lawton. 2006. Young Teenagers' Perceptions of their Own and Others' Bodies: A Qualitative Study of Obese, Overweight and 'Normal' Weight Young People in Scotland. *Social Science and Medicine* 62(2): 396–406.

Zubaida, S. and R. Tapper. eds. 1994. *Culinary Cultures of the Middle East*. London: Tauris.

Part V
THE SOCIOLOGY OF THE SELF

CHAPTER 21
Sociology of the Body and Embodiment

Carla A. Pfeffer

In 2009, Sociology of the Body and Embodiment was granted official recognition as a section by the American Sociological Association.[1] The section mission is described as follows:

> The aim of the Section on the Sociology of the Body and Embodiment is to support and encourage sociological scholarship on a wide range of embodied dynamics including human and non-human bodies, morphology, human reproduction, anatomy, body fluids, biotechnology, genetics; but also theories of embodiment, virtual bodies, productivity of bodies, changing bodies, life course and the body, body and spirit/soul, unequal bodies, micro and macro sociological analysis of the political, and social and individual bodies.[2]

Today, the section boasts more than 300 dues-paying active members. In addition to

[1] Given space constraints, this chapter focuses on sociology of the body and embodiment in the United States.
[2] See www.asanet.org/asa-communities/sections/body-and-embodiment, accessed December 21, 2016.

the disciplinary recognition of sociology of the body and embodiment, the growing visibility of this subdisciplinary area at the turn of the twenty-first century is also revealed by the growth of overviews, readers, and edited collections on body and embodiment studies (e.g., Bobel and Kwan 2011; Cregan 2012; Howson 2013; Lorber and Moore 2011; Malacrida and Low 2008; Moore and Kosut 2010; Turner 2012; Waskul and Vannini 2006). While disciplinary recognition of the section is rather recent, the history of sociology of the body and embodiment reaches farther back.

Sociology of the body and embodiment emerged to fill gaps in existing theoretical and empirical scholarship. As Turner writes, "there exists a theoretical prudery with respect to human corporeality which constitutes an analytical gap at the core of sociological inquiry" (2008: 33). In order to understand the emergence of sociology of the body and embodiment, one must first consider the origins of sociology itself. One of the key contributions of sociology as a discipline, and a central motivating factor for its creation, is the insistence that human experience is neither preordained nor rooted solely in physiology or psychology. Rather than social inequalities being generated and reproduced through divine ordination or a natural biological essence or set of thought patterns shared among members of particular groups, sociologists argue that inequalities are largely determined through the structures and institutions of society and through the interactions of these structures, institutions, and members of society. In this way, sociologists have differentiated themselves from clergy, physicians, biologists, and psychologists.[3]

Yet in arguing for the structuring power of human interaction in concert with social systems, institutions, and structures, sociologists sometimes lose sight of the very bodies involved in these social processes. A central critique of sociology, therefore, may be that it has tended to sideline the body and embodiment as it has made the case for the profound influence of the social. It has also been argued that many theories of society have a "cognitive bias," focusing on social actors' rationales, thinking, and mental calculations as if these were located somewhere outside of the body, or as if bodies were incidental to these cognitive processes (Turner 1984). As such, sociology of the body and embodiment is, at its core, a sociology that critically attends to the material – the various ways in which bodies are utilized, consuming, disciplined, formed, shaped, exploited, pleasurable, humiliating, communicating, liberated, enslaved, and profane (see also Frank 2010).

In the United States, work around sociology of the body and embodiment began to emerge in the 1970s and 1980s, galvanized by gains of the civil rights and feminist social movements of the 1960s. Each of these movements was centered in powerful discourse about the social importance of revaluing bodies. The Black power and feminist movements, respectively, advanced "Black is beautiful" and "our bodies, ourselves"[4] cultural politics that sought to revalue and center forms of the body and embodiment that had been denigrated and used to both justify and fuel racist and sexist sentiments. The proliferation of scholarship on sociology of the body and embodiment began in earnest in the 1990s. In many ways, sociology of the body and embodiment may be said to be an interdisciplinary or even transdisciplinary affair – drawing on scholars and scholarship across the disciplines and subdisciplines of history, philosophy, cultural studies, anthropology, biology, gender studies, medicine, racial and ethnic studies, fat studies, and disability studies (to name but a few).

Just as sociology of the body and embodiment is not mono-disciplinary, there is also no singular theoretical, empirical, or methodological approach for sociological-relevant studies of the body and embodiment. However, several key approaches or frameworks do tend to predominate. Some of these include symbolic interaction and ethnomethodology (Kessler and McKenna 1978; Waskul and Vannini 2006); human perception and phenomenology (Merleau-Ponty 1962); postmodern and deconstructionist (Foucault 1975; Haraway 1990); bodily capital and carnal sociology (Bourdieu 1986; Wacquant 1995; 2006; 2015); and feminist and queer approaches (Bobel and Kwan 2011; Bordo 1993; Lorber and Moore 2011; Pausé et al. 2014). While an extensive overview of each of these approaches is outside the scope of this brief overview of sociology of the body and embodiment,[5] I include citations for further study and exploration. In the following sections, I detail the ways in which sociology of the body and embodiment has helped us to understand some of the particular ways

---

[3] See the second chapter, "Sociology and the Body," of Turner's (2008) text, *The Body & Society*, for a more comprehensive overview of the emergence of the subdiscipline.

[4] This sentiment was ultimately parlayed into the popular and best-selling feminist text, *Our Bodies, Ourselves* (Boston Women's Health Book Collective. 2011. New York, NY: Simon & Schuster).

[5] See Turner (2008) for an excellent overview of some of these epistemological, methodological, and theoretical strands.

in which the body shapes (and is shaped by) society across a number of structuring domains.

Body and Embodiment across Particular Domains

While I focus on an overview of several key domains across which sociology of the body and embodiment has been concentrated, one alternative approach would be to consider the various social institutions ripe for focused sociological analyses of the body and embodiment. Some of the key social institutions that are illuminated through sociological analysis of the body and embodiment include (but are not limited to) culture, media and technology, family, work, medicine and health care, religion, education, and politics and government. Further, when engaging with the domains informed by sociological analyses of the body and embodiment, the various social institutions I have mentioned, and others, are always implicated.

While I explore the particular domains of sex, gender, and sexuality; race; social class; and disability and body size in this chapter, this should not be taken to imply that these are the only domains of relevance for scholars of sociology of the body and embodiment. Rather, they offer a sampling or a "taste" of just some of the domains across which scholarship on sociology of the body and embodiment has concentrated and expanded. Further, not all of the scholars or scholarship presented below derives exclusively from sociology or sociologists. I present this work to offer examples of the types and variety of scholarship from which sociologists draw and build upon to expand theoretical and empirical understandings of the body and embodiment in their own work.

Sex, Gender, and Sexuality

Scholarship at the intersection of sex, gender, sexuality, and the body and embodiment has moved the discipline of sociology (as well as others) forward in at least three major ways. First, sociologists have highlighted the potential perils of universalizing particular bodies and embodiments. For example, by understanding male physiology as universal, advancements in medicine and health care fail to consider how differences between male and female pathophysiology may mean that men's and women's bodies display symptoms of illness differently or respond differentially – qualitatively and quantitatively – to medications (Clarke et al. 2010). Yet just as some scholars have warned about universalizing male bodies and experiences, so too have they criticized over-emphasis of the relative distinctions between male and female bodies and embodiments (Fausto-Sterling 2000), and of ignoring significant historical and cultural trends that mark shifts in cultural expectations for embodiment among members of various sex and gender groups (Immergut 2010).

This second major contribution has focused on analysis of "Mars and Venus"-type assessments of the perceived differences between men and women wherein men and women are perceived as so different from one another that they might as well be considered from other planets. Michael Kimmel (2012) refers to this as the "interplanetary theory of gender." Sociologists, however, have drawn upon biological evidence showing that while male and female biology and physiology may be distinct, there is generally more overlap than distinction (Fausto-Sterling 2000).

Moreover, where perceived differences do exist, many may be said to follow social construction feedback loops wherein members of particular groups receive repeated messages about their bodies or embodiments and come to engage with their bodies in ways that conform to these messages (Dworkin and Wachs 2009; Young 1980). For example, Iris Marion Young (1980) explores how "throwing like a girl" is less indicative of biological incapacity and more indicative of the ways in which social and cultural beliefs about girls' and women's inferior strength and sportsmanship (notice even the gendering of that term), relative to boys' and men's, shape girls' and women's bodies and embodiment. By examining myriad cultural practices, such as foot binding (Mernissi 2014), genital cutting (Wade 2011), depilation (Fahs and Delgado 2011; Immergut 2010), and dieting (Germov and Williams 1996), sociologists have examined how social and cultural mediation of the body and embodiment practices are often gendered in particular ways.

A third contribution that sociologists have made is to propose sex, gender, and sexuality as, at least in part, socially constructed. While sociological understandings initially paved the way for understanding gender as the social and cultural corollary of biological sex, more recent sociological analysis underscores just how actively we often work to construct sex as well. By considering the practices of genital surgeries on intersex infants (Davis 2015; Preves 2003), male circumcision (Carpenter 2010), and transsexual embodiment (Connell 2011; Williams et al. 2013), sociology of the body prompts us to consider the social and cultural malleability of even some of the most taken-for-granted aspects of biology and identity.

Sociological studies find that body and embodiment practices are of particular importance among members of lesbian, gay, and bisexual communities. In normative and heteronormative sexual fields (see Green 2013), wherein members who are perceived as the same sex are assumed to be searching exclusively for "opposite-sex" partners for traditional forms of sex and sexuality, members of sexual minority communities have often relied upon embodied signaling techniques – the use of differently-colored and positioned handkerchiefs or "flagging," wearing hairstyles and clothing most commonly associated with the "other" sex, wearing a corset or other bondage gear, displaying tattoos, and adorning one's body in leather or rainbows (Kosut 2010). In this way, we begin to see possibilities for the performance of identities and social group membership that may be displayed on and through the body without necessarily emerging intrinsically from it.

Race

Sociology of the body and embodiment has also prompted more careful consideration of the historical, social, and cultural construction of race. While often considered a biologically determined category, many sociologists have long considered race primarily a social and cultural construction (Desmond and Emirbayer 2009; Omi and Winant 1986). Recent analyses of the human genome have confirmed that racial groups have very little basis in biology,[6] and are largely rooted in social perceptual and attributional processes (Fullwiley 2007). Sociological analyses of "passing" have revealed how social structures grant differential access and privilege to those bearing particular phenotypes and that access is a largely perceptual process (Pfeffer 2014; Renfrow 2004). In this way, those who are born with skin shades and other phenotypic forms of embodiment that are perceived to align with those of majority status groups may be able to access privilege despite parentage or ancestral connection to those from minority status groups.

Recent work by Asia Friedman re-locates the workings of identity-based group membership in perceptual processes. Friedman (2013; American Sociological Association 2015) interviewed blind individuals to discern how they make attributions of others' gender and race. She found that, unlike for sighted persons, the perceptual processes that underlie how blind people assign gender and race are deliberate, rather than rapidly formed in response to a cursory glance. These processes essentially require more fully embodied perceptual awareness drawing from a broader array of the human senses. Friedman provides evidence for the possibility of becoming less certain about the gender and racial attributions we make on a daily basis, opening up possibilities to view these categories as more social than biological, with boundaries that are far more

---

[6] See popular media coverage at www.nytimes.com/2000/08/22/science/do-races-differ-not-really-genes-show.html, accessed December 5, 2016.

permeable than they are often presumed to be.

In sociological work on Black sexuality, Collins (2005) details some of the embodied intersectional practices of historical and contemporary racism and sexism in the United States and their differential effects on Black women and men. Drawing historical linkages between slavery, lynching, and mass incarceration of Black men, as well as rape, domestic violence, and increasing incarceration of Black women, Collins convincingly argues that practices of embodied and gendered racism have shifted form, not disappeared. Gilman (2010) traces the historical trajectory and physiognomy of the "racial nose," highlighting the ways in which medical and cultural authorities often serve as gatekeepers for determining which bodily contours get to "count" as cultured, denigrated, inferior, and superior.

Social Class

Sociological studies of social class have long focused on the material conditions of everyday life; scholarship in this vein expands its analysis into the realm of body and embodiment to consider how the work that we do quite literally shapes and is shaped by and through our bodies. Tracing the role of industrialization in shaping the contours of working-class laborers' bodies across the nineteenth and early twentieth centuries, Slavishak (2008) finds spines twisted, lungs blackened, and limbs amputated as industry carved the way for embodied consumerism. Workers must now purchase products – stimulants, painkillers, prostheses – to support their transformed embodiments (see also Pine 2010).

The convergence of sociological studies of the body and embodiment and social class has also revealed how social class is often read through the body vis-á-vis one's clothing, hairstyle, makeup, language choices, and even comportment. Indeed, some bodies may be said to manifest greater "bodily capital" than others. The concept of non-monetary "capital" was elaborated by Pierre Bourdieu (1986). Bourdieu's thinking and writing on capital were later extended by his students – one of the most notable being Loïc Wacquant. Wacquant outlines a theory of "bodily capital," a form of social currency whereby some bodies and forms of embodiment are perceived as (and become) more or less valuable than others (Wacquant 1995; 2010).

Even within the same occupation we see manifestations of differential bodily capital (Hutson 2013). For example, at the intersection of gender, class, race and ethnicity, sexuality, and body and embodiment, Mary Nell Trautner (2005) finds differential styles of makeup application and clothing choices among strippers at higher-status versus lower-status strip clubs. Similarly, Kimberly Kay Hoang (2015) finds forms of class stratification in embodiment practices among female sex workers and their male clients located across different types of "hostess bars" in Saigon. In each of these instances, social class is something that is not naturally or biologically emergent, but that nevertheless shapes, adorns, and transforms the body in ways that are then culturally "read" by others through processes of everyday social and commercial exchange.

Disability and Body Size

Sociological theorizing on the body and embodiment has been particularly powerful in its intersection with disability and disability studies. Prior to the emergence of disability studies, much sociological work focused on disability, social policy, and the law, addressing fundamental structural access issues, as well as stigma and discrimination (Turner 2009). While these remain fundamentally important areas of sociological inquiry, they tend to simultaneously erase the actual bodies of those with disabilities and fail to consider how disabilities arise less from bodies themselves and more from the limiting ways in which buildings, workplaces, homes, and public spaces are built and structured (McLaughlin and Coleman-Fountain 2014). Recent work, however, by scholars such as Friedman (2013) serve as examples of methodologically re-centering the experiences and perspectives of those with disabilities (in Friedman's case, blindness) to provide deeper understanding of the taken-for-granted assumptions that imbue seemingly-mundane (yet highly consequential) social processes like gender and racial attribution and meaning-making.

Like scholarship on disability, much scholarship on body size has tended to situate various types of bodies as problematic rather than address the structural and systemic challenges faced by those with bodies that are not normatively valued. Fat studies and fat rights have had a developmental trajectory paralleling that of disability studies and disability rights. Specifically, fat studies and disability studies challenge the notions that fat and disabled bodies are problematic per se. Sociologists who study fatness often do so from the perspective of minority stress and high obesity rates, linking them to the structural unavailability of healthy affordable foods in minority communities. Sociologists who study fatness from a fat studies perspective (see Boero 2012; Saguy 2014[2012]), however, tend to critique or resist labels such as "obesity," on the grounds that they reveal medicalization of what could alternately be considered natural variation in body size. They also draw upon epidemiological and public health literatures (e.g., Flegal et al. 2013) that challenge assumed linkages between fatness and mortality, as well as highlight the stigma and discrimination faced by people with larger body sizes across the arena of interpersonal relationships, employment, education, and public accessibility (see Puhl and Brownell 2001; Puhl and Heuer 2009).

In addition to its interface with studies of fatness, sociology of the body attends to groups considered underweight and socially problematic as well. For example, sociologists have studied members of pro-anorexia and pro-bulimia ("pro-ana," "pro-mia") groups to develop sharper understandings of social and interpersonal processes connected to body ideals, impact of cultural body expectations and norms, internet community building (Boero and Pascoe 2012; Richardson and Cherry 2011), and social distancing (Ettore 2010). Additional fruitful connections between sociology of the body and embodiment and body size (and shape) can be found in research on body image (Pfeffer 2008) and plastic surgery (Gagné and McGaughey 2002) to name just a few areas.

While sociology of the body and embodiment is a comparatively young subdiscipline, its impact is already being felt. Offering a corrective to sociology's tendency to theorize in abstraction by situating the body both critically and materially, sociology of the body and embodiment begins to mend the dualistic schisms between self and society, body and culture, nature and nurture, body and mind, and identity and attribution. Sociology of the body and embodiment reflects a twenty-first century resistance toward singular classifications and approaches. Rather, it offers intersectional analytic perspectives and modes of inquiry that are every bit as complex, diverse, expansive, and perplexing as bodies themselves.

References

American Sociological Association. 2015. Study Investigates Whether Blind People Characterize Others by Race. *Sciencedaily*, August 25, 2015. Available at www.sciencedaily.com/releases/2015/08/150825083610.htm, accessed December 5, 2016.

Bobel, Chris and Samantha Kwan. eds. 2011. *Embodied Resistance: Challenging the Norms, Breaking The Rules*. Nashville, TN: Vanderbilt University Press.

Boero, Natalie C. 2012. *Killer Fat: Media, Medicine, and Morals in the American Obesity Epidemic*. New Brunswick, NJ: Rutgers University Press.

Boero, Natalie and C. J. Pascoe. 2012. Pro-Anorexia Communities and Online Interaction: Bringing the Pro-Ana Body Online. *Body and Society* 18(2): 27–57.

Bordo, Susan. 1993. *Unbearable Weight: Feminism, Western Culture, and the Body*. Berkeley, CA: University of California Press.

Bourdieu, Pierre. 1986. The Forms of Capital. In *Handbook of theory and Research for the Sociology of Education*. Edited by John Richardson New York, NY: Greenwood, 241–258.

Carpenter, Laura M. 2010. On Remedicalisation: Male Circumcision in the United States and Great Britain. *Sociology of Health and Illness* 32(4): 613–616.

Clarke, Adele, Laura Mamo, Jennifer Ruth Fosket, Jennifer R. Fishman, and Janet K. Shim. eds. 2010. *Biomedicalization: Technoscience, Health, and Illness in the U.S.* Durham, NC: Duke University Press.

Collins, Patricia Hill. 2005. *Black Sexual Politics: African Americans, Gender, and the New Racism*. New York, NY: Routledge.

Connell, Cati. 2011. The Politics of the Stall: Transgender and Genderqueer Workers Negotiating the Bathroom Question. In *Embodied Resistance: Challenging the Norms, Breaking the Rules*. Edited by Chris Bobel and Samantha Kwan. Nashville, TN: Vanderbilt University Press, 175–185.

Cregan, Kate. 2012. *Key Concepts in Body and Society*. Thousand Oaks, CA: Sage Ltd.

Davis, Georgiann. 2015. *Contesting Intersex: The Dubious Diagnosis*. New York, NY: New York University Press.

Desmond, Matthew and Mustafa Emirbayer. 2009. What Is Racial Domination? *Du Bois Review* 6(2): 335–355.

Dworkin, Shari L. and Faye Linda Wachs. 2009. *Body Panic: Gender, Health, and the Selling of Fitness*. New York, NY: New York University Press.

Ettore, Elizabeth. 2010. *Culture, Bodies and the Sociology of Health*. Burlington, VT: Ashgate Publishing Co.

Fahs, Breanne and Denise A. Delgado. 2011. The Specter of Excess: Race, Class, and Gender in Women's Body Hair Narratives. In *Embodied Resistance: Challenging the Norms, Breaking the Rules*. Edited by Chris Bobel and Samantha Kwan. Nashville, TN: Vanderbilt University Press, 13–25.

Fausto-Sterling, Anne. 2000. *Sexing the Body: Gender Politics and the Construction of Sexuality*. New York, NY: Basic Books.

Flegal, Katherine M., Brian K. Kit, Heather Orpana, and Barry I. Graubard. 2013. Association of All-Cause Mortality with Overweight and Obesity Using Standard Body Mass Index Categories: A Systematic Review and Meta-Analysis. *Journal of the American Medical Association* 309(1): 71–82.

Foucault, Michel. 1975. *Discipline and Punish: The Birth of the Prison*. New York, NY: Random House.

Frank, Arthur. 2010. The Body's Problems with Illness. In *The Body Reader: Essential Social and Cultural Readings*. Edited by Lisa Jean Moore and Mary Kosut. New York, NY: New York University Press, 31–47.

Friedman, Asia. 2013. *Blind to Sameness: Sexpectations and the Social Construction of Male and Female Bodies*. Chicago, IL: University of Chicago Press.

Fullwiley, Duana. 2007. Race and Genetics: Attempts to Define the Relationship. *Biosocieties* 2(2): 221–237.

Gagné, Patricia and Deanna McGaughey. 2002. Designing Women: Cultural Hegemony and the Exercise of Power among Women Who Have Undergone Elective Mammoplasty. *Gender and Society* 16(6): 814–838.

Germov, John and Lauren Williams. 1996. The Epidemic of Dieting Women: The Need for a Sociological Approach to Food and Nutrition. *Appetite* 27(2): 97–108.

Gilman, Sander L. 2010. The Racial Nose. In *The Body Reader: Essential Social and Cultural Readings*. Edited by Lisa Jean Moore and Mary Kosut. New York, NY: New York University Press, 201–227.

Green, Adam Isaiah. 2013. *Sexual Fields: Toward a Sociology of Collective Social Life*. Chicago, IL: University of Chicago Press.

Haraway, Donna J. 1990. *Simians, Cyborgs and Women: The Reinvention of Nature*. New York, NY: Routledge.

Hoang, Kimberly Kay. 2015. *Dealing in Desire: Asian Ascendancy, Western Decline, and the Hidden Currencies of Global Sex Work*. Oakland, CA: University of California Press.

Howson, Alexandra. 2013. *The Body in Society: An Introduction*. Cambridge, UK: Polity.

Hutson, David J. 2013. Your Body Is Your Business Card: Bodily Capital and Health Authority in the Fitness Industry. *Social Science and Medicine* 90: 63–71.

Immergut, Matthew. 2010. Manscaping: The Tangle of Nature, Culture, and Male Body Hair. In *The Body Reader: Essential Social and Cultural Readings*. Edited by Lisa Jean Moore and Mary Kosut. New York, NY: New York University Press, 287–304.

Kessler, Suzanne and Wendy McKenna. 1978. *Gender: An Ethnomethodological Approach.* Chicago, IL: University of Chicago Press.

Kimmel, Michael. 2012. *The Gendered Society.* New York, NY: Oxford University Press.

Kosut, Mary. 2010. Extreme Bodies/Extreme Culture. In *The Body Reader: Essential Social and Cultural Readings.* Edited by Lisa Jean Moore and Mary Kosut. New York, NY: New York University Press, 184–200.

Lorber, Judith and Lisa Jean Moore. 2011. *Gendered Bodies: Feminist Perspectives.* 2nd edn. New York, NY: Oxford University Press.

Malacrida, Claudia and Jacqueline Low. eds. 2008. *Sociology of the Body: A Reader.* New York, NY: Oxford University Press.

McLaughlin, Janice and Edmund Coleman-Fountain. 2014. The Unfinished Body: The Medical and Social Reshaping of Disabled Young Bodies. *Social Science and Medicine* 120: 76–84.

Merleau-Ponty, Maurice. 1962. *Phenomenology of Perception.* New York, NY: Routledge.

Mernissi, Fatema. 2014. The Western Woman's Harem. In *The Kaleidoscope of Gender: Prisms, Patterns, and Possibilities.* 4th edn. Edited by Joan G. Spade and Catherine G. Valentine. Thousand Oaks, CA; Sage.

Moore, Lisa Jean and Mary Kosut. eds. 2010. *The Body Reader: Essential Social and Cultural Readings.* New York, NY: New York University Press.

Omi, Michael and Howard Winant. 1986. *Racial Formation in the United States: From the 1960s to the 1980s.* New York, NY: Routledge.

Pausé, Cat, Jackie Wykes, and Samantha Murray. 2014. *Queering Fat Embodiment.* Hampshire, England: Ashgate Publishing Co.

Pfeffer, Carla A. 2008. Bodies in Relation – Bodies in Transition: Lesbian Partners of Trans Men and Body Image. *Journal of Lesbian Studies* 12(4): 325–345.

Pfeffer, Carla A. 2014. I Don't Like Passing as a Straight Woman: Queer Negotiations of Identity and Social Group Membership. *American Journal of Sociology* 120(1): 1–44.

Pine, Jason. 2010. Embodied Capitalism and the Meth Economy. In *The Body Reader: Essential Social and Cultural Readings.* Edited by Lisa Jean Moore and Mary Kosut. New York, NY: New York University Press, 164–183.

Preves, Sharon E. 2003. *Intersex and Identity: The Contested Self.* New Brunswick, NJ: Rutgers University Press.

Puhl, Rebecca and Kelly D. Brownell. 2001. Bias, Discrimination, and Obesity. *Obesity* 9(12): 788–805.

Puhl, Rebecca M. and Chelsea A. Heuer. 2009. The Stigma of Obesity: A Review and Update. *Obesity* 17(5): 941–964.

Renfrow, Daniel G. 2004. A Cartography of Passing in Everyday Life. *Symbolic Interaction* 27(4): 485–506.

Richardson, Abigail and Elizabeth Cherry. 2011. Anorexia as a Choice: Constructing a New Community of Health and Beauty through Pro-Ana Websites. In *Embodied Resistance: Challenging the Norms, Breaking the Rules.* Edited by Chris Bobel and Samantha Kwan. Nashville, TN: Vanderbilt University Press, 119–129.

Saguy, Abigail. 2014[2012]. *What's Wrong with Fat?* New York, NY: Oxford University Press.

Slavishak, Edward. 2008. *Bodies of Work: Civic Display and Labor in Industrial Pittsburgh.* Durham, NC: Duke University Press.

Trautner, Mary Nell. 2005. Doing Gender, Doing Class: The Performance of Sexuality in Exotic Dance Clubs. *Gender and Society* 19(6): 771–788.

Turner, Bryan S. 1984. *The Body and Society.* 1st edn. Thousand Oaks, CA: Sage.

Turner, Bryan S. 2008. *The Body and Society.* 3rd edn. Thousand Oaks, CA: Sage.

Turner, Bryan S. 2009. Disability and the Sociology of the Body. In *Handbook of Disability Studies.* Edited by Gary L. Albrecht, Katherine Seelman, and Michael Bury. Thousand Oak, CA: Sage, 252–267.

Turner, Bryan S. ed. 2012. *The Routledge Handbook of the Body.* New York, NY: Routledge.

Wacquant, Loïc. 1995. Pugs at Work: Bodily Capital and Bodily Labour among Professional Boxers. *Body and Society* 1(1): 65–93.

Wacquant, Loïc. 2006. *Body and Soul: Notebook of an Apprentice Boxer.* New York, NY: Oxford University Press.

Wacquant, Loïc. 2010. Crafting the Neoliberal State: Workfare, Prisonfare, and Social Insecurity. *Sociological Forum* 25(2): 197–220.

Wacquant, Loïc. 2015. For a Sociology of Flesh and Blood. *Qualitative Sociology* 38(1): 1–11.

Wade, Lisa. 2011. The Politics of Acculturation: Female Genital Cutting and the Challenge of building Multicultural Democracies. *Social Problems* 58(4): 518–537.

Waskul, Dennis D. and Phillip Vannini. eds. 2006. *Body/Embodiment: Symbolic Interaction and the Sociology of the Body*. Hampshire, England: Ashgate Publishing Co.

Williams, Colin, Martin S. Weinberg, and Joshua G. Rosenberger. 2013. Trans Men: Embodiments, Identities, and Sexualities. *Sociological Forum* 28(4): 719–741.

Young, Iris Marion. 1980. Throwing Like a Girl: A Phenomenology of Feminine Body Comportment Motility and Spatiality. *Human Studies* 3(2): 137–156.

CHAPTER 22

The Sociology of Emotion

Kathryn J. Lively

Introduction

Prior to the formal development of the sociology of emotion, the study of emotion had, for the most part, been left to the purview of psychologists. With few exceptions, psychological scholarship on emotion focused closely on cognitive and neurological processes as predictors of emotional experience, without concern for the social environments in which individuals are embedded. In particular, psychologists have concerned themselves with how emotions relate to cognition and personality and, to a lesser degree, social and physical health, without taking into consideration the degree to which every aspect of emotion – from its initial constitution to its consequence – is profoundly social (see Lewis et al. 2015 for a recent review of the field). Over the last four decades, however, sociological scholarship on emotion has begun to fill this gap.

Sociological observations reveal that feelings are not only social constructs, but are also socially patterned and play a vital role in social life. Hochschild (1983), for one, likens emotions to senses that signal what is personally relevant about surrounding events. Building upon this definition, Thoits (1989: 317–342) proposed a four-factor model, which suggests that emotion is comprised of four interrelated factors: physiology, cognition, expression, and labels. Notably, these four factors are interdependent and most sociologists assume a change in one may lead to a change in the others, providing multiple pathways for emotion management. While recognizing the utility of Thoits's approach for organizing existing scholarship on emotion, Lively and Heise (2014: 51–76) have recently redefined emotion as "responses to events that are linked with corporeal manifestations." Their streamlined definition allows for the possibility of ineffable emotions – emotions for which there are no culturally shared labels, but which can nonetheless be found in newspaper photos, religious paintings, and computer simulations.

Theoretical Foundations

Sociological interest in emotion is not new. Marx (1988) wrote eloquently about alienation, just as Weber (1958) did of disenchantment and Durkheim (1951) of anomie. While each was valuable in understanding a discrete emotional syndrome, these early treatises did little to elucidate the broader social-emotional processes that characterize social life (Smith-Lovin 1995: 118–148).

In 1975, American sociologists called for a study of emotion as a social process in its own right. In that same year, Arlie Hochschild (1975: 2–3) argued that a purely cognitive view of human life was not sufficient for sentient beings. Her insistence that emotion was socially patterned was partly explained by her concept of feeling rules, i.e., culturally and historically variable norms defining what should be felt in various situations. This relatively simple insight led to a spate of studies on particular emotions, including grief (Lofland 1985: 71–90), love (Cancian 1987), anger (Stearns and Stearns 1989) and sympathy (Clark 1997), that documented the ways in which feelings are both culturally and historically situated.

Concurrently, Kemper (1978) argued that two fundamental dimensions – power and status – determine *all* emotions, regardless of context. Here, "social power" refers to one's ability to force another's compliance against their will, whereas, "social status" refers to favors freely given. When individuals experience the degree of status or power they expect during a social interaction, they are predicted to feel content or happy. Experiences of excesses or deficits along these dimensions, however, result in certain distressful emotions depending on whether one attributes the cause to one's self or others, as well as the relationship between actors. For instance, if an individual loses status, as a result of his or her incompetence, embarrassment is expected. However, if he or she loses status as a result of another power they expect during a social interaction, they are predicted to feel content or happy.

Taken together, these early theories gave rise to what are collectively known as the cultural and structural perspectives within the sociology of emotion (Lively and Weed 2014: 202–207). Scholars affiliated with the cultural perspective are more likely to be concerned with the set of symbols and meaning that people create or use to regulate their emotions, as well as their behaviors and interactions (Swidler 2003). In contrast, those more aligned with the structural perspective are more attentive to individuals' locations in social structures – that is, one's position within a social network or as a set of status positions that grant access to various levels of power, prestige, or other resources (Lawler and Thye 1999: 217–244; Ridgeway 2011). Although the cultural and structural perspectives are often viewed as distinct (Simon and Nath 2004: 1137–1176), most sociologists agree that social structure and culture are complementary (Heise 2007; Hochschild 1983; Ridgeway 2011). Consequently, most sociological studies of emotion contain elements of both culture and structure (Lois 2013; Lively and Powell 2006: 17–38; Pierce 1995).

Today the sociology of emotions is a formally recognized section of the American Sociological Association. There have been numerous reviews of the field (Thoits 1989: 317–318; Smith-Lovin 1995: 118–148; Stets and Turner 2008: 32–46; Turner and Stets 2006: 25–52), including two full-length handbooks (Stets and Turner 2007; 2014) and a series of volumes dedicated to social perspectives on emotion (e.g., Franks and Gecas 1992). Moreover, several social-psychological theories within sociology have been expanded to make considerations of emotion more central (Smith-Lovin 1990: 238–270; Ridgeway and Johnson 1990: 1198–1212; Lively and Heise 2014: 51–76; Stets 2005: 39–56; Lawler and Thye 1999: 217–244; Lively et al. 2010: 358–379; Hegvdegt and Parris 2014: 103–126; among others), and sociologists routinely contribute to the *Handbook of Emotion* (Lewis et al. 2008; 2015).

Role-Taking, Characteristic, and Structural Emotions

In addition to contributing to psychological debates about the nature of primary versus secondary emotions (e.g., evolutionarily important and cross-culturally universal emotions versus those acquired through socializing agents (Kemper 1987)), sociologists also drew analytic attention to a relatively new category of emotions. According to Shott (1979: 1317–1334), role-taking emotions – embarrassment, shame, guilt, as well as other-directed empathic emotions of sympathy and pride – arise from individuals' ability to engage in the social-psychological process of role-taking. Unlike primary emotions, which are critical for individual survival, role-taking emotions are imperative for the survival of social life. While role-taking – the capacity to see oneself as others do and to use their anticipated responses to guide further conduct (Mead 1967) – was originally introduced as a cognitive process (MacKinnon 1994), Shott, like Hochschild, argued that cognition alone was not enough to motivate and to sustain normative social control. Instead, she suggests that individuals' desire to avoid negative emotions (including shame and embarrassment) and to experience positive ones (such as pride and sympathy) encourages them to engage in self-control, which translates, writ large, into social control. (See also Turner and Stets's (2007: 544–566) recent elaboration of moral emotions.)

Sociologists also make a distinction between characteristic and structural emotions (Heise 2007; Kemper 1987). Characteristic emotions are those feelings that arise when an individual's social role identity is perfectly confirmed (Lively and Heise 2014: 51–76). Characteristic emotions rarely occur during the course of real social interactions, but are useful in that they serve as the basis of emotion norms – the culturally shared beliefs people have about what emotions they should be feeling (e.g., brides should be happy, mourners should be sad).

Structural emotions, in contrast, are those feelings that arise during the course of social interactions and may depart from characteristic emotions within just a few interactional turns. For instance, although most people know they *should* feel sad at a funeral, it is not uncommon to see mourners smiling, or even laughing, during a funeral or wake (Lively and Heise 2014: 51–76).

Emotional Socialization

Emotional socialization refers to the processes through which members of a society learn the expectations, rules, practices, and consequences of emotional experience and its display (Johnson 1992: 183–202). Young children are taught about emotions both explicitly and implicitly, most often by parents and teachers. For example, Pollak and Thoits (1989: 22–34) found that children attending a therapeutic daycare center for those with emotional difficulties were taught explicitly how to link emotion words ("sad" or "angry") to physiological experiences (an upset stomach) and events (being dropped off at school). The goal, rather than to teach students to manage their emotions in appropriate ways, was to get children to understand the causes of their emotions, to express them properly, and to understand their consequences. Leavitt (1994) documented analogous messages (as well as lessons involving emotion management) in her study of non-therapeutic daycare centers.

Although adults tend to be the primary agents of emotional socialization for young children (Johnson 1992: 183–202), by adolescence, teens are active in their own and others' socialization processes (Corsaro 2005: 231–247). Simon et al. (1992: 29–46) report that adolescent girls created new, and sometimes contradictory, norms about romance, while also mirroring norms from the dominant culture. Although the girls policed one another via gossip, name calling, and, in some cases, shunning, some (especially those with high social status) successfully resisted these norms through the strategic use of humor (also see Thorne 1993). Emotional socialization continues throughout the life course, as evidenced by studies of medical students (Smith and Kleinman 1989: 56–69), mortuary science students (Cahill 1999: 101–105), service workers

(Hochschild 1983; Leidner 1993), professionals (Pierce 1995), and black students attending predominantly white colleges (Jackson 2013: 61–71).

Emotion Management

One of the most-studied phenomena within the sociology of emotion is the act of emotion work, or as it is more widely known, emotion management (for a recent review, see Lively and Weed 2014: 202–207). Emotion management refers to the strategies individuals use to bring their feelings in line with existing emotion norms (Hochschild 1979: 551–575). Techniques used to manage emotions include surface acting, to mask or enhance the expression of emotion; and deep acting, wherein the actual emotion is changed (Hochschild 1983).

Empirical studies reveal that the four factors of emotion identified by Thoits (1989: 317–342) are potential points where emotion management can occur. Specifically, individuals can manage their emotions not only by reframing the meaning of a situation (e.g., re-envisioning a problematic passenger as a frightened child, or oneself as a gracious hostess, in order to cultivate positive emotions (Hochschild 1983)), but also by changing their emotional expression (Thoits 1995: 85–109), the labels they use to describe their feelings (Ritchie and Barker 2006: 584–601), or their physiological state (Simon and Nath 2004: 1137–1176).

One distinction sociologists make when studying emotion management is the difference between *intrapersonal* and *interpersonal* emotion management. Whereas intrapersonal emotion management refers to the attempts individuals make in order to bring their own emotions in line with existing feeling norms, and which may have an indirect effect on others, interpersonal emotion management refers to individuals' attempts to directly affect the emotions of others.

Empirical studies illustrate how emotion management specialists – such as therapists (Francis 1997: 153–171), psychodrama leaders (Thoits 1995: 85–109), and social movement activists (Britt and Heise 2000: 252–268) – use interpersonal emotion strategies to influence the emotions of others directly. For example, the therapists in Francis's (1997: 153–171) study of the newly divorced or bereaved helped participants cognitively reframe their own identities, as well as the identities of their former/departed spouses, in ways that led to more positive emotions.

Many interpersonal emotion management strategies involve moving subjects through numerous emotions, leading some scholars to conclude that making several moves between emotions that are experientially near, or similar in terms of one or more dimensions of affective meaning, is easier than making one big leap between two relatively distant or dissimilar emotions (Lively and Heise 2004: 1109–1136; also see Gengler 2014). Indeed, political leaders often move their constituents out of distress and into pride by first invoking fear and anger (Wasielewski 1985: 207–222; also see Britt and Heise 2000: 252–268).

Notably, interpersonal emotion management also occurs informally among friends, coworkers, and loved ones. Staske, for example, documents the collaborative emotion management that occurs among friends and lovers during intimate talk (1996: 111–135). Similarly, Lively (2000: 32–63) illustrates how coworkers routinely engage in reciprocal emotion management in backstage areas, out of the earshot of troublesome employers or clients. Hochschild's (1989) account of dual earner couples further reveals how husbands and wives *co-create* family myths in order to manage individual and shared emotions (also see Jackson 2013).

Emotional Labor

When emotion management is sold for a wage, it becomes emotional labor (Hochschild 1983). For instance, waitresses are paid to "be nice" regardless of insults and are paradoxically asked to be genuine (Erickson 2011). Bill collectors, on the other hand, are taught to be angry, mean, and impatient, in order to bring about fear and compliance in debtors (Hochschild 1983). Unlike "emotion management," which typically occurs in individuals' private lives and has a "use value," "emotional labor" has a "monetary value" and typically benefits the corporation by whom the actor is employed or the customers, clients, or patients with whom the actor is engaged.

In addition to documenting the types of emotional labor performed by individuals from every point on the occupational prestige scale (Wharton 2009: 147–165), sociologists have also investigated the socio-emotional effects of its performance (Hochschild 1983; Leidner 1993). In one of the most systematic attempts to understand this relationship, Wharton and Erickson conducted numerous survey-based studies, where they controlled for a variety of factors, including level of autonomy, self-directed work, and client contact (see Wharton 1993: 205–232; 2009: 147–165 for a review of this literature). Similarly, Erickson and Ritter (2001: 146–163) investigated the effects of three dimensions of emotional labor. They found that managing agitated feelings was more likely to increase feelings of burnout and inauthenticity, whereas managing positive or negative emotions were not.

Although emotional labor has been associated with a variety of jobs, it is worth noting that the demands to provide emotional labor are often gendered and raced. Role identities, such as professional (Wingfield 2010: 251–268), professorial (Bellas 1999: 96–110), or attorney (Harlow 2003; Pierce 1995), which are marked by social characteristics such as black or female are typically held to a higher standard of emotional labor than those which are unmarked (Lively and Heise 2014: 51–76). Hochschild (1983) argued that women (and, by extension, racial and ethnic minorities) have lower "status shields" than (white) men. Individuals with lower status shields are more likely to experience the brunt of others' negative emotions, have their own emotions criticized, and be required to engage in more emotional labor.

Originally, emotion management and emotional labor were theoretically distinct, with emotion management occurring in the private sphere and emotional labor occurring in the public sphere. There is an increasing interest – especially among scholars also interested in the relationship between emotion and stress – in the emotion management that occurs voluntarily in the workplace (Lively 2000: 32–63; Sloan et al. 2013: 343–372) and the emotional labor that occurs at home, even without the benefit of a paid wage (Lois 2013). As a result of this increasing overlap, some scholars have argued for the adoption of a more general term such as emotional regulation, which would capture these processes regardless of context or wage-status (see Grandey et al. 2013).

Emotional Deviance

In addition to studying how culture and social structure shape emotional experience and behavior, sociologists are also interested in the ways in which individuals and their emotions deviate from cultural and structural expectations. In an attempt to better understand the relationship between emotion and mental health problems, Thoits (1985: 221–249) coined the term "emotional deviance." Building on Becker's (1963) labeling theory of deviance, Thoits argues that individuals are often labeled – by self and others – as mentally ill, when they are unable to bring their emotions in line with pre-existing emotion rules or norms. According to this perspective, emotional deviance is likely to arise from multiple roles, role transitions, and unrealistic role demands.

In her recent study of homeschooling mothers, Lois (2013) found that homeschooling mothers were often labeled as emotionally deviant by mothers who sent their children to schools outside of the home. Non-homeschoolers tended to view homeschoolers as emotionally selfish, over-dependent upon their children, arrogant, etc. Instead of seeking professional help, as

Thoits predicted (1985), most homeschooler moms turned to other homeschoolers for help in reframing their emotions as consistent with being "good" mothers.

Identity, Emotion, and Social Structure

According to sociologists, our sense of self – our identity – is connected to social structures and institutions (MacKinnon and Heise 2010; also see Stryker and Serpe 1994: 16–35; Burke 1991: 836–849). In part, this is because identities are embedded in social roles. The emotional aspects of identity work are, in effect, commitments to role performances. When actors conform to the emotional and behavioral expectations of social roles, they are managing their own sense of self and they are also reifying the institutions and organizations in which these roles are embedded. For example, when individuals enact the emotional and behavioral expectations of a physician they are also reifying the institution of medicine (MacKinnon and Heise 2010). In addition, they are perpetuating the relative status positions of physicians and patients, and physicians and other health care providers.

According to *affect control theory* (ACT), individuals create events that confirm their fundamental affective sentiments regarding themselves, others, and settings (Heise 2007). Moreover, when they find themselves in situations that disconfirm these sentiments, they feel "deflection," which is often experienced as emotion. Fundamental sentiments capture a gut sense about how we "feel" about something and are distinguished in terms of Evaluation (how good or bad something is), Potency (how powerful or weak something is), and Activation (how lively or quiescent something is). These dimensions of affective meaning have been documented across numerous cultures and, within a single culture, represent shared meaning regarding identities, behaviors, settings, attributes, and emotion (Heise 2007). Using a cybernetic model, ACT predicts that when transient sentiments contradict fundamental sentiments, individuals are motivated to alter their behavior in order to minimize deflection and reduce the likelihood of re-identification of self, other, or both. Notably, many of the theory's predictions have been verified using ethnographic (Francis 1997: 153–177), survey based (Lively and Powell 2006: 17–38), and experimental methods (Robinson et al. 1994: 175–190), across a wide range of social contexts (e.g., support groups, intimate relations, and mock juries).

Identity control theory, as articulated by Burke and Stets (Burke 1991: 836–849; Stets 2005: 39–56) also illustrates that emotions are implicated when individuals' identities are disconfirmed. Unlike ACT, which calculates deflection using culturally shared affective meaning of social roles, behaviors, and settings, identity control theory is focused primarily on the correspondence between individuals' self-conceptions and others' reactions to their identity performances (Granberg 2006: 106–126). Burke and Harrod's (2005: 359–374) analysis of identity processes among intimate couples, for example, reveals that individuals within committed relationships are happier when their partner's evaluations of them match their own, compared to individuals at the beginning stages of relationships, who would rather their partner see them as slightly better than they see themselves.

Emotions and Theories of Equity, Justice, and Exchange

Other social-psychological theories have grown to incorporate emotion, including equity theory (Walster et al. 1978), justice theory (Hetgvedt and Parris 2014: 103–126), and exchange theory (Lawler 2001: 321–352; Lawler and Thye 1999: 217–244); they, like the identity theories (Heise 1979, 2006; Burke 1991: 836–849), each detail the co-constitutive relationship between emotion and social structure.

Equity theory (Walster et al. 1978) predicts that individuals are likely to experience negative emotion when they perceive an inequity in their interactions with others. Originally, the theory predicted that individuals would experience some form of distress, whether they were under-benefited or over-benefited. However, later scholars specified that anger was more likely in the former case, whereas shame was more likely experienced in the latter (Hegtvedt and Killian 1999: 269–303). Studies using surveys of college students as well as individuals in long-term romantic couples, reveals a variety of emotions, including positive ones, that are implicated in both the projections and perceptions of inequity (Sprecher 1986: 309–321; Lively et al. 2010: 358–379).

The *justice framework* is generally concerned with two social processes: procedural justice and distributive justice (see Hegtvedt and Parris 2014: 103–126). Whereas the former focuses on the means by which outcomes are distributed, the latter is more concerned with the actual allocation of outcomes, often taking into account such issues as need, equity, and equality. Generally speaking, people are happy when they feel as if procedural decisions are just and outcomes seem fair. They are less happy, however, when they believe the procedures to be unfair and the outcomes – as a result – fail to meet their expectations. Moreover, even when individuals receive less than they expected, their negative feelings are somewhat alleviated if they believe the procedure governing the decision is fair (Hegtvedt and Killian 1999: 269–303), or, if the decision-maker is legitimate (Clay-Warner 2006: 207–227).

Finally, *exchange theory*, too, has also made advances in conceptualizing the role of emotions in exchange interactions. A framework for a number of more specific theories (e.g., the theory of social commitments (Lawler et al. 2009), the relational cohesion theory (Lawler and Yoon 1996: 89–108) and the affect theory of social exchange (Lawler 2001: 321–352), exchange theory, at its most basic, suggests that individuals who perceive equity in their social arrangements, who see these arrangements as inherently just, and who believe their contributions are successful, are happier with their outcomes, experience more group cohesion, and are more affectively committed to ongoing exchanges. Conversely, individuals who feel that their costs outstrip their rewards, their contributions are not valued, or the exchange is not successful, are likely to exit the exchange – whether within the context of a friendship, a marriage, or a job, or a small task-focused group – especially in light of better viable alternatives.

As with theories of identity, these perspectives on equity, justice, and exchange reveal that emotions are shaped by existing social and structural arrangements. They also illustrate emotions' ability to contribute to and disrupt the very conditions that gave rise to them initially. Equity theory, justice theory, and exchange theory all rely on the assumption that it is the *perception* of equity, fairness, or net gains over the course of an interaction that affect emotions, rather than the actual, obdurate conditions in which the individuals are actually embedded.

Conclusion

Since its introduction nearly forty years ago, the sociology of emotion has highlighted the emotional processes that arise from and contribute to social life. These processes range from individual-level identity confirmation (Heise 1979; 2007; Burke 1991: 836–849), to organizational behavior (Van Maanen and Kunda 1989: 43–103), to widespread social change (Gould 2009; Jasper 2014: 208–213; Taylor 1996). At a practical level, emotion scholarship has shed light into how criminal sentencing decisions are made (Robinson et al. 1994: 175–190), why individuals with stigmatized identities join social support groups (Schrock et al. 2004: 61–81) and social movements (Britt and Heise 2000: 252–268; Gould 2009), what motivates participation in risky (Lois 2003) or painful (Newmahr 2011) play, and how individuals and organizations alike engage in temporal emotion work that manipulates time in order to manage emotions and manages emotion in order to manipulate time (Lois 2013; Mullaney and Shope 2012).

During the same period, the sociology of emotion established itself as an entity independent from other disciplines with interests in emotion. Recent scholarship seeks to forge a more interdisciplinary path that will allow sociological insight to contribute to broader discussions of emotion – discussions which incorporate understanding originating from such diverse fields as psychology, biology, and cognitive neuroscience (Simon and Lively 2008: 1543–1568; Schnittker 2008: S233–S259; Rogers et al. 2014: 93–99). Moreover, emotion scholars are on the cusp of forging new multi-methodological research designs (Lively 2015), which will allow them to capture each of the four factors of emotion both in isolation and in tandem, and to better understand the genesis and the consequences of human emotions.

References

Becker, Howard. 1963. *Outsiders: Studies in the Sociology of Deviance*. New York, NY: Free Press.

Bellas, Marcia. 1999. Emotional Labor in Academia: The Case of Professors. *Annals of the American Academy of Political and Social Science* 561: 96–110.

Britt, Lori and David R. Heise. 2000. From Shame to Pride in Identity Politics. In *Self, Identity, and Social Movements*. Edited by Sheldon, Timothy J. Owens, and R. W. White. Minneapolis, MN: University of Minnesota Press.

Burke, Peter J. 1991. Identity Processes and Social Stress. *American Sociological Review* 56: 836–849.

Burke, Peter J. and Michael M. Harrod. 2005. Too Much of a Good Thing? *Social Psychology Quarterly* 68: 359–374.

Cahill, Spencer E. 1999. Emotional Capital and Professional Socialization: The Case of Mortuary Science Students (and Me). *Social Psychology Quarterly* 62: 101–116.

Cancian, Francesca M. 1987. *Love in America: Gender and Self-Development*. Cambridge: Cambridge University Press.

Clark, Candace. 1997. *Misery and Company: Sympathy in Everyday Life*. Chicago, IL: University of Chicago Press.

Clay-Warner, Jody. 2006. Procedural Justice and Legitimacy: Predicting Negative Emotional Reactions to Workplace Injustice. *Advances in Group Processes* 23: 207–227.

Corsaro, William A. 2005. Collective Action and Agency in Young Children's Peer Cultures. In *Studies in Modern Childhood: Society, Agency and Culture*. Edited by Jens Qvortrup. Basingstoke: Palgrave Macmillan.

Durkheim, Emile. 1951. *Suicide: A Study in Sociology*. New York, NY: Free Press.

Erickson, Karla. 2011. *The Hungry Cowboy: Service and Community in a Neighborhood Restaurant*. Jackson MI: University Press of Mississippi.

Erickson, Rebecca J. and Christian Ritter. 2001. Emotional Labor, Burnout, and Inauthenticity: Does Gender Matter? *Social Psychology Quarterly* 64: 146–163.

Francis, Linda E. 1997. Ideology and Interpersonal Emotion Management: Redefining Identity in Two Support Groups. *Social Psychology Quarterly* 60: 153–171.

Franks, David and Viktor Gecas. eds. 1992. *Social Perspectives on Emotion*. Vol. 1. Greenwich, CT: JAI Press.

Gengler, Amanda M. 2014. Preemptive Emotion Work among Families of Seriously Ill Children. *American Sociological Association Annual Meetings*. San Francisco, CA.

Gould, Deborah. 2009. *Moving Politics: Emotion and ACT UP's Fight against AIDS*. Chicago, IL: University of Chicago Press.

Granberg, Ellen M. 2006. "Is That All There Is?": Possible Selves, Self-Change, and Weight Loss. *Social Psychology Quarterly* 69: 109–126.

Grandey, Alicia, James A. Diefendorff, and Deborah Rupp. eds. 2013. *Emotional Labor in the 21st Century: Diverse Perspectives on Emotional Regulation at Work*. New York, NY: Psychology Press/Routledge.

Harlow, Roxanna. 2003. "Race Doesn't Matter, But…": The Effect of Race on Professors' Experiences and Emotion Management in the Undergraduate College Classroom. *Social Psychology Quarterly* 66: 348–363.

Hegtvedt, Karen A. and C. Killian. 1999. Fairness and Emotions: Reactions to the Process and Outcomes of Negotiations. *Social Forces* 78: 269–303.

Hegtvedt, Karen and Christine L. Parris. 2014. Justice Theory and Emotions. In *Handbook of Sociology of Emotion*. Vol. 2. Edited by Jan E.

Stets and Jonathon H. Turner. New York, NY: Springer.

Heise, David R. 1979. *Understanding Events: Affect and the Construction of Social Action.* New York, NY: Cambridge University Press.

Heise, David R. 2007. *Expressive Order: Confirming Sentiments in Social Actions.* New York, NY: Springer.

Hochschild, Arlie Russell. 1975. The Sociology of Feeling and Emotion: Selected Possibilities. *Sociological Inquiry* 45: 2–3.

Hochschild, Arlie Russell. 1979. Emotion Work, Feeling Rules, and Social Structure. *American Journal of Sociology* 85: 551–575.

Hochschild, Arlie Russell. 1983. *The Managed Heart: Commercialization of Human Feeling.* Berkeley, CA: University of California Press.

Hochschild, Arlie Russell (with Anne Machung). 1989. *The Second Shift: Working Parents and the Revolution at Home.* New York, NY: Viking.

Jackson, Brandon. 2013. The Bonds of Brotherhood: Emotional and Social Support among College Black Men. *The ANNALS of the American Academy of Political and Social Science* 642: 61–71.

Jasper, James M. 2014. Constructing Indignation: Anger Dynamics in Protest Movements. *Emotion Review* 6: 208–213.

Johnson, Cathryn. 1992. The Emergence of the Emotional Self: A Developmental Theory. *Symbolic Interaction* 15: 182–202.

Kemper, Theodore D. 1978. *A Social Interactional Theory of Emotions.* New York, NY: John Wiley and Sons.

Kemper, Theodore. 1987. How Many Emotions Are There? Wedding the Social and Autonomic Components. *American Journal of Sociology* 93(2): 263–289.

Lawler, Edward J. 2001. An Affect Theory of Social Exchange. *The American Journal of Sociology* 107: 321–352.

Lawler, Edward J. and Shane R. Thye. 1999. Bringing Emotions into Social Exchange Theory. *Annual Review of Sociology* 25: 217–244.

Lawler, Edward J. and Jeongkoo Yoon. 1996. Commitment in Exchange Relations: Test of a Theory of Relational Cohesion. *American Sociological Review* 61: 89–108.

Lawler, Edward J., Shane R. Thye, and J. Yoon. 2009. *Social Commitments in a Depersonalized World.* New York, NY: Russell Sage.

Leavitt, Robin Lynn. 1994. *Power and Emotion in Infant-Toddler Day Care.* Albany, NY: State University of New York Press.

Leidner, Robin. 1993. *Fast Food, Fast Talk: Service Work and the Routinization of Everyday Life.* Berkeley, CA: University of California Press.

Lewis, Michael, Jeannette M. Haviland-Jones, and Lisa Feldman Barrett. eds. 2008. *The Handbook of Emotions.* 3rd edn. New York, NY: The Guildford Press.

Lewis, Michael, Jeannette M. Haviland-Jones, and Lisa Feldman Barrett. eds. 2015 *The Handbook of Emotions.* 4th edn. New York, NY: The Guildford Press.

Lively, Kathryn J. 2000. Reciprocal Emotion Management: Working Together to Maintain Stratification in Private Law Firms. *Work and Occupations* 27: 32–63.

Lively, Kathryn J. 2015. Commentary on "Methodological Innovations from the Sociology of Emotions – Methodological Advances." *Emotion Review* (doi:10.1177/1754073914555924).

Lively Kathryn J. and David R. Heise. 2004. Sociological Realms of Emotional Experience. *American Journal of Sociology* 109: 1109–1136.

Lively, Kathryn J. and David R. Heise. 2014. Emotions in Affect Control Theory. In *Handbook of Sociology of Emotions.* Vol. 2. Edited by Jan E. Stets and Jonathon H. Turner. New York, NY: Springer.

Lively, Kathryn J. and Brian Powell. 2006. Emotional Expression at Work and at Home: Domain, Status or Individual Characteristics? *Social Psychology Quarterly* 69: 17–38.

Lively, Kathryn J. and Emi A. Weed. 2014. Emotion Management: Sociological Insight into What, How, Why, and to What End? *Emotion Review* 6: 202–207.

Lively, Kathryn J., Lala C. Steelman, and Brian Powell. 2010. Equity, Emotion, and Household Division of Labor. *Social Psychology Quarterly* 73: 358–79.

Lofland, Lynn H. 1985. The Social Shaping of Emotion: The Case of Grief. *Symbolic Interaction* 8: 171–190.

Lois, Jennifer. 2003. *Heroic Efforts: The Emotional Culture of Search and Rescue Volunteers.* New York, NY: New York University Press.

Lois, Jennifer. 2013. *Home Is Where The School Is: The Logic of Homeschooling and the Emotional Labor of Mothering.* New York, NY: New York University Press.

MacKinnon, Neil J. 1994. *Symbolic Interactionism as Affect Control.* Albany, NY: State University of New York Press.

MacKinnon, Neil J. and David R. Heise. 2010. *Self, Identity, and Social Institutions.* New York, NY: Palgrave.

Marx, Karl. 1988. *The Economic and Philosophic Manuscripts and the Communist Manifesto.* New York, NY: Prometheus Books.

Mead, Herbert G. 1967. *Mind, Self, and Society: From the Standpoint of a Social Behaviorist.* Edited by C. W. Morris. Chicago, IL: University of Chicago Press.

Mullaney, Jamie L. and Janet H. Shope. 2012. *Paid to Party: Working Time and Emotion in Direct Home Sales.* New Brunswick, NJ: Rutgers University Press.

Newmahr, Staci. 2011. Playing on the Edge: Sadomasochism, Risk, and Intimacy. Bloomington, IN: University of Indiana Press.

Pierce, Jennifer L. 1995. *Gender Trials: Emotional Lives in Contemporary Law Firms.* Berkeley, CA: University of California Press.

Pollak, Lauren Haurte and Peggy A. Thoits. 1989. Processes in Emotional Socialization. *Social Psychology Quarterly* 52: 22–34.

Ridgeway, Cecilia. 2011. *Framed by Gender: How Gender Inequality Persists in the Modern World.* New York, NY: Oxford University Press.

Ridgeway, Cecilia L. and Cathryn Johnson. 1990. What Is the Relationship between Socio-Emotional Behavior and Status in Task Groups? *American Journal of Sociology* 95: 1189–1212.

Ritchie, Ani and Meg Barker. 2006. "There Aren't Words for What We Do or How We Feel So We Have to Make Them Up": Constructing Polyamorous Languages in a Culture of Compulsory Monogamy. *Sexualities* 9: 584–601.

Robinson, Dawn T., Lynn Smith-Lovin, and Olga Tsoudis. 1994. Heinous Crime or Unfortunate Accident?: Effects of Remorse on Responses to Mock Criminal Confessions. *Social Forces* 73: 175–190.

Rogers Kimberly B., Tobias Schröder, and Christian Von Scheve. 2014. Dissecting the Sociality of Emotion: A Multi-Level Approach. *Emotion Review* 6: 93–99.

Schnittker, Jason. 2008. Happiness and Success: Genes, Families, and the Psychological Effects of Socioeconomic Position and Social Support. *American Journal of Sociology* 114(Supplement): S233–S259.

Schrock, Doug P., Daphne Holden, and Lori Reid. 2004. Creating Emotional Resonance: Interpersonal Emotion Work and Motivational Framing in a Transgender Community. *Social Problems* 51: 61–81.

Shott, Susan. 1979. Emotion and Social Life: A Symbolic Interactionist Analysis. *American Journal of Sociology* 84: 1317–1334.

Simon Robin W. and Kathryn J. Lively. 2008. Sex, Anger and Depression. *Social Forces* 88: 1543–1568.

Simon Robin W. and Leda E. Nath. 2004. Gender and Emotion in the U.S.: Do Men and Women Differ in Self-Reports of Feelings and Expressive Behavior? *American Journal of Sociology* 109: 1137–1176.

Simon, Robin W., Donna Eder, and Cathy Evans. 1992. The Development of Feeling Norms Underlying Romantic Love among Adolescent Females. *Social Psychology Quarterly* 55: 29–46.

Sloan Melissa M., Renae N. Evenson, and Ashley B. Thompson. 2013. Counting on Coworkers: Race, Social Support, and Emotional Experiences on the Job. *Social Psychology Quarterly* 76: 343–372.

Smith, Allen C., III and Sherryl Kleinman. 1989. Managing Emotions in Medical School: Students' Contacts with the Living and the Dead. *Social Psychology Quarterly* 52: 56–69.

Smith-Lovin, Lynn. 1990. Emotion as the Confirmation and Disconfirmation of Identity: An Affect Control Model. In *Research Agendas in the Sociology of Emotions.* Edited by Theodore D. Kemper. Albany, NY: State University of New York Press.

Smith-Lovin, Lynn. 1995. The Sociology of Affect and Emotion. In *Sociological Perspectives on Social Psychology.* Edited by Karen S. Cook, Gary Alan Fine, and James S. House. New York, NY: Allyn and Bacon.

Sprecher, Susan. 1986. The Relation between Inequality and Emotions in Close Relationships. *Social Psychology Quarterly* 49: 309–321.

Staske, Shirley A. 1996. Talking Feelings: The Collaborative Construction of Emotion in Talk between Close Relational Partners. *Symbolic Interaction* 19: 111–135.

Stearns, Carolyn Z. and Peter N. Stearns. 1989. *Anger: The Struggle for Emotional Control in America's History.* Chicago, IL: University of Chicago Press.

Stets, Jan E. 2005. Examining Emotions in Identity Theory. *Social Psychology Quarterly* 68: 39–56.

Stets, Jan E. and Jonathon H. Turner. eds. 2007. *Handbook of the Sociology of Emotion*. Vol. 1. New York, NY: Springer.

Stets, Jan E. and Jonathon H. Turner. 2008. The Sociology of Emotion. In *Handbook of Emotions*. Edited by Michael Lewis, Jeannette M. Haviland-Jones, and Lisa Feldman Barrett. 3rd edn. New York, NY: Guilford.

Stets, Jan E. and Jonathon H. Turner. eds. 2014. *Handbook of the Sociology of Emotion*. Vol. 2. New York, NY: Springer.

Stryker, Sheldon and Richard T. Serpe. 1994. Identity Salience and Psychological Centrality: Equivalent, Overlapping, or Complementary Concepts. *Social Psychology Quarterly* 57: 16–35.

Swidler, Ann. 2003. *Talk of Love: How Culture Matters*. Chicago, IL: University of Chicago Press.

Taylor, Verta. 1996. *Rock-a-by Baby: Feminism, Self-Help and Post-Partum Depression*. New York, NY: Routledge.

Thoits, Peggy A. 1985. Self-Labeling Processes in Mental Illness: The Role of Emotional Deviance. *American Journal of Sociology* 92: 221–249.

Thoits, Peggy A. 1989. The Sociology of Emotions. *Annual Review of Sociology* 15: 317–342.

Thoits, Peggy A. 1995. Managing the Emotions of Others. *Symbolic Interaction* 19: 85–109.

Thorne, B. 1993. *Gender Play: Girls and Boys in School*. New Brunswick, NJ: Rutgers University Press.

Turner, Jonathon H. and Jan E. Stets. 2006. Sociological Theories of Human Emotions. *Annual Review of Sociology* 32: 25–52.

Turner, Jonathon H. and Jan E. Stets. 2007. Moral Emotions. In *Handbook of the Sociology of Emotions*. Vol. 1. Edited by Jan E. Stets and Jonathon H. Turner. New York, NY: Springer.

Van Maanen, J. and Gideon Kunda. 1989. Real Feelings: Emotional Expression and Organizational Culture. *Research in Organizational Behavior* 11: 43–103.

Walster, E., G. W. Walster, and Elaine Berscheid. 1978. *Equity: Theory and Research*. New York, NY: Allyn and Bacon Inc.

Wasielewski, Patricia L. 1985. The Emotional Basis of Charisma. *Symbolic Interaction* 8: 207–222.

Weber, Max. 1958. *The Protestant Ethic and the Spirit of Capitalism*. New York, NY: Charles Scribner.

Wharton, Amy S. 1993. The Affective Consequences of Service Work. *Work and Occupations* 20: 205–232.

Wharton, Amy S. 2009. The Sociology of Emotional Labor. *Annual Review of Sociology* 35: 147–165.

Wingfield, Adia H. 2010. Are Some Emotions Marked "Whites Only"? Racialized Feeling Rules in Professional Workplaces. *Social Problems* 57: 251–268.

CHAPTER 23
The Sociology of Friendship

James Vela-McConnell

Despite how central friendship is to our social lives, it has only recently emerged as a focused area of study within sociology. Unlike the family, the study of friendship is not yet widespread enough to warrant the creation of its own section or division within the American Sociological Association. Moreover, in a world where "friend" has become a verb and many people can be "friended" online who might not actually be friends off-line – and are instead acquaintances, colleagues, professional contacts, and even strangers – there is a greater sense of ambiguity over what counts as a friend in the first place. To blur the lines even further, there are some friends who might be considered a part of one's family. Regardless of these ambiguities, there are important reasons for studying friendship from a sociological perspective, not the least of which is that friendships are socially patterned, making them inherently sociological in nature (Spencer and Pahl 2006). With this focus in mind, we will examine the sociological perspective on friendship with a particular eye toward understanding why it is such an important sociological topic.

Friendship and the Fabric of Society

Within contemporary society, an increasing number of relationships are characterized by contractual arrangements between the parties involved. Work and business relations, familial and even neighborhood relations are governed by contracts, specifying both the rights and obligations of the individuals concerned. If these contracts are broken, there are legal procedures and policies designed to protect the aggrieved party, highlighting how the state has a vested interest in the stability of these relationships. The fact that the state oversees such relations reflects an unstated measure of the importance placed on them. They are seen as fundamental to the fabric of society and so are guaranteed special protections.

In contrast, friendships are completely voluntary in nature and are characterized by a distinct absence of contractual arrangements. Even in cases where one friend borrows money from another, any agreement is likely to be entirely verbal and based on one's "word." A friend may even be offended at the prospect of a contract in such a situation. Unlike most ongoing relationships, friendships are freely entered into, maintained, and terminated. These relationships are strictly private in the sense that they enjoy no state recognition; nor is there a perceived need to protect them with legal procedures and policies. Unlike marriage or signing a mortgage or lease agreement, there are no public social rituals associated with friendship, though there are likely to be many private ones between the friends themselves, such as the exchange of gifts and other symbols of the relationship (Rubin 1985). Essentially, it seems that friendships are not deemed important to the fabric of society.

Such a viewpoint, however, is without merit, for friendships are essential to the social fabric. Indeed, friendships are integral to establishing large networks of social ties. These ever-widening networks are exactly what comprise the fabric of society. Sociologist Georg Simmel (Wolff 1950) argued that dyadic relationships – those between two people – represent the building blocks of society, for it is within these dyads that social relations begin. Every larger group is comprised of numerous dyadic relationships organized into interlocking social webs. For Putnam (2000), friendship represents an informal social connection, one that is of central importance given its function in connecting individuals into much larger social networks. In this way, patterns of friendships bring people together into ever-larger networks, weaving together the fabric of society.

Anthropologists have long recognized the importance of friendship networks in creating social cohesion (Eve 2002). They note that friendships are based on a sense of reciprocity between the two individuals, best symbolized by the exchange of gifts or favors. Such a social bond is formed with an eye toward ensuring the relationship will continue, for if one gives a gift an obligation to reciprocate is created. Ideally, the reciprocity between individuals becomes generalized beyond the dyadic relationship extending outward to include others through the creation of what might be termed "bridging ties." Such generalized reciprocity fosters a sense of trust that "lubricates social life," especially when it extends out and includes a diverse group of people (Putnam 2000). In this way, friendships – like other relationships – serve to foster the social cohesion that holds society together. Insofar as our interactions and relationships begin to follow predictable patterns, we create social order. Hence, the popular sentiment that friendships are less fundamental to society than formally recognized and state-protected relationships is misguided.

The Nature of Friendships

But what is it that characterizes friendships? As already noted, they are completely voluntary and without contractual obligations, which means that the sense of connection is one that emerges from and is sustained by the relationship itself. These relationships are *chosen* rather than *given*, as familial relations are (Spencer and Pahl 2006). Perhaps of more importance, friendships are egalitarian in nature. Friends recognize one another as equals (Pahl 2000; Bell 1981). Neither party is dependent upon the other. While support is often provided, each recognizes that the other may be called upon to provide that support and there is an expectation that such support will be shared. In addition, this egalitarian quality results from a sense of mutual respect and acceptance that implies each person equally values the other (Allan and Adams 1998). When there is a power disparity within a relationship, the sense of reciprocity is out of balance and one member feels a greater sense of obligation toward the member with greater power, making the relationship less voluntary. In the context of friendships, such an imbalance leads to resentment and contempt, undermining the friendship or even its possibility (Rude 2009). In this way, the egalitarian and voluntary natures of friendship are intimately tied to one another.

With an eye toward distinguishing friendships from other intimate – typically familial – relationships and highlighting their purely voluntary and egalitarian natures, friendship is understood to be "an active and freely chosen platonic relationship between two equals demonstrating a high degree of commitment toward each other and relating to one another in a variety of ways" (Vela-McConnell 2011: 23). Even with this definition in mind, there are many ways in which to organize our sociological understanding of friendship. One may focus on the patterns of entering and exiting friendships or on friendship careers or trajectories in terms of how they develop.

For example, it is possible to differentiate among types of friendship. Spencer and Pahl (2006) distinguish between simple and complex friendships. Friends relate to one another in a variety of ways based on the type and degree of attachment between the members. Sometimes a friend is a useful contact, someone who can do a favor for us, or someone with whom we can just have fun. Such relationships may be considered "simple friendships" in that there is only one form of interaction that takes place. Friendships typically begin as simple friendships based on shared interests or exchanging favors and many of these never grow into deeper relationships. When people are able to connect at a deeper level, developing a sense of commitment, their friendship may grow. "Complex friendships" arc multifaceted in that the friends relate to one another in a variety of ways. For example, they can have fun together, provide help when needed, become confidants and even soul mates.

Given that our networks of friends change over time, it is also helpful to distinguish between current and ongoing friendships and those that are more episodic in nature or those that exist largely in the past. "Active friendships" are those in which there is regular contact between the friends and a strong sense of presence in each other's lives. Such friends provide us with a sense of identity and connection. Over time, however, there are life course changes and events that occur – such as moving to another part of town or the country, changes in one's socio-economic status, a new job or retirement, or starting a family – that lead us to connect with new people even as we disengage from some friends. Some active friendships may then become "latent," meaning the frequency of contact diminishes while maintaining a sense of presence in one another's lives continues. If that sense of presence is strong enough, it is relatively easy for the friends to "pick up where they left off." Other friendships no longer exist as such and so may be considered "historical friendships" because there is no contact between the members. Even among these friendships, there may be a sense of presence in our lives given that they played a role in shaping our biography. We may look back at them with a sense of nostalgia and they may evoke a sense of connection with who we once were (Spencer and Pahl 2006).

Regardless of the type of friendship or its degree of intimacy, these relationships are embedded within a larger social and cultural context. As such, friendships are subject to societal norms and trends. Moreover, they tend to reflect existing social structures and hierarchies. For the sociologist, what this means is that the study of friendship and friendship patterns reveals much about the structure of society.

Friendship as a Social Barometer

In June of 2006, a study published by the *American Sociological Review* made national headlines with the news that the size of Americans' circle of friends was shrinking (American Sociological Association 2006). Researchers found that the number of people in the United States who have no one they consider to be a confidant more than doubled from 10 percent in 1985 to 24.6 percent in 2004 (McPherson et al. 2006). The study included a number of different relationships among those considered to be confidants; if one isolates friendships, those survey respondents who consider a friend to be one of their confidants dropped from 73.2 percent in 1985 to 50.6 percent in 2004. Clearly, something happened to friendships among Americans over the course of those twenty years.

There are a number of sociologists who are concerned that the fabric of society is wearing thin. As such, friendships represent a "social barometer" reflecting deeper social patterns and trends. This concern with the breakdown in social and civic engagement goes all the way back to Alexis de Tocqueville (1889). Much more recently, Robert Putnam argued there is ample evidence indicating that friendships and other social connections are deteriorating, threatening the social fabric of society. Today, we are far less likely to spend time at home with friends than we were thirty or forty years ago. Putnam concludes that, "visits with friends are now on the social capital endangered species list" (2000: 100). Given the importance of these relationships in fostering the voluntary social bonds that hold society together, this decline is an admittedly critical indicator of the erosion of social cohesion.

In addition, friendship patterns tend to reflect the system of stratification in our society in that people are more likely to befriend those very much like themselves in terms of race, class, gender, sexual orientation, etc. – what is known as "status homophily" (McPherson et al. 2001). In other words, differentiation based on status places a check on the establishment of friendships such that these networks are largely restricted to those of similar status. Given that friendship is characterized in part by its egalitarian nature, the prevalence of homophily within these relationships underscores the fact there is social pressure to avoid potential friendships between those of differing status. Narrowing the range of our friendship possibilities places limits on the possible variety of social bonds making up the fabric of society and the underlying social cohesion.

Why is homophily common within friendships? Many would point to individual preferences and choices. Evidence suggests, however, that such an explanation is problematic. Instead, it is important to keep in mind the social context: the options available to us are constrained by opportunities we have to meet diverse others, opportunities that are limited by the arrangement of our physical and social environments (De Souza Briggs 2002). Within that social context, individuals make what Feld calls "focused choices" (1982).

While we live in a heterogeneous society, our neighborhoods continue to be highly segregated by class (Dwyer 2010), race (Wright et al. 2014), and even sexual orientation, age, and religion. The same holds true for many institutions and organizations. Schools, for example, tend to reflect the demographics of the area in which they are located, and public schools in particular are increasingly segregated (Orfield 2008). We are also segregated within our work environments and even our voluntary organizations, particularly with regard to gender and level of education (McPherson et al. 2001; Rotolo and Wilson 2007). Such segregation limits our opportunities to meet and engage in regular interaction with people from different backgrounds and statuses.

Given these constrained options, it should come as no surprise that our social networks are disproportionately homogenous. This constrains our opportunities to form friendships with diverse others. In fact, the lack of diversity within a social network is the strongest predictor of friendship homophily. As noted by Feld, "people tend to choose their friends from among those with whom they have regular contact in one or another of their focused activities; the set of people who are available through these foci tends to direct their choices to individuals with particular personal characteristics" (1982: 797). Our choices are constrained by the diversity of the groups in which we participate and the resulting pattern of homophily is largely "induced" rather than specifically chosen by individuals.

It is clear that our social context – the neighborhoods we inhabit, our work, school, and other institutional environments and our social networks – plays a significant role in patterns of friendship homophily by constraining our opportunities to meet and interact with diverse others as equals. When we do have the opportunity to befriend those who are different, our own choices tend to reinforce the homophilous pattern (Feld 1982). The choices we make are often based on the social boundaries created by our own prejudices and stereotypes of those who are different. Much like strangers, those who are different are considered to be socially distant from ourselves (Wolff 1950). Those with whom we share similarities are also those with whom we are most likely to establish social bonds and create group solidarity. The similarities allow a sense of "we-ness" to develop, opening the door for the creation of what Gordon Allport (1954) describes as an "in-group." Once such a sense of connectedness with similar others emerges, there is a corresponding separation from those who are different: the "out-group." At a most basic level, there is a tendency to perceive such differences as possible threats to the in-group and it is this perception – or misperception – that opens the door for prejudice and social distance. The social distance that shapes our individual choices and the spatial distance that constrains our friendship options to begin with are mutually reinforcing. For example, social distance may produce patterns of neighborhood segregation even in the absence of housing discrimination (Fossett 2006a; 2006b). Moreover, such segregation patterns reinforce and increase the social distance between groups (White et al. 2005).

The consequences of both social context and individual choice on friendship patterns are well established. We are most likely to establish and maintain friendships with those who are demographically similar to ourselves, though such homophily is not equally distributed. For example, those in positions of privilege tend to have the most homogenous social networks (McPherson et al. 2006). The pattern of friendship homophily is strongest for race and ethnicity, though it appears to be decreasing over time. Race and ethnicity are followed by age and gender. In the case of gender homophily, the pattern has remained stable over time (McPherson et al. 2006). Class-based friendship, when measured in terms of education and occupation, is just as strong as gender homophily. When measured by wealth, class homophily patterns are even stronger (McPherson et al. 2001). There has been far less research focusing on friendship patterns and sexual orientation; but the existing research indicates that the same pattern of friendship homophily is present (Nardi 1992a; Nardi 1992b; Price 1999).

Patterns of friendship homophily both reflect and reinforce the system of stratification in our society. If friendships represent a sort of "social barometer" measuring the health and cohesiveness of society, then sociologists have cause for concern. The social divisions within society are strong and run deep. The range of friendship ties is narrow and, as the number of those who have friends they consider to be confidants diminishes, the consequences for the fabric of society are worrisome. Nevertheless, there appears to be some cause for optimism as our social networks slowly begin to diversify. For example, the percentage of adults in the United States who had at least one person of another race in their social network increased from 8.9 percent in 1985 to 15.4 percent in 2004 (McPherson et al. 2006). A 2013 survey indicated that 25 percent of whites had a least one person of color in their social network (Public Religion Research Institute 2014). While the percentage is still small, it suggests that cracks are forming in the segregation patterns described above. As social networks begin to diversify, opportunities for diverse friendships will also increase.

Strengthening the Fabric of Society

As already discussed, friendships are fundamentally egalitarian in nature. To the extent that friendships are formed outside of the typical patterns just described, they pose a challenge to the system of stratification. There is reason to believe that, as with marriage patterns, friendship segregation may be decreasing (Vela-McConnell 2011), suggesting that diverse friendships may counteract the trend toward social disintegration lamented by sociologists like Robert Putnam. As these egalitarian relationships across lines of stratification increase in number, a pattern of interpersonal relations emerges and becomes a tacit public statement calling into question – at its most fundamental level – the current system of stratification.

Putnam (2000) suggests that two conditions must be met in order to realize the potential of friendships – and diverse friendships in particular – to strengthen the cohesion of society. First, if our social context limits our opportunities to meet diverse others, we need to adjust that context in order to maximize the opportunities available. This requires promoting diversity and integration within the structures of society, particularly in our neighborhoods and social institutions. Because it requires addressing long-established patterns of segregation within neighborhoods, schools, churches, work environments, and our own social circles, this is perhaps the most challenging hurdle to overcome.

The second condition provides more cause for optimism. As prescribed by contact theory (Allport 1954), once individuals are presented with the opportunity to meet diverse others, they are better able to re-evaluate and set aside any prejudice, anxiety, or fear they have toward diverse others and bridge the differences between them. Changing the social context to allow increasing contact between diverse groups of people is in itself insufficient. In keeping with the egalitarian nature of friendships, such contact must be between those with equal status. More importantly, diverse groups of people should work together "in the pursuit of common goals" in order to allow the members of these groups to recognize that they have common interests and a common humanity. Integration of this sort "creates a condition where friendly contacts and accurate social perceptions can occur" (Allport 1954: 272). Pettigrew (1998) described this condition as "friendship potential." Moreover, because friendships encourage a much greater depth of connection, the positive effects of reducing prejudice are heightened (Barlow et al. 2009). These effects even extend beyond the individuals within these friendships (Bousfield and Hutchison 2010), generalizing to the entire out-group, not just the individual friend who is a part of the out-group. Overall, contact with diverse others not only enhances knowledge and reduces anxiety, but also augments the ability to take the perspective of and empathize with those who are different (Pettigrew and Tropp 2006); and it is our ability to role take and empathize with others that is key to establishing the sense of connectedness that holds society together (Vela-McConnell 1999).

As noted above, contact theory rests on the fundamental requirement that the parties be of equal status. The egalitarian nature of friendships makes these relationships especially important in terms of challenging the systems of stratification that keep those of different races, genders, and sexual orientations apart. The pursuit of equality that characterizes friendship represents an ethical practice of friendship as well as a political practice and outcome such that the equality of these relationships has much potential for creating social change: "Standing as equals embodies a challenge to hierarchical social structures. The tendency of friendships toward equal treatment is therefore a fundamental political potential...It flies in the face of the status quo" (Rawlins 2009: 194).

Conclusion

Friendships, as dyadic relationships, are key building blocks of society, fundamental to the social fabric. Social cohesion begins at the micro-level of dyadic relationships. The bonding ties that characterize friendships are clearly evident within homogenous social groups. The challenge is to generalize these ties beyond such social groups into "bridging ties" that connect diverse groups of people together, strengthening social cohesion at the macro-level (Putnam 2000). Furthermore, each friendship occurs within over-lapping social circles, allowing diverse friendships to serve as role models that influence ever-widening and over-lapping social circles.

Strong social bonds characterize enduring friendships forming the basis of the network of social ties upon which all our institutions rest. Friendship patterns that conform to the divisions within society based on race, class, gender, sexual orientation, and other forms of marginalization indicate that the foundation of society is fractured. A strong social fabric requires bringing together the diverse peoples who comprise society. To the extent that we choose to befriend those from different status levels and consider them to be our equals, our friendships pose a challenge to the existing system of stratification. Friendships that bridge different groups, establishing ties among them, play a key role in creating what Pahl (2000) described as a "truly friendly society."

Given how fundamental these purely voluntary and egalitarian relationships are, the study of friendship represents a lens through which sociologists may examine the health of society itself. Friendships provide us with a strong sense of connection with the world around us, embedding us within ever-widening social networks. When these social ties decrease in number and become increasingly homogenous, it is right to worry about the problems of social isolation, disconnection, and the breakdown of society. As these friendships – and the social bonds they represent – increase and diversify, sociologists can rest assured that the social cohesion that holds society together is getting stronger. And all of us can enjoy our friends not only for who they are but what they represent: our connection with the fabric of society.

References

Allan, Graham and Rebecca G. Adams. 1998. Reflections on Context. In *Placing Friendships In Context*. Edited by Rebecca G. Adams and Graham Allan. Cambridge: Cambridge University Press.

Allport, Gordon. 1954. *The Nature of Prejudice*. Reading, MA: Addison-Wesley Publishing Company.

American Sociological Association. 2006. Americans' Circle of Close Friends Shrinking, New Study Shows. *Science Daily*. June 23. Available at www.sciencedaily.com/releases/2006/06/060623093533.htm, accessed December 5, 2016.

Barlow, Fiona Kate, Winnifred R. Louis, and Miles Hewstone. 2009. Rejected! Cognitions of Rejection and Intergroup Anxiety as Mediators of the Impact of Cross-Group Friendships on Prejudice. *British Journal of Social Psychology*. 48: 389–405.

Bell, Robert R. 1981. *Worlds of Friendship*. Beverly Hills, CA: Sage.

Bousfield, Catherine, and Paul Hutchison. 2010. Contact, Anxiety, and Young People's Attitudes and Behavioral Intentions towards the Elderly. *Educational Gerontology*. 36: 451–466.

De Souza Briggs, Xavier. 2002. *Social Capital and Segregation: Race, Connections, and Inequality in America*. Report. John F. Kennedy School of Government, Harvard University.

Dwyer, Rachel E. 2010. Poverty, Prosperity, and Place: The Shape of Class Segregation in the Age of Extremes. *Social Problems*. 57: 114–137.

Eve, Michael. 2002. Is Friendship a Sociological Topic? *European Journal of Sociology*. 43: 386–409.

Feld, Scott L. 1982. Social Structural Determinants of Similarity among Associates. *American Sociological Review*. 47: 797–801.

Fossett, Mark. 2006a. Ethnic Preferences, Social Distance Dynamics, and Residential Segregation: Theoretical Explorations Using Simulation Analysis. *Journal of Mathematical Sociology*. 30: 185–274.

Fossett, Mark. 2006b. Including Preference and Social Distance Dynamics in Multi-Factor Theories of Segregation. *Journal of Mathematical Sociology*. 30: 289–298.

McPherson, Miller, Lynn Smith-Lovin, and James M. Cook. 2001. Birds of a Feather: Homophily in Social Networks. *Annual Review of Sociology*. 27: 415–444.

McPherson, Miller, Lynn Smith-Lovin, and Matthew E. Brashears. 2006. Social Isolation in America: Changes in Core Discussion Networks over Two Decades. *American Sociological Review*. 71: 353–375.

Nardi, Peter M. 1992a. Sex, Friendship, and Gender Roles among Gay Men. In *Men's Friendships*. Edited by Peter M. Nardi. Newbury Park, CA: Sage.

Nardi, Peter M. 1992b. That's What Friends Are For: Friends as Family in the Gay and Lesbian Community. In *Modern Homosexualities: Fragments of Lesbian and Gay Experience*. Edited by Ken Plummer. New York, NY: Routledge.

Orfield, Gary. 2008. Race and Schools: The Need for Action. *Civil Rights Project/Proyecto Derechos Civiles*. University of California – Los Angeles, NEA Research Visiting Scholars Series, Spring 2008. Vol. 1b. January 1, 2014. Available at www.nea.org/home/13054.htm, accessed December 5, 2016.

Pahl, Ray. 2000. *On Friendship*. Cambridge: Polity Press.

Pettigrew, Thomas F. 1998. Intergroup Contact Theory. *Annual Review of Psychology*. 49: 65.

Pettigrew, Thomas F. and Linda R. Tropp. 2006. A Meta-Analytic Test of Intergroup Contact Theory. *Journal of Personality and Social Psychology*. 90: 751–783.

Price, Jammie. 1999. *Navigating Differences: Friendships between Gay and Straight Men*. Binghamton, NY: Haworth Press Inc.

Public Religion Research Institute. 2014. *Analysis: Race and Americans' Social Networks*. August 28. Available at www.prri.org/research/race-religion-political-affiliation-americans-social-networks/, accessed December 21, 2016.

Putnam, Robert D. 2000. *Bowling Alone: The Collapse and Revival of American Community*. New York, NY: Simon and Schuster.

Rawlins, William K. 2009. *The Compass of Friendship: Narratives, Identities, and Dialogues*. Newbury Park, CA: Sage.

Rotolo, Thomas and John Wilson. 2007. Sex Segregation in Volunteer Work. *The Sociological Quarterly*. 48: 559–585.

Rubin, Lillian B. 1985. *Just Friends: The Role of Friendship in Our Lives*. New York, NY: Harper and Row, Publishers.

Rude, Jesse D. 2009. Interracial Friendships in Context: Their Formation, Development, and Impact. Thesis, University of California – Davis.

Spencer, Liz and Ray Pahl. 2006. *Rethinking Friendship: Hidden Solidarities Today*. Princeton, NJ: Princeton University Press.

de Tocqueville, Alexis. 1889. *Democracy in America*. London: Longman, Green and Co.

Vela-McConnell, James A. 1999. *Who Is My Neighbor? Social Affinity in a Modern World*. New York, NY: State University of New York Press.

Vela-McConnell, James A. 2011. *Unlikely Friends: Bridging Ties and Diverse Friendships*. Lanham, MD: Lexington Books.

White, Michael J., Ann H. Kim, and Jennifer E. Glick. 2005. Mapping Social Distance: Ethnic Residential Segregation in a Multiethnic Metro. *Sociological Methods and Research*. 34: 173–203.

Wolff, Kurt H. 1950. *The Sociology of Georg Simmel*. New York, NY: The Free Press of Glencoe.

Wright, Richard, Mark Ellis, and Steven Holloway. 2014. Neighbourhood Racial Diversity and White Residential Segregation in the United States. In *Social-Spatial Segregation: Concepts, Processes and Outcomes*. Edited by Christopher D. Lloyd, Ian G. Shuttleworth, and David Wong. Cambridge: Polity Press.

Part VI

THE SOCIOLOGY OF THE LIFE COURSE

CHAPTER 24

The Sociology of Children

Gertrud Lenzer

Why is there a Sociology of Children and Youth and when did it come into existence? What are its theoretical and methodological premises and mission? And how does it relate to the "Sociology of Childhood," to "Children's Studies" and "Childhood Studies?" These are some of the questions this chapter attempts to answer.

The need for a sociological subdiscipline with a central focus on children became clear in May 1985 with the publication of *Children in Poverty*. Issued by the US House of Representatives Committee on Ways and Means, it reported a major and significant increase in child poverty in the United States. Entire institutional governmental domains,[1] legal systems, and bureaucracies existed with foci on children, such as those with emphasis on "child protection" and "juvenile justice." In the economy, the world of business and the economy at large, children and youth had become a major market sector. Sociology, though, had no subfield dedicated to a focus on children.

The Development of the Sociology of Children

How was it that sociology had forgotten about children?[2] Not only sociology, but also anthropology, economics, political science, and other disciplines lacked a special focus on children.[3] Finally, in the article "Is There Sufficient Interest to Establish a Sociology of Children?" in the August 1991 issue of *Footnotes*,[4] the Newsletter of the

---

[1] The United States Children's Bureau was founded in 1912 and later became a part of the United States Department of Health and Human Services' Administration for Children and Families. Every state has its own Office of Children and Family Services, even though the names may slightly vary.

[2] Similar questions were also raised by Ambert (1986) and Thorne (1987).

[3] There existed, however, other fields which focused on children. Historically, both psychology and education had such special fields as "child psychology," "child development" and pedagogy and the medical professions had pediatrics.

[4] Vol. 19(6): 8.

American Sociological Association (ASA), members of the US sociological community were asked whether they held the establishment of a new section in the "Sociology of Children" desirable or even necessary. This inquiry was supported in a letter by then President-Elect of the ASA, James S. Coleman, that accompanied the inquiry in *Footnotes*, even though he previously held the position in private conversations that sociology was already addressing children in its subfields of the "Sociology of Education," the "Sociology of the Family," and the "Sociology of Generations."

In response to the publication of the *Footnotes* article, letters came in welcoming and supporting the establishment of a Sociology of Children section within the American Sociological Association. Many respondents indicated that they had experienced major difficulties in finding a disciplinary home in sociology for their research and articles on children. Only one respondent wrote to express his conviction that such a new field was not desirable for the field of sociology.

In light of such widespread support from inside the discipline, the requisite signatures from ASA members were gathered[5] and there was quick approval of the Sociology of Children section as a new "Section-in-Formation" by the executive body of the American Sociological Association in January 1992. The rapidly increasing number of signatories justified the full formation of the Section by May 1992 and the inclusion of the Section of the Sociology of Children in the annual meetings of the Association in August 1992 at which the bylaws for the new section were written and its first section officers elected. The history of this spontaneous – as it were – creation and development of the 31st ASA Section of the Sociology of Children is in and of itself of special historical significance. With the establishment of the section, the Sociology of Children was formally institutionalized as the first academic and professional organization internationally with a focus on children.

The original bylaws of the Sociology of Children section focused on children as a generational cohort and social class from age zero to eighteen. This specification was based on both effective definitions within US law and international jurisprudence. The binding legal definitions of what constitutes a child in society are of importance. In the United States all laws, regulations, and national statistics commonly define a child as being under the age of eighteen. As for international jurisprudence, the bylaws used Article 1 of the UN Convention on the Rights of the Child (UNCRC), according to which "a child means every human being below the age of 18 years unless, under the law applicable to the child, majority is attained earlier." In 2000, the title of the section was changed to the Sociology of Children and Youth.

The Development of the Sociology of Childhood

The idea of a Sociology of Childhood emerged in Europe at around the same time but it took several years before national sociological associations in Europe established respective sections.[6] Due to an initiative by European sociologists, signatures were gathered there and in the United States for the establishment of a Working Group on the Sociology of Childhood within the International Sociological Association (ISA). This ISA Working Group, which came into existence in the early part of the 1990s, subsequently achieved the status of a Research Committee on the Sociology of Childhood and exists now as Research Committee 53[7] with its own sessions at ISA international congresses.

---

[5] Sociological colleagues such as Barrie Thorne, Doris Entwisle, and numerous others helped with the collection of signatures.

[6] For example, the German section of the Sociology of Children and Childhood was only established in the German Sociological Association in 1995.

[7] Interestingly enough, within the ISA there also exists the Research Committee on Youth, RC 34, which was founded in 1975.

The Historical Background

The emergence of interest in children and young people among sociologists occurred within a larger historical framework and context. Beginning in 1979, the Year of the Child, and over the following ten years, the universal human rights treaty for children was drafted. The UNCRC was adopted by the UN General Assembly and was opened for signature on November 20, 1989 and it came into force on September 2, 1990. Today, all governments and countries – with the exception of the United States – have ratified the Convention and are state parties to it. Moreover, 1991 marked the publication of the final report of the national US Commission on Children: *Beyond Rhetoric: A New Agenda for Children and Families*. This was the report of a United States Commission created by President Ronald Reagan and Congress in 1987, which focused on children, very much like previous national commissions going back to 1909 and periodic commission reports until 1970.[8] This renewed interest in children – both globally and nationally – is of significance when it comes to the establishment of scholarly institutions such as the ASA and ISA sections focusing on children.

In light of these developments and in hindsight, the historical emergence of the subfield of the Sociology of Children was part of a growing phenomenon in which children increasingly appeared in public consciousness in the academy and many other quarters. During this period, other disciplines, such as history and anthropology also developed special foci on children and young people. In other words, sociology was only one of the humanities and social science disciplines which "discovered" this class of hitherto neglected human beings. However, the subfield of the Sociology of Children in the United States was the first to become organizationally institutionalized and active.

The Interdisciplinary Field of Children's Studies

In addition to the creation of the Sociology of Children subfield, the year 1991 also saw the initiation of the interdisciplinary field of Children's Studies. The founders of this interdisciplinary field maintained that individual disciplines would capture only particular aspects of children and bring about a fragmented and disjointed picture. The challenge was to establish an academic and scholarly field – across disciplines – which would address children as a generational cohort and the individual child in her/his fullness.

The interdisciplinary field of Children's Studies, as a separate and integrated field of study, was founded at Brooklyn College of the City University of New York in autumn 1991. In 1994, it became fully instituted with an interdisciplinary degree.[9] This new field of Children's Studies encompassed all

---

[8] It was in 1909, under President Theodore Roosevelt, that the first White House Conference on Care of Dependent Children was convened to improve the conditions of dependent and neglected children. Six more White House conferences on children and youth followed in 1919, 1929, 1939, 1950, 1960, and in 1970.

[9] Since there was no precedent anywhere – neither in the United States nor abroad – it took some time to convince the academic administration to support such a new interdisciplinary field of study and research. From the beginning, Children's Studies was a free-standing program and existed independent from any department. The new and interdisciplinary field was also announced in *ChildNews*, the Newsletter of the ASA section of the Sociology of Children in 1992. The Children's Studies Program has flourished over the years and hundreds of students are registered every semester and graduate with a Children's Studies degree. The courses offered include "Perspectives on Childhood," "The Human Rights of Children: A Transnational Development," "History of Children, Public Policy and Law in the United States," "Child Well-being in a Global World: Focus on the United States," "Children and Education," "Children and the Law," "Children in Crisis," "Child Abuse and Neglect," "Interdisciplinary Perspectives on Children and Disability: Local, National, and International Development," "Children, Government, Policy and Advocacy in New York State," "Children of New York," "The Professional and Performing Child: Past and Present Issues," "Applied Research in Children's

children from birth to eighteen years of age and included all fields in the humanities, social and medical sciences, and law.

The vision for this new interdisciplinary and interdepartmental field of study was based on the insight that children from birth forward represent in every society a distinct socio-cultural class and generational cohort. From its beginnings, the field of Children's Studies made the ontological claim that children must be viewed in their fullness as human beings in all their civil, political, social, economic and cultural dimensions, and in their human transhistorical condition. The human rights of children provide the overarching framework for Children's Studies. Other universities, such as Eastern Washington University and York University in Canada, followed suit and soon after introduced their own children's studies degree program.[10]

During this same period, in 1996, the Children's Rights Centre of the University of Ghent, Belgium, under the leadership of Professor Eugeen Verhellen, introduced an annual series of International Interdisciplinary Courses on Children's Right. From these conferences also emerged an international network of universities and faculty in Europe focusing on the study of children's rights. The proceedings of the conferences were published under the title of *Ghent Papers on Children's Rights*.

The Sociology of Children and Youth

The ASA Section of the Sociology of Children and Youth has over 400 members and

Studies," and a "Professional Exploration Internship." Courses from other departments in the social sciences and humanities include "The History of Childhood," "Literature for Young People," "The Black Child and the Urban Education System," "Health and Nutrition Sciences – Child Development," "Introductory Child Psychology," "Family and Influences on Child Health," "Psychological and Developmental Disorders of Childhood," "Cognitive Development," "The Family," "The Sociology of Children," "Speech and Language Development," "The Performance of Children's Literature," "The Puerto Rican, Latino, and Caribbean Child in New York City."
[10] See Lenzer 2001.

holds numerous sessions at the annual meetings of the ASA. In terms of research and teaching, the field is large and widely diversified with regard both to topics and theoretical perspectives. It covers a rich variety of subjects ranging from studies of gender, schooling, and health to socialization, parental relations to children, and peer group analyses. It also makes use of a range of methodologies including sociopsychological methods, life course analyses, and developmental and longitudinal research methods.

The book series of the ASA, the *Sociological Studies of Children and Youth* (SSCY), now published by Emerald Books,[11] contains nineteen volumes as of 2015. The volumes in this annual series include such titles as *Soul of Society: A Focus on the Lives of Children and Youth* (Warehime 2014), *Child Labor in Global Society* (Close 2014), *Youth Engagement: The Civic-Political Lives of Children and Youth* (Nenga and Taft 2013), *Children and Youth Speak for Themselves* (Johnson 2010), and *Technology and Youth: Growing up in a Digital World* (Claster and Blair 2015). Other examples of the variety of topics can be gained from the session topics of the national meetings of the ASA and sessions of the Sociology of Children and Youth Section in August 2013. They include such topics as "The Changing Transition to Adulthood: Developing Skills, Capacities and Orientations for Success," "Social Class and the Early Life-Course," "Social Connections and Adolescent Development," "Digital Youth: Young People, New Media and Social Change," and "Youth and Troubled Economic Times." As these examples demonstrate, the topics come from different social interests in the conditions of today's children, adolescents, and youth, pursue specific research endeavors, and use a variety of methods, and theoretical perspectives.

Perhaps one of the most influential American publications on children in recent

[11] The journals *Childhood* (Sage) and *Children & Society* (Wiley) serve as the two major international and scholarly publications for research on children and childhood. Rutgers University Press also has a Childhood Studies series of books.

years is Annette Lareau's *Unequal Childhoods: Class, Race, and Family Life* (2003). It analyzes how parents of different social classes socialize their children. Middle-class parents practice "concerted cultivation." Lareau notes:

> *middle-class parents who comply with current professional standards and engage in a pattern of cultivation deliberately try to stimulate their children's development and foster their cognitive and social skills. Working-class and poor parents, by contrast, tend to undertake the "accomplishments of natural growth," leaving their children much more to their own devices. The result is that poor children have more free time, while middle-class children's time is organized by multiple activities. The commitment among working-class and poor families to provide comfort, food, shelter, and other basic support requires ongoing effort, given economic challenges and the formidable demands of child rearing. But it stops short of the deliberate cultivation of children and their leisure activities that occur in middle-class families. For working-class and poor families, sustaining children's natural growth is viewed as an accomplishment. [These different practices lead to]* the transmission of differential advantages *to children (2003: 5, emphasis in original).*[12]

Since theories of socialization have been rejected by some European proponents of Childhood Studies, Handel, Cahill and Elkin published *Children and Society: The Sociology of Children and Childhood Socialization* (2007) as a rejoinder. They insist on the merit of theories of socialization and claim that "many of these earlier works continue to provide a basic foundation for our current knowledge and understanding" (2007: ix).[13]

---

[12] In *Our Kids: The American Dream in Crisis* (2015), Robert Putnam also deals with the transmission of differential advantages, arguing that it has led to increasing inequality in US society.

[13] See also Gerald Handel's earlier writings on socialization, such as his 1988 edited volume on *Childhood Socialization*. Also, throughout the history of sociology, virtually all introductory texts to sociology have contained sections on socialization.

The Sociology of Childhood and Childhood Studies

The Sociology of Childhood and Childhood Studies, as developed in Europe, represent fields anchored in sociology. According to its founders and major representatives, "childhood" is perceived as a social institution and embedded in the structural realities of society. One major tenet of this literature makes the claim that childhood and the child are "social constructs – an idea which in this literature is being used like a trope. Allison James and Alan Prout explain it in the following way in their *Constructing and Reconstructing Childhood* (1997):

> *The title encapsulates what we feel to be the nature of the social institution of childhood: an actively negotiated set of social relationships within which the early years of human life are constituted. The immaturity of children is a biological fact of life but the ways in which this immaturity is understood and made meaningful is a fact of culture. It is these facts of culture which may vary and which can be said to make of childhood a social institution. It is in this sense, therefore, that one can talk of the social construction of childhood and also, as it appears in this volume, of its re- and deconstruction. In this double sense, then, childhood is both constructed and reconstructed both for children and by children (James and Prout 1997: 1).*

Other publications which advance a similar perspective include *Childhood Matters* (Qvortrup et al. 1994) and the *Palgrave Handbook of Childhood Studies* (Qvortrup et al. 2009). It is the "agentic child" (James 2009: 37) which occupies a key role in the paradigm of childhood studies. Thus, childhood is not seen as a period of life but "is understood as a permanent form of any generational structure" (Qvortrup 2009: 23).

Some of the central ideas of the Sociology of Childhood and Childhood Studies – which by now have become in many instances the same and are indistinguishable in the literature – have to do with their major objections to the scholarly fields of child development and socialization. One pervasive objection has to do with the notion presumably inherent in these theories which considers children as "becoming" and under the influence of adults, without agency of their own. In contrast, some of the key authors of the sociology of childhood and childhood studies propose that childhood is a structural social entity – a generational structure – in which children do have agency. Particularly, Leena Alanen's contributions to the generational theories of childhood are of importance (Alanen 2009).[14]

The Future of Children Disciplines

For the Sociology of Children and Youth as well as for Childhood Studies, the question arises as to their methodological and philosophical focus on "childhood" versus "children" as a framework. As the American Sociology of Children and Youth demonstrates, the focus on "children and youth" as a social class and generational cohort in every society provides a more general framework within which "childhood" posits a special sub-category for investigation. The dilemma created by making "childhood" the framework of a disciplinary field led, for example, to a conference convened in 2011 by a major Childhood Studies Department on the topic of "Multiple Childhoods." The self-evident postulate that there is more than one "childhood" clearly demonstrated the predicament of a Sociology of Childhood and of Childhood Studies.[15]

In brief, the real contributions of the Sociology of Childhood lie in its understandings that children have "agency" and are not simply the recipients of their upbringing by adults, or the agency of adults. Children must be viewed as contributors to the process of growing up instead of as not-yet-adults. That widely shared, one-way perspective was in need of correction. The theoretical emphasis upon the agency of the child also corresponds to the right of participation as articulated in the UNCRC, which identifies the child as a subjective rights-holder in society in addition to her/his human rights to provision and protection.

It is the right to being protected and provided for, however, which marks the general condition of children in any society. The inequality of children in relation to the power of the adult generation leads to the need for provision and protection of children in any social configuration of children and adults. These are unacknowledged yet normative realities which follow from the biological difference between children and adults in any social setting and lie at the very bottom of any sociological or historical analysis.

The childhood paradigm as a subset of social structures cannot capture these realities. It is itself a historically bounded conception and therefore not an empirical or theoretical tool to analyze the relations of power, responsibilities, and interdependencies between the generations in any social configuration. The historical reality of children as a minority group,[16] both in terms of age and social circumstances, must be addressed. In fact, the theoretical category of "agency" as a central concept related to children in childhood sociology disguises their lack of de facto power and self-determination. It hypostatizes a normative assumption contained in the theoretical model.

It appears then that both disciplines – the Sociology of Children and Youth and the Sociology of Childhood – are in need

---

[14] To learn more about the international development of the Sociology of Childhood, see "Childhood Sociology in 10 countries," in *Current Sociology*, in March 2010, portraying the state of the sociology of childhood and children in each.

[15] This reminded the author of an autobiography by an African American student: "The Old Man in a Jungle Gym," in which he pointed out that he had no childhood and by the time he would be able to enjoy a jungle gym he was going to be a grown man.

[16] It might be of interest to mention in this context that Elisabeth Young-Bruehl in her recent book, *Childism: Confronting Prejudice against Children* (2012: backcover) postulates that "prejudice exists against children as a group and that it is comparable to racism, sexism, and homophobia. This prejudice – childism – legitimates and rationalizes a broad continuum of acts that are not 'in the best interests of children,' including the often violent extreme of child abuse and neglect."

of further clarifications and that they would substantively gain from a theoretically more unified approach and an articulation of the methodological premises underlying both.

References

Alanen, Leena. 2009. Generational Order. In *The Palgrave Handbook of Childhood Studies*. Edited by Jens Qvortrup, William A. Corsaro, and Michael Sebastian Honig. New York, NY: Palgrave Macmillan, 159–174.

Ambert, Anne Marie. 1986. Sociology of Sociology: The Place of Children in North American Sociology. *Sociological Studies of Child Development* 1(1): 11–31.

Claster, Patricia Neff and Sampson Lee Blair. 2015. *Technology and Youth: Growing Up in a Digital World*. Sociological Studies of Children and Youth, Vol. 19. Bingley, UK: Emerald Group Publishing Limited.

Close, Paul. ed. 2014. *Child Labour in Global Society*. Sociological Studies of Children and Youth, Vol. 17. Bingley, UK: Emerald Group Publishing Limited.

Congressional Research Service and the Congressional Budget Office. 1985. *Children in Poverty*. Committee on Ways and Means. 99th Congress, 1st Session. Washington, DC: US Government Printing Office.

Handel, Gerald. 1988. ed. *Childhood Socialization*. New York, NY: Aldine de Gruyter.

Handel, Gerald, Spencer E. Cahill, and Frederick Elkin. 2007. *Children and Society: The Sociology of Children and Childhood Socialization*. Los Angeles, CA: Roxbury.

James, Allison. 2009. Agency. In *The Palgrave Handbook of Childhood Studies*. Edited by Jens Qvortrup, William A. Corsaro, and Michael Sebastian Honig. New York, NY: Palgrave Macmillan, 34–45.

James, Allison and Alan Prout. eds. 1997. *Constructing and Reconstructing Childhood: Contemporary issues in the sociological study of childhood*. 2nd edn. London: Routledge.

Johnson, Heather Beth. 2010. *Children and Youth Speak for Themselves*. Sociological Studies of Children and Youth, Vol. 13. Bingley, UK: Emerald Group Publishing Limited.

Lareau, Annette. 2003. *Unequal Childhoods: Class, Race, and Family Life*. Berkeley, CA: University of California Press.

Lenzer, Gertrud. 1991. Is there Sufficient Interest to Establish a Sociology of Children? *Footnotes. Newsletter of the American Sociological Association* 19(6): 8.

Lenzer, Gertrud. 2001. Children's Studies: Beginnings and Purposes. *The Lion and the Unicorn* 25: 181–186.

Nenga, Sandi Kawecka and Jessica K. Taft. eds. 2013. *Youth Engagement: The Civic-political Lives of Children and Youth*. Sociological Studies of Children and Youth, Vol. 16. Bingley, UK: Emerald Books.

Putnam, Robert D. 2015. *Our Kids: The American Dream in Crisis*. New York, NY: Simon & Schuster.

Qvortrup, Jens. 2009. Childhood as a Structural Form. In *The Palgrave Handbook of Childhood Studies*. Edited by Jens Qvortrup, William A. Corsaro, and Michael Sebastian Honig. New York, NY: Palgrave Macmillan, 21–33.

Qvortrup, Jens, Marjatta Bardy, Giovanni Sgritta, and Helmut Wintersberger. eds. 1994. *Childhood Matters: Social Theory, Practice and Politics*. Aldershot: Avebury.

Qvortrup, Jens, William A. Corsaro, and Michael Sebastian Honig. eds. 2009. *The Palgrave Handbook of Childhood Studies*. New York, NY: Palgrave Macmillan.

Thorne, Barrie. 1987. Revisioning Women and Social Change: Where are the Children? *Gender and Society* 1(1): 85–109.

US Commission on Children. 1991. *Beyond Rhetoric: A New Agenda for Children and Families*. Washington, DC: US Government Printing Office.

Warehime, Mary Nicole. ed. 2014. *Soul of Society: A Focus on the Lives of Children and Youth*. Sociological Studies of Children and Youth, Vol. 18. Bingley, UK: Emerald Group Publishing Limited.

Young-Bruehl, Elisabeth. 2012. *Childism: Confronting Prejudice against Children*. New Haven, CT: Yale University Press.

Sociology of Aging

Elizabeth W. Markson and Peter J. Stein

This chapter focuses on the major theoretical approaches to aging and how these theories have guided social research and social policy on aging. Of course, theories and models of aging are shaped by the culture and historical context in which they are made. Likewise, social policies related to aging change over time and from society to society.

Was there a "Golden Age" for the Elderly?

A common belief is that somewhere, in the past or in some distant society, the elderly were venerated and respected precisely because they were old. Alas, there has probably never been a "golden age" in which elders were automatically respected or loved (Nydegger 1985). Rather, power and prestige among the elderly have been largely due to their ability to control goods, knowledge, and other resources.

Power not Veneration in Gerontocracy

A society in which elders – usually men – are in control is called a gerontocracy.

For example, in the Samburu of Northern Kenya the power of elder men came from the belief that their curse has religious power. If an elder cursed a junior for disrespect of any kind, divine punishment resulted. This power was dominated by fathers whose sons remained in the household both before and after their marriage. Absolute obedience and complete devotion to parents and the lower ranking of younger people was the rule. This type of family organization allowed elders to keep a monopoly over timing of marriage and the number of wives for their sons (Spencer 1965).

In colonial America, on the other hand, power among the elderly did not come automatically. The retired, the poor, and widows without husbands or children were often segregated from the rest of society and dependent upon others for support (Haber 1983). Although some historians (e.g., Fischer 1977) claimed that a firmly established gerontocracy existed in colonial America, others (Demos 1978; Smith 1978) argue that any high status the elderly achieved was due to their control over valued resources. More important than chronological age was economic power (Haber 1983). Those old men and women who were poor and dependent upon the goodwill of their relatives and the community did not enjoy high status (Haber and Gratton 1994).

In the early years of the United States, some portrayed the last years in life as the "good old age" of virtue, health, independence, and salvation. Others viewed it as the "bad old age" of sin, disease, dependency, premature death, and damnation (Cole 1992: 161–162). These two opposing views have shaped social theories about aging and old age and continue to do so today.

Old Age as Dependence

Negative views of old age – the concept of "bad old age" – were preponderant during the nineteenth century. The American physician George Miller Beard (1874), collecting material from the biographies of famous older people through history, computed the mean age at which these men and women accomplished their major works. He concluded that "seventy percent of the work of the world is done before forty-five and eighty percent before fifty" (Beard 1874, cited in Cole 1992: 165). Similarly in 1905, Sir William Osler, the most influential physician of his time, decided to retire at age 55 from the medical faculty of Johns Hopkins, commenting that "men above forty years of age" are useless. He apparently then decided he was an exception and went on to accept a position at Oxford University that he held until his death at age seventy (Cohen 2012).

Social scientists, while analyzing various issues of the nineteenth century, such as the increasing number of poor people, overcrowded labor markets, and growing numbers of unskilled workers in the United States, hypothesized that the elderly declined in status and fell into poverty almost universally. They were the inevitable casualties of an industrial society. Old age began to be defined by social scientists, reformers, and physicians alike as a social problem, directly linked to poverty and ill health (Haber 1983: 46). The connection between dependent old age and living in an institution for the poor seemed clear: "Generations grew up with 'a reverence for God, the hope of heaven, and the fear of the poorhouse'" (Haber and Gratton 1994: 122). From this perspective, old age was not only related to physical and mental decline but also a social problem associated with modernization and industrialization.

Macro- and Micro-Theories on Aging

Much of the research on aging during the first half of the twentieth century accepted the belief that being elderly was an explicitly or tacitly undesirable state in an individualistic, activist society such as the United States. Theories on aging during this era reflected two themes: a focus on the society and its relationship to individuals – macro-theories – and a focus on individuals as they grew old – micro-theories.

Early Micro-Theories

ACTIVITY THEORY

The basic premise of activity theory is that the individual who ages best is one who maintains his or her usual activities as long as possible. The theory uses data drawn from the Kansas City Studies of Adult Life, a ten-year landmark study of midlife and old age (Cavan et al. 1949; Neugarten 1964). According to activity theory, people aged sixty-five and older are not very different from people in midlife. Social researchers emphasized activity and individual life satisfaction as hallmarks of normal (versus pathological) old age. Continued activity in old age preserves self-concept and ensures higher levels of life satisfaction (Cavan et al. 1949; Hadler 2011). Defying one's age by keeping busy and staying as active as possible are the keys to a good old age.

Although activity theory is intuitively appealing to Americans who value individualism and personal independence, studies have failed to show that activity is integral to life satisfaction. One test conducted in three racially and socio-economically mixed retirement communities found that informal social supports provided by friendships are important for life satisfaction in old age, but having a high level of activity is not (Longino and Kart 1982).

CONTINUITY THEORY

Another theory that focuses on the individual is continuity theory. As originally stated by Neugarten (1964), this approach holds that personality remains stable with aging. People continue to use the adaptive mechanisms they have developed throughout adulthood to diagnose situations, chart future courses, and adapt to change in later life.

But is the self ageless? The answer is yes and no. In one sense, the self is ageless because it is continuous throughout our lives, no matter what our ages or how we physically change (Kaufman 1995). Upon seeing their reflections in the mirror, some people in their eighties and nineties say that they are surprised at how old they look; they never thought of themselves as enveloped in such aged bodies. Others state that they do not feel radically different than they did when they were younger. This perception has been termed the mask of aging: "the awareness of an experiential difference between the physical processes of aging, as reflected in outward appearance, and the inner or subjective 'real self' which paradoxically remains young" (Hepworth 1991: 93). This provides support for continuity theory.

But the view that "the self is ageless" also denies the importance of life experience and physical changes. As modern music composer John Cage commented: "I now see that the body is part and parcel of the whole being. There isn't a split...When I was younger, I mistreated the body because I thought the mind was what I was really dealing with. But as I get older I see that I'm dealing quite straightforwardly with the body and that I must keep it in good working order as long as I can" (quoted in Berman and Goldman 1992: 31).

Continuity of the self is thus not agelessness but a dynamic tension between change and constancy. Andrews elaborates on this point: "Time and time again, old people say they experience the aging process as a continuation of being themselves: their lives are ongoing. But this is not 'agelessness.' People see value in the years they have lived; without them they have no history, they have no genuine self" (Andrews 2000: 316). Continuity theory has an intuitive appeal because it emphasizes that personality, problem solving, and personal preferences do not change with aging but remain relatively constant throughout adulthood.

Early Macro-Theories on Aging

Micro-theories focus on the individual rather than on the society in which people grow old. By contrast, macro-theories focus on how the structures of society influence individual life trajectories, statuses, and roles in later life.

DISENGAGEMENT THEORY

Challenging the individualistic activity perspective, sociologist Elaine Cumming and psychologist William Henry also used data from the Kansas City Study to develop disengagement theory, a macro-theory, centering on the smooth functioning of a society rather than on individual adjustment or attitudes (Cumming and Henry 1961). From this perspective, individual lives are played out in and governed by a society with a pre-existing set of norms that maintain societal continuity and stability. As people age, they become less competent and will weigh the society down unless they disengage from vital social roles. Disengagement is "an inevitable mutual withdrawal" between the aged person and society. The elderly, because of their impending deterioration and death, either choose to occupy fewer statuses or are forced out of them. For example, the older man who chooses to retire from his job or the older middle-management executive who is "reorganized out" of the company against her will have disengaged from social roles. Both have probably also reduced their social life space – the extent and frequency of social contact with others. And their retirement from employment has made room for younger workers.

Disengagement theory also introduced the concept of "age-as-leveler," which assumes that once an individual becomes old, other differences such as race, ethnicity, social class, and gender become irrelevant. This was based on earlier research on aging which concluded that old age is almost always characterized by poor physical health and economic problems. The age-as-leveler assumes that old age is somewhat like a giant mixer where everyone is blended into one bland substance or leveled out (Ferraro 2007; Calasanti 2008).

The notion of age-as-leveler ignored the effect that membership in the social hierarchies of social class, gender, and race/ethnicity has on the many ways in which people grow old. Both disengagement theory and activity theory, which argues that an individual can age optimally by maintaining his or her usual activities as long as possible and finding substitute statuses and roles for relinquished ones, were based on relatively homogenous, middle-class, primarily white samples of elders.

Disengagement theory remains important for several reasons. First, it called attention to aging not as confined to the individual but as socially patterned where accepted social norms govern withdrawal of the elderly from vital social roles. Second, it challenged a major premise of activity theory that successful old age was a continuation of middle age – by proposing that old age was a distinct life stage characterized by activities different in quantity and quality than those of earlier life.

Disengagement theory made perhaps the first explicit recognition of gender differences in aging (Cumming 1963). Studies of gender and its complex connections to aging, inequality, and the life-span have come more recently and are discussed below. Disengagement theory with its focus on society, social roles, social norms, and social structure stimulated other macro-theory development during the 1970s and onward – Dowd's exchange theory, Rose's subculture of aging, and Riley's age stratification are but a few. Given space constraints, we will here briefly review age stratification theory.

AGE STRATIFICATION

Age stratification became an influential macro-theory, developed by Matilda White Riley and her associates (Riley et al. 1972). Age stratification proposes that it is both theoretically and practically useful to think of members of a society as stratified on the dimension of age, just as by social class. Calling attention to the importance of birth cohort, Riley emphasized the significance of the period in history in which we live and its interaction with our chronological age. For example, members of the large baby boom cohorts born in the decades following World War II faced greater competition for jobs than did smaller cohorts born during the Great Depression years of the 1930s. This shaped their perspective on employment and other key aspects of life. This "cohort effect" can also be seen in the differing impact of the Great Depression on various generations. Those who were growing up in the 1930s have never forgotten the fear of unemployment and instant poverty, and it still shows in their strong support of Social Security. Their children, however, have only vague memories of that fear and are less committed to preserving the safety net, while their grandchildren have been willing to risk part of their old age benefits in the stock market, the very institution whose collapse led to the Great Depression (Elder 1974).

Age stratification is especially useful to show that some of the presumably fixed, built-in life stages that have been proposed by social scientists and physicians alike reflect the experiences of a particular cohort (Riley et al. 1972; Calasanti and Slevin 2001; Ferraro and Shippee 2009). Thus, great caution must be used in making sweeping generalizations about "normal aging". As Riley stated: "Because society changes, members of different cohorts, born at different times, age in different ways…[Hence,] the lives of those who are growing old today cannot be the same as the lives of those who grew old in the past or of those who will grow old in the future" (Riley et al. 1999: 333). And, because the population sixty-five+ now contains several distinct cohorts, some born in the early years of the twentieth century and others in the 1940–1960 years, we cannot speak of "the elderly" as an undifferentiated mass. How one ages physically, opportunities and obstacles encountered, and concerns in old age vary from one birth cohort to another. Changes in education, income, life styles, the timing of marriage and parenthood, and dramatic developments for women, mean that people born in the 1990s will enter old age with very different resources and expectations than previous cohorts.

Combining Macro and Micro Perspectives

LIFE COURSE

The micro and macro frameworks are imperfect because aging occurs in a specific context and is influenced by historical as well as individual events. Increasingly, a number of frameworks combine both individual and social perspectives. For example, the life course approach focuses on individuals, the different patterns of their lives from birth to death, and the differential effects of membership in a specific birth cohort. This approach assumes that the meaning of age in any society is socially constructed and formulated by the society and the period of history in which people live (Quadagno 2014). Adding to the age stratification approach, life course research emphasizes both the importance of birth cohort and the intertwining of gender, social class, and historical events. These theorists also note that, in order to understand the complexity of the life course, we need to distinguish between predictable and "relatively durable strains" of daily life: scheduled and transitional life events like graduation from high school and college, courtship and marriage, childbirth, and less expected, unscheduled events such as job loss, shutting down or moving one's workplace, war, environmental catastrophes, etc.

Also important in the life course is the timing of life transitions, events, and behaviors in a person's life (Elder 1998). For example, some people may become grandparents at forty, others at sixty or even eighty. The timing of this event is a milestone in "becoming old" for most people. Norms identify appropriate ages for most transitions, such as marriage, retirement, and so forth (B. Neugarten 1964; D. Neugarten 2006). The marriage of two fifteen-year-olds, for example, would be considered an "off-time" event in the United States and probably would have very different social and economic consequences for their life courses than marrying "on-time" at age twenty-five.

At the socio-structural level, our birth cohort and socio-historical events also shape life opportunities and lifestyles (Dannefer and Uhlenberg 1999). Although members of each birth cohort share a common backdrop of social and historical events, each person's life chances will differ. The concept of life chances, as defined by Max Weber (1978[1922]) refers to the likelihood of having a particular lifestyle shaped by our socioeconomic position – the social and economic resources available. Thus one's ability to attain "success," will be shaped by both individual ability to command economic resources and personal attributes and also by the size of one's birth cohort and the life chances or opportunities available to each birth cohort (Stein and Taylor-Jones 2010).

The life course approach also emphasizes the importance of early life experiences, environmental and socio-historical factors, and social class, race, and ethnicity to explain the dramatic heterogeneity and diversity in growing old (Butler 1963; Cain 1964; Heinz and Marshall 2003; Markson and Stein 2012).

Power and Inequality and Aging

During the past few decades, a theoretical shift has occurred, setting new directions for examining old age. Social theorists have turned their critical lenses inward, examining previous assumptions about aging. In doing so, they have focused on such issues as power and inequality, gender, economic systems, and ageism.

Interest in power, inequality, and the interplay among race, social class, and ethnicity was in part a response to the age-as-leveler assumption. The concept of "double jeopardy" responded to this assumption. It was initially applied to the odds faced by elderly African Americans as both old and members of an oppressed minority group (Talley 1956; Calasanti 1993; Calasanti and King 2014). Double jeopardy has been subsequently expanded to focus attention on lifestyles and problems faced by other people in old age – women, gays, lesbians, and ethnic groups experiencing multiple forms of discrimination.

Nonetheless, as Dresse et al. (1997) point out, focus on social disadvantage has unintendedly led to a deficit thinking mentality that once again portrays disadvantaged elders as victims, ignoring the strengths that disadvantaged groups also possess. Instead, strong social supports from family, friends, and religion, values in African American culture emphasizing old age as a natural process, and satisfaction over having survived a lifetime of discrimination and economic disadvantage tend to lead to very old African Americans having higher levels of life satisfaction than other elderly Americans (Johnson 1995; Ladner 2000).

Gender

Gender and its relationship to aging and inequality are late comers to age theories. Estes (2006) developed the following four premises of a "critical feminist perspective" on aging: (1) the experiences of women across the life course are socially constructed; (2) the life experiences and problems of older women are not the product of individual behavior and decisions; (3) women's disadvantage cumulates across the life course; and (4) marginalization of women results from life-long oppressions of race, ethnicity, class, and sexuality. Building on this perspective, other social gerontologists have looked at the impact of gender inequality over the life-span and its persistent influence in old age (Calasanti and Slevin 2001; Calasanti 2010). For example, at age sixty-five and older, women face greater financial insecurity with poverty rates almost double (11.9 percent vs. 6.6 percent) and incomes just 57 percent that of older men (US Department of Health and Human Services 2014). This income differential reflects the gender gap in pay throughout the life course, resulting in lower lifetime salaries, lower Social Security benefits and decreased probability in receiving a private pension in retirement.

Political Economy of Aging

Focus on the political economy of aging has expanded awareness of the importance of social structure and membership in social hierarchies. The political economy perspective on age stresses how socio-economic institutions affect individuals over the life course and their social and economic well-being in old age. Theorists utilizing the political-economic perspective on aging are concerned about whether capitalism as a productive social system can be reconciled with the needs of the elderly (Schulz and Binstock 2006). The British sociologist Chris Phillipson (2008), arguing that the priorities of capitalism almost always make social and individual needs less important than the search for profits, suggested that the elderly are likely to be caught between the need for better services and the steady decline of facilities and cuts in their standard of living imposed by the most powerful social classes.

A leading American spokesperson for the political economy approach to aging has been Carroll Estes who, with her associates, proposed that the course of the aging process is conditioned by each individual's location in the social structure and the economic and social factors that affect that position (Estes 1979; Minkler and Estes 1991). According to Estes (2013), medical professionals have a disproportionate say in how we define old age and how resources for older people will be allocated: Those who control definitions of aging in effect control access to old age benefits such as medical care, as well as the personal and public costs of care and the structure of health care delivery. Currently, public money and professional effort are disproportionately expended on institutional (hospital and nursing home) medical services for the elderly (Estes 2013). Social programs designed to benefit the elderly reflect a definition of health care that is the product of the professional dominance of medicine and a guarantee of a profitable medical care industry (Hadler 2011). They have not only created an "aging establishment" that regulates the distribution of social resources to the elderly but also have often benefited business interests more than the interests and needs of older people (Gawande 2014).

Critical Theory

Recently, critical theory has also challenged older theories and assumptions in social gerontology. Of particular interest to critical theory is how gerontologists have separated their work on elders' lives from those doing the living (Estes 2013). The result has been that the elderly become the "other," objects rather than subjects of study. Critical theory emphasizes social justice and focuses on applying social research toward human betterment, especially the condition of those with less power – minorities, people of color, women, and elderly people (Moody 1988; Ray and Cole 2008). As Harry Moody (1993: xv), a leading spokesperson for the critical approach in aging has emphasized: "Above all, critical gerontology is concerned with the problem of emancipation from all forms of domination ... identifying possibilities for emancipatory social change, including positive ideals for later life" (see also Walker 2006; Ray, et al, 2008).

Ageism

All sociologists are keenly aware of the social issue of ageism. As defined by Robert Butler (1969), a psychiatrist who introduced the term, ageism is the "systematic stereotyping of and discrimination against people because they are old, just as racism and sexism accomplish this with skin color and gender." It involves two kinds of activities: discrimination, denying persons opportunities because they are old, and prejudice, negative stereotypes about older people (Quadagno 2014). Such prejudice stereotypes older people as either useless, poor, frail, burdensome, and powerless, or as cute, adorable, and automatically wise. As noted above, while the term may be new, ageism is a social issue that has existed throughout history.

When people use negative stereotypes, they practice age discrimination. Similar to race and gender discrimination, age discrimination takes many forms (Quadagno 2014). It often happens in the workplace, when employers refuse to hire or promote older workers (Ray and Cole 2008; Stein 2009). Ageism also occurs in health care, especially in the differential treatment for elderly patients compared with younger adults (Quadagno 2014).

While ageism is transmitted in many ways, it is constantly reinforced via television, books, magazines, and in films. The relationship between sexism and ageism can be seen in portrayals of older women and men in the media. Women have much shorter careers on film and fewer roles as they age – they tend to be evaluated for their sexual attractiveness much more so than men – a double standard of aging (Markson and Taylor 2000).

Conclusion

While there is currently no single "grand" theory that explains all aspects of aging, various theories provide useful roadmaps to navigate disparate research findings (Marshall and Bengston 2011). Sociologists of aging continue to develop theoretical and conceptual approaches which will help us understand the process of aging and the diversity of aging groups over the life course. As the average life-span lengthens and many, particularly Global North societies and Japan, continue to increase their elderly populations, such research has never been more vital to understanding society.

References

Andrews, Molly. 2000. The Seductiveness of Agelessness. *Ageing and Society* 19(3): 301–318.

Beard, George Miller. 1874. *Legal Responsibility in Old Age* New York, NY: Russells.

Berman, Phillip L. and Connie Goldman. 1992. *Ageless Spirit*. New York, NY: Ballantine Books.

Butler, Robert. 1963. The Life Review: An Interpretation of Reminiscence in the Aged. *Psychiatry* 26: 65–76.

Butler, Robert. 1969. Age-Ism: Another Form of Bigotry. *Gerontologist* 9: 243–246.

Cain, Leonard. 1964. Life Course and Social Structure. In *Handbook of Modern Sociology*. Edited by Robert Faris. Chicago, IL: Rand McNally, 272–309.

Calasanti, Toni. 1993. Bringing Diversity in: Toward an Inclusive Theory of Retirement. *Journal of Aging Studies* 7(2)(invited, Special Issue): 133–150.

Calasanti, Toni. 2008. Gender and Class Relations in the Struggle for Old-Age Security. *Journal of Aging* 2(December): 238–250.

Calasanti, Toni. 2010. Gender and Applied Research on Aging. *Gerontologist* 50(6)(50th anniversary issue): 1–15.

Calasanti, Toni and Neal King. 2014. Intersectionality and Cultural Gerontology. In *Handbook of Cultural Gerontology*. Edited by Julia Twigg and Wendy Martin. London: Routledge.

Calasanti, Toni and Kathleen Slevin. 2001 Gender, Social Inequalities, and Aging. Walnut Creek, CA: Alta Mira Press.

Cavan, Ruth Shonle, Ernest W. Burgess, Herbert Goldhamer, and Robert Havighurst. 1949. *Personal Adjustment in Old Age*. Chicago, IL: Science Research Associates.

Cohen, Patricia. 2012. A Sharper Mind, Middle Age and Beyond. *The New York Times*, January 19: 20. Available at www.nytimes.com/2012/01/22/education/edlife/a-sharper-mind-middle-age-and-beyond.html, accessed January 22, 2012.

Cole, Thomas. 1992. The Journey of Life: A Cultural History of Aging in America. New York, NY: Cambridge University Press.

Cumming, Elaine. 1963. Further Thoughts on the Theory of Disengagement. *International Social Science Journal* 15: 377–393.

Cumming, Elaine and William Henry. 1961. *Growing Old: The Process of Disengagement*. New York, NY: Basic Books.

Dannefer, Dale and Peter Uhlenberg. 1999. Paths of the Life Course: A Typology. In *Handbook of Theories of Aging*. Edited by Vern Bengston and K. Warner Schaie. New York, NY: Springer, 306–326.

Demos, John. 1978. *Old Age in Early New England*. In *The American Family in Socio-Historical Perspective*. Edited by Milton Gordon. New York, NY: St. Martin's, 220–256.

Dressel, Paula, Michele Minkler, and Irene Yen. 1997. Gender, Race, Class, and Aging: Advances and Opportunities. *International Journal of Health Services* 27(4): 579–600.

Elder, Glen. 1974. *Children of the Great Depression*. Chicago, IL: University of Chicago Press.

Elder, Glen. 1998. The Life Course as Developmental Theory. *Child Development* 69(1): 1–12.

Estes, Carroll. 1979. *The Aging Enterprise*. San Francisco, CA: Jossey-Bass.

Estes, Carroll. 2006. Critical Feminist Perspectives, Aging, and Social Policy. In *Aging, Globalization and Inequality: The New Critical Gerontology*. Edited by Jan Baars, Dale Dannefer, Christopher Phillipson, and Alan Walker. Amityville, New York, NY: Baywood, 81–101.

Estes, Carroll. 2013. *Health Policy: Crisis and Reform*. 6th edn. Burlington, MA: Jones & Bartlett.

Ferraro, Kenneth. 2007. The Gerontological Imagination. In *Gerontology: Perspectives and Issues*. Edited by Janet Wilmoth and Kenneth Ferraro. New York, NY: Springer, 325–342.

Ferraro, Kenneth and Tetyana Shippee. 2009. Aging and Cumulative Inequality: How Does Inequality Get Under the Skin? *Gerontologist* 49: 333–343.

Fischer, David. 1977. *Growing Old in America*. New York, NY: Oxford University Press.

Gawande, Atul. 2014. *Being Mortal: Medicine and What Matters in the End*. Holt: Henry & Co.

Haber, Carole. 1983. *Beyond Sixty-Five: The Dilemma of Old Age in America's Past*. Cambridge: Cambridge University Press.

Haber, Carole and Brian Gratton. 1994. *Old Age and the Search for Security: An American Social History*. Bloomington, IN: University of Indiana.

Hadler, Nortin. 2011. *Rethinking Aging: Growing Old and Living Well in an Overtreated Society*. Chapel Hill, NC: University of North Carolina Press.

Heinz, Walter and Victor Marshall. 2003. *Social Dynamics of the Life Course*. New York, NY: DeGruyter.

Hepworth, Michael. 1991. Positive Aging and the Mask of Age. *Journal of Educational Gerontology* 6(2): 93–101.

Johnson, Coleen. 1995. Determinants of Adaptation of Oldest Old Black Americans. *Journal of Aging Studies* 9(3): 231–244.

Kaufman, Sharon. 1995. *The Ageless Self: Sources of Meaning in Late Life*. Madison, WI: University of Wisconsin Press

Ladner, Joyce. 2000. *The Ties that Bind: Timeless Values for African American Families*. New York, NY: John Wiley and Sons.

Longino, Charles and Cary Kart. 1982. Explicating Activity Theory: A Formal Replication. *Journal of Gerontology* 37: 713–722.

Markson, Elizabeth and Peter Stein. 2012 *Social Gerontology: Issues and Prospects*. San Diego, CA: Bridgepoint.

Markson, Elizabeth and Carol Taylor. 2000. The Mirror Has Two Faces. *Ageing and Society* 20(2): 137–160.

Marshall, Victor and Vern Bengtson. 2011. Theoretical Perspectives on the Sociology of Aging. In *Handbook of the Sociology of Aging*. Edited by Jacqueline Angel and Richard Settersten. New York, NY: Springer.

Minkler, Meredith and Carroll Estes. eds. 1991. *Critical Perspectives on Aging*. New York, NY: Baywood.

Moody, Harry. 1988. *Abundance of Life: Human Development Policies for an Aging Society*. New York, NY: Columbia University Press.

Moody, Harry. 1993. Overview: What Is Critical Gerontology and Why Is It Important? In *Voices and Visions of Aging: Toward a Critical Gerontology*. Edited by Thomas R. Cole, W. Andrew Achenbaum, Patricia L. Jakobi, and Robert Kastenbaum. New York, NY: Springer, xv-xli.

Neugarten, Bernice. 1964. *Personality in Middle and Late Life*. New York, NY: Atherton.

Neugarten, Dail. 2006. *The Meanings of Age: Selected Papers of Bernice L. Neugarten*. Chicago, IL: University of Chicago Press.

Nydegger, Corinne. 1985. Family Ties of the Aged in Cross-Cultural Perspective. In *Growing Old in America*. Edited by Beth Hess and Elizabeth Markson. New Brunswick, NJ: Transaction, 71–85.

Phillipson, Christopher 2008. Authoring Aging: Personal and Social Constructions. *Journal of Aging Studies* 22: 163–168.

Quadagno, Jill. 2014. *Aging and the Life Course*. 6th edn. New York, NY: McGraw- Hill.

Ray, Ruth and Thomas Cole. eds. 2008. Coming of Age: Critical Gerontologists Reflect on their Own Aging. *Journal of Aging Studies* 22(2): 97–209.

Riley, Matilda, Marilyn Johnson, and Anne Foner. 1972. *Aging and Society*. Vol. 3: A Sociology of Age Stratification. New York, NY: Russell Sage.

Riley, Matilda, Anne Foner, and John Riley. 1999. The Aging and Society Paradigm. In *Handbook of Theories of Aging*. Edited by Vern Bengtson and K. Warner Schaie. New York, NY: Springer, 327–343.

Schulz, James and Robert Binstock. 2006. *Aging Nation: The Economics and Politics of Growing Older in America*. Westport, CT: Praeger Publishers.

Smith, Donald. 1978. Old Age and the "Great Transformation": A New England Case Study. In *Aging and the Elderly: Humanistic Perspectives in Gerontology*. Edited by Stuart Spicker, Kathleen Woodward, and David van Tassel. Atlantic Highlands, NJ: Humanities Press, 285-302.

Spencer, Paul. 1965. *The Samburu: A Study of Gerontocracy in a Nomadic Tribe*. Reprinted with a new preface, 2004. London: Routledge.

Stein, Peter. ed. 2009. *Report of the Forum on North Carolina's Aging Workforce*. Chapel Hill, NC: UNC Institute on Aging.

Stein, Peter and Althea Taylor-Jones. 2010. Economics of Aging. *Governor's Conference on Aging*. Raleigh, Chapel Hill, NC.

Talley, Thomas. 1956. The Negro Aged. *Newsletter, Gerontological Society*, December 6.

US Department of Health and Human Services. 2014. *Profile of Older Americans: 2014 Profile*. Washington, DC.

Walker, Alan. 2006. Reexamining the Political Economy of Aging: Understanding the Structure/Agency Tension. In *Aging, Globalization and Inequality: The New Critical Gerontology*. Edited by Jan Baars, Dale Dannefer, Christopher Phillipson, and Alan Walker. Amityville, New York, NY: Baywood, 59–80.

Weber, Max 1978[1922]. *Economy and Society*. Berkeley, CA: University of California Press.

The Sociology of Death and Dying

Ruth McManus

Any account of the sociology of death and dying is always going to be partial. However, it is hoped that readers will engage with this account in the spirit that is intended – as one of many possible roadmaps through a dynamic terrain. This entry is not an exhaustive review of names and publications in the sociology of death and dying, as these are readily available. Instead, this review offers a conceptual overview of the subfield's main concerns and strategies from its earliest inception to today. I hope the route taken offers both information and insight into the wide-ranging subdiscipline that is the sociology of death and dying.

Death cannot be ignored, it is socially exigent. We are born, we live, we die, and we do so together, as humans are social beings. This means that death plays a pivotal role in our practice as social beings. How we constitute death, i.e., the specific forms that death practices take, are implicated in the way we make and remake the social world. Regardless of how we feel at the time, when confronted with death we invariably draw upon systematic yet incredibly complex social processes. From making funeral arrangements ourselves to watching funerals in blockbusters (see Oz 2007) we are engaged in death practices that forge and recast social relationships. What the living do with, to, and for the dead is articulated through diverse social institutions made up of patterned practices and processes that vary across time, place, and culture.

Sociologists describe, interpret, explain, critique and evaluate the social. When focusing on death, we must pay attention to the ongoing interplay between societal formations (systems of social organization), social change (history), social institutions (infrastructure), and social identities (selfhood) to make sense of death-related human activity. As death is present in all of these social domains and its presence varies in form and purpose, it becomes possible to understand the myriad and complex ways that death is socially mediated.

Roots of the Sociology of Death and Dying

As a subdiscipline of sociology, the sociology of death and dying orients itself on the relationship between death and society.

Accounts of its emergence reveal a dual-layered origin story. On the one hand, its first seeds were cast at the birth of the discipline when the grand theorists were seeking the laws of society. Emile Durkheim developed his account of the laws of society through an empirical study of suicide (Durkheim 1897). Marx, Durkheim, and Weber all offered foundations for the sociology of death and dying through their theorizations of rites and rituals in society. Marx's (1970[1844]) argument, that as the "opium of the people," religious beliefs and rites – including death and funeral rites – supported exploitative relations is tempered by Durkheim's maxim in *The Elementary Forms of Religious Life* that death prompts social solidarity (Durkheim 1995[1912]). The collective force of belief in social organization is extended by Weber's insights into the role of Puritan belief in the emergence of capitalist accumulation in *The Protestant Ethic and Spirit of Capitalism* (Weber 1904[1958]).

As society always responds to death, "society also shapes *responses* to death. This insight is at the core of the sociology of death, which shows how social factors drive all manner of death practices, from palliative care, to funerals, to grief norms, to collective remembrance of the dead..., to the politics and ethics of managing ancient human remains" (Walter 2014: 33). Sociology's foundational theorists represent the earliest conceptual formulations of death as key to the laws of society. Their thought laid the groundwork for the sociology of death and dying's driving focus: the significance of death in modernist societies.

The Establishment of the Subfield

While sociological interest in death and dying is linked to the birth of the discipline itself, there is general agreement that there was a tipping point in the middle of the twentieth century when debates about death and society gathered sufficient momentum to generate a critical mass of scholarship. Linked to post-World War II mainstreaming of social science disciplines in Western academies, the role of death in the constitution of society was first publicly discussed in two studies that focused on, respectively, death as a rite of passage and death as a source of collective representations (or shared worldviews). Arnold van Gennep (2004[1960]) showed that as a rite of passage, death rites repair damage to specific social relations affected by death. And Robert Hertz (2004[1960]) suggested that these mortuary rituals embodied significant collective life transitions through which society was embodied.

Initiated by Kephart's empirical study of status after death (Kephart 1950), the sociological study of death practices gained critical purchase in such classics as Fulton's *Death and Identity* (1965), Glaser and Straus's *Time for Dying* (1968), and Gorer's *The Pornography of Death* (1955). In their own ways, each posed the defining question for this emerging subdiscipline: "What is the relationship between death and society in modern society?" In line with broader trends in the discipline, responses to this question were no longer framed as attempts at generating the laws of society. Instead, the diversity articulated a broader disciplinary struggle over sociological paradigms (Morgenbesser 1970; Teddlie and Tashakkori 2009) and revealed the growing maturity of diverse sociological approaches replete with their distinctive sociological epistemologies, ontologies, and methodologies.

Various sociologists generated structural-functionalist (Lifton 1983; Mellor 1993), critical realist (Elias 1985), interactionist (Becker 1973), and discursive (Armstrong 1987) explanations for death in modernity. Mellor's macro-oriented approach explains death-denial as the driving force for modern society. His theory is based on the premise that because modern societies are founded on science and reason, we are always questioning what we know and so are chronically insecure. To cope with this dread, modern societies are organized in such a way as to bracket out or sequester aspects that intensify this self-doubt. For Mellor, death is always a potential challenge to our everyday meaningfulness, and consequently a challenge to our elaborate social frameworks, so in modern society we have bracketed off death by hiding it away in lonely hospital beds. While Elias sees society and individuals inextricably interwoven in a continuous, contingent figuration process, he also understands modern society as a particularly individualizing and isolating outcome of universal forces that undergird a civilizing process of social development (Elias 1978; Elias et al. 1998). The outcome of this process is to encourage an alienated, solitary dying (Kellehear 2014). "Never before have people died as noiselessly and hygienically as today in these societies, and never in social conditions so much fostering solitude" (Elias 1985: 85).

In Becker's case, outlined below, we can see the influence of symbolic interactionism. Becker emphasizes that the ongoing personal experiences of death as socially invisible mean that the symbolic meanings associated with death are oriented toward fear of the unknown. Armstrong develops his theory of death in modern society by taking a discursive approach to understanding the social world (Armstrong 1987). This perspective approaches current death practices as elaborations of particular regimes of truth with associated institutions, infrastructure, symbolic referents, and habituated responses to particular events that have come to be known as dying (also see Prior 1989). Armstrong deals directly with the issue of sequestration. He explains that the conventional debate over whether death is hidden in contemporary society misses the mark. He argues that these transforming death practices have arisen because there has been a succession of different ways of knowing, a succession of different regimes of truth or death discourses rather than a profound transformation in the constitution of society.

The Death-Denial Thesis

Despite the diversity of sociological approaches, one particular presumption came to dominate the majority of accounts about death – that modern society is death denying. The death-denial thesis claims that modern society's death practices are marked by a discomfiting contradiction: On the one hand, the personal experience of death is of loneliness and isolation in hospital wards surrounded by professionals, while at the same time modern funeral rites are marked, especially in America, by their lavishness and ostentation. The tension lying at the heart of this contradiction stems from the fact that modern society is marked by growing secularization and, consequently, it has become impossible for modern individuals to hide the existential contradiction that defines humanity. This capacity to think symbolically in a finite body is experienced as a fear, or terror, of death and is "the mainstream of human activity" in that it fuels the pursuit of heroism, which is at the core of all social activity (Becker 1973: xi).

A deep concern rooted in the denial-of-death thesis is that modern societies are profoundly damaged because, through urbanization and individualization, people are no longer able to re-knit their communities in the face of loss in time-honored ways, where death rituals bound relations across families and neighborhoods. Norbert Elias, in *The Loneliness of the Dying* (1985), lambasts the resulting isolation of the dying as the ultimate alienation, and describes fine funerary accoutrements as the galling frippery of the mass commercialism of modern capitalist economies, so deftly decried in Jessica Mitford's *The American Way of Death* (Mitford 1963).

Just as accepted truths have been questioned in the discipline at large, the sociology of death and dying also offers a series of meta-reflections on the dominance of the denial-of-death thesis (see for instance Clark 1994; Kearl 1989; Seale 1998; Walter 1994). Summing up these reflections and critiques, Howarth (2007) argues that the mid-twentieth-century explanations of modern death as death denying were children of their times. While still often the go-to position for those looking to criticize rather than analyze people's death practices, the thesis of death-denial rests on an argument that tends to over-generalize the behaviors and beliefs of those who corroborate the thesis, and neglects death and dying experiences that do not conform to it. Unable to grapple with demands for inclusivity and complexity, and seen as ideologically driven rather than substantively accurate, it is no longer a sufficient explanation for the relationship between death and society in the late twentieth and early twenty-first centuries.

The Sociology of Death Today

The increasingly anachronistic character of the denial-of-death thesis serves to highlight that twenty-first century social relations have qualitatively shifted. As advanced modern societies are marked by a world of global markets, radical-fundamentalist politics, and real-time global communication, new trends in death practices are increasingly visible and in need of analysis. These change rapidly and include, for instance, the snowclone "death whisperers" in Australia who seek to support people as they die by making sure they are comfortable in themselves and can cope with fears and consider choices in the time they have got left (Legge 2011); pro-sumer activity (where prospective consumers are involved in the design, manufacture, or development of a product or service) in funeral arrangements (Schafer and McManus 2015); and Skype-enabled online ancestor veneration where "busy relatives can purchase graveside offerings for the dead by the mouseclick. Cemetery staff bring the items to the tombs and [live stream or] send videos or photos of the display by e-mail" (Brennan 2014: 31). A plurality of sociological accounts is emerging apace.

While death and dying scholars still try to explain the continuing trend toward individualization in advanced modern times, their explanations differ from those of previous decades. For example, Walter explains it as a series of new social movements, such as the rise of the hospice movement and the growing practice of arranging one's own funeral that are reviving interest in and attention to death (Walter 2005). Kellehear (2007) suggests that contemporary dying (what he calls cosmopolitan death) is drawn-out, shameful, and socially unsupported because contemporary societies have lost a clear sense of the social process of dying and so leave the dying alone, fevered, and demented. McManus (2013) argues that contemporary deaths are deeply inscribed by collective relations forged within globalization. In these new relations the dying and dead become more explicitly a resource or commodity that is utilized to service the needs of the living in a variety of globally interconnected ways.

Today, death can be used for potential benefits harnessed through, for example, organ harvesting, martyrdom for global politics, a new market for cross-country end of life care organizations, or calls to legalize euthanasia in order to reduce the cost burden of aging populations (among other reasons). Perhaps the growing pluralism of contemporary life can be incorporated into a theoretically pluralistic sensibility of death and dying.

Whether death and dying are seen as gaining revived interest, shameful experiences, and/or harnessed for various gains, current sociological theories about death and society offer explanations. The theories and debates among them carry the hallmark of a maturing subdiscipline with its own defining questions, concerns, and canon that makes valuable contributions to the sociology mother-ship. The sociology of death and dying examines past, informs current, and explores emergent forms of the collective organization and management of death and in doing so is a productive conduit between the substantive, disputative discipline of sociology, the interdisciplinary field of death studies, and the public domain.

Much like those in many other academic subjects, sociology of death and dying scholars are a dispersed web of small nodes of scholars who connect across wide, digitally hosted networks that materialise through conferences, edited collections, special editions of journals, and edited books. The majority of their current research focuses on modernity and individualization. Looking at death and dying through the lens of globalization has allowed them to develop more complex accounts and new theories of the place of death in advanced modernity.

The Sociology of Death and Dying and Interdisciplinary Death Studies

The subfield of death and dying is of value to interdisciplinary death studies. As a movement, interdisciplinary death studies (including scholars across the social and life sciences) are replete with sociological ideas and influences. Contemporary accounts of its emergence continually note the need for and influence of sociological concerns (see for instance Howarth 2007; Stillion and Attig 2014). The world's first (and, currently, only) Professor of Death Studies, Tony Walter, is a sociologist at Bath University in England.

Combining and incorporating sociological knowledge about death and dying with other disciplines (such as psychology) and areas (such as disaster studies) enables us to gain a coherent understanding of complex issues that are beyond the ability of any one discipline to address comprehensively or resolve adequately. For instance, Robben (2014) combines anthropological, sociological, and psychological insights into the memorialisation of mass deaths in ways that help develop an understanding of collective grieving applicable to other mass death situations and so inform disaster planning and recovery efforts.

Today, there exists an extensive professional network of death studies scholars, professionals, and practitioners. This is catalogued in Stillion and Attig's *Death Dying and Bereavement* (2014) and embodied in the growing number of institutional centers such as the Centre for Death and Society (Bath, UK) and the Antipodean Society for Death Studies. A growing network of international conferences in the Americas, Antipodes, and Eastern Europe signal a globalization of death scholarship networks, a broader circulation of ideas and debates, a networked knowledge space, professional support, and growing career opportunities for death studies scholars and professionals.

Benefits of the Subfield for Society

Distinct from the larger interdisciplinary field of death studies, the sociology of death and dying benefits society in a variety of ways. Specifically, it advances knowledge on how, why, and on what terms death practices are collectively organized in a given time and place. It is able to note changes in societal practices, emerging trends, and social concerns. In doing so, it can contribute data to assist in social planning, public policy, and public debate. It can also help shape the direction of public debates away from emotive toward considered, empirically informed reflections on significant social issues such as end of life care, euthanasia, and health provision systems. For example, research on the provision (or inadequate provision) of end of life care can help guide emergent health policies (Clark 2013). Likewise, social research on beliefs and expectations on the cost of funerals can influence national debates on funeral grant support (McManus and Schafer 2014). It can also contribute to political movements and policies to change attitudes and practices to create fairer and more equitable death experiences within and across societies.

Understanding death and the dying process is indispensable for the understanding and planning of society and developing adequate solutions to problems and concerns. On an individual level, it can help individuals better understand their relationship with society and with death and how both can change over time. Also, classes in sociology of death and dying, now offered in most sociology programs, give students a way to engage conceptually with a fundamental aspect of life at a time when they do not have to be in the thick of it emotionally.

Conclusion: A Community of Scholars across Generations and a Rising Subfield

Sociology Professor Michael Kearl dropped dead of a heart attack while walking across his campus in March of 2015. He had just been working on symbols of mortality (Kearl 2015). Three months later, anthropologist Dr. Cyril Schafer died suddenly of an aneurism at lunchtime in Dunedin, New Zealand. We had been co-writing a piece on death and consumerism (Schafer and McManus 2015). I owe a big debt to both these men. To me, our professional relationships capture the essence of the sociology of death and dying. On the one hand, Michael's manuscript reviews pushed for sociological depth through his demands for empirical substantiation and conceptual coherence. On the other hand, Cyril and I were a small interdisciplinary team that sought broader insights from the synthesis of both our disciplines. Their combined depth and breadth speaks to Emile Durkheim's adage: "the character of the collectivity outlasts the personalities of its members" (Durkheim 2002[1961]: 62). Their untimely deaths help crystalize the shift from specific people researching ideas and practices to a dynamic collective entity we may call the sociology of death studies, made up of a generationally shifting network of scholars, practitioners, and professionals, who seek to examine the social aspects of death and dying.

References

Armstrong, David. 1987. Silence and Truth in Death and Dying. *Social Science and Medicine* 24(8): 651–657.

Becker, Ernest. 1973. *The Denial of Death*. New York, NY: The Free Press.

Brennan, Michael John. 2014. *The A–Z of Death and Dying: Social Medical and Cultural Aspects*. USA: ABC-CLIO.

Clark, David. 1994. *The Sociology of Death: Theory, Culture, Practice*. Sociological Review Monograph. Oxford: Blackwell.

Clark, David. 2013. *Transforming The Culture of Dying: The Work of the Project on Death in America*. Oxford: Oxford University Press.

Durkheim, Emile. 1897. *Suicide: A Study in Sociology*. New York, NY: Free Press.

Durkheim, Emile. 1995[1912]. *The Elementary Forms of Religious Life*. New York, NY: The Free Press.

Durkheim, Emile. 2002[1961]. *Moral Education: A Study in the Theory and Application of the Sociology of Education*. Mineola, New York, NY: Dover Publications Inc.

Elias, Norbert. 1978. *What Is Sociology?* Columbia, OH: Columbia University Press.

Elias, Norbert. 1985. *The Loneliness of the Dying*. Oxford: Blackwell.

Elias, Norbert, Stephen Mennell, and Johan Goudsblom. 1998. *On Civilization, Power, and Knowledge: Selected Writings*. Chicago, IL and London: The University of Chicago Press.

Fulton, Robert. 1965. *Death and Identity*. New York, NY: Wiley.

Glaser, Barney and Anselm Strauss. 1968. *Time for Dying*. Chicago, IL: Aldine Publishing Company.

Gorer, Geoffrey. 1955. The Pornography of Death. *Encounter* 49–52.

Hertz, Robert. 2004[1960]. *Death and the Right Hand*. London: Routledge.

Howarth, Glennys. 2007. *Death and Dying: A Sociological Introduction*. Cambridge: Polity Press.

Kearl, Michael K. 1989. *Endings: A Sociology of Death and Dying*. New York, NY, and Oxford: Oxford University Press.

Kearl, Michael K. 2015. The Proliferation of Skulls in Popular Culture: A Case Study of How the Traditional Symbol of Mortality Was Rendered Meaningless. *Mortality* 20: 1.

Kellehear, Allan. 2007. *A Social History of Dying*. Cambridge: Cambridge University Press.

Kellehear, Allan. 2014. *The Inner Life of the Dying Person*. Columbia, OH: Columbia University Press.

Kephart, W. M. 1950. Status after Death. *American Sociological Review* 15: 635–643.

Legge, Kate. 2011. The Death Whisperers. *The Australian* (Weekend Edition). Sydney: News Corp Australia.

Lifton, Robert Jay. 1983. *The Broken Connection: On Death and the Continuity of Life*. New York, NY: Basic Books Inc.

Marx, Karl. 1970[1844]. *A Contribution to the Critique of Hegel's Philosophy of Right*. Cambridge: Cambridge University Press.

McManus, Ruth. 2013. *Death in a Global Age*. London, New York, NY: Palgrave Macmillan.

McManus, Ruth and Cyril Schafer. 2014. Final Arrangements: Examining Debt and Distress. *Mortality* 19(4): 379–397.

Mellor, Phillip A. 1993. Death in High Modernity: The Contemporary Presence and Absence of Death. In *The Sociology of Death*. Edited by D. Clark. Oxford: Blackwell/The Sociological Review, 11–30.

Mitford, Jessica. 1963. *The American Way of Death*. London: Hutchinson.

Morgenbesser, Sidney. 1970. Is It a Science? In *Sociological Theory and Philosophical Analysis*. Edited by D. Emmet and A. MacIntyre. London: Macmillan, 20–35.

Oz, Frank. 2007. *Death at a Funeral*. UK P. 90m 25s, released November 2.

Prior, Lindsay. 1989. *The Social Organisation of Death: Medical Discourse and Social Practices in Belfast*. Basingstoke: Macmillan.

Robben, Antonius. 2014. Massive Violent Death and Contested National Mourning in Post-Authoritarian Chile and Argentina: A Sociocultural Application of the Dual Process Model. *Death Studies* 38(5): 335–345.

Schafer, Cyril and Ruth McManus. 2015. Authenticity, Informality and Privacy in Contemporary New Zealand Post-Mortem Practices. In *Death in a Consumer Culture*. Edited by S. Dobscha. USA: Routledge.

Seale, Clive. 1998. *Constructing Death: The Sociology of Dying and Bereavement*. Cambridge: Cambridge University Press.

Stillion, Judith and Thomas Attig. 2014. *Death, Dying and Bereavement: Contemporary Perspectives, Institutions and Practices*. New York, NY: Springer.

Teddlie, Charles and Abbas Tashakkori. 2009. Paradigm Issues in Mixed Methods. In *Foundations of Mixed Methods*. Edited by C. Teddlie and A. Tashakkori. New York, NY: Sage, 83–105.

Van Gennep, Arnold. 2004[1960]. *The Rites of Passage*. London: Routledge.

Walter, Tony. 1994. *The Revival of Death*. London: Routledge.

Walter, Tony. 2005. Three Ways to Arrange a Funeral: Mortuary Variation in the Modern West. *Mortality* 10(3): 173–192.

Walter, Tony. 2014. Sociological Perspectives in Death, Dying and Bereavement. In *Death, Dying and Bereavement: Contemporary Perspectives, Institutions and Practices*. Edited by J. Stillion and T. Attig. New York, NY: Springer, 31–44.

Weber, Max. 1904[1958]. *The Protestant Ethic and the Spirit of Capitalism*. New York, NY: Charles Scribner.

Part VII
CULTURE AND BEHAVIOR

CHAPTER 27
The Sociology of Consumption

Stanley Blue

Introduction

During the second half of the twentieth century there was a rapid growth in the subdiscipline of the Sociology of Consumption. Consumption is now well established as a central topic for sociologists and others seeking to address a number of contemporary and pressing global issues, such as sustainability and health. The Sociology of Consumption is armed with a range of concepts that are capable of conceptualizing how resource intensive and unhealthy ways of consuming might be shifted, but contemporary patterns of consumption persist, as discourses about the autonomy of the individual and the power of technological innovation continue to dominate. In this chapter, I trace the development of this subdiscipline to show that the Sociology of Consumption has much to offer those seeking to shape ways of living and consuming. I begin by saying something more broadly about the field, and then give more detail on the development of key approaches and positions: (1) "mass culture," (2) "consumer culture," (3) distinction and taste, and (4) more recent developments. I conclude by arguing that ideas from these positions would better inform approaches to "real world" issues, through the example of sustainable consumption.

The Field of the Sociology of Consumption

Until the middle of the twentieth century, consumption was not a key topic in the social sciences. Instead, the so-called "forefathers" of sociology, like Marx and Weber, addressed consumption only indirectly. Veblen's *The Theory of the Leisure Class* (2001[1899]) was the first work to engage with the notion of consumption in its own right. He studied how middle classes in the United States at the turn of the century distinguished themselves from those who were less well-off through overt displays of wealth, or "conspicuous consumption." Veblen's work prompted critical and ongoing debates about the relationships between class and consumption.

Despite this demonstration of the economic significance of consumption, for a large part of the twentieth century work in this area remained limited. It was only in the 1960s and 1970s that academic scholars really began to study the process and content of consumption itself. Here I follow Warde's (2015) comprehensive review of the field and his identification of three distinct periods of development. The first is from classic sociological work until the 1980s, where work focused on the production of "mass culture." The second is from the 1980s until the turn of the century, where writers influenced by the "cultural turn" in sociology drew attention to the creative potential of "consumer culture." The third period of development takes us to the present day, where more recent approaches have combined previous arguments to study both the economic and cultural aspects of consumption.

Each of these various approaches emphasizes different elements of consumption and deals with the notion of consumption differently. Because of this, it is difficult to provide one single coherent definition of consumption that might be accepted by proponents of each position. However, Campbell gives as good a description of the concept as any:

> *a simple working definition, [is] one that identifies consumption as involving the selection, purchase, use, maintenance, repair and disposal of any given product or service. (Campbell 1995: 101–102)*

While consensus over a more narrow definition of consumption might be difficult to achieve, the field of the Sociology of Consumption is now well recognized as an important and broad domain of sociological enquiry. It deploys socio-theoretical concepts to study the particularities of consumption, but it also draws on empirical work to develop key sociological theories about consumption. In particular, three key themes emerge.

The first is the question of how to imagine "the consumer" or the consuming subject. Gabriel and Lang (1995) show that different approaches to the study of consumption (i.e., different periods of development) imagine and define the consuming subject differently. For example "the consumer" can be considered variously as: chooser, communicator, explorer, identity-seeker, hedonist, artist, victim, rebel, activist, and citizen. These representations, respectively, position the consuming subjects differently in terms of their autonomy and their use of consumption as an expression of identity (see Aldridge 2003: 16).

These different views of the consuming subject relate to classic sociological questions about how to understand the social subject: as homo-economicus or homo-sociologicus (see Vaisey 2008). Within the field of the Sociology of Consumption, some approaches consider individuals as capable of making autonomous and rational decisions in light of their own personal self-interest (homo-economicus). Others recognize and emphasize the interdependence of individuals, that people have shared norms and values as well as shared understandings, and that social institutions shape social action and therefore patterns of consumption (homo-sociologicus). The Sociology of Consumption is both informed by and speaks back to these questions about the social subject.

A second key theme that emerges is the way in which different approaches conceptualize the acquisition, appropriation, and appreciation (the "three As") of goods and services (see Warde 2010). Acquisition is about how goods and services are obtained through different kinds of social and economic exchanges. Appropriation is about what people do with goods once they acquire them. And appreciation is about how things gain and lose value.

The final theme deals with a number of cross-cutting issues that plot consumption against a number of antinomies, or opposites, such as relationships between economy and culture, materialism and idealism, structure and agency, optimism and pessimism, etc.

It should be noted that the study of consumption has a significantly different tradition in the United States than it does in the United Kingdom and Europe. American studies have tended to be much less critical of capitalism and have instead focused on the role of the consumer. For example, Zukin and Smith Maguire's (2004) review paper defines consumption simply as "a process of choosing goods," (2004: 173) viewing consumption as tied to a tradition of consumer behavior rather than examining how consumption is constitutive of social relations. In what follows, I discuss the three periods of historical development outlined by Warde (2015) to show how each of these approaches tackles different key themes in the Sociology of Consumption (i.e., the consuming subject, the three As, and positioning antinomies).

Mass Culture

After World War II, countries in the West experienced a long boom. New industrial methods for the mass production and distribution of goods and increased wages created strong economic growth, improving quality of life for many and at the same time developing new kinds and increased levels of consumption. These changes in production, consumption, and affluence were intriguing sites of investigation across a range of disciplines. A revival of Marxist thought at that time meant that studies of changes in social order focused on production, the accumulation of capital, and class antagonisms. Consumption itself was never the focus of study, and neither was the minutiae of how people went about their activities of consumption. Instead, changes in consumption were understood as a result of macro-economic changes in the way in which things were produced.

The most well recognized sociological contribution to the study of consumption during this period is work by the Frankfurt School and particularly their critique of "mass culture." Fleeing the persecution, oppression, and horrors of Nazi Germany, members of the Frankfurt School made their way to the United States, where they were confronted with the results of radical shifts in forms of production – not only in the production of goods, but of culture as well! They considered the abundant new forms of popular entertainment to have been produced by a "culture industry" meant to domesticate, distract, and dupe the masses into accepting capitalist relations of production and the socio-economic inequalities that resulted.

For the members of the Frankfurt School, new forms of popular entertainment and art were now mass produced in the same way that cars and jeans were produced in the factory. They claimed that the routines of artists and entertainers had become structured by economic ownership in that they had taken on the character of the factory floor assembly line. Adorno and Horkheimer describe this as: "the synthetic, planned method of turning out...products (factory-like not only in the studio but, more or less, in the compilation of cheap biographies, pseudo documentary novels, and hit songs...)" (1979[1937]: 163). They argued that this production of a mass culture had three important consequences for the ways that people consume.

First, they argued that it resulted in standardized, "safe," and passive forms of consumption. They write:

> As soon as the film begins, it is quite clear how it will end, and who will be rewarded, punished, or forgotten. In light music, once the trained ear has heard the first notes of the hit song, it can guess what is coming and feel flattered when it does come. (1979[1937]: 125)

The culture industry produces entertainment that repeats the same tropes, stories, and passive politics that distract the working class from recognizing their position as oppressed and dupes them into consuming entertainment products that satisfy and reaffirm popular, widely held, and false understandings of the way that the world is.

The second consequence is that it leads to the loss of individuality, spontaneity, and choice. Rather than providing a wealth of products from which to choose to represent our own identities, we purchase the product or commodity which has been mass produced for "our type." When it comes to consumption, the Frankfurt School scholars claim that choice and spontaneity are illusions. Instead, people consume repetitively in the supermarket, on the high street, and in the pub, replicating the automation of the workplace and the standardization of the assembly line.

The final consequence for Adorno and Horkheimer is that all art and the avant-garde is reduced into kitsch mass culture. For the Frankfurt School, themselves lovers of opera, high culture, and the avant-garde, the production of consumption leads to great works of art no longer being judged on their content or on their ability to challenge dominant ways of thinking. Instead art is judged on how well it conforms to the prescribed formulas set out by the culture industry, so that it might become a best-seller or "go platinum."

This period of the Sociology of Consumption positioned the consuming subject as a dupe and as a victim of mass culture, tricked into ways of consuming that were presented as emancipatory. The Frankfurt School's analysis attributes little to no autonomy to individuals in their consumption choices or at least argues that these choices are only pseudo-choices that have limited political significance. This model of "the consumer" is fully aligned with the model of homo-sociologicus, positioning the social subject as interdependent, with norms and behaviors rooted in shared norms and values which are organized and produced by economic, social, and cultural institutions.

This approach has significant consequences for understanding how goods and services are acquired, appropriated, and appreciated. For the Frankfurt School, goods and services are acquired through the volume and distribution of goods made available and they are disposed of through built-in obsolescence (changes in fashion trends, new facilities on mobile phones etc.). They are not acquired as part of an expression of individual taste or through a managed display of identity. Goods are appropriated as alienating and domesticating products of mass consumption, and they are appreciated through a framework of "false needs" (see Marcuse 2002[1964]).

This approach to consumption sits on one side of a set of antinomies within the field of the Sociology of Consumption. It is pessimistic rather than optimistic about the role of consumption in human endeavors; it emphasizes economy, structure, and materialism over culture, agency, and idealism; and it deals mostly in theoretical or abstract accounts of consumption rather than in empirical studies. It is a thesis of manipulation, domination, and control that calls for the study of the material and economic conditions of production, rather than the study of cultural meanings in order to get at processes of consumption.

Consumer Culture

During the 1980s, however, the field of the Sociology of Consumption was transformed. Consumption went from being a secondary concern, after primary considerations of capitalist production, to a central and organizing feature of the social order. This shift coincided with a decline in neo-Marxist approaches in the fashion of the Frankfurt School amidst strong critiques of economistic explanations of consumption. It also coincided with the development of semiotic studies about the meaning of consumption, a recognition of the important role of culture, and the rise of postmodernism. All of these developments were part and parcel of a broader "cultural turn" happening at that time in the social sciences.

Scholars in what became known as cultural studies were critical of the idea of a powerful and independent culture industry. They argued that consumption could not be reduced to a blanket mass culture. For them, the acquisition of goods was not only about use value and exchange value but, importantly, about symbolic value and the meaning of goods. These studies claimed that the absence of attention to symbolic meaning left Adorno, Horkheimer, et al. incapable of understanding the creative potential of mass consumption. They were also critical of Adorno and Horkheimer's style of grand and abstract theorizing about consumption, arguing that consumption needed to be understood empirically through observations of how people actually went about purchasing goods (e.g., Douglas 1996).

These cultural studies scholars proposed that studies of consumption should focus attention toward the symbolic nature of goods and services in order to understand the meanings behind consumption, understanding consumption choices not merely as instrumental but as expressive of emotions and desires, of individual agency and choice. This work analyzed social and symbolic exchange by studying how the consumption of signs, symbols, and images created and communicated social meaning. The result was a recognition of the virtues of a mass consumption that allowed individuals to communicate different personal and social identities, that provided different kinds of entertainment, and that developed intellectual stimulation and innovation.

In particular, Featherstone's work on *Consumer Culture and Postmodernism* (1991), emphasized a much more positive view of consumption as "consumer culture," one that sought to understand everyday social interaction as navigated through consumption as the expression of self-identity. Moving away from theses of manipulation and control, authors like Featherstone (1991), Giddens (1991), and Slater (1997) challenged the determinism of previous studies of macro-economic phenomena, shifting emphases from rules and order toward choices and freedom. These authors viewed the idea that there was no choice but to choose as liberating. Being able to choose how, when, and what to consume was central to freedom of expression and self-identity.

As such, the Sociology of Consumption became concerned with understanding how symbolically significant goods were acquired in the pursuit of distinct "lifestyles." Featherstone writes:

> *Rather than unreflexively adopting a lifestyle, through tradition or habit, the new heroes of consumer culture make lifestyle a life project and display their individuality and sense of style in the particularity of goods, clothes, experiences...they design together into a lifestyle.* (1991: 86)

Advocates of "consumer culture" emphasized the agency of individuals in designing and displaying their own lifestyles while at the same time they examined how and why consumption became the arena for this kind of work.

This approach to understanding the role of consuming subjects as designers of their own lifestyles stands in opposition to understanding "the consumer" as a victim or a dupe. In reaction to and criticism of those modern and neo-Marxist theories of capitalist production, cultural studies attributes to "the consumer" a much larger degree of agency, recognizing them variously as: chooser, communicator, explorer, identity-seeker, and, potentially, as activist. "The consumer," at least within postmodern theories of "consumer culture," is understood more or less as an active, rational actor, rather than as a passive dupe; as independent homo-economicus, rather than interdependent homo-sociologicus.

This position therefore, has ways of understanding how goods and services are acquired, appropriated, and appreciated that are significantly different from the Frankfurt School approach. Rather than being gained only through economic exchange, goods and services are acquired through symbolic exchange, through the communication and expression of self-identity. Rather than being taken on as domesticating and alienating products of mass consumption, goods and services are appropriated through processes of decommodification, singularisation, and personalisation. And rather than being seen through a framework of "false needs," objects are appreciated through a symbolic framework of pleasure, satisfaction, hedonism, and meaning.

Cultural studies can more or less be positioned in opposition to the Frankfurt School when it comes to the study of consumption. Cultural studies emphasizes culture, idealism, and agency over economy, materialism, and structure. It is much more optimistic, seeing in consumption the potential for creativity, play, and the opportunity for self-expression. And it provides detailed empirical studies about the micro-social interactions and sites of consumption that constitute a plurality of modes of identification and belonging.

Having outlined these first two opposing positions, it will be important to say something about the contribution of Pierre Bourdieu's work to the Sociology of Consumption before moving on to a discussion of more recent developments in the field.

Distinction and Taste

Although his worked preceded, and was in many ways the target of, arguments within cultural studies, no discussion of the Sociology of Consumption could ignore the important contribution to the field made by Pierre Bourdieu, particularly in *Distinction* (1984). Rather than providing either an economistic account of the top-down production of mass culture or emphasizing the potential creativity of culture through the expression of different lifestyles, Bourdieu was one of the first theorists to engage seriously with both the cultural and economic spheres, adding the central concept of "cultural capital" as a marker of class position to the traditional distinguisher of economic capital or wealth. Again, Bourdieu's account was not one of consumption itself but of how "taste" operates as a mechanism for maintaining, reproducing, and struggling over class inequalities.

Through the use of the concept of "habitus," the idea that one develops embodied dispositions, competences, skills, and responses depending on experiences of being brought up and living a particular class position, Bourdieu argues that people develop a practical and semi-conscious sense of their likes and dislikes. These tastes (informed by the habitus) become a critical mechanism for distinguishing between social groups, between the "us" and "them." According to Bourdieu, because the working classes are constrained by lower endowments of economic *and* cultural capital, they develop a taste for those goods which are available to them, seeing them as necessary and functional, and they reject those which are unavailable, seeing them as extravagant. Upper classes on the other hand distance themselves from such "tastes for necessity" and instead develop a "taste for the superfluous" (e.g., abstract art). Struggles over what counts as necessary and what counts as superfluous consumption then act as the subconscious battleground for social and cultural distinction.

Bourdieu's argument that dominant classes establish the legitimacy of taste as part of the process of reproducing and representing class distinctions has, however, been contested. Thirty years on, it is questionable whether there is still a similar relationship between socio-economic and cultural inequalities in the same way. Some argue that consumption has become much more open and less restricted by class. One powerful exposition of this argument is the cultural omnivore thesis (see Peterson and Kern 1996). The term was developed to explain a lack of relationship between high social status and the consumption of high culture in the United States. A number of empirical studies show that economically privileged and well-educated groups across several countries engage in a number of different activities of disparately high and low taste. These groups are "cultural omnivores," capable of consuming anything and everything. Yet, while the evidence may demonstrate a dissolution of the links between high status and the consumption of high culture, the reasons for this are contested. Rather than implying a greater appreciation of different cultural objects, omnivorousness may instead simply be a new marker of distinction. These debates continue and offer fertile ground for thinking about the relationship between class and consumption.

More Recent Developments

While the cultural turn enriched the study of consumption, it also stands accused of over-emphasizing certain aspects of consumption while neglecting others. Investigations of the political economy of consumption, of the relationship between consumption and class, and of material inequalities were side-lined in favor of analyses of specific examples of different modes of personal identity creation. Cultural studies emphasized analyses of the symbolic meaning of certain goods but obscured the material role of objects and technologies within processes of consumption. A great deal of this work focused on conspicuous consumption and on consumption as displays of identity, while ordinary, routine, and everyday consumption was ignored.

Recent developments in the Sociology of Consumption have attempted to respond to these gaps and balance some of the more extreme antinomies between culture and economy, structure and agency, production and consumption, materialism and idealism. Without leaving these orienting distinctions behind, more recent contributions have incorporated understandings of meaning with understandings of the material conditions of consumption and have engaged with understandings of macro-economic phenomena alongside and in relation to micro-situations of consumption.

One significant development can be seen in the revival of the political economy of consumption. Developed alongside and in response to a focus on consumer culture, Fine and Leopold (1993) link macro-economic processes with more micro and situated acts of consumption. Rather than maintaining a distinction between spheres of production and consumption to understand how one might affect or organize the other, Fine and Leopold suggest shifting from a vertical analysis to a horizontal one, in order to think about systems of provision. This analytical move emphasizes studying the links between consumption and production and between distribution and retail in order to explain socio-economic changes and changes in consumption more broadly. Such analyses focus on the commodity as the embodied unity of social and economic processes that reveals distinct relationships between the material and cultural practices that underpin the production, distribution, circulation, retail, and consumption of the specific commodities concerned. Following Appadurai's (1981) suggestion to "follow the things," studies in this vein (e.g., Cook 2004) usually start with cultural understandings of consumption and then work back along the commodity chain, often through an ethnography of various stages of the commodity's production and consumption.

Nevertheless, despite seeking to link production and consumption, such work arguably still focuses on production (i.e., provision). The process of working backward, or starting with "the things," demotes cultural understandings of social change and consumption in favor of processes higher up the supply chain, such as regulatory frameworks, policy, and production.

Other contributions have sought to bridge the divide between economy and culture by focusing specifically on the role of objects. Instead of conceiving of goods as the alienating products of mass culture or studying them for their cultural meanings, more recent work has complicated understandings of how "things" are incorporated and adapted to social processes. Actor network theory (ANT) (see Latour 2005) ascribes agency to things so that, for example, shopping trolleys (Cochoy 2009) and market devices (Callon et al. 2007), play a significant role in shaping the performance of shopping in the supermarket (i.e., they permit people to shop for more items at once) and the organization of markets. The importance of such an analysis shows that objects are not appropriated simply at will, but form part of socio-technical arrangements that matter for the construction of social relationships and for social action.

Following what has been described as the "practice turn" in contemporary social theory (Schatzki et al. 2001), proponents of "theories of practice" have argued that studies of consumption can provide a more careful account of the relationship between production and consumption, between structure and agency, between systems and lifestyles and between humans and things, by taking social practices as the central unit of analysis. Theories of practice provide a particular development in understanding the role of objects in processes of consumption, by focusing on how goods are used in the accomplishment of social habits and routines that are based on shared understandings of how particular activities should be done (see Warde 2005). As such they provide an important insight into ordinary, mundane, and everyday consumption (Gronow and Warde 2001) and the "inconspicuous consumption" (Shove and Warde 2002) of water, energy, food, etc. Through an approach which is organized neither around individual choices nor around social structures but around the emergence and decline of social practices like cooking, washing, shopping, etc., theories of practice show that consumption of goods and services can effectively be understood as an outcome of the ongoing organization and reproduction of the social practices that make up everyday life. This kind of approach, in particular, has been very successfully applied in the area of environmental sustainability.

Sustainable Consumption

The debates outlined above about how to understand the consumer, about the relationship between production and consumption, and about how to understand how goods and services are acquired, appropriated, and appreciated are important scholarly contributions to sociological theory. They are also fundamentally important for applied approaches to "real life" social issues, not least of all to questions of sustainability. By now it is clear that unsustainable consumption is a major cause of environmental degradation. It is not consumption per se that is the culprit, but the high levels of resource consumption that are associated with so-called "consumer cultures." For example, if the United Kingdom is to meet its 2050 carbon reduction targets, the patterns of consumption that constitute people's daily lives need to change and change much more quickly than they are currently.

The challenge of finding a path toward a more sustainable future requires radically different ways of living and consuming to take hold in developed nations. This is clearly no small adjustment, but policy continues to focus on ecological modernization, technological fixes and influencing consumer behavior – or getting individuals to make "greener" choices. Such policies are based on limited understandings of the processes of consumption, its relationship to systems of provision and production, and a limited, portfolio model of the consuming subject as homo-economicus, which paints consumers as independent individuals who make rational choices. Any irrational behaviors are seen as consequences of inefficiencies, something going wrong, or misaligned attitudes and values. At bottom, this approach continues to understand consumption as little more than purchasing behavior. Policy responses that follow, therefore, involve intervening in prices and incentives, with social marketing campaigns to correct "information deficits" and attempts to foster attitudinal changes in order to tinker with and adjust contemporary ways of living. Crucially though, such approaches to individualizing risk and responsibility are not working at anything like the required rate of change.

The Sociology of Consumption has much to bring to these debates. It can offer "big theories" of social order and change (e.g., the Frankfurt School). It can complicate narratives about individual choice as being about lifestyle and cultural meaning (e.g., Featherstone). It can deal with technologies, infrastructures, and networks (Callon,

Latour), the role of the state and systems of provision (Fine and Leopold), and account for embedded social routines, habits and ordinary, everyday consumption (Gronow and Warde).

Conclusion

The Sociology of Consumption is a diverse and contested field. This should be seen as a strength and not a weakness. Currently, policy-makers tackling social issues that are the outcomes of patterns of consumption (e.g., health and sustainability) rely on a handful of concepts about identity, the individual, consumer choice, and consumer society. It should be clear from the above that consumption is not about individuals going shopping for things that are provisioned through the market. For sociologists, consumption is about the organization and reproduction of ways of life. Some understand these ways of life as being dependent upon social structures and institutions. To change patterns of consumption, these structures need to be at the center of discussions about consumption. For others, ways of life are expressions of meanings and discourses. Such accounts identify social concerns, conventions, meanings, and judgments as potential targets of intervention. From the perspective of an emerging body of work, consumption is an outcome of the practices that people do, that make up everyday life. For these authors, sources of change in patterns of consumption lie in the development of the organization of social practices.

Different approaches will be more appropriate and successful depending on the research topic and the kinds of questions asked. But, significantly, each approach contributes important concepts, ideas, and insights that can be employed to better study, understand, and potentially shift the processes and mechanisms of consumption embedded into contemporary ways of living.

References

Adorno, Theodor W. and Max Horkheimer. 1979[1937]. *Dialectic of Enlightenment.* Translated by J. Cumming. London: Verso.

Aldridge, Alan. 2003. *Consumption.* Cambridge: Polity.

Appadurai, A. ed. 1981. *The Social Life of Things: Commodities in Cultural Perspective.* Cambridge: Cambridge University Press.

Bourdieu, Pierre. 1984. *Distinction: A Social Critique of the Judgement of Taste.* London: Routledge and Kegan Paul.

Callon, Michel, Yuval Millo, and Fabian Muniesa. 2007. *Market Devices.* Oxford: Blackwell.

Campbell, Colin. 1995. The Sociology of Consumption. In *Acknowledging Consumption: A Review of New Studies.* Edited by D. Miller. London: Routledge.

Cochoy, Franck. 2009. Driving a Shopping Cart from STS to Business, and the Other Way Round: On the Introduction of Shopping Carts in American Grocery Stores (1936–1959). *Organization* 16(1): 31–55.

Cook, Ian. 2004. Follow the Thing: Papaya. *Antipode* 36(4): 642–664.

Douglas, Mary. 1996. *Thought Styles: Critical Essays on Good Taste.* London: Sage.

Featherstone, Mike. 1991. *Consumer Culture and Postmodernism.* Thousand Oaks, CA: Sage.

Fine, B. and E. Leopold. 1993. *The World of Consumption.* London: Routledge.

Gabriel, Yiannis and Tim Lang. 1995. *The Unmanageable Consumer: Contemporary Consumption and its Fragmentation.* London: Sage.

Giddens, Anthony. 1991. *Modernity and Self-Identity: Self and Society in the Late Modern Age.* Cambridge: Polity.

Gronow, Jukka and Alan Warde. 2001. *Ordinary Consumption.* New York, NY: Routledge.

Latour, Bruno. 2005. *Reassembling the Social: An Introduction to Actor-Network-Theory.* New York, NY: Oxford University Press.

Marcuse, Herbert. 2002[1964]. *One-Dimensional Man: Studies in the Ideology of Advanced Industrial Society.* London: Routledge.

Peterson, Richard A. and Roger M. Kern. 1996. Changing Highbrow Taste: From Snob to Omnivore. *American Sociological Review* 61(5): 900–907.

Schatzki, Theodore, Karin Knorr-Cetina, and Eike von Savigny. 2001. *The Practice Turn in Contemporary Theory*. Abingdon, Oxford: Taylor and Francis Group.

Shove, Elizabeth and Alan Warde. 2002. Inconspicuous Consumption: The Sociology of Consumption, Lifestyles and the Environment. *Sociological Theory and the Environment: Classical Foundations, Contemporary Insights* 230: 51.

Slater, Don. 1997. *Consumer Culture and Modernity*. Cambridge: Polity.

Vaisey, Stephen. 2008. Socrates, Skinner, and Aristotle: Three Ways of Thinking about Culture in Action. *Sociological Forum* 23(3): 603–613.

Veblen, Thorstein. 2001[1899]. *The Theory of the Leisure Class*. Modern Library Classics. New York, NY: Modern Library.

Warde, Alan. 2005. Consumption and Theories of Practice. *Journal of Consumer Culture* 5(2): 131–153.

Warde, Alan. 2010. *Consumption*. Thousand Oaks, CA: Sage.

Warde, Alan. 2015. The Sociology of Consumption: Its Recent Development. *Annual Review of Sociology* 41(1): 117–134.

Zukin, Sharon and Jennifer Smith Maguire. 2004. Consumers and Consumption. *Annual Review of Sociology* 30: 173–197.

CHAPTER 28
The Sociology of Leisure and Recreation

Robert A. Stebbins

Leisure is a commonsense term whose etymologic roots date to Roman times and the Latin verb *licere*. In everyday parlance, leisure refers both to the time left over after work and non-work obligations – often called free time – and to the way we spend that time. Scientific attempts to define the idea have revolved, in considerable part, around the problems generated by this simplistic definition.

Scientifically speaking, leisure is uncoerced, contextually framed activity engaged in during free time, which people want to do and, using their abilities and resources, actually do in either a satisfying or a fulfilling way (or both) (this, the most recent version of this definition, comes from Stebbins 2012: 4). Note, in this regard, that boredom occurring in free time is an uncoerced state, but it is not something that bored people *want* to experience. Therefore, it is not leisure; it is not a positive experience, as just defined.

Two common elements in the standard definitions of leisure – "choice" and "freely chosen activity" (e.g., Kelly 1990: 21) – have, obviously, been avoided in the foregoing definition. And for good reason, since the two have come in for some considerable criticism. Juniu and Henderson (2001: 8), for instance, say that such terms cannot be empirically supported, since people lack significant choice because "leisure activities are socially structured and shaped by the inequalities of society" (see also Shaw 2001: 186–187). True, experiential definitions of leisure published in recent decades, when they do contain reference to choice, tend to refer to perceived, rather than objective, freedom to choose. The definers recognize thus that various conditions, many of them unperceived by leisure participants and unspecified by definers, nevertheless constrain choice of leisure activities. Juniu and Henderson argue that these conditions are highly influential, however, and that defining leisure even as perceived choice tends to underplay, if not overlook, their true effect.

But what would happen to human agency in the pursuit of leisure were we to abandon mentioning in definitions of leisure the likes of "choice" and "freely chosen"? It would likely be lost, were it not for the principle of lack of coercion. Behavior is un-coerced when people make their own leisure. Un-coerced, people believe they are doing something they are not pushed to do, something they are not disagreeably obliged to do. Emphasis is on the acting individual, which retains human agency in the formula. This in no way denies that there may be things people want to do but cannot do because of numerous constraints on choice (e.g., aptitude, ability, socialized leisure tastes, knowledge of available activities, accessibility of activities). In other words, when using our definition of leisure, whose central ingredient is lack of coercion, we must be sure to frame such use in relevant structural, cultural, and historical context. This context is also the appropriate place for discussing choice and its constraints.

Lack of coercion to engage in an activity is a quintessential property of leisure. No other sphere of human activity can be exclusively characterized by this property. Moreover, note that some workers, including professionals, consultants, craft workers, some small business entrepreneurs, and paid-staff in volunteer organizations, find their jobs so profoundly fulfilling that they closely approach this ideal. They work at "devotee occupations" (Stebbins 2014[2004]).

Where does recreation fit in all this? The word is often used as a synonym for leisure, though the latter term is far more prevalent in the modern scientific literature. In keeping with this trend I will speak mostly about leisure. The idea of recreation is most distinctive when referring to activity done in free time, which, after work, refreshes and restores a person to return to work again (Godbey 1999: 12–13). Of course, some leisure can accomplish the same thing, though that term fails to underscore this function as clearly as the term recreation.

The Rise of Leisure in the West

In the following discussion of the rise of the idea and pursuit of leisure, the Protestant ethic serves as the principal orientation that, until the later part of the nineteenth century, inspired the dominant attitude toward leisure in parts of the West, particularly the United States. That orientation, as reflected in the Protestant ethic and the work ethic that succeeded it, was that, in general, leisure is to be scorned. In fact the Protestant ethic was particularly strict (Weber 1930). Waste of time – sloth – be it in sociability, idle talk, luxury, or excessive sleep, was considered the worst of sins. Bluntly put, unwillingness to work was held as evidence of lack of grace. Sport received a partial reprieve from this fierce indictment, but only so far as it regenerated physical efficiency leading to improved productivity at work. Thus, sport served as recreation.

By the mid-nineteenth century in Europe and North America, leisure had, with the weakening of the Protestant ethic, gained a margin of respectability. Gelber (1999: 1) observed that "industrialism quarantined work from leisure in a way that made employment more work-like and non-work more problematic. Isolated from each other's moderating influences, work and leisure became increasingly oppositional as they competed for finite hours." Americans, according to Gelber, responded in two ways to the threat posed by leisure as potential mischief caused by idle hands. Reformers tried to eliminate or at least restrict access to inappropriate activity, while encouraging people to seek socially approved free-time outlets. Hobbies and other serious leisure pursuits were high on the list of such outlets. In short, "the ideology of the workplace infiltrated the home in the form of productive leisure" (Gelber 1999: 2).

If, in the later nineteenth century, the Protestant ethic was no longer a driving force for much of the working population, its surviving components in the work ethic were. Cross (1990: 87) and Russell (2013: 22) concluded for the United States and Britain, respectively, that, during much of this century, employers and upwardly mobile employees looked on "idleness" as threatening industrial development and social stability. The reformers in their midst sought to eliminate this "menace" by, among other approaches, attempting to build bridges to the "dangerous classes" in the new cities and, by this means, to transform them in the image of the middle class. This led to efforts to impose (largely rural) middle-class values on this group, while trying to instill a desire to engage in rational recreation – in modern terms, serious leisure – and consequently to undertake less casual leisure (these latter two forms are discussed in the next section).

But times have changed even more. Applebaum (1992: 587) writes that "with increases in the standard of living, consumerism, and leisure activities, the work ethic must compete with the ethic of the quality of life based on the release from work." And as the work ethic withers further in the twenty-first century, in face of widespread reduction of work opportunities (e.g., The Economist 2014), leisure is slowly, but inexorably it appears, coming to the fore. In other words leisure has, since mid-nineteenth century, been evolving into a substantial institution in its own right. At first leisure was poor and under-developed, standing in pitiful contrast next to its robust neighbor of work. But the dual ideas that work is inherently good and that, when it can be found, people should do it (instead of leisure) are now being increasingly challenged.

Beck (2000: 125) looks on the near future as a time when a significant portion of work will be done without remuneration:

> The counter-model to the work society is based not upon leisure but upon political freedom; it is a multi-activity society in which housework, family work, club work and voluntary work are prized alongside paid work and returned to the center of public and academic attention. For in the end, these other forms remained trapped inside a value imperialism of work, which must be shaken off.

Beck calls this work without pay "civil labor." Some of it, however, especially club work and voluntary work, is also leisure, for it fits perfectly our definition of the serious pursuits set out below.

Leisure in Society

The issue of the place of leisure in society is the oldest in the field of sociology – its most pervasive, its most enduring. Yet it all started in philosophy, where Aristotle first weighed in favorably on the matter (leisure is the goal of work) and the concept has captivated philosophers ever since. It greatly worried the Puritans and, as noted, gained Weber's attention. Veblen (1899) introduced the dimension of leisure inequality in his famous analysis of the upper classes and their conspicuous consumption of leisure goods and services. Others conceptualized leisure as one of society's several institutions. This, often functionalist, approach was taken by, among others, Parker (1976: 28–30) and Kaplan (1975: 28–31), and consisted of identifying and describing the distinctive roles, norms, and values of this institution.

Another analytic stance has been to examine critically the fit of leisure in society. Such analyses have tended to proceed from either a neo-Marxist or a cultural perspective or a combination of both. For example, Rojek (1985) and Clarke and Critcher (1986) viewed leisure as part of the hegemonic apparatus used by the ruling classes in capitalist society to keep the rest properly attuned to their work roles. Later, Rojek (2000), in calling attention to the nature and extent of deviant leisure, challenged the conventional wisdom that leisure invariably conforms to dominant social norms.

Time

Concern with the available amount of leisure time has, since the 1970s, been another enduring interest. One of the most pressing questions in this area has been whether, in subsequent decades, such time is increasing and, if so, for whom and in which areas of activity. As background for their own work, Cushman et al. (2005: 6–10) summarized five international comparative studies of time use. Dating from 1972 (Szalai 1972), such studies have been conducted exclusively in the West. In the

West, however, varying definitions of leisure have made it difficult to mount valid cross-national comparisons. In general it may be concluded, nevertheless, that leisure time has increased up through the 1980s, with declines becoming evident in the 1990s. But there is no clear trend in participation, with some activities becoming more popular and others becoming less so (Cushman et al. 2005: 285). Still, Dumazedier (1988) discerned between 1968 and 1988 a Western trend toward increased cultural leisure, especially "educational activities," broadly conceived of today as any of the serious leisure activities.

Overall, research does support the claim that, in the United States, after-work time of many people has been growing both in amount and significance (Robinson and Godbey 1997). But, oddly, this research also suggests that some people feel more rushed than ever (Zuzanek 1996: 65). In recent years, employees have worked longer hours as demands for doing more with fewer workers have increased. This group of reluctantly overworked employees is shrinking as more and more of their positions are lost in the nearly universal rush to organize as much work as possible along electronic lines.

Types of Leisure

Yet another way to consider leisure in society is to classify its many forms. The primeval typology has been, and remains in many quarters, the enduring dichotomy of work and leisure, which, as part of her general warning about typologies in leisure research, Samdahl (1999: 124) says is over-simplistic. Nonetheless, classifications of leisure are uncommon. The few efforts of this nature tend to be narrowly focused, usually revolving around classification of leisure lifestyles (e.g., Kelly 1999: 144–147). And yet, the broader tendency to rely on undifferentiated lists of leisure activities – the prevailing way the field approaches its subject matter – masks the many ways activities can be lumped together for fruitful analysis and generalization. Obviously, watching television or taking a nap, on the one hand, and climbing a mountain or knitting a quilt, on the other, involve different motives, return different benefits to the participant, and take place in different social and geographic contexts.

To avoid missing their various essential features, all classifications should be grounded in ongoing exploratory research. This is indeed the empirical foundation of the most widely accepted classification of leisure activities at present, namely, the serious leisure perspective (SLP). It is the theoretic framework that synthesizes three main forms of leisure – i.e., the serious pursuits (serious leisure and devotee work), casual leisure, and project-based leisure – showing, at once, their distinctive features, similarities, and interrelationships (for its empirical underpinning see Stebbins 1992; 1997; 2005; 2015[2007]; Elkington and Stebbins 2014). More precisely the SLP offers a classification and explanation of all known leisure activities and experiences, as these two are framed in the social-psychological, social, cultural, geographical, and historical conditions in which each activity and accompanying experience take place (see SLP Diagram, available at www.seriousleisure.net).

Serious leisure is systematic pursuit of an amateur, hobbyist, or volunteer activity that participants find so interesting and fulfilling that, in the typical case, they launch themselves on a (leisure) career centered on acquiring and expressing its special skills, knowledge, and experience. Devotee work, as mentioned already, is serious leisure sufficiently remunerative to be a livelihood. Casual leisure (e.g., taking a nap, light conversation, sightseeing) is immediately intrinsically rewarding, relatively short-lived pleasurable activity requiring little or no special training to enjoy it. It is fundamentally hedonic, engaged in for the significant level of pure pleasure found there. Project-based leisure (e.g., preparing a genealogy, organizing a fiftieth wedding anniversary celebration, being a one-off volunteer at an arts festival) is a short-term, moderately complicated, either one-shot or occasional, though infrequent, creative undertaking carried out in free time (Stebbins 2005). It requires considerable planning, effort, and sometimes skill or knowledge, but for all that it is neither serious leisure nor intended to develop into such. Nor is it casual leisure.

The Meaning and Motivation of Leisure

What motivates people to participate in certain leisure activities rather than others has fascinated a great number of philosophers and social scientists from Aristotle to the present. This is an enormously complicated issue, which helps explain why it is still in the course of being examined. Sociology retains its generalized approach to leisure through studying the meaning of leisure for those who partake of it, an interest it shares with social psychology. There is a vast literature here, a substantial amount of it concerned with the idea of "leisure experience." Such experience is commonly studied by examining its quality, duration, intensity, and memorability. Examining leisure satisfaction – an interest of psychologists – constitutes another way of assessing the meaning of leisure (Mannell 1999: 235–252). And, from still another angle, Shaw (1985) has applied the sociological conceptualization of meaning – the definition of the situation – in her study of the meaning of work and leisure in everyday life. She found that activities defined as leisure by her respondents were freely chosen, intrinsically motivated, and pursued outside of work (see also Samdahl 1988: 29). Shaw's highly influential article may still be the most cited work in all leisure research.

This concept of meaning relates to leisure in society, because meaning at this level is, in significant part, shaped by the role leisure plays socially as well as by the way society evaluates that role. For instance, an amateur orchestra provides the local community with classical music, an art form valued highly by many of those there who go in for high culture. Moreover, knowing the meaning a thing, activity, experience, or situation has for an individual is tantamount to understanding that person's motivation with reference to that thing, activity, and so on. Sociologists have long treated such meaning as a key element in the motivation of behavior (for a partial review of this literature, see Albas and Albas 2003).

Specialization in the Sociology of Leisure

In this section we will include as scholarly works on leisure, only those books, chapters, and articles that concentrate primarily on this subject. Examinations of leisure of this depth using a sociological perspective were sporadic until approximately the beginning of the 1950s, the aforementioned work of Veblen was a notable exception. So was that of Lundberg et al. (1969) who examined leisure in an American suburb, which was to become the first of a handful of community studies in the United States in which leisure was a main point of analysis. Following Lundberg et al. were, among others, studies by Vidich and Bensman (1968) on small town leisure and by Hollingshead (1975) on youth and leisure in a small Midwestern city. The primary goal in these investigations was to describe the place of leisure in the American local community.

By contrast David Riesman focused on the leisure interests of the masses. His (1961) observations on the decline of the work ethic in the United States and the rise there of the "other-directed man," ushered in an era of work-leisure comparisons and a lasting debate about this basic typology. Shortly thereafter, analyses appeared on mass leisure (e.g., Larrabee and Meyerson 1958) and on the ways work and leisure are related. Apropos the latter, Kando and Summers (1971: 83–86) formulated and tested two celebrated hypotheses about "spillover" (work is similar to leisure) and "compensation" (work is separate or different from leisure), though neither was convincingly confirmed (Kelly 1987: 147–153). In Britain, Parker (1971) wrote about the future of work and leisure as they influence each other. This line of thought continues (e.g., Haworth 1997; Stebbins 2014[2004]), for the relationship between the two is complicated and ever changing.

From approximately the early 1980s, the sociological study of leisure began to add various specialties, two of which are covered below. These specialties did not, however, eclipse the broader interest of leisure in society, which has continued apace.

Symbolic Interactionism

John R. Kelly is the most prominent and prolific representative of symbolic interactionism in the sociology of leisure, in particular, and the interdisciplinary field of leisure studies, in general. The fullest expression of his interactionist ideas was set out in *Leisure Identities and Interactions* (1983), in which he examined interaction in leisure activities as a main field for identity development throughout the life course. Using the example of amateurs (serious leisure enthusiasts whose activity has a professional counterpart), he observed that leisure can be most substantial (i.e., pursued with skill, knowledge, effort) and that such leisure typically becomes the basis for a valued personal as well as social identity. Leisure in this sense – the serious pursuits – tends to become a vital part of a person's life, a true "central life interest" (Dubin 1992).

In fact, this leisure identity may be as, or even more, central to people than their work identities. But leisure identities, like identities in other spheres of life, are fashioned in interaction with like-minded folk, such as other members of a serious pursuit (e.g., orchestra, club, team). Moreover, the centrality of leisure for a person may change over the life course, owing to greater (or fewer) family or work obligations, for instance, with retirement being a period when leisure involvements and associated identities may flourish, often as never before (Stebbins 2013). Furthermore, evidence suggests that today's children and young people will become a different leisure generation compared with their predecessors (Roberts 2013).

Gender and the Feminist Perspective

Shaw (2003: 200) writes that research in the 1970s touched on the issue of gender mostly by breaking down rates of leisure participation according to sex of participant. Enlightened by the feministic perspective, many female researchers in leisure viewed this demographic approach as highly skewed, as for instance, in omitting the woman's unique experience of leisure and the unique problems she faces trying to have it. Meanwhile, other female leisure scholars took interest in the issue of gender. They have pursued such questions as the gendered nature of leisure for both sexes and how leisure behavior influences gender beliefs and ideologies (Shaw 2003: 202).

The feminists and gender specialists share the constructionist approach to human stereotyping in the domain of leisure. They are also mutually concerned with identifying and explaining the constraints on pursuing particular kinds of leisure imposed by such conditions as age, class, gender, and geographic location. Harrington et al. (1992), while recognizing that constraints on leisure may be either personal or environmental, studied a sample of Ontario women to learn how women themselves perceive such constraints. They found, for example, that the need to find childcare in order to engage in a leisure activity discouraged some of their sample from participating in the activity.

Henderson and Bialeschki (1999) describe the beginnings of the feminist approach to understanding leisure. "Researchers focused attention on leisure and recreation issues for women and have provided ways to challenge the predominantly androcentric perspectives of leisure research prior to the mid-1980s" (167). Examples include works by Bella (1989) and Henderson (1990).

The feminist program in the sociology of leisure has led to, among many other interests, that of *resistance*, which today serves as another key sensitizing concept in this area. The idea may have come to the sociology of leisure by way of Donnelly's (1988) discussion of it in female sport and exercise. Thus some women resist dominant views (often shared by both men and women) of what is appropriate leisure for their sex.

Organizational Basis of the Sociology of Leisure

Although few academic units in sociology offer a leisure and recreation curriculum, cultural sociology has in recent decades for some sociologists become the center of the sociology of leisure. In their eyes this supports their claim that in sociology itself the sociology of leisure is alive and well. This claim rests on a misunderstanding of the nature of leisure, however, for much of leisure falls well beyond the scope of cultural sociology. That is, leisure is far broader than the consumption of fine and popular art, sports events, the mass media of entertainment, and the like (Stebbins 2009), even while each forms an important part of the sociology of culture. Indeed, much of leisure cannot be conceived of as cultural (in this consumptive sense), as seen in the active pursuit of amateur, hobbyist, and volunteer interests, certain "non-cultural" casual leisure activities (e.g., napping, sociable conversation), and such undertakings in free-time as short-term projects. For similar reasons, the sociology of sport may not be regarded as synonymous with the sociology of leisure.

So where, then, does the sociology of leisure hang its scholarly hat? It turns out that its vestiary is now located almost exclusively in departments and similar academic units variously named "Leisure Studies," "Leisure and Recreation," "Recreation and Park Administration," "Sport, Leisure, and Physical Education," "Parks, Leisure, and Tourism Studies," and "Recreation and Tourism Management." Here lies the contemporary hub of this specialty. Sociologists in these units, along with colleagues inclined toward sociology, identify with the interdisciplinary field of Leisure Studies and its several research centers and professional associations scattered across the world.

Furthermore, leisure studies is also a field of practice, with considerable research and application devoted to such practical matters as leisure counseling, leisure education, delivery of leisure services, and development and management of parks and recreational centers. Additionally, there are strong ties with tourism and events studies, therapeutic recreation, information science, and arts and science administration. Leisure sociology helps inform these diverse applications and is, of course, further shaped by them. The sociology of leisure since the early 1970s has, by and large, come of age theoretically and empirically in this interdisciplinary arena.

The sociology of leisure is advancing. It has become a vibrant subdiscipline of its own, even if organizationally alienated from mainstream sociology. In the twenty-first century, as leisure gains equal standing with work, as issues related to work/life balance, quality of life, and well-being grow in importance, lurking in the background is the question of sociologists in sociology departments again playing a prominent role in an area of academic study that sprang from their discipline.

References

Albas, Cheryl A. and Daniel C. Albas. 2003. Motives. In *Handbook of Symbolic Interactionism*. Edited by Larry T. Reynolds and Nancy J. Herman-Kinney. Walnut Creek, CA: Altamira.

Applebaum, Herbert. 1992. *The Concept of Work: Ancient, Medieval, and Modern*. Albany, NY: State University of New York Press.

Beck, Ulrich. 2000. *The Brave New World of Work*. Cambridge: Polity.

Bella, Leslie. 1989. Women and Leisure: Beyond Androcentrism. In *Understanding Leisure and Recreation: Mapping the Past, Charting the Future*. Edited by Edgar L. Jackson and Thomas L. Burton. State College, PA: Venture.

Clarke, John and Chas Critcher. 1986. *The Devil Makes Work: Leisure in Capitalist Britain.* Champaign, IL: University of Illinois Press.

Cross, Gary. 1990. *A Social History of Leisure since 1660.* State College, PA: Venture.

Cushman, Grant, A. J. Veal, and Jiri Zuzanek. eds. 2005. *Free Time and Leisure Participation: International Perspectives.* Wallingford: CABI.

Donnelly, Peter. 1988. Sport as a Site for "Popular" Resistance. In *Popular Cultures and Political Practices.* Edited by Richard Gruneau. Toronto: Garamond.

Dubin, Robert. 1992. *Central Life Interests: Creative Individualism in a Complex World.* New Brunswick, NJ: Transaction.

Dumazedier, Joffre. 1988. *Révolution culturelle du temps libre 1968–1988.* Paris: Méridiens Klincksieck.

The Economist. 2014. Special Report: The World Economy. 4 October.

Elkington, Sam and Robert A. Stebbins. 2014. *The Serious Leisure Perspective: An Introduction.* London: Routledge.

Gelber, Steven M. 1999. *Hobbies: Leisure and the Culture of Work in America.* New York, NY: Columbia University Press.

Godbey, Geoffrey. 1999. *Leisure in Your Life: An Exploration.* 5th edn. State College, PA: Venture.

Harrington, Mareen, Don Dawson, and Pat Bolla. 1992. Objective and Subjective Constraints on Women's Enjoyment of Leisure. *Loisir et société/Society and Leisure* 15: 203–222.

Haworth, John T. ed. 1997. *Work, Leisure, and Well-Being.* London: Routledge.

Henderson, Karla A. 1990. Anatomy Is Not Destiny: A Feminist Analysis of the Scholarship on Women's Leisure. *Leisure Sciences* 12: 229–239.

Henderson, Karla A. and M. Deborah Bialeschki. 1999. Makers of Meanings: Feminist Perspectives on Leisure Research. In *Leisure Studies: Prospects for the Twenty-First Century.* Edited by Edgar L. Jackson and Thomas L. Burton. State College, PA: Venture.

Hollingshead, August B. 1975. *Elmtown's Youth and Elmtown Revisited.* 2nd edn. New York, NY: Wiley.

Juniu, Susana and Karla A. Henderson. 2001. Problems in Researching Leisure and Women: Global Considerations. *World Leisure Journal* 43: 3–10.

Kando, Thomas M. and William C. Summers. 1971. The Impact of Work on Leisure. *Pacific Sociological Review* 14: 310–327.

Kaplan, Max. 1975. *Leisure: Theory and Policy.* New York, NY: Wiley.

Kelly, John R. 1983. *Leisure Identities and Interactions.* London: George Allen and Unwin.

Kelly, John R. 1987. *Freedom to Be: A New Sociology of Leisure.* New York, NY: Macmillan.

Kelly, John R. 1990. *Leisure.* 2nd edn. Englewood Cliffs, NJ: Prentice-Hall.

Kelly, John R. 1999. Leisure Behaviors and Styles: Social, Economic, and Cultural Factors. In *Leisure Studies: Prospects for the Twenty-First Century.* Edited by Edgar L. Jackson and Thomas L. Burton. State College, PA: Venture.

Larrabee, Eric and Rolf B. Meyerson. eds. 1958. *Mass Leisure.* Glencoe, IL: Free Press.

Lundberg, George A., Mirra Komarovsky, and Mary A. McInerny. 1969. *Leisure: A Suburban Study.* 2nd edn. New York, NY: Agathon.

Mannell, Roger C. 1999. Leisure Experience and Satisfaction. In *Leisure Studies: Prospects for the Twenty-First Century.* Edited by Edgar L. Jackson and Thomas L. Burton. State College, PA: Venture.

Parker, Stanley R. 1971. *The Future of Work and Leisure.* New York, NY: Praeger.

Parker, Stanley R. 1976. *The Sociology of Leisure.* London: George Allen and Unwin.

Riesman, David. 1961. *The Lonely Crowd: A Study of the Changing American Character.* rev. edn. New Haven, CT: Yale University Press.

Roberts, Ken. 2013. Leisure and the Life Course. In *Routledge Handbook of Leisure Studies.* Edited by Tony Blackshaw. London: Routledge.

Robinson, John P. and Geoffrey Godbey. 1997. *Time for Life: The Surprising Ways Americans Use Their Time.* University Park, PA: Pennsylvania State University Press.

Rojek, Chris. 1985. *Capitalism and Leisure Theory.* London: Tavistock.

Rojek, Chris. 2000. *Leisure and Culture.* New York, NY: Palgrave.

Russell, Dave 2013. The Making of Modern Leisure: The British Experience c. 1850 to c. 1960. In *Routledge Handbook of Leisure Studies.* Edited by Tony Blackshaw. London: Routledge.

Samdahl, Diane M. 1988. A Symbolic Interactionist Model of Leisure: Theory and Empirical Support. *Leisure Studies* 10: 27–39.

Samdahl, Diane M. 1999. Epistemological and Methodological Issues in Leisure Research. In *Leisure Studies: Prospects for the Twenty-First Century*. Edited by Edgar L. Jackson and Thomas L. Burton. State College, PA: Venture.

Shaw, Susan M. 1985. The Meaning of Leisure in Everyday Life. *Leisure Sciences* 7: 1–24.

Shaw, Susan M. 2001. Conceptualizing Resistance: Women's Leisure as Political Practice. *Journal of Leisure Research* 33: 186–201.

Shaw, Susan M. 2003. Gender. In *Encyclopedia of Leisure and Outdoor Recreation*. Edited by John M. Jenkins and John J. Pigram. London: Routledge.

Stebbins, Robert A. 1992. *Amateurs, Professionals, and Serious Leisure*. Montreal: McGill-Queen's University Press.

Stebbins, Robert A. 1997. Casual Leisure: A Conceptual Statement. *Leisure Studies* 16: 17–25.

Stebbins, Robert A. 2005. Project-Based Leisure: Theoretical Neglect of a Common Use of Free Time. *Leisure Studies* 24: 1–11.

Stebbins, Robert A. 2009. *Leisure and Consumption: Common Ground, Separate Worlds*. New York, NY: Palgrave Macmillan.

Stebbins, Robert A. 2012. *The Idea of Leisure: First Principles*. New Brunswick, NJ: Transaction.

Stebbins, Robert A. 2013. *Planning Your Time in Retirement: How to Cultivate a Leisure Lifestyle to Suit Your Needs and Interests*. Lanham, MD: Rowman and Littlefield.

Stebbins, Robert A. 2014[2004]. *Between Work and Leisure: The Common Ground of Two Separate Worlds*. New Brunswick, NJ: Transaction (paperback edn. with new preface).

Stebbins, Robert A. 2015[2007]. *Serious Leisure: A Perspective for Our Time*. New Brunswick, NJ: Transaction (paperback edn. with new introduction).

Szalai, Alexander. ed. 1972. *The Use of Time: Daily Activities of Urban and Suburban Populations in Twelve Countries*. The Hague: Mouton.

Veblen, Thorstein. 1899. *The Theory of the Leisure Class*. New York, NY: Macmillan.

Vidich, Arthur J. and Joseph Bensman. 1968. *Small Town in Mass Society: Class, Power, and Religion in a Rural Community*. rev. edn. Princeton, NJ: Princeton University Press.

Weber, Max. 1930. *The Protestant Ethic and the Spirit of Capitalism*. Translated by Talcott Parsons. New York, NY: Charles Scribner.

Zuzanek, Jiri. 1996. Canada. In *World Leisure Participation: Free Time in the Global Village*. Edited by Grant Cushman, A. J. Veal, and Jiri Zuzanek. Wallingford: CAB International.

Popular Culture

Dustin Kidd, Jennifer Kim, and Amanda Turner

Popular culture refers to representations that are consumed by a mass audience, often because they are created through a process of mass production. In its most basic form, popular culture simply refers to widely shared images, ideas, and objects – the culture of the people. However, in contemporary parlance, it typically refers to a specific kind of people's culture: that produced by the institutions of the mass media. This mass media culture can include books, television, news media, advertisements, films, music, clothing, games, and much more.

The term popular culture can refer either to the meaningful *products* that the mass media disseminates, or it can refer to widely shared *processes* of engaging with ideas. In most social science research, the study of popular culture refers to processes by which people produce or consume mass media objects. As sociologist Wendy Griswold (1994) has suggested, sociological analysis of culture should include studies of the products themselves, processes of production and consumption, and an understanding of the social world in which the objects, their production processes, and their consumption processes are situated. In addition, we must also consider the role that various institutions play as gatekeepers that create limitations on what can be produced and how, what can be consumed and how, and how cultural objects should be interpreted.

The sociology of popular culture sits at the crossroads of two major subfields in the discipline: economic sociology and cultural sociology. Economic sociology provides the tools for understanding such issues as (1) the labor market that produces popular culture, including artists, writers, directors, producers, and technicians; (2) the commodification of cultural objects, including the assignment of particular market values to cultural goods; (3) the role of cultural objects as a tool for the advertisement of other commodities; and (4) the consumption of cultural objects by audiences who are understood first and foremost as consumers.

Cultural sociology helps us to understand such issues as (1) the decision-making processes that lead to particular kinds of representations; (2) the role of cultural objects as carriers of meanings; (3) the interpretation of cultural objects by audiences that are understood first and foremost as active agents who are able to shape the meanings they take from those objects; and (4) the ways that audiences then deploy these meanings as they act in their everyday lives as citizens of the social system.

The sociology of popular culture intersects with many outside fields, as well. Most importantly, it is in conversation with the humanities in its goal to understand the meanings of cultural products. It is also in dialog with media studies in its efforts to understand the processes by which mass representations are made and consumed.

Major Theoretical Approaches

Leo Lowenthal (1950; 1984) championed a humanistic approach to the study of culture, emphasizing historical and philosophical approaches. Popular culture in and of itself was less the problem for Lowenthal than the technological advances of mass production, part and parcel of the rapid economic, social, and cultural changes endemic to the historical growth of capitalism. Of primary concern was the moral, psychological, and social durability of the autonomous individual. The view of mass culture as oppressive to the individual has its roots in the "mass culture critique," which states that popular culture is characterized by mass production and wide availability. The impact of this mass culture on consumers, according to the critique, is that it renders them submissive to powerful economic and political forces. In this regard, popular culture is distinctly different from high culture which, according to the mass culture critique, sustains creativity and cultivates aesthetic appreciation (Horkheimer and Adorno 2002; Marx and Engels 2000).

Rather than engaging in questions over the boundaries between "high" and "low" culture or entertaining assumptions that popular culture is incapable of the levels of aesthetic achievement and human edification found in high culture, Herbert Gans's *Popular Culture and High Culture* (1975) instead advocates for an equality of all forms of cultural expression. Gans replaces cultural hierarchy with various "taste publics" engaging in distinct "taste cultures." Noting the unfortunate tendency by scholars to unduly denigrate popular culture, Gans offers several conceptual and analytical considerations for the study of cultural participation and production. He distinguishes values from practices and, in turn, makes a distinction between consumers (taste publics) and the goods they consume (taste cultures). Gans places the emphasis on how individuals make use of taste cultures to make choices, however limited. He notes the empirical problem of discretely isolating a taste culture, given its invariable overlap with other cultural orientations and practices. For instance, some popular films receive critical praise, placing them in an ambiguous taste culture. Finally, Gans offers the recognition that popular culture is distinct both from "lived culture" *and* its complement.

Paul DiMaggio (1977: 1997) draws from research by economists and psychologists, lending both theoretical and empirical gravitas to an often timid and disparate collection of work. Through cross-disciplinary explorations, he illuminates and clarifies several aspects of culture: (1) historically negative evaluations of popular culture did not consider the role of the marketplace and the nature of cognitive processes; (2) past views of mass culture as oppressive are not supported; and (3) perspectives that rely only on socialization as the source of cultural transmission are too limited. DiMaggio gives due consideration to economic factors like market structure, which can range from oligopolistic to competitive. Cultural pluralism indicates more variety in the "cultural economy" than the mass culture theory would posit, and suggests a need for a renewed attention to issues of audience agency.

Major Methodological Approaches

Content Analysis

Content analyses of popular culture provide researchers with insight into the content of a television show, movie, song, or other cultural object and may be either quantitative or qualitative. In general, research questions focusing on representation or the prevalence of messages are best suited to quantitative content analyses, whereas questions involving meanings and context may be better suited for qualitative research.

Quantitative content analysis is often used to provide descriptive statistics about the relative under-representation of particular identity groups. Examples of this are relative racial representations on prime-time TV (Hunt 2003) or the gender of characters in children's books (McCabe et al. 2011). Some argue that content analysis is necessarily quantitative and focused on objectively measuring the messages in popular cultural content (Neuendorf 2002).

In qualitative content analyses, the focus shifts from counts and prevalence to description, themes, and meaning. These analyses may allow themes to emerge from the coding of data (Emerson 2002), and methods such as ethnographic content analysis (Altheide and Schneider 2013) may combine qualitative observation with a quantitative protocol.

Ethnography

Ethnography is used to study the meanings of actions and interactions of people in particular settings. As such, it may be best suited for examining the production and consumption of popular culture. Production ethnographies provide rich, observational accounts of the production process of various forms of popular culture. Studies such as those by Joshua Gamson (1998) or Laura Grindstaff (2002), both of whom study daytime talk shows, give detailed accounts of production processes, workplace dynamics, and inequalities. Ethnography allows scholars to study the moment of consumption.

As examples, researchers have studied how gender roles within a family shape individuals' relationships to computer and television consumption (O'Keeffe 2009) and the ways that social relationships have formed from playing online video games (Taylor 2006).

Interviews and Focus Groups

Interviews and focus groups provide another way to qualitatively assess meaning-making, in either an individual or group setting. Interviews and focus groups allow researchers to question individuals directly about their behaviors and are well suited to studying production and consumption. Interviews with producers of popular cultural objects are rare, and focus groups even more so. Some examples that utilize these methods are Gamson's (1998) and Grindstaff's (2002) use of interviews with producers of daytime talk shows to supplement their larger ethnographic projects, and Gitlin's (1983) interviews with creators of prime-time television shows. The lack of production studies utilizing interviews and focus groups is unsurprising, given the relative difficulty of gaining access to production staff. Interviews and focus groups are much more common with audiences. For example, JoEllen Shively (1992) uses both to explore the different meanings that Anglos and American Indians created when experiencing the same Western movie. Thomas Linneman (2008) uses focus groups to examine how audiences make sense of gendered language on the gay-themed television show *Will and Grace*.

Surveys

Surveys ask respondents to share their thoughts, feelings, and opinions in response to a questionnaire, allowing them either to select answers from a list or provide open-ended replies. As with interviews and focus groups, this method is well suited for the study of both audiences and producers. Evan Cooper (2003) uses survey questionnaires to unpack how audiences relate to characters in the show *Will and Grace* and how that sense of relating to a character interacts with the audience members' relationship to the themes of sexual identity and diversity. Researchers may gain a greater number of responses using surveys than other methods. In some cases, a survey researcher might utilize secondary data to explore popular culture. For instance, Bethany Bryson (1996) uses data from the General Social Survey to analyze the relationship between musical dislikes and symbolic exclusion.

Case Studies

Case studies allow researchers to explore thoroughly a single (or small number) of cultural objects, production sites, or audiences. They may utilize a mixture of qualitative and quantitative methods, with their distinguishing characteristic being the depth they bring to an analysis. Case studies may range in scope. Some studies focus on a medium of popular culture, such as Paul Lopes's 2006 work on comic books. Some studies examine a particular genre, like David Grazian's 2004 case study of blues music in Chicago. Finally, some studies focus on a particular audience segment, such as Elisabeth Hayes's 2007 analysis of video game players.

Production Studies

Production studies comprise any research that focuses on the institutions, people, or processes by which cultural content is produced. Studies show that ownership of media production is increasingly concentrated in the hands of a few corporations that are increasingly integrated in horizontal (McChesney 1999) and vertical (Peterson and Berger 1975) dimensions. Horizontal integration refers to expanding a company's control of the market field. Vertical integration refers to expanding a company's control of the production and distribution processes.

A related issue is that board members for major entertainment and media companies serve as executives for other companies, or as policy-makers, creating corporate interlocks (Thornton et al. 2006). These interlocks have the effect of reducing economic competition between major media outlets.

Ownership and creation of cultural objects continues to be largely consolidated in the hands of white men. Maryann Erigha (2015) argues that, in cultural production, there are three aspects of minority underrepresentation: numerical representation – the relative presence and roles of groups on- or off-screen; the quality of representation – the types of roles available for actors; and centrality of representation – how close marginalized groups are to the "core of the industry."

Within production studies, institutional analyses focus on organizations and those they employ, often using organizational reports and written records. For example, Denise Bielby and William Bielby (1996) use employment records from the Writers' Guild of America West to explore longitudinally career development barriers faced by women writers of feature films. Todd Gitlin (1983) uses a combination of observation and interviews with workers at various levels of production to argue that the stories in prime-time television are told by a relatively small group of "insiders." Similarly, Grindstaff (2002) worked behind-the-scenes at two daytime television talk shows, observing how producers influence the non-celebrity guests on these shows, bolstering her observations with interviews. She argues that while such shows increase the numerical representation of individuals and stories not generally visible, the production process shapes them into culturally familiar forms which reproduce stereotypes and inequality. These findings reflect the earlier research of Gamson (1998), who conducted interviews with creators of daytime talk shows. Interviews are also a primary source of information in Duffy's (2014) research on the production of women's magazines. Duffy argues that shifts toward digital content are changing labor conditions, creative decision-making, and workplace hierarchies and dynamics in a previously female-dominated industry.

For those interested in carrying out research in the area of production studies, access can be a problem. Those who have gained entry, however, have provided deep insights into the creative processes of telling stories and making culture.

Content Studies

Sociology has been critiqued by many scholars for its failure to address the content of cultural objects (Wolff 1992). The critique arises from the sociology of art, but it also applies to the sociology of popular culture. A growing number of scholars have been taking content seriously and treating it as a dynamic element of social structure. Although audiences have agency in how they make meaning out of a cultural work, their agency is structured by the elements of the work itself. The possible interpretations may be influenced by the creative decision-making of the artist but they are also influenced by context elements which may change over time. For example, the television show *All in the Family*, and its lead character Archie Bunker, have become cultural reference points for discussions of racist images on television. However, when the show first aired, it was identified as racially progressive because of creator Norman Lear's desire to expose racial divides and to make issues of race part of the national discourse. The changing context of racial politics in the United States helped to alter the meaning of the show. But the context alone cannot determine the meaning. It is the relationship between the content and the context that matters. *All in the Family* demands a racial analysis, regardless of the context, because race is a central theme in the show.

Sociological analyses of popular culture are increasingly focused on questions of content. How do themes and representations influence beliefs and actions? What kinds of structural shifts result in changes to content? Political scientist Murray Edelman has explored the question of how content influences action in his book *From Art to Politics*, arguing that "works of art are the essential catalysts of support for a course of political action, and sometimes for several (perhaps contradictory) courses" (Edelman 1995: 10). Identifying the exact mechanisms by which cultural objects influence political action is the difficult part. However, some of those mechanisms are coming into greater focus. For instance, case studies have unveiled the impact that cultural objects can have on social movements (Kidd 2007). Similarly, studies of cognition have revealed the impacts of cultural consumption on social action (DiMaggio 1997).

Reception Studies

Reception studies shift the focus from cultural objects to the audiences that consume them. Contemporary work in reception studies acknowledges the issues of power raised by earlier critics of mass culture, while also suggesting less deterministic views of cultural influence and agency (Grindstaff and Turow 2006). Contrary to Horkheimer and Adorno's (2002) hypothesis, audiences are active and engaged in constructing, unpacking, and reconstructing meanings attached to race, gender, and sexuality, as well as social issues like poverty, health care, and marriage (Fiske 1992). But popular culture also functions as entertainment. It presents familiar cultural narratives and styles drawn from the dominant culture and uses them to tell stories that give distraction and pleasure (Gray 1995). As a site of images, messages, and identities, television and other forms of popular culture provide audiences with both choices (of ideas, styles, and commodities) and conventions (Gans 1975; Hirsch and Newcomb 1983).

Analysis of television and other media formats may help to explain the messages embodied in the cultural content and the use of those messages by members of the audience (Shively 1992). Films, or visual images in general, function as "symbolic vehicles of meaning" because they project particular images of human behavior to a hypothetically complicit audience. Narratives of the human condition project on both the "big" and "small" screen, ranging from the comic, dramatic, and romantic. The trajectory of these images can take various forms – from reinforcing previously held beliefs and behavior to reflecting current cultural realities. In his anthropological analysis of films, Weakland (1995) evaluates several previous studies on films, compiling the significant points to consider. He argues that the underlying consideration should be constant recognition of the cultural contexts of both the film and of the researcher conducting the reading. Although content is important, hasty conclusions about the meaning of the material should be avoided.

Through a combination of content analysis and ethnographic research conducted in Holland, Ien Ang (1993) elicited responses via letters from viewers of the television show *Dallas* and concluded that popular culture is indeed a mechanism for constructing social meaning; viewers consumed the product, reacted to its influence, and entered into a process of meaning-making. Similarly complex findings regarding race and racial identities were echoed in Sut Jhally and Justin Lewis's (1992) study of *The Cosby Show*; Manthia Diawara's (1988) study of black male responses to racially charged films; JoEllen Shively's (1992) analysis of white and Native American interpretations of films from the "western" genre; and Jacqueline Bobo's (2002) examination of audience responses to *The Color Purple*.

Gatekeepers

A growing body of sociological literature has focused on the role of cultural intermediaries, who stand between cultural producers and audiences. These intermediaries – typically referred to as gatekeepers – can influence everything from cultural access to how cultural objects are interpreted. Gatekeepers can include critics, distributors, reviewers, awards, and other systems or professionals who work in fields that involve curating the cultural landscape. In their study of racial depictions in children's picture books, Bernice A. Pescosolido, Elizabeth Grauerholz, and Melissa A. Milkie (1997) found that gatekeepers play a very important role in shaping the kind of racial imagery that children consume. High culture gatekeepers, like the Caldecott Awards, had consistently more black images across the twentieth century than children's books in general. By comparison, *Little Golden Books*, which might be seen as a low culture gatekeeper, had wider fluctuations from the overall pattern, with more black representations in some periods and fewer in others.

Cultural Controversies

At times, popular culture becomes the locus of significant controversy, usually due to content deemed inflammatory. Examples of controversy-inducing content include Robert Mapplethorpe's homoerotic photography, Martin Scorsese's film *The Last Temptation of Christ*, the Super Bowl incident when Justin Timberlake exposed Janet Jackson's breast, Madonna's video for the song "Justify My Love," and the Candice Bergen situation comedy *Murphy Brown*, to name just a few. In these events, typically the content resonates with a broader social fault line that involves changing social mores. These can include issues of sexuality, gender, religion, race, politics, conceptions of the family, or any issue around which there is an ongoing battle to change or defend a particular social institution. Although these battles are typically in place before popular culture enters into the fray, cultural representations can function like a switch in the train tracks that changes the direction of the battle. When Vice President Joseph Biden announced his support for gay marriage, he specifically identified watching gay representations on the television show *Will and Grace* as a pivotal experience in the evolution of his beliefs on the issue. Artists and other kinds of cultural producers often deliberately create content that takes a stance on social issues as a way to use their platform to steer social change.

Popular culture often becomes controversial when it exposes taken-for-granted assumptions about the social order. For example, Amy Binder's studying of debates (both in the media and in Congress) about the controversial content of both rap and heavy metal reveals that when discussing threats to "our kids" most commenters were referencing white youth. People who disapproved of heavy metal saw it as a direct threat because of the impact it could have on children's morals. People who disapproved of rap saw it as an indirect threat, because people who listen to rap might be influenced toward violent behavior. The controversy exposed the assumption that "our kids" means "white kids." Studying these controversies allows social scientists to examine issues of social change and the maintenance of symbolic boundaries. Over time, these controversies can alter social mores. Content that is controversial in one decade may be mundane in another.

Conclusion

Popular culture is often misunderstood as mere entertainment. While the entertainment function of popular culture should not be discounted and deserves serious sociological attention, popular culture must also be understood as more than entertainment. It is also a process by which people acquire meaningful stories that help them make sense of the complex world around them. It informs the decisions that people make as they interact with their families and friends, their careers, the marketplace, and the political system. The production processes of popular culture, and the careers associated with various gatekeeper positions, are institutions composed of a labor force that should be taken as seriously as any other, as they determine who is able to create and tell the stories that shape widely held understandings of the social world. Popular culture is now a major source of social norms, and it constitutes some of the major tools for shaping social boundaries. While popular culture is often a mechanism that holds social systems in place, it can also be a powerful tool for social change. Sociologists in this subfield help us to understand its influence on individuals, various demographic groups, and society as a whole.

References

Altheide, David L. and Christopher J. Schneider. 2013. *Ethnographic Content Analysis from Qualitative Media Analysis*. Thousand Oaks, CA: Sage.

Ang, Ien. 1993. Dallas and the Ideology of Mass Culture. In *Cultural Studies Reader*. Edited by Simon During. London: Routledge.

Bielby, Denise D. and William T. Bielby. 1996. Women and Men in Film: Gender Inequality among Writers in a Culture Industry. *Gender and Society* 10: 248–270.

Bobo, Jacqueline. 2002. *Black Women as Cultural Readers*. New York, NY: Columbia University Press.

Bryson, Bethany. 1996. "Anything But Heavy Metal": Symbolic Exclusion and Musical Dislikes. *American Sociological Review* 61: 884–899.

Cooper, Evan. 2003. Decoding "Will and Grace": Mass Audience Reception of a Popular Network Situation Comedy. *Sociological Perspectives* 46: 513–533.

Diawara, Manthia. 1988. Black Spectatorship: Problems of Identification and Resistance. *Screen: The Journal of the Society for Education in Film and Television* 29: 66–78.

DiMaggio, Paul. 1977. Market Structure, the Creative Process, and Popular Culture: Toward an Organizational Reinterpretation of Mass-Culture Theory. *Journal of Popular Culture* 11: 436–452.

DiMaggio, Paul. 1997. Culture and Cognition. *Annual Review of Sociology* 23: 263–287.

Duffy, Brooke Erin. 2014. *Remake, Remodel: Women's Magazines in the Digital Age*. Urbana, IL: University of Illinois Press.

Edelman, Murray. 1995. *From Art to Politics: How Artistic Creations Shape Political Conceptions*. Chicago, IL: University of Chicago Press.

Emerson, Rana A. 2002. "Where My Girls At?": Negotiating Black Womanhood in Music Videos. *Gender and Society* 16: 115–135.

Erigha, Maryann. 2015. Race, Gender, Hollywood: Representation in Cultural Production and Digital Media's Potential for Change. *Sociology Compass* 9: 78–89.

Fiske, John. 1992. *Television Culture*. London: Methuen and Co.

Gamson, Joshua. 1998. *Freaks Talk Back: Tabloid Talk Shows and Sexual Nonconformity*. Chicago, IL: University of Chicago Press.

Gans, Herbert J. 1975. *Popular Culture and High Culture: An Analysis and Evaluation of Taste*. New York, NY: Basic Books.

Gitlin, Todd. 1983. *Inside Prime Time*. Berkeley, CA: University of California Press.

Gray, Herman. 1995. *Watching Race: Television and the Struggle for Blackness*. Minneapolis, MN: University of Minnesota Press.

Grazian, David. 2004. The Production of Popular Music as a Confidence Game: The Case of the Chicago Blues. *Qualitative Sociology* 27: 137–158.

Grindstaff, Laura. 2002. *The Money Shot: Trash, Class, and the Making of TV Talk Shows*. Chicago, IL: University of Chicago Press.

Grindstaff, Laura and Joseph Turow. 2006. Video Cultures: Television Sociology in the "New TV" Age. *Annual Review of Sociology* 32: 103–125.

Griswold, Wendy. 1994. *Cultures and Societies in a Changing World*. Thousand Oaks, CA: Pine Forge Press.

Hayes, Elisabeth. 2007. Gendered Identities at Play: Case Studies of Two Women Playing Morrowind. *Games and Culture* 2: 23–48.

Hirsch, Paul and Horace Newcomb. 1983. Television as Cultural Forum: Implications for Research. *Quarterly Review of Film Studies* 8: 45–55.

Horkheimer, Max and Theodor W. Adorno. 2002. *Dialectic of Enlightenment*. Translated by E. Jephcott. Edited by G. S. Noerr. Stanford, CA: Stanford University Press.

Hunt, Darnell. 2003. *Prime Time in Black and White: Not Much Is New for 2002*. Los Angeles, CA: Ralph J. Bunche Center for African American Studies at UCLA.

Jhally, Sut and Justin Lewis. 1992. *Enlightened Racism: The Cosby Show, Audiences, and the Myth of the American Dream*. Boulder, CO: Westview Press.

Kidd, Dustin. 2007. Harry Potter and the Functions of Popular Culture. *The Journal of Popular Culture* 40: 69–89.

Linneman, Thomas J. 2008. How Do You Solve a Problem Like Will Truman? The Feminization of Gay Masculinities on *Will and Grace*. *Men and Masculinities* 10: 583–603.

Lopes, Paul. 2006. Culture and Stigma: Popular Culture and the Case of Comic Books. *Sociological Forum* 21: 387–414.

Lowenthal, Leo. 1950. Historical Perspectives of Popular Culture. *American Journal of Sociology* 55: 323–332.

Lowenthal, Leo. 1984. *Literature and Mass Culture*. New Brunswick, NJ: Transaction Books.

Marx, Karl and Friedrich Engels. 2000. *The Communist Manifesto*. In *Karl Marx: Selected Writings*. Edited by David McLellan. Oxford: Oxford University Press.

McCabe, Janice, Emily Fairchild, Liz Grauerholz, Bernice A. Pescosolido, and Daniel Tope. 2011. Gender in Twentieth-Century Children's Books: Patterns of Disparity in Titles and Central Characters. *Gender and Society* 25: 197–226.

McChesney, Robert. 1999. *Rich Media, Poor Democracy: Communication Politics in Dubious Times*. Urbana, IL: University of Illinois Press.

Neuendorf, Kimberly A. 2002. *The Content Analysis Guidebook*. Thousand Oaks, CA: Sage.

O'Keeffe, Margaret. 2009. Remote Control and Influence: Technocultural Capital as a Species of Cultural Capital. *Irish Journal of Sociology* 17: 38–55.

Pescosolido, Bernice A., Elizabeth Grauerholz, and Melissa A. Milkie. 1997. Culture and Conflict: The Portrayal of Blacks in U.S. Children's Picture Books through the Mid- and Late-Twentieth Century. *American Sociological Review* 62: 443–464.

Peterson, Richard A. and David G. Berger. 1975. Cycles in Symbol Production: The Case of Popular Music. *American Sociological Review* 40: 158–173.

Shively, JoEllen. 1992. Cowboys and Indians: Perceptions of Western Films among American Indians and Anglos. *American Sociological Review* 57: 725–734.

Taylor, T. L. 2006. *Play between Worlds: Exploring Online Game Culture*. Cambridge, MA: MIT Press.

Thornton, Bridgett, Britt Walters, and Lori Rouse. 2006. Corporate Media Is Corporate America: Big Media Interlocks with Corporate

America and Broadcast News Media Ownership Empires. In *Censored 2006: The Top 25 Censored Stories*. Edited by Peter Phillips and Project Censored. New York, NY: Seven Stories Press.

Weakland, John H. 1995. Feature Films as Cultural Documents. In *Principles of Visual Anthropology*. Edited by Paul Hockings. Berlin: Mouton De Gruyter.

Wolff, Janet. 1992. Excess and Inhibition: Interdisciplinarity in the Study of Art. In *Cultural Studies*. Edited by Lawrence Grossberg, Cary Nelson and Paula Treichler. New York, NY: Routledge.

CHAPTER 30
The Sociology of Art

Alain Quemin

Introduction

Sociology of art is a subdiscipline of sociology that analyzes art as a social phenomenon. It examines the arts – both popular forms and high art – as a special category of cultural production in society. From a symbolic interactionist perspective, sociology of art can be defined as examining the socio-cultural context in which collective practices pertinent to the production, distribution, and consumption of the art take place and interact.

For several decades after the founding of sociology as a discipline, sociology of art was not really identified as a distinct field in the vast domain that emerged as sociology of culture, probably the widest subfield of sociology. In the 1960s, however, there began a movement to establish the sociology of art as a distinct subfield in sociology – a process that has been achieved to varying degrees across countries. After tracing the main lines of the discipline's development internationally from the end of the nineteenth century until now, we will present the two main theoretical perspectives that now guide the domain. Then, we will briefly describe what the sociology of art covers today.

Unlike descriptions of sociology of art in many other books – even if this restriction is generally unconscious – *this chapter will adopt a proper international perspective on the domain, as opposed to focusing upon one national conception of the subfield*. Several useful and informative handbooks and readers are available that can offer a much more developed presentation of sociology of art in the English language (Deinhard 1970; Wolff 1981; Foster and Blau 1989; Zolberg 1990; Inglis and Hughson 2002; Alexander 2003; Tanner 2003; Rothenberg 2014), but also in other important languages for the social sciences such as French (Moulin 1986; Heinich 2001; Péquignot 2013; Quemin and Villas Bôas 2016), German (Danko 2012), or Brazilian Portuguese (Quemin and Villas Bôas 2016). The large number of books available that explore sociology of art is a clear indicator of the strong development of the domain, especially since the 1980s. The aspects of the sociology of art that relate to the sociology of culture (especially popular culture), as well as most works that deal with music and those related to consumer behavior or to leisure, will not be included within this chapter, as all these domains are already covered within this handbook.

Toward the Emergence of the Present Conception of Sociology of Art

The very beginnings of the sociology of art date back in Europe to the emergence of sociology as a discipline (Quemin and Villas Bôas 2016). Culture and the arts were already present in the writings of the earliest European sociologists. The first book to associate sociology and art in its title is credited to a French author who is generally overlooked today, Jean-Marie Guyau (1854–1888), who in *L'art au point de vue sociologique* ("Art from a Sociological Perspective") (Guyau 1889) tried to explain works of art from their material conditions of production only. This was at a time when Emile Durkheim (1858–1917), the founding father of French sociology, had made sociology fashionable in France. Still, Guyau was much more a philosopher than a sociologist. Although Emile Durkheim himself wrote very little on art, he created a section in *L'année sociologique* ("The Sociological Yearly"), founded in 1896, that was devoted to "aesthetic sociology." Among other authors, Durkheim's nephew, Marcel Mauss (1872–1950), contributed to this particular section. Durkheim also played a role in the later development of the sociology of art, in so far as he had a major influence over Charles Lalo (1877–1953), a philosopher who was a specialist in the aesthetics domain. In 1927, Charles Lalo published *L'art et la vie sociale* ("Art and Social Life") (Lalo 1927).

During the early phases of the development of sociology, German economist, political activist, philosopher, and sociologist Karl Marx (1818–1883) wrote very little on art. However, with his perspective that culture and ideas reflect the economic base of society – its mode of production – he contributed to a very important current that would later see art as a major object of concern for sociologists. Another pioneer of German sociology, Max Weber (1864–1920) wrote a text on the sociology of music (Weber 1921) in which he underlined the rationalization process of music. Still, this was rather peripheral to Weber's overall work which demonstrated more concern for the economy. German sociologist and philosopher Georg Simmel (1858–1918) also wrote about art in several of his texts.

Until the first half of the twentieth century, many texts published on art were characterized by some disciplinary uncertainty: Was it *real* sociology or was it more aesthetics? Art history or philosophy of art? Among the most illustrative cases of this uncertainty about the sociological dimension of these works is that of French art historian Pierre Francastel (1900–1970). His status as a sociologist of art is still debated today, even though Francastel coined the phrase "sociology of art " and held the first chair in this domain (in the sociology of the visual arts at the École Pratique des Hautes Etudes that was created in Paris in 1948).

In Germany the same uncertainty prevailed. Sociology of art had undergone significant development but mostly with a very Marxist perspective in the Frankfurt school (some prominent figures were Max Horkheimer (1895–1973), Walter Benjamin (1892–1940), Theodor W. Adorno (1903–1969), and Jürgen Habermas (born 1929)). However, in the past decade this Marxist tradition, that also included other European authors such as Georg Lukacs (1885–1971) and Lucien Goldmann (1913–1970), has lost most of its influence with the development of a radically revised sociology of art in Germany now rooted in the French and American traditions.

In France, the sociology of art emerged in its present form in the 1960s.[1] The most influential work there was Pierre Bourdieu (1930–2002) and Alain Darbel's *L'amour de l'art* (*The Love of Art*) (Bourdieu et al. 1997[1969]), which was published in France

---

[1] In her recent handbook on the sociology of art, German sociologist Dagmar Danko pays much attention to France when she presents the development of the domain (Danko 2012).

in 1966 and played a central role in the social debate about the democratization of art. An earlier book on the social practice of photography, *Un art moyen. Essai sur les usages sociaux de la photographie* ("Photography: A Middle-Brow Art"), was published one year earlier, in 1965 (Bourdieu et al. 1996).

Raymonde Moulin (born 1924) first published *Le marché de la peinture en France* ("The French Art Market") in 1967 (Moulin 1987[1967]), and this was to play a decisive role in the institutionalization of the sociology of art. Bourdieu and Moulin's works on art benefited from the creation of a ministry for cultural affairs in France in 1959. Famous writer and Minister André Malraux held the position for ten years and did a great deal to promote cultural democratization. In the United States, Harrison C. White and Cynthia A. White had published a major book, *Canvases and Careers*, with a similar socioeconomic approach to Raymonde Moulin on art markets and institutions (White and White 1993[1965]) two years earlier, but the intellectual context in the United States was less open, then, to the sociological study of the arts.

At that time, even in France, sociology of art was still a burgeoning sociological domain; its full development was to arrive later, under the double influence of the institutionalization of the discipline and a greater social and political concern for culture and the arts in the 1980s. In 1981, François Mitterrand, a left-wing president, was elected and his first government did much to promote culture and the arts. It both deepened cultural democratization policies and adopted a more inclusive approach to the arts, far beyond the traditional limits of high art. In this very favorable context, in 1985, the first French congress of sociology of art[2] was organized in Marseilles and was chaired by Raymonde Moulin (Moulin 1986).

The French tradition that took form from the 1960s until its total institutionalization in the middle of the 1980s quickly influenced some other national traditions, particularly that in the United States. American precursors in the sociology of art were often fluent in French and could follow the development of a proper sociology of art in France from its very beginning, long before the most important works were translated from French into English.[3] For example, Vera Zolberg, Priscilla Ferguson, and Diana Crane played a major role in the international diffusion of sociology of art. And Howard S. Becker learned French in order to be able to read Raymonde Moulin's first book (Moulin 1987[1967]) even before it was translated from French into English.

The sociology of art research committee of the International Sociological Association (founded in 1949) was created in 1979 and strongly influenced by French and English speaking sociologists of art. The European Sociological Association (created in 1992) has a proper research network in the sociology of the arts that was established in 1999. The American Sociological Association, however, still has no section on the sociology of art, and activities dealing with the sociology of art are still included in the sociology of culture section. And still, today, most "regional" and other national sociological associations have research committees that mix culture and the arts such as the Latin American Sociological Association and the national sociological associations in France, Germany, Spain, Brazil, and Japan.

Two Main Theoretical Contributions to the Sociology of Art

When listing the most noticeable works that have helped define the sociology of art subfield, British-based sociologist Marta Herrero (Herrero 2013) mentions two main

---

[2] Four thematic sessions were organized during the conference: "Cultural policies and institutions," "Artistic occupations and art markets," "Publics and aesthetic perception," and "Is a sociology of works of art possible?"

[3] Although Pierre Bourdieu wrote many of his most important books in the 1960s, most of his oeuvre was not translated from French into English until the 1990s.

theoretical contributions: Becker's (1982) symbolic interactionist analysis of art world and artistic activity as the outcome of collective action and Bourdieu's publications on various aspects of artistic and cultural production and consumption (Bourdieu 1984[1979]; 1991; 1996[1993]). German sociologist of art Dagmar Danko (2012) distinguishes three authors: Bourdieu, Becker, and German Niklas Luhmann (1927–1998) (the latter's influence seems overrated and is mostly limited to the German national context). American sociologist Julia Rothenberg presents Bourdieu and Becker as the two main sociologists in this domain (Rothenberg 2014). From a French perspective, Bourdieu, Raymonde Moulin (Moulin 1986; 1987[1967]; 1992), and Becker would probably be considered the most important contributors to the sociology of art, the first two of them being extensively mentioned by Bruno Péquignot (Péquignot 2013). These few examples listed above help illustrate that Bourdieu and Becker are universally seen as formative figures in the sociology of art.

Pierre Bourdieu (1930–2002)

Although Bourdieu's main concern throughout his career was the sociology of culture, with a strong emphasis on sociology of culture and education (especially during the 1960s), his contributions to sociology in general and to sociology of art are absolutely essential to the discipline and subfield. Even today, more than ten years after his death, Bourdieu remains the most internationally quoted sociologist.

Bourdieu wrote five major books that relate to the sociology of art domain; two of them were initially published in French in the 1960s – *Photography: A Middle-Brow Art* (Bourdieu et al. 1996) and *The Love of Art* (Bourdieu et al. 1997[1969]). *Distinction: A Social Critique of the Judgment of Taste* (Bourdieu 1984[1979]), which was published in French in 1979, expands beyond the sociology of art into the sociology of culture. *The Rules of Art: Genesis and Structure of the Literary Field* (Bourdieu 1996[1993]) was the last book to be published while Bourdieu was still alive. *Manet: Une révolution symbolique* (Bourdieu 2013), was released more than ten years after Bourdieu died and consists of transcripts of the lectures that he gave at Collège de France from 1998 until 2000.

In the English speaking world, and hence in international sociology appreciative of the central position of American sociology today, Bourdieu's *The Love of Art* is far less influential than Bourdieu's *The Rules of Art*. Still, the former is an impressive work, less marked by a theoretical perspective and based much more on empirical data. It played an essential contribution to the development of the sociology of art and influenced museums (through visitors' surveys) and public policies. The main findings of *The Love of Art* remain valid today, the most important being its establishment of the factor that influences most artistic practices (especially in the high culture domain) – the level of an individual's education.

The strong emphasis on the theoretical dimension probably explains the success of *The Rules of Art* among sociologists of art, as all main Bourdieusian concepts were mobilized in order to explain the transformations of the French literary world during the second half of the nineteenth century and to understand the success of French writer Flaubert. In order to do this, Bourdieu developed an analysis that combined his main concepts of *habitus*, *field*, and *capital*.

Bourdieu defines *habitus* as a matrix of perceptions, appreciations, and actions. Habitus influences, among other things, the social tastes and practices of the different classes that are determined by the volume of *capital* that they hold and also by the structure of that capital (economic, cultural, social, and symbolic capital). In the arts domain, cultural capital matters most. The habitus of the dominant class (as opposed to the dominated class) consists as a way of evaluating and consuming culture that Bourdieu calls the "aesthetic disposition" and that expresses and makes distinct its privileged position in social space (Bourdieu 1984[1979]).

The concepts of habitus and capital are associated with a third concept, that of the field. Bourdieu defines a field as a network of objective relations between positions, which itself conditions the habitus that can also be defined as the system of mental and physical dispositions individuals develop while operating in a particular field. Hence, what could be seen as individual is always fundamentally social. In the particular case of artists, instead of viewing their practices as based on individual cognitive processes, Bourdieu's theory considers the *field*, the social space of conflict and competition in which artists struggle for control over the various types of *capital*, as well as the *habitus* in its fundamentally social dimension.

The artistic field is generally the site of struggles, such as those between traditional modes of production and aesthetic values on the one hand and artistic innovation on the other and between commercial art and high art values (Bourdieu 1996[1993]: 40). Struggles also involve such fundamental issues as determining the distinction between art and non-art. While established artists generally favor continuity and reproduction, newcomers are likely to seek difference, rupture, or even revolution (Bourdieu 1996[1993]) in order to establish themselves in the most enviable positions in the field. Hence, newcomers will often use difference and distinctive marks in order both to make their names and disqualify their predecessors. Traditional competitors are conventional, less daring, and less innovative.

Howard S. Becker (Born 1928)

Although Becker, an American sociologist, had already made major contributions in sociological domains such as the sociology of work, sociology of deviance, and sociological methods, making him one of the most prominent members of the Chicago School of sociology and symbolic interactionism, he focused upon the sociology of art in a very influential book *Art Worlds* (Becker 1982) and has been very active in the domain since that time.

Becker's analyses focus on cooperation in the art world. Although art historians and critics often conceive of art as an individual activity and praise the genius of exceptionally talented individuals in the production of art works, Becker unveils the collective dimension that underlies all artistic activities. Rather than being spontaneous, works of art result fundamentally from a *collective* work process (Becker 1974) involving not only artists but also supporting personnel such as assistants, critics, and museum personnel (who play a major role in identifying works as art), gallerists (who are central in the valorization of works of art), collectors, etc. Although the *collaborative* nature of art worlds is more obvious in some areas (e.g., orchestras and theater groups) than others, it exists in any artistic domain. Becker insists that the institutional structures and social interactions through which these art worlds are created and reproduced should be studied. Both Bourdieu and Becker have provided sociologists studying the arts with rich case studies and helpful analytical tools.

The Sociology of Art Today

The Influence of Social Class on Art Practices and Consumption

From a Marxist perspective, a common class position generates a similar understanding of the world, which is expressed in art production and art forms. More generally, through shaping identity, social class or group membership affects an individual's aesthetic preferences and more generally his or her "taste" (Bourdieu 1984[1979]; Lamont and Fournier 1992; Peterson and Kern 1996; Halle 1996; DiMaggio 1991). Critical theorists like Theodor Adorno (1903–1969) and Max Horkheimer (1895–1973) adopted a very judgmental perspective of art, maintaining that commercially produced culture was a powerful tool used by elites in order to produce conformity among the people and to neutralize them.

Bourdieusian theory demonstrates some similarity with the Marxist view, although the influence of Max Weber is also evident. In this perspective, class belonging is mediated through field effects. In 2004, a survey conducted in the United States for the National Endowment for the Arts revealed that education (positively associated with income) is more strongly related to attendance at arts events than any other factor (National Endowment for the Arts 2008). Graduate degrees remain strong predictors of arts participation, thus confirming Bourdieu and his collaborators' main finding in *The Love of Art* (Bourdieu et al. 1997[1969]). The contribution of that survey on the public of visual arts museums has become central to visitors' studies and to public policies aimed at reducing social inequalities.

In a highly regarded ethnographic survey, American sociologist David Halle (Halle 1996) studied how people of different social classes – from those in working-class districts to people in bourgeois neighborhoods in New York City – use art in order to decorate their homes. While calm (relaxing) landscapes can be found in all types of neighborhoods, abstract art can be found in upper-class homes only. Household artistic decoration is also influenced by race and religion.

On the other hand, American sociologist Richard A. Peterson (1932–2010) stressed that the traditional association of the masses with commercial culture and elites with high art no longer holds. Audiences for popular and high art forms now overlap, with cultural consumers today being "cultural omnivores" with no exclusivity in their cultural tastes (Peterson 1992: Peterson and Kern 1996).

The Influence of Gender in the Arts

Gender, like social class, plays a major role in social life and is socially shaped (Butler 1990). Since the 1970s, gender issues have become much more important in the social sciences. Today, no less than 5,000 colleges and universities in the United States alone offer programs and courses in women and gender studies (Rothenberg 2014), a domain in which sociology plays a major part. Empirical research demonstrates that within the arts domain, as in other professions and occupations, women's careers suffer from the existence of gender bias. For example, women are discriminated against through the expectations of gatekeepers of the art world, exclusion from male dominated social networks, and glass ceilings, be it in the domain of music (DeNora 1995: Buscatto 2007) or the visual arts (Nochlin 1971; Simioni 2008).

Race, Ethnicity, and the Arts

Just like gender, race is socially constructed. Racial categories are created and maintained through social processes and social interactions called racialization that can also be observed and analyzed in the art world. Some emblematic features of African American culture such as jazz music and the relationship between black power and the arts in the 1960s have been studied by historians and sociologists. Other art practices are also associated with African Americans. For instance, Patricia Banks studied the collecting practices of black art collectors and showed an important affective dimension related to their racial identity in their choices of buying art produced by artists of African descent (Banks 2010). In his study of the decoration of American homes in New York City, David Halle showed that people of African descent were more likely to hang African masks on their walls (Halle 1996). In his analysis of the creation of art institutions in Boston by the Anglo elite in the late 1800s and early 1900s, Paul DiMaggio showed how art institutions were used by people descending from early immigrants to secure their own cultural standards and impose them on more recent immigrants (DiMaggio 1991). Most recently, collections in major art museums that focus solely or primarily upon works by artists of European descent have been questioned and criticized.

Art, Politics, and the Economy

Even in a free market economy, governments play a major role in distributing resources such as grants, stipends, subsidies, awards, and access to exhibition venues that they manage and control. They can also intervene directly in the arts and censor them, although usually artists integrate self-censorship into their work. Over the past couple of decades, institutions of high culture, such as museums, theaters, and orchestras, have gone through a key evolution in terms of "managerialization"; an organizational shift that enhances the power of the administrators (DiMaggio 1991) that cultural policies have expanded (Rodrìguez Moratò 2003; 2007; 2012).

The art market has mainly been studied in the visual arts. For example, Harrison White and Cynthia White effectively analyzed the art dealer gallery system and showed how the development of a commercial gallery system in Paris contributed a great deal to the success of the impressionist painters (White and White 1993[1965]). Moulin also studied the French art market at the time of the impressionists and looked at how it developed subsequently and was then reorganized in the early 1980s (Moulin 1987[1967] and 1992). Diana Crane brought an important contribution with her analysis of the New York visual arts scene in the 1940s and 1950s (Crane 1987). These works on the socio-economy of the art market were more recently expanded by various sociologists, including Alain Quemin (Quemin 2006 and 2013a and 2013b), Sari Karttunen (Karttunen 1998) and Olav Velthuis (Velthuis 2005).

The Territorial Dimension of Art: The Arts, the City, and Globalization

The spatial dimension of art is an important domain of research that developed very distinctly under the influence of the topic of globalization starting in the 1990s. Prior to this, sociologists of art focused primarily on art's relationship to the city. For example, Crane investigated the factors that led to changes in the visual arts world of New York City from 1940 to 1985 (Crane 1989). After studying the decoration of American homes in New York City, Halle (1996) developed a fascinating longitudinal study with Elisabeth Tiso on the spatial dimension of the distribution of contemporary art in New York City. Continuing the work of Sharon Zukin (who had studied the transformations of SoHo under the influence of the presence of artists' lofts and the contemporary art galleries (Zukin 1982)), they analyzed the move of contemporary art galleries that were previously concentrated in SoHo to the new art district of West Chelsea in the early 1990s (and the development of such urban megaprojects in the Far West Side of Manhattan as the High Line) (Halle and Tiso 2014). Rising real estate prices led many art galleries to move from SoHo to Chelsea. That specific kind of art related activity completely redeveloped that part of the city (Rothenberg 2012; Halle and Tiso 2014).

Other important contributions include the theses of Richard Florida. Florida stressed that the presence of high numbers of creative workers, the "creative class," can lead to the economic development of territories and cities (Florida 2003; 2005). Thus, cities should adopt policies that foster the arts in order to attract the kind of professionals that will benefit urban and economic development.

A second element of the study of art in its territorial dimension relates to the topic of "globalization" (Ortiz 1997). For example, George Ritzer described the "McDonaldization" of society (Ritzer 2004) whereby uneven cultural flows among countries spread Western norms worldwide. On the other hand, anthropologist Arjun Appadurai focused on cultural hybridization produced by globalization (Appadurai 1996). Crane (2002) proposed an interesting synthesis of existing theories on globalization and the arts (cultural imperialism, cultural flows/networks, reception theory, and cultural policy strategies). Empirical studies on both literature (Heilbron 2010; Sapiro 2008) and the visual arts (Quemin 2006; 2013a and 2013b) clearly show that the international diffusion of art is characterized by uneven flows among countries and that, even in an era of supposed globalization and the erasure of national borders, some nations clearly dominate others. For instance, in most activities of the visual arts like art fairs (Quemin 2013a) or careers of artists (Quemin 2013b), the United States generally comes first by far, followed by a very small group of countries which include Germany and the United Kingdom.

Art and Work

Becker probably offers the best illustration of how artists and their works are produced through specific historical processes, institutions, and social arrangements (Becker 1982). It should also be stressed that Bourdieu's analysis in terms of field and habitus previously presented in this chapter also offers an analytical grid in order to explain artistic work and the artistic creation process within a sociological perspective (Bourdieu 1996[1993]). Many other researchers who study art from a sociological perspective focus on the production process of art (Zukin 1982; Crane 1987), especially those who examine artists (Moulin 1987[1967] and 1992; Menger 1999; Buscatto 2007; Simioni 2008; Quemin 2013b).

A Sociology of Works of Art

For years, many sociologists have shied away from studying works of art in order to distinguish their field of study from more established disciplines like art history, aesthetics, or literary criticism that all place works of art at their core (Zolberg 1990). They also kept their distance with a somewhat reductionist approach to works of art from the perspective of the Frankfurt school. However, works of art are social facts and, as such, can be studied sociologically. The real challenge is to find the appropriate angle to sociologically analyze them.

In terms of studying works of art from a sociological perspective, the United States is clearly more advanced than France. Long before Lévy and Quemin convinced French-speaking sociologists that sociology of works of art was possible (Lévy and Quemin 2007), the American sociologist of culture and literature Wendy Griswold offered an exceptional contribution in that domain (Griswold 1987). Her metaphor of the cultural diamond (Griswold 2012) presents some analogies with Becker's approach, in so far as the emphasis is put on social processes rather than individual creativity. Griswold demonstrates the conception of cultural production in terms of four points of a diamond: producers or creators, cultural objects, receivers, and the vast social world. Each point of the diamond can be connected to any other point through the lines that shape its perimeter or through the lines that bisect its interior. In this general frame of analysis, her sociology of works is remarkable. Unlike Griswold, who mostly analyzed literature, a narrative form of art that makes sociological analysis somewhat easier, French sociologist Jean-Claude Passeron examined works in even more challenging domains such as the visual arts (Passeron 1991).

Once again, it should be noted that Bourdieu's theory offers a specific perspective from which to study works of art. Whereas authors inspired by Marxist theory generally tended to explain works of art (belonging to the superstructure) in relation to the production mode (that is to say, the infrastructure) of the society in which they emerge, Bourdieu insisted on the mediation of the *field* in order to explain works of art properly from a sociological perspective (Bourdieu 1996[1993]).

Conclusion

Although in some countries, the autonomization process of the sociology of art is still under way, in other countries the domain is already a distinct subfield with proper research networks or committees devoted to the sociology of art in national sociological associations. Moreover, many books have been published within the domain, including handbooks and readers, and some of the most important journals of sociology regularly publish articles in the sociology of art, be it in generalist reviews such as *International Sociology, European Societies, The American Sociological Review, The American Journal of Sociology* or *Theory and Society*, or in specific scientific journals that are devoted to the sociology of (culture and) the arts such as *Poetics, Journal of Empirical Research on Culture, the Media and the Arts, Cultural Sociology*, or French journal *Sociologie de l'art*.

Today, the body of knowledge produced by scholars in the sociology of art is extensive and has created a vibrant and growing field within the discipline of sociology. The seven domains that we briefly presented clearly show that this subfield is not isolated from the rest of sociology and that works produced by sociologists of art – on social class, gender, race, globalization, and other themes – contribute to the development of the overall discipline. Moreover, research conducted by sociologists in this subfield can benefit society in many ways, as can be seen in its use in visitors' surveys and cultural public policies.

References

Alexander, Victoria Dean. 2003. *Sociology of the Arts: Exploring Fine and Popular Forms*. Alden: Blackwell.

Appadurai, Arjun. 1996. *Modernity at Large: Cultural Dimensions of Globalization*. Minneapolis, MN: University of Minnesota Press.

Banks, Patricia A. 2010. Black Cultural Advancement: Racial Identity and Participation in the Arts amongst the Black Middle Class. *Ethnic and Racial Studies* 33(2): 272–289.

Becker, Howard S. 1974. Art as Collective Action. *American Sociological Review* 39(6): 767–776.

Becker, Howard S. 1982. *Art Worlds*. Berkeley, CA: University of California Press.

Bourdieu, Pierre. 1984[1979]. *Distinction: A Social Critique of the Judgment of Taste*. London: Routledge and Kegan Paul.

Bourdieu, Pierre. 1991. *The Love of Art: European Art Museums and Their Public*. Stanford, CA: Stanford University Press.

Bourdieu, Pierre. 1993. *The Field of Cultural Production: Essays on Art and Literature*. New York, NY: Columbia University Press.

Bourdieu, Pierre. 1996[1993]. *The Rules of Art: Genesis and Structure of the Literary Field*. Stanford, CA: Stanford University Press.

Bourdieu, Pierre. 2013. *Manet. Une révolution symbolique*. Paris: Seuil.

Bourdieu, Pierre, Luc Boltanski and Robert Castel. 1996. *Photography: A Middle-Brow Art*. Stanford, CA: Stanford University Press.

Bourdieu, Pierre, Alain Darbel, and Dominique Schnapper. 1997[1969]. *The Love of Art: European Art Museums and Their Public*. London: Polity Press.

Buscatto, Marie. 2007. *Femmes du jazz. Musicalités, féminités, marginalités*. Paris: CNRS Éditions.

Butler, Judith. 1990. *Gender Trouble: Feminism and the Subversion of Identity*. New York, NY: Routledge.

Crane, Diana. 1987. *The Transformation of the Avant-Garde: The New York Art World, 1940–1985*. Chicago, IL: Chicago University Press.

Crane, Diana. 1989. Reward Systems in Avant-Garde Art: Social Networks and Stylistic Change. In *Art and Society: Readings in the Sociology of Arts*. Edited by A. W. Foster and J. R. Blau. Albany, NY: State University of New York Press.

Crane, Diana. 2002. Culture and Globalization: Theoretical Models and Emerging Trends. In *Global Culture: Media, Arts, Policy and Globalization*. Edited by D. Crane, N. Kawashima, and K. Kawasaki London: Routledge, 1–25.

Danko, Dagmar. 2012. *Kunstsoziologie*. Bielefeld: Transcript Verlag.

Deinhard, Hanna. 1970. *Meaning and Expression: Toward a Sociology of Art*. Boston, MA: Beacon Press.

DeNora, Tia. 1995. *Beethoven and the Construction of Genius: Musical Politics in Vienna, 1792–1803*. Berkeley, CA: University of California Press.

DiMaggio, Paul. 1991. Cultural Entrepreneurship in Nineteenth-Century Boston: The Creation of an Organizational Base for High Culture in America. In *Rethinking Popular Culture. Contemporary Perspectives in Cultural Studies*. Edited by Mukerji Shandra and Shudson Michael. Berkeley, CA: University of California Press, 374–397.

Florida, Richard. 2003. Cities and the Creative Class. *City & Community* 2(1): 3–19.

Florida, Richard. 2005. *Cities and the Creative Class*. New York, NY: Routledge.

Foster, Arnold W. and Judith R. Blau. 1989. *Art and Society: Readings in the Sociology of Arts*. Albany, NY: State University of New York Press.

Griswold, Wendy. 1987. The Fabrication of Meaning: Literary Interpretation in the United States, Great Britain and the West Indies. *American Journal of Sociology* 92: 1077–1117.

Griswold, Wendy. 2012. *Cultures and Societies in a Changing World*. Thousand Oaks, CA: Sage.

Guyau, Jean-Marie. 1889. *L'art au point de vue sociologique*. Paris: Alcan.

Halle, David. 1996. *Inside Culture: Art and Class in the American Home*. Chicago, IL: University of Chicago Press.

Halle, David and Elisabeth Tiso. 2014. *New York's New Edge: Contemporary Art, the High Line and Urban Megaprojects on the Far West Side*. Chicago, IL: Chicago University Press.

Heilbron, Johan. 2010. Towards a Sociology of Translation: Book Translations as a Cultural World System. In *Critical Readings in Translation Studies*. Edited by Mona Baker London: Routledge, 304–316.

Heinich, Nathalie. 2001. *La sociologie de l'art*. Paris: La découverte.

Herrero, Marta. 2013. Sociology and Art Markets. *European Societies* 15(2): 155–161.

Inglis, David and John Hughson. 2002. *The Sociology of Art*. Basingstoke: Palgrave.

Karttunen, Sari. 1998. How to Identify Artists? Defining the Population for "Status-of-the-Artist" Studies. *Poetics* 26(1): 1–19.

Lalo, Charles. 1927. *L'art et la vie sociale*. Paris: Doin.

Lamont, Michèle and Marcel Fournier. 1992. *Cultivating Differences: Symbolic Boundaries and the Making of Inequality*. Chicago, IL: Chicago University Press.

Lévy, Clara and Alain Quemin. 2007. Une sociologie des oeuvres sous conditions. *L'Année sociologique* 57(1): 207–236.

Menger, Pierre-Michel. 1999. Artistic Labor Markets and Careers. *Annual Review of Sociology* 25: 541–574.

Moulin, Raymonde. 1987[1967]. *The French Art Market: A Sociological View*. New Brunswick, NJ: Rutgers University Press.

Moulin, Raymonde. ed. 1986. *Sociologie de l'art*. Paris: La documentation française.

Moulin, Raymonde. 1992. *L'artiste, l'institution et le marché*. Paris, Flammarion.

National Endowment for the Arts. 2008. 2008 Survey of Public Participation in the Arts. Available at www.arts.gov/sites/default/files/2008-SPPA.pdf, accessed December 13, 2016

Nochlin, Linda. 1971. Why have there been no Great Women Artists? In *The Feminism and Visual Culture Reader*. Edited by Amelia Jones. New York, NY: Routledge, 229–233.

Ortiz, Renato. 1997. *Mundializacion y cultura*. Buenos Aires: Alianza.

Passeron, Jean-Claude. 1991. *Le raisonnement sociologique: L'espace non poppérien du raisonnement naturel*. Paris: Nathan.

Péquignot, Bruno. 2013. *Sociologie des arts*. Paris: Armand Colin.

Peterson, Richard A. 1992. Understanding Audience Segmentation: From Elite and Mass to Omnivore and Univore. *Poetics* 21(4): 242–258.

Peterson, Richard A. and Roger M. Kern. 1996. Changing Highbrow Taste: From Snob to Omnivore. *American Sociological Review* 61(5): 900–907.

Quemin, Alain. 2006. Globalization and Mixing in the Visual Arts: An Empirical Survey of "High Culture" and Globalization. *International Sociology* 21(4): 522–550.

Quemin, Alain. 2013a. International Contemporary Art Fairs in a "Globalized" Art Market. *European Societies* 15(2): 162–177.

Quemin, Alain. 2013b. *Les stars de l'art contemporain: Notoriété et consécration artistiques dans les arts visuels*. Paris: Editions du CNRS.

Quemin, Alain and Glaucia Villas Bôas. eds. 2016. *Art et société: Recherches récentes et regards croisés Brésil*. France: ouvrage en ligne, 31 March.

Ritzer, George. 2004. *The McDonaldization of Society*. Thousand Oaks, CA: Pine Forge Press.

Rodrìguez Morató, Arturo. 2003. The Culture Society: A New Place for the Arts in the Twenty-First Century. *Journal of Arts Management, Law and Society* 32(4): 243–256.

Rodrìguez Morató, Arturo. ed. 2007. *La sociedad de la cultura*. Barcelona: Ariel.

Rodrìguez Morató, Arturo. 2012. The Culture Society: A Heuristic for Analyzing Cultural Change in the Global Age. In *Sociology Today: Social Transformations in a Globalizing World*. Edited by Arnaud Sales. London: Sage.

Rothenberg, Julia. 2012. Selling Art to the World in Chelsea. *Visual Studies* 27(3): 277–294.

Rothenberg, Julia. 2014. *Sociology Looks at the Arts*. New York, NY: Routledge.

Sapiro, Gisèle. ed. 2008. *Translatio: Le marché de la traduction en France à l'heure de la mondialisation*. Paris: Editions du CNRS.

Simioni, Ana Paula. 2008. *Profissão Artista: Pintoras e Escultoras Brasileiras, 1884–1922*. São Paulo: EDUSP/ FAPESP.

Tanner, Jeremy. ed. 2003. *The Sociology of Art: A Reader*. New York, NY: Routledge.

Velthuis, Olav. 2005. *Talking Prices: Symbolic Meanings of Prices on the Market for Contemporary Art*. Princeton, NJ: Princeton University Press.

Weber, Max. 1921. *Die rationalen und soziologischen Grundlagen der Musik*. Munich: Drei Masken-Verlag.

White, Harrison and Cynthia A. White. 1993[1965]. Canvases and Careers: *Institutional Change in the French Painting World*. Chicago, IL: Chicago University Press.

Wolff, Janet. 1981. *The Social Production of Art*. New York, NY: New York University Press.

Zolberg, Vera L. 1990. *Constructing a Sociology of the Arts*. New York, NY: Cambridge University Press.

Zukin, Sharon. 1982. *Loft Living: Culture and Capital in Urban Change*. Baltimore, MD: Johns Hopkins University Press.

The Sociology of Music

Pamela M. Hunt

Scholars from a wide range of disciplines (e.g., history, philosophy, anthropology, aesthetics, and semiotics) have studied music. Substantive topics within the field of "musicology," a broad perspective that encompasses most scholarly research on the topic, range from the study of music theory and composition of music to examinations of musical performances. Sociologists have studied music from a variety of perspectives. Just a few of the more recent approaches to the sociological study of music include the examination of music subculture formation and persistence (Haenfler 2004; Hall and Jefferson 1976; Hunt 2014), the recognition of music as identity (DeNora 2000), and the consumption of music as a form of cultural taste or preference (Bourdieu 1984).

From what social scientists have examined with regard to music, I propose the following definition. The sociology of music is the study of the content, production, and consumption (including uses and reception) of music and its influence on the interactions and social relations of individuals and groups in society. As I note later, music is considered by social scientists to be both an object and an action (Roy and Dowd 2010). That is, music is an observable entity as well as a collective production.

History and Overview

The sociological study of music is not new. Some of sociology's founding fathers, including Max Weber and Georg Simmel, conducted research on, and proposed theory about, music. Further, scholarly interest in music has been central to the work of several prominent social scientists of the twentieth century, including Theodor Adorno, Pierre Bourdieu, and Howard Becker. In this brief history, I review some of the most notable sociological studies of music, including the examination of music for its communicative properties (e.g., Simmel 1968[1882]), as a victim of the rationalized, modern, capitalistic world (Adorno 1973[1949]; Weber 1958[1921]), for its part in the world of subcultures and drugs (e.g., Becker 1973[1963], Thornton 1995; Hunt 2014), and as an art form for which varying groups have a "taste" (Bourdieu 1984).

One of the earliest sociological analyses of music came from Georg Simmel (1968[1882]). Simmel argued that, like spoken language, music, whether vocal or instrumental, is a form of communication. He added that, although instrumental music is a special form of communication providing emphasis to regular speech patterns, vocal music is even more intricate and direct in its expression of human emotion. This is not to discount instrumental music; being less precise, it has the ability to be more inclusive than vocal music. Simmel tied these ideas to the social world more specifically by arguing that social groups tend to appreciate distinct music styles. There are two reasons for these differences: (1) The meaning of music (and any sound pattern, for that matter) is constructed through the learned emotions of a social group. A group's use of emotive language and the permitted and prohibited emotions within their culture influence the content and construction of music that they create and consume. (2) Access to various technical skills needed to produce certain types of music is specific to social groups. Some groups have access to skills, lessons, instruments, and performance arenas to which other groups are not privy. Etzkorn (1964) suggests that Simmel's analysis of these varying social processes may have been the impetus for the discussion of taste groups in later analyses of the sociology of culture (e.g., Bourdieu 1984).

Max Weber also engaged in the sociological study of music. It is a lesser known line of Weber's research, but it remains much in tune with his desire to uncover the basis for rationalization in several arenas of social life. Specifically, Weber used music to investigate rationalization within the realm of culture. He proposed that, as a cultural object, music was rationalized by the Roman Catholic Church in the Middle Ages (1958[1921]). Weber suggested that the increase of choral singing in the church, the development of modern musical instruments, and the notation of music – all three the creation of the modern organized society – are evidence of the rationalization of music. He argued that during this time musical instruments became standardized in shape, sound, and production, and that the once ephemeral creation of sound emanating from a musician/singer was replaced by standardized choral harmonies and the standardization of musical performance (via the creation of music notation). All of this, combined with the infusion of capitalism, Weber argued, led to the increasing publication, or commodification, of music.

Adorno's (1941; 1973[1949]) analysis of music closely resembles that of Weber's, an increasing reproach of popular music. That is, while Adorno praises pioneering music, he seems partial to less commercialized forms. For example, the routinization of popular "hit" records and their commodification, something Frith (1996) would later take pride in researching, was perceived by Adorno as detrimental to the state of the art form.

Building on Simmel's recognition of music's role in creating group distinctions and Weber's proposal that capitalism and rationalization commodified music, later scholars examined how music creates and maintains social distinctions. For example, Bourdieu (1984) proposed such theoretical concepts of cultural capital, field, and habitus in his examination of society's production and contextualization of art forms such as music. Bourdieu took a particularly Marxist stance on the connection between the social and the aesthetic. He theorized that the ruling class of a society creates the cultural preferences for art and that members of this social class make use of the types of "capital" they acquire as a way to distinguish themselves from members of "lower" social classes.

Between the 1950s and 1990s, many sociologists took to ethnography (e.g. Becker 1973[1963]; Faulkner 1971) to explore music and sociology. For instance, ethnographers from the Centre for Contemporary Cultural Studies in England began studying youth subcultures and the influence of music on the lives of subculture members (Hall and Jefferson 1976; McRobbie and Garber 1975; Willis 1978; Hebdige 1979). These scholars especially noted social class and rebellion from mainstream society as the driving forces behind the subcultural production and consumption of music. In fact, Thornton (1995) expanded upon Bourdieu's concept of cultural capital and applied it to subcultures. She noted that – parallel to Bourdieu's findings – cultural capital is used to distinguish some people from others. "Authentic" subculture members measure their worth by the "subcultural capital" they acquire (Thornton 1995). Later ethnographers focused less on similarities within subcultures (e.g., social class, age) and more on the potential differences within subcultures (Andes 1998; Fox 1987; Haenfler 2004; Hunt 2008; Sardiello 1994; Thornton 1995; Wood 2003).

In the past few decades, sociologists have continued to examine the relationship between music and society/culture. The most recent contributions include studies that examine the performance of sexuality, gender, and race in music lyrics (e.g., Walser 1993), the use of music as a bridge in forming and maintaining community (e.g., Gardner 2004), music as political participation (Turino 2008) and the backdrop to social movements (Roy 2010), the appropriation of music within particular genres (e.g., Rodriguez 2006), and the effect of music on the creation and maintenance of social distinctions (e.g., Bryson 1996). In the following section, I use some of these studies to illustrate how the study of music is intrinsically connected to sociology. Specifically, I review how the creation, performance, and consumption of music are tied to several fundamental sociological concepts, such as identity, stratification, and social change.

Key Aspects

Symbolic interactionism (SI) is one of the major theoretical paradigms in sociology, and is a perspective rooted in the traditions of pragmatism, interpretivism, and social psychology. Within the sociological analysis of music, SI has been used to study musicians of all genres, as well as to examine the interrelationship between music and identity. Blumer, the father of SI, proposed that interaction is facilitated by the use of shared meanings (1969). That is, we give meaning to the objects in our social environment. Music is no exception. It is a social creation that influences our interactions, personal identity and group allegiances, tastes/preferences, emotions, and perception of the greater culture or society in which we live. Music is a cultural and collective production. It is something humans "do" (Roy and Dowd 2010). It is created by people living within the conventions and boundaries of a particular culture (Becker 1982). As such, music has the potential to bring people together or to keep people apart.

Identity

As a form of interaction and communication, music provides a medium through which people generate meaning. These meanings enable us to relate to ourselves as well as to other people. That is, the creation or consumption of music is part of the process by which we create, maintain, or change our identity (Fox 1987; Haenfler 2004). The type of music we produce, listen to, and purchase presumably represents who we are and what we value. Typically, these values are the result of belonging to a social group. For example, members of the straightedge music subculture value clean living, vegetarianism, staying positive, and protecting the environment (Haenfler 2004). The lyrics of the music to which these members listen promote these values (Haenfler 2004). Similarly, the punk subculture values the DIY (Do It Yourself) approach to living, and the music encourages this lifestyle (Bennett 2006). Other notable studies of music's creation and maintenance of group identities include those investigating race (Douglass 2009[1845]), gender (DeNora 2002; LeBlanc 1999; Walser 1993), and religious or spiritual affiliation (Wuthnow 2003).

One of the consequences of identifying with, and thus categorizing, particular music styles is the creation and reinforcement of social distinctions. Social psychologists have found time and again that even arbitrary categorization of people into groups creates an "us" versus "them" mentality. This mentality consists of what social psychologists term the accentuation effect, the tendency to exaggerate the similarities of one's in-group and to overstate the differences between our in-group and some relevant out-group (Tajfel 1981). As a result, we stereotype the out-group and discriminate our treatment of them versus "us" (our in-group). Preference for music has the ability to establish such an arbitrary in-group/out-group mentality, even if music preference is the only (or one of the main) distinctions between the groups. Members of music subcultures often join them with the goal of distinguishing themselves from some out-group.

Yet, not all members of a particular group or culture are homogenous. Music subculture researchers have noted that group identity is a valued commodity – one that can be imitated or authentically internalized and personified. Often, members evaluate each other with regard to the authenticity of their subcultural identity. There are members who embody the values and beliefs of the group, and are therefore considered the "true" or "authentic" members. These members are held in high contrast to "poseurs" (Wilson 2006). The result is often a within-group status hierarchy, which is a fundamental topic in the next key aspect of the sociology of music.

Social Stratification

The study of stratification is a central component within the discipline of sociology. Weber's discussion of the standardization of music instrumentation is one of the earliest studies to discuss how music is involved in the process of social hierarchies and distinctions. Weber argued that the ability to learn about, acquire, and play a musical instrument is not a privilege given to all (1958[1921]). Cultural and financial resources allow some but not others access to this advantage. Bourdieu's (1984) later discussion of taste in art forms and art as a form of cultural capital also addresses these social distinctions.

In addition, the sociological study of music illustrates social stratification through the examination of music that conveys oppression and other interactional and structural inequities. For example, rap and hip hop emerged as a political stance against institutional discrimination based on race (Binder 1993; Watkins 2001). In addition, other scholars, such as those researching punk music and those examining the performance of race, gender, and sexuality within the music world, have discussed how music provides an opportunity to critique conventional society (Bennett 2006; Rodriguez 2006; Whitely 2013).

Social Bonds

Although the production and consumption of music has the ability to create and sustain social divides, it can also build social bonds, and has the capacity to generate sympathy (Cruz 1999; Roy and Dowd 2010). For example, times of tragedy or misfortune call for the healing power of music. That is, in times of cultural/society crisis, music is created, performed, and received as an affirmation that humans can come together. In the 1980s, examples of this included live concerts to benefit organizations such as amfAR (The American Foundation for AIDS Research), Farm Aid (a movement to help family farms thrive), and USA for Africa. In the aftermath of 9/11, residents of New York and New Jersey pled for Bruce Springsteen to write music to help the nation heal, as he had done for particular cities in the Rust Belt in decades past, and he responded with the album *The Rising* (Yates 2005).

In another example of how music creates social bonds, Durkheim's concept of collective effervescence has been connected to studies of music sociology (1995[1912]). Several music subculture researchers note a heightened sense of group membership during the performance or listening to music

(Hunt 2013). This emotional energy (Collins 2004) created during live musical performances enhances feelings of social solidarity (Hunt 2013; Sardiello 1994). These experiences are described by members as moments of collective consciousness, and are said to provide connections beyond words.

Conclusion

The sociological study of music offers a perspective from which we might understand both the connections we make with one another and the disconnecting boundaries we build. That is, by simply calling attention to social bonds and social distinctions, the study of music becomes useful to sociology. As an expression of social injustice, a medium for social change, and a channel through which we can define racial, ethnic, gender, and sexual identities (among others), music is critical to many subfields within, as well as to the general study of, sociology.

Music often suggests the proscriptive and prescriptive norms within social groupings and social institutions. Unlike most other art forms, music is present in and critical to most institutions within society. The messages carried by music within religion, organizations, and the family, for example, consist of important pieces of cultural information. For instance, within religious settings, music is used to build community, to express emotion and transmit beliefs at general gatherings and during various rites of passage within social institutions (e.g., funerals, weddings). In this vein, music has the power to indicate the kind of society we currently are and the type of society we may wish to become. Within cultures, music can forge social bonds (Gardner 2004; Hunt 2013). Between cultures, music has the ability to exclude and separate individuals (Bourdieu 1984; Bryson 1996; Haenfler 2004).

Within varying life stages, music is used to convey angst, anger, love, and celebration. It can also spark nostalgia, and subsequently have a powerful influence on people decades after it is first produced and/or consumed. Across generations, music is often linked to the desire for social change. During the most notable time in the United States' history for social movements, music played a critical role in conveying fear and emotion. It was produced after the deaths of Malcom X, Huey Newton, Martin Luther King, Jr., and many others during the Civil Rights Movement, to express the confusion and agitation at what seemed to be the termination of the crusade for the rights of blacks and other racial minorities. Music was produced during the anti-Vietnam War movement that reflected the growing anger from youth and young adults. Music continues to deliver the emotions of women of all races and colors in the fight for women's rights (Roy 2010).

In sum, the study of music is fundamental to the study of sociology. Scholars have examined the sociological significance of music in many ways, including the content of the music (e.g., lyrics, notation, instrumentation), the creation, performance, and consumption of music, and the relationship between music, identity, and social interaction. Sociologists have noted the usefulness of music in studying stratification and inequality, the creation and maintenance of social bonds as well as social rifts, critiques of conventional society, and the power of social movements. From the increasing number of books and articles published on the subject, the sociological study of music will no doubt continue. As a valued object and collective process, and as a ubiquitous representation of culture and society, music is a subject that is sure to endure within the realm of sociology.

References

Adorno, Theodor W. 1941. On Popular Music. *Studies in Philosophy and Social Sciences* 9: 17–48.

Adorno, Theodor W. 1973[1949]. *Philosophy of Modern Music*. Translated by Anne G. Mitchell and Wesley W. Bloomster. New York, NY: Continuum.

Andes, Linda. 1998. Growing Up Punk: Meaning and Commitment Careers in a Contemporary Youth Subculture. In *Youth Culture: Identity in a Postmodern World*. Edited by Jonathan Epstein. Malden, MA: Blackwell, 212–231.

Becker, Howard S. 1973[1963]. *Outsiders: Studies in the Sociology of Deviance*. New York, NY: Free Press.

Becker, Howard S. 1982. *Art Worlds*. Berkeley, CA: University of California Press.

Bennett, Andy. 2006. Punk's Not Dead: The Continuing Significance of Punk Rock for an Older Generation of Fans. *Sociology* 40: 219–235.

Binder, Amy. 1993. Constructing Racial Rhetoric: Media Depictions of Harm in Heavy Metal and Rap Music. *American Sociological Review* 58: 753–767.

Blumer, Herbert. 1969. *Symbolic Interactionism: Perspective and Method*. Englewood Cliffs, NJ: Prentice-Hall.

Bourdieu, Pierre. 1984. *Distinction: A Sociological Critique of the Judgement of Taste*. Cambridge: Cambridge University Press.

Bryson, Bethany. 1996. Anything But Heavy Metal: Symbolic Exclusion and Musical Dislikes. *American Sociological Review* 61: 884–899.

Collins, Randall. 2004. *Interaction Ritual Chains*. Princeton, NJ: Princeton University Press.

Cruz, Jon. 1999. *Culture on the Margins: The Black Spiritual and the Rise of American Cultural Interpretation*. Princeton, NJ: Princeton University Press.

DeNora, Tia. 2000. *Music in Everyday Life*. Cambridge: Cambridge University Press.

DeNora, Tia. 2002. Music into Action: Performing Gender on the Viennese Concert Stage, 1790–1810. *Poetics* 30: 19–33.

Douglass, Frederick. 2009[1845]. *Narrative of the Life of Frederick Douglass, an American Slave*. Oxford: Oxford University Press.

Durkheim, Emile. 1995[1912]. *Elementary Forms of Religious Life*. Translated by Karen Elise Fields. New York, NY: Simon and Schuster.

Etzkorn, K. Peter. 1964. Georg Simmel and the Sociology of Music. *Social Forces* 43(1): 101–107.

Faulkner, Robert R. 1971. *Hollywood Studio Musicians: Their Work and Careers in the Recording Industry*. Chicago, IL: Aldine-Atherton.

Fox, Kathryn. 1987. Real Punks and Pretenders: The Social Organization of a Counterculture. *Journal of Contemporary Ethnography* 16: 344–370.

Frith, Simon. 1996. *Performing Rights: On the Value of Popular Music*. Cambridge, MA: Harvard University Press.

Gardner, Robert Owen. 2004. The Portable Community: Mobility and Modernization in Bluegrass Festival Life. *Symbolic Interaction* 27: 155–178.

Haenfler, Ross. 2004. Rethinking Subcultural Resistance: Core Values of the Straight Edge Movement. *Journal of Contemporary Ethnography* 33: 406–436.

Hall, Stuart and Tony Jefferson. 1976. *Resistance through Rituals: Youth Subcultures in Post-War Britain*. Working Papers in Cultural Studies. London: Hutchinson.

Hebdige, Dick. 1979. *Subculture: The Meaning of Style*. New York, NY: Methuen.

Hunt, Pamela M. 2008. From Festies to Tourrates: Examining the Relationship Between Jamband Subculture Involvement and Role Meanings. *Social Psychology Quarterly* 71(4): 356–378.

Hunt, Pamela M. 2013. Not Fade Away: Ritual Solidarity and Persistence in an Ephemeral Community. In *Music Sociology: Examining the Role of Music in Social Life*. Edited by Sara Towe Horsfall, Jan-Martijn Meij, and Meghan Probtsfield. Boulder, CO: Paradigm Publishers, 158–165.

Hunt, Pamela M. 2014. *Where the Music Takes You: The Social Psychology of Music Subcultures*. San Diego, CA: Cognella Academic Publishing.

LeBlanc, Lauraine. 1999. *Pretty in Punk: Girls' Gender Resistance in a Boys' Subculture*. Piscataway, NJ: Rutgers University Press.

McRobbie, Angela and Jenny Garber. 1975. Girls and Subcultures. In *Resistance through Rituals: Youth Subcultures in Post-War Britain*. Edited by Stuart Hall and Tony Jefferson. Routledge, London.

Rodriguez, Jason. 2006. Color-Blind Ideology and the Cultural Appropriation of Hip-Hop. *Journal of Contemporary Ethnography* 35: 645–668.

Roy, William G. 2010. *Reds, Whites and Blues: Social Movements, Folk Music, and Race in America*. Princeton, NJ: Princeton University Press.

Roy, William G. and Timothy J. Dowd. 2010. What is Sociological about Music. *Annual Review of Sociology* 36: 183–203.

Sardiello, Robert. 1994. Secular Rituals as Popular Culture: A Case for Grateful Dead Concerts and Deadhead Identity. In *Adolescents* and Their Music: If it's Too Loud, You're Too Old*. Edited by Jonathan Epstein. New York, NY: Garland, 115–140.

Simmel, Georg. 1968[1882]. Psychological and Ethnological Studies on Music. In *The Conflict in Modern Culture and Other Essays*. Translated by K. Peter Etzkorn. New York, NY: Teachers College, Columbia University, 98–140.

Tajfel, Henri. 1981. Social Stereotypes and Social Groups. In *Intergroup Behavior*. Edited by Jonathan. C. Turner and Howard. Giles. Oxford: Blackwell, 144–167.

Thornton, Sarah. 1995. *Club Cultures: Music, Media, and Subcultural Capital*. Middletown, CT: Wesleyan University Press.

Turino, Thomas. 2008. *Music as Social Life: The Politics of Participation*. Chicago, IL: University of Chicago Press.

Walser, Robert. 1993. *Running with the Devil: Power, Gender, and Madness in Heavy Metal Music*. Hanover, CT: Wesleyan University Press.

Watkins, S. Craig. 2001. A Nation of Millions: Hip Hop Culture and the Legacy of Black Nationalism. *Communication Review* 4: 373–398.

Weber, Max. 1958[1921]. *The Rational and Social Foundations of Music*. Translated and Edited by Don Martindale, Johannes Riedel and Gertrude Neuwirth. Carbondale, IL: Southern Illinois Press.

Whiteley, Sheila. 2013. *Women and Popular Music: Sexuality, Identity and Subjectivity*. New York, NY: Routledge.

Willis, Paul E. 1978. *Profane Culture*. Routledge, London.

Wilson, Brian. 2006. *Fight, Flight, or Chill: Subcultures, Youth and Rave into the Twenty-First Century*. Ontario: McGill-Queen's University Press.

Wood, Robert. 2003. The Straightedge Youth Sub-Culture: Observations on the Complexity of Sub-Cultural Identity. *Journal of Youth Studies* 6: 33–52.

Wuthnow, Robert. 2003. *All in Sync: How Music and Art Are Revitalizing American Religion*. Berkeley, CA: University of California Press.

Yates, Bradford. 2005. Healing a Nation: Deconstructing Bruce Springsteen's The Rising. Paper presented at the Glory Days Symposium, Monmouth, NJ, September.

Part VIII

SOCIOLOGY'S IMPACT ON SOCIETY

CHAPTER 32

Public Sociology

Laura Nichols

Public sociology refers to the application and uses of sociology beyond the academy. The term has been used very broadly to describe any sociological theory, methods, research findings, or commentary by sociologists that are consumed (and, ideally, used) by non-sociologists. Its central aim is "to correct – that is, to make better, social conditions for the betterment of humanity" (Hanemaayer and Schneider 2014: 5). Public sociology has also been referred to more specifically as an approach sociologists use to participate in public discussions about social issues as "public intellectuals" (Burawoy 2005).

Every day sociologists are engaging with groups, communities, and organizations to actively help improve social conditions by applying the results of research and what we know about how society operates. Whether it is sociologists

- showing how the dynamics between nurses and doctors in hospitals impact patient care (Apesoa-Varano and Varano 2014);

- advising government organizations such as the National Aeronautics and Space Administration on how organizational culture in an era of technological prowess can lead to bad decision-making at NASA (Consultant 2008; Vaughan 1997);
- conducting interviews and making observations to design and implement a new technology driven by user needs and interests (Kelly and Farahbakhsh 2013);
- blogging about how programs that provide safe facilities to inject illegal drugs save lives and public dollars (Boeri 2015); or
- providing research that informs court cases about issues such as affirmative action (Ancheta 2012),

sociologists use scientific methods and principles in ways that influence programs, organizations' policies, and outcomes.

The public use and application of sociological ideas, methods, and findings have always been part of the discipline of sociology, but the perceived value of public sociology to the discipline has varied given the context and geographic location (for examples see Wang 1981 and Webster 2004). The specific term "public sociology" has been newly popularized in the early twenty-first century, gaining its greatest use just before, during, and after Michael Burawoy's presidency of the American Sociological Association (ASA) in 2004. In his presidential address, Burawoy (2005) presented a four-field approach as an attempt to capture the varied work and positions of all sociologists. As one of the four fields – professional, critical, policy, and public sociology – Burawoy defined public sociology as distinct from other types of sociology that engage with people outside of academe (policy and critical sociology). According to Burawoy's conceptualization, policy or applied sociologists respond to the research needs of clients, while critical sociologists use their academic positions to criticize the state, markets, or other institutions that are often not questioned or problematized as part of the status quo. In Burawoy's four-field conceptualization, public sociologists work as public intellectuals to bring sociological findings to audiences outside of academia. However, since Burawoy's presidency, the term public sociology has taken on a broader meaning, including all types of engagement with publics (ASA Task Force 2005).

This chapter focuses on public sociology in its broadest definition, as the sharing of sociological lessons with publics beyond sociologists, and includes a range of activities from publishing opinion pieces to daily work in government, organizations, court rooms, classrooms, and communities around the world. Because many of the published works about public sociology are in response to the US-based Burawoy and the ASA, this chapter privileges the North American context. However, it must not be forgotten that public sociology has been and is being debated and practiced all over the world. Public sociology is flourishing in South Africa, Finland, China, Hungary, France, Russia, Portugal, Brazil, Germany, Taiwan, Lebanon, and England among other places (Burawoy 2008). Canada, in particular, has many sociologists writing about the value of public sociology (see Hanemaayer and Schneider 2014). For many, there is not a distinction between a professional or academic sociology and a public sociology; they are one and the same. Thus, the centrality of public sociology varies substantially depending on the country of one's training and employment, with public sociology being the usual way of doing sociology in many parts of the world (Kennedy 2009).

Other disciplines are also determining how to integrate the academic and public aspects of their work. For example, applied anthropologists are trying to determine whether to consider themselves part of a separate field or to integrate across specializations (Johnston 2012). Writing on the topic of public criminology, Loader and Sparks (2011) do not prescribe what they think academic criminologists should do or even how they should act in relation to a public criminology. However, they encourage a "sensibility or disposition, a way of being in and relating to public life...Criminology's public role is most coherently and convincingly described as...contributing to a better politics of crime and its regulation" (116–117).

Types of Public Sociologies and Public Sociologists

Public sociologists work in higher education (although not always in sociology departments) as well as in non-academic positions (Spalter-Roth 2007). About a quarter of all Ph.D. sociologists in North America work outside of higher education (Spalter-Roth 2007). No matter the occupational context, public sociologists use sociological tools to understand how society works *and* communicate their findings to various publics to have an impact on society. There are many specific types of sociology that fall under the public sociology umbrella. These include applied and clinical sociology and social engineering as well as work as teachers and public intellectuals.

Of the various types of public sociologists, applied and clinical sociologists have the greatest number of publications and conference papers, and likely the most practitioners.[1] They work in a variety of areas including most types of organizations across business, government, and the non-profit/non-governmental sectors. These include health, law and criminal justice, military, marketing, education, demography, housing, etc. Some full-time academics also engage with community groups and conduct research as part of their work.

Applied sociologists typically conduct research in the form of program evaluations, needs assessments, asset mapping, and policy analysis. They usually adapt common sociological methods and analysis to fit the research questions and needs of organizations, communities, and policy-makers. (To learn more, see Chapter 34 in this volume.)

Clinical sociologists use their knowledge of demographics, systems theories, organizational theory, group theory, and social psychology to advise and direct individuals, groups, and organizations using interventions (Fritz 2008). A certification process exists to certify clinical sociologists as professionals in the field. (To learn more, see Chapter 35 in this volume.)

Social engineers take a larger, macrosystems approach, often reimagining how societies could work in ways dramatically different from what currently exists. Turner (1998) describes the social engineering done by sociologists as being concerned with "tearing down" and rebuilding existing structures and systems. The work of Erik Olin Wright (2010) on "real utopias" and some futurists could be categorized as social engineering in that they imagine, as in the case of Wright, how a completely different type of system (socialism) could be implemented that ultimately changes all parts of society.

Some have also argued that teaching and writing textbooks, especially at the undergraduate level, is a form of public sociology, giving students the knowledge and skills to take a structural, ecological, critical view of the world and social issues (Prentice 2014). DeCesare (2009) states that high school students are a growing audience for public sociology. And there are a growing number of textbooks that help students see the application of sociology to communities and organizations (for examples see Korgen and White 2015 and Nyden et al. 2011). More and more fields, such as medicine, health care, and social work, see the sociological perspective and approach to issues and problems as valuable. For example, the 2015 Medical College Admission Test (MCAT) recently added a required equivalent of one US semester each of introductory psychology and sociology for premedical students applying to medical school admission (Med School Pulse 2015). In addition, some disciplines with an applied or practitioner focus, such as marketing, management, criminal justice, communication, ethnic studies, and environmental studies, often apply sociological concepts, methods, and theories in a more public way than traditional sociology departments.

Being a public intellectual is also a way that sociologists working in academe have contributed as public sociologists. Mainly via editorials, blogs, and public lectures, public intellectuals generally bring a critical, reflexive take on social issues and discuss them in ways that allow for public understanding and consumption. For example, Philip Cohen uses his blog, Family Inequality (familyinequality.wordpress.com), to discuss issues and present new data about subjects both within and outside of the academy, C. N. Le's Asian-Nation (www.asian-nation.org/) website provides a sociological perspective on the Asian American experience and The Society Pages (http://thesocietypages.org/) provides lay and academic readers alike with a wide range of current and accessible sociological research.

For Martinelli (2008), such interaction with publics is extremely important, but

---

[1] For a full discussion and definitions of many types of public and applied sociology see Zevallos 2009. The website and blog were initially supported by the Australian Sociological Association.

he argues that sociologists must still keep a "critical distance" so as not to lose an "autonomy of judgment" and slip into ideology. Discussions about the role of public intellectuals are often where division between the roles of "value-free science" and "value-laden political activism" collide. Brick (2011) shows that C. Wright Mills, known for popularizing the idea of the "sociological imagination" for a mass audience, gains relevance and attention during times when what he terms the "radical left" are ineffectual in mainstream politics. And Collins (2013) argues that intellectual activism must not back away from, but embrace and engage with politics. While discussions about the role of public sociology in the professional academy can break down because of fears that such work results in a loss of the scientific approach, sociologists continue to engage in activities that make research accessible for public consumption and discussion. The call for a more robust engagement often speaks to sociologists eager to bring to bear the knowledge and tools of social science to inform and imagine new possibilities.

In terms of training in the different types of public sociology, the American Sociological Association's *Guide to Graduate Departments in Sociology* (ASA 2014), which includes 196 US and eighteen international departments, does not list all the types of public sociology, or even the term "public sociology," itself, as specializations in its index. However, Applied Sociology/Evaluation Research is indexed and the guide lists forty-four departments with such a specialization. Policy Analysis is another such program indexed, and found in fourteen departments, and Public Policy is a third specialization in thirteen departments (there is overlap among the three areas).

Today, most graduate sociology programs and professional associations around the world train and support sociologists to work as academics producing research to advance theory, methods, and substantive findings for other sociologists. The reality, though, is that many sociologists with graduate training in sociology are spending most of their post-graduate careers teaching and/or doing research that reaches non-sociologists.

Recognizing the advantages for both the discipline and individual sociologists, more graduate programs are adding courses and programs in public sociology. Just the first two pages resulting from a Google search of "graduate studies in public sociology" reveals public sociology graduate programs at Indiana University, Humboldt University, Rice University, American University, Salem State University, George Mason University, the University of California at Berkeley, Boston College, Syracuse University, and the University of Illinois at Chicago. Some faculty advertise themselves as public sociologists on their Web sites. In addition, many traditionally trained academic sociologists are teaching themselves how to write for a public audience to make their research more accessible.

Public Sociology in Historical Perspective

Throughout history, sociologists have contributed to society by identifying how social structures – large and small, formal and informal – impact individuals, groups, neighborhoods, and societies (for an overview see Perlstadt 2005). Emile Durkheim, Max Weber, and Karl Marx – generally known as the founding theorists of sociology – provided public analyses of the rapid social changes of the mid-to-late nineteenth century and early twentieth century. For example, religion, as a dominant institution during that time, was one of the foci of these early sociologists. Durkheim showed that the larger cultural and structural components of the religion to which one belonged could determine one's likelihood of suicide. Weber and Marx took a more critical look at religion, with Weber arguing that the similar values and ideals of capitalism and Protestantism allowed both to flourish and Marx noting religion's role in dulling individual agency and collective consciousness.

These earliest sociologists were public sociologists in that their work not only advanced the social scientific perspective, but also took a critical view of dominant systems within society (Du Bois 1903). In Europe, social scientists as public intellectuals appeared to be acting in direct response to the role that philosophers played in society. Said Marx, "Philosophers have only interpreted the world in different ways, but the point is to change it" (quoted in Bodemann 1978: 388).

However, "the search for scientific legitimacy led many sociologists in the early decades of the [American Sociological] society to want to put as much distance as possible between its historical roots in social reform and its aspiration to status as an academic discipline" (Gollin 1989: 57). There has always been a tension between an academic or, in Burawoy's term, "professional" sociology that aims to promote the "pure" academic scientific model that takes place primarily in the realm of academe and is consumed by other academics, contrasted against a more public, applied, or clinical sociology which happens primarily outside of academe and is consumed by non-sociologists.[2]

In the 1960s, applied sociology became a more regularly acknowledged part of professional sociology associations. In 1962, the theme of the annual ASA conference was "The Uses of Sociology." The volume published after the conference on the theme focused primarily on applied sociology, helping to define the roles and types of clients and sociologists and the nature of their interactions in an organizational context (Lazarsfeld et al. 1967).

The 1970s saw particular attention paid to the use of sociology in policy, and in the 1980s applied and clinical sociology further evolved, forming smaller specialized professional associations that help keep public sociologists within the discipline of sociology. Today public sociologists, especially those working in the health sciences, are involved in "translational research" to translate the results of scientific research for practical use (Wethington 2010).

In 1989, Herbert Gans called for sociologists to pay more attention to the larger "lay" public who would benefit from knowing the results of sociological inquiry (Gans 1989). In 2004, Michael Burawoy (2005) traveled the world and spoke of the need to institutionalize public sociology into the discipline. Agger (2007) termed this a campaign of branding public sociology.

The institutionalization of public sociology has stalled many times since the inception of the discipline. The early years saw a backlash against the presumed politicization of the discipline by Marx in favor of a more objective science. In more recent years, Burawoy's description of critical sociology has put off many sociologists (Zussman et al. 2007), especially the notion that sociologists know what is best for society. As Christensen (2013: 40) asks, "from where do we (sociologists) inherit the moral high ground?" For others, the fear is that the adoption of public sociology as a form of sociology accepted by the discipline will result in the abandonment of sociology as scientifically based, subsequently resulting in a lack of respect for the field (Tittle 2004).

Despite the criticisms, there have always been practicing sociologists and proponents of a more accessible sociology (Agger 2007). As noted earlier, the earliest sociologists were public sociologists. Today, many argue that society's persistent social problems necessitate an integration of professional/academic and public sociologies (Calhoun 2007) and that such a merger would both unify the discipline and make its value to society more obvious to all (Jeffries 2009).

Products and Publications

One area of disconnect between the academic and practicing parts of sociology is

---

[2] Interestingly, the accountability and assessment demands that have now reached higher education institutions have caused administrators in postsecondary institutions to draw on the assistance of social scientists within their universities to measure outcomes.

the sharing of work. The lengthy review and publication processes of traditional outlets of academic sociology do not align with the need to share research results with publics in a timely way. Also, public sociologists often write reports, policy briefs, or opinion pieces that are not read or seen as valuable by academic sociologists. Some have attempted to ameliorate this problem by creating journals that uphold the scholarly expectations of peer review for work that has a more public focus. For example, in June of 1990 the first issue of *Sociological Practice Review* was published. The last issue was published in October of 1992. In 1999, the journal: *Sociological Practice: A Journal of Clinical and Applied Sociology* was established, and it published issues until 2002. In 2007, the Association of Applied and Clinical Sociology launched the *Journal of Applied Social Science*, which publishes two issues a year.

The ASA's creation of the journal *Contexts* in 2002 was an attempt to popularize and extend the influence of sociology beyond colleges and universities. Other professional associations have launched journals or parts of journals dedicated to public sociology, including the *Journal of Public and Professional Sociology* in 2005 and *Social Currents*, the official journal of the Southern Sociological Society, which dedicates some of its space in each issue to "short, theoretical, agenda-setting contributions and brief, empirical and policy-related pieces." In terms of books, however, sociologists have not managed to gain a wide public following. Gans (1997) conducted a study looking at sales of books by sociologists and found that very few had sold over 50,000. Longhofer et al. (2010) did a similar study in 2010 and found results similar to Gans.

In a search for various types of public sociology in the ProQuest library database Sociological Abstracts, the term "applied sociology" results in 2,937 books, conference papers, or journal articles starting as far back as the 1930s.[3] A search of the term "clinical sociology" results in 971 books, conference papers, and articles. In contrast, a search of the more recently created term "public sociology" gave 369 results with the earliest citation in the 1960s. The term "applied sociology" is connected to fifty dissertations or theses; "clinical sociology" to none; and "public sociology" to seven, the first in 1998 and the other six not until 2007 or later, all evoking Burawoy.

The Future of Public Sociology

Current social conditions are optimal for the expansion of a more public sociology. The combined circumstances of an occupational demand for people who know what to do with data with a reduction in the proportion of full-time faculty at universities (Weissmann 2013) means that more and more sociologists will likely work outside of sociology departments. Colleges and universities are also under pressure to make sure that their graduates are employed. Sociologists and others trained in social science fields have options beyond academe. As noted above, graduate programs have begun to respond, with more offering public sociology courses and areas of concentration. The Commission on the Accreditation of Programs in Applied and Clinical Sociology (CAPACS) has researched and created standards that represent best practices and necessary components for accreditation for bachelor, master's, and doctoral programs to train students in applied and/or clinical sociology. And the Research Committees on Clinical Sociology and Community Research that are part of the International Sociological Association provide a dynamic venue for sharing among public sociologists all over the world.

Realizing the need for more "hands-on" training and experience for college students has resulted in colleges looking to offer more pedagogical approaches that use project-based learning, "flipped classrooms," and community-based learning experiences. These strategies are already in line with the way courses in public sociology are taught. The explosion of service learning in colleges and calls for civic engagement training for high school and college students are also

---

[3] Search took place on January 26, 2015.

similar to the aims and approaches of public sociology courses that actively engage sociological research with community and organizational issues and problems.

Further, the proliferation of print and Web sites that publish opinion pieces and other outlets for widespread dissemination of research beyond traditional journal articles and books as well as online courses via Massive Open Online Courses (MOOCs) provide easily accessible avenues for academics to reach a broader public. More organizations are being formed with the purpose of bringing academic research necessary to solve complicated, persistent, and long-standing public issues into the public realm. For example, at the clinical level organizations such as PART (Practice and Research Together; www.partcanada.org/about-part) work to make research easily accessible to practitioners; and numerous policy centers and think tanks both at universities and independent organizations work to conduct research that will inform policy decisions and implementation.

Sociologist Craig Calhoun, while president of the Social Science Research Council, advocated for a social science where applied and pure research inform one another and are not pitted against each other as separate enterprises. Says Calhoun (2004), "[s]ometimes work undertaken mainly out of intellectual curiosity or to solve a theoretical problem may prove practically useful. At least as often, research taking up a practical problem or public issues tests the adequacy of scientific knowledge, challenges commonplace generalizations and pushes forward the creation of new, fundamental knowledge" (14). As our societies and connections with one another in a global context become more complex, there is a need, as public sociologist Donald Light (2005) says, for sociologists and other social scientists to "de-mythologize and democratize knowledge" (650).

Further, the increased call for accountability in education, government, and other organizations has resulted in demand for data to drive decision-making (Haskins 2014; P/PV 2011). Fields typically seen as separate from the social sciences, such as engineering and finance, are realizing the need to better understand the human dimensions of their work and the problems they are trying to solve (Bastow et al. 2014). Globally, organizations are struggling to measure impact. Journalism programs are reimagining their curricula to figure out how to best train future reporters in the age of big data and digital technology (Weiss and Royal 2013). And Web-based information seeking has resulted in reams of qualitative and quantitative data that many without research skills are uncertain how to analyze. Sociologists are well trained to contribute to such work, especially in ways that are participatory (such as that theorized and practiced by scholars like Patricia Hill Collins (2007)) and in which sociologists "pursue original ideas that result from looking at society from new angles – especially bottom-up ones" (Gans 2010: 88). As a result, sociology programs need to actively train students to be able to transfer their sociological theory and methods knowledge to work in business, non-governmental and governmental organizations, widening the occupational choices of sociologists and also spreading sociological knowledge for the good of many.

Public sociology puts sociologists in the middle of the complicated "unscripted problems" facing organizations, communities, and societies in a globalized context. It demands that sociologists ask the kinds of questions raised in these complex contextual realities (Calhoun 2007; Gans 2010; Jeffries 2009) and produce theory and research that can be utilized by various publics and decision-makers to address them. Social conditions in the twenty-first century are ripe for the growth of public sociology and the influence of the work of public sociologists on society.

References

Agger, Ben. 2007. *Public Sociology: From Social Facts to Literary Acts*. Lanham, MD: Rowman and Littlefield Publishers.

Ancheta, Angelo N. 2012. Brief of the American Educational Research Association et al. as Amici Curiae in Support of Respondents.

Available at www.americanbar.org/content/dam/aba/publications/supreme_court_preview/briefs_2015_2016/14-981_amicus_resp_AmericanEducationalResearchAssociationEtAl.authcheckdam.pdf, accessed December 13, 2016.

Apesoa-Varano, Ester Carolina, and Charles S. Varano. 2014. *Conflicted Health Care: Professionalism and Caring in an Urban Hospital.* Nashville, TN: Vanderbilt University Press.

ASA. 2014. *Guide to Graduate Departments in Sociology.* Washington, DC: ASA.

ASA Task Force. 2005. *Public Sociology and the Roots of American Sociology: Re-Establishing our Connections to the Public.* Washington, DC: American Sociological Association Available at www.asanet.org/sites/default/files/savvy/images/asa/docs/pdf/TF%20on%20PS%20Rpt%20(54448).pdf, accessed December 7, 2016.

Bastow, Simon, Patrick Dunleavy, and Jane Tinkler. 2014. *The Impact of the Social Sciences.* London: Sage.

Bodemann, Y. Michal. 1978. A Problem of Sociological Praxis: The Case for Interventive Observation in Field Work. *Theory and Society* 5(3): 387–420.

Boeri, Miriam. 2015. Safe Injection Facilities: More than Just a Place to Shoot Drugs. *The Conversation.* March 4. Available at http://theconversation.com/safe-injection-facilities-more-than-just-a-place-to-shoot-drugs-36386, accessed December 7, 2016.

Brick, Howard. 2011. C. Wright Mills, Sociology, and the Politics of the Public Intellectual. *Modern Intellectual History* 8(2): 391–409.

Burawoy, Michael. 2005. For Public Sociology. *American Sociological Review* 70: 4–28.

Burawoy, Michael. 2008. Open the Social Sciences: to Whom and for What? *Portuguese Journal of Social Science* 6: 137–146.

Calhoun, Craig. 2004. *Toward a More Public Social Science.* New York, NY: Social Science Research Council.

Calhoun, Craig. ed. 2007. *Sociology in America: A History.* Chicago, IL: University of Chicago Press.

Christensen, Tony. 2013. No Path to Paradise: Deconstructing the Promise of Public Sociology. *American Sociologist* 44: 23–41.

Collins, Patricia Hill. 2007. Going Public: Doing the Sociology that Had No Name. In *Public Sociology: Fifteen Eminent Sociologists Debate Politics and the Profession in the Twenty-First Century.* Edited by D. Clawson, R. Zussman, J. Misra, N. Gerstel, and R. Stokes. Berkeley, CA: University of California Press.

Collins, Patricia Hill. 2013. Truth-Telling and Intellectual Activism. *Contexts* 12(1): 36–39.

Consultant. 2008, May. Interview: Diane Vaughan. www.consultingnewsline.com/Info/Vie%20du%20Conseil/Le%20Consultant%20du%20mos/Diane%20Vaughan%20(English).html. Retrieved March 17, 2015.

Decesare, Michael. 2009. Presenting Sociology's four "Faces": Problems and Prospects for the High School Course. In *Handbook of Public Sociology.* Edited by Vincent Jeffries. Lanham, MD: Rowman and Littlefield Publishers.

Du Bois, W. E. B. 1903. *The Souls of Black Folk.* New York, NY: AC McClurq.

Fritz, Jan. M. ed. 2008. *International Clinical Sociology.* New York, NY: Springer.

Gans, Herbert J. 1989. Sociology in America: The Discipline and the Public American Sociological Association. *American Sociological Review* 54: 1–16.

Gans, Herbert J. 1997. Best-Sellers by Sociologists: An Exploratory Study. *Contemporary Sociology* 26: 131–135

Gans, Herbert J. 2010. Making Sociology More Socially Useful. *Contexts* 9: 88.

Gollin, Albert E. 1989. History of Applied Sociology: Some Interpretive Notes. *Sociological Practice* 7(1): 57–61.

Hanemaayer, Ariane and Christopher J. Schneider. eds. 2014. *The Public Sociology Debate: Ethics and Engagement.* Toronto: UBC Press.

Haskins, Ron. 2014. Social Programs that Work. *New York Times.* December 31.

Jeffries, Vincent. 2009. ed. *Handbook of Public Sociology.* Lanham, MD: Rowman and Littlefield Publishing Group Inc.

Johnston, Barbara Rose. 2012. Applied Anthropology. *Oxford Bibliographies.* Available at www.oxfordbibliographies.com/view/document/obo-9780199766567/obo-9780199766567-0002.xml, accessed December 13, 2016.

Kelly, Benjamin and Khosrow Farahbakhsh. 2013. Public Sociology and the Democratization of Technology: Drawing on User-Led Research to Achieve Mutual Education. *American Sociologist* 44: 42–53.

Kennedy, Michael D. 2009. On Public Sociology and Its Professional, Policy, and Critical

Complements in America and the Post Communist World. *Academic Studies from Lviv Sociological Forum*.

Korgen, Kathleen O. and Jonathan M. White. 2015. *The Engaged Sociologist: Connecting the Classroom to the Community*. 5th edn. New York, NY: Sage.

Lazarsfeld, Paul F., William H. Sewell, and Harold L. Wilensky. eds. 1967. *The Uses of Sociology*. New York, NY: Basic Books Inc.

Light, Donald W. 2005. Contributing to Scholarship and Theory through Public Sociology. *Social Forces* 83: 1647–1654.

Loader, Ian and Richard Sparks. 2011. *Public Criminology?* London: Routledge.

Longhofer, Wesley, Shannon Golden, and Arturo Baiocchi. 2010. A Fresh Look at Sociology Bestsellers. *Contexts* 9(2): 18–25.

Martinelli, Alberto. 2008. Sociology in Political Practice and Public Discourse. *Current Sociology* 56(3): 361–370.

Med School Pulse. 2015. What Is Changing on the MCAT 2015? Available at www.medschoolpulse.com/2014/08/25/changing-mcat-2015/, accessed March 18, 2015.

Nyden, Philip, Leslie Hossfeld, and Gwendolyn Nyden. 2011. *Public Sociology: Research, Action, and Change*. New York, NY: Sage.

Perlstadt, Harry. 2005. Applied Sociology. In *21st Century Sociology: A Reference Handbook*. Vol. 2. Edited by C. Bryant and D. Peck. Thousand Oaks, CA: Sage.

P/PV. 2011. Priorities for a New Decade: Making (More) Social Programs Work (Better). *Public/Private Ventures*. February 25. Available at http://ppv.issuelab.org/resource/priorities_for_a_new_decade_making_more_social_programs_work_better, accessed December 7, 2016.

Prentice, Susan. 2014. Reflections on the Theory and Practice of Teaching Public Sociology. In *Public Sociology Debate: Ethics and Engagement*. Edited by A. Hanemaayer, C. Schneider and M. Burawoy. Toronto: UBC Press.

Spalter-Roth, Roberta. 2007. Sociologists in Research, Applied, and Policy Settings: Bringing Professionals in from the Cold. *Journal of Applied Social Science* 1(2-4): 4–18.

Tittle, Charles R. 2004. The Arrogance of Public Sociology. *Social Forces* 82(4): 1639–1643.

Turner, Jonathan H. 1998. Must Sociological Theory and Sociological Practice Be So Far Apart?: A Polemical Answer. *Sociological Perspectives* 41(2): 243–258.

Vaughan, Diane. 1997. *The Challenger Launch Decision: Risky Technology, Culture, and Deviance at NASA*. Chicago, IL: University of Chicago Press.

Wang, Kang. 1981. Sociology: Past and Present. *Chinese Sociology and Anthropology* 13: 3–19.

Webster, Edward. 2004. Sociology in South Africa: Its Past, Present, and Future. *Society in Transition* 35: 27–41.

Weiss, Amy Schmitz and Cindy Royal. 2013, July 26. At the Intersection of Journalism, Data Science, and Digital Media: How Can J-Schools Prep Students for the World They're Headed Into? *Nieman Lab*. Available at www.niemanlab.org/2013/07/at-the-intersection-of-journalism-data-science-and-digital-media-how-can-j-schools-prep-students-for-the-world-theyre-headed-into/.

Weissmann, Jordan. 2013. The Ever-Shrinking Role of Tenured College Professors. *The Atlantic* April 13.

Wethington, Elaine. 2010. What Is Translational Research? *Evidence-Based Living*. Cornell University. Available at. http://evidencebased-living.human.cornell.edu/2010/08/18/what-is-translational-research/, accessed February 21, 2017.

Wright, Erik Olin. 2010. *Envisioning Real Utopias*. New York, NY: Verso.

Zevallos, Zuleyka. 2009. What Is Applied Sociology. Available at http://sociologyatwork.org/about/what-is-applied-sociology/, accessed December 7, 2016.

Zussman, Robert, Dan Clawson, Joya Misra, Naomi Gerstel, Randall Stokes and Douglas Anderton. eds. 2007. *Public Sociology: Fifteen Eminent Sociologists Debate Politics and the Profession in the Twenty-First Century*. Berkeley, CA: University of California Press.

Humanist Sociology

Woody Doane

Humanist sociology can be defined as a *value-oriented* sociology that is explicitly directed toward expanding individual and human potential and pursuing social justice. As such, humanist sociology is set in direct contrast to the value-neutral or "objective" perspective that has historically dominated American sociology. In this chapter, I will discuss the roots of humanist sociology, the mid-twentieth-century "crisis" of sociology and the rise of humanist and critical perspectives, the emergence of an overtly humanist sociology in the Association for Humanist Sociology, and the impact of humanist sociology and its future prospects.

The Roots of Humanist Sociology

The roots of humanist sociology (and humanism in general) can be traced back to the Enlightenment, the eighteenth-century European philosophical movement that emphasized progress and rationality over traditional religious authority, and the evolution of classical liberalism, with its focus upon *individual* rights and freedoms. This also gave rise to ideas about the potential improvement or even perfectibility of humankind. These developments coincided with the English, American, and French revolutions, the emergence of bourgeois democracies and the idea that government exists to protect individual liberty and to advance the common good, the Industrial Revolution, and the rise of the modern nation-state. Politically, this was manifest in such documents as the 1776 United States *Declaration of Independence*, with its statement of "inalienable rights" to "life, liberty, and the pursuit of happiness" and the 1789 French *Declaration of the Rights of Man* and its emphasis on equality and the "natural rights" of man.

A related significant (and concurrent) development was the Scientific Revolution, the rapid expansion of knowledge in the physical sciences and the application of this knowledge to technological innovation via the Industrial Revolution. In addition to the dramatic social changes that it brought about, the Scientific Revolution also had profound influence upon the emerging discipline of sociology. As humans expanded their knowledge of the scientific laws governing natural phenomena, it occurred to social theorists such as Henri Saint-Simon and Auguste Comte that a "science of man" or "social physics" could identify – using scientific methods of observation and measurement – the "natural laws" of social order and social change. For Comte, this "positive philosophy" or "positivism" would in turn provide a blueprint for social betterment. As sociology continued to evolve, the quest for scientific status led sociologists to continue to desire to emulate the natural sciences. In his book *The Rules of Sociological Method*, French sociologist Emile Durkheim (1964 [1895]) gave primacy to the "objective" reality of *"social facts"* and the unbiased application of the scientific method. One of the earliest and most influential sociology textbooks in the United States, Robert E. Park and Ernest Burgess's 1,000 page *Introduction to the Science of Sociology* emphasized scientific rigor and the importance of "disinterested investigation." Such perspectives were very influential in shaping the evolution of sociology as an academic discipline.

Ironically, the same European/Western societies that gave birth to the humanism of the Enlightenment simultaneously engaged in an unprecedented global project of conquest, colonialism, and racialized enslavement. The expansion of capitalism as an economic system led to a dynamic world-economy as well as extensive dislocation, disruption, and inequality. And Europe and the world experienced social upheaval, revolutions, conflict, and two world wars. In response to these events, social critics – and, arguably, humanist sociologists – such as Karl Marx, W. E. B. Du Bois, and Jane Addams analyzed and attempted to ameliorate social problems stemming from capitalism and racism and worked to improve the human condition (Scimecca and Goodwin 2003). While not explicitly humanist, these scholars emphasized humanist concerns such as individual liberation and social justice. Such perspectives, however, remained at the margins of the discipline of sociology.

The Crisis of Mainstream Sociology and the Humanist/Critical Critique

By the middle of the twentieth century, the ascendancy in the United States of a "positivist" mainstream sociology seemed complete. Sociologists worked to affirm the status of their discipline as a "science" where "objective" practitioners based in universities produced new knowledge that was useful to politicians and policy-makers. This was reflected in the words of William Ogburn (cited in Dale and Kalob 2011: 73), who in his 1929 American Sociological Society (predecessor to the American Sociological Association (ASA)) presidential address stated that "sociology as a science is not interested in making the world a better place." Use of the "scientific method," hypothesis testing, survey research, and statistical analysis buttressed sociology's scientific credentials. Government and foundation funding for large-scale research was expanding. As Alvin Gouldner (1970) observed, this meant that mainstream sociology, with its corporate orientation and institutionalization in academia, had become increasingly well-entrenched in American society.

Yet, within a few years, this same sociology was in a state of crisis due to what critics described as its removal from human affairs. In his book *The Sociological Imagination*, C. Wright Mills (1959) decried the irrelevance of both "grand theory" and "abstracted empiricism." By the 1960s, sociology faced criticism for failing to foresee the rebellion of African Americans embodied in the Civil Rights Movement – a situation acknowledged by C. Everett Hughes (1963) in his ASA presidential address. In the face of the post-world War II decolonization of the Global South and the African American uprising of the mid-twentieth century, works such as Franz Fanon's (1963) *The Wretched of the Earth*, Paolo Freire's (1970) *Pedagogy of the Oppressed*, and Stokely Carmichael and Charles Hamilton's (1967) *Black Power* proved far more engaging to a new generation of critical and humanist scholars.

This ferment reached to the very core of mainstream sociology – the ASA. By the late 1960s, groups of sociologists had established the Sociology Liberation Movement (later the Radical Caucus), a black caucus, and a women's caucus – all of which posed challenges to the sociological establishment. The ASA annual meetings in the late 1960s and early 1970s were often tumultuous, as ideological and disciplinary disputes played out in the convention hall. Perhaps the culmination of this process was at the 1968 ASA meeting in Boston, when insurgents demanded to insert a speaker in a plenary session who then castigated "fat cat sociologists" who were profiting by "studying downward" (individuals and groups at the margins of society) at the behest of corporations, government, and funding agencies (Nicolaus 1968). These conflicts continued over the next few years, but eventually dwindled away by the 1980s (Oppenheimer et al. 1991).

The Emergence of an Explicitly Humanist Sociology: The Association for Humanist Sociology

In the wake of the social upheaval of the 1960s and the ongoing criticism of mainstream sociology, the mid-1970s saw the emergence of an explicitly humanist sociology. In 1976, noted sociological critic Alfred McClung Lee, his wife Elizabeth Briant Lee, and a group of sociologists (including, among others, Charles Flynn) founded the Association for Humanist Sociology (AHS) at a meeting in Oxford, Ohio (Miami University). Ironically, Alfred Lee had just concluded a term (1975–1976) as President of the ASA, an office to which he was elected as a write-in candidate following an insurgent campaign. Lee's term as president of the ASA had a limited long-term impact on the organization, as most of his proposals were contested by the ASA Council and by the staff of the organization (Galliher and Galliher 1995). Interestingly, the Lees had also played lead roles in establishing another important sociological organization, the Society for the Study of Social Problems (SSSP) in 1950–1951 (SSSP currently presents an annual Lee Founders' Award) and Al Lee served as the second president of the organization in 1953–1954. While appreciative of the contributions of SSSP, the Lees chose to found AHS because they believed that the SSSP had become too close to the sociological mainstream (Galliher and Galliher 1995; Lee and Lee 1976).

At the inaugural conference, Al Lee (1977) presented his vision for "A Different Kind of Sociological Society." He criticized the ASA for being controlled by elites from prestigious universities and for never reflecting the needs of American society, as part of the power structure of society, and "as part of the problems sociologists should be probing." Lee's goal for the AHS was clear: it should attract *"those whose dedication is to a sociology committed to the service of humanity."* In other words, the purpose of humanist sociology is to use sociological research and analysis to promote individual freedom and the social betterment of humanity. Lee is also very clear about whom humanist sociologists should oppose: the "power manipulators," the "plutocrats," and the "colonialist and neocolonialist" exploiters. These themes resonate throughout humanist sociology: from the first textbook (Scimecca 1995[1981]), to early theoretical works (Goodwin 1983), to more recent AHS presidential addresses (Doane 2000; Dolgon 2011a).

Lee's critique of mainstream sociology and his vision for humanist sociology are more completely articulated in his two books, *Toward Humanist Sociology* (Lee 1973) and *Sociology for Whom* (1978). As described by Lee and others (Goodwin 1983; Du Bois and Wright 2002), humanist sociology emphasizes the following principles:

- Rejection of "objective" or "value-neutral" sociology. This is at the core of humanist sociology. As a perspective that emphasizes the service of humankind, humanist sociology rejects the claim that sociologists must be "value-free" scientists. Lee (1978: 88) emphasizes that *all* scientists – even those who claim to be "value-free" – are embedded in a larger social context of "competition and conflict" between groups with different or even diametrically opposed interests and that this "consciously or unconsciously" shapes theory and research. Moreover, the perspective of each sociologist is also shaped by his or her social location and experience in terms of class, race, ethnicity, gender, sexuality, religion, institutional affiliation, and other social connections. Lee and other humanist sociologists harshly criticize mainstream sociology for virtuously claiming to be neutral and objective while actually working in support of existing institutional arrangements and structures of power; that is, by studying individuals, groups, and conditions defined as "deviant" or as "social problems" by social elites. And, if sides must be taken, the choice for humanist sociologists is clear: to be a voice for freedom, social justice, and the betterment of humanity, "to serve people, not their manipulators" (Lee 1978: 93).

- Emphasis upon human agency. Humanist sociology rejects a rigid determinism – the suggestion that humans are inexorably bound by social or natural laws. Instead, the humanist perspective views individuals as social actors who make choices and construct social reality. According to the AHS website (cited in Dolgon 2011b: 33; see also www.humanist-sociology.org), humanist sociology views people "not merely as products of social forces, but also as shapers of social life, capable of creating social orders in which everyone's potential can unfold." Humanist sociology also rejects extreme positivism in theory and research; instead it valorizes multiple ways of knowing and a wide range of research methods. In teaching and practice, humanist sociology emphasizes the importance of understanding and empathizing with people who are different (Lee 1978). Yet humanist sociology also recognizes the role that social forces play in shaping human behavior. Goodwin (1983) approvingly cites Mills's (1959) "sociological imagination" and the need to understand how social forces shape life chances. For humanist sociologists, then, this means that one essential task is to lift the veil that masks how institutional and cultural forces circumscribe the day-to-day existence of individual humans and to dispel the myths that are used by elites to manipulate the masses.

As an organization, the AHS was intentionally created as the antithesis of the ASA. For Lee (1978: 221), the AHS was founded as "a society of cooperative friends in search of social knowledge" as opposed to a bureaucratic organization serving the interests of careerism and corporate sociology. While it had many of the trappings of a traditional scholarly society – an annual meeting, a journal, and a newsletter – AHS also instituted a number of practices that reflected humanist values and ran counter to those of mainstream sociological organizations. Both articles in the AHS journal, *Humanity and Society*, and presentations at the annual meeting are expected to be preceded by a "reflexive statement" that describes the author's value orientation with respect to the issues being discussed – as opposed to a "value-neutral" standpoint. Manuscripts submitted to *Humanity and Society* for possible publication do not undergo the "double blind" anonymous review process employed by most academic journals, but instead are reviewed using an open process designed to facilitate dialog between the reviewers and the author. As long time AHS members Chet Ballard (2002) and Jerold Starr (2002) have observed, annual meetings are also designed to be different: presenters are strongly encouraged to talk about their research rather than read a paper, sessions are organized to be inclusive and to promote dialog (with presenters and attendees often sitting in a large circle together), status differences (e.g., between senior scholars and graduate students) are downplayed, meetings of the board of directors are open to all AHS members, and major issues are decided by a referendum of all members. Both Ballard and Starr also highlighted what they experience as the sense of community at AHS annual meetings, a spirit of camaraderie and commitment to shared values that make each conference an important personal and professional experience.

At the same time, it is important to underscore that there is not a unitary vision among humanist sociologists and AHS members regarding the contours or practice of humanist sociology. Ballard (2002: 45) describes those attracted to AHS as including "Marxists, anarchists, symbolic interactionists, therapists, experimental teaching advocates, clinicians, spiritualists, and grassroots organizers." Similarly, Starr (2002: 63) divides early AHS members into three groups: humanist theorists, Marxists, and community organizers/applied sociologists. This diversity could be both a source of strength and a source of conflict, especially with regard to the content of *Humanity and Society*. AHS members also vary in terms of the relative value of spontaneity versus structure with respect to the annual meeting. As Ballard (2002) notes, some of these disagreements have even led to resignations from the organization.

Humanist Sociology: Impact and Future Prospects

After nearly four decades, I believe that it is possible to speak of a humanist/critical movement in sociology. The idea of a humanist "movement" incorporates both the AHS as a unique organization and other forms of humanism within the larger discipline of sociology. This leads to two questions. First, what is the current impact of humanist sociology upon the discipline? And second, what are the future prospects for a humanist sociology?

The AHS has persisted for more than forty years as an organizational haven for those who practice a value-oriented brand of sociology in pursuit of social justice.

Humanity and Society continues to publish critical scholarship and in 2011 saw the publication of a volume of some of the best work that has appeared in its pages (Dolgon and Chayko 2011). AHS annual meetings remain strong and vibrant, with plenary sessions featuring such activists as Medea Benjamin, Diane Wilson, Jim Hightower, Tim Wise, Dolores ("Granny D") Haddock, and Nadine Smith. "Activist cafes" bring humanist sociologists and local activists together for strategic discussions. And regular sessions continue to highlight humanist theory, critical social issues, and humanist pedagogy and practice. This organizational space and professional community has played an important role in maintaining an alternative to mainstream sociology and in some ways – especially with respect to pedagogy and activism – it has broadened the boundaries of humanist sociology from the 1970s (Dale and Kalob 2011).

Nevertheless, the more things change, the more they remain the same. The AHS and *Humanity and Society* continue to exist on the margins of the discipline. Much of the institutional control of sociology remains in the hand of the disciplinary elite that Lee (1977) criticized at the first AHS annual meeting (see, for example, a similar critique by Feagin 1999). AHS membership and annual meeting attendance have not appreciably increased since the 1980s and the lack of size and organizational resources make it difficult for the organization to retain the connections with local activists that are established at annual meetings or to establish a visible national presence (Doane 2000). The footprints of an explicitly humanist sociology remain relatively faint.

On the other hand, if we speak of a humanist sociology writ large – of a larger movement of humanist and critical sociologists – then the footprints are much deeper. There are a range of organizations, many with roots back to the 1960s, that practice a sociology that works toward social change and social justice – for example, the Association of Black Sociologists, Sociologists for Women in Society, the Section on Marxist Sociology of the ASA, the

Association for Applied and Clinical Sociology, and Sociologists Without Borders. The SSSP has expanded its role as a source for critical research on social problems (Hess 1999). The journal *Critical Sociology* (the successor to *The Insurgent Sociologist* that emerged from the Sociology Liberation Movement in the late 1960s and early 1970s) continues as an outlet for alternative and critical scholarship. And the past decades have seen the emergence of new subfields – e.g., critical race studies, LGBT studies, women's studies, environmental sociology, critical criminology – that provide important critiques of social structures and social problems as well as new methods such as participatory action research (Stoecker 2005) and more engaged forms of ethnography. It is fair to say that it has become more acceptable to practice more critical sociology and to blend scholarship and activism – especially outside of elite universities. The sociological center has definitely moved, and the efforts of humanist and critical sociologists have played a key role in this process.

The effects of this movement even reached into the center of the mainstream, the ASA. In 2000, ASA president Joe Feagin, a noted critical race scholar, used his presidential address to assert that "we sociologists must vigorously engage issues of social justice or become largely irrelevant to the present and future course of human history" (2001: 6). Also in 2001, Feagin and Hernan Vera (joined in later editions by Kimberley Ducey) published *Liberation Sociology* in which they articulated a vision of a sociology whose purpose is "not just to research the social world but also to assist in changing it in the direction of expanded human rights, participatory democracy, and social justice" (Feagin et al. 2015[2001]: 1). The history and practice of "liberation sociology" that is outlined in this book covers essentially the same ground as the description of humanist/critical sociology that is outlined in this chapter.

In 2004, another ASA president, Michael Burawoy, exhorted sociologists to return to a "public sociology" (this was the theme of the 2004 ASA annual meeting) and outlined a historical path similar to that of humanist sociology and liberation sociology. In his presidential address, Burawoy (2005: 7–8) described two types of public sociology: "traditional" public sociology, in which sociologists provide commentary on public issues, and "organic" public sociology, in which sociologists work in collaboration with groups, organizations, or social movements to address social problems. Burawoy's vision of "public sociology" in some ways parallels Lee's call for humanist sociologists to engage with public issues, but it conspicuously lacks Lee's directive to serve the people instead of power elites. Interestingly, while Burawoy's call for "public sociology" received considerable attention and support among sociologists, it also evoked criticism from sociologists who feared that sociology was descending into leftist partisanship (see the discussion in Dale and Kalob 2011: 83–84) and moving away from its "scientific" status.

While this expansion of humanist (critical, liberation) sociology can be seen – from a humanist perspective – as a positive development, the future expansion of humanist sociology faces significant obstacles. The first barriers are within the academy itself. The reward structure may have shifted slightly in the direction of a humanist or public sociology, but publications (in prestigious outlets) and grants are still the coin of the realm, especially in elite and doctoral institutions. Moreover, the pressures of the academic job market and institutional status have led to the bar being raised in terms of the publication expectations for initial appointment and for tenure. A significant number of sociologists will continue to adopt a critical or humanist approach (including liberation sociology and public sociology), yet as Chris Dale and Dennis Kalob (2011) observe, most of this will continue to take place in academic settings and not as activists or change agents – except for a small minority generally located in less prestigious institutions. At the end of the day, most sociologists, including humanist sociologists, are academics more than activists, and are more comfortable in the classroom or the conference room than in the streets. But in keeping with Alfred McClung Lee's vision for humanist sociology, social critics do play a key role in uncovering systems of oppression, dispelling myths, and raising consciousness.

Finally, there are larger social forces that threaten the future prospects for humanist and critical sociology. Higher education in the United States has been undergoing a number of changes as a result of the fiscal crises of state governments and the corporatization of universities. Lee (1978) observed that, despite the pressures for conformity, the system of academic tenure can create space for independent and creative scholarship. Yet over the past few decades, higher education has seen a decline in the number of full-time, tenure-track faculty and an increase in the number of part-time or contingent faculty – and, as advocated by some outside of the academy, there is the increasing possibility of replacing large segments of the professoriate with technology, including Massive Open Online Courses (MOOCs). This trend is exacerbated by the emphasis on career preparation or "professional" fields and a decline in the traditional liberal arts that serve as the source for humanist inquiry and critique. Added to this is the growing conservative assault on higher education, one that is supported by a view of college professors as "tenured radicals" and by organizations such as the American Council of Trustees and Alumni (ACTA) and the National Association of Scholars. In recent years, governors and legislators have proposed limitations on tenure, increased teaching loads for faculty, and funding cuts that would severely handicap research in the social sciences and humanities. Such policies, if enacted, would certainly restrict opportunities for the practice of humanist sociology.

In short, the forecast for the future is contradictory. On one hand, the acceptance of humanist sociology appears to be expanding. On the other hand, the space for practicing humanist sociology appears to be contracting. Yet, in conflict and crisis are the seeds of opportunity. From climate change to social conflict to economic dislocation, humanity faces a seemingly increasing array of crises. In such a world, the need for critical perspectives and the dispelling of myths is great. If sociology (and social science in general) is to remain viable, it needs to increase its relevance to human needs and the human condition. If human freedom and social justice are the ultimate goals for society, then humanist sociology has an important role to play.

References

Ballard, Chet. 2002. An Epistle on the Origin and Early History of the Association for Humanist Sociology. *The American Sociologist* 33(4): 37–61.

Burawoy, Michael. 2005. For Public Sociology. *American Sociological Review* 70: 4–28.

Carmichael, Stokely and Charles V. Hamilton. 1967. *Black Power: The Politics of Liberation in America*. New York, NY: Vintage.

Dale, Chris and Dennis Kalob. 2011. Embracing Social Activism: Sociology in the Service of Social Justice and Peace. In *Pioneers of Public Sociology: 30 Years of Humanity and Society*. Edited by Corey Dolgon and Mary Chayko. Cornwall-on-Hudson, NY: Sloan, 71–96.

Doane, Ashley W. 2000. Confronting Structures of Power: Toward a Humanist Sociology for the 21st Century. *Humanity and Society* 24: 612–625.

Dolgon, Corey. 2011a. Don't Celebrate, Organize! A Public Sociology to Fan the Flames of Discontent. In *Pioneers of Public Sociology: 30 Years of Humanity and Society*. Edited by Corey Dolgon and Mary Chayko. Cornwall-on-Hudson, NY: Sloan, 419–429.

Dolgon, Corey. 2011b. My Twenty Cents Worth on Paradigms. In *Pioneers of Public Sociology: 30 Years of Humanity and Society*. Edited by Corey Dolgon and Mary Chayko. Cornwall-on-Hudson, NY: Sloan, 33–34.

Dolgon, Corey and Mary Chayko. eds. 2011. *Pioneers of Public Sociology: 30 Years of Humanity and Society*. Cornwall-on-Hudson, NY: Sloan.

Du Bois, William and R. Dean Wright. 2002. What is Humanistic Sociology? *The American Sociologist* 33(4): 5–36.

Durkheim, Emile. 1964[1895]. *The Rules of Sociological Method*. Edited by George E. G. Catlin.

Translated by Sarah A. Solovay and John H. Mueller. 8th edn. New York, NY: Free Press.

Fanon, Frantz. 1963. *The Wretched of the Earth*. Translated by Constance Farrington. New York, NY: Grove Press.

Feagin, Joe R. 1999. Soul-Searching in Sociology: Is the Discipline in Crisis? *Chronicle of Higher Education*, October 15, 1999: B4-B6.

Feagin, Joe R. 2001. Social Justice and Sociology: Agendas for the Twenty-First Century. *American Sociological Review* 66: 1–20.

Feagin, Joe R., Hernan Vera, and Kimberley Ducey. 2015[2001]. *Liberation Sociology*. 3rd edn. Boulder, CO: Paradigm.

Freire, Paolo. 1970. *Pedagogy of the Oppressed*. Translated by Myra Bergman Ramos. New York, NY: Bloomsbury Academic.

Galliher, John F. and James M. Galliher. 1995. *Marginality and Dissent in Twentieth-Century American Sociology: The Case of Elizabeth Briant Lee and Alfred McClung Lee*. Albany, NY: State University of New York Press.

Goodwin, Glenn. 1983. Toward a Paradigm for Humanistic Sociology. *Humanity and Society* 7(3): 219–237.

Gouldner, Alvin W. 1970. *The Coming Crisis of Western Sociology*. New York, NY: Basic Books.

Hess, Beth B. 1999. Breaking and Entering the Establishment: Committing Social Change and Confronting the Backlash. *Social Problems* 46: 1–12.

Hughes, C. Everett. 1963. Race Relations and the Sociological Imagination. *American Sociological Review* 28: 879–890.

Lee, Alfred McClung. 1973. *Toward Humanist Sociology*. Englewood Cliffs, NJ: Prentice-Hall.

Lee, Alfred McClung. 1977. A Different Kind of Sociological Society. *Humanity and Society* 1(1): 1–11.

Lee, Alfred McClung. 1978. *Sociology for Whom?* New York, NY: Oxford University Press.

Lee, Alfred McClung and Elizabeth Briant Lee. 1976. The Society for the Study of Social Problems: Parental Recollections and Hopes. *Social Problems* 24: 4–14.

Mills, C. Wright. 1959. *The Sociological Imagination*. New York, NY: Oxford University Press.

Nicolaus, Martin. 1968. Fat Cat Sociology: Remarks at the American Sociological Association Convention. Available at www.colorado.edu/Sociology/gimenez/fatcat.html, accessed December 7, 2016.

Oppenheimer, Martin, Martin J. Murray, and Rhonda Levine. eds. 1991. *Radical Sociologists and the Movement: Experiences, Lessons, and Legacies*. Philadelphia, PA: Temple University Press.

Park, Robert E. and Ernest W. Burgess. 1969[1921]. *Introduction to the Science of Sociology*. 3rd edn. Chicago, IL: University of Chicago Press.

Scimecca, Joseph A. 1995[1981]. *Society and Freedom: An Introduction to Humanist Sociology*. 2nd edn. Chicago, IL: Nelson-Hall.

Scimecca, Joseph A. and Glenn A. Goodwin. 2003. Jane Addams: The First Humanist Sociologist. *Humanity and Society* 27: 143–157.

Starr, Jerold. 2002. The Association for Humanist Sociology: A Personal Celebration. *The American Sociologist* 33(4): 62–65.

Stoecker, Randy. 2005. *Research Methods for Community Change: A Project-Based Approach*. Thousand Oaks, CA: Sage.

CHAPTER 34
Applied Sociology and Sociotechnics

Harry Perlstadt

Applied Sociology is the oldest term for using sociology. During the twentieth century, however, applied sociology segmented into the sociological areas discussed in the neighboring chapters on Sociology's Impact on Society: Public Sociology, Humanist Sociology, Clinical Sociology, and Teaching Sociology. These, along with Sociotechnics, are collectively referred to as Sociological Practice, which can be defined as using sociology to purposefully improve social conditions in society, social organizations, communities, and/or social groups (Abrams 1985: 181). This chapter will focus on applied sociology and sociotechnics.

Andrew Abbott (1988) distinguished between scientific researchers who develop a body of abstract knowledge and professional practitioners who attempt to interpret and apply that knowledge. To some extent, the history of applied sociology and sociotechnics has been embroiled in clarifications and disputes over jurisdictions between the academic discipline of scientific sociology and the professional practice of sociology. In the United States, the tension between scientific objectivity and the practical objectives of social reform was manageable. This was not the case, however, in Britain where social research was traditionally based outside universities and delayed the acceptance of sociology as a scientific academic discipline (Harley 2012).

Sociologists in the United States prefer the term applied sociology while the European equivalent is sociotechnics. Applied sociology first appeared in an 1892 publication of the Brooklyn New York Ethical Association entitled *Man and the State: Studies in Applied Sociology*. The association was dedicated to the scientific study of ethics, politics, economics, sociology, religion, and philosophy. It considered sociology to be the science of social evolution à la Herbert Spencer, whose 1873 *The Study of Sociology* was the first book with the term "sociology" in its title. The Ethical Association sought to study and discuss the pressing problems of politics and statesmanship confronting the people of the United States (Perlstadt 2006).

Applied sociology uses sociological knowledge and methods to answer research questions or problems as defined by a funding agency or client rather than the researcher (Steele and Price 2007: 4). The primary concern of applied sociologists is less with making a contribution to academic scholarship and more on having a direct influence on clients, stakeholders, or decision-makers (Freeman and Rossi 1984: 572–573). Place of employment is not the crucial determinant for identifying applied sociologists. Sociologists in academic departments, research institutes and centers, and professional schools (medicine, nursing, law, architecture, criminal justice, and education) have conducted non-basic research sponsored by government agencies, private foundations, and businesses. This is despite the claim by Lazarsfeld, Sewell, and Wilensky (1967: xxii) that a Ph.D. in sociology did not really train students for employment outside academia.

Applied Sociology in Britain and the United States

Auguste Comte (1961[1853]: 129), the founder of sociology, divided it into statics, which was the core of sociology, and dynamics, which concerned the continuous progress and gradual development of humanity. He envisioned a "corps of positivist priests" trained as sociologists, who would not possess any temporal power but would provide useful scientific knowledge and social advice in all affairs of civil life (Barnes 1948). They would suggest action to the civil authorities but would never undertake such action on their own responsibility or initiative. It appears that Comte's applied sociologist would be neither a basic researcher nor social activist/interventionist, but rather occupy a translational role between the two.

Philip Abrams (1985: 182; 1968: 7ff) wrote that sociology could be useful if it attempted to close the gap between social knowledge and social action. He identified several interwoven strands in early British sociology: political economy, social statistics, amelioration, and social evolution.

Unlike in the United States, sociology did not become a recognized academic discipline in Britain until the 1950s (Soffer 1982). Nevertheless, the practice of sociology did exist in Britain outside academia in government bureaucracies in the form of "applied administrative research" (McLaughlin 2005: 17).

Although not known as sociologists or sociotechnicians, nineteenth-century *political economists* believed research was needed to verify the natural laws of society – the Invisible Hand and individual self-interest – that could guide social legislation. Malthus thought that disagreements would prove to be the result of an inadequate study of facts rather than conflicts over values or interests. What was needed was neither a laissez-faire nor an interventionist government but an informed government that would apply that knowledge to benefit society. *Social statisticians* sought to gather and evaluate facts on social conditions which could be utilized by government decision-makers (Abrams 1968: 9). This was epitomized in Charles Booth's 1897 *Life and Labour of the People of London*, which used statistics, maps, and case studies.

Amelioration sought to change social conditions related to drunkenness, prostitution, and poverty. The solution, found in the Victorian era moral philosophy of utilitarian Christianity, was to design reforms that would strengthen the moral development of the individual. Absent social theory, research focused on "moral statistics" to support legislation on temperance, sexual conduct, prisons, schools and public health.

Social evolution originated in Herbert Spencer's view that survival of the fittest was the primary and most efficient mechanism of progress. Spencer proposed a universal theory of evolution and stages of development and held that "the greatest purpose of sociology was … to impress upon men the fatuity of efforts to accelerate the improvement of their condition by legislative measures" (Abrams 1968: 73).

Meanwhile in the United States, Lester Ward, who became the first president of the American Sociological Association (ASA) in 1906, published *Dynamic Sociology or Applied Social Science* in 1883. He supported Comte's idea that government can directly improve the conditions of society in a conscious or telic manner if the legislators will only become social scientists or gain acknowledge of the nature and means of controlling social forces and be willing to apply this knowledge (Barnes 1948: 183).

When Congress commissioned a nationwide survey on the slums of great cities in 1893, Florence Kelley and others conducted a door-to-door survey in the Hull House district in Chicago (Perlstadt 2006). Following the lead of Booth, they created a set of maps and papers showing the nationality, wages, and employment history of each resident. In the preface, Jane Addams wrote that the contents are recorded observations, "chiefly directed, not toward sociological investigation, but to constructive work" (Residents of Hull House (1895: vii–viii)). Addams, who co-founded the Hull House settlement, was a charter member of the ASA and published in the *American Journal of Sociology*.

Seba Eldridge wrote *Problems of Community Life: An Outline of Applied Sociology* in 1915. In a review, Robert E. Park declared that it may be "valuable for club discussions or as an aid to the investigations of amateur sociologists. It has no merits as a work of science" (Park 1915). Eldridge, who would later join the University of Kansas sociology department, had done little more than compile a list of problems broken down by their causes, the philanthropies, social reform groups, and municipal agencies providing services, and possible methods to improve the social condition.

In his ASA presidential address, William Ogburn (1930: 300–301) declared that "sociology as a science is not interested in making the world a better place in which to live, ... in leading the multitudes or in guiding the ship of state." He wanted to ensure that scientific methods would be the basis for applied research and to distance it from ethics, religion, social philosophy, journalism, and propaganda. The scientific sociologist would collect data on significant social problems in order to discover new knowledge and relationships which could then be used by executives, leaders, and social workers.

Podgórecki and Sociotechnics

During the first half of the twentieth century, Comte's "corps of positivist priests" became "social engineers," which took on an ominous and decidedly negative connation as practiced under Nazi and Soviet totalitarian regimes (Perlstadt 2006). In response, Polish sociologist Adam Podgórecki (1966; 1996) coined the term *sociotechnics*, which became an area of interest within the Social Engineering Section of the Polish Sociological Association (Podgórecki 1979: 274). It was widely adopted in Europe after he helped form the International Sociological Association's Research Committee 26 on Sociotechnics in 1971. Podgórecki went on to develop a theory of purposive and directed social change, essentially a paradigm for planned social action in democratic and liberal societies in which sociotechnics deals with matters of just and rational social changes.

Given his experiences with the cycle of repression and reform in postwar Communist Poland (Hogsbro et al. 2009: 44), it is not surprising that Podgórecki (1996: 48–49) was concerned about the values and ethics of social engineering and sociotechnics. He identified three types of values: data, operatives and values proper. *Data values* are social statistics similar to Durkheim's social facts and can document the social reality in the group, organization, community or society. *Operative values* determine the variables, target populations, outputs, outcomes and impacts that are to be included in the socio-technical equations or what might be called the program's logic model.[1] The

---

[1] A logic model is used to evaluate the effectiveness of a program. It is presented as a series of boxes or matrix that links outcomes (both short- and long-term) with the theoretical assumptions/principles of the program, its inputs, activities/processes, and outputs.

independent variables generate expected or predictable effects on a selected social problem or public issue, e.g., privatization policies, immigration reform, or climate change. Finally what he termed *values proper* are the normative guides or professional ethics for sociotechnicians, which enabled Podgórecki to label sociotechnicians who do not follow these ethics and produce or support a repressive political doctrine as having succumbed to the dark side á la Darth Vader, the villain in *Star Wars*.

Podgórecki (1996: 26–27) listed four types of social engineering: sociotechnics proper; self-made social engineering; quackish social engineering; and "dark" social engineering. *Sociotechnics proper* provides a method to seek effective ways and means to achieve aims. It is based on a given accepted system of values as well as a usable set of methodologically tested propositions or hypotheses describing and explaining human behavior. *Self-made social engineering* presumes the accumulated wisdom of the given profession or agency to be verified knowledge about the effectiveness of specific social actions. *Quackish social engineering* does not depend on tested and relevant theoretical frameworks but attempts to implement ideologies or social philosophies. Finally, *"dark" social engineering*, as practiced in Nazi Germany and the Soviet Union, can be consciously used to produce harm.

Podgórecki then described five meta models of sociotechnics: classical, clinical, intervention, solicitant, and articulative. *Classical sociotechnicians* submit scientifically sound findings to their sponsors. With permission, they may publish selected results and a final report, but they are not interested in its practical fate. They are consultants, who like Comte's "corps of positivist priests" provide independent opinions but would never undertake action on their own responsibility or initiative. *Clinical sociotechnicians* have a more collaborative relationship helping their clients better understand the agency's goals and desired outcomes. They are often hired when the need for research is imposed on an agency or organization and are able to press for changes as a byproduct of their research.

Intervention sociotechnicians initiate proposals to intervene in various social groups, organizations, or societies. One type of interventionist is an independent social pressure group of experts and professional scholars who hold certain socio-political attitudes and values, e.g., Union of Concerned Scientists. A second is an authoritarian regime that utilizes social science findings to manipulate and eventually subjugate groups with "dark force" sociotechnicians acting as agents. A third presents data to unmask a social program or initiative showing that seemingly beneficial goals stated by governments or powerful organizations are not what they seem to be and/or do not lead to the desired outcomes.

The *Solicitant sociotechnican* is usually an outside change agent who is hired to turn an organization or program around. They have little if any motivation for social service and seek sponsors who value their expertise. They pass over to the "dark side" when they help keep the citizenry under control in authoritarian societies or sell their services to corporations seeking to exploit their workforce. Finally the *Articulative sociotechnican* works with clients to bring to the surface underlying values for mission statements and strategic planning purposes. After weighting and prioritizing these values, the clients then identify goals and action plans to fulfill their mission and vision.

Abrams on the Uses of Sociology

Between them, Podgórecki and Abrams provide the basis for a Sociology of Sociotechnics. Whereas Podgórecki's paradigm is based primarily on experiences in Communist Poland, Abrams derived his perspective on sociology and sociotechnics from the history of sociology in Britain and his interest in closing the gap between social knowledge and social action. Abrams (1985: 183–185) identified different uses of sociology: (1) social engineering, consisting of policy science and sociotechnics; (2) enlightenment in the form of clarification or advocacy; and (3) education.[2]

Policy science is a strong engineering model that hopes to close the gap between knowledge and action by creating an authoritative body of social knowledge for planning a concerted effort to build a better society. This model views politics as inherently irrational and seeks to create a new combination of social scientists and policy-makers whose decisions are universal, impartial and rational. This combines Podgórecki's clinical sociotechnican with Comte's "corps of positivist priests."

For Abrams, *Sociotechnics* is a relatively weak engineering model. Sociotechnicians prefer to negotiate with policy-makers, provide social intelligence (e.g., needs assessments and evaluations) or give advice on data gathering and analysis. Applied sociologists have pioneered evaluation research (Patton 2015), and, according to Hougland (2015), sociologists conducting evaluations should ensure that stakeholders and program administrators understand the rationale for sociologically based measures and explanations, i.e. Podgórecki's operative values.

Sociotechnicians point out conflicts of values or overriding interests in a social program that may produce unintended consequences. They consider themselves as technical functionaries to decision-makers. However, their scientific skepticism may occasionally lead them to challenge the policy and policy-makers, at which point they become "an alarmingly political animal" (Abrams 1985: 184). This combines Podgórecki's clinical sociotechnican who presses for changes as a byproduct of their research, and the third type of interventionist who unmasks the shortcomings of social action programs.

Clarification is a strong but passive version of sociology as enlightenment (see Janowitz 1970). Sociologists reformulate social issues by challenging or elucidating assumptions or misconceptions and changing the language of public discourse about the problem. They publish their conclusions in scholarly journals or books, and their contribution is judged on its merits. Occasionally it may eventually become general knowledge. Closing the gap between knowledge and action is seen as a political matter best left to others. This model resembles Podgórecki's classical sociotechnican in its scholarly orientation and avoidance of politics.

Advocacy shares the basic enlightenment view that the relationship between knowledge and action is complex. Therefore, the sociological advocate may promote a preferred reading of the sociological evidence and may enter a partnership with policy-makers who favor that way of interpreting the data. Apparently aware of Podgórecki's intervention sociotechnican, Abrams cautions that it is important to bring empirical evidence to the support of a good cause.

Finally the *Educational* use of sociology holds that sociology has a body of authoritative knowledge and an array of methods and techniques for social inquiry and analysis. Both can be widely disseminated to the next generation through textbooks and lectures to help them understand and solve social problems in a rational, efficient, and sensitive manner.

A Sociology of Sociotechnics

Sociotechnics can be practiced at the micro-, meso-, and macro-levels of operations (Podgórecki 1996: 45–47), but sociological theory and methods are not always required. For example, sociological theory and data might not be needed to solve the *micro-level* problem of reducing waiting time for elevators by having a group of floors served by a different set of elevators. On the *meso-* or *sectoral level*, improving the status of women in the work force could take into account the sociological concept of reducing relative deprivation. The solution of raising women's salaries to parity with men,

---

[2] The reader is invited to compare Podgórecki's and Abram's types of sociotechnics and uses of sociology with the topics covered in other chapters in Part VIII of this handbook.

however, requires data but not much sociological imagination or theory.

The *macro-* or *state/society level*, however, would require sociological theories and hypotheses that are international in scope, for example, grand theory or world systems, or self-made socio-technical theories accounting for the apparently spontaneous strategies in a specific society. To this end, Podgórecki et al. (1996) present a set of case studies, covering among others, Nixon and the Watergate scandal; Jaruzelski's imposition of martial law in an attempt to crush Solidarity, the first non-Communist trade union in Eastern Europe; and lessons from the Canadian anti-smoking campaign of the late 1980s, as building blocks for a sociology of sociotechnics.

If Podgórecki was trying to construct a sociology of sociotechnics, Abrams held a more skeptical view. He argued that the most useful thing sociotechnic research accomplished was to discredit the assumptions on which yesterday's sociotechnics was based (Abrams 1985: 186–190). For example, starting in the 1830s, many assumed that collecting data from social statistics and surveys and then presenting them uncontaminated by theory would validate religious and ideological postulates thereby opening the way for government to implement appropriate policies. The data and findings, however, revealed the existence of complicated social structures and challenged the laissez-faire atomistic model of society which focused on individual morality and responsibility. Throughout most of the nineteenth century, data collected by British social statisticians revealed that poverty was not the result of moral or personal weakness.

This ambiguity over the usefulness of sociotechnics existed into the twentieth century. In 1963, the British Secretary of State for Education and Science established the Heyworth Committee, which was charged with reviewing social science research being done in government departments, universities, and other institutions and suggesting a funding regime for social research (Blume 1987; King 1997). The committee met with groups of academics and users/consumers of sociology including government officials, industry leaders, town planners, and social service administrators.

While some academics valued the study of social science as an end in itself, a majority thought that it could contribute to planning a better society or at least averting major policy disasters. The users/consumers were somewhat disappointed with the existing work of social scientists, but attributed this partly to their own inability to guide the work of social scientists and partly to the preference of social scientists to investigate problems that interested themselves rather than their potential clients. The final report recommended a strong commitment to social research for policy-making, while expressing significant reservations about its practicality. Abrams (1985: 191) concluded that the report was widely labeled by disappointed politicians and administrators as "useless." In essence, attempts to use social knowledge for sociotechnical purposes served to reveal the limits of sociotechnics.

I suggest that Abrams did not distinguish *sociological* theories, for example, role, reference group, and resource mobilization, from *social* theories such as political ideologies, religious tenets, and ethical principles that underlie government, business, or educational policies intended to guide decision-makers. Sociologists test sociological theories and hypotheses to generate abstract knowledge about social groups, communities, organizations, and society, while applied sociologists and sociotechnicians test the assumptions embedded in policies, initiatives and demonstration projects intended to achieve some positive benefit or avoid some negative effect. By highlighting false assumptions and documenting what works, applied research provides a guide for the next round of policy and programs.

Abrams (1985: 188–189) proposed that sociotechnics flourishes best when a dominant consensus exists about social objectives. For example, during a war or economic depression, government will demand social intelligence to develop policies and attain its goals. In Britain, sociologists participated in wartime social surveys, creating a central statistical office and developing national health coverage. In the United States, Samuel Stouffer et al. (1949) conducted a series of large-scale surveys for the US Army during World War II to document the attitudes of soldiers in order to inform personnel and related policies.

These government uses of sociology led to the increasing use of sociologists on advisory committees and commissions and in research positions in government, business, and non-profits/non-governmental organizations. Abrams (1985: 202) observed, however, that although some sociological studies and concepts are recognized as valuable by society, they often become commonsense and are no longer perceived as sociological, while sociology itself is often thought to be either laughable or subversive. This view is supported by Halsey (1994: 132) who noted that Conservative politicians (Tories) and the media consider sociology to be "a polysyllabic plague promoting the subversion of the political order" (i.e., promoting social change over the status quo).

Applied sociology or sociotechnics, which seeks to improve society through empirical research, is a type of critical sociology in that it focuses on the need for and means to attain social change. The findings may show a policy or program is effective and efficient, reveal inconvenient outcomes or side-effects, or conclude that the effort failed. US examples include the evaluation of the Affordable Care Act/Obamacare (Collins et al. 2015) and an examination of whether or not community boards in New York City neighborhoods engage all stakeholders in meaningful or sustained ways (Hum 2010).

Such findings may dispel illusions, reformulate the social problem, or change the language of public discourse about the problem. I contend that when this happens, applied sociologists and sociotechnics create cognitive dissonance for those who sincerely and strongly hold an ideological or pragmatic view on the problem and its solution (Perlstadt 2013). This cognitive dissonance is then relieved by either denigrating sociology or ignoring and quickly forgetting what the findings revealed.

Furthering Applied Sociology and Sociotechnics

In my opinion, the future of applied sociology lies in two directions: improving the training of sociologists for employment outside traditional research oriented academic departments and building a body of knowledge and case studies on sociotechnics, i.e. a sociology of sociotechnics.

In the United States, sociologists with terminal masters degrees are those most likely to enter sociological practice. They work in institutional research offices at colleges and universities, or are employed in research positions in business, non-profit, and government agencies (Van Vooren and Spalter-Roth 2011). Many sociology departments recognize that a growing proportion of their graduates pursue careers that are in applied, clinical, or public settings rather than in teaching or basic research. The Commission on the Accreditation of Programs in Applied and Clinical Sociology (CAPACS) recognizes graduate and undergraduate programs that provide high-quality training in sociological practice.

Professional schools utilize case studies to familiarize students with the processes and problems of practice. The cases in Podgórecki et al. (1996) are just the beginning. US cases that could be added include Alexander Hamilton empowering the executive branch and stabilizing federal finances; Isidore Falk's work on the Committee on the Costs of Medical Care and the Social Security Administration; Daniel Patrick Moynihan and the war on poverty; and on the dark side, Project Camelot, a counter-insurgency study to analyze the society and culture of Latin America.

Finally, one case that contributed to both sociology and human relations management was conducted at the Hawthorn Plant of the Western Electric Company from 1927 to 1932 (Landsberger 1958). The researchers observed workers in three test rooms and discovered the experimenter or Hawthorn effect, whereby behavior changes when people are observed or receive unanticipated attention. They also found that group dynamics, including work group norms and social interactions, impact worker productivity.

While sociology as a discipline may have difficulty being appreciated in an era of individualism and political conservatism, the practice of sociology has much to contribute. The movement toward evidence-based decision-making will require that applied sociologists and sociotechnicians conduct research to test social theories and assumptions before developing and implementing social policies and programs.

References

Abbott, Andrew. 1988. *The System of Professions: An Essay on the Division of Expert Labor.* Chicago, IL: University of Chicago Press.

Abrams, Philip. 1968. *The Origins of British Sociology, 1834–1914.* Chicago, IL: University of Chicago Press.

Abrams, Phillip. 1985. *The Uses of British Sociology.* In *Essays on the History of British Sociological Research.* Edited by Martin Bulmer. Cambridge. Cambridge University Press, 1831–1981.

Barnes, Harry Elmer. 1948. *An Introduction to the History of Sociology.* Chicago, IL: University of Chicago Press.

Blume, Stuart S. 1987. Social Science in Whitehall: Two Analytic Perspectives. In *Social Science Research and Government: Comparative Essays on Britain and the United States.* Edited by Martin Bulmer. Cambridge: Cambridge University Press.

Booth, Charles. 1897. *Life and Labour of the People of London.* New York: MacMillan and Co.

Collins, S. R., P. W. Rasmussen, S. Beutel, and M. M. Doty. 2015. *The Problem of Underinsurance and how Rising Deductibles Will Make It Worse – Findings from the Commonwealth Fund Biennial Health Insurance Survey,* The Commonwealth Fund. Available at www.commonwealthfund.org/publications/issue-briefs/2015/may/problem-of-underinsurance, accessed December 7, 2016.

Comte, Auguste. 1961[1853]. Society and Government. In *Theories of Society: Foundations of Modern Sociological Theory.* Edited by Talcott Parsons, Edward Shils, Kasper D. Naegele, and Jesse R. Pitts. New York, NY: Free Press of Glencoe.

Eldridge, Selba. 1915. *Problems of Community Life: An Outline of Applied Sociology.* New York, NY: Thomas Y. Crowell.

Freeman, Howard E. and Peter H. Rossi. 1984. Furthering the Applied Side of Sociology. *American Sociological Review* 49(4): 571–580.

Halsey. A. H. 1994. Sociology as Political Arithmetic. *British Journal of Sociology* 48: 427–444.

Harley, Kristin. 2012. Sociology's Objects, Objectivity and Objectives: Successes and Failures in Establishing the Discipline in America, England and Australia before 1945. *Journal of Sociology* 48: 410–426.

Hogsbro, Kjeld, Hans Pruijt, Nikita Porrovsky, and George Tsobanoglou. 2009. Sociological Practice and the Sociotechnics of Governance. In *ISA Handbook in Contemporary Sociology.* Edited by Ann Denis and Devorah Kalek Fishman. Thousand Oaks, CA: Sage.

Hougland, James G. Jr. 2015. Sociology as a Partial Influence on Evaluation Research. *American Sociologist.* On line DOI 10.1007/S12108-015-9273-X.

Hum, Tarry. 2010. Planning on Neighborhoods with Multiple Publics: Opportunities and Challenges for Community-Based Nonprofit Organizations. *Journal of Planning Education and Research* 29: 461–477.

Janowitz, Morris. 1970. *Political Conflict.* Chicago, IL: University of Chicago Press.

King, Desmond. 1997. Creating a Funding Regime for Social Research in Britain: The Heyworth Committee on Social Studies and the Founding of the Social Science Research Council. *Minerva* 35: 1–26.

Landsberger, Henry A. 1958. *Hawthorne Revisited.* Ithaca, New York, NY: The New York State School of Industrial and Labor Relations.

Lazarsfeld. P. F., W. H. Sewell, and H. L. Wilensky. 1967. *The Uses of Sociology.* New York, NY: Basic Books.

McLaughlin, N. 2005. Canada's Impossible Science: Historical and Institutional Origins of the Coming Crisis in Anglo-Canadian Sociology. *Canadian Journal of Sociology/Cahiers Canadiens De Sociologie* 30: 1–40.

Ogburn, W. F. 1930. The Folkways of Scientific Sociology. *Scientific Monthly* 30: 300–306.

Park, Robert, E. 1915. Reviewed Work: *Problems of Community Life. An Outline of Applied Sociology*. By Seba Eldridge. *American Journal of Sociology* 21: 121.

Patton, Michael Quinn. 2015. The Sociological Roots of Utilization-Focused Evaluation. *American Sociologist*. On line DOI 10.1007/S12108-015-9275-8.

Perlstadt, Harry. 2006. Applied Sociology. In *21st Century Sociology: A Reference Handbook*. Vol. 2. Edited by Clifton D. Bryant and Dennis L. Peck. Thousand Oaks, CA: Sage.

Perlstadt, Harry. 2013. Political Ideology, Party Identification and Perceptions of Health Disparities: An Exploratory Study of Cognitive and Moral Prejudice. In *Social Determinants, Health Disparities and Linkages to Health and Health Care: Research in the Sociology of Health Care*. Vol. 31. Social Determinants. Edited by Jennie Jacobs Kronenfeld. Bingley, UK: Emerald Group Publishing Ltd.

Podgórecki, Adam. 1966. *Zasady Socjotechniki* ("Principles of Sociotechnics"). Warszawa: Wiedza Powszechna.

Podgórecki, Adam. 1979. Definition and Scope of Sociotechnics. In *Multi-Dimensional Sociology*. Edited by Adam Podgórecki and Maria Łoś. London, Routledge and Kegan Paul.

Podgórecki, Adam. 1996. Sociotechnics: Basic Concepts and Issues. In *Social Engineering*. Edited by A. Podgórecki, J. Alexander, and R. Shields. Kingston: Ontario: McGill-Queen's Press.

Podgórecki, A., J. Alexander, and R. Shields. 1996. *Social Engineering*. Kingston: Ontario: McGill-Queen's Press.

Residents of Hull House. 1895. *A Presentation of Nationalities and Wages in a Congested District of Chicago, Together with Comments and Essays on Problems Growing Out of the Social Conditions*. New York, NY: Thomas Y. Crowell.

Soffer, Reba N. 1982. Why Do Disciplines Fail? The Strange Case of British Sociology. *The English Historical Review* 97: 767–802.

Spencer, Herbert. 1873. *The Study of Sociology*. London: H. S. King.

Steele, Steven F. and Jammie Price. 2007. *Applied Sociology: Terms, Topics, Tools and Tasks*. 2nd edn. Belmont, CA: Thomson Wadsworth Publishing.

Stouffer, Samuel A., E. A. Suchman, L. C. Devinney, S. A. Star, and R. M. Williams, Jr. 1949. *Studies in Social Psychology in World War II: The American Soldier*. Vol. 1. Adjustment during Army Life. Princeton, NJ: Princeton University Press.

Van Vooren, Nicole, and Roberta Spalter-Roth. 2011. *Sociology Master's Graduates Join the Workforce*. Washington, DC: The American Sociological Association.

Ward, Lester. 1883. *Dynamic Sociology or Applied Social Science*. New York, NY: D. Appleton and Company.

CHAPTER 35

Clinical Sociology

Jan Marie Fritz

Clinical sociology, one of the fields that pairs science and action, is a humanistic, creative and multidisciplinary endeavor that seeks to improve the quality of people's lives (e.g., Fritz 1985; Fritz 2008: 1; Fritz and Rhéaume 2014). Clinical sociologists assess situations and attempt to understand issues and/or reduce problems through analysis and intervention. Clinical analysis is the critical assessment of beliefs, policies, and/or practices with an interest in improving the situation. Intervention, the creation of new systems as well as the change of existing systems, is based on continuing analysis.

Clinical sociologists usually work in a collaborative way. For example, Jean-Philippe Bouilloud, who is with ESCP Europe (an international business school), employs the "clinical tradition of co-construction of solutions" as well as role-playing when he works with companies (Fritz 2012: 399). And French sociologist Vincent de Gaulejac uses two main approaches in his research and intervention – "organizing groups of involvement and retrieval in which participants work on their life history" and "organidromes" (in which participants analyze the causes "of conflict structures at work or in social life") (Fritz 2012: 399).

Clinical sociologists work at various levels – from the individual to the global. Even though clinical sociologists each tend to specialize in one or two levels of intervention (e.g., marriage counseling, community consulting, national policy development), the practitioner will move among a number of the levels (e.g., individual, small group, organization, community, society, inter-societal, global) in order to analyze and/or intervene.

Clinical sociologists work in many different capacities. They are, for example, scholar-practitioners,[1] policy-makers, action researchers, community organizers, consultants, sociotherapists, mediators, focus-group facilitators, social policy implementers, and administrators. Judith Blau, for instance, was a university professor when she founded the Human Rights

---

[1] Scholar-practitioners study/write about topics (frequently while holding university positions) and also undertake some kind of practice (clinical or applied work).

Center in the town of Carrboro, North Carolina (Fritz and Rhéaume 2014) and Italy's Association of Clinical Sociology "runs a house for people with social problems and two multifunctional centers for children" (Gargano 2008: 155).

The next section discusses the history of clinical sociology with an emphasis on its international settings. The following sections are about clinical sociology developments in the United States and the theories and research methods used by clinical sociologists.

The History of Global Clinical Sociology

Clinical sociology is as old as the field of sociology, and its roots are found in many parts of the world. Clinical sociology can be traced back to the fourteenth-century work of the Arab scholar and statesperson Abd-al-Rahman ibn Khaldûn (1332–1406) (Fritz 1985). Ibn Khaldûn held many positions including secretary of state to the ruler of Morocco and chief judge of Egypt.

Auguste Comte (1798–1857), Emile Durkheim (1858–1917), and Karl Marx (1818–1883) are frequently identified as precursors to or initial figures in the development of sociological practice (Fritz 2008). Comte, a French scholar, believed that the scientific study of societies would provide the basis for social action. Harry Perlstadt (2007: 342–343) notes Comte's "translational role" between basic research and "activists/interventionists." Emile Durkheim's work on the relation between levels of influence (e.g., social in relation to individual factors) led Alvin Gouldner (1965) to write that "more than any other classical sociologist (Durkheim) used a clinical model." Karl Marx, as Alfred McClung Lee noted in 1979, brought to his written work "the grasp of human affairs only possible through extensive involvement in praxis..., social action,...agitation, and...social organization" (Lee 1979).

The first use of the term "clinical sociology" was in Spain in 1899 (Fritz and Rhéaume 2014), but some of the best examples of continuous work in the field come from France, French Canada, and Italy. French is the language of many of the current international clinical sociology conferences, and many publications clearly linked to clinical sociology have appeared in Quebec, Canada, and France. French-speaking clinical sociologists emphasize clinical analysis and frequently focus on the relationship between psychology and sociology. They established a solid international network in sociology; have done an excellent job of attracting psychologists and professionals in other fields to their network; and have an extensive publication record. This record includes writing by the Van Bockstaeles and their colleagues (1963); Enriquez (1997); Enriquez et al. (1993); Gaulejac and Roy (1993); and Sevigny (1997).

During the last twenty years, Italians have hosted sociological practice conferences and workshops, offered a graduate program in clinical sociology, established associations of clinical sociologists and professional sociologists and published clinical sociology books and articles (e.g., Tosi and Battisti (1995); Luison (1998); Corsale (2008)).

Clinical sociology is also found in other parts of the world. Of particular interest are developments in China (Li 1999), Greece (e.g., Rigas and Papadaki 2008), Brazil (Takeuti and Niewiadomski 2009), Japan (e.g., Noguchi 2008), and Malaysia (Wan 2004a). Mexico, Brazil, France, Canada, Italy, the United States, Spain, Greece, Japan, Uruguay, and South Africa are among those countries that have hosted international conferences in clinical sociology. The *Indian Journal of Applied and Clinical Sociology* should be mentioned here, as well as the particularly large number of sociology students that study clinical sociology at the University of Johannesburg and North West University in South Africa.

The international development of clinical sociology is supported primarily by three organizations. The International Sociological Association (ISA) is home to the clinical sociology division (RC46) that was organized in 1982 at the ISA World Congress in Mexico City as well as the division on sociotechnics/sociological practice (RC26). Other major influences are the clinical sociology section of the Association internationale des sociologues de la langue française (AISLF, International Association of French Language Sociologists) and the clinical sociology division of l'Association française de sociologie (l'AFS, the French Sociology Association). All these groups hold conferences and encourage publication. The clinical sociology division of the ISA, for example, has co-sponsored a book about teaching clinical sociology (Fritz 2006) and developed a book about effective community intervention (Fritz and Rhéaume 2014).

The History of Clinical Sociology in the United States

Sociology in the United States emerged as a discipline in the 1890s at a time when the nation was struggling with issues of democracy, capitalism, and social justice. Frustration led to public protests and the development of reform organizations. In this climate, it is not surprising that many of the early sociologists were scholar-practitioners interested in reducing or solving the pressing social problems that confronted their communities.

Albion Small, chair of the Department of Sociology at the University of Chicago and founding editor of *The American Journal of Sociology*, published "Scholarship and Social Agitation" in 1896. Small thought the primary reason for the existence of sociology was its "practical application to the improvement of social life" (Timasheff and Theodorson 1976: 2). In Small's (1896: 564) words:

> Let us go about our business with the understanding that within the scope of scholarship there is first science, and second something better than science. That something better is first prevision by means of science, and second intelligent direction of endeavor to realize visions. I would have American scholars, especially in the social sciences, declare their independence of do-nothing traditions. I would have them repeal the law of custom which bars marriage of thought with action. I would have them become more profoundly and sympathetically scholarly by enriching the wisdom which comes from knowing with the larger wisdom which comes from doing.

Clinical Sociology as a Concept

While many of the first sociologists in the United States were interested in practice, the earliest known proposal using the words "clinical sociology" was put forward by Milton C. Winternitz, a physician who was dean of the Yale School of Medicine from 1920 through 1935 (Fritz 1989). At least as early as 1929, Winternitz began developing a plan to establish a department of clinical sociology within Yale's medical school.[2] Winternitz wanted each medical student to have a chance to analyze cases based on a medical specialty as well as a specialty in clinical sociology. Winternitz thought of medicine as a social science and that "obtaining the data in regard to the individual in relation to society must be considered of just as great importance to the (medical) student as obtaining a physical history" (Fritz 1989). One of his most forceful statements in support of the field appeared in his 1930–1931 annual report which stated, in part: "Not only in medicine and in law, but probably in many other fields of activity, the broad preparation of the clinical sociologist is essential..."

---

[2] Winternitz vigorously sought financial backing for his proposal for many years from the Rosenwald Fund, but was unable to obtain support for a department of clinical sociology. He did note, however, the success of a course in the medical schools' section on public health that was based on the clinical sociology plan.

The first discussion of clinical sociology by a sociologist was Louis Wirth's (1931a) article, "Clinical Sociology," in *The American Journal of Sociology*. That same year, Wirth (1931b) also wrote a career development pamphlet which stated:

> The various activities that have grown up around child-guidance clinics, penal and correctional institutions, the courts, police systems, and similar facilities designed to deal with problems of misconduct have increasingly turned to sociologists to become members of their professional staffs.

Wirth "urged (sociology students) to become specialists in one of the major divisions of sociology, such as social psychology, urban sociology ... or clinical sociology."

In 1931, Saul Alinsky was a University of Chicago student enrolled in Ernest Burgess's clinical sociology course. Three years later, Alinsky's (1934) article, "A Sociological Technique in Clinical Criminology," appeared in the *Proceedings of the Sixty-Fourth Annual Congress of the American Prison Association*. Alinsky, best known now for his work in community organizing, was, in 1934, a staff sociologist and member of the classification board of the Illinois State Penitentiary.

In 1944, the first formal definition of clinical sociology appeared in H. P. Fairchild's *Dictionary of Sociology*. The author, Alfred McClung Lee, wrote, in part, that clinical sociology "reports and synthesizes the experiences of (a) social psychiatrists with functional problems of individual adaptation and (b) societal technicians with functional problems of institutional adjustments." Lee was one of the founders of the Society for the Study of Social Problems, the Association for Humanist Sociology, and the Clinical Sociology Association. He was also president of the American Sociological Association from 1976 to 1977.

Edward McDonagh's "An Approach to Clinical Sociology" was published in 1944. McDonagh, who later became the chair of the Department of Sociology and Dean of Social and Behavioral Sciences at Ohio State University, proposed establishing social research clinics that would use groups to study and solve problems.

In 1946, George Edmund Haynes's "Clinical Methods in Interracial and Intercultural Relations" was included in *The Journal of Educational Sociology*. Haynes was a co-founder of the National Urban League (1910) and the first African American to hold a US government sub-cabinet post. His 1946 article, written while he was executive secretary of the Department of Race Relations at the Federal Council of the Churches of Christ in America, discussed the department's urban clinics. The clinics were designed to deal with interracial tensions and conflicts by developing limited, concrete programs of action.

The First University Courses

The first clinical sociology course was taught by Ernest W. Burgess at the University of Chicago in the late 1920s (Fritz 2008). The university catalogs did not include a description of the clinical sociology course, but it was always listed under the social pathology grouping. The courses in this section dealt with topics such as criminality, punishment, criminal law, organized crime, and personal disorganization.

Many students enrolled in these first clinical sociology courses were placed in child guidance clinics. Clarence E. Glick, for instance, was the staff sociologist at the Lower North Side Child Guidance Clinic, and Leonard Cottrell was the clinical sociologist at the South Side Child Guidance Clinic.

Two other universities – Tulane University and New York University – offered clinical sociology courses in the 1930s (Fritz 2008). The Tulane University course was designed to give students the opportunity to learn about behavior problems and social therapy.

The New York University course, taught by Harvey Warren Zorbaugh, provided undergraduate and graduate preparation for visiting teachers, educational counselors, clinicians, social workers, and school guidance administrators. This course was part of a program which focused on the solution of educational problems and other social dilemmas. Zorbaugh, a faculty member in the School of Education, co-taught a "Seminar in Clinical Practice" in 1930. The course was intended to qualify students as counselors or advisers dealing with behavioral difficulties in schools. From 1931 through 1933, the clinical practice course, titled "Seminar in Clinical Sociology," was open to graduate students who were engaged in writing theses or conducting research projects in educational guidance and social work.

Zorbaugh, author of *The Gold Coast and the Slum: A Sociological Study of Chicago's Near North Side* (1929) and "Sociology in the Clinic" (1939), had been involved with clinics since at least 1924, when Clifford Shaw and Zorbaugh organized two sociological clinics in Chicago. Zorbaugh was associate director of the Lower North Child Guidance Clinic in 1925 and also a founder, in 1928, of New York University's Clinic for the Social Adjustment of the Gifted. Zorbaugh was director of this clinic for intellectually gifted and talented preadolescent children at its inception and was actively involved in its work for over fifteen years. The clinic gave graduate students the opportunity to have supervised experiences in teaching, clinical diagnosis, and treatment of children.

During the 1953–54 academic year, Alvin W. Gouldner taught a "Foundations of Clinical Sociology" course at Antioch College in Ohio (Fritz 2008). The college bulletin provided the following description of the course:

> A sociological counterpart to clinical psychology with the group as the unit of diagnosis and therapy. Emphasis on developing skills useful in the diagnosis and therapy of group tensions. Principles of functional analysis, group dynamics, and organizational and small group analysis examined and applied to case histories. Representative research in the area assessed.

Contemporary Developments

While publications mentioning clinical sociology appeared at least every few years after the 1930s, the number of publications increased substantially after the founding of the Clinical Sociology Association in 1978 (Fritz 2008). The Association, which later became the Sociological Practice Association, made publications a high priority, particularly in its early years. The *Clinical Sociology Review* and the theme journal, *Sociological Practice*, were published by the Association beginning in the early 1980s. These annual journals were eventually replaced by *Sociological Practice: A Journal of Clinical and Applied Sociology*, a quarterly publication.

The Clinical Sociology Association/Sociological Practice Association had a central role in the development of American clinical sociology (Fritz 2008). The Association helped make available the world's most extensive collection of teaching, research, and intervention literature (e.g., Fritz 2001; Straus 2004) under the label of clinical sociology and, in the 1980s, introduced the only clinical sociology certification process.

The Sociological Practice Association and the Society for Applied Sociology merged in 2005. The name of the new association – the Association for Applied and Clinical Sociology (AACS) – once again gave name recognition to clinical sociology. AACS (www.aacsnet.net), sponsor of the *Journal of Applied Social Science*, continues to make certification available to clinical and applied sociologists from the United States and other countries at both the M.A. and Ph.D. levels.

The Sociological Practice Association and the Society for Applied Sociology also put in place a commission to accredit practice programs. The Commission on the Accreditation of Programs in Applied and Clinical Sociology (www.sociologycommission.org) developed standards for the accreditation of clinical, applied, sociological practice and engaged public sociology programs at the undergraduate, master's and doctoral levels. Sociological practice is the "umbrella term," for applied (research for practical purposes) and clinical (analysis and intervention) programs. Engaged public sociology refers only to those public sociology programs that meet the standards for sociological practice, applied or clinical programs.

Theories and Research Methods

Clinical sociologists with graduate-level degrees frequently have training in more than one discipline (e.g., psychology, public policy, management) and a great deal of experience in working with intervention teams whose members have a variety of backgrounds. Because of this, clinical sociologists integrate and use a broad range of theoretical approaches[3] and, if they conduct research or collaborate with researchers, also have exposure to or use a range of research methods.

Research Methods

Clinical sociologists who conduct research use a wide variety of research methods and techniques such as participatory action research,[4] geographic information systems, evaluations, focus-group analysis, and surveys. But clinical sociologists probably are best known for their case studies. Case studies involve systematically assembling and analyzing detailed, in-depth information about a person, place, event, or group. This methodological approach involves many techniques such as document analysis, life histories, in-depth interviews, and participant observation.

Sometimes the cases are directly related to intervention work (e.g., a critical evaluation of program outcomes) and sometimes they are analyses of situations (real or based on reality) that will be of assistance to policy-makers and administrators who are considering interventions. An example of that kind of work is the analysis of the tobacco control interventions in "Well City" (Fritz et al. 2000), which includes a list of lessons/ intervention considerations.

Those clinical sociologists who conduct research may do so before beginning an intervention project to assess the existing state of affairs, during an intervention, and/or after the completion of the intervention to evaluate the outcomes. For some clinical sociologists, the research activity is an important part of their own clinical work. Other clinical sociologists prefer to concentrate on the interventions and leave any research to other team members.

Theories and Models

Clinical sociologists, in good part because of their interdisciplinary training and work experience, use a wide range of theories. Clinical sociologists use existing theory to formulate models (guidelines) that will be helpful in identifying and understanding issues and identifying strategies to reduce or solve problems. Clinical sociologists have shown that practice can have an influence on existing theories and help in the development of new ones.

Each of the areas of practice can have its own theories and models. It might be useful to briefly discuss one area of practice – mediation – to begin to understand the complexity of choosing appropriate theories and models (Fritz 2014). Mediation is defined here as a flexibly-structured, creative process in which one or more impartial individuals assist disputants (Fritz 2004; Fritz 2014).

Stage models are frequently used for organizational and community disputes.

---

[3] For example, South African Tina Uys (2015) says she is "eclectic" in terms of the theoretical approaches she uses regarding whistleblowing, her area of specialization.

[4] French-Canadian Robert Sevigny (Fritz 2012), for instance, has been a consultant for a range of organizations and notes that his own work "has always been on the qualitative side" with an emphasis on "participation and communication." He says he has used "a participatory or action research approach whenever possible." And Emma Porio (Fritz 2012), a clinical sociologist from the Philippines, says she "favors (participatory research) as her approach to housing, social justice and other urban issues."

While a seven-stage model[5] is popular in the United States, other models may have from three to twelve stages. There may be differences, at times, in the order of the stages (e.g., a mediation conducted once a week may find events during the week require that a previous stage needs to be reopened for discussion) or the length of time devoted to certain stages (e.g., if an unexpected site visit needs to be included in the mediation). There will also be differences in the way and extent that mediators and organizations that hire mediators rely on the models.

The models used by mediators from the United States are related to their approaches to mediation (e.g., participant-centered, solution-oriented, transformative, narrative, and humanist/integrated process) (Fritz 2004). The models and these approaches are grounded in a range of theories (e.g., biological, psychological, social, land based).

Dispute intervention can lead to theories, models, and intervention strategies being adjusted as the work proceeds. New or refined models, theories, and intervention strategies are seen as a normal part and/or outcome of the creative mediation process.

Conclusion

It is clear there is global interest in clinical sociology. While there is a common core (e.g., conceptual framework, acceptance of a wide range of theories and research methods), there are differences. First, in some countries, clinical sociologists are more interested in providing analyses to policy-makers and the public (e.g., France) than in undertaking intervention (e.g., the United States) and there can be differences in their areas of focus.[6] Second, in certain circumstances, practitioners may usually introduce themselves as *sociological* practitioners, clinical *sociologists*, public *sociologists* or applied *sociologists*, while in other settings, the labels practitioners use may be connected to the work they do (e.g., analyst, consultant, policy researcher, therapist) rather than to the discipline of sociology. The latter approach can make it difficult to easily recognize the sociological practice tradition in a country. Finally, it must be noted that while scholar-practitioners in certain areas of the world (the United States, French Canada, and France) have had important roles in the development of clinical sociology, there are now many other national and regional influences (e.g., South Africa, Uruguay) that will help shape the future of this global specialization.

References

Alinsky, Saul. 1934. A Sociological Technique in Clinical Criminology. In *Proceedings of the Sixty-Fourth Annual Congress of the American Prison Association* (September 17–21), 167–178.

Beer, Jennifer E. with Eileen Stief. 1997. *The Mediator's Handbook*. Gabriola Island, British Columbia, Canada: New Society Publishers.

Corsale, Massimo. ed. 2008. Monographic Section on Health and Illness Problems Faced by Clinical Sociologists. *International Revue of Sociology* 18(3): 415–517.

Enriquez, Eugene. 1997. The Clinical Approach: Genesis and Development in Western Europe. *International Sociology* 12(2) (June): 151–164.

Enriquez, Eugene, Gilles Houle, Jacques Rhéaume, and Robert Sevigny. eds. 1993. *L'analyse clinique dans les sciences humaines*. Montreal: Editions Saint-Martin.

Fritz, Jan Marie. 1985. *The Clinical Sociology Handbook*. New York, NY: Garland.

Fritz, Jan Marie. 1989. Dean Winternitz, Clinical Sociology and the Julius Rosenwald Fund. *Clinical Sociology Review* 7: 17–27. Available at http://digitalcommons.wayne.edu/csr/vol7/iss1/4, accessed December 7, 2016.

Fritz, Jan Marie. ed. 2001. *The Clinical Sociology Resource Book*. 5th edn. Washington, DC: American Sociological Association Teaching Resources Center and the Sociological Practice Association.

---

[5] See, for instance, Beer with Stief's model (1997) in which the seven stages are opening, listening to each party, discussion, deciding on topics, identifying possible options, decisions, and written agreement.

[6] For instance, clinical sociology in Japan focuses on health, illness and disability.

Fritz, Jan Marie. 2004. Derrière la magie: Modèles, approches et théories de médiation (Behind the Magic: Mediation Models, Approaches and Theories). *Esprit Critique*. 6(3)(Ete).

Fritz, Jan Marie. 2006. L'approccio al conflitto (Approaching Conflict). In *La Mediazone come strumento di intervento sociale (Mediation as an Instrument of Social Intervention*. Edited by Lucio Luison and Jan Marie Fritz. Milano, Italy: Francoangeli.

Fritz, Jan Marie. 2008. *International Clinical Sociology*. New York, NY: Springer.

Fritz, Jan Marie. 2012. Practicing Sociology: Clinical Sociology and Human Rights. In *Handbook of Sociology and Human Rights*. Edited by David Brunsma, Keri Smith, and Brian Gran. Boulder, CO: Paradigm, 394–401.

Fritz, Jan Marie. ed. 2014. *Moving Toward a Just Peace: The Mediation Continuum*. Dordrecht/Heidelberg/New York, NY/London: Springer.

Fritz, Jan Marie and Jacques Rhéaume. eds. 2014. *Community Intervention*. Dordrecht/Heidelberg/New York, NY/London: Springer.

Fritz, Jan Marie, Paula Bistak, and Christopher Auffrey. 2000. The Bumpy Road to a Tobacco-Free Community: Lessons from Well City. *Sociological Practice* 2(2)(June): 113–126.

Gargano, Giuseppe. 2008. Art and Science in Italian Clinical Sociology. In *International Clinical Sociology*. Edited by Jan Marie Fritz. New York, NY: Springer, 153–169.

Gaulejac, Vincent De, and Shirley Roy. eds. 1993. *Sociologies Cliniques*. Paris: Hommes et Perspectives.

Gouldner, Alvin. 1965. Explorations in Applied Social Science. *Social Problems* 3(3)(January): 169–81. Reprinted (5–22) in Alvin Gouldner and S. M. Miller. eds. *Applied Sociology*. New York, NY: Free Press.

Haynes, George E. 1946. Clinical Methods in Interracial and Intercultural Relations. *The Journal of Educational Sociology*. 19(5)(January): 316–325.

Lee, Alfred McClung. 1944. Sociology, Clinical. In *Dictionary of Sociology*. Edited by H. P. Fairchild. New York, NY: Philosophical Library, 303.

Lee, Alfred McClung. 1979. The Services of Clinical Sociology. *American Behavioral Scientist* 22(4): 487–511.

Li, De. 1999. Reconstructing Chinese Sociology: A Quest for an Applied Science. *Sociological Practice: A Journal of Clinical and Applied Research* 1(4): 273–284.

Luison, Lucio. ed. 1998. *Introduczione alla sociologia clinica: teorie, metodi e tecniche di intervento*. Milano: Francoangeli.

McDonagh, Edward C. 1944. An Approach to Clinical Sociology. *Sociology and Social Research* 27(5)(May–June): 376–383.

Minardi, Everardo and Stefano Cifiello. 2005. *Ricercazione: Teoria e metodo del lavoro sociologico*. Milano: Francoangeli.

Noguchi, Yuji. 2008. Clinical Sociology in Japan. In *International Clinical Sociology*. Edited by Jan Marie Fritz. New York, NY: Springer, 72–81.

Perlstadt, Harry. 2007. Applied Sociology. In *21st Century Sociology Reference Handbook*. Vol. 2. Edited by Clifton D. Bryant and Dennis L. Peck. Thousand Oaks, CA, London, and New Delhi: Sage, 342–352.

Rigas, Anastasia-Valentine and Adriani Papadaki. 2008. Psychosocial Interventions and the Rehabilitation of Drug Users in Greece. In *International Clinical Sociology*. Edited by Jan Marie Fritz. New York, NY: Springer, 15–134.

Sevigny, Robert. 1997. The Clinical Approach in the Social Sciences. *International Sociology*. 12(2)(June): 135–150.

Small, Albion W. 1896. Scholarship and Social Agitation. *The American Journal of Sociology*. 1(5)(March): 564–582.

Straus, Roger A. ed. 2004. *Using Sociology: An Introduction from the Applied and Clinical Perspectives*. 3rd edn. New York, NY: General Hall.

Takeuti, Norma Missae and Christophe Niewiadomski. 2009. *Reinvencoes do sujeito social: teorias e praticas biograficas* ("Reinvention of the Social Subject"). Porto Alegre, Brazil: Sulina.

Timasheff, Nicholas S. and George A. Theodorson. 1976. *Sociological Theory, Its Nature and Growth*. New York, NY: Random House.

Tosi, Michelina and Francesco Battisti. eds. 1995. *Sociologia clinica e sistemi socio-sanitari: dalle premesse epistemologiche allo studio di casi e interventi*. Milano: Francoangeli.

Uys, Tina. 2015. Interview. June 30.

Van Bockstaele, Jacques, Maria van Bockstaele, Colette Barrot, and Cl. Magny. 1963. Travaux de sociologie clinique: quelques conditions d'une intervention de type analytique en sociologie. *L'Annee Sociologique*. Paris: Presses Universitaires De France.

Winternitz, Milton C. 1930. Practical Study of Social Relations: Plan for Graduate Department of Clinical Sociology at Yale. Report. Yale University Archives, School of Medicine, Records of Dean. YRG-27-A-5-9. Box 174, Folder 3608.

Wirth, Louis. 1931a. Clinical Sociology. *American Journal of Sociology* 37: 49–66.

Wirth, Louis. 1931b. Sociology: Vocations for Those Interested in It. Pamphlet. Vocational Guidance Series, No. L. Chicago, IL: University of Chicago. Louis Wirth Collection, University of Chicago, Department of Special Collections. Box LVI, Folder 6.

Zorbaugh, Harvey Warren. 1929. *The Gold Coast and the Slum: A Sociological Study of Chicago's Near North Side*. Chicago, IL: The University of Chicago Press.

Zorbaugh, Harvey Warren. 1939. Sociology in the Clinic. *Journal of Educational Sociology*. 12(6)(February): 344–351.

Teaching Sociology: Creating a Citizenry with a Sociological Imagination

Kathleen S. Lowney

Their names are burned into our short-term memory – Michael Brown and Ferguson, Missouri; Eric Garner and New York City; Trayvon Martin, George Zimmerman, and Sanford, Florida – and the list continues to grow. We know, as sociologists, that the list of young men, primarily racial minorities, killed by law enforcement officers or individuals claiming self-defense, such as George Zimmerman did, could go on and on. Some of our students are coming to sociology classes in this post-Trayvon Martin era angry, with a newly awakened or reinvigorated sense of discrimination (Kingkade 2015). They are struggling to process their feelings of being unsafe, of worrying about their friends and for themselves, and are disillusioned with the promises of how American society is supposed to work. Other students – often upper class and white – come to our classrooms feeling pressured to see and then renounce privilege that they do not feel or believe they have. They, too, can be angry, but for quite different reasons. And thanks to many recent news stories (see e.g., Bennett 2014; Sander 2014) many female students are concerned about the rate of sexual assault on campus (both reported and unreported) and wonder how safe they are both on and off campus. Add to those feelings the fact that many of our students are struggling to afford college and wondering if their degrees will be "worth it" economically, and teaching – let alone teaching sociology – can be an enormous intellectual and emotional challenge for professors today.

It is easy to feel isolated when we try to engage students in our classrooms while tackling some of the most complex social problems of our time. Luckily, our discipline has a thriving community of scholar-teachers who have engaged in the scholarship of teaching and learning for nearly half a century, and I encourage all of us to engage with this community. The American Sociological Association (ASA) Section on Teaching and Learning sponsors numerous teaching-oriented sessions at the annual meeting; the ASA used to publish syllabi collections and now has taken that idea online, in the Teaching Resources and Innovations Library for Sociology (TRAILS); there are lively online resources such as Sociological Images (https://thesocietypages.org/socimages/); Facebook groups such as Teaching with a Sociological Lens and Shared Teaching Resources for Sociology. More formalized research on the scholarship of teaching and learning can be found in the ASA's sole pedagogically oriented journal, *Teaching Sociology*. These resources allow faculty to find activities which can engage, challenge, and advance our students' understanding of sociological concepts. In the rest of this chapter I want to focus on introductory sociology classes – often offered in the general education curriculum for social science credit. These students – and not just sociology majors – can be ambassadors of the sociological way of thinking if we can get them to engage their sociological imaginations early and often in class.

How do we help our students to process the content we want them to learn, to grow intellectually and emotionally, given the stresses they bring to our classrooms? How can we use those worries in a sensitive, pedagogically appropriate way, as we help students to learn to think sociologically about the society and world they inhabit? And how do we effectively encourage them to bring sociological insights to their future careers, given the data that so many of our students see higher education as little more than a box to check on the path to a career? Those of us teaching general education sociology classes, such as Introduction to Sociology or Social Problems, know that most of our students will never take another sociology class. What do we want them to take away as representative of our discipline, its insights, its way of thinking about the social world?

One of the first concepts that most Introduction to Sociology and Social Problems textbooks discuss is the sociological imagination. Here is how the book I happen to be using this year talks about the concept (Ferris and Stein 2015: 13, emphasis in original):

> One of the classic statements about the sociological perspective comes from C. W. Mills (1916–62), who describes a quality of mind that all great social analysts seem to possess: the **sociological imagination**. By this, he means the ability to understand "the intersection of biography and history" or the interplay of self and the world; this is sociology's task and its "promise."

This linkage between private issues and public problems represents the bedrock analytical contribution sociology offers to our students and to the academic world. But sociology teachers know that helping our students to see how to make those analytical connections is not necessarily pedagogically easy. US popular culture is saturated with psychological explanations of deviant (and less often "good") behavior and our students have grown up internalizing those messages (Abt and Seesholtz 1994; Gamson 1998; Janis 1980; Lowney 1999; Peele 1995; Rapping 1996). They have seen, for example, Dr. Phil McGraw advocate intense one-on-one therapy and rehabilitation for drug addicts, racists, and bullies. If only I had a dollar for the number of times students in class have repeated Dr. Phil's signature question, "How's that working for you?", which he asks the person who needs "fixing" on his show every day! Many students, not surprisingly, come to see the "fix the person" (or at least "control the person's 'bad' behavior through drug-based modification") approach that much of modern psychology offers as being the sole way to deal with these issues. They will vociferously argue that bullies need counseling, that drug addicts need to get clean and work a 12-step program … and all will be okay with society.

So when sociology instructors push back against that perspective by urging them to see the connections between the private issues and public problems – how fixing one "problematic person" rarely challenges the structures of oppression, and that systematic changes are what is most needed now – we are asking them to challenge deeply held values and beliefs about how their world – if not THE world – works. How, then, can we use our disciplinary content to take our students on an intellectual journey which culminates in their being able to ask these kinds of questions?

A Pedagogical Process for Teaching the Sociological Imagination

Introducing the Concept

To ensure that students truly understand this core disciplinary concept, we cannot teach it on one day and then move on. It must be woven into nearly each class meeting, each assignment, every text, and every video clip we show. It needs to be a key – if not THE – pedagogical learning outcome around which our courses are structured. A "one [day] and done" approach to the sociological imagination is unlikely to create enough opportunities for students to comprehend the profoundly different way of seeing social life embedded in this concept (e.g., Huisman 2010; Packard 2013; Rubin 2012). Instead, we need to practice good pedagogy and use backward design (Lowry et al. 2005; Sample 2013; Wiggins and McTighe 1999; 2011) to create courses which focus on creating and then honing their sociological imaginations. At the end of the course, how should your students be able to exhibit to you (and possibly to outside evaluators/assessors) that they understand the sociological imagination?

Building Students' Ability to Move beyond the Personal

Introducing the sociological imagination early in the course is a good start, but do not expect many students to "get it" after one day in class and perhaps reading 1–2 pages about it in the text. As a faculty member, we have to exemplify this new way of thinking continuously. On the first day of a face-to-face class, the instructor might ask about how students' days have gone thus far. It is highly likely that tales of parking problems, lack of child care, hassles with authorities in their lives, and long lines at various campus offices (e.g., the bookstore and financial aid) will come forth. Perhaps if you are teaching one of the larger sections that many institutions are creating in bad economic times, students will publicly lament being in a class that size and wonder if they can learn as well in a big class. You can work with such comments! They are great to use as a foundation for building their sociological imaginations. Many an individual's story will be seconded by others in the room. So the student who first shared the story understands that "it happened to others, too" – something many of them did not consider before. That is the moment when we as a class can begin to talk about social patterns. Why might the bookstore respond to an individual student's question in a patterned way, especially during the busy first week of class? Or why might campus police be less than sympathetic to "but I'm running late to my first class so, just today, I am parking in a spot designated as for those with disabilities" excuse? Why are major-specific classes smaller than general education classes, for the most part? Helping the student move ever so slightly away from personal experience (personal issues) to beginning to see patterns (public problems), can be a good first step in developing their sociological imaginations.

Faculty will need to reinforce these intellectual first steps. Have a wide variety of personal problems in your teaching repertoire and ask students to think about how they might be linked to social patterns and public problems. Good pedagogy (Armstrong 2010; Bean 2001; Central Washington University n.d.; Day 1989; Grauerholz et al. 2013; Hudd and Bronson 2007; Kebede 2009; Massengill 2011; Picca et al. 2013) means some of these exercises should be written. Ask each student to write individual answers for five minutes. Urge them to just keep writing and get all their thoughts down. Then break into Think-Pair-Share groups (ideally of just two people) and have them first read what the other has written and then to talk together about their writing. Let them know that you will be calling on some students (volunteers or announce which pairs in advance) to share with the class. Some students will start writing right away, but many others need time to ponder your question, to write-to-think. Give them that time if you want their best work!

Every now and then, add one of the more complex examples, like racism, sexism, classism, religious discrimination, or ableism, but do not solely focus on those topics just yet. Students have more deeply held views on those topics, and might be less able (or willing) to think sociologically about them just yet. Remember, the pedagogical goal is for students to develop their sociological imagination over the course of the term, not by any one day. If instructors scaffold using the sociological imagination with exercises of greater complexity, most students can get to the desired learning outcome by the end of the term.

Expanding Their Knowledge: The Social Construction of Reality

When students are gaining some confidence with seeing patterns in the social world, then expanding their sociological toolkit to include the social construction of reality can be a pedagogically useful next step. Understanding that every social group creates its own norms, beliefs, intellectual legitimations, and material cultural objects can deepen their analytical skills. This concept can be deeply disturbing to some students, for what they have been told is "enduring forever" or "is best for everyone, everywhere" (e.g., religious norms, political and economic policies) has now been directly challenged. The social construction of reality can feel – at least initially for some students – like a blunt object, smashing their worldview into bits. Let them push back, let them process this new understanding – and yes, let them resist if they wish, within classroom management limits.

Good pedagogy now shifts from providing examples to asking a lot of questions for students to consider: Why might a group construct their values and norms in this way? What benefits accrue with such a construction? Once they feel more comfortable with the concept, push them toward nuancing it. Who gets rewarded (and who does not) under a particular social construction? Here we as instructors can begin discussions of status and privilege which we will come back to in much more depth later on in the course.

It is at this point in the course when I show a visual image, three times, and ask students to go on an intellectual journey with me. The image is the Twin Towers in New York City, with smoke streaming from them, on September 11, 2001. Remember most of our current students were quite young on that day; many have no clear recollection of that terrorist attack except that it was an unusual day at school and adults seemed sad and worried. The first slide asks, "What is the social construction of this image to most Americans?" Individually, students write for a few minutes and then plan a Think-Pair-Share activity. The room gets quite animated; they are very willing to talk about this. Then we come together as a class. The second slide has the exact same image, but the question is different: "What is the social construction of this image to most al Qaeda members?" This time, the room feels quite different. Many struggle to write anything down and the pairs are much quieter, more subdued. When we come back together, I address that immediately, by asking them why this was a harder question than the first one. Hardly anyone wants to talk at first but then one student will usually say something like, "I knew what you wanted me to say, but it felt so wrong thinking like a terrorist, that I was uncomfortable." What a brave – and wonderfully rich – sociological statement. We can build on it; discussing why it is more difficult to think like a member of a group that seems quite different from our own group; how the word "terrorist" has been socially constructed in the United States and across the globe, recently and historically. They are coming to understand the conceptual power of the social construction of reality and how thinking like a sociologist can sometimes be difficult. Then I show the visual again, with the words, "What is the social construction of this image to a citizen of Iceland" (or Canada, or the Maldives or some other nation)? I think this third question can help students to see that the social constructive process is not always an "us or them"/"with us or against us" type of dichotomy.

Deepening Their Experience Further: Culture

It is at this point that the class and I turn to a thorough examination of culture as a social construction. We have talked about culture since the first day of class, but now we have some analytical tools with which to study culture sociologically. We begin with language, values, norms, and sanctions. These concepts flow naturally out of the social construction of reality. Once they understand cultures are different, students are curious about how groups construct culture and form; beliefs (religious, political, scientific). Do not think your examples have to be all that "other," either, to be pedagogically sound. Try showing the periodic table of the elements as a visual and ask about the values which undergird it. Ask about the scientific norms which shape the order of the elements. You are likely to have some science majors who will weigh in with the norms (but in case not – answers are easily Googled!). Or put on-screen a sheet of music and ask them about the symbols, language, and norms involved.

Begin to introduce the concept of social structure, status, and social stratification now. Students will want to know how different groups rank and reward individuals. Define the concepts and have them draw the social structure in one or two groups to which they belong. Plant the seeds for later learning now. Then move to a US subculture or counterculture and eventually to a different society completely. There are many sociological studies which can serve as excellent examples for these discussions (e.g., Chambliss 1988; Gelder 2005; Lowney 1995; Thompson 2009).

You might notice that as the examples get more distant from the cultural practices of most students, they may struggle more to see culture as a social construction, understandable from within its own perspective. When many students seem to want to judge another culture and its social construction, it is time for the next pair of concepts.

Ethnocentrism and Cultural Relativism

Part of the sociological perspective we want to be sharing with students is that sociologists are curious. We question everything and everyone but should practice cultural relativism when we do. Different groups construct their social worlds as they like and, as cultural observers, we need to not judge them based on our own society's culture. I suggest you note that cultural relativism is a norm of the *profession of sociology* and part of its ethical mandates, just as the life sciences have norms about how to treat ethically the species they study. Perhaps this is even the place to introduce the ethical codes of our discipline (however, others may want to hold off and pair ethical codes with research methods). Usually one or more students ask if it is *really* possible to be completely culturally relativistic when studying another group, given the power of socialization into one's own culture. Again, getting this question is a pedagogical success; your students are thinking carefully about the sociological perspective and what it means to do sociology.

With these conversations, students are beginning to view the world – hesitantly, perhaps – via their sociological imagination. They – and you – are now ready to tackle how social structure – while initially merely a social construction – has taken on the power to shape the life chances of individuals and groups. They are more able to see how private issues are not simply due to individuals' selfishness, deviance, lack of willpower, or sinfulness – but shaped in large part by the ways power, privilege, and resources are constructed and distributed in a particular group or society. They are more public problems than private issues, needing collective answers rather than private therapy or rehabilitation. As Hironimus-Wendt and Wallace (2009: 77) put it:

> *We routinely teach our students that social issues are not the result of bad choices*

made by a subset of misguided individuals, nor the result of natural forces beyond our collective control. Social issues arise when dysfunctional social arrangements (environments) limit the range of choices available to individuals into either a subset of primarily bad choices, or no good choices at all.

After you and your students unpack social structures' systems of oppression and the legitimations which support them, they are now ready to ask questions about issues related to social class, race and ethnic discrimination, sexism, and so on. Moreover, you and they have taken an intellectual journey which has given them tools not only to ask – but begin to *answer* their questions about power, privilege, and the unjust distribution of resources within a group and between groups.

Media examples (both locally and beyond) often work well. Hurricane Katrina examples of "looting" versus "finding" supplies can be excellent conversation starters (e.g., Jones 2011; Ralli 2005). Or ask students to watch local news and code stories which air during the first ten minutes of the broadcast for a week. Have them code stories for type of activity (e.g., political, crime, weather, etc.) and if the story states racial identifiers of any person in the story (or uses photographs which could imply race) (Gilliam and Iyengar 2000; LeDuff 2007). What patterns did they find? What are the possible implications of those patterns on public policy? Citizens' views of each other? Law enforcement's view of the people they serve and protect? etc. When students can begin to ask these kinds of questions, they are beginning to engage their sociological imaginations.

Do not think that you and they have to solve society's problems as you discuss and analyze these topics. Think locally. Are there issues on your campus and in your community that can be analytic prompts? Students are acutely aware that they embody far lower rungs of a campus's social structure than the administration and faculty. They often have grievances based on these power differentials that they want to – need to – share. Few, though, realize that together, as an organized group, they have the power to effectively encourage administrators to address (at least some) of their concerns. Understanding the power of organized people is also an important part of teaching the sociological imagination.

Why Helping Our Students to "Commit Sociology" Must Be Important to Our Discipline

The public, and hence our students and their parents, increasingly hears that sociology is – or may be – a discipline in crisis (Feagin 1999) or irrelevant (Patterson 2014). From Canadian Prime Minister Stephen Harper's now famous statement in response to an alleged terror plot to attack a Canadian passenger train that "[t]his is not the time to commit sociology" (Campion-Smith 2013) to nearly 50 percent of Freakonomics.com readers offering advice to college and university presidents that the discipline of sociology is the social science which should be eliminated because it is "no longer as relevant to the mission of research and education" (Venkatesh 2012), to sociologists who teach about sexuality being called before my state's legislature (Georgia) and asked to justify teaching entire classes about oral sex and prostitution to college students during times of economic belt-tightening (Stombler 2009) (erroneous "facts," as it turned out), sociology's reputation needs repair.

Like it or not, the general public tends to think in a more psychological manner, while the ruling elite seems deeply enamored with economics (Rojas 2007). If we are able to get students to see the connections between macro-level social forces and individuals' lives then we are creating a body public which might think differently about crime, poverty, war, climate change, overpopulation, racism, and the myriad of other social problems which face the United States and the world. That means, however, that we need to spend more than one day in class, more than just a few pages in a "big book textbook," on the concept of the sociological imagination. We need to nudge and push students throughout the semester to see these connections in their daily lives, in the lives of others with whom they are less familiar, and throughout society.

The sociological imagination needs to become the center of our introductory courses. It is the key insight students must take from our classes. Our society need more citizens who can look beyond themselves and their social locations to see the connections between social structure and individuals' lives of wealth and privilege or poverty and the struggle – and the diminishing life chances between these two. Educating citizens *is* the promise of sociology. It allows students to understand people as embedded within social structure and to better comprehend why they make the choices that they do – good and bad ones.

Amanda Moore McBride and Eric Mlyn's (2015) recent commentary on why "Innovation Alone Won't Fix Social Problems" asked:

> Where are we teaching our students to assess community needs, as well as community assets and ideas? Where are we teaching our students (not just encouraging them) to work in groups, debate issues, compromise, use the tools of political action, and commit to a cause for the long term? Where are we teaching our students about the political and social processes and infrastructures that are necessary to make an idea a reality?

If we are doing our pedagogical and disciplinary jobs correctly, one answer to their questions should be: in our sociology classes, where we teach students to use their sociological imaginations to see, analyze, and begin to solve social problems.

References

Abt, Vicki and Mel Seesholtz. 1994. The Shameless World of Phil, Sally, and Oprah: Television Talk Shows and the Deconstructing of Society. *Journal of Popular Culture* 28: 171–191.

Armstrong, Jeanne. 2010. Designing a Writing Intensive Course with Information Literacy and Critical Thinking Learning Outcomes. *Reference Services Review* 38: 44–57.

Bean, John C. 2001. *Engaging Ideas: The Professor's Guide to Integrating Writing, Critical Thinking, and Active Learning in the Classroom*. San Francisco, CA: Jossey-Bass.

Bennett, Jessica. 2014. The Problem with Frats Isn't Just Rape: It's Power. *Time.Com*. December 3. Available at http://time.com/3616158/fraternity-rape-uva-rolling-stone-sexual-assault/, accessed February 11, 2015.

Campion-Smith, Bruce. 2013. Prime Minister Stephen Harper Rejects 'Sociology' Talk in Wake of Terror Plots. TheStar.Com. April 25. Available at www.thestar.com/news/canada/2013/04/25/prime_minister_stephen_harper_rejects_sociology_talk_in_wake_of_terror_plots.html, accessed February 14, 2015.

Central Washington University. n.d. Writing across the Curriculum's Frequently Asked Questions about Writing across the Curriculum. Available at www.cwu.edu/general-education/writing-across-curriculum, accessed June 20, 2014.

Chambliss, William J. 1988. The Saints and the Roughnecks. In *Down to Earth Sociology*. Edited by James D. Henslin. 5th edn. New York, NY: The Free Press, 188–202.

Day, Susan. 1989. Producing Better Writers in Sociology Classes: A Test of the Across-the-Curriculum Approach. *Teaching Sociology* 17(4): 458–464.

Feagin, Joe R. 1999. Soul-Searching in Sociology: Is the Discipline in Crisis? *The Chronicle Review*. October 15. Available at http://chronicle.com/article/soul-searching-in-sociology-/27716/, accessed January 23, 2015.

Ferris, Kerry and Jill Stein. 2015. *The Real World: An Introduction to Sociology*. 4th edn. New York, NY: W.W. Norton.

Gamson, Joshua. 1998. *Freaks Talk Back: Tabloid Talk Shows and Sexual Nonconformity*. Chicago, IL: University of Chicago Press.

Gelder, Ken. 2005. *The Subcultures Reader*. 2nd edn. New York, NY: Routledge.

Gilliam, Franklin D., Jr. and Shanto Iyengar. 2000. Prime Suspects: The Influence of Local Television News on the Viewing Public. *American Journal of Political Science* 44: 560–573.

Grauerholz, Liz, Joanna Eisele, and Nicole Stark. 2013. Writing in the Sociology Curriculum:

What Types and How Much Writing Do We Assign? *Teaching Sociology* 41: 46–59.

Hironimus-Wendt, Robert J. and Lora Ebert Wallace. 2009. The Sociological Imagination and Social Responsibility. *Teaching Sociology* 37: 76–88.

Hudd, Suzanne S. and Eric Franklyn Bronson. 2007. Moving Forward Looking Backward: An Exercise in Recursive Thinking and Writing. *Teaching Sociology* 35: 264–273.

Huisman, Kimberly. 2010. Developing a Sociological Imagination by Doing Sociology: A Methods-Based Service-Learning Course on Women and Immigration. *Teaching Sociology* 38: 106–118.

Janis, Irving. 1980. The Influence of Television on Personal Decision-Making. In *Television and Social Behavior*. Edited by S. B. Withey and R. P. Ables. Hillsdale, NJ: Laurence Erlbaum, 161–189.

Jones, Van. 2011. Black People "Loot" Food... White People "Find" Food. *Huffington Post Politics*. May 25. Available at www.huffingtonpost.com/van-jones/black-people-loot-food-wh_b_6614.html, accessed February 1, 2015. [Note: This is an updated story, but Huffington Post says original was posted 12/31/1969, which is clearly an error, given that it deals with Hurricane Katrina.]

Kebede, Alem. 2009. Practicing Sociological Imagination through Writing Sociological Autobiography. *Teaching Sociology* 37: 353–368.

Kingkade, Tyler. 2015. College Student Survey Suggests We've Made Little Progress Eliminating Racism. *Huffington Post Live*. February 7. Available at www.huffingtonpost.com/2015/02/07/college-student-survey-race_n_6632854.html, accessed February 10, 2015.

LeDuff, Kim Maria. 2007. *Tales of Two Cities: How Race and Crime Intersect on Local TV News in Indianapolis and New Orleans*. A Dissertation Submitted in Partial Fulfillment of the Requirements for the Degree of Doctor of Philosophy in the School of Journalism. Indiana University.

Lowney, Kathleen S. 1995. Teenage Satanism as Oppositional Youth Subculture. *Journal of Contemporary Ethnography* 23: 453–481.

Lowney, Kathleen S. 1999. *Baring Our Souls: TV Talk Shows and the Religion of Recovery*. New York, NY: Aldine De Gruyter.

Lowry, Janet Huber, Carla B. Howery, John P. Myers, Harry Perlstadt, Caroline Hodges Persell, Diane Pike, Charles H. Powers, Shirley A. Scritchfield, Cynthia M. Siemsen, Barbara Trepagnier, Judith Ann Warner, and Gregory Weiss. 2005. *Creating an Effective Assessment Plan for the Sociology Major*. Washington, DC: American Sociological Association.

Massengill, Rebekah Peeples. 2011. Sociological Writing as Higher-Level Thinking: Assignments that Cultivate the Sociological Imagination. *Teaching Sociology* 39: 371–381.

McBride, Amanda Moore and Eric Mlyn. 2015. Commentary: Innovation Alone Won't Fix Social Problems. *The Chronicle of Higher Education*.February 2. Available at http://chronicle.com/article/innovation-alone-won-t-fix/151551/, accessed February 3, 2015.

Packard, Josh. 2013. The Impact of Racial Diversity in the Classroom: Activating the Sociological Imagination. *Teaching Sociology* 41: 144–158.

Patterson, Orlando. 2014. How Sociologists Made Themselves Irrelevant. *The Chronicle Review*. September 1. Available at http://chronicle.com/article/how-sociologists-made/150249/, accessed February 7, 2015.

Peele, Stanton. 1995. *Diseasing of America: How We've Allowed Recovery Zealots and the Treatment Industry to Convince Us We Are Out of Control*, with a new preface. New York, NY: Lexington.

Picca, Leslie H., Brian Starks, and Justine Gunderson. 2013. "It Opened My Eyes": Using Student Journal Writing to Make Visible Race, Class, and Gender in Everyday Life. *Teaching Sociology* 41: 82–93.

Ralli, Tania. 2005. Who's a Looter? In Storm's Aftermath, Pictures Kick Up a Different Kind of Tempest. *The New York Times*. September 5. Available at www.nytimes.com/2005/09/05/business/05caption.html?_r=0, accessed February 7, 2015.

Rapping, Elayne. 1996. *The Culture of Recovery: Making Sense of the Self-Help Movement in Women's Lives*. Boston, MA: Beacon Press.

Rojas, Fabio. 2007. Why Does Sociology Have Such a Bad Reputation? Available at https://orgtheory.wordpress.com/2007/07/19/why-does-sociology-have-such-a-bad-reputation/, accessed February 1, 2015.

Rubin, Beth. 2012. Shifting Social Contracts and the Sociological Imagination. *Social Forces* 91: 327–346.

Sample, Mark. 2013. Planning a Class with Backward Design. *The Chronicle of Higher*

Education. May 31. Available at http://chronicle.com/blogs/profhacker/planning-a-class-with-backward-design/33625, accessed June 28, 2013.

Sander, Libby. 2014. Colleges Are Reminded of Federal Eye on Handling of Sexual-Assault Cases. *The Chronicle of Higher Education.* February 11. Available at http://chronicle.com/article/colleges-are-reminded-of/144703/, accessed January 25, 2015.

Stombler, Mindy. 2009. In the Hot Seat. *The Chronicle of Higher Education.* May 1. Available at http://chronicle.com/article/in-the-hot-seat/44821, accessed February 4, 2015.

Thompson, William E. 2009. Pseudo-Deviance and the "New Biker" Subculture: Hogs, Blogs, Leathers, and Lattes. *Deviant Behavior* 31: 89–114.

Venkatesh, Sudhir. 2012. The Verdict Is In: Sociology and Political Science Deserve the Hatchet. July 12. Available at http://freakonomics.com/2012/07/12/the-verdict-is-in-sociology-and-political-science-deserve-the-hatchet/, accessed February 3, 2015.

Wiggins, Grant and Jay McTighe. 1999. What Is Backward Design? flec.ednet.ns.ca. Available at www.flec.ednet.ns.ca/staff/what%20is%20backward%20design%20etc.pdf, accessed September 12, 2012.

Wiggins, Grant and Jay McTighe. 2011. *The Understanding by Design Guide to Creating High-Quality Units.* Alexandria, VA: Association for Supervision and Curriculum Development.

Part IX

RELATED FIELDS

CHAPTER 37

Criminology

Kaitlyn Clarke, Philip D. McCormack, and Larry J. Siegel

While the association between sociology and criminology remains strong and relevant, it is a misnomer to describe criminology as merely a branch or sub-area within the sociological universe. Though most, if not all, definitions of sociology contain terms such as *social institutions, social networks, social groups* and so on, criminology takes on a broader perspective. Criminology today is an independent field of study that takes an integrated, multidisciplinary approach to the study of criminal behavior and the efforts being made to control and deter its occurrence. Scholars who define themselves as **criminologists** hold degrees in a variety of diverse fields, and while sociology still stands out, many criminologists hold advanced degrees in **criminal justice**, political science, law, psychology, public policy, economics, and the natural sciences. Nor is it uncommon to see a criminologist holding a degree in biology or neuropsychology and conducting research on the genetic basis of crime or the relationship between brain structure and criminal activity. Some of the pre-eminent scholars in the field hold degrees in economics and social psychology. All are equally accepted; there is no single path to becoming a criminologist.

It is equally inappropriate to categorize criminology as a sub-area within the growing academic study of criminal justice, a field of study which now contains thousands of programs across the United States. There are numerous programs that title themselves as the School, College or Department of Criminology and Criminal Justice or some such iteration. Nonetheless, although the fields may seem similar, and people often confuse the two or lump them together, there are major differences between the two. Criminology explains the etiology, extent, and nature of crime in society, whereas criminal justice refers to the study of the operations of agencies of social control – police, courts, and corrections. While criminologists are mainly concerned with identifying the suspected causes of *crime,* criminal justice scholars spend their time identifying effective methods of *crime control.*

Since both fields are crime-related, there is of course some overlap. Some criminologists devote their research to justice and social control and are concerned with how the agencies of justice operate, how they influence crime and criminals, and how justice policies shape crime rates and trends. Criminal justice experts often want to design effective programs of crime prevention or rehabilitation and, to do so, must develop an understanding of the nature of crime and its causation. Whether the integration of criminal justice and criminology makes academic sense or is a cost-saving marriage of convenience that makes university administrators happy is, in the end, a matter of personal perception.

History of Criminology

The fact that criminology is not merely a branch of sociology or criminal justice, as some wrongfully believe, is aptly illustrated by the intellectual shifts that have occurred during the 300-year history of the field. For example, its earliest roots can be traced to political philosophy and biology rather than social science. Criminologists usually point to the writings of an Italian scholar, Cesare Beccaria (1738–1794), as being one of the first attempts to develop a systematic understanding of why people commit crime. In his 1764 classic, *On Crimes and Punishment*, Beccaria offered a utilitarian approach to explain why people commit crimes: criminal activity promises to bring wealth, vengeance, prestige, and other rewards with a minimum of effort. Why, then, are not all people criminals given crime's attractiveness? There is a downside that must be taken into consideration: the threat of criminal punishment. Crime will only occur when people come to the conclusion, after a brief period of calculation, that their law violations will bring an immediate reward with a minimal threat of expected punishment. Crime, therefore, should be the expected outcome when punishment is distant, slow, and ineffective. Who commits crime? Why, we all would if we dared, but most of us do not; we are just too afraid of the consequences.

Beccaria's (1974[1764]) writing had a great deal of influence on criminal law and was influential in shaping the formulation of legal codes. However, his work was superseded by the development and application of the scientific method to the study of behavior. The first attempts now seem rather farcical. In the late eighteenth century, physiognomists studied the facial features of criminals and concluded that the shape of the ears, nose, and eyes and the distances between them were associated with anti-social behavior. They were joined by phrenologists, who concluded that the shape of the skull and bumps on the head were linked to criminal behavior. An Italian physician, Cesare Lombroso (1835–1909), known today as the "father of criminology," reported on his studies of the cadavers of executed criminals in an effort to determine scientifically how criminals differed from non-criminals. Lombroso (1876) was soon convinced that serious and violent offenders had inherited criminal traits and that these "born criminals" suffered from "atavistic anomalies" which meant that physically they were throwbacks to more primitive times when people were savages. By the beginning of the twentieth century, American authors were discussing "the science of penology" and "the science of criminology." While today we scoff at these attempts as being both primitive and unscientific, efforts to link anti-social behavior to biological anomalies have never been stronger. Criminologists worldwide are now studying the varying effects of such biological factors as dietary intake (Schoenthaler and Bier 2000), hormonal imbalance (Boyd 2000), and hereditary effects on criminality (Caspi et al. 2002), and the field has taken notice of their claims that the true cause of crime has an individual rather than social source (Beaver and Connelly 2015).

Sociology began having a significant effect on criminologists when, in his study of suicide, Emile Durkheim (1897) found that one presumed cause was a result of the breakdown of the social standards necessary for regulating behavior. He helped popularize the term "anomie" or normlessness to signify a period when common values and common meanings are no longer widely understood or accepted. Because their replacements have not been developed, the populaces begin to acquire a psychological state characterized by a sense of futility, despair, lack of purpose, and feelings of personal emptiness: this is anomie. In his 1893 *Division of Labor*, Durkheim also found that role confusion occurred amidst a shift from a small, rural society, which he labeled "mechanical," to the more modern "organic" society with a large urban population, division of labor, and personal isolation. An anomic society is in chaos, experiencing moral uncertainty and an accompanying loss of traditional values. Durkheim's conceptualization was eventually brought to the forefront of criminology by American sociologist Robert Merton (1938), when he argued that in contemporary society anomie was achieved by the disjunction of valued social goals (e.g., financial success, power, possessions) and the means available to reach them (e.g., vocational and educational achievement.) Crime becomes the inevitable outcome when people believe that they can never achieve the American Dream with the methods they have at their disposal. In a society that stresses the financial success goal first among all others, failure to achieve it is a precursor of desperate measures. Theft, drug dealing, and violence are merely alternative tools used to achieve socially acceptable ends. It is the greater emphasis on ends rather than means that creates the stress that leads to a breakdown in the regulatory structure of society and releases people from bonds they may have had with the social order.

Sociology Takes the Forefront

The primacy of sociological positivism was secured by research begun in the early twentieth century by Robert Ezra Park (1864–1944), Ernest W. Burgess (1886–1966), Louis Wirth (1897–1952), and their colleagues in the Sociology Department at the University of Chicago. The scholars who taught in this program created what is still referred to as the **Chicago School** in honor of their unique style of doing research (Park 1915; Park et al. 1925; Wirth 1928). These urban sociologists examined how neighborhood conditions, such as poverty levels, influenced crime rates. They found that social forces operating in urban areas created a crime-promoting environment; some neighborhoods were "natural areas" for crime. In urban neighborhoods with high levels of poverty, the fabric of critical social institutions, such as the school and the family, come undone. Their traditional ability to control behavior was undermined, and the outcome was a high crime rate.

Research conducted by two Chicago School sociologists, Clifford R. Shaw and Henry McKay, has had the most enduring influence on the field. Shaw and McKay (1942) explained crime and delinquency within the context of the changing urban environment and ecological development of the city. They saw that Chicago had developed into distinct neighborhoods (natural areas), some affluent and others wracked by extreme poverty. These poverty-ridden **transitional neighborhoods** suffered high rates of population turnover and were incapable of inducing residents to remain and defend the neighborhoods against criminal groups. Subsequent changes in population composition, disintegration of traditional cultures, diffusion of divergent cultural standards, and gradual industrialization dissolved neighborhood culture and organization. The continuity of conventional neighborhood traditions and institutions was broken, leaving people feeling displaced and without a strong or definitive set of values.

The development of teenage law-violating groups is an essential element of misbehavior in slum areas. When neighborhoods become disorganized and informal, social controls break down and gangs provide a form of stability in a normless environment. By placing gang youth in conflict with existing middle-class norms, the resulting value conflict further separates the delinquent gang member from conventional society; the result is a more solid embrace of deviant goals and behavior.

But the field did not rest here. Because the Chicago School focus seemed rather narrow, criminology took a turn toward social psychology during the 1930s and 1940s. Crime was present in small towns and rural areas, not just big cities. What could explain its universality? Scholars began to link criminal behavior to disruption in socialization, and focused their research on the association between critical elements of social life and development – education achievement, the quality of family life, and the intensity of peer relations – and criminal behavioral choices.

One position, championed by the preeminent American criminologist Edwin Sutherland (1939), is that people learn criminal attitudes and behaviors and that crime is a learned experience. People interact with significant others who hold and/or admire deviant values, and constant exposure without counter pressure enculturates them in a delinquent way of life. Counterbalancing this view, the social control theory approach's best known proponent, Travis Hirschi, held that people are able to engage in anti-social behavior when their bond to significant others is frayed or torn, freeing them from social control, and opening the path to crime. Criminality is both fun and profitable. People do not learn to commit crime, Hirschi (1969) suggested. In contrast, they have to be taught to color within the lines, stay within legal boundaries and forego today's pleasures for tomorrow's rewards. Without the proper guidance, the path to criminality is left open. Those without a bond to significant others were immune to control and free to violate the law.

While Hirschi's Social Bond Theory (Hirschi 1969) dominated the field for some time, another group of criminologists was influenced by the social upheaval of the late 1960s. Fueled by the Vietnam War, the development of an anti-establishment counterculture movement, the Civil Rights Movement, and the women's movement, these so-called radical criminologists began to analyze the social/economic conditions in the United States that promoted class conflict and crime. What emerged from this intellectual ferment was a critical criminology that indicted the economic system for producing the conditions that support a high crime rate. Crime was viewed as one of many social ills caused by a rapacious capitalist system based on greed; sexism, racism, and classism are other problems caused by capitalism.

Criminal Careers

In 1972, Marvin Wolfgang, Robert Figlio, and Thorsten Sellin published their groundbreaking book, *Delinquency in a Birth Cohort*, which highlighted the fact that relatively few people (6 percent of every birth cohort) commit lots of crime and are responsible for more criminal acts than all the rest. Not only are they active, but they are hard to deter, immune to the effects of punishment (which only makes them commit more crime), and non-responsive to the ravages of time (they continue to commit crime as they grow older while the rest of us sink into a comfortable middle age). These chronic offenders are the real problem, not the teens who shoplift from Walmart or get into a fight at school. The Wolfgang research spurred interest in criminal careers. Why do some people commit a single crime and desist from illegal activities while others become repeat, chronic offenders who never stop?

Another trend was theory integration, research that integrated sociological, biological, psychological, and economic elements into a complex developmental view of crime causation. A number of important research efforts followed the careers of known delinquents in order to identify the factors that predicted persistent offending. Now, rather than focus on the criminal act, criminologists began to devote their attention to criminal careers. This focus has helped moved the field further from the sociological ambit, focusing more now on human agency or the ability people have to make choices and control their own destiny.

Where We Are Today

As the field has matured and evolved, criminology has become a stand-alone area of study much like psychology and sociology. As in those social sciences, there are several sub-areas that exist within the broader arena of criminology. Criminologists may specialize in one of them in the same way in which psychologists might specialize in child development, perception, personality, psychopathology, or social psychology. What sub-areas of scholarship fall under the criminological umbrella?

Criminal Statistics. The sub-area of criminal statistics/crime measurement involves calculating the amounts and trends of criminal activity. How much crime occurs annually? Who commits it? When and where does it occur? Which crimes are the most serious? This activity usually involves formulating advanced techniques for collecting and analyzing relevant data sources, ranging from data mining to survey instrument creation.

One major effort is to gain a valid and accurate count of criminal activity. While traditionally criminologists relied on police data, they know that barely half of all crimes are actually reported. To measure criminal activity not reported to the police by victims, survey instruments have been developed and research protocols created that estimate the percentage of people who commit crimes but escape detection by the justice system (James and Council 2008; Lauritsen and Rezey 2013).

Socio-legal Studies. Socio-legal studies is a sub-area of criminology concerned with the role that social forces play in shaping criminal law and the role of criminal law in shaping society. Criminologists interested in socio-legal studies might investigate the history of legal thought in an effort to understand how the legal conceptualization of criminal acts (such as theft, rape, and murder) evolved into their present form and the processes by which those criminal acts are punitively addressed. Much of the research is policy-oriented. When someone like Dzhokhar Tsarnaev, one of the brothers who committed the Boston Marathon bombing, is sentenced to death for his crime, socio-legal scholars may want to determine whether such harsh punishment encourages or discourages similar acts, the context in which deaths sentences are given, or if the application of law is equal for all individuals. The end result would be an analysis of how legal mandates (e.g., criminal sentences) are distributed and if those mandates require redress.

Theory Development. Criminologists also explore the causes of crime. Some who have a psychological orientation view crime as a function of personality, development, social learning, or cognition. Others investigate the biological correlates of antisocial behavior and study the biochemical, genetic, and neurological linkages to crime. Those with a sociological orientation look at the social forces producing criminal behavior, including neighborhood conditions, poverty, socialization, and group interaction. Pinning down "one true cause" of crime remains a difficult problem. Criminologists are still unsure why, given similar conditions, some people choose criminal solutions to their problems, whereas others conform to accepted social rules of behavior.

Understanding and Describing Criminal Behavior. Another sub-area of criminology involves research on specific criminal types and patterns: violent crime, theft crime, public order crime, organized crime, and so on. Numerous attempts have been made to describe and understand particular crime types. Marvin Wolfgang's (1958) study, *Patterns in Criminal Homicide*, is a landmark analysis of the nature of homicide and the relationship between victim and offender. Wolfgang discovered that, in many instances, victims caused or precipitated the violent confrontation that led to their deaths, spawning the term *victim precipitated homicide*.

Edwin Sutherland's (1940) analysis of business-related offenses also helped coin a new phrase, **white-collar crime**, to describe economic crime activities of the affluent. Criminologists are constantly broadening the scope of their inquiries because new crimes and crime patterns are constantly emerging. Whereas fifty years ago they might have focused their attention on rape, murder, and burglary, now they also may be looking at stalking, cybercrime, terrorism, and hate crimes. For example, a number of criminologists are now doing research on terrorism and the terrorist personality in order to discover why some young people are motivated to join terror groups.

Penology. The study of penology involves efforts to control crime through the correction of criminal offenders; it is the area of criminology closest to the study of criminal justice. Some criminologists advocate a therapeutic approach to crime prevention that relies on the application of rehabilitation services. They direct their efforts at identifying effective treatment strategies for individuals convicted of law violations, relying on, for example, community sentencing rather than prison. Others argue that crime can be prevented only through the application of formal social control, through such measures as mandatory sentences for serious crimes and even the use of capital punishment as a deterrent to murder.

Victimology. As noted above, criminologists recognize that the victim often plays a critical role in the criminal process and that the victim's behavior is often a key determinant of crime. Victimology involves the use of victim surveys to measure the nature and extent of criminal behavior and to calculate the actual costs of crime to victims, calculating probabilities of victimization risk, studying victim culpability in the precipitation of crime, and designing services for crime victims, such as counseling and compensation programs.

Criminologists who study victimization have uncovered some startling results. For one thing, criminals have been found to be at greater risk of victimization than noncriminals. This finding indicates that rather than being passive targets who are "in the wrong place at the wrong time," victims may themselves be engaging in a high-risk behavior, such as crime, that increases their victimization risk and renders them vulnerable to crime.

Areas of Overlap

Does all this mean that there is an insurmountable schism between criminology and sociology? Hardly. While criminology has branched out in a number of directions independent from sociology, the sociological tradition is still alive and well in the field. The influence of sociology is especially noticeable in the recent focus on ecological conditions that produce high crime rates in socially disorganized areas, and in areas of contemporary research that emphasize the association of community deterioration and economic decline with criminality but place less emphasis on value conflict. Contemporary social ecologists believe that crime rates are associated with community deterioration – disorder, poverty, alienation, disassociation, and fear or perception of crime – rather than culture conflict. According to what is popularly known as the "broken windows" model (Wilson and Kelling 1982), neighborhoods with a high percentage of deserted houses and apartments experience high crime rates; abandoned buildings serve as a "magnet for crime." Areas in which houses are in poor repair, boarded up, and burned out, whose owners are best described as slumlords, are also the location of the highest violence rates and gun crime.

Broken windows fuel despair and further undermine the ability of communities to police themselves, to produce informal social controls. In disorganized neighborhoods that suffer social and physical incivilities, residents experience unruly youths, trash and litter, graffiti, abandoned storefronts, burned-out buildings, littered lots, drunks, vagabonds, loiterers, prostitutes, noise, congestion, angry words, dirt, and stench. As a result, people dread leaving their homes at night and withdraw from community life.

The presence of such incivilities, especially when accompanied by relatively high crime rates, convinces residents that their neighborhood is dangerous and that they should leave as soon as they are able. The most stable and hardworking community members flee. Those who can move to more affluent neighborhoods find that their lifestyles and life chances improve immediately. They will then try to convince family and friends to join them in these new areas, creating further population shifts. Those who cannot leave find themselves surrounded by a constant influx of new residents. In response to this turnover, a culture may develop that dictates to neighborhood youths standards of dress, language, and behavior that are in opposition to those of conventional society. Neighborhoods most at risk for increased crime contain large numbers of single-parent families and unrelated people living together, have changed from owner-occupied to renter-occupied units, and have lost semi-skilled and unskilled jobs (hence the growing number of discouraged workers who are no longer seeking employment). These ecological disruptions strain existing social control mechanisms and undermine their ability to control crime and delinquency.

One of the strongest voices for the effect of ecology on crime rates is Harvard sociologist William Julius Wilson (1997), who has poignantly described how working- and middle-class families flee inner-city areas where poverty is pervasive, resulting in a poverty **concentration effect** in which the most disadvantaged population is consolidated in the most disorganized urban neighborhoods. Poverty concentration has been associated with income and wealth disparities, nonexistent employment opportunities, inferior housing patterns, and unequal access to health care. As the working and middle classes move out to the suburbs, they take with them their financial and institutional resources and support. The people left behind have an even tougher time coping with urban decay and conflict and controlling youth gangs and groups; after all, the most successful people in the community have left for "greener pastures." Businesses are disinclined to locate in poverty-stricken areas and banks become reluctant to lend money for new housing or businesses. Unemployment rates skyrocket, destabilizing households, and unstable families are likely to produce children who use violence and aggression to deal with limited opportunity. Large groups or cohorts of people of the same age are forced to compete for relatively scarce resources.

All is not bleak, however. Poverty itself is not a precursor to community disorganization and crime. In areas with high levels of poverty, communities with high levels of cohesion, social control, and social integration – where people know one another and develop interpersonal ties – may still develop *collective efficacy:* a mutual trust, a willingness to intervene in the supervision of children, and the maintenance of public order. Cohesion among neighborhood residents, combined with shared expectations for informal social control of public space, promotes collective efficacy. Residents in these areas enjoy a better life because the fruits of cohesiveness can be better education, health care, and housing opportunities. Some elements of collective efficacy operate on the primary, or private, level and involve peers, families, and relatives. These sources exert informal control by either awarding or withholding approval, respect, and admiration. Other elements of community collective efficacy involve the use of local institutions to control crime and provide for institutional social control. Stable neighborhoods are also able to arrange for external sources of social control. If they can draw on outside help and secure external resources – a process referred to as public social control – they are better able to reduce the effects of disorganization and maintain lower levels of crime and victimization.

These recent efforts to identify the community level processes that impact on local area crime rates amply show that the sociological tradition within criminology is still vital; that the two fields can amiably coexist and support each other as the effort to understand the forces that shape and control human behavior marches steadily on.

References

Beaver, Kevin M. and Eric Connelly. 2015. Key Findings from Biosocial Research and What They Mean for the Future of Criminology. In *The Routledge International Handbook of Biosocial Criminology*. Edited by M. Delisi and M. Vaughn. New York, NY: Routledge, 46–56.

Beccaria, Cesare. 1974[1764]. *Dei delitti e delle pene* ("On Crimes and Punishment"). Reprinted in 1995 in *On Crimes and Punishment and Other Writings: Cesare Beccaria*. Edited by R. Bellamy. Translated by R. Davies with V. Cox and R. Bellamy. Cambridge: Cambridge University Press.

Boyd, Neil. 2000. *The Beast Within: Why Men Are Violent*. New York, NY: Greystone Books.

Caspi, Avshalom, Joseph McClary, Terrie E. Moffitt, Jonathan Mill, Judy Martin, Ian W. Craig, Alan Taylor, and Richie Poulton. 2002. Role of Genotype in the Cycle of Violence in Maltreated Children. *Science* 297: 851–854.

Durkheim, Emile. 1893. *The Division of Labor in Society*. New York, NY: Free Press.

Durkheim, Emile. 1897. *Suicide: A Study in Sociology*. New York, NY: Free Press.

Hirschi, Travis. 1969. *Cause of Delinquency*. Berkeley, CA: Free Press.

James, Nathan and Logan R. Council 2008. *How Crime in the United States Is Measured*. Washington, DC: Congressional Research Service.

Lauritsen, Janet L. and Maribeth L. Rezey. 2013. *Measuring the Prevalence of Crime with the National Crime Victimization Survey*. Washington DC: US Department of Justice, Bureau of Justice Statistics.

Lombroso, Cesare. 1876. *L'uomo delinquente*. Turin: Fratelli Bocca.

Merton, Robert K. 1938. Social Structure and Anomie. *American Sociological Review* 3(5): 672–682.

Park, Robert E. 1915. The City: Suggestions for the Investigation of Human Behavior in the City Environment. *American Journal of Sociology* 20(5): 577–612.

Park, Robert E., Ernest W. Burgess, and Roderick D. McKenzie. 1925. *The City: Suggestions for the Study of Human Nature in the Urban Environment*. Chicago, IL: University of Chicago Press.

Schoenthaler, Stephen J. and Ian D. Bier. 2000. The Effect of Vitamin – Mineral Supplementation of Juvenile Delinquency among American Schoolchildren: A Randomized, Double-Blind Placebo-Controlled Trial. *Journal of Alternative and Complementary Medicine* 6: 7–17.

Shaw, Clifford R. and Henry D. McKay. 1942. *Juvenile Delinquency and Urban Areas*. Chicago, IL: University of Chicago Press.

Sutherland, Edwin H. 1939. *Principles of Criminology*. 3rd edn. Philadelphia, PA: Lippincott.

Sutherland, Edwin H. 1940. White-Collar Criminality. *American Sociological Review* 5(1): 1–12.

Wilson, Wilson J. 1997. *When Work Disappears: The World of the New Urban Poor*. New York, NY: Knopf.

Wilson, James Q. and George Kelling. 1982. Broken Windows. *The Atlantic Monthly*, March: 29–38.

Wirth, Louis. 1928. *The Ghetto*. Chicago, IL: Phoenix.

Wolfgang, Marvin E. 1958. *Patterns of Criminal Homicide*. Philadelphia, PA: University of Pennsylvania Press.

Wolfgang, Marvin E., Robert M. Figlio, and Thorsten Sellin. 1972. *Delinquency in a Birth Cohort*. Chicago, IL: University of Chicago Press.

CHAPTER 38
Criminal Justice Studies

Gennifer Furst

The Field of Criminal Justice Studies

The field of criminal justice studies examines the three parts of the criminal justice system: the police (law enforcement), courts (the judicial system), and corrections (punishment or penology). Criminal justice is related to criminology, the study of the causes of crime; when we know the causes of crime we can then develop mechanisms to control and prevent crime via the criminal justice system. Generally, criminal justice is considered applied or practical in that it focuses primarily on understanding and improving the criminal justice system, rather than on the roots of criminal behavior. The relationship between the two disciplines will be discussed further below.

The Field

The goal of the criminal justice system is to respond to and prevent violations of the law. In principle, then, the criminal justice system reflects the morals of a society. However, criminal justice system personnel tend to have a high level of discretion and a low level of accountability. Individual workers have the power to make many decisions that greatly impact suspects and defendants without being held responsible for the consequences of those decisions. For example, discretion can lead to troubling patterns of differential treatment of people based on extra-legal factors such as race. Evidence for this can be seen in the disproportionate number of black males in the United States who have been exonerated, meaning they were found to be innocent after having been wrongly incarcerated (Innocence Project 2016).

The criminal justice system in the United States is vast and multi-tiered with local (municipal), county, state, and federal levels. After the terror attacks of 9/11, the criminal justice system grew dramatically and the federal government created the Department of Homeland Security and changed Immigration and Nationalization Services (INS) to Immigration and Customs Enforcement (ICE). Much of federal law enforcement is now focused on issues of terrorism. At the same time, the federal levels rely on local law enforcement to share information and responsibilities. Local officials also have access to many federal-level tools. Military weapons, used to fight in wars overseas, have been given to local law enforcement agencies, changing how police officers in many communities deal with disturbances (see Landler 2014).

Most crimes do not fall under the purview of the federal system but are under state and local jurisdictions. As a result, most law enforcement occurs at the local level. Two hundred and sixty billion dollars is spent each year on criminal justice; most of the money is spent on state and local incarceration (Brennan Center for Justice 2015; National Association for the Advancement of Colored People 2014), and the majority of criminal justice personnel are employed at the local level.

The US has 5 percent of the world's population but 25 percent of the world's incarcerated people (National Association for the Advancement of Colored People 2014). In 2013, in the United States, approximately 6.9 million adults (about one in thirty-five) were under some form of correctional supervision, including 2.2 million in prison and jail (about one in 110) and about 4.8 million in the community but under supervision of probation or parole (about one in fifty-one) (Glaze and Kaeble 2014). The US incarceration rate is much higher than in other developed nations, with an incarceration rate of 716 (per 100,000 people), compared to 148 in England, 130 in Australia, ninety-eight in France, and seventy-nine in Germany (Walmsley 2014). Approximately 18 percent of all incarcerated people are females (Glaze and Kaeble 2014).

The Sequence of Events in the Criminal Justice System

The criminal justice system is often described as a sequence of events, starting with a criminal act. The criminal activity can be viewed by the police or discovered through investigation or informants. Sometimes the victim reports the crime. Most crime is not reported, however, and contributes to what is known as the dark figure of crime that makes the exact rate of crime impossible to calculate (for a discussion see Bosick et al. 2012). After law enforcement personnel establish that a crime has been committed, they seek to identify and arrest a suspect or suspects. The suspect(s) may be arrested at the scene of the crime or found after an investigation. Sometimes no suspect is found, while other times the suspect who was arrested was found not to be involved and released.

The police are the most visible component of the criminal justice system. Once a person is arrested, the process proceeds to the court system which is less visible and less understood by the public. After a suspect is arrested, the police present information about the events surrounding the crime to the prosecutor who determines if formal charges will be brought by the court. If not charged, the suspect is released. If charged, the suspect is brought before a judge for an initial appearance, usually within twenty-four to forty-eight hours of arrest. At the initial appearance, also known as an arraignment, the judge explains the charges to the accused who then enters a plea of guilty or not guilty. The judge determines if there is probable cause, or reasonable or sufficient grounds, to detain the person before the trial. If the crime is not serious or if the accused is judged not to be a flight risk, the judge will set bail or release the person on his/her own recognizance. If detained, the accused will be brought to the county jail for pretrial detention. When the crime is a misdemeanor, or minor offense, the judge may decide guilt or innocence at the initial hearing and determine the punishment, such as a fine.

Because of variations in state court systems, the sequence of events surrounding how cases are adjudicated varies somewhat throughout the country. Sometimes, a person will be assigned a lawyer at an initial appearance. Regardless of the state, however, any accused person who can be punished with incarceration if found guilty is eligible to receive a public defender. The judge will also generally make a decision regarding pretrial release at the initial appearance. While beyond the scope of the present piece, pretrial detention is a significant issue, as the majority of people in jail are there prior to being found guilty. The practice is expensive, disproportionately affects the poor and people of color, and contradicts the principle of innocent until proven guilty (see Freiburger et al. 2010).

After the arraignment, a preliminary hearing takes place, during which the judge decides whether the prosecutor has shown probable cause, or sufficient evidence, to put the accused on trial. The government, or prosecutor, presents evidence and can call witnesses to testify, while the defense tries to create doubt sufficient enough to cause the judge to dismiss the case. Some jurisdictions only use a preliminary hearing when the crime is a felony, while others use a grand jury indictment system. A grand jury hears only evidence from the government and decides whether the case should be heard in court. A grand jury can also be used by the government to investigate criminal activity as a way of opening a criminal case. Rather than using law enforcement to respond to a complaint of a crime reported by a member of the public, the government relies on a grand jury indictment; this method is most frequently used in complex cases involving, for example, drugs, gangs, embezzlement, and conspiracies. After the indictment is issued, a law enforcement agency apprehends the suspects.

All defendants have the right to a jury trial if accused of a crime that can be punished by incarceration. Some states have created the right to a jury trial in all criminal prosecutions regardless of the possible punishment. A felony is punishable by a year or more in a state or federal prison, while a misdemeanor is punishable by less than one year in a local jail. Alternately, the defendant can request a bench trial at which only the judge hears and decides the case. People most likely to opt for a bench trial are those accused of particularly violent crimes who hope to avoid shocking a jury, and law enforcement officers charged with unlawful activities related to their jobs who hope judges are more understanding than members of the public of the challenges they face. Some states use six-person juries while some use twelve; federal juries are comprised of twelve members.

The vast majority of cases, more than 95 percent, are settled with a guilty plea from the defendant (Reaves 2013). The adjudication of the case can result in an acquittal or conviction. In all trials except capital offenses, where the jury determines whether the defendant should be executed, the judge determines the punishment after a conviction. The defendant can petition for an appeal or review of the case after the trial is completed. In death penalty cases, the appeal is automatic. Sentencing, which can be decided during a separate hearing, is determined while considering mitigating circumstances, which reduce culpability, and aggravating circumstances, which increase the seriousness of the offense. In addition, the local probation authority is usually responsible for the pre-sentencing investigation which outlines the defendant's criminal history as well as other characteristics such as mental health needs, substance abuse history, marital status and military record. A victim impact statement comes from the victim or victim's family and describes the effects of the crime.

There are a number of sentencing possibilities. In order of decreasing severity they are: the death penalty (in some states), incarceration, probation, fines, and restitution. As noted earlier, punishment for committing a felony is incarceration in a state or federal prison, for a year or more, and a misdemeanor is punishable by up to one year in a local jail. Probation allows the convicted person to remain in the community while abiding by conditions such as drug testing, curfew, and residence requirements. Restitution generally refers to the offender paying monetary compensation to the victim, often for lost or damaged property or medical or legal costs. Intermediate sanctions, which are less restrictive than incarceration but more serious than probation, include house arrest, electronic monitoring, and community service. Many states have mandatory minimum sentences for certain crimes, such as felony murder and drug offenses. Determinate sentences require the offender to serve a specific term, while with an indeterminate sentence a parole board determines when an offender is released from confinement. Similar to probation, parole has restrictions, such as requirements of employment and substance abuse treatment. Approximately two-thirds of all offenders recidivate and return to prison.

The Juvenile Justice System

Juvenile offenders are processed similarly to adults, but with a few key differences. Unlike adults, juveniles can commit status offenses, which are offenses only because of the accused's age, such as drinking alcohol or running away from home. Unlike adults, juveniles can be referred to the court system for behavioral issues by parents, social service agencies, or schools. While states have different statutes that determine juvenile court jurisdiction, most states treat offenders under eighteen as juveniles. When a juvenile commits an offense considered especially heinous, however, a child as young as fourteen can be processed through the adult system through a waiver. A juvenile processed through the adult court system may be sentenced to a juvenile or adult carceral facility for punishment.

Unlike adults, juveniles accused of committing delinquent acts, not crimes, have their cases heard in civil – not criminal – court. Juveniles are not guaranteed a jury trial but retain other due process rights such as having the right to cross-examine witnesses. Juvenile court judges are afforded greater discretion than in adult courts. A juvenile whose case is informally processed may, for example, be ordered to participate in counseling, write an essay, or engage in community service. Juvenile courts have a wider variety of sentencing options including ordering a juvenile to participate in programs such as those designed to prevent shoplifting or underage drinking. Juvenile courts can also remove children from their homes for placement in foster homes or treatment facilities. After being released from a facility, a juvenile can be assigned to aftercare services such as family counseling and anger management designed to help ease the transition back to the community. A juvenile who violates the requirements of aftercare can be returned to the juvenile detention center or be transferred to the adult criminal justice system.

History of the Criminal Justice System

Contemporary American law can be traced back thousands of years. The Babylonian King Hammurabi (1792–1750 BCE), in Mesopotamia (today, Southern Iraq) created the first set of written rules, or laws. The central features of modern American law can be traced to the rule of Henry II (1154–1189). The King of England sent his royal judges to the villages of his kingdom where they heard about the violations that had taken place since their last appearance. The judges traveled a circuit, deciding the cases based on the local customs and standards of conduct. According to the principle of *stare decisis*, to let the decision stand, the judges established precedents which were then used to decide future cases. The local rules developed into a system of common law where what was usual, or common, in a locale was used as a legal standard. The judges' decisions were published and the legal rulings and precedents became the foundation of the English legal system. Under common law, crimes were divided into two types: *mala in se* and *mala prohibitum*. Crimes that are *mala in se* are inherently evil, such as rape or murder, while *mala prohibitum* offenses were behaviors made illegal due to a law that was passed. Behaviors deemed *mala prohibitum*, such as drug and alcohol use, may change over time with variations in social norms.

The legal system, which the criminal justice system in the United States enforces, is based on common law. The federal government codified statutes for *mala in se* offenses. New statutes are added, for *mala prohibitum* crimes, as society changes and can vary among states. For example, statutes prohibiting speeding differ across the country. Crimes that use computers, such as stealing credit card numbers and illegally downloading movies, have been created and refined as technology has advanced.

While a crime is committed against an individual or corporation, in the US criminal justice system, the government, whether at the state or federal level, represents the victim. In this sense, the crime is treated as if it has damaged society as-a-whole. The lawsuit, or litigation, is filed against the defendant by the government, the prosecution. In a civil case, the plaintiff, a private entity such as a person or a corporation, files a lawsuit against another private party using tort law. While a criminal case is punishable with the loss of liberty (incarceration or execution), a civil lawsuit is punishable by monetary compensation. Since the possible outcome of a criminal case is more serious than paying damages, the burden of proof is higher than in a civil litigation. The defendant is assumed innocent and the prosecution must prove guilt beyond a reasonable doubt, commonly thought of as 99 percent certainty. In a civil suit the burden is generally on the plaintiff who must show guilt with a preponderance of the evidence, at least 51 percent. In some civil cases, the standard is "clear and convincing evidence," which is more than preponderance of the evidence but less than beyond a reasonable doubt.

While the United States has a long history of crime and violence, the criminal justice system did not always have the reach it has currently. During the first decades of the nation, law enforcement consisted of night watchmen and constables, peace officers who patrolled for suspicious activity. The Industrial Revolution and the rise of cities in the early nineteenth century brought rapid changes and increased social disorganization and crime. The peace officers were not able to respond adequately to the concomitant increase in crime in the cities and were replaced, over time, by formal police forces (Thale 2004). The city of Boston created the first police department in the United States in 1838; New York followed in 1844, and Philadelphia in 1854.

Early police forces were associated with corruption and abuse of power. Police officers received little training and were largely viewed as unprofessional. They were known for using violence to enforce the will of the political party in power and to control the growing immigrant population. In 1893, the International Association of Chiefs of Police (IACP) was created in order to increase the professionalization of the field. One of their recommendations was to create civil service exams to replace the political favoritism and bribery that pervaded police hiring at the time.

In 1931 President Herbert Hoover created the National Commission of Law Observance and Enforcement, known as the Wickersham Commission. The Commission's report on the state of the criminal justice system in the United States revealed a complex system of procedures and policies and loosely connected agencies that did not communicate.

The American Bar Foundation (ABF), created in 1952 as an independent, non-profit research agency, was the first to use the term "criminal justice system" to describe the association between the various agencies that respond to crime and process offenders. According to the first reports of the ABF, much of the criminal justice system – from police investigations to criminal prosecutions – went unobserved by the public and largely unmonitored. The foundation's research also highlighted the high levels of discretion used by criminal justice employees.

In 1965, President Lyndon Johnson convened the President's Commission on Law Enforcement and Administration of Justice, comprised of academics, lawyers, and criminal justice practitioners, to study the system as a whole and make recommendations for reform. One of the outcomes of the Crime Commission was the Safe Streets and Crime Control Act of 1968, which created federal funding for state and local crime control programs. At the federal level, the legislation funded the National Institute of Law Enforcement and Criminal Justice (NILECJ), a research organization renamed the National Institute of Justice (NIJ) in 1979. The NIJ continues to support innovative programs and evaluation of criminal justice work. The Crime Control Act also created the Law Enforcement Assistance Administration (LEAA), which provided funding for criminal justice programs. While the LEAA was dissolved after fourteen years, its work continues through the NIJ and the Bureau of Justice Assistance (BJA).

Criminal Justice Studies, Criminology, and Sociology

Two main debates surround the field of criminal justice: whether it is distinct from criminology and whether it is a separate discipline from sociology. While criminology is the study of crime as a social phenomenon, criminal justice is broader and includes research on law, punishment, social control, victimization, capital punishment, practitioner ethics, and organizational issues such as management and politics. Traditionally, criminology has "enjoyed a privileged status over criminal justice because of its reputation for having a more scientific, empirical approach compared to the practical and applied" nature of criminal justice (Steinmetz et al. 2014: 358).

Roots in Sociology

The work of Emile Durkheim (1964[1893]), a founder of sociology, examined how the Industrial Revolution and other large-scale social change influenced the rural people who flocked to newly growing cities. The rise of cities brought new social problems and changed the collective norms and values of the people, what Durkheim called the collective conscience. Rapid social change, such as what occurred with the Industrial Revolution, led to anomie or confusion about the new social norms. Violations of the collective conscience, or crimes, are an inevitable part of society and even serve important functions. Crime can contribute to social change as people challenge laws and the norms and values of society are reassessed. In addition, crime can increase social cohesion as people bond against a common enemy. Durkheim also recognized that crime would create jobs as people were needed to control and respond to it. His work is the foundation for the study of crime as a structural phenomenon.

Robert Merton (1938) built on Durkheim's work about anomie. For Merton, though, anomie was the strain that occurred when culturally prescribed norms are unachievable using the culturally acceptable means. Merton developed a typology of five reactions to anomie: conformity, innovation, ritualism, retreatism, and rebellion. The most common form of adaptation is conformity; conformists use traditional ways to achieve material success. They will earn an education and work hard. In contrast, innovators reject the traditional ways of achieving success and instead use alternative, often criminal, means.

The rise of cities also influenced the work of other sociologists. At the University of Chicago, Robert Park and Ernest Burgess (1925) were the first urban sociologists and studied the effect of the environment on crime. They developed the concentric zone theory and found that each of the zones moving out from the center of a city had unique characteristics and patterns of crime. Zone two, immediately outside the central business district at the epicenter of the city, had the highest levels of crime. It was also where recent immigrant groups settled and was marked by deteriorated housing, factories, and abandoned buildings. Clifford Shaw and Henry McKay (1942) argued that many of the characteristics of zone two, including high levels of poverty, unemployment, and population turnover, lead to a breakdown of social norms. Their concept of social disorganization described these neighborhoods as having lower levels of informal social control, such as a sense of community, and, thus, higher rates of crime.

The Rise of Criminal Justice Studies

Criminal justice studies began with the so-called "college cop movement" and was often regarded as practical criminology (Morn 1980). Here also began the distinction between the academic and prestigious (criminology) versus the applied (criminal justice). August Vollmer, chief of police in Berkeley, California was the first administrator to require college training for police officers in order to increase the professionalization of policing. He helped establish the School of Criminology at the University of California at Berkeley in 1916. One of his students, O. W. Wilson, went on to establish the first police science degree at Wichita State University in 1937. In 1941, Wilson and six other men who taught police science and administration held the founding meeting of the National Association of College Police Training Officials, which focused on practical policing. It was this organization that was renamed the American Society of Criminology (ASC) in 1956. As sociological criminologists became active in the ASC and gained dominance, practitioners left and established the International Association of Police Professors in 1963, which was later renamed the Association of Criminal Justice Studies (ACJS). In 1965, the City University of New York established the College of Police Science (COPS), later renamed John Jay College of Criminal Justice, after the first Supreme Court Chief Justice. These originally all-male organizations saw the integration of women by the late 1960s.

Today, the ACJS is associated with applied criminal justice and the ASC with academia. According to survey research, members of the ACJS are more likely to be criminal justice practitioners who focus on teaching and advising undergraduate and master's level students, and spend less time on research. Members of the ASC, meanwhile, report spending more time conducting research and teaching in doctoral programs (Sorensen et al. 1994).

The legitimacy of criminal justice studies was declared by Todd Clear in his 2001 Presidential Address to ACJS in which he asserted that academic criminal justice was an area of study and had "come of age" (Clear 2001: 726). Criminal justice, he argued, is deserving of an "accepted place at the scholarly table" (711). He bases his argument on two indicators: a significant number of graduates earning advanced degrees in criminal justice and criminal justice scholars who publish at rates similar to those from established social science disciplines such as sociology. He suggests the path of academic criminal justice mirrors that of sociology, which itself struggled for the "respect of the older, established social sciences" (723).

Academics do not seem ready to draw a distinction between criminology and criminal justice. Some academic departments have established criminology and criminal justice (CCJ) departments, signaling the unification rather than bifurcation of the discipline (Wrede and Featherstone 2012). In fact, the Association of Doctoral Programs in Criminology and Criminal Justice (ADPCCJ), an organizing body whose goal is to "work to advance the study of crime and justice" is "open to all institutions that currently have or are developing a doctoral program in criminology, criminal justice, or a closely related discipline" (Brennan et al. 2014: 1). In 2014, the ADPCCJ had forty-two member programs, most were criminal justice programs but CCJ programs outnumbered criminology programs. The ASC's list of MA programs includes criminal justice, criminology, and programs in other related fields. The list, organized according to state, does not differentiate between criminal justice and criminology programs. Complicating the issue further is the growth of master's level programs in narrowly defined areas such as Emergency Management and Terrorism.

Recently, Steinmetz and colleagues (2014) examined the distinction between criminal justice and criminology. They examined the curricula of thirty-five members of the ADPCCJ and found most programs required a class in criminology, but not in criminal justice. In order to address the claim than criminology is more scholarly and rigorous than criminal justice, they examined the publications of the ten most prestigious CCJ journals, as determined by the Institute for Scientific Information Journal Citation Reports. While articles about criminology-related topics outnumbered those about criminal justice, the number was not significantly greater. They conclude without defining the nature of the relationship between criminal justice and criminology and recommend additional research on the relationship between the two.

While the boundaries between criminal justice and criminology are not clear, the majority of scholars do agree the reliance of criminology and criminal justice on sociology has dissolved. As discussed above, the roots of criminal justice studies are found in the work of sociologists in the first half of the twentieth century. In 1951, the bestselling textbooks in the field were authored by sociologists (Wrede and Featherstone 2012). However, by the late 1970s, CCJ courses had begun to "shift...out of departments of sociology" (Cressey 1978: 173 cited in Wrede and Featherstone 2012: 105). And "while there is no exact date provided as to when the chains binding CCJ to sociology began to loosen, it seems apparent that the beginnings of emancipation" were present by 1990 (Wrede and Featherstone 2012: 105). Wrede and Featherstone point to the Stanford University Press publication of *A General Theory of Crime*, by Gottfredson and Hirschi (1990), the most cited CCJ researcher between 1986 and 2000, as another sign of the strength of a separate CCJ discipline (Cohn and Farrington 2007). Wellford's (1991) piece in *The Criminologist*, the official ASC newsletter, highlighted the need for additional CCJ doctoral programs in order to train discipline-specific academics. In addition, Cullen's 1995 piece in *ACJS Today*, its official newsletter, criticized "academics, particularly sociologists, who suggest that CCJ is merely a technical field or that it is dependent upon other disciplines" (Wrede and Featherstone 2012: 106).

Wrede and Featherstone (2012) provide an updated exploration of the "placement of CCJ academia" (108). While the ADPCCJ has forty-two members, The SocioLog, an online resource for Sociology, lists 137 doctoral programs in Sociology in North America, (www.sociolog.com/us_links/phd_soc.html). Not surprisingly, they find significantly fewer students earn Ph.D. degrees in CCJ compared to sociology, but significantly more students earn degrees in CCJ than in sociology at the bachelor's and master's levels. Overall, the number of CCJ degrees earned between 1999 and 2009 grew exponentially compared to sociology. For example, at the master's level, the number of CCJ degrees increased by 134 percent, while the number of sociology degrees decreased by 21 percent. The authors also examined the departmental affiliation of CCJ doctoral programs and found that all but three of the twenty-five programs they included in their analysis were housed in independent departments, separate from sociology. The faculty in CCJ departments are more likely to hold a doctorate in CCJ than in sociology. They cite Abbott (2001) who argues that "academic fields transition into disciplines 'once they hire mainly Ph.D.'s in their own field'" (139 cited in Wrede and Featherstone 2012: 120). It seems clear, then, that CCJ has parted ways from sociology.

Conclusion: Criminal Justice Studies Today

While the founders of the field were sociologists, the field of criminal justice today is its own established discipline, connected primarily with criminology rather than sociology. Scholars in the field of criminal justice use a range of social science tools to analyze criminal justice systems. Formal study of the criminal justice system, from a variety of perspectives, is crucial if its policies and programs are to be effective and just. Likewise, given the control the criminal justice system wields on people's lives, proper training of criminal justice system personnel is also vital. The field of criminal justice studies, in helping to provide both, carries out an essential service for the larger society.

References

Abbott, Andrew. 2001. *Chaos of Disciplines*. Chicago, IL: University of Chicago Press.

Bosick, Stacey J., Callie Marie Rennison, Angela R. Gover, and Mary Dodge. 2012. Reporting Violence to the Police: Predictors through the life course. *Journal of Criminal Justice*. 40: 441–451.

Brennan Center for Justice. 2015. Solutions: American Leaders Speak Out on Criminal Justice. Available at www.brennancenter.org/sites/default/files/analysis/Solutions_American_Leaders_Speak_Out_On_Criminal_Justice.pdf, accessed December 13, 2016.

Brennan, Pauline, Gaylene Armstrong, and Natasha Frost. 2014. Association of Doctoral Programs in Criminology and Criminal Justice (ADPCCJ) 2014 Survey Report, January 15, 2104. Available at www.adpccj.com/documents/2014survey.pdf, accessed December 13, 2016.

Clear, Todd. 2001. Has Academic Criminal Justice Come of Age? *Justice Quarterly*. 18: 709–726.

Cohn, Ellen G. and David P. Farrington. 2007. Changes in Scholarly Influence in Major American Criminology and Criminal Justice Journals Between 1986 and 2000. *Journal of Criminal Justice Education* 8: 6–34.

Cressey, Donald R., 1978. Criminological Theory, Social Science, and the Repression of Crime. *Criminology*. 16: 171–191.

Cullen, Frank. 1995. Fighting Back: Criminal Justice as an Academic Discipline. *ACJS Today*. 13: 1, 3.

Durkheim, Emile. 1964[1893]. *The Division of Labor in Society*. New York, NY: Free Press.

Freiburger, Tina L., Catherine D. Marcum, and Mari Pierce. 2010. The Impact of Race on the Pretrial Decision. *American Journal of Criminal Justice*. 35: 76–86.

Innocence Project. 2016. *DNA Exonerations Nationwide*. Available at www.innocenceproject.org/dna-exonerations-in-the-united-states/, accessed December 13, 2016.

Glaze, Lauren E. and Danielle Kaeble. 2014. Correctional Populations in the United States, 2013. January 18, 2014. Available at www.bjs.gov/content/pub/pdf/cpus13.pdf, accessed December 13, 2016.

Gottfredson, Michael R. and Travis Hirschi. 1990. *A General Theory of Crime*. Stanford, CA: Stanford University Press.

Landler, Mark. 2014. Obama Offers New Standards on Police Gear in Wake of Ferguson Protests. January 15, 2014 *The New York Times*. Available at www.nytimes.com/2014/12/02/us/politics/obama-to-toughen-standards-on-police-use-of-military-gear.html, accessed December 13, 2016.

Merton, Robert. 1938. Social Structure and Anomie. *American Sociological Review* 3: 672–682.

Morn, Frank. 1980. *Academic Disciplines and Debates: An Essay on Criminal Justice and Criminology as Professions in Higher Education*. Monograph prepared for the Joint Commission on Criminology and Criminal Justice Education and Standards.

National Association for the Advancement of Colored People. *Criminal Justice Fact Sheet*. January 15, 2014. Available at www.naacp.org/pages/criminal-justice-fact-sheet, accessed December 13, 2016.

Park, Robert and Ernest Burgess. 1925. *The City*. Chicago, IL: University of Chicago Press.

Reaves, Brian A. 2013. Felony Defendants in Large Urban Counties, 2009. January 18, 2014. Bureau of Justice Statistics. Available at www.bjs.gov/index.cfm?ty=pbdetail&iid=4845, accessed December 13, 2016.

Shaw, Clifford and Henry McKay. 1942. *Juvenile Delinquency in Urban Areas*. Chicago, IL: University of Chicago Press.

Sorensen, Jonathan R., Allen G. Widmayer, and Frank R. Scarpitti. 1994. Examining the Criminal Justice and Criminological Paradigms: An Analysis of ACJS and ASC Members. *Journal of Criminal Justice Education*. 5: 150–166.

Steinmetz, Kevin F., Brian P. Schaefer, Rolando V. Del Carmen, and Craig Hemmens. 2014. Assessing the Boundaries Between Criminal Justice and Criminology. *Criminal Justice Review*. 39: 357–376.

Thale, Christopher. 2004. Assigned to Patrol: Neighborhoods, Police, and Changing Deployment Practices in New York City before 1930. *Journal of Social History*. 37: 1037–1064.

Walmsley, Roy. 2014. World Prison Population List. 10th edn. International Centre for Prisons Studies. January 15, 2014. Available at www.prisonstudies.org/news/more-1035-million-people-are-prison-around-world-new-report-shows, accessed December 13, 2016.

Wellford, Charles F. 1991. Graduate Programs in Criminology and Criminal Justice. What Are Our Needs? *The Criminologist* 16: 3–4.

Wrede, Clint and Richard Featherstone. 2012. Striking Out On Its Own: The Divergence of Criminology and Criminal Justice from Sociology. *Journal of Criminal Justice Education*. 23: 103–125.

CHAPTER 39
Social Work

Kathleen McInnis-Dittrich

Deeply rooted in the sociological tradition, social work has prospered as well as struggled as a profession and an academic discipline. In a direct services capacity, social work plays a vital role in providing health and mental health services and supporting children, families, and older adults facing life challenges. As a provider of indirect or macro interventions, social workers can be found in community organizing, social service agency administration, social planning and policy development, and most recently as part of the social innovation movement. Yet, the social work profession is not exclusively qualified to provide services in any of those areas. With the proliferation of similar professionals such as mental health, family and marriage counselors, social innovators and managers from the business community, and policy wonks from political science and economics, social work faces an occupational encroachment that threatens its future as a viable profession. Or does it? This chapter begins with a discussion of social work as a profession exploring its value base and the two methods of practice (direct and indirect services) and the theoretical underpinnings of both approaches.

Critics have suggested that in order to survive as a profession and to be respected as an academic discipline, a fundamental overhaul of social work education and social work research is needed (Stoesz et al. 2010). This argument is explored briefly in the second part of this chapter. The expansion in the sheer number of social work programs in the last fifteen years at the bachelor's and master's level has created a glut of new graduates with substantial student debt, employed at salaries embarrassingly below comparably educated peers. The increase in these programs has resulted in a huge growth in doctoral education as academics are needed to teach in the BSW and MSW programs. While tenure and promotion decisions in colleges and universities are often based on research productivity, does social work employ sufficiently rigorous empirical standards to be taken seriously by other academic disciplines? The chapter concludes with a look at the social, economic, and demographic challenges the profession faces in the twenty-first century.

Social Work: A Values-Based Profession

Social work can be described as a helping profession that uses an eclectic social sciences knowledge base to inform strategic interventions with individuals, groups, communities, organizations, and political systems. These interventions, ideally designed with the input and consent of the target systems, are aimed at enhancing psychosocial functioning and "creating social conditions that support communities in need" (National Association of Social Workers 2015). Consistent with the definition of a profession, social work is obligated to respect the public trust, perform services in the public interest, and regulate its members by establishment and enforcement of a code of ethics (Hillman 2005). These professional responsibilities are reflected in its value base.

The National Association of Social Worker Code of Ethics (2015) identifies six core values of the profession. The first value is that of *service*, a commitment to helping people in need and addressing social problems. Regardless of field of practice, service is considered an obligation of all social workers. In that sense, social work is both a profession and an avocation. A second value is that of *social justice*. While concern about the deleterious effects of unequal treatment and inadequate access to opportunities for vulnerable populations is certainly not the sole propriety of social work, this concern does form a major guiding value that informs practice in every context of social work practice.

A belief in the *dignity and worth* of every person and its corollary of *self-determination* comprise the third core value of the social work profession. Regardless of what an individual or community has done (or failed to do) in creating a social problem to be addressed, all client systems have inherent value and should be given the right to actively participate in developing their own capacities. However, the right to choose does not always lead to what others perceive as the right choice. The *importance of human relationships* is a fourth value of the profession. Relationships provide the support people (and communities) need to function and thrive. The fifth value of *integrity* and sixth value of *competence* are essential to social work's status as a profession. Basic honesty, trustworthiness, and a commitment to maintaining the highest levels of professional conduct are values common to many other professions such as law and medicine. These values are codified in the National Association of Social Workers' Code of Ethics, which serves as both private guide and public statement about social work.

Methods and Theories of Social Work Practice

Social work practice methods are generally divided into direct and indirect services to client systems. Direct practice focuses on individual (and group) behaviors that contribute to the development and maintenance of social problems. The field of indirect social work practice, often referred to as macro practice, works toward remediating socio-cultural and political conditions that maintain dysfunctional or oppressive social systems. Indirect practice focuses on larger systems such as neighborhoods, organization, communities, and political systems.

The Common Theoretical Base for Social Work

The foundation of social work as both a profession and as an academic discipline is a solid understanding of the "person-in-environment" as a dynamic phenomenon. Physiological, psychological, emotional, behavioral, and social domains form the contexts for human behavior and the biopsychosocial perspective. Social systems theory is the most widely agreed upon theoretical foundation for the social work profession. It addresses the blend of psychological, sociological, cultural, economic, and political forces that affect the functioning of both individuals and society

Regardless of the size of a client system, human behavior is seen as the result of the interaction and interrelationship between complex systems. Systems theory as used by social work, is an extension of the concept of individual biological systems (Barker 2013; Von Bertalanffy 1968). A social system (similar to the human body as an individual system) is a functioning whole with interrelated parts such as individuals, families, communities, and organizations, each a system in its own way.

By their nature, systems strive to achieve homeostasis, or a stable state, for maximum efficiency, functioning, and well-being (Longres 1995). Paradoxically, however, systems need both to achieve a stable state and to grow and evolve. A system needs continuous input from other systems to thrive and grow. When a change occurs in one system, all other systems are affected. The systems perspective is an essential part of the social worker's attention to "person-in-environment." For example, to understand and therefore identify solutions to a child's under-achievement in school, one must look at the school in the neighborhood context, the economic health of the community, and the influence of state and federal educational policies in addition to concerns about individual abilities, emotional and family stability, and the quality of teaching.

Direct Practice

Direct practice is aimed at developing, implementing and evaluating intervention with individuals, families, or groups. These settings include child welfare agencies promoting child protection, foster care, adoption, and juvenile justice. Direct practitioners can also be found in hospitals, health and mental health centers, correctional settings, substance abuse and geriatric care settings.

Social work roles in these settings most often involve working with clients to identify the problem that brings them into the professional helping system and devise an action plan to solve the problem or facilitate access to services to meet needs. While not all social problems are unique to the poor, social workers in direct practice are most likely to work with people with low incomes or other vulnerable populations such as older adults, refugees, immigrants, persons who have been incarcerated, or those struggling with homelessness.

Clinical Social Work

Clinical social workers, a subset of direct services, practice primarily in mental health clinics or as private psychotherapists. According to the National Association of Social Workers, there over 200,000 clinical social workers who provide more mental health services than psychiatrists, psychologists, and psychiatric nurses combined (2015). The increase has been influenced by improvement in clinical education of social workers, the choice of social work as a less expensive option for mental health treatment, and the emergence of clinical social work as a more prestigious segment of the profession. Clinicians are usually required to have at least a Master of Social Work (MSW) and licensing at the level of Licensed Independent Clinical Social Worker (LICSW). While exact requirements for this highest level of licensing vary by state, most states require two to three years of post-master's experience and intensive professional supervision. The authorization to engage in private practice (and the ability to bill private and public health insurance) is highly regulated by states and is contingent on strict enforcement of education and licensing requirements.

Some critics within and outside the profession have identified direct practitioners (and community organizers from indirect practice) as the "real social workers" reflecting the profession's origins in Settlement House and Charity Organization Society work. Are clinical social workers, who may treat those unsympathetically called "the worried well" really social workers?

Or have they abandoned the original mission of the profession (Specht and Courtney 1994)? The answer to that question may well be both yes and no. Yes, clinical social work feels far from the work in the trenches of social injustice originally envisioned as social work's domain, specifically if one assumes clinical social work treats more economically privileged populations. Yet, many clinical social workers *are* working with vulnerable low-income populations who have long suffered from a lack of mental health services. Clinical social work is more lucrative financially than many areas of the profession and is a huge attraction for students who want to be mental health practitioners yet are not competitive with applicants to clinical psychology programs. The discussion on this issue has waned in the profession since it was first raised by Harry Specht and Mark Courtney two decades ago but it has not been resolved.

Theoretical Models in Direct Practice

Direct social work practice allows social workers to tailor therapeutic work to reflect their own theoretical beliefs about the etiology and resolution of emotional and psychiatric problems. The theory base of direct practice borrows heavily from psychology and psychiatry as reflected in the adoption of traditional theories of human behavior such as Sigmund Freud's psychodynamic theory and Erik Erikson's psychosocial development theory. B. F. Skinner's behavior theory and Albert Bandura's social learning theory have also become mainstays of social work practice. These theories reflect the belief that behavior can be changed either by encouraging or discouraging certain behaviors or providing opportunities to learn new behavior.

Direct service practitioners cast a wide net for theories, in addition to the traditional perspectives, to guide practice, which is both a strength and a challenge for the profession. For example, current direct services approaches include family and internal family systems theories, cognitive-behavior theory, problem solving theory, strengths-based approaches, solution-focused approaches to behavior change, and narrative theory to name just a few. A broad range of theoretical orientations appeals to the interests and abilities of a variety of clients and social workers. However, this smorgasbord of theoretical constructs combined with even more esoteric theories such as postmodernism and constructivism is considered by some to be a threat to the theoretical integrity of the profession and the academic discipline (Thyer 2010; Tucker 2000).

Indirect Practice

Indirect social work focuses on larger systems such as neighborhoods, communities, organizations, and political systems. The intent of indirect or macro practice is to affect change in social, cultural, and political systems, thus improving the quality of life for a broader range of clients than is afforded by direct practice. As community organizers, social workers help communities identify and solve community level problems such as a lack of affordable housing, neighborhood safety, or recreational opportunities for children and youth. Community organizers may also engage in collective organizing around a cause such as immigration, police-community relationships, or prison reform.

Administration or management of social service organizations is another component of indirect social work. While not the exclusive purview of social work, mid- and executive-level management by social workers involves managing budgets, program planning, and human resources in agencies that provide the services to clients. Other macro areas of practice are policy development, community planning and development, legislative and political advocacy, and the newest addition to the profession, social innovation.

Social Innovation

Social innovation, as practiced by the social work profession, is a concentrated effort to propose new approaches to solving social problems resulting in transformative social change. Social innovation encompasses the concept of social enterprise that "applies commercial strategies to maximize improvement in human and environmental well-being" (Dover and Lawrence 2012). Such an approach uses the power of the marketplace to advance social, environmental, and social justice agendas.

For example, "innovations" may include new ways of developing resources used to fund social programs such as a for-profit enterprise within a non-profit social service agency that subsidizes the cost of service delivery, the development and adoption of new programs to meet existing needs, and new programs that produce better outcomes. Customizing existing service models for new populations or envisioning new organizational structures to provide services are two other approaches considered "innovations" in this area of macro social work. New services, new organizations, new products, new approaches to resource development, new paradigms of service delivery, or new models of service delivery are all considered social innovation (Pitt-Catsouphes and Berzin 2012). To be considered a social innovation, ideas and programs should have the potential to transform the problem, have the possibility of being sustainable and replicable, and hold the promise of enhancing social justice. The focus on social justice and problem transformation are what social work claims as its unique contribution to social innovation, which is also demonstrated in business and government.

Theoretical Models in Indirect Practice

Indirect or macro social work practice uses many mainline sociological theories about social change and community interaction. For example, systems theory is frequently applied to understanding and managing an organization in much the same way that social work applies systems theory to understanding an individual or a family. Organizations seek to maintain homeostasis but are constantly challenged by positive and negative interactions among components within the organization. Anticipating how any decision or program will affect other components of the organization is considered smart management.

Human relations theory and contingency theory are approaches commonly used by social workers in administration in much the same way these theories guide business management. Managers need to focus on the people in the organizational structure rather than the structure itself by considering individual motivation, group motivation, and leadership. If employees' needs for recognition, praise, achievement, and satisfaction are met in the context of doing their jobs, the organization will be efficient and effective in carrying out its mission. Contingency theory suggests that organizational decisions should be based on the specific situation in the organizational content, or "it depends," rather than relying on a single theory of management when organizational circumstances vary so dramatically.

Community organizers and social planners often use conflict theory as a framework for understanding the communities they work with and for adjusting power structures to help residents solve their own community problems. Community members struggle to maximize their benefits and access to resources with those who hold power over those resources, creating inherent conflict. These change efforts can be achieved by altering social and political institutions through public protest, political activism, education, and raising individual and group consciousness. A correlate to conflict theory is power-dependency theory which suggests that those who hold resources (banks, governments, and businesses) acquire power by transferring money and goods to people who cannot reciprocate. Dependency is created and maintained by this unequal social exchange. Altering power structures in the relationship between a community and outside institutions is the only way to break the cycle of dependency.

Consistent with conflict theory is empowerment theory, also frequently employed by community organizers and social planners. Disadvantaged communities do not have adequate resources and experience social problems because they are not empowered (or do not believe they are empowered) to affect change in the community. As a result, they suffer the consequences of oppression, inequality, and social stratification, which include substandard housing, health care, education, and psychosocial well-being. Empowerment theory suggests that developing an awareness of individual power (and consequently community power) through collective action, community awareness, and political access are the steps to addressing social injustice.

Social Work as an Academic Discipline

Social Work Education

Social work education moved from the apprentice model of learning by doing in the Settlement Houses and Charity Organization Societies into the university setting in the early 1900s, consistent with the growth in the number of middle-class individuals attending college (Boyle et al. 2009). Bachelor of Social Work (BSW) programs typically last the normal duration of an undergraduate degree. Most MSW programs require basic, first-year foundation courses in practice, social welfare policy, diversity, human behavior in the social environment, and research methods as prerequisites for more advanced course work in either direct or indirect services during the second year of study. Students take courses and are placed in concurrent field education placements (or practicums) both years of coursework under the supervision of experienced, licensed social workers. Two years is the typical length of the educational program for MSW programs but part-time programs may extend that training to as long as four years.

Too Many Social Work Programs?

The Council on Social Work Education (CSWE) is the accrediting body responsible for approving social work programs at both the bachelor and master's level since 1952. Currently, there are 502 bachelor and 234 master's social work programs in the United States with twelve bachelor's and sixteen master's programs still in "candidacy," the step preceding full accreditation (Council on Social Work Education 2015). This compares with 351 bachelor's and eighty-nine master's program in 1985 (Rubin 1986). The wisdom of accrediting this exponential growth in social work programs during a period of political conservatism, economic instability, and spiraling tuition costs is questionable. Stoesz et al. (2010) suggest that the proliferation of social work programs may be more of a financial incentive for CSWE than a proactive consideration of the correlation between supply and demand of social workers in the American economy. While social work has a projected job growth rate of 19 percent between 2012 and 2022, what constitutes the demand for graduates of CSWE accredited programs versus the more generic category of "human services" is not clearly delineated (Bureau of Labor Statistics 2015a).

Inadequate Salaries

The sheer number of social workers in the marketplace likely relates to the slow growth of social work salaries. Compared to cohorts in nursing and education, social workers earn considerably less despite similar educational requirements. The *median* salary for a social worker (not defined as either BSW or MSW) was $44,200 in 2012, meaning half of all social workers make less than $44,200! This is considerably lower than the median salary for nurses ($65,470) or teachers ($55,360) according to the Bureau of Labor Statistics (Bureau of Labor Statistics 2015b; US News and World Report 2015). Although it is unlikely that individuals are drawn to any of these fields for the monetary rewards, substantial student loan debt adds to the inadequacy of low salaries. The average student loan debt for all graduating college seniors in 2012 was $29,400, up from $23,450 in 2008 (The Institute for College Access and Success 2014).

The combination of low salary and high student debt raises the question of whether social work is losing the best and brightest students because the profession is simply not a viable economic choice. Are persistently low salaries a question of too much supply and not sufficient demand or is there a more subtle dynamic at work? A majority of social workers in direct service roles are women who continue to be paid less than men for similar work in many fields (Pew Research Center 2015). Likely, the combination of sex discrimination, the aversion the profession seems to have toward union organization (Stoesz et al. 2010), and the profession's implicit acceptance of such meager salaries may all have some influence on salary levels.

Social Work as an Academic Discipline

Social work in the academy has tried since the early 1990s to develop a sustainable research infrastructure to encourage and promote high-quality research. In 1994, the Society for Social Work Research (SSWR) was established by a group of social work researchers in an attempt to preserve research for its own value rather than as a neglected component of the Council on Social Work Education. While the infrastructure now exists to promote social work research, a credible research agenda for the profession from which it can generate its own knowledge base has not emerged. Social work continues to be dependent on other disciplines such as sociology, psychology, economics, and political science for the theoretical constructs for research.

Evidenced Based Practice (EBP) or the application of practice methods and approaches whose effectiveness is supported by mainstream research methods is the profession's attempt to gain empirical credibility (Gambrill 1999). In other words, how does the social work profession through either direct or indirect practice know that interventions are effective? The logical platform for empirical testing of these interventions is the academic setting through a program of rigorous scientific testing.

One might assume that social work academics would embrace the opportunity to show that "the work of social work" accomplishes what it proposes to do. However, EBP has not been adopted universally within the academy. Some of this resistance may in fact be due to the acceptance of postmodern and social constructivist theories which stand in opposition to more positivistic theories (Thyer 2010). These theories espouse that there are different ways of knowing, that knowledge is a relative construct, difficult to define and therefore impossible to measure. There is no objective reality and to understand what challenges people, one must enter their consciousness and assess the reality that has been constructed resulting in alternative paradigms of human experience. It is not a surprise that social work research based on this theoretical orientation is rejected by other social scientists. David Tucker (2000) calls this the "anything goes" view of knowledge, where any theoretical perspective is accepted rather than the pursuit of a more consistent "problematic, an integrated framework of concepts, propositions and practice that together define the intellectual problems of a field" (Tucker 2000: 239). More rigorous doctoral level research training, better role models and mentoring for young scholars, and higher standards for judging whether research is publication worthy are suggestions for ameliorating this problem (Stoesz et al. 2010).

Challenges to Social Work in the Twenty-First Century

While it is still early in the twenty-first century, there are at least five areas that will affect social work as a profession and as an academic discipline. It is yet to be seen how well social work will meet these challenges as part of its effort to continue to survive and thrive both as a profession and an academic discipline.

The first challenge to social work (as well as government and economics) is the growing influence of global citizenship on both social and economic contexts. The dominance of Western nations is fading as Global South nations gain in economic and social influence (United Nations Development Program 2013). Dramatic changes in political structures in Central America and Africa have produced significant waves of immigrants and refugees who will force policy reform. The United States and other wealthy nations are struggling to determine how to handle immigrants and refugees already in the country without legal status. Nations are desperately trying to balance service provision to its own citizens with a humane response to migrating individuals and families.

Stubborn and growing socio-economic inequality in the United States poses a second challenge to social work. Even for middle-class families, expensive housing, the astronomical costs of higher education and medical care threaten even those who have "followed the rules" with employed heads of household and home ownership. The Great Recession of 2008 challenged everybody's assumptions of who was safe from the devastations of unemployment and home foreclosure. High poverty rates persist among populations of color, older adults, and persons with disabilities (US News and World Report 2014). While education levels have risen dramatically in the past century, the number of young adults with inadequate education or skills to offer a tech-savvy society continues to grow despite overwhelming efforts to focus on job training and vocational education.

Demographic changes present a third challenge to the profession. With a rapidly aging society, one in five residents of the United States will be over the age of sixty-five by 2030 (Administration on Aging 2012). The fastest growing segments of the aging population are older adults of color (specifically Latino) and those over the age of eighty-five years. The demands this population will make on housing and health care services is unimaginable, yet social work with older adults is one of the smallest special-interest groups within the profession.

A fourth challenge to social work will be the changing health care system, which includes accessing health care and paying for it. While the Affordable Care Act promises the availability of health care coverage to all Americans, it cannot promise that there will be health care providers available in all parts of the country (Supplemental Health Care 2012). Will there be health care providers who accept patients with Medical Assistance or Medicare? Will "affordable" health care plans have such high deductibles and co-pays that they are unusable to persons with low incomes? Will mental health services, so crucial to many vulnerable populations, be accessible in numbers sufficient to meet demand? Will the social work profession be prepared to continue to be the largest provider of mental health services? And, if so, at what cost to its mission to serve the most vulnerable and oppressed populations?

Finally, technology, including the internet and social media, will challenge the social work profession. How can the profession benefit from the movement toward electronic medical records without contributing to the violation of privacy and confidentiality of a vulnerable population? What roles do social media play in the development and maintenance of mental health problems? Does technology show promise in terms of expanding access to remote mental health services through telemedicine? How can community organizers and social advocates harness the energy of social media to enhance organizing efforts within communities struggling with social injustice?

Despite the challenges facing the profession and its role as an academic discipline, social work will survive and thrive, though perhaps in a much different form from today. The pressing problems of poverty, discrimination, unemployment, child protection, substance abuse, and many others show little likelihood of abating without continuing societal attention. The persistence of acute and chronic mental health issues will likely continue to be treated by clinical social workers as valuable members of the mental health profession. Social workers in conjunction with colleagues in business and other disciplines offer promise to the dynamic field of social innovation. The challenge to the field will be to face its own limitations and define the professional journey ahead.

References

Administration on Aging. 2012. Aging statistics: Future growth. Available at www.aoa.acl.gov/Aging_Statistics/Profile/2013/4.aspx, accessed December 8, 2016.

Barker, Robert L. 2013. *The Social Work Dictionary*. 6th edn. Washington, DC: National Association of Social Workers.

Boyle, Scott, Grafton Hull, Janna Hurn Mather, Larry Lorenzo Smith, and, O. William Farley. 2009. *Direct Practice in Social Work*. 2nd edn. Boston, MA: Pearson.

Bureau of Labor Statistics. 2015a. *Occupational Outlook Handbook, 2014–2015 Edition: Community and Social Services Workers*. Washington DC: US Department of Labor. Available at www.bls.gov/ooh/community-and-social-service/social-workers.htm, accessed December 13, 2016.

Bureau of Labor Statistics. 2015b. *Occupational Outlook Handbook, 2014–2015 Edition: Health Care, Registered Nurses*. Washington DC: US Department of Labor. Available at www.bls.gov/ooh/healthcare/registered-nurses.htm, accessed December 8, 2016.

Council on Social Work Education. 2015. Accreditation. Alexandria, VA: CSWE Available at www.cswe.org/Accreditation.aspx, accessed December 8, 2016.

Dover, Graham and Thomas Lawrence. 2012. The Role of Power in Nonprofit Innovation. *Nonprofit and Voluntary Sector Quarterly* 41: 6: 991–1013.

Gambrill, Eileen. 1999. Evidence-Based Practice: An Alternative to Authority-Based Practice. *Families in Society* 80: 4: 341–350.

Hillman, Amy J. 2005. Reflections on Service Orientations, Communities and Professionals. *Academy of Management Journal* 48: 2: 185–188.

Longres, E. John. 1995. *Human Behavior in the Social Environment*. Itasca, IL: F. E. Peacock.

National Association of Social Workers. 2015. *Code of Ethics*. Washington, DC: National Association of Social Workers. Available at www.socialworkers.org/pubs/code/default.asp, accessed December 8, 2016.

Pew Research Center. 2015. On Equal Pay Day: Key Facts about the Gender Pay Gap. Available at www.pewresearch.org/fact-tank/2015/04/14/on-equal-pay-day-everything-you-need-to-know-about-the-gender-pay-gap/, accessed December 13, 2016.

Pitt-Catsouphes, Marcie and Stephanie Berzin. 2012. *Leading the Way: Social Innovation in Massachusetts*. Chestnut Hill, MA: Boston College Center on Social Innovation. Available at http://bc.edu/schools/gssw/csi/about/keyareas/investigate.html, accessed December 8, 2016.

Rubin, Alan. 1986. *Statistics on Social Work Education in the United States: 1985*. Alexandria, VA: CSWE.

Specht, Harry and Mark Courtney. 1994. *Unfaithful angels*. New York, NY: Free Press.

Stoesz, David, Howard Jacob Karger, and Terry Carrilio. 2010. *A Dream Deferred: How Social Work Education Lost Its Way and What Can Be Done*. New Brunswick, NJ: Transaction Publishers.

Supplemental Health Care. 2012. Patient Care Forum: The Patient Protection and Affordable Care Act: A Snapshot of Pros and Cons.

Available at www.supplementalhealthcare.com/blog/2012/patient-protection-and-affordable-care-act-snapshot-pros-and-cons, accessed December 8, 2016.

The Institute for College Access and Success. 2014. Quick Facts about Student Debt. Available at http://ticas.org/sites/default/files/pub_files/Debt_Facts_and_Sources.pdf, accessed December 8, 2016.

Thyer, Bruce. 2010. The Council on Social Work Education and the National Association of Social Workers: A Concerned Critique. In *A Dream Deferred: How Social Work Education Lost Its Way and What Can Be Done*. Edited by David Stoesz, Howard J. Karger, and Terry Carrilio. New Brunswick, NJ: Transaction Publishers, 175–196.

Tucker, David. 2000. Eclecticism Is Not a Free Good: Barriers to Knowledge Development in Social Work. In *Social Work at the Millennium: Critical Reflections on the Future of the Profession*. Edited by June Gary Hopps and Robert Morris New York, NY: The Free Press, 225–248.

US News and World Report. 2014. Solving America's Inequality Puzzle. Available at www.usnews.com/opinion/articles/2014/03/28/america-has-regressed-in-income-inequality-and-social-mobility, accessed December 8, 2016.

US News and World Report. 2015. High School Teacher: Salary. Available at http://money.usnews.com/careers/best-jobs/high-school-teacher/salary, accessed December 8, 2016.

United Nations Development Program. 2013. "Rise of South" Transforming Global Power Balance, Says 2013 Human Development Report. Available at www.undp.org/content/undp/en/home/presscenter/pressreleases/2013/03/14/-rise-of-south-transforming-global-power-balance-says-2013-human-development-report.html, accessed December 8, 2016.

Von Bertalanffy, Ludwig. 1968. *General Systems Theory*. rev. edn. New York, NY: George Braziller.

CHAPTER 40

Social Psychology

Laurie T. O'Brien, Stefanie Simon, and Caroline Tipler

Many scholars trace the birth of social psychology back to Normal Triplett's (1898) empirical studies of social facilitation effects with children reeling in fishing line (e.g., Allport 1954). Although this account has subsequently been criticized as an "origin myth" (see Haines and Vaughan 1979), there is widespread agreement that social psychology as an empirical field is just over one hundred years old. At the time of its conception, social psychology was widely viewed as a field lying at the intersection of two larger parent disciplines – sociology and psychology. As we will see, social psychology has since developed along somewhat independent trajectories in the fields of psychology and sociology. In fact, Cartwright (1979) and others use the terms sociological social psychology and psychological social psychology to differentiate between social psychology conducted in the sociological tradition and social psychology conducted in the psychological tradition.

We begin by discussing definitions of social psychology, the history of social psychology, and how social psychology came to develop separately within sociology and psychology. Next, we discuss methodological approaches to social psychology within the disciplines of sociology and psychology and how different methodological tools have contributed to the independent trajectories of social psychology within its two parent disciplines. We then identify several areas of study common to both approaches, and we end with a discussion of the benefits of bridging the divide between psychology and sociology.

Defining Social Psychology

One of the most frequently used definitions of social psychology was provided by Gordon Allport who said that "social psychology is the scientific attempt to explain how the thoughts, feelings, and behaviors of individuals are influenced by the actual, imagined, or implied presence of other human beings" (Allport 1954: 5). This rather individualistic definition focuses on the "ABCs" of psychology – affect, behavior, and cognition – with the added caveat that social psychology is the study of how the

ABCs of psychology are subject to social influence from other people. In comparison, Cartwright (1979) offered a definition of social psychology that more squarely situates the field between psychology and sociology. He defined social psychology as the "branch of the social sciences which attempts to explain how society influences the cognition, motivation, development, and behavior of individuals and, in turn, is influenced by them" (Cartwright 1979: 91).

Cartwright's definition retains the focus on affect, behavior, and cognition but is distinct from Allport's definition in two key ways. First, rather than a narrow focus on how other "human beings" influence the individual, Cartwright's use of the term "society" opens the study of social psychology to include how social institutions, organizations, and other social contexts influence the individual. Second, Cartwright's definition focuses on the *reciprocal* relationship between the individual and society, recognizing that not only does society influence the individual, but the individual influences society. In this way, Cartwright offers a definition of social psychology that can be more easily adopted by sociologists and social psychologists alike.

There is room for flexibility in how scholars define social psychology, although definitions that vary in their breadth may be more or less useful for scholars in different areas. In our view, the most useful definitions of social psychology incorporate three elements: (1) a recognition that social psychology is a science; (2) a focus on affect, behavior, and cognition; and (3) a statement of the reciprocal influence between individuals on the one hand and other individuals, groups, social contexts, and social institutions on the other hand.

History of Social Psychology

In 1908, the first two textbooks on social psychology were published, one by a psychologist (McDougall 1921[1908]) and one by a sociologist (Ross 1908). At its inception, social psychology was an interdisciplinary field situated between sociology and psychology. Today, however, many social psychologists are largely unaware of the sociological roots of social psychology and the historical relationship between the two fields (Oishi et al. 2009). Several scholars have lamented the divide between social psychology in the psychological and sociological traditions, a divide that has grown over the years (Eagly and Fine 2010; Cartwright 1979; House 1977; Oishi et al. 2009). How did this divide come to be?

In the beginning of the twentieth century, psychological social psychology and sociological social psychology were nearly indistinguishable (Allport 1954). World War II is often viewed as the historical event that had the largest impact on the development of the field (Cartwright 1979; House 1977). The social upheaval created by the war influenced both the topics that social psychologists chose to study and the demographic composition of the field. Many scholars were fleeing Europe for the United States at a time when social psychology was in its formative years, defining its topic of study and improving its methodological tools. The United States government recruited social psychologists to help identify solutions to the social problems faced by a country at war and, in the process, helped to establish social psychology as a legitimate field of scientific inquiry that deserved public funding. At this time and in the years that followed the war, many prominent social psychologists worked in interdisciplinary programs, publishing their work in both sociological and psychological journals (Oishi et al. 2009). However, after World War II, social psychology began to align itself more with psychology.

A number of prominent interdisciplinary programs began to be dismantled during the second half of the twentieth century (Berkowitz 1999; Oishi et al. 2009). In addition, the traditional departmental structure in universities forced social psychologists to declare themselves as either psychologists or sociologists (Berkowitz 1999). As a result, American social psychologists in particular became more identified with psychology and adopted the experimental methodology and outlook on science dominant in psychology departments (Berkowitz 1999; Danziger 2000; Rozin 2001). The founding of the Society of Experimental Social Psychology in 1965 was a watershed moment in social psychology that reflected a growing move toward viewing the experiment as the gold standard of research (Oishi et al. 2009). The focus on experimental methodology helped contribute to psychological social psychology's drift from sociology, as experimental methods are not well suited for investigating many sociological phenomena. Moreover, the focus on laboratory experiments is also believed to have contributed to an individualistic focus in psychological social psychology on intrapersonal phenomena (e.g., cognitive processes including attitudes) and immediate situational context as opposed to a more distal macro-level focus on social institutions (Cartwright 1979; Deutsch 1999). In so far as the pressure to obtain grant funding drives researcher decisions about topics of study (Berkowitz 1999; Cartwright 1979), the relatively greater availability of funding in the biomedical sciences as compared to sociology may have also helped push psychological social psychology away from sociology and toward neuroscience, public health, and related fields. Since 1965, social psychologists have become increasingly unlikely to publish their research in sociology journals (Oishi et al. 2009).

Shortly after the one hundred year anniversary of the publication of the first social psychology textbooks, a social psychology conference with both psychologists and sociologists was held at Northwestern University in an attempt to bridge the divide between the fields (Eagly and Fine 2010). An issue of *Social Psychology Quarterly* (2010, Vol. 73, No. 4) was dedicated to rebuilding the lost connection between sociology and psychology. *Personality and Social Psychology Review* also published an excellent paper advocating for increased dialog between psychology and sociology (Oishi et al. 2009). We consider this to be a positive development that reflects a growing awareness of both what sociology can offer to psychology and what psychology can offer to sociology.

Meta-theoretical and Methodological Approaches

Different meta-theoretical and methodological approaches in psychology and sociology have also contributed to the distancing of sociology from psychological social psychology. Sociological perspectives tend to focus on social structures and the collective and are concerned with how societies develop and function. As a result, sociologists tend to view institutions, organizations, and other collective phenomena as a fundamental level of analysis in their research. Psychological perspectives, in contrast, are markedly individualistic in focus, particularly within the United States (Berkowitz 1999; Oishi et al. 2009; Scherer 1993). Most psychological social psychologists view the individual as the fundamental level of analysis.

In the early days of social psychology, researchers more commonly used a broad array of methodologies including case studies, surveys, and field and laboratory experiments. Over time, however, experiments in general, and laboratory experiments in particular have come to be viewed as the gold standard of research among psychological social psychologists (Cialdini 2009; Danziger 2000; Wilson et al. 2010). This emphasis on experimental research has led psychological social psychologists to increasingly focus on effects that are proximal (i.e., located in the immediate situation) and decomposable (i.e., could be separated into distinct components and analyzed in isolation, see Danziger 2000). Psychological social psychologists are primarily interested in understanding the thoughts, feelings, and behavior of the individual and use a variety of assessment techniques including self-report, reaction-times, and behavioral observations (Baumeister et al. 2007). More recently, psychological social psychologists have increasingly begun to expand their repertoire of assessment techniques to include measures such as functional magnetic resonance imaging (fMRI, e.g., Van Bavel et al. 2008), electroencephalography (EEG, e.g., Amodio et al. 2004), cardiovascular reactivity (e.g., Blascovich et al. 2001), and hormonal assays (Dickerson and Kemeny 2004).

In comparison, social psychologists working within the sociological tradition are more likely to focus on a higher level of analysis and more frequently study thoughts, feelings, and behavior on an aggregated level. Although this focus on an aggregated level of analysis may limit the inclusion of measurement techniques such as fMRI or EEG, it allows a focus on phenomena that may only emerge at a group-level (Oishi et al. 2009). Experiments are less common among sociological social psychologists, who rely more frequently on surveys and qualitative methodologies such as interviews and ethnography (e.g., Glaser and Strauss 2009).

Areas of Common Interest

Despite the fact that social psychologists working in the psychological and sociological traditions may use different methodological approaches, they are interested in many of the same topics (Eagly and Fine 2010). In this next section, we highlight social-psychological research in four areas of interest to both psychologists and sociologists: culture, gender, emotion, and the self and identity. Although there are many other areas of common interest (e.g., racism, social class, cognition, attitudes, aggression, prosocial behavior), we chose to focus on these four areas as illustrative of topics that can bridge what has become a growing divide between psychology and sociology.

Culture. There are a number of similarities between psychological and sociological approaches to culture. Psychological social psychologists, for example, conceive of humans as a cultural species (e.g., Heine and Norenzayan 2006). According to this notion, every action humans engage in is shaped by cultural context. Individuals are not "hard-wired" with psychological processes that emerge independently of cultural context; instead, individuals possess cognitive capacities that emerge and develop in adaptive and flexible ways to the particular environments in which they mature. Similarly, cultures emerge and develop according to the inter-person interactions and person-environment interactions they can afford their constituents. Sociological social psychologists offer a near identical account of culture: individuals cannot be understood separately from their cultural contexts and cultural contexts cannot exist apart from individuals (e.g., Miyamoto and Eggen 2013; Ridgeway 2006).

While in the past, psychological social psychologists focused almost exclusively on WEIRD contexts (i.e., Western, educated, industrialized, rich, and democratic; Henrich at al. 2010), they now appreciate that many social-psychological phenomena vary significantly across cultural context. Similarly, while sociological social psychologists originally suggested that each individual, group, and society could possess only a single culture defined as a system of integrated and unified beliefs, values, and norms (e.g., Parsons 1949), they have begun to appreciate that individuals can acquire multiple cultural frameworks which they may flexibly employ or unconsciously activate (Schnittker 2013; Ridgeway 2006).

Despite this move toward a greater appreciation of cultural complexity, many psychological social psychologists continue to organize cultures into individualist and collectivist types (e.g., Triandis 1995; 2001). The core assumption of individualism (typically attributed to Western societies like the United States) is that people are independent of one another, whereas the core assumption of collectivism (typically attributed to Eastern societies like Japan) is that people are fundamentally interconnected with the members of their groups (Oyserman et al. 2002). The distinction between individualism and collectivism can trace its history to theories proposed by sociologists (e.g., Durkheim 1933[1893]). For example, Weber (1958[1905]) discussed the growing emphasis on personal interest and self-reliance that emerged in the West following Protestantism. More recently, Hofstede (1980) can be credited with stimulating a flurry of research among psychologists and sociologists alike when he identified individualism-collectivism as one of the four dimensions of cultural variation.

Social psychologists have identified differences between individuals from individualist and collectivist societies in the domains of self-perception (more independent vs. more interdependent; Markus and Kitayama 1991), cognition and perception (more analytic vs. more holistic; Masuda and Nisbett 2001), and emotion (more expressive vs. more inhibited; Matsumoto et al. 2008), among others. However, both psychological and sociological social psychologists increasingly emphasize that cultural tendencies toward individualism and collectivism can be flexibly activated or overridden (by cues in the environment, for instance). For example, Japanese exhibit more self-enhancing behaviors when exposed to American "situations" (success and failure scenarios recounted by Americans) and Americans exhibit more self-critical behaviors in response to Japanese "situations" (success and failure scenarios generated by Japanese; Kitayama et al. 1997). This research and others like it suggests that truly understanding what it means to be a cultural species requires integrating perspectives that emphasize individual psychological processes (psychological social psychology) and perspectives that emphasize socio-cultural contexts (sociological social psychology).

Gender. The terms "gender" and "sex" have long been studied as distinct causes of men's and women's behavior – with gender used more frequently to refer to cultural distinctions and sex used more frequently to refer to biological distinctions between men and women (e.g., Haig 2004; Unger 1979). However, recently gender researchers have begun to recognize the complexity of these interwoven terms. Specifically, biological (i.e., sex) differences between men and women may emerge as a product of the division of labor in societies and a system of gender practices that include cultural beliefs and institutional structures, as well as gendered interpersonal interactions and gendered understandings of the self (Wood and Eagly 2010; Wood and Ridgeway 2010). Thus, the topic of gender is inherently multilevel – including the individual-level and societal-level causes – and calls for an interdisciplinary perspective which examines the influence of gender at the individual, relational, and societal level.

A large focus of social-psychological research on gender is to understand and eliminate gender inequality. Gender role beliefs are an important contributor to gender inequality and exert influence, in part, by shaping gender identities and gender expectations (Wood and Eagly 2009). Gender role beliefs are rooted in society's division of labor, where people observe men and women taking part in different activities (Eagly et al. 2000). From these observations, people develop beliefs about attributes and personality traits that are reflected in stereotypes about men and women. For example, men are believed to be more agentic (assertive, dominant) than women, and women are thought to be more communal (concerned with others) than men (Bakan 1966). These gender role beliefs specify both what women typically do (descriptive) and what women ought to do (prescriptive; Prentice and Carranza 2002; Spence and Helmreich 1978).

Gender roles lead people to expect men to be masculine and fill masculine roles and women to be feminine and fill feminine roles (i.e., doing gender; West and Zimmerman 1987). Women who do not meet gender expectations are viewed with negative, hostile beliefs, whereas women who do meet gender expectations are viewed positively with benevolent beliefs (Glick and Fiske 2001). A major concern among psychological social psychologists is how gender expectations and stereotypes influence women's performance in culturally masculine domains. Specifically, women often underperform men when they feel at risk of confirming negative stereotypes about their gender group in culturally masculine domains such as math or leadership, but perform equally well when they do not feel at risk of confirming negative stereotypes (i.e., stereotype threat; Hoyt and Simon 2011; Spencer et al. 1999; Davies et al. 2005).

While both sociologists and psychologists recognize that gender operates through structural influences on men and women, in practice, researchers typically address a single piece of the gender puzzle. Because gender is a multi-level phenomenon, an interdisciplinary approach that does not limit theoretical and empirical investigations to a specific level of analysis would be fruitful (Wood and Ridgeway 2010). Specifically, because there are many causes of gender differences and gender inequality (Ridgeway and Smith-Lovin 1999), interventions should focus on gender issues at all levels to promote social change, from individual to structural. Sociologists have begun to explore ways to reduce gender inequality through status and organizational interventions, whereas psychologists have focused on understanding the circumstances under which negative gender role beliefs are more or less likely to be applied (Harkness and Hall 2010). However, researchers have yet to explore the intersections of these areas. Thus, both social and psychological social psychologists could benefit from a focus on interdisciplinary gender research.

Emotion. The study of emotion has a long history in psychology (e.g., James 1884), although dispute as to the precise nature of emotions continues among social psychologists to this day. In practice, emotions are defined as complex constructs comprised of a number of other psychological phenomena: thoughts, feelings, physiological changes, expressions, and behavioral inclinations (e.g., Cosmides and Tooby 2000: 93; see also Rogers and Robinson 2014). Importantly, some researchers distinguish emotions (e.g., anger) from moods (e.g., boredom) and affective dispositions (e.g., generalized anxiety; Scherer 2005; Smith-Lovin 1995; Thoits 1989).

In addition to defining emotions, emotion researchers also seek to determine emotions' universality. Sociological social psychologists, for example, have debated the number of emotions or facial expressions that are culturally universal and the extent to which displayed and felt emotions are shaped by the society in which people live (e.g., Hochschild 1983; Kemper 1987). While some psychological social psychologists argue that the *capacity* to produce, identify, and experience emotions is identical across cultures, they acknowledge cultural differences in "display rules," or the rules designed to govern when and to what extent specific emotional *expressions* are appropriate (Ekman and Friesen 1969). For example, Japanese and American subjects displayed virtually identical expressions of disgust, fear, and sadness in response to stress-inducing videos (bodily mutilation) as compared to neutral films (nature scenes) when alone (i.e., in private; Ekman 1972; Friesen 1972). However, while Americans continued to express negative emotionality when an experimenter was present in the room (i.e., in public), the Japanese subjects masked their negative feelings with smiles.

Sociological social psychologists similarly identify "emotion norms," but bisect them into "expression rules" (similar to display rules) and "feeling rules" that prescribe the "range, duration, intensity, and targets" of *felt* emotions (Hochschild 1979; Thoits 2004: 360). In support of the feeling rules perspective, Japanese not only report that *expressing* certain emotions is less appropriate than Americans (Matsumoto et al. 2008), but they also report *feeling* emotions more briefly and less intensely than Americans (Matsumoto et al. 1988). An emphasis on interdisciplinary research could further elaborate the extent to which experienced and expressed emotions are shaped by innate versus external/cultural influences, or some combination thereof.

Another area ripe for interdisciplinary research concerns the extent to which emotions are informed by bodily changes vs. cognitive appraisals. Older theories of the role of physiology in emotion argued that bodily changes were necessary (though not always sufficient) to produce the subjective experience of emotion (e.g., James 1884; Schachter and Singer 1962). This idea has recently experienced a resurgence in psychology due to the emerging theory of embodiment, which proposes that the processing and recalling of events involves simulation of the event through the sensory systems (Niedenthal 2007; Niedenthal et al. 2009). For example, emotion recognition is impaired when people are unable to mimic the expressions on others' faces (Neal and Chartrand 2011).

This emphasis on sensory experiences in emotional processing may appear contradictory to sociology's emphasis on symbolic interactionism (where one's understanding of reality is structured through a comparatively abstract understanding of interpersonal interactions; Blumer 1969), but it is actually complementary. While symbolic interactionism emphasizes the influence of top-down processes (where cognitive processes like mental representation shape one's current perception of reality), embodiment emphasizes bottom-up processing (where bodily experiences shape understanding of reality). From this perspective, embodiment may actually offer a mechanism by which social structures can shape individual emotional experiences. For example, theories of embodiment help explain how individuals come to structure their understanding of abstract culturally generated emotion symbols: by utilizing the physical domain to better understand them (Lakoff and Johnson 1999).

The self and identity. As with emotion, social psychology's interest in the self can be traced back to William James (1950[1890]) who described the self as a something that gives individuals a sense of continuity. James's conceptualization of the self is reflected in contemporary "neo-Jamesian" (Swann and Bosson 2010) social-psychological research that views the self as multidimensional – consisting of many motivational forces and a large social element. This "neo-Jamesian" conceptualization of the self is also heavily influenced by sociologists Cooley (1902) and Mead's (1934) symbolic interactionism emphasizing the importance of others in self-knowledge.

Self-knowledge can be explicit (i.e., controllable and deliberate) or implicit (i.e., uncontrollable and automatic). While people can report their explicit self-knowledge, implicit self-knowledge is often accessed indirectly by observing automatic behaviors (e.g., Greenwald and Banaji 1995). Discrepancy between people's implicit and explicit self-knowledge (i.e., a more positive explicit than implicit view) can result from a defensive strategy to present oneself in a self-aggrandizing manner (e.g., Bosson et al. 2003; Jordan et al. 2003).

Social psychologists have distinguished between personal self-knowledge and social self-knowledge (e.g., Tajfel and Turner 1986). Whereas personal self-knowledge consists of individual traits and characteristics, social self-knowledge consists of the social groups that individuals belong to and their feelings about those groups. Social identities, or individuals' social self-knowledge pertaining to knowledge of their memberships in social groups, have a profound influence on thoughts, behaviors, and emotion (Mackie et al. 2008; Turner et al. 2006). Social identity theory has provided social psychologists with an influential framework for understanding how self-processes are related to social situations and the broader social structure. For example, people join groups to serve a self-enhancement motive: in order to perceive themselves positively and distinctively (e.g., Abrams and Hogg 1988; Brewer and Kramer 1985). Social identities also help to reduce uncertainty (e.g., Hogg and Mullin 1999), give the world a sense of coherence (Ellemers and Van Knippenberg 1997), and protect people from the existential fear of their inevitable death (Castano et al. 2002).

Sociological and psychological perspectives both recognize the self as existing within and as being influenced by society (Deaux and Martin 2003; Stets and Burke 2000). Research that investigates the motivation for having and maintaining an identity, a question central to identity theories within both fields, would benefit from an interdisciplinary approach from sociologists and psychologists. While the plethora of motivations for identities is a testament to the interest in this area, as Deaux and Burke (2010) point out, there has been little work to compare the strength of various motives.

Identity change is another area of identity research that would benefit from interdisciplinary work (Cantwell and Martiny 2010). Identity changes are often a natural and important part of life (Robins et al. 2005) and can be sparked by societal shifts. For example, the Civil Rights and Women's Liberation movements brought upon changes in the socio-cultural expectations of groups that were historically disadvantaged in the United States, that in turn gradually influenced the identities of African Americans and women in the United States. As the United States becomes increasingly culturally diverse, identity change will continue to be an important area of research. Specifically, in intergroup situations, the need for a positive social identity and positive distinctiveness both help define one's identity in a given context. Understanding how these identities might change over time calls for integration of sociological and psychological perspectives (Cantwell and Martiny 2010).

Conclusion: Learning from Each Other

Although social psychology was originally conceived as an interdisciplinary field at the juncture of sociology and psychology, over the years much of the research being conducted within the field, particularly in the United States, has drifted toward psychology, with its stronger emphasis on individualism and experimental methodology. However, there are many opportunities for rebuilding the lost connection between social psychology and sociology. For example, recent developments in the measurement of implicit attitudes and the inclusion of physiological indices of psychological constructs have led to a number of important theoretical advances (Greenwald 2012). As technology to deploy implicit measures over the internet has become available, it is now possible to conduct the large-scale, societal-level analyses favored by sociologists with implicit psychological measures. Moreover, many social psychologists could benefit from sociology's lessons about the influences of society, institutions, and more distal social influences on the individual, even when these influences are hard to study with experiments in the laboratory. Rediscovering the lost connection between sociology and social psychology holds the promise of stimulating important theoretical and methodological advances in both fields. A promising sign of a renewed interest in bridging the gap between social psychology and sociology has begun to be set forth by several scholars (e.g., Oishi et al. 2009; Eagly and Fine 2010). We view this as a positive development as scholars in both fields have much to learn from each other.

References

Abrams, Dominic and Michael A. Hogg. 1988. Comments on the Motivational Status of Self-Esteem in Social Identity and Intergroup Discrimination. *European Journal of Social Psychology* 18: 317–334.

Allport, Gordon. 1954. The Historical Background of Modern Social Psychology. In *Handbook of Social Psychology*. Vol. 1. Edited by Lindzey Gardner. Reading, MA: Addison-Wesley, 3–56.

Amodio, David M., Eddie Harmon-Jones, Patricia G. Devine, John J. Curtin, Sigan L. Hartley, and Alison E. Covert. 2004. Neural Signals for the Detection of Unintentional Race Bias. *Psychological Science* 15: 88–93.

Bakan, David. 1966. *The Duality of Human Existence: Isolation and Communion in Western Man*. Boston, MA: Beacon.

Baumeister, Roy F., Kathleen D. Vohs, and David C. Funder. 2007. Psychology as the Science of Self-Reports and Finger Movements: Whatever Happened to Actual Behavior? *Perspectives on Psychological Science* 2: 396–403.

Berkowitz, Leonard. 1999. On the Changes in U.S. Social Psychology: Some Speculations. In *Reflections on 100 Years of Experimental Social Psychology*. Edited by Aroldo Rodrigues and Robert V. Levine. New York, NY: Basic Books, 158–169.

Blascovich, Jim, Wendy Berry Mendes, Sarah B. Hunter, Brian Lickel, and Neneh Kowai-Bell. 2001. Perceiver Threat in Social Interactions with Stigmatized Others. *Journal of Personality and Social Psychology* 80: 253–267.

Blumer, Herbert. 1969. *Symbolic Interactionism: Perspective and Method*. Englewood Cliffs, NJ: Prentice-Hall.

Bosson, Jennifer K., Ryan P. Brown, Virgil Zeigler-Hill, and William J. Swann. 2003. Self-Enhancement Tendencies among People with High Explicit Self-Esteem: The Moderating Role of Implicit Self-Esteem. *Self and Identity* 2: 169–187.

Brewer, Marilyn B. and Roderick M. Kramer. 1985. The Psychology of Intergroup Attitudes and Behavior. *Annual Review of Psychology* 36: 219–243.

Cantwell, Allison M. and Sarah E. Martiny. 2010. Bridging Identities through Identity Change. *Social Psychology Quarterly* 73: 320–321.

Cartwright, Dorwin. 1979. Contemporary Social Psychology in Historical Perspective. *Social Psychology Quarterly* 42: 82–93.

Castano, Emanuele, Vincent Yzerbyt, Maria-Paola Paladino, and Simona Sacchi. 2002. I Belong, Therefore, I Exist: Ingroup Identification, Ingroup Entitativity, and Ingroup Bias. *Personality and Social Psychology Bulletin* 28: 135–143.

Cialdini, Robert B. 2009. We Have to Break Up. *Perspectives on Psychological Science* 4: 5–6.

Cooley, Charles H. 1902. *Human Nature and the Social Order*. New York, NY: Charles Scribner.

Cosmides, Leda and John Tooby. 2000. Evolutionary Psychology and the Emotions. In *Handbook of Emotions*. Edited by Michael Lewis and Jeannette Haviland-Jones. New York, NY: Guildford Press, 91–115.

Danziger, Kurt. 2000. Making Social Psychology Experimental: A Conceptual History, 1920–1970. *Journal of the History of the Behavioral Sciences* 36: 329–347.

Davies, Paul G., Steven J. Spencer, and Claude M. Steele. 2005. Clearing the Air: Identity Safety Moderates the Effects of Stereotype Threat on Women's Leadership Aspirations. *Journal of Personality and Social Psychology* 88: 276–287.

Deaux, Kay and Peter Burke. 2010. Bridging Identities. *Social Psychology Quarterly* 73: 315–320.

Deaux, K. and Daniela Martin. 2003. Interpersonal Networks and Social Categories: Specifying Levels of Context in Identity Processes. *Social Psychology Quarterly* 66: 101–117.

Deutsch, Morton 1999. A Personal Perspective on the Development of Social Psychology in the Twentieth Century. In *Reflections on 100 Years of Experimental Social Psychology*. Edited by Aroldo Rodrigues and Robert V. Levine. New York, NY: Basic Books, 1–34.

Dickerson, Sally S. and Margaret E. Kemeny. 2004. Acute Stressors and Cortisol Responses: A Theoretical Integration and Synthesis of Laboratory Research. *Psychological Bulletin* 130: 355–391.

Durkheim, Emile. 1933[1893]. *The Division of Labour in Society*. Glencoe, IL: Alexander Street Press LLC.

Eagly, Alice and Gary Alan Fine. 2010. Bridging Social Psychologies: An Introduction. *Social Psychology Quarterly* 73: 313–315.

Eagly, Alice H., Wendy Wood, and Amanda B. Diekman. 2000. Social Role Theory of Sex Differences and Similarities: A Current Appraisal. In *Developmental Social Psychology of Gender*. Edited by Thomas Eckes and Hanns M. Trautner. Mahwah, NJ, US: Lawrence Erlbaum Associates Publishers, 123–174.

Ekman, Paul. 1972. Universals and Cultural Differences in Facial Expressions of Emotion. In *Nebraska Symposium on Motivation, 1971*. Vol. 19. Edited by J. K. Cole. Lincoln, NB: University of Nebraska Press, 207–283.

Ekman, Paul and Wallace V. Friesen. 1969. The Repertoire of Nonverbal Behavior: Categories, Origins, Usage, and Coding. *Semiotica* 1: 49–98.

Ellemers, Naomi and Ad van Knippenberg. 1997. Stereotyping in Social Context. In *Social Psychology of Stereotyping and Group Life*. Edited by Russell Spears, Penelope J. Oakes, Naomi Ellemers, and Alexander S. Haslam. Malden, MA: Blackwell, 208–235.

Friesen, Wallace V. 1972. Cultural Differences in Facial Expressions in a Social Situation: An Experimental Test of the Concept of Display Rules. Unpublished Doctoral Dissertation, University of California, San Francisco.

Glaser, Barney G. and Anselm L. Strauss. 2009. *The Discovery of Grounded Theory: Strategies* for *Qualitative Research*. New Brunswick. NJ: Transaction Publishers.

Glick, Peter and Susan T. Fiske. 2001. An Ambivalent Alliance: Hostile and Benevolent Sexism as Complementary Justifications for Gender Inequality. *American Psychologist* 56: 109–118.

Greenwald, Anthony G. 2012. There Is Nothing so Theoretical as a Good Method. *Perspectives on Psychological Science* 7: 99–108.

Greenwald, A. G. and M. R. Banaji. 1995. Implicit Social Cognition: Attitudes, Self-Esteem, and Stereotypes. *Psychological Review* 102: 4–27.

Haig, David. 2004. The Inexorable Rise of Gender and the Decline of Sex: Social Change in Academic Titles, 1945–2001. *Archives of Sexual Behavior* 33: 87–96.

Haines, Hilary and Graham M. Vaughan. 1979. Was 1898 a "Great Date" in the History of Experimental Social Psychology? *Journal of the History of the Behavioral Sciences* 15: 323–332.

Harkness, Sarah K. and Deborah L. Hall. 2010. The Future of the Gender System: An Interventionist Approach. *Social Psychology Quarterly* 73: 339–340.

Heine, Steven J. and Ara Norenzayan. 2006. Toward a Psychological Science for a Cultural Species. *Perspectives on Psychological Science* 1(3): 251–269.

Henrich, Joseph, Steven J. Heine, and Ara Norenzayan. 2010. Most People Are Not WEIRD. *Nature* 466(7302): 29.

Hochschild, Arlie Russell. 1979. Emotion Work, Feeling Rules, and Social Structure. *American Journal of Sociology* 85: 551–575.

Hochschild, Arlie Russell. 1983. *The Managed Heart: Commercialization of Human Feeling*. Berkeley, CA: University of California Press.

Hofstede, Geert. 1980. *Culture's Consequences: International Differences in Work-Related Values*. Beverly Hills, CA: Sage.

Hogg, Michael A. and Barbara-A. Mullin. 1999. Joining Groups to Reduce Uncertainty: Subjective Uncertainty Reduction and Group Identification. In *Social Identity and Social Cognition*. Edited by Dominic Abrams and Michael A. Hogg. Malden, MA: Blackwell Publishing, 249–279.

House, James S. 1977. The Three Faces of Social Psychology. *Sociometry* 40: 161–177.

Hoyt, Crystal L. and Stefanie Simon. 2011. Female Leaders: Injurious or Inspiring Role Models for Women? *Psychology of Women Quarterly* 35: 143–157.

James, William. 1884. What Is an Emotion? *Mind* 9: 188–205.

James, William. 1950[1890]. *The Principles of Psychology*. New York, NY: Dover.

Jordan, Christian H., Steven. J. Spencer, Mark P. Zanna, Etsuko Hoshino-Browne, and Joshua Correll. 2003. Secure and Defensive High Self-Esteem. *Journal of Personality and Social Psychology* 85: 969–978.

Kemper, Theodore D. 1987. How Many Emotions Are There? Wedding the Social and the Autonomic Components. *American Journal of Sociology* 93(2): 263–289.

Kitayama, Shinobu, Hazel Rose Markus, Hisaya Matsumoto, and Vinai Norasakkunkit. 1997. Individual and Collective Processes in the Construction of the Self: Self-Enhancement in the United States and Self-Criticism in Japan. *Journal of Personality and Social Psychology* 72(6): 1245–1267.

Lakoff, George and Mark Johnson. 1999. *Philosophy in the Flesh: The Embodied Mind and Its Challenge to Western Thought*. New York, NY: Basic Books.

Mackie, Diane M., Eliot R. Smith, and Devin G. Ray. 2008. Intergroup Emotions and Intergroup Relations. *Social and Personality Psychology Compass* 2: 1866–1880.

Markus, Hazel R. and Shinobu Kitayama. 1991. Culture and the Self: Implications for Cognition, Emotion, and Motivation. *Psychological Review* 98(2): 224.

Masuda, Takahiko and Richard E. Nisbett. 2001. Attending Holistically Versus Analytically: Comparing the Context Sensitivity of Japanese and Americans. *Journal of Personality and Social Psychology* 81(5): 922.

Matsumoto, David, Tsutomu Kudoh, Klaus Scherer, and Harald Wallbott. 1988. Antecedents of and Reactions to Emotions in the United States and Japan. *Journal of Cross-Cultural Psychology* 19(3): 267–286.

Matsumoto, David, Seung Hee Yoo, and Johnny Fontaine. 2008. Mapping Expressive Differences around the World: The Relationship Between Emotional Display Rules and Individualism Versus Collectivism. *Journal of Cross-Cultural Psychology* 39(1): 55–74.

McDougall, William. 1921[1908]. *An Introduction to Social Psychology*. Boston, MA: Luce.

Mead, George. H. 1934. *Mind, Self and Society*. Chicago, IL: University of Chicago Press.

Miyamoto, Yuri and Amanda Eggen. 2013. Cultural Perspectives. In *Handbook of Social Psychology*. Edited by John Delamater and Amanda Ward. 2nd edn. New York, NY: Springer Science+Business Media, LLC, 595–624.

Neal, David T. and Tanya L. Chartrand. 2011. Embodied Emotion Perception Amplifying and Dampening Facial Feedback Modulates Emotion Perception Accuracy. *Social Psychological and Personality Science* 2: 673–678.

Niedenthal, Paula M. 2007. Embodying Emotion. *Science* 316(5827): 1002–1005.

Niedenthal, Paula M., Piotr Winkielman, Laurie Mondillon, and Nicolas Vermeulen. 2009. Embodiment of Emotion Concepts. *Journal of Personality and Social Psychology* 96(6): 1120–1136.

Oishi, Shigehiro, Selin Kesebir, and Benjamin H. Snyder. 2009. Sociology: A Lost Connection in Social Psychology. *Personality and Social Psychology Review* 13: 334–353.

Oyserman, Daphna, Heather M. Coon, and Markus Kemmelmeier. 2002. Rethinking Individualism and Collectivism: Evaluation of theoretical Assumptions and Meta-Analyses. *Psychological Bulletin* 128(1): 3–72.

Parsons, Talcott. 1949. *The Structure of Social Action*. New York, NY: Free Press.

Prentice, Deborah A. and Erica Carranza. 2002. What Women Should Be, Shouldn't Be, Are Allowed to Be, and Don't Have to Be: The Contents of Prescriptive Gender Stereotypes. *Psychology of Women Quarterly* 26: 269–281.

Ridgeway, Cecilia L. 2006. Linking Social Structure and Interpersonal Behavior: A Theoretical Perspective on Cultural Schemas and Social Relations. *Social Psychology Quarterly* 69(1): 5–16.

Ridgeway, Cecilia L. and Lynn Smith-Lovin. 1999. The Gender System and Interaction. *Annual Review of Sociology* 25: 191–216.

Robins, Richard W., Erik E. Noftle, Kali H. Trzesniewski, and Brent W. Roberts. 2005. Do People Know How Their Personality Has Changed? Correlates of Perceived and Actual Personality Change in Young Adulthood. *Journal of Personality* 73: 489–521.

Rogers, Kimberly B. and Dawn T. Robinson. 2014. Measuring Affect and Emotions. In *Handbook of the Sociology of Emotions*. Vol. 2. Edited by Jan E. Stets and Jonathan H. Turner. New York, NY: Springer, 283–306.

Ross, Edward A. 1908. *Social Psychology: An Outline and Source Book*. New York, NY: Macmillan.

Rozin, Paul. 2001. Social Psychology and Science: Some Lessons from Solomon Asch. *Personality and Social Psychology Review* 5: 2–14.

Schachter, Stanley and Jerome Singer. 1962. Cognitive, Social, and Physiological Determinants of Emotional State. *Psychological Review* 69(5): 379.

Scherer, Klaus R. 1993. Two Faces of Social Psychology: European and North American Perspectives. *Social Science Information* 32: 515–552.

Scherer, Klaus R. 2005. What Are Emotions? And How Can They Be Measured? *Social Science Information* 44(4): 695–729.

Schnittker, Jason. 2013. Social Structure and Personality. In *Handbook of Social Psychology*. Edited by John Delamater and Amanda Ward. 2nd edn. New York, NY: Springer, 89–115.

Smith-Lovin, Lynn. 1995. The Sociology of Affect and Emotion. In *Sociological Perspectives on Social Psychology*. Edited by Karen S. Cook, Gary Alan Fine, and James S. House. Boston, MA: Allyn and Bacon, 118–148.

Spence, Janet T. and L. Robert Helmreich. 1978. *Masculinity and Femininity: Their Psychological Dimensions, Correlates, and Antecedents*. Austin, TX: University of Texas Press.

Spencer, Steven J., Claude M. Steele, and Diane M. Quinn. 1999. Stereotype Threat and Women's Math Performance. *Journal of Experimental Social Psychology* 35: 4–28.

Stets, Jan E. and Peter J. Burke. 2000. Identity Theory and Social Identity Theory. *Social Psychology Quarterly* 63: 224–237.

Swann, William J. and Jennifer K. Bosson. 2010. Self and Identity. In *Handbook of Social Psychology*. Vol. 1. Edited by Susan T. Fiske, Daniel T. Gilbert, and Lindzey Gardner. 5th edn. Hoboken, NJ: John Wiley and Sons Inc, 589–628.

Tajfel, Henri. and John C. Turner. 1986. The Social Identity Theory of Intergroup Behavior. In *Psychology of Intergroup Relations*. Edited by Stephen Worchel and W. G. Austin. Chicago, IL: Nelson-Hall, 7–24.

Thoits, Peggy A. 1989. The Sociology of Emotions. *Annual Review of Sociology* 15: 317–42.

Thoits, Peggy A. 2004. Emotion Norms, Emotion Work, and Social Order. In *Feelings and*

Emotions: The Amsterdam Symposium. New York, NY: Cambridge University Press, 359–378.

Triandis, Harry Charalambos. 1995. *Individualism and Collectivism: New Directions in Social Psychology.* Boulder, CO: Westview Press.

Triandis, Harry Charalambos. 2001. Individualism-Collectivism and Personality. *Journal of Personality* 69(6): 907–924.

Triplett, Norman. 1898. The Dynamogenic Factors in Pacemaking and Competition. *American Journal of Psychology* 9: 507–533.

Turner, John C., Katherine J. Reynolds, Alexander S. Haslam, and Kristine E. Veenstra. 2006. Reconceptualizing Personality: Producing Individuality by Defining the Personal Self. In *Individuality and the Group: Advances in Social Identity.* Edited by Tom Postmes and Jolanda Jetten. Thousand Oaks, CA: Sage, 11–36.

Unger, Rhoda. K. 1979. Toward a Redefinition of Sex and Gender. *American Psychologist* 34: 1085–1094.

Van Bavel, Jay J., Dominic J. Packer, and William A. Cunningham. 2008. The Neural Substrates of In-Group Bias: A Functional Magnetic Resonance Imaging Investigation. *Psychological Science* 19: 1131–1139.

Weber, Max. 1958[1905]. *The Protestant Ethic and the Spirit of Capitalism.* New York, NY: Charles Scribner.

West, Candace and Don H. Zimmerman. 1987. Doing Gender. *Gender and Society* 1: 125–151.

Wilson, Timothy D., Elliot Aronson, and Kevin Carlsmith. 2010. The Art of Laboratory Experimentation. In *Handbook of Social Psychology.* Vol. 1. Edited by Susan T. Fiske, Daniel T. Gilbert, and Lindzey Gardner. 5th edn. Hoboken, NJ: John Wiley and Sons, 629–667.

Wood, Wendy and Alice H. Eagly. 2009. Gender Identity. In *Handbook of Individual Differences in Social Behavior.* Edited by Mark R. Learly and Rick H. Hoyle. New York, NY: Guilford Press, 109–125.

Wood, Wendy and Alice H. Eagly. 2010. Gender. In *Handbook of Social Psychology.* Vol. 1 Edited by Susan Fiske, Daniel T. Gilbert, and Lindzey Gardner. 5th edn. Hoboken, NJ: John Wiley and Sons, 629–667.

Wood, Wendy and Cecilia L. Ridgeway. 2010. Gender: An Interdisciplinary Perspective. *Social Psychology Quarterly* 73: 334–339.

CHAPTER 41
Sociology of Translation

Rafael Schögler

This chapter offers an overview of the creation and development of sociology of translation. It then discusses some of its key foci. It concludes by noting the subfield's contributions to sociology and the society as a whole.

Translation Studies

Sociology of translation is deeply rooted in the field of translation studies. This interdisciplinary academic field, established in the 1950s and 1960s, deals with the phenomenon of translation in all of its diversity, including written, spoken (interpreting), interlingual, and intralingual translation. It deals with issues related to such topics as localization, transcultural communication, and cognitive processes. Initially, the field developed from the linguistic interest in the structure of languages, equivalence and – more specifically – Bible translation. The failure to achieve rules or algorithms to reach equivalence between source and target languages as well as the lack of success in developing (useful) machine translation tools based on this kind of research led to a diversification of interests.

The second step in the development of translation studies was to reject the "sacred" status of the original and turn toward the target text, i.e. the translation itself. Through dealing with the functions of translations in their target environment and by describing norms directing the translation process, researchers began studying cultural and social aspects that influence translations. Translators began to be viewed as experts who actively participate in the selection, translation, and reception of the texts they translate. This new perspective on translation required a reorientation of the object of research, the methods used, and the theoretical foundations that deal with questions regarding social norms and understandings of culture and power in the context of inter- and intralingual translation.

This new perspective has been labeled the cultural and sociological turn in translation studies (see Wolf 2006). In the early 2000s, sociology of translation turned into an established paradigm of translation studies that now coexists with linguistic, cultural, cognitive, and psychological research on translation. This turn to the social dimension of translation was predicted much earlier. In a speech in 1978, James S. Holmes mentioned the "development of a field of translation sociology" (reprint see Holmes 2000) as a possible direction for the discipline. And although in the late 1990s Gerald Parks (1998) voiced doubts about the accessibility of analytic tools available to translation studies scholars, the field did thrive. The research program was initiated through the collaboration of sociologists, cultural, literary, and translation studies scholars (for a summary of early developments in translation sociology see Wolf 2003 and 2007, for recent writing on the sociological turn see Angelelli 2012).

Positioning Sociology of Translation Within Sociology

As noted above, sociology of translation developed outside the core discipline of sociology. Although many of the researchers contributing to the field of sociology of translation were (and are) not formally trained as sociologists, their expertise and knowledge of sociological theory and, at least for some, also methodology is thorough. Institutionally, research in sociology of translation mainly takes place in departments of translation studies. In these departments, sociologists of translation work together with fellow colleagues trained in linguistics or comparative literature. At the same time, scholars affiliated with departments of translation studies collaborate with sociologists and other social scientists in interdisciplinary projects, cross-departmental efforts, and international networks. Most publications in sociology of translation take place in specialized journals (such as *Translation and Interpreting Studies*) and book series (e.g., *Benjamin's Translation Library* or *Representation-Transformation: Translating across Cultures and Societies*). However, some broader sociological journals such as *Current Sociology* or the French *Actes de la Recherche en Sciences Sociales* (see special issue on the circulation of ideas with contributions from Pierre Bourdieu, Gustavo Sorá and Victor Karady: Heilbron and Sapiro 2002) also publish papers on translation.

Sociology of translation is strongly dominated by research in comparative literature and translation studies, which explains the focus on studies on literary translation. However, translation is also the object of research in other subfields of sociology such as the sociology of science and historical sociology. In both of these subfields, translations are not the phenomenon of interest per se but an element that needs to be taken into account, either to further the understanding of knowledge-making or to explain specificities in the history of sociology or in the development of certain concepts and the problems of translating sociological thought in general (e.g., the translation of Max Weber's work into English, see, e.g., Tribe 2012 or Schögler 2012).

Translation as a Social Practice

What does it actually mean to understand translation as a social practice? Over the past two decades, researchers mainly affiliated with departments of translation studies or literature have focused on an array of questions that best exemplify for what translation as a social practice stands. The focus can be differentiated among work on the actors, the process, and the products of translation (see Wolf 2003). For instance, in research dealing with the **actors**, one important topic has been the submissiveness of translators in accepting certain norms and taking a subservient position in negotiating their role (Simeoni 1998). Other researchers have looked at questions relating to the professional status of specific occupational groups, such as conference or public service interpreters, legal or literary translators (see Sela-Sheffy and Shlesinger 2009; 2010). A topic of recurring interest is the visibility of translators (on the translator's invisibility see Venuti 2008) and related questions such as the recognition of the translator's work or the position of translators in the social strata compared to, for example, literary authors. The sociopolitical ideology of translators in the context of their professional behavior has also been studied in manifold ways (see e.g., Ben-Ari 2012; Pokorn 2014). The power of translation can be seen in the active and creative role that translators can take in manipulating texts – not least to challenge hegemonic or totalitarian powers (see Tymoczko and Gentzler 2002).

This leads us to a second dimension, which is the act of **translating** as a social practice. From a sociological perspective, this means that research focuses on micro-, meso- and macro-structural factors that influence translation or vice versa. On the micro-level, one can find the study of social interactions such as the interplay between the interpreter and his or her clients or between translators and authors. Historic research, such as Wolf's extensive study of translation in the Habsburg monarchy (Wolf 2015), focuses on the role, presentation, and representation of translators. The meso-level can best be exemplified by studies dealing with censorship authorities, like Uribarri's research on the Franco regime in Spain (Uribarri 2008; 2013) or Thomson-Wohlgemuth's (2007) work on censorship and different forms of self-censorship in the German Democratic Republic. The macro-level influences tend to be more difficult to grasp and are not usually studied separately from the other dimensions. For example, some of those who have analyzed macro-level influences have looked at structural elements, such as understanding translation as an element in a larger societal development such as globalization (e.g. Pöckl 2011; Sapiro 2008; 2009), internationalization, and digitalization (Cronin 2013) or concentrated on translation flows and related items, i.e. the amount of works, usually books, translated from one language into another, networks of publishers, authors, and translators etc.

The third object of study is the **product**, the translations, perceived as cultural artefacts with an agency of their own. Translations are studied as elements shaping change in their target (and source) fields. Seeing translation as a social practice opened the doors for questions relating to institutions, politics, and ethics of translation. Also, feminist and postcolonial approaches contributed to theoretical, empirical, and practical endeavors that formed what sociology of translation is today. Sociology of translation thus has not only produced a plethora of data and theoretical writings, but also serves as impetus for a transformation of the practice of translation as well as the position of translators and translator training.

Feminist translation is a good example of the interconnectedness of practice, training and research. By analyzing gender specific items in translations of, for example, Simone de Beauvoir (e.g., Simons 1983; Butler 1986 but also, later, Von Flotow 2000; 2009), scholars can create an awareness of the manipulation of texts by hegemonic canons in the target culture, the societal pressures on translators, and the cultural effects at work in the reception of translations. These analyses led to the implementation of activist/feminist translation strategies. In rewritings of either existing translations or of original texts, translators actively and deliberately manipulate the text to represent a feminist perspective and to counter hegemonic understandings of literary, political, or ideological canon.

Feminist approaches to translation focused a spotlight on the power of hegemonic discourse in the production of translations and had an impact on translator training. Students in modern translator training are made aware of and confronted with the power of hegemonic discourse in the production of translations in general and feminist issues more specifically. They are shown that it is the translator's decision to accept certain discourses, counter them, or construct new ones. The power of discourses is particularly prevalent in postcolonial (for a deconstruction of British colonial literature, see, e.g., Niranjana 1992) or totalitarian settings. It is also found in hegemonic forms of popular culture, which "dictate" certain translatorial norms. These norms can be countered by translating differently (e.g., changing the role or socio-cultural backgrounds of certain characters or – more visibly – explaining the history of a certain concept in paratexts).

From a sociological point of view, community or public service interpreting is a particularly promising research field. This form of oral translation refers to the practice of interpreting in communicative settings between public authorities of one kind or another and a second client, such as in police or medical interpreting (see, e.g., Kainz et al. 2011). An important distinction from other forms of interpreting that makes it interesting for sociology is the – often blatant – imbalance of power between the actors involved. This can either be due to disparities of power between the clients, such as a policeman and an arrested person and/or a client and the interpreter (e.g., a child might be called to translate between a doctor and his mother). For an overview of research on this topic see Urpi (2012) or Hale (2007).

Summing up, researchers who focus on translation as a social practice examine the selection, production, distribution, and reception of translation. They take into account the **actors** (not only the translators) involved in translation, the **processes** (what happens when translating, what kind of manipulative forces act on translation), and the **product** (the translations); see Wolf (2003). There is a close relationship between certain strands of sociological theory and sociology of translation. The theoretical perspectives, concepts, and theories are used to explain and understand social structure, power, agency, and social interaction related to translation processes.

Theory in the Sociology of Translation

Whereas most empirical research in the sociology of translation has been conducted outside traditional departments of sociology, the theoretical groundwork is deeply rooted in contemporary sociological theory. This ties together sociology and sociology of translation on many levels, as the use of sociological theory contributes to its reception, interpretation, and development.

There are four dominant theoretical strands in sociology of translation. First, and most prominently, it draws on Bourdieu's cultural sociology and the conception of habitus, field, and capital as will be shown in detail below. Second, some sociology of translation scholars take into account symbolic interactionist views, especially Goffman's dramaturgic approach. Sela-Sheffy (2014), for example, connects Bourdieu to Goffman's micro-sociological view on social interactions to explain the agency of translators. By looking at Israeli literary translators, Sela-Sheffy elaborates on identity work and highlights how negotiations between translators and other actors are situation-dependent. Goffman's work helps her to focus on negotiations in social interactions, enables her to take into account the intentions and self-perceptions of actors, and allows her to differentiate between relatively homogeneous groups. This would be a more difficult task working with just Bourdieu's habitus concept.

The third strand of research follows Luhmann and sees translation "as a social systemic phenomenon based on its nature, which is mediation" (Tyulenev 2010: 351). This perspective notes that autopoiesis (self-reproduction) of the system of translation takes place in its communicative events, which are "drawing on prior translational operations and anticipating future translational operations" (Tyulenev 2010: 362). Understanding translation as a system has, according to Tyulenev (2010: 369), the advantage of being able to observe translation in relation to its environment, other social systems, or as a subsystem (see Hermans 1999 for an early interpretation of Luhmann in translation studies and Tyulenev 2009 and 2012 for more recent efforts to implement this theoretical strand).

The last dominant theoretical strand is actor network theory (ANT), which was developed by Callon, Latour, and others in the context of science studies. Akrich et al. (2006) refer to the terms translation and translation sociology in their writings. However, they focus not on the transfer between languages but on how networks form and how agency (the possibilities and limits of actions) and objectives are negotiated in (scientific) innovation processes. For ANT researchers, agency is not necessarily restricted to human beings but also includes non-humans, which are referred to as actants.

Buzelin (2005) and others tried to connect Bourdieusian theory with Latour's Actor-Network approach in translation studies. ANT presupposes that the way artefacts come into existence is as important as the products themselves, as the production processes are not random but follow certain logics (though these logics do not predefine the actions of different actors). This approach thus focuses on "tracing the genesis of products called translations" (Buzelin 2005: 215) and the negotiations among different types of human actors and non-human actants. Actors include publishers, copy-editors, and translators, whereas non-human actants can be IT equipment or dictionaries that contribute in the negotiation of knowledge production when translating.

Bourdieu and Translation Sociology

Bourdieu's cultural sociology is certainly among the most significant concepts used in the sociology of translation. Bourdieu's idea of **habitus** was perhaps the first element of his cultural sociology that found its way into translation studies. Put simply, habitus refers to a set of dispositions and predispositions that both shape and are shaped by social structure. It frames the scope of action of actors and entails the understanding of power relations in specific societal fields. (See Chapter 10 in Volume 1 of this handbook.) The idea of a professional translator's habitus was first introduced when Simeoni (1998) described it as "to become a translator in the West today is to agree to becoming nearly fully subservient" (Simeoni 1998: 12), i.e., serving clients, publics, texts, or languages. This, according to Simeoni, is the result of centuries of translators acting out their low-status position in comparison to authors and of the low status translations have compared to their source texts.

Simeoni's interpretation is highly contested, not least because subsequent empirical research on the self-perception of translators showed that they do not feel subservient, invisible, or powerless. Quite to the contrary, many translators are aware of their power to shape the mediation process. More important than this internal debate, however, is the idea of focusing on translators, on their social background and their worldviews, and understanding translators as a collective with a shared history. All of this has remained an important impetus for sociological inquiries into translation. For example Vorderobermeier (2014) recently edited a volume fully dedicated to the concept of the translator's habitus.

The conceptualization of **field** is another recurring topic in the sociology of translation. Bourdieu's fields are to be understood as fields of power or battlefields where different actors compete for social positions and the power to define the rules of the game of a specific societal field. These fields – i.e. the literary, political, scientific fields – operate relatively autonomously from one another in the sense that the rules and credentials of one field do not necessarily apply to the others. Credentials, in Bourdieu's theory, come in the forms of different types of **capital** – cultural, economic, social, and symbolic. The first and primary question for sociology of translation was to decide whether such a relatively autonomous field exists for translation itself. The answer to that question remains unsettled.

Gouanvic states that "far from constituting a field of their own, translated texts are submitted to the same objective logic as indigenous texts of the target space" (2002: 160), thus disputing the existence of a field of translation. Wolf argues that "translated texts are inscribed by various configurations which make them belong to different specific fields" (2007: 21). In that regard, she also remains doubtful that translation produces relatively autonomous fields. In contrast to Gouanvic, however, she acknowledges that it is not only the target field that is important in framing translations. Inghilleri (2003) argues that the specific cultural, and more particularly linguistic, capital of translators does indeed produce a field where translators battle over norms, translation strategies, and social positions. This view is more favorable to a field of translation, without negating the possibility that this field may be dominated by other societal spheres.

The initial use of the field concept in sociology of translation is usually linked to Gouanvic and his studies of the literary field. Gouanvic's (see 1999; 2005) work on the creation and translation of science fiction literature in France form the beginning of an engagement with the conception of field. Gouanvic takes the position that any translated work needs to follow the logics of the target field to acquire legitimation. At the same time, he acknowledges that translations have the power to transform the rules of the game. In his study of science fiction translations from English to French between 1945 and 1960, he concludes that it was mainly the work of three French intellectuals who established a relatively autonomous field of literary communication by translating, producing critiques, and editing the works. Gouanvic shows that they were aware of the overarching cultural and field specific rules in which they operated. The actors had to negotiate their position – and the position of science fiction – in the much broader French literary field.

Kaindl (2004 and later), making use of Bourdieu's work, looks at the translation of comic books, exploring the lack of translation norms when translating into German, compared to when translating for the US or French market. The lack of comic culture in Germany, or more generally the lack of a certain (literary) field in a target culture, could be identified as an important element in the production process, or "chaotic" early translations of this genre.

Sociological studies of translation in the literary field do not stop at questions concerning translators, cultural norms influencing translation, or the reception and influence of translation on genres or national literary fields. Also broader questions connected with the selections and production conditions are addressed. As mentioned above, ideological and political conditions influence the selection (as well as the production and reception) of translations in totalitarian systems. Researchers have also examined gatekeepers to translations in democratic societies from a variety of angles. For example, French sociologist Sapiro (2010) examines contextualizing factors by focusing on the function of the globalizing literary book market. Other researchers then expanded this study of the role of publishing houses, the impact of subsidies and prizes for translations, and the logics of editors to the translation of texts in the social sciences and humanities (Sapiro et al. 2014; Sapiro and Popa 2008).

The relationship of different languages to each other comprises another aspect of understanding translation as a phenomenon taking place in global power structures. Heilbron (2000), a historical sociologist, understands translation as a cultural world-system and argues that "international communication about books depends on the centers in the international system" (Heilbron 2000: 17). This sociological perspective on translations puts flows of translation and the role of translation within language groups into the limelight. In short, the analysis of translation flows is a structural analysis that tries to show the relationship, patterns, and relative importance of different languages in translation. As flows of translation are uneven, they can very well be represented in a core-periphery model.

The main impediment to this kind of research is the availability of data. Thus, for practical reasons, the main focus is on book translation. Printed books are easily identifiable entities for the analysis of translation flows. A powerful tool for such an undertaking is the UNESCO database of translations, Index Translationum, which was first created in 1932 and set up as a digital database in 1979. As Heilbron (2000) shows, the Index can be used to study how many languages a work has been translated into, how some languages are more important on the translation market than others, and how translations developed in a country or a language over time.

Conclusion

We have established that sociology of translation deals with the phenomenon of translation as a social practice. While this aspect of translation has been relevant in some other subfields of sociology, such as historical sociology, sociology of translation established translation as an object of research in itself. By studying selection mechanisms, production processes, and the distribution and reception of translation, this subfield contributes to the sociological understanding of cultural transfer and the transfer of ideas and social change in general. In doing so, it adds to our sociological understanding of historical developments in multilingual and multicultural societies that heavily rely on translation to form, control, and reform cultural and political landscapes.

Although most research in sociology of translation can be found in Europe where the discipline of translation studies is more institutionalized than elsewhere, sociology of translation has also found adherents in Canada, China, and the United States. Future efforts in the sociology of translation should aim at an even closer collaboration between researchers affiliated with the discipline of translation studies and those in sociology in order to continue the exchange of theoretical ideas and methodological procedures.

Sociology of translation contributes to society by offering insights into the mediating function of translation in the circulation of ideas and culture in a globalized world. It also helps unveil the lasting influence of hegemonic discourses, cultural policy, and censorship by analyzing, monitoring, and deconstructing translations in a historical perspective. The feminist and postcolonial translations described above and the historical reappraisal of translations in Francoist Spain and the ongoing circulation of these once censored works provide examples of such efforts. Moreover, sociology of translation adds to our understanding of intercultural communication practices in a world of migration, global communication, and economic globalization by studying practices, conditions, and power relations in community interpreting. Finally, sociology of translation continues to shape translator training and the professional self-perception of translators by revealing the complexities and emphasizing the cultural aspects of this endeavor.

References

Akrich, Madeleine, Michel Callon, and Bruno Latour. 2006. *Sociologie de la traduction: Textes fondateurs*. Paris: Presses de l'École des Mines.

Angelelli, Claudia V. 2012. The Sociological Turn in Translation and Interpreting Studies. *Translation and Interpreting Studies* 7(2): 125–128.

Ben-Ari, Nitsa. 2012. Political Dissidents as Translators, Editors, and Publishers. *Translation and Interpreting Studies* 7(2): 144–160.

Butler, Judith. 1986. Sex and Gender in Simone de Beauvoir's Second Sex. *Yale French Studies* 72: 35–49.

Buzelin, Hélène. 2005. Unexpected Allies. How Latour's Network Theory Could Complement Bourdieusian Analyses in Translation Studies. *The Translator* 11(2): 193–218.

Cronin, Michael. 2013. *Translation in the Digital Age. New Perspectives in Translation Studies*. London: Routledge.

Gouanvic, Jean-Marc. 1999. *Sociologie de la traduction. La science-fiction américaine dans l'espace culturel français des années 1950*. Arras: Artois Presses Université.

Gouanvic, Jean-Marc. 2002. The Stakes of Translation in Literary Fields. *Across Languages and Cultures* 3(2): 159–168.

Gouanvic, Jean-Marc. 2005. A Bourdieusian Theory of Translation, or the Coincidence of Practical Instances. *The Translator* 11(2): 147–166.

Hale, Sandra B. 2007. *Community Interpreting. Research and Practice in Applied Linguistics*. Basingstoke: Palgrave Macmillan.

Heilbron, Johan. 2000. Translation as a Cultural World System. *Perspectives* 8(1): 9–26.

Heilbron, Johan and Gisèle Sapiro. eds. 2002. La circulation internationale des idées. *Actes de la recherche en sciences sociales*. Special issue, 145.

Hermans, Theo. 1999. *Translation in Systems: Descriptive and Systemic Approaches Explained*. Translation Theories Explained 7. Manchester: St. Jerome Publishing.

Holmes, James S. 2000. The Name and Nature of Translation Studies. In *The Translation Studies Reader*. Edited by Lawrence Venuti. London, New York, NY: Routledge, 172–185.

Inghilleri, Moira. 2003. Habitus, Field and Discourse: Interpreting as a Socially Situated Activity. *Target* 15(2): 243–268.

Kaindl, Klaus. 2004. *Übersetzungswissenschaft im interdisziplinären Dialog: Am Beispiel der Comicübersetzung*. Studien zur Translation 16. Tübingen: Stauffenburg-Verlag.

Kainz, Claudia, Erich Prunč, and Rafael Y. Schögler. eds. 2011. *Modelling the Field of Community Interpreting. Questions of Methodology in Research and Training*. Wien, Berlin: Lit-Verlag.

Parks, Gerald. 1998. Towards a Sociology of Translation. *Rivista internazionale di tecnica della traduzione* 3: 25–35.

Pöckl, Wolfgang. 2011. Seitenblicke auf die Globalisierung. In *Translation – Sprachvariation – Mehrsprachigkeit: Festschrift für Lew Zybatow zum 60. Geburtstag*. Edited by Wolfgang Pöckl, Ingeborg Ohnheiser, and Peter Sandrini. Frankfurt am Main, Wien: Peter Lang, 527–541.

Pokorn, Nike K. 2014. The Godless World of Winnetou: The Ideologial Imperative in Socialism. In *Translationswissenschaftliches Kolloquium III: Beiträge zur Übersetzungs- und Dolmetschwissenschaft (KölnGermersheim)*. Edited by Barbara Ahrens, Silvia Hansen-Schirra, Monika Krein-Kühle, Michael Schreiber, and Ursula Wienen. Publikationen des Fachbereichs Translations-, Sprach- und Kulturwissenschaft der Johannes-Gutenberg-Universität Mainz in Germersheim. Frankfurt am Main: Lang, 97–118.

Niranjana, Tejaswini. 1992. *Siting Translation: History, Poststructuralism, and the Colonial Context*. Berkeley, CA: University of California Press.

Sapiro, Gisèle. ed. 2008. *Translatio: Le marché de la traduction en France à l'heure de la mondialisation*. Paris: CNRS Éditions.

Sapiro, Gisèle. ed. 2009. *Les contradictions de la globalisation éditoriale*. Paris: Nouv. Monde Éditions.

Sapiro, Gisèle. 2010. Globalization and Cultural Diversity in the Book Market: The Case of Literary Translations in the US and in France. *Poetics* 38(4): 419–439.

Sapiro, Gisèle and Ioana Popa. 2008. Traduire les sciences humaines et sociales: logiques éditoriales et enjeux scientifiques. In *Translatio. Le marché de la traduction en France à l'heure de la mondialisation*. Edited by Gisèle Sapiro. Paris: CNRS Éditions, 107–138.

Sapiro, Gisèle, Alejandro Dujovne, Marcello Frisani, Jill A. McCoy, Heber Ostroviesky, Hélène Seiler-Juilleret, and Gustavo Sorá. 2014. Sciences humaines en traduction: Les livres français aux États-Unis, au Royaume-Uni et en Argentine. Available at www.institutfrancais.com/sites/default/files/sciences_humaines-en_traduction.pdf, accessed December 9, 2016.

Schögler, Rafael Y. 2012. Übersetzungsstrategien und Übersetzungsfelder: Die Übersetzungen von Max Webers Die protestantische Ethik ins Englische. *Österreichische Zeitschrift für Geschichtswissenschaft* 23(3): 127–160.

Sela-Sheffy, Rakefet. 2014. Translators' Identity Work: Introducing Micro-Sociological Theory of Identity to the Discussion of Translators' Habitus. In *Remapping Habitus in Translation Studies*. Edited by Gisella M. Vorderobermeier. Amsterdam, New York, NY: Rodopi, 43–55.

Sela-Sheffy, Rakefet, and Miriam Shlesinger. eds. 2009. Profession, Identity and Status: Translators and Interpreters as an Occupational Group. Special issue of *Translation and Interpreting Studies* 4(2).

Sela-Sheffy, Rakefet, and Miriam Shlesinger. eds. 2010. Profession, Identity and Status: Translators and Interpreters as an Occupational Group. Special issue of *Translation and Interpreting Studies* 5(1).

Simeoni, Daniel. 1998. The Pivotal Status of the Translator's Habitus. *Target* 10(1): 1–39.

Simons, Margaret A. 1983. The Silencing of Simone de Beauvoir. Guess What's Missing from "The Second Sex". *Women's Studies International Forum* 6(5): 549–564.

Thomson-Wohlgemuth, Gaby. 2007. On the Other Side of the Wall: Book Production, Censorship and Translation in East Germany. In *Modes of Censorship and Translation: National Contexts and Diverse Media*. Edited by Francesca Billiani. Manchester: Jerome Publishing, 93–116.

Tribe, Keith. 2012. Max Weber: The Works. *Economy and Society* 41(2): 282–298.

Tymoczko, Maria and Edwin Gentzler. 2002. *Translation and Power*. Amherst, MA: University of Massachusetts Press.

Tyulenev, Sergey. 2009. Why (not) Luhmann? On the Applicability of Social Systems Theory to Translation Studies. *Translation Studies* 2(2): 147–162.

Tyulenev, Sergey. 2010. Is Translation an Autopoietic System? *Monografías de Traducción e Interpretación* 2: 345–371.

Tyulenev, Sergey. 2012. *Applying Luhmann to Translation Studies: Translation in Society*. New York, NY: Routledge.

Uribarri, Ibon. 2008. Translations of German philosophy and Censorship. In *Translation and Censorship in Different Times and Landscapes*. Edited by Teresa Seruya and Maria L. Moniz. Newcastle-upon-Tyne: Cambridge Scholars Publishing, 103–118.

Uribarri, Ibon. 2013. Philosophical Collections, Translation and Censorship. In *Translation in Anthologies and Collections: (19th and 20th Centuries)*. Edited by Teresa Seruya, Lieven D'hulst, Alexandra Assis Rosa, and Maria Lin Moniz. Amsterdam: John Benjamins, 247–258.

Urpi, Mireia V. 2012. State of the Art in Community Interpreting Research: Mapping the Main Research Topics. *Babel* 58(1): 50–72.

Venuti, Lawrence. 2008. *The Translator's Invisibility: A History of Translation*. London: Routledge.

Von Flotow, Luise. 2000. Translation Effects. How Beauvoir Talks Sex in English. In *Contingent Loves: Simone de Beauvoir and Sexuality*. Edited by Melanie Hawthorne. Charlottesville, VA: University Press of Virginia, 13–33.

Von Flotow, Luise. 2009. This Time "the Translation is Beautiful, Smooth, and True": Theorizing Retranslation with the Help of Beauvoir. In *Translation in French and Francophone Literature and Film*. Edited by James Day. Amsterdam: Rodopi, 35–49.

Vorderobermeier, Gisella M. ed. 2014. *Remapping Habitus in Translation Studies*. Amsterdam, New York, NY: Rodopi.

Wolf, Michaela. 2003. Übersetzer/innen – Verfangen im sozialen Netzwerk? Zu gesellschaftlichen implikationen des übersetzens. In *Studia Germanica Posnaniensia XXIX. Probleme des literarischen Übersetzens*. Edited by Maria Krysztofiak-Kaszynska. Poznań: Wydawnictwo Naukowe UAM, 105–119.

Wolf, Michaela. ed. 2006. *Übersetzen – translating – traduire: Towards a "social turn"?* Vienna, Berlin: Lit-Verlag.

Wolf, Michaela. 2007. Introduction: The Emergence of a Sociology of Translation. In *Constructing a Sociology of Translation*. Edited by Michaela Wolf and Alexandra Fukari. Amsterdam, Philadelphia, PA: John Benjamins, 1–36.

Wolf, Michaela. 2015. *The Habsburg Monarchy's Many-Languaged Soul: Translating and Interpreting, 1848–1918*. Translated by Kate Sturge. Amsterdam, Philadelphia, PA: John Benjamins.

CHAPTER 42

Women and Gender Studies: Its Origins and Intersections with Sociology

Angela Hattery and Earl Smith

The field of women's studies *officially* began in 1969, when Cornell University offered the first women's studies course. That said, philosophers and scholars in a variety of disciplines have been writing about issues of concern to women since at least the mid-eighteenth century. What is most interesting about their writings and perspectives is how similar they are to the concerns being addressed by women and gender studies scholars in the early years of the twenty-first century. This chapter will explore the perspectives of the early philosophers, the development of the formal field of women and gender studies, including the "waves," and its integration with the formal discipline of sociology.

Early Philosophers

Beginning in the Enlightenment era, philosophers of the social world, both men and women, in part as a response to the Protestant Reformation (Russell 1946: 492–494), began to think and write about individual actors and their interactions in the social world. During this time, philosophers were critical of rigid structures, such as the Catholic Church, which left very little room for individual interpretation and action. Not surprisingly then, the ideas born of the Enlightenment period extended not only the focus on the individual, but also on new ways of organizing the social world. Many European countries experienced revolutions that pushed back on the traditional rule of aristocracies, and democracy was born.

It is not really surprising then, that it is during this era that philosophers who were already focused on "the individual" articulated and debated gender differences, for example, the distribution of individual traits. Men were thought to be blessed with traits such as rationality whereas women were thought to be somewhat inferior based on their predominant trait: emotionalism. This distinction was critically important in assigning not only specific traits to men and women but also in designating different spheres and opportunities for men and for women.

Private/Public Split

Simultaneous with the rise of Enlightenment philosophy in the United States and Europe came the Industrial Revolution. Thus, as philosophers were debating the traits of men and women and their overall "constitution," the world they were living in was rapidly changing. Among the most important changes was the movement of "work" from the private sphere to the public sphere. This movement had significant and lasting implications for gender roles and gender relations that would continue to be among the top concerns for feminists well into the twenty-first century.

For the vast majority of human history, work and family were organized in the "private" sphere. For millions of years humans lived in a subsistence economy. (The majority of people living in Africa and parts of Asia, the South Pacific and Central and South America lived in a subsistence economy well into the twentieth century and there are pockets where populations continue to live in this economic system.) Subsistence economies are characterized primarily as those in which food and other resources are limited to the minimum amount needed to subsist; there is no ability – for a variety of reasons – to accumulate resources, including food. Thus, the work of staying alive and passing one's genes onto the next generation involved a complex system of hunting and gathering. There is much debate about the gendered division of labor in these economies (Tanner 1982). The degree to which labor was rigidly divided likely depended on a variety of factors associated with the environment. For example, as environmental pressures changed the availability of plant food as well as access to animals, labor would likely adjust accordingly. Despite variations that may have existed, one thing is commonly agreed upon and that is that subsistence economies required high levels of cooperation. No one person, and often not even a single family group, was able to provide for all of their nutritional needs, and thus individuals and families developed high levels of cooperation that increased the likelihood that babies would survive and grow up to pass on a group's genes.

As humans became more efficient in hunting and gathering and gained mastery over migration patterns and plant growth in particular, they were able to domesticate both animal and plant sources of food. Along with this came the ability to produce more food than was required. Humans innovated mechanisms for preserving food resources and accumulating the extra for periods of austerity. This led to the dawn of the agricultural period that dominated human economies for more than 10,000 years (continuing today in some less economically developed societies).

Much like subsistence economies, agriculture-based economies required a great deal of human labor and cooperation. Though family groups grew larger as more and more babies survived into adulthood and life expectancy extended, cooperation remained the primary strategy for survival. Even the modern family farm requires most family members to contribute regularly to the work of the farm in order for it to remain economically viable.

The Industrial Revolution ushered in an entirely new form of work that transformed not only labor but also family and gender relations. For the most part, men became laborers in factories and mines and other industries while women worked at home, both taking care of the family and continuing to engage in farm and piece-work related economic production. This public-private split (Padavic and Reskin 2002) is considered to be one of the most important factors behind the gendered division of labor and the gender inequality we still see in many post-industrial economies today. Specifically, this split resulted in assigning the majority of the work of the home to women and the ability to earn a wage to men. Today we see the vestiges of this division in things like the persistent gendered wage gap (Padavic and Reskin 2002) and the "second shift" (Hochschild 1989).

Social philosophers of the Enlightenment era were transfixed by the Industrial

Revolution and the impact, mostly negative, that they both observed and predicted it would have on social life and gender and families in particular. For example, Friedrich Engels, Karl Marx's co-author, wrote in his *Origins of the Family* (Engels and Leacock 1972[1889]) that the Industrial Revolution required particular gendered arrangements that created inequality that favored men and disadvantaged women. Engels considered this exploitation in the family to be akin to the exploitation of the worker, by the owner, that he and Marx described in *The Communist Manifesto*. Women's dependency on men for economic support left them open to exploitation in the home; in other words, the husband could demand his wife's labor be used in any way he saw fit and there was little she could do about it. Specifically, Engels argued that the economic power men derived from earning wages allowed them to exploit the labor of their wives, making the work of the home entirely their responsibility.

Engels was not the only philosopher who argued that men's economic power generated significant gender inequality in the home. Both Emma Goldman (1972) and Charlotte Perkins Gilman (1898) also argued that marriage, and motherhood in particular, kept women from achieving true equality. They argued that if women could not be economically self-sufficient then they would be forever dependent on men. This kind of vulnerability had significant consequences, including women not being able to leave unsatisfying or even harmful marriages, domestic violence, pressure to marry, and the kinds of exploitation Engels described. Further, they both understood clearly that part and parcel to women's economic independence was their ability to control their reproductive lives and, if they chose, to eschew motherhood. More than 200 years later, feminist are still making the same arguments: that economic dependency leaves women vulnerable and that a critical aspect of attaining economic security is the ability to control one's reproductive life.

Waves

Many people associate the beginning of feminism (the first wave), or "the women's movement" with the suffrage movement of the late nineteenth and early twentieth centuries. As a result, women like Susan B. Anthony and Elizabeth Cady Stanton are considered the founders of feminism even though, as we have just argued, feminists had been contributing to the discourse for at least a century prior to the suffrage movement. Obviously, the primary goal of the suffrage movement was winning the right to vote for women. Ironically, the right to vote, granted in 1920 by the nineteenth amendment to the US Constitution, was predicated on the Enlightenment concept that women were "irrational." Among the debates around women's suffrage some argued that because women were "irrational" they would simply vote like their fathers or their husbands (who were "rational"); the 80 percent of women who were married would simply "double their husband's vote." Therefore, giving women the vote would result in no significant impact. (Ironically, gender is one of the key variables that predicts local, regional, and national elections today: Moses and Hartmann 1995.)

Many fewer people are as familiar with Margaret Sanger who, at the same time as the suffragists were agitating, was a fierce advocate for birth control and reproductive rights. Sanger got caught up, sadly, on the wrong side of the eugenics movement of that time, which may in part explain why she is lesser known. But, much like her foremothers before her, she reminds us that reproductive issues are both hotly contested and at the core of gender equality. We and others would argue that this is precisely why reproductive issues are so hotly contested (Luker 1984).

Activism

Perhaps because of the nature of the suffrage movement, feminism has always been strongly associated with activism. And, this relationship continued to be developed during subsequent waves of the feminist movement. Feminist activism died down a bit during the middle part of the twentieth century and came back as a major force in the 1960s and 1970s. Often referred to as the sexual revolution – which largely has to do with the continued movement for access to reproductive rights – the "second wave" feminist movement of the 1960s and 1970s is most often associated with women like Gloria Steinem and Betty Friedan. The two main areas of focus for second wave feminists were labor force participation and sexual liberation.

Labor Force Participation

Though many people make the assumption that women did not really enter the labor force in any significant numbers until the 1970s, in fact, the period in which women were *not* in the formal labor market is actually quite limited (Coontz 1992). After the United States industrialized in the early part of the twentieth century, and in response to the Great Depression, women found many more opportunities for paid labor (Gordon 1988). Women worked in factories and did piece-work (ironing, laundry) and women of color, particularly African American women, worked as domestics in the households of millions of whites. During World War II, when the men were shipped off to fight in both Europe and Asia, women's labor, especially white women's labor, was needed to keep the factories and the war machine churning. Rosie the Riveter ("We can do it!") became the image to recruit women into these jobs. In droves, women entered jobs that had previously been reserved for men. And, they were successful; they earned money and they developed the self-confidence that they could do all kinds of work, including work typically associated with men.

The period following World War II was a challenge for America because the jobs women had taken during the war had been promised to the men returning from war. In order to convince women to return to homemaking while their husbands and brothers returned to work, a powerful ideology was manufactured and pushed out: the glories of homemaking! A perusal of the advertisements of this period reveals that companies sought to seduce women into what is really tedious work (housekeeping) by glamorizing it and linking homemaking with caring for one's family. Women's magazines and afternoon television commercials showed women vacuuming in formal wear, suggesting that their husbands would find them more attractive if they kept a clean house. As a result of the efforts to push women out of jobs and promote a specific ideology of a "good wife and mother" the number of women (mostly confined to white women) leaving the labor market to become homemakers rose dramatically.

The second wave feminist movement was in large part a reaction to this relatively abrupt change in women's status; women's labor force participation was at its height in the early to mid-1940s and plummeted to its lowest just a few years later. Second wave feminists from Simone de Beauvoir to Betty Friedan to Gloria Steinem understood, as Engels and Gilman and Perkins had before them, that women's labor force participation was essential to gender equality.

Reproductive Control/Sexual Revolution

A second force that significantly shaped second wave feminism involved birth control. As noted previously, before her unfortunate connection to the horrors of the eugenics movement, Margaret Sanger recognized that gender equality hinged on women being able to control their reproductive lives. At the time, disseminating any information about contraception was illegal, but Sanger challenged this by printing leaflets and mailing them (a violation of federal law) in an attempt to move the conversation around contraception forward. Eugenicists were both friend and foe of Sanger. They co-opted her information on contraception and sterilization in order to restrict births among "undesirables" (namely people of color and immigrants) and they sought to ban the distribution of information regarding contraception to white middle-class women whom they encouraged to increase their birth rates.

The pressure on white women to increase their birth rates was clearly political (eugenicists were worried about the United States becoming increasingly "less white") but also needs to be understood in the context of industrialization. Scholars of economic development (e.g., Malthus 2016) had noted for more than one hundred years previously that birth rates are largely driven by the economy, what Malthus called the "J Curve". Birth rates are high in subsistence economies because infant mortality rates are staggering, but because death rates are also high, there is relatively no growth in population. In agricultural economies, birth rates stay high (labor is a necessity) but death rates fall and, as a result, population growth is steep. Families in industrial economies need less labor and thus birth rates fall. Because death rates also continue to decline, the population stabilizes and may even decline. Thus, women in the industrializing United States were looking for ways to reduce their fertility and Margaret Sanger was, in some ways, responding to a predictable trend.

Second wave feminists understood, as Gilman and Perkins had before them, that being able to control their reproductive lives was central to gender equality. It was legal to pay women less than men and to hire men instead of women. Many employers feared women would leave work to have babies (and never return as they were lured into the glories of homemaking) and believed (wrongly, especially for non-white women) that their incomes were supplemental and not necessary for the family.

Simultaneously, in response to many social forces, including the Vietnam War, a sexual revolution was underway. It goes without saying that contraception and reproductive control were essential to women participating in any capacity in the sexual revolution or "free love" movement. Thus, though we often focus on the legalization of abortion and the famous Roe v. Wade case as the hallmark of second wave feminism, it is clear that this was only the most visible of the concerns for women seeking equality in the 1960s and 1970s.

In the late 1960s and early 1970s, women's studies began to be formalized as a field of study. This codification was a result of an interesting interplay between scholars and activists and set the tone for one central element of women's studies today: activism and community engagement.

Though many different voices were important during the second wave, Gloria Steinem, founder of MS Magazine, was one of the voices that brought discussions of feminists to the mainstream. One of the hallmarks of the 1970s feminist movement was the consciousness-raising groups. Women from all backgrounds, on college campuses, in bars, and in each other's living rooms, came together to explore their experiences. As one can imagine, many different kinds of issues were discussed – from the division of household labor to the wage gap to experiences with abortion – but one of the issues that gained tremendous exposure was violence against women, both rape and domestic violence.

Many credit the consciousness-raising groups and the work that came out of these as moving not only the conversation but the laws significantly forward with regards to both of these critical issues. For example, at the time, domestic violence was legal, there were no shelters, and it was nearly impossible for a woman to escape her abuser. Women in these consciousness-raising groups began taking women into their homes and this "shelter movement" was the beginning of a systematic approach to combating domestic violence. Additionally, this type of activism resulted in changes in the law. Domestic violence was finally outlawed in the mid-1980s, and eventually sweeping approaches, such as the Violence Against Women Act 1994, were enacted.

The Third Wave and Identity Politics

In the 1990s, a "third" wave of feminism emerged, driven largely by young women who used new techniques like "zines" and "blogging" (Baumgardner and Richards 2000). Self-proclaimed third wave feminists made several serious and well-founded critiques of their second wave mothers. They argued that the feminist movement, going all the way back to the suffrage movement, was a largely white, middle-class, heterosexual movement. In doing so, they pointed out that the movement itself was both by and for middle class, heterosexual, white women and that it largely excluded women of color and lesbians and ignored their needs and goals.

Feminist scholars, mostly black women, took these concerns and developed a series of theoretical perspectives that forced feminism to stretch to accommodate these critiques. What began as Black Feminist Theory, birthed by scholars like Patricia Hill Collins, Alice Walker, Audre Lord, and bell hooks, was again transformed, in response to other marginalized identities and systems, and became intersectional theory (see the work of Kimberlé Crenshaw, Maxine Baca Zinn, and Bonnie Thorton Dill). Though mainstream now, much of the scholarship of feminists of color was initially published by presses *they created*; among the most famous was The Kitchen Table Press.

Today, there remain tensions in the feminist movement that continue to hinge on expanding understandings of sex, gender, sexual identity, and gender identity and other marginalized identities; much of the tension can be characterized as generational, with third and post-wave feminists believing their second wave mothers are antiquated and too conservative. Many women and gender studies programs have recently struggled or are continuing to struggle with the tension between inclusion related to gender identity and gender oppression. Specifically, there is pressure to expand women and gender studies programs to incorporate masculinity studies and transgender studies. And, yet there are some who fear that in becoming too expansive, women's issues will be lost. Others contend that the expansion is good as long as at the core remain discussions of power and privilege and the ways in which gender inequality remains a central form of oppression.

What is most interesting is that despite all of the tension, the issues concerning feminists remain largely the same: equal pay, equality at home, reproductive justice, and violence.

Development of the Formal Field

The whole point of this chapter has been to demonstrate that feminist scholarship and activism has been going on since at least the Enlightenment era. The scholarship was primarily in certain disciplines, including philosophy (as noted), the humanities (especially English), and sociology. The field of women's studies began to be formalized when the first courses were taught under the official designation; Cornell University is noted as the first, offering a course in women's studies in 1969. Just a year later, the first two programs in women's studies were developed, at SUNY-Buffalo and San Diego State College (now San Diego State University). And, less than a decade later, in the 1970s, the first scholarly journal dedicated to feminist scholarship, *Feminist Studies*, was born and the National Women's Studies Association was founded.

Today there are more than 600 programs in women's studies, and sixteen universities offer the Ph.D. in women's studies, with Emory University establishing the first doctoral program in 1990. That said, many universities still offer only a major (or in many cases only a minor) in women and gender studies and no degree program at the graduate level. As a result, the majority of scholars and activists working in the field of women and gender studies earn their primary degree, with a focus on gender, in a related field such as history, English, sociology, anthropology, and other humanities and social science fields.

There are both pros and cons to this situation. One of the strengths is that the field remains entirely interdisciplinary as scholars working in different home disciplines, with different training, and with different methodological approaches, are in conversation around the issues most pressing to the field, including identity, power, and intersectionality. There are two significant downsides to this situation. First, because the majority of scholars and activists earn their degrees in a home discipline while taking courses in women and gender studies programs – typically a minimum coursework requires a course in feminist theory – the specific training in women and gender studies may be uneven. Second, scholars working in women and gender studies may feel that the colleges and universities who employ them do not take the field seriously enough to invest in a stand-alone program. Their colleagues may feel similarly and thus many women and gender studies scholars find that they are required to teach core courses in their primary discipline – like theory or methods – and that they are required to publish at least some of their work in journals that are mainstream in their discipline. What this means is that routinely women and gender studies scholars find themselves having to explain their work to their colleagues when they are considered for tenure and to editors of mainstream journals who may not fully understand how their work "fits." All of that said, many women and gender studies scholars find that they are able to infuse gender studies into their traditional disciplinary courses – even courses such as theory and methods – and mainstream publications such that they are able to reach an even broader audience with their work.

From the women's studies program perspective, which is very often reliant on affiliate faculty, with few or no faculty with appointments in the women's studies program itself, there are also upsides and downsides. The major benefit is the interdisciplinary nature of the faculty. Working alongside each other and co-teaching, faculty with training in history, English, sociology, and anthropology have an opportunity to learn from their colleagues with a different disciplinary perspective who study and teach about the same issues, for example, violence against women. The downside is that affiliate faculty have obligations to their home departments, and thus it can be challenging to administer a women's studies program with few to no permanent staff.

Women's Centers

One unique aspect of women's studies programs is their relationship with women's centers. Much like the consciousness-raising groups women formed in their homes and workplaces and places of worship, many colleges and universities had women's centers long before they had academic programs. These centers provided women (and men) a place to find support and learn more about the issues facing them. Often women's centers were precursors to student affairs programs that addressed rape, domestic violence, and women's health. Faculty, staff, and students involved in women's centers tended to be the driving force behind the development of women's studies curricula and ultimately academic programs. Women's centers are also often the mechanism by which the activist element of women's studies gets operationalized. Women's centers are often engaged directly with community partners – women's health centers, domestic violence shelters – and these relationships, along with those between individual faculty and the community – facilitate and reinforce the importance of activism to the field of women's studies.

It is important not to overlook the unique nature of this relationship between academic and extra-curricular programming because it exists in almost no other field of study. Even racial and ethnic "area" studies, such as African American Studies or Chicano Studies rarely have the same kind of relationship with the related student affairs office (Office of Multicultural

Affairs). The primary difference seems to be that women's studies *faculty* were and remain heavily invested in women's centers, while similar offices addressing racial and ethnic issues were more often started by student affairs professionals with little involvement by the faculty.

At George Mason University, we are part of a unique Women and Gender Studies program. What makes this program exceptional is the special relationship between the academic program and the women's center on campus. The founding mothers of the program envisioned it as a three-legged stool, with the three legs being teaching, research, and activism. They wisely understood that in order to maintain such a delicate and important balance, there needed to be structural support for all three activities in a way that would be seamless and integrated. Their solution was to design and seek support, successfully, for a fully integrated program. What is now the Women and Gender Studies Program at George Mason is dually funded with dual reporting lines to both the College of Humanities and Social Sciences (the academic home) and University Life (the student affairs home). This dual funding and dual reporting results in a program that completely embodies the integrated approach. Courses are deliberately designed to take advantage of center programming and vice versa. Courses are sometimes taught in the center. Students, faculty, and staff use the center to meet, to hold events, and in many other ways that facilitate the faculty, staff, student interaction that is the hallmark of women's centers. In addition, we have relationships with the community such that our partners often hold their meetings in the center which further facilitates activism and research.

Integration with Sociology

Sociology has long been a discipline ripe for scholars interested in women's studies issues, though the support for gender research has not always been there. This is especially interesting given the fact that many founders of the discipline, like Jane Addams, were in fact doing gender research and that much of the discipline of sociology is focused on inequalities. That said, it took nearly the entire twentieth century for the discipline to diversify in terms of both areas of concern and the scholars holding leadership positions. (In this regard women and feminist sociology have had significantly more success than scholars of color, who remain remarkably underrepresented among the leading scholars and among those holding leadership positions in the discipline.)

In response to encountering discrimination as individuals and as scholars doing research on gender, a group of women, including Alice Rossi, founded a women's caucus. At the 1969 annual meeting of the American Sociological Association, they confronted the leadership at the business meeting with a set of demands. The group met over the next two years, in the winter, and in 1971 Sociologists for Women in Society (SWS) was born. SWS was founded, much like consciousness-raising groups and other activist groups, as a place for women to find support, mentoring, and objective feedback on their teaching and research. Frustrated by the lack of gender diversity at the regional and national levels, SWS nurtured their own leaders, and by the late 1980s and early 1990s they were successfully getting feminist sociologists elected to the leadership of regional and national associations. Frustrated by the obstacles they faced getting feminist scholarship published in the top mainstream journals (*American Sociological Review, American Journal of Sociology*), in 1989 SWS members founded a new journal, *Gender and Society*, devoted entirely to the dissemination of feminist scholarship. In 2014, *Gender and Society* is considered a top journal in both sociology (16/134) and women and gender studies (2/40, right behind *Signs*).

SWS remains a strong organization, which leaves one wondering to what degree feminist studies has or has not become mainstream in the larger discipline of sociology. Will feminist sociology become like other mainstream subspecialties – economic sociology, family sociology – or will it remain the case that organizations like SWS are still needed to ensure that women and feminist scholars of all genders have access to leading the organization and having their research published in mainstream journals? Given the incredible successes of both SWS and *Gender and Society*, there is reason to believe that by the mid twenty-first century feminist sociology will not only become part of mainstream sociology but will become central to the discipline itself.

In conclusion, the discipline of women's studies, though it only became formalized in the late 1960s and early 1970s, has played a significant role in the development of theoretical thought since at least the late eighteenth century. It has influenced many disciplines, including the field of sociology. With the focus in the field of sociology on inequalities, women's studies is both a natural "fit" and a leader in shaping the discipline. The intentional marriage of intellectual inquiry and activism in women and gender studies allows for the discipline to influence and contribute both to areas of scholarly inquiry and social movements.

References

Baumgardner, Jennifer, and Amy Richards. 2000. *Manifest A: Young Women, Feminism, and the Future*. New York, NY: Farrar, Straus and Giroux.

Coontz, Stephanie. 1992. *The Way We Never Were: American Families and the Nostalgia Trap*. New York, NY: BasicBooks.

Engels, Friedrich and Eleanor Burke Leacock. 1972[1889]. *The Origins of the Family, Private Property, and the State, in the Light of the Researches of Lewis H. Morgan*. New York, NY: International Publishers.

Hochschild, Arlie Russell (with Anne Machung). 1989. *The Second Shift: Working Parents and the Revolution at Home*. New York, NY: Penguin Books.

Gilman, Charlotte Perkins. 1898. *Women and Economics*. Boston, MA: Small, Maynard and Co.

Goldman, Emma. 1972. The Tragedy of Women's Emancipation. In *Emma Speaks: Selected Writings and Speeches by Emma Goldman*. Edited by Alix Kates Shulman. New York, NY: Vintage Press

Gordon, L. 1988. *Heroes of their Own Lives*. New York, NY: Penguin.

Luker, Kristin. 1984. *Abortion and the Politics of Motherhood*. Berkeley, CA: University of California Press.

Malthus, Thomas. 2016. *An Essay on the Principle of Population*. London: CreateSpace Independent Publishing Platform.

Marx, Karl and Friedrich Engels. 2015. *The Communist Manifesto*. London: CreateSpace Independent Publishing Platform.

Moses, Claire Goldberg and Heidi I. Hartmann. 1995. *U.S. Women in Struggle: A Feminist Studies Anthology*. Chicago, IL: University of Illinois Press.

Padavic, Irene and Barbara F. Reskin. 2002. *Women and Men at Work*. 2nd edn. Thousand Oaks, CA: Pine Forge Press.

Russell, Bertrand. 1946. *History of Western Philosophy*. London: George Allen and Unwin.

Tanner, Nancy. 1982. *On Becoming Human*. Cambridge: Cambridge University Press.

Index

Cambridge Handbook of Sociology Volume 2
Locators in *italic* refer to figures
Locators in **bold** refer to tables

ABC of psychology (affect, behavior, cognition), 387–388
Abrams, Philip, 331, 333–334, 335
abstract liberalism framework, color-blind racism, 22
abuse of animals, 98. *See also* animal sociology
academic sociology. *See* institutionalization of sociology; journals
academic tenure, 328
accountability
  criminal justice system personnel, 367
  governmental, 319
acquisition, sociology of consumption, 266, 267–268
action groups, antivivisectionist, 100
activism. *See also* social movements
  environmental justice, 193
  feminist perspectives, 409–410
  food, 200
  public sociology, 315–316
activity theory, sociology of aging, 247–248
actor network theory (ANT)
  consumption, 271
  risk, 136
  science and technology, 170–171
  translation, 403
actors, social practice of translation, 400, 402
Addams, Jane, 332
Adorno, Theodor
  art, 297

  consumption, 267–268
  music, 305
  popular culture, 285, 288–289
advocacy, sociotechnics, 334
affect. *See also* emotion
  feminist perspectives, 78
  social psychology, 387–388
  violence, 182–183
affect control theory (ACT), emotion, 223
affirmative action, racial discrimination, 7
Affordable Care Act, 154, 336, 384
age, and friendship, 233
age-as-leveler concept, 248–249. *See also* aging
age stratification theory, 249–250
ageism, 252
agency
  children, 243–244
  humanist sociology, 325
  leisure, 275–276
aging, sociology of, 246, 252–253
  ageism, 252
  critical theory, 252
  dependence in old age, 247
  gender perspectives, 251
  gerontocracy, 246–247
  macro/micro-theories, 247–250
  political economy, 251–252
  power structures, 250–251
Alinsky, Saul, 342

All in the Family television show, 288
Allport, Gordon, 387–388
amelioration, applied sociology/sociotechnics, 331
American Bar Foundation (ABF), 371
American Dream, 361
American Psychiatric Association (APA), 149
American Society of Criminology (ASC), 373
American Sociological Association (ASA), 295
Ancient world
    Athens city-state, 51–52
    criminal justice, 370
And We are Not Saved: The Elusive Quest for Racial Justice (Bell), 30
animal behavior, sociobiology, 156–162
animal rights, 100–102
Animal Rights Crusade (Jasper and Nelkin), 101–102
animal sociology, 95, 102
    animal testing, 100
    classical sociological tradition, 95–97
    companion animals, 97–98
    entertainment animals, 100–101
    farm animals, 98–99
    symbolic interactionism, 97
    vegetarianism, 101–102
    wildlife, 99–100
anomie
    criminal justice studies, 372
    criminology, 360–362
anonymity, visual sociology, 125–126
anthropological perspectives
    cultural symbolic approach to risk, 131
    friendship, 230
    popular culture, 288–289
    sociobiology, 156, 157
anti-oppression counter-frames, systemic racism, 16
anti-vivisectionist action groups, 100
Apache peoples, environmental justice, 192
apartheid, South Africa, 44–45
Appeal to the Coloured Citizens of the World (Walker), 16
applied sociology, 330–331
    Abrams' contribution, 333–334, 335
    future directions, 336–337
    Podgórecki's contribution, 332–333
    public sociology, 315
    sociology of, 334–336
    in UK/USA, 331–332
appreciation of goods and services, 266, 267–268
appropriation of goods and services, 266, 267–268
art, sociology of, 293–294, 300–301
    Becker, 295, 297
    Bourdieu, 296–297
    gender perspectives, 298
    historical perspectives, 294–295
    political economics perspective, 298–299
    race/ethnicity, 298
    social class, 297–298
    spatial perspectives, 299–300
    works of art, 300
articulative sociotechnics, 333

Asian American label, racial formation theory, 7–8
Association for Applied and Clinical Sociology (AACS), 343
Association for Humanist Sociology (AHS), 324–326
Association of Criminal Justice Studies (ACJS), 373
Athens city-state, Ancient Greece, 51–52

backstage racism, 14, 23
Beauvoir, Simone de, 74
Beccaria, Cesare, 360
Beck, Ulrich, 130, 132–134
Becker, Howard S., 295, 297
beekeeping, colony collapse disorder, 99
behavior, social psychology, 387–388
behavioral genetics, 160–161
Bell, Derrick, 30, 31
Bentley, Arthur F., 52, 53
Beyond Rhetoric: A New Agenda for Children and Families (US Commission on Children), 241
Bible translation, 399–400
biological perspectives, sociobiology, 156–162. *See also* ecological perspectives
biomedical model of mental distress, 153
biotechnology, 100
birds, urban, 99–100. *See also* animal sociology
birth control, women's studies, 4, 5–6
black categorizations, 6
black feminist ideology, 84–86, 413
Black Feminist Thought (Collins), 84
Black Pete, systemic racism example, 17
black power movement, 210. *See also* racism/racial perspectives
black sexuality, sociology of the body, 213
Blauner, Robert, 32–33
Blumer, Herbert, 200–202
body size, 213–214. *See also* embodiment
Bonilla-Silva, Eduardo, 9, 22, 23
Booth, Charles, 331
Bourdieu, Pierre
    art, 294, 296–297, 300
    Distinction, 270–271
    food, 204
    music, 305
    translation, 402, 403–405
Braverman, Harry, 43
breeding, zoo animals, 101
broken windows model, criminology, 364–366
Burawoy, Michael, 44, 313–314, 317, 327
Burgess, Ernest W., 361, 372–373

Cage, John (composer), 248
Calhoun, Craig, 319
Canada, human development index (HDI), 108–113, 114
candidate-selection process, class-dominance theory of power, 63
capabilities concept
    environmental justice, 191
    human development index, 107
CAPACS (Commission on the Accreditation of Programs in Applied and Clinical Sociology), 318, 336

capital concept
  art, 296–297
  translation, 403–404
Capital (Marx), 42, 45
captive breeding, zoo animals, 101
career criminals, 362–363
Carroll, William, 48
Cartwright, D., 388
case study methodology, popular culture, 287
Catholic church. *See also* religion, sociology of
  environmental justice, 192
  music, 305
  women's studies, 408
causality, strong programme of scientific knowledge, 169–170
characteristic emotions, 220
Chicago School
  criminology, 361–362
  violence, 181–182
child and youth well-being index (CWI), 115, 114–115
children, sociology of, 239–245
Children and Society: The Sociology of Children and Childhood Socialization (Handel, Spencer, Cahill and Elkin), 243
Children in Poverty (US House of Representatives Committee on Ways and Means), 239
Chin, Vincent, 7–8
CITES treaty (Convention on International Trade in Endangered Species of Wild Fauna and Flora), 101
cities, concentric zone theory, 372–373
citizenship, critical race theory, 35
Civil Rights Cases (1883), 12–13
civil rights movement, color-blind racism, 21
civilizing processes, sociology of violence, 179
clarification, sociotechnics, 334
class. *See* social class
class-dominance theory of power, 60–61, 67
  contrast with Marxist theory, 67
  union movement, 64–67
  US applicability, 61–64
classical sociotechnics, 333
classical perspectives. *See also* Comte; Du Bois; Durkheim; Gilman; Marx; Mead; Simmel; Spencer; Weber
  animal sociology, 95–97
  clinical sociology, 340
  and critical race theory, 32–33
  death and dying, 256–257
  food, 200–202, 204
  public sociology, 316–317
Clear, Todd, 373
climate change
  environmental justice, 194–195
  green Marxism, 47–48
clinical social work, 379–380
clinical sociology, 334–335, 339, 345
  conceptualizations, 341–342
  contemporary developments, 343–344
  historical perspectives, 340–341
  institutionalization, 342–343
  methodology, 344
  public sociology, 315
  theoretical foundations/models, 344–345
Clinical Sociology Association, 343–344
clinical sociotechnics, 333
coalition of anxiety, risk society, 133
CoBRAS measure, color-blind racism, 23–24
coercion, sociology of leisure, 275–276
cognition, social psychology, 387–388
cohesion of society, and friendship, 233–234
collaborative research, visual sociology, 122, 124–125
collective action, anti-vivisectionist, 100
collective conscience, 372
collective effervescence, sociology of music, 307
collective efficacy, criminology, 365
collective power, 60–61. *See also* class-dominance theory of power
collectivism, 390–391
college cop movement, 373
College of Police Science (COPS), 373
colonialism, feminist perspectives, 75
colony collapse disorder, beekeeping, 99
color-blind racism, 21–26, 32
Comcast example, pluralism, 56–57
Commission on the Accreditation of Programs in Applied and Clinical Sociology (CAPACS), 318, 336
commodification of nature, 47
Communist Manifesto (Marx), 4, 42
community care, mental illness, 152
community interpreting, sociology of translation, 402
companion animals, 97–98
competence, social work core values, 378
composite social indictors, 107. *See also* child and youth well-being index; human development index
comprehensive emergency management (CEM) framework, sociology of disasters, 141
Comte, Auguste, 322–323
  applied sociology/sociotechnics, 331
  clinical sociology, 340
concentration effect, poverty, 365
concentric zone theory, cities, 372–373
The Condition of Postmodernity (Harvey), 46
conflict theory, social work, 381
confrontation-tension fear (*ct/f*) barrier, violence, 182–183
consciousness-raising groups, feminist, 6
consent, for visual sociology research, 125–126
Constructing and Reconstructing Childhood (James and Prout eds.), 243
Consumer Culture and Postmodernism (Featherstone), 269
consumption, sociology of, 265, 273
  cultural studies, 268–270
  field of study, 265–267
  food sociology, 204
  mass culture, 267–268
  recent developments, 271–272
  sustainability, 272–273
  taste and distinction, 270–271

content analysis, popular culture, 286, 288
contingency theory, social work, 381
continuity theory, sociology of aging, 248
Convention on International Trade in Endangered Species of Wild Fauna and Flora (CITES), 101
core values, social work, 378
corruption, criminal justice system, 371
Council on Social Work Education (CSWE), 382
counter-storytelling, critical race theory, 34
Crane, Diana, 299
Creating Mental Illness (Horwitz), 149
Crenshaw, Kimberlé, 84–85
criminal justice studies, 374–375
   and criminology, 359, 372, 373–374
   field of study, 367–368
   historical perspectives, 370–372
   institutionalization, 373–374
   juvenile offenders, 370
   sequence of events, 368–370
   sociology of, 372–373
Criminal Statistics, 363
criminalization, of mental illness, 152
criminologists, 359
criminology, 359–360, 364–366, 372–373
   contemporary developments, 363–364
   criminal careers, 362–363
   and criminal justice studies, 359, 372, 373–374
   historical perspectives, 360–361
   public sociology, 314
   sociology of, 361–362
critical race theory (CRT), 15–16, 30–36
critical sociology, 317, 326–327. *See also* humanist sociology
critical theory of aging, 252
cultural perspectives
   environmental justice, 192
   place of leisure in society, 277
   popular culture, 284–285
   risk, 130–132
   social psychology, 390–391
   teaching sociology, 352
cultural relativism, teaching sociology, 352–353
cultural studies, 268–270. *See also* consumption, sociology of
Cumming, Elaine, 248–249

Dahl, Robert A., 53, 57
Dallas television show, 289
dark social engineering, 333
data values, sociotechnics, 332–333
death and dying, sociology of, 256–261
Decade for Women (1975 to 1985), 75
decentralization/fragmentation
   mental illness services, 152–154
   response to disasters, 142
definitions
   child, 240
   clinical sociology, 342
   consumption, 266
   emotion, 218

   humanist sociology, 322
   leisure, 275–276
   mental health and illness, 148–150
   music sociology, 304
   nature of violence, 178–179
   party of the dominant class, 62
   power, 56
   public sociology, 313–314
   risk, 130
   social indicators, 106
   social psychology, 387–388
   sociobiology, 156
de-individualization, slaughter of animals, 98
Delinquency in a Birth Cohort (Wolfgang, Figlio and Sellin), 362–363
Democrats Party, US, 63–64
demographic changes, role of social work, 384
denial, death, 258–259
denial, sociology of disasters, 141
dependence in old age, 247. *See also* aging
deviance, emotional, 222–223
deviance generalization hypothesis, animal abuse, 98
Diagnostic and Statistical Manual (DSM), American Psychiatric Association, 149
difference, feminist perspectives, 75
dignity, social work core values, 378
Dilemma of Mental Health Policy: Radical Reform or Incremental Change? (Grob and Goldman), 153–154
DiMaggio, Paul, 285
disability studies, 213–214
Disaster Research Center, Ohio State University, 140
disasters, sociology of, 139
   chief research areas/findings, 141
   companion animals, 98, 142
   emergency management, 145
   environmental justice, 193–194
   future directions, 144
   historical perspectives, 139–141
   mitigation strategies, 143–144
   preparedness for disasters, 141–142
   recovery from disasters, 142–143
   resilience, 143, 144
   response to disasters, 142
   vulnerability analyses, 144
   warning systems, 144–145
disease branding, medical model of mental distress, 153
disengagement theory, sociology of aging, 248–249
Disneyization, of zoos, 101
Distinction (Bourdieu), 270–271
distinction, sociology of consumption, 270–271
distinctions, sociology of music, 306–307
distributional approach, environmental justice, 191
distributive power, 60–61. *See also* class-dominance theory of power
division of labor
   class-dominance theory of power, 61
   private vs. public spheres of work, 3–4
Division of Labor (Durkheim), 360–361
divorce, social support, 151
dogfighting, 100
dogs, pet, 97. *See also* companion animals

"Doing Gender" (West and Zimmerman), 79
domestic labour, Marxist feminism, 45
domestic violence, 183–184, 411
Domhoff, G. William, 57
Douglas, Mary, 130–132, 201
dramaturgic approach, translation, 402
dual systems theory, Marxist feminism, 45
Du Bois, W. E. B., 32–33
Durkheim, Emile
 art sociology, 294
 clinical sociology, 340
 criminal justice studies, 372
 criminology, 360–361
 death and dying, 256–257
 The Rules of Sociological Method, 323
 Suicide, 148
 totemic principle, 96
dying. *See* death and dying, sociology of
Dynamic Sociology or Applied Social Science (Ward), 331–332

Eating Together (Julier), 203–204
ecological perspectives
 criminology, 361, 364–366
 Marxism and social class, 47–48
 violence sociology, 181–182
economic power networks, 60–61. *See also* class-dominance theory of power
economic sociology, popular culture, 284–285
Edelman, Murray, 288
edgework approach, sociology of risk, 135–136
education measures, human development index, 108
educational contexts
 color-blind racism, 24
 critical race theory, 34
 public sociology, 315, 318–319
 sociotechnics, 334
egalitarianism
 friendship, 230–231
 grid-group typology of risk, 131–132
Eisenhower administration, union movement, 66
elders, respect for, 246. *See also* aging
Eldridge, Seba, 332
Elias, Norbert, 179, 181–182, 200–202, 258
elite theory vs. pluralism, 53
elite whites
 feminist methodologies, 86
 popular culture, 287
 privilege, 15, 18–19
 social psychology, 390
embodiment, 209–214
 aging, 248
 emotion, 392–393
emergency management, disasters, 145
emotion, 218, 224–225. *See also* affect
 characteristic and structural emotions, 220
 emotion management, 221
 emotional deviance, 222–223
 emotional labor, 221–222
 emotional socialization, 220–221
 equity theory, 223–224

exchange theory, 224
 identity and social structures, 223
 justice framework, 224
 role-taking emotions, 219–220
 social psychology, 392–393
 sociobiology, 159–160
 theoretical foundations, 218–219
emotional regulation, 222
empirical focus, pluralism, 53–54
Employee Representation Plans, union movement, 64–65
employment. *See* work/employment
empowerment theory, social work, 382
Engels, Friedrich, 3–4, 45
Enlightenment, 322–323, 408, 409
entertainment animals, animal rights, 100–101
environmental crises, green Marxism, 47–48
environmental justice (EJ), 188, 195
 climate change, 194–195
 institutionalization, development and growth, 189–191
 justice theories, 191–192
 movement, 188–189
 natural disasters, 193–194
 religion/spirituality, 192–193
environmental privilege, 192. *See also above*
equity theory, sociology of emotion, 223–224
Estes, Carroll, 251–252
ethics, visual sociology, 125–126
ethnicity-based theories of race, 5. *See also* racism/racial perspectives
ethnocentrism, teaching sociology, 352–353
ethnographic perspectives, 121
 music, sociology, 305–306
 popular culture, 286
 visual sociology, 121, 124–125
eugenics movement, 410, 411
Europe
 art, 294–295
 consumption, 266–267
 systemic racism, 16–17
European Sociological Association, 295
evidenced based practice (EBP), social work, 383. *See also* science and technology
evolutionary perspectives, sociobiology, 159
evolutionary psychology, 156, 157
expanded mode of production approach, Marxist feminism, 45
experimental methodology, social psychology, 389
expert panels, objective social indicators research, 106
experts, authority of
 disasters, 143
 risk, 130
 science and technology, 172, 173–174
expressive violence, 179

Faces at the Bottom of the Well: The Permanence of Racism (Bell), 30
families/family sociology
 critical race theory, 35
 food sociology, 202–204

farm animals, 98–99, 100
fat studies/fat rights, 213–214. *See also* embodiment
fatalism, grid-group typology of risk, 131–132
Feagin, Joe, 33–34, 327
Featherstone, Mike, 269, 374
Federal Emergency Management Agency (FEMA), 140
Feeding the Family (De Vault), 203–204
feminism, 73–74, 79–80. *See also* gender sociology; women's studies
  activism, 410–411
  contribution to sociology, 78–79
  critical race theory, 31, 35
  difference, 75
  embodiment, 210
  emerging ideas, 78
  identity, 74–75
  intersectionality, 75–76, 83
  leisure, 280–281
  Marxism and social class, 45–46
  postmodern, 77–78
  standpoint theory, 76–77, 83
  vegetarianism, 101–102
  waves of, 410, 413
feminist methodologies, 82–84, 89
  intersectionality, 83, 84–86
  non-print media, 87–88
  sexuality and queer studies, 88–89
  third world, 86–87
Feminist Methods in Social Research (Reinharz and Davidman), 83–84
The Feminine Mystique (Friedan), 82
fertility, sociobiology, 157, 159, 161–162
field concept
  art, 296–297, 300
  translation, 402, 403–404
Fischler, Claude, 201
Florida, Richard, 299
focus groups, popular culture, 286
Fogo Process, participatory video, 123–124
food activism, 200
food scares, 202
food, sociology of, 199–205
Footnotes article, sociology of children, 239
Foster, John Bellamy, 47
Foucault, Michael, 134–135, 149
four-factor model of emotion, 218, 221
four-network theory of power, 60–61. *See also* class-dominance theory of power
fragmentation. *See* decentralization/fragmentation
Francastel, Pierre, 294
France
  art, 294–295
  clinical sociology, 340
Frankfurt School, 267–268, 269–270
Fraser, Nancy, 45
free-market principles, color-blind racism, 22
friendship, sociology of, 229–235
Fritz, Charles E., 139–141
From Art to Politics (Edelman), 288
Fukushima nuclear accident (2011), 173
functionalist theories. *See* structural functionalism

funding policies, mental illness, 152–154
funeral arrangements, 259

gang culture, criminology, 361–362
Gans, Herbert, 285
gatekeepers
  popular culture, 289
  translation, 404
Gender Inequality Index (GII), 108
gender sociology, 79. *See also* feminism
  aging sociology, 251
  art sociology, 298
  embodiment, 211–212
  emotional labor, 222
  environmental justice, 190, 194–195
  feminist methodologies, 84
  food sociology, 203–204
  friendship sociology, 233
  leisure sociology, 280–281
  sex roles, 79
  social constructionism, 159
  social practice of translation, 401
  social psychology, 391–392
  social work salaries, 382–383
  vegetarianism, 101–102
  violence sociology, 183–184
Gendering Bodies (Crawley, Foley, and Shehan), 79
generational theories of childhood, 243–244
genetic engineering, farm animals, 100
genetics, sociobiology, 158, 160–161
genocide, sociology of violence, 184–185
geographical models. *See* spatial perspectives
George Mason University, women's studies, 415
Germany
  art sociology, 294–295
  systemic racism example, 16–17
gerontocracy, 246–247. *See also* aging
Gilman, Charlotte Perkins, 4
global citizenship, role of social work, 384
global comparisons, human development index (HDI), 109–113
global life satisfaction, quality-of-life research, 106–107
globalization
  art sociology, 299–300
  Marxism and social class, 48
  risk society, 133
goals commissions approach, objective social indicators, 106
Goffman, Erving, 402
Goldman, Emma, 4
Gouanvic, Jean-Marc, 404
Gouldner, Alvin W., 343
government policy. *See* policy initiatives
governmentality, sociology of risk, 134–135
Great Depression, union movement, 66–67
green Marxism, 47
grid-group typology of risk, 131, 132
Griswold, Wendy, 300
group identity, sociology of music, 307–308
group selection, 158
Guyau, Jean-Marie, 294

habitus concept
  art, 296–297
  consumption, 270–271
  translation, 402, 403
Halle, David, 298
Handbook for the Study of Mental Health (Scheid and Brown), 150
happiness. *See* social indicators and quality-of-life research
Harlan, Justice John Marshall, 12–13
Harvey, David, 46
Haynes, George Edmund, 342
HDI (human development index), 107–113, 114, 116–117
health care systems, role of social work, 384
health measures, human development index, 107
heat wave deaths, environmental justice, 194–195
heavy metal rock music, 290
Henry, William, 248–249
HEP (Human Exemptionalist Paradigm), 96–97
Heyworth Committee, 335
hierarchy, grid-group typology of risk, 131–132
Hirschi, Travis, 362
historical materialism, 42
history of sociology. *See also* classical perspectives
  art sociology, 294–295
  criminal justice, 370–372
  criminology, 360–361
  disasters, 139–141
  humanist sociology, 322–323
  Marxism and social class, 42
  public sociology, 316–317
  social psychology, 388–389
  women's studies, 408
hobbies, 276. *See also* leisure, sociology of
Holocaust, 184–185
homemaking, women's studies, 409
homeschooling, 222–223
homo-economicus/homo-sociologicus, 266, 269
Horkheimer, Max, 267–268, 285, 288–289, 297
human development index (HDI), 107–113, 114, 116–117
Human Exemptionalist Paradigm (HEP), 96–97
human relations theory, social work, 381
human relationships, social work core values, 378
humanist sociology, 322
  Association for Humanist Sociology, 324–326
  critique of mainstream sociology, 323–324
  future directions, 326–328
  historical perspectives, 322–323
  principles of, 324–325
hunting, wildlife, 99–100
Hurricane Katrina
  companion animals, 98
  environmental justice, 194–195
  teaching sociology, 353
hyper-ghettoization, violence, 182

Ibn Khaldûn, Abd-al-Rahman, 340
identity
  consumption as expression of, 266, 269–270, 271
  emotion sociology, 223
  feminist perspectives, 74–75
  leisure sociology, 280
  music sociology, 306–307
  social psychology, 393–394
identity-based group membership, 212–213
identity control theory, 223
ideological networks of power, 60–61. *See also* class-dominance theory of power
idleness, 276. *See also* leisure, sociology of
If You Tame Me (Irvine), 97
images. *See* visual sociology
immigrant populations
  critical race theory, 35
  impacts of industrialization. *See* environmental justice
  role of social work, 384
impartiality, strong programme of scientific knowledge, 169–170
in prison-based animal training programs, 98
incarceration rates, US prisoners, 368
Index Translatonium (UNESCO database), 404–405
indicators of social change approach, 106
indigenous peoples, impacts of industrialization. *See* environmental justice
individualism, 131–132, 390–391
industrial revolution
  humanist sociology, 322–323
  private vs. public spheres of work, 3–4
inequality
  aging, 250–251
  embodiment, 210
  environmental, 192. *See also* environmental justice
  role of social work, 384
Inequality-Adjusted HDI (IHDI), 108
in-groups
  friendship sociology, 232–233
  music sociology, 306–307
innovations, social, 381
institutionalization of sociology. *See also* journals
  children's sociology, 240
  clinical sociology, 342–343
  criminal justice studies, 373–374
  death and dying, 257–258, 260
  disasters sociology, 139–141
  embodiment, 209
  environmental justice, 189–191
  feminist perspectives, 82
  humanist sociology, 328
  leisure, 281
  public sociology, 316, 317
  science and technology, 166–167
  social work, 382–383
  teaching sociology, 353–354
  women's studies, 413–414
instrumental violence, 179
integrity, social work core values, 378
intellectual activism, 315–316
interdisciplinarity
  children's studies, 241–242
  death and dying sociology, 260
  embodiment, 210
  environmental justice, 189

interdisciplinarity (cont.)
  food sociology, 200, 202
  humanist sociology, 326
  social psychology, 388–389
  translation studies, 399–400
  violence sociology, 178
interest convergence theory, 31, 33–34
interest groups
  class-dominance theory of power, 62–63
  pluralism, 55–56
international perspectives. *See also* globalization
  art, 293–294
  clinical sociology, 340–341
International Sociological Association, 295, 341
International Visual Sociology Association, 119
internet, feminist methodologies, 87–88
interpersonal emotion management, 221
interplanetary theory of gender, 211
intersectionality
  critical race theory, 31, 32
  embodiment, 213
  feminist methodologies, 83, 84–86
  feminist perspectives, 75–76
  impacts of industrialization, 190. *See also* environmental justice
  systemic racism, 15
intervention model of sociotechnics, 333
interviews, popular culture, 286
intrapersonal emotion management, 221
Introduction to the Science of Sociology (Park and Burgess), 323
Irvine, Leslie, 97
"Is There Sufficient Interest to Establish a Sociology of Children?" *Footnotes*, 239
Italy, clinical sociology, 340

James, William, 393
Johnson administration, 371
John Jay College of Criminal Justice, 373
journals
  art sociology, 300–301
  clinical sociology, 343–344
  disasters sociology, 141
  feminist, 82–83
  humanist sociology, 325, 326
  mental health and illness, 150
  public sociology, 317–318
  social indicators and quality-of-life research, 106
justice, environmental. *See* environmental justice
justice framework, sociology of emotion, 224
juvenile offenders, criminal justice, 370

Kelley, Florence, 332
Kelly, John R., 280
The Kitchen Table Press, 413
Kuhn, Thomas, 169

labeling theory
  mental illness, 149–150
  racial formation theoretical framework, 7–8
labor, emotional, 221–222

labor force participation, women's studies, 411
laboratory animals, animal testing, 100
Labour and Monopoly Capital (Braverman), 43
laissez-faire atomistic model of society, 335
laissez faire racism. *See* color-blind racism
Lalo, Charles, 294
LatCrit, 31. *See also* critical race theory
Latino groups, color-blind racism, 26
law of uneven development, 46–47
lay experts, 130, 172, 173–174
Lee, Alfred McClung, 324–326, 342
Lefebvre, Henri, 46
legitimation of the status quo, color-blind racism, 22
Leisure Identities and Interactions (Kelly), 280
leisure, sociology of, 275–276
  gender and feminist perspectives, 280–281
  in-depth studies, 279–280
  institutionalization, 281
  meaning and motivational studies, 279
  place of leisure in society, 277
  symbolic interactionism, 280
  time pressure, 277–278
  typologies, 278–279
  Western societies, 276–277
liberation sociology, 327–328. *See also* humanist sociology
Licensed Independent Clinical Social Worker (LICSW), 379
Life and Labour of the People in London (Booth), 331
life chances concept, 250
life course sociology
  children sociology, 239–245
  death and dying sociology, 239–245
  life course approaches to aging, 250. *See also* aging
life satisfaction, global, 106–107
lifestyles, sociology of consumption, 269
Limits to Capital (Harvey), 46
Lisbon earthquake example, disasters, 139
living standards measures, human development index, 108
locally unwanted land uses (LULUs), 188. *See also* environmental justice
The Loneliness of the Dying (Elias), 258
Lowenthal, Leo, 285
Luhmann, N., 402
Luxton, Meg, 45
Lyng, Stephen, 135–136

macro-level theories
  aging, 248–250
  racial formation theoretical framework, 8–9
  social practice of translation, 401
  sociotechnics, 334–336
macro social work practice, 380–382
Madness and Civilization (Foucault), 149
The Making of the English Working Class (Thompson), 43–44
male dominance, class-dominance theory of power, 61
Malthus, Thomas Robert, 331, 412
Man and the State: Studies in Applied Sociology (Brooklyn New York Ethical Association), 330

Man-Made Disasters (Turner), 129
marriage, women's studies, 4
Mars, interplanetary theory of gender, 211
Marx, Karl and Marxism. *See also* social class, Marxist perspectives
   animal sociology, 95–96
   art sociology, 294, 297–298
   clinical sociology, 340
   death and dying, 256–257
Marxist feminism, 45–46
Marx's Ecology (Foster), 47
masculinity discourses, violence, 183–184
mask of aging, continuity theory, 248
mass culture. *See* popular culture
massive open online courses (MOOCs)
   humanist sociology, 328
   public sociology, 319
McBride, Amanda Moore, 354
McDonagh, Edward, 342
McDonaldization, 101, 299–300
McKay, Amy, 57
McKay, Henry, 361
Mead, George Herbert, 96
media responses to disasters, 142. *See also* social media platforms
media studies, sociology of risk, 136
mediation, clinical sociology, 344–345
Medical College Admission Test (MCAT), 315
medical model of mental distress, 153
mega risks, risk society, 132–133
Mellor, P. A., 257–258
Mennell, Stephen, 201
mental health and illness, 148, 154
   definitions, 148–150
   role of social work, 379–380, 385
   service delivery/policy, 152–154
   social context of, 150–151
Mental Health Parity and Addictions Act (2008), 153
Merton, Robert, 361, 372
Mertonian school of science and technology, 167–169
meso-level theories
   social practice of translation, 401
   sociotechnics, 334–335
methodology
   clinical sociology, 344
   color-blind racism, 23–24
   popular culture, 286–289
micro-level theories
   aging, 247–248
   racial formation theoretical framework, 8–9
   social practice of translation, 401
   sociotechnics, 334–335
micro-aggressions, critical race theory, 34–35
military networks of power, 60–61. *See also* class-dominance theory of power; war
mirror neurons, 160
mitigation strategies, disasters, 143–144
Mitterrand, François, 295
Mlyn, Eric, 354
modern racism. *See* color-blind racism

Moore, Wendy Leo, 34
motivational studies, leisure, 279
Moulin, Raymonde, 295
Mount Graham, environmental justice, 192
movements, social. *See* social movements
multiculturalism, feminist methodologies, 83
Multidimensional Poverty Index (MPI), 108
multinational corporations, power structures, 56–57
music, sociology of, 304–308

National Association of Social Workers' Code of Ethics, 378
National Comorbidity Survey, US, 149
National Institute of Justice (NIJ), 372
National Institute of Law Enforcement and Criminal Justice (NILECJ), 372
National Labor Board (NLB), union movement, 64–65
National Labor Relations Act (1935), 64, 67
National Labor Relations Board (NLRB), 65
National Longitudinal Survey of Youth, 35
National Opinion Research Center (NORC), 140
nation-based theories, race, 6
native peoples, environmental justice, 192
natural disasters. *See* disasters, sociology of
Natural Hazards Research and Applications Information Center, 140
natural world/nature, environmental justice, 190
neoconservative perspectives, post-racialism, 33
Neo-Kuhnian school, science and technology sociology, 169
neoliberalism, Marxist feminism, 45–46
neo-Marxist perspectives, place of leisure in society, 277
Netherlands
   human development index, 108–114
   systemic racism example, 17
network analysis, transnational class theory, 48
networks of power, 60–61. *See also* class-dominance theory of power
   United States applicability, 61–64
networks of social ties, 230
neurosociology, 159–160
New Ecological Paradigm (NEP), 96–97
new imperialism, 46–47
New Perspectives on Environmental Justice (Stein), 190–192
Newfoundland island, Fogo community, 123–124
Nixon administration, union movement, 66
Nordlinger, Eric, 57–58
normlessness. *See* anomie
nuclear power, risk society, 133
nutrition, health sciences, 202

Obama administration, and racism, 14, 23
Obamacare, 154, 336, 384
obesity. *See* body size
objective social indicators, 105–107
objects, sociology of consumption, 271
Ogburn, William, 323, 332
old age, dependency, 247. *See also* aging
Omi, Michael, 5–10, 17–18, 33

On Crimes and Punishment (Beccaria), 360
operative values, sociotechnics, 332–333
opinion-shaping processes, class-dominance theory, 63
Origins of the Family (Engels), 4, 45
The Other Price of Britain's Oil (Carson), 129
out-groups
    friendship sociology, 232–233
    music sociology, 306–307

Paradoxes of Gender (Lorber), 79
Park, Robert Ezra, 361, 372–373
PART (Practice and Research Together), 319
participatory parity, environmental justice, 191
participatory practices
    science and technology sociology, 171–172
    social construction of participation, 172–173
participatory research methods, visual sociology, 122
participatory videos, visual sociology, 121, 123–124
party of the dominant class, 62. *See also* class-dominance theory of power
Passeron, Jean-Claude, 300
Patterns in Criminal Homicide (Wolfgang), 363
pedagogical processes, 350–353. *See also* teaching, sociology
Pellow, David, 102
penology, 360, 364
person-in-environment systems, social work, 378–379
pesticides, sociology of risk, 129, 130
Peterson, Richard, 298
pets
    disasters sociology, 141
    dogs, 97. *See also* companion animals
pharmaceutical drugs, medical model of mental distress, 153
photo elicitation, visual sociology, 121, 123
photo voice, visual sociology, 123
photography, 120. *See also* visual sociology
phrenologists, 360
physiognomy, 360
Pinker, Steven, 179
pluralism, 51–53, 58
    active exercise of power, 56–57
    critiques, 57–58
    vs. elite theory perspective, 53
    empirical focus, 53–54
    interest groups and the public, 55–56
    power structures, 54
Podgórecki, Adam, 332–333
police forces, historical perspectives, 371
policy initiatives. *See also* pluralism
    applied sociology/sociotechnics, 336
    art sociology, 298–299
    color-blind racism, 24–25
    critical race theory, 31
    mental illness, 153–154
    racial formation theoretical framework, 7–8
policy-planning process, class-dominance theory of power, 63
policy science, 334
political consumers, 133

political economics perspective
    aging, 251–252
    applied sociology/sociotechnics, 331
    art, 298–299
    consumption, 271
political networks of power, 60–61. *See also* class-dominance theory of power
Polsby, Nelson, 53
popular culture, 284–285, 290
    controversies of, 289–290
    consumption, 267–268
    gatekeepers, 289
    mass culture, 267–268
    methodology, 286–289
    theoretical foundations, 285
Popular Culture and High Culture (Gans), 285
positive philosophy/positivism
    criminology, 361–362
    humanist sociology, 322–323
postmodern feminist perspectives, 77–78
post-racialism, and critical race theory, 32, 33
poverty
    applied sociology/sociotechnics, 335
    concentration effect, 365
    feminist perspectives, 75
    role of social work, 384
power elites, 62
power structures. *See also* class-dominance theory of power
    aging sociology, 246–247, 250–251
    participatory research methods, 122
    pluralism, 54, 56–57
    popular culture, 288–289
    standpoint theory, 76–77
    translation sociology, 404
    violence sociology, 183–184
power-dependency theory, social work, 381
The Practice of Eating (Warde), 204
practice turn, sociology of consumption, 272
pregnancy example, governmentality, 134
prisoners, incarceration rates, 368
private vs. public spheres, women's studies, 3–4
privilege
    critical race theory, 34
    environmental, 192. *See also* environmental justice
    racial, 9–10, 15, 18–19, 25. *See also* racism/racial perspectives
processes, social practice of translation, 402
products, social practice of translation, 401, 402
production studies, popular culture, 287–288
profession of social work, 377, 382–383
profession of sociology, teaching, 352
Protestant ethic, 276–277
psychology, ABC of, 387–388. *See also* evolutionary psychology; mental health and illness; social psychology
public exhibition/ethnography, visual sociology, 125
public service
    delivery/policy, mental illness, 152–154
    social work core values, 378
    translation, 402

public sociology, 313–314
　future directions, 318–319
　historical perspectives, 316–317
　publications, 317–318
　typology, 314–316
public vs. private spheres, women's studies, 3–4

quackish social engineering, 333
qualitative research. *See also* visual sociology
　color-blind racism, 23
　feminist, 83
　popular culture, 286
quality-of-life research. *See* social indicators
quantitative research
　color-blind racism, 23–24
　feminist, 83
　popular culture, 286
queer studies. *See also* sexuality studies
　environmental justice, 190
　feminist methodologies, 88–89

RaceCrits, 30–31. *See also* critical race theory
racial formation theory (RFT), 5–10
　and critical race theory, 33
　and systemic racism, 10, 17–18
Racial Oppression in America (Blauner), 32–33
racial project concept, 6, 17–18
racialization, 6
racism/racial perspectives
　affirmative action, 7
　art sociology, 298
　color-blind, 21–26, 32
　embodiment, 212–213
　emotional labor, 222
　environmental, 190, 193. *See also* environmental justice
　friendship sociology, 233
　Marxism and social class, 44–45
　popular culture, 289
　systemic. *See* systemic racism theory
Racism Without Racists (Bonilla-Silva), 22, 23
rape, 184
Rawls, John, 191–192
Reagan Administration, union movement, 66
reception studies, popular culture, 288–289
recognition, excluded groups, environmental justice, 191
recordings, visual sociology, 121
recovery, from disasters, 142–143
recovery, from mental illness, 152
recreation, 276. *See also* leisure, sociology of
reflexivity
　feminist methodologies, 85
　strong programme of scientific knowledge, 169–170
refugees, role of social work, 384
relationships. *See* human relationships, social work core values
relativism, teaching sociology, 352–353
religion, sociology of
　environmental justice, 192–193
　ideological networks of power, 60–61
　music, 308

representative democracy, 52
Reproducing Racism: White Space, Elite Law Schools, and Racial Inequality (Moore), 34
reproductive success, sociobiology, 157, 159, 161–162
reproductive rights, 408. *See also* birth control, women's studies
Republican party, United States, 63–64
resilience, disasters, 143, 144
resistance, sociology of leisure, 280–281
resistance movements. *See* social movements
respect for elders, 246. *See also* aging
Riesman, David, 279–280
Riley, Matilda White, 249–250
risk, sociology of, 129–130, 136–137
　and culture, 130–132
　edgework approach, 135–136
　governmentality, 134–135
　grid-group typology, *131*, 132
　risk society, 132–134
Risk and Culture (Douglas and Wildavsky), 130–132
risk management/risk aversion, 135
The Risk Society (Beck), 130
rite of passage, death as, 257–258
Roberts, Chief Justice John, 51, 52
role-taking emotions, 219–220
Roosevelt Administration, 64–65
The Rules of Sociological Method (Durkheim), 322–323

Safe Streets and Crime Control Act (1968), 372
salaries, social work, 382–383
Samson the bull, animal sociology, 99
Sanger, Margaret, 410, 411–412
scapegoats, racial, 7–8
Scheff, Thomas, 183
schizophrenia, 149. *See also* mental health and illness
"Schools for Africa" posters, 16–17
science and technology, 166–167, 174–175
　actor network theory, 170–171
　Mertonian school, 167–169
　Neo-Kuhnian school, 169
　participatory practices, 171–172
　social construction of participation, 172–173
　social constructionism, 170, 171
　sociology of, 170, 171
　strong programme of scientific knowledge, 169–170
　thematic development, 168
　third wave argument, 172
　under-determination of scientific knowledge, 174, 173–174
scientific method, use in sociology, 323
scientific revolution, 322–323. *See also* industrial revolution
SCOT (social construction of technology), 170, 171. *See also* science and technology; social constructionism
segregation, color-blind racism, 24–25
self-determination, social work core values, 378
selfhood, animals, 97
self-made social engineering, 333
self/self-knowledge, social psychology, 393–394
self-sociology, 209–214. *See also* identity

serious leisure perspective (SLP), 278–279
service. *See* public service
sex roles, feminist perspectives, 79. *See also* gender sociology
sexual harassment, 83
sexual revolution, women's studies, 411–412
sexual violence, 184
sexuality studies
   embodiment, 211–212
   environmental justice, 190
   feminist methodologies, 84, 88–89
shame theory, sociology of violence, 183
Shaw, Clifford R., 361
shelter movement, women's studies, 412
Silent Spring (Carson), 129
Simmel, Georg
   food sociology, 200–202
   music sociology, 305
slaughter of animals, animal sociology, 98–99
Small, Albion, 341
Snowden, Don, 123–124
social barometer, friendship as, 231–233
social bond theory
   criminology, 362
   music sociology, 307–308
social causation, mental illness, 150–151
social class. *See also below*; class-dominance theory of power
   art sociology, 297–298
   class formation, 43–44
   class structure, 43
   color-blind racism, 25–26
   embodiment, 213
   friendship sociology, 233
   mental illness, 150–151
   and pluralism, 55–56
   and race, 6
   socialization of children, 242–243
   taste and distinction, 270–271
social class, Marxist perspectives, 41–43, 48–49
   class as a social relation, 43
   class formation, 43–44
   and class-dominance theory of power, 67
   ecological perspectives, 47–48
   feminist perspectives, 45–46
   globalization, 48
   racial perspectives, 44–45
   spatial dimensions, 46–47
   structural theories, 43
social construction of technology (SCOT), 170, 171
social constructionism
   childhood, 243
   cultural symbolic approach to risk, 131
   feminist perspectives, 77–78
   hunting wildlife, 99
   leisure, 280–281
   participation, 172–173
   popular culture, 289
   race, 6, 10, 31, 33, 35, 44
   and sociobiology, 159
   teaching sociology, 351–352
Social Darwinism, 157–158

Social Dimensions of Disaster emergency management guide, 145
social engineering, 315, 332–333, 334
social evolution, applied sociology/sociotechnics, 331
social exclusion, and environmental justice, 191
social hierarchies, color-blind racism, 25
social indicators and quality-of-life research, 105, 116–117
   child and youth well-being index, 114–115, 115
   composite, 107
   human development index, 107–113, 114
   objective and subjective, 105–107
social innovation, social work, 381
social justice
   feminist methodologies, 85
   social work core values, 378
social media platforms
   disaster warning systems, 144–145
   feminist methodologies, 87–88
   response to disasters, 142
   role of social work, 384–385
   visual sociology, 126–127
social movements
   critical race theory, 32–33
   environmental justice, 188–189
   humanist sociology, 326–328
   music sociology, 308
   systemic racism, 13
social network analysis, transnational class theory, 48
social patterns, teaching sociology, 350
social practices
   sociology of consumption, 272
   translation sociology, 400–402
social problems
   companion animals, 97–98
   farm animals, 98–99
   wildlife, 99–100
social psychology, 387, 394
   definitions, 387–388
   historical perspectives, 388–389
   meta-theoretical and methodological approaches, 389–390
   overlaps with sociology, 390–394
social reaction, mental illness, 150–151
social selection, mental illness, 150–151
social statistics, applied sociology/sociotechnics, 331
social stratification, music sociology, 307. *See also* social class
social structures. *See* structural perspectives/structuralism
social support, mental illness, 151
social theories, and sociological theories, 335
social work, 377
   clinical social work, 379–380
   core values, 378
   direct practice, 379–380
   future directions, 384–385
   indirect practice, 380–382
   institutionalization, 382–383
   research, 383
   social innovation, 381
   theoretical foundations, 378–379, 380, 381–382

socialization, emotional, 220–221
socialization of children
    and agency of the child, 243–244
    criminology, 362
    and social class, 242–243
Society for Social Work Research (SSWR), 383
Society of Experimental Social Psychology, 388–389
society-centered perspective, pluralism, 57–58
sociobiology, 156–162
socio-economic status. *See also* social class
    impacts of industrialization. *See* environmental justice
    and sociobiology, 157, 160, 161–162
socio-legal studies, criminology, 363
sociological imagination, teaching, 349, 350–353
The Sociological Imagination (Wright Mills), 323
Sociological Practice Association, 343–344
sociological theories
    and social psychology, 390–394
    and social theories, 335
Sociologists for Women in Society (SWS), 415
Sociology for Whom (Lee), 324
Sociology Liberation Movement, 324
Sociology of Children and Youth section, American Sociological Association, 239–245
sociology of scientific knowledge (SSK), 170, 171. *See also* science and technology
sociotechnics proper, 333. *See also* applied sociology
solicitant sociotechnics, 333
The Souls of Black Folk (Du Bois), 32–33
South Africa, apartheid, 44–45
Southern Democrats Party, United States, 63–64
spatial perspectives
    art sociology, 299–300
    impacts of industrialization. *See* environmental justice
    Marxism and social class, 46–47
special-interest processes, class-dominance theory, 62–63
Species Survival Plan (1981), 101
speciesism, animal sociology, 101
Spencer, Herbert, 331
spillover effect, slaughter of animals, 99
spiritual perspectives, environmental justice, 192–193. *See also* religion, sociology of
SRT. *See* systemic racism theory
SSK. *See* sociology of scientific knowledge
stage models, clinical sociology, 344–345
standpoint theory, feminist perspectives, 76–77, 83
state-centered perspectives, pluralism, 57–58
state-perpetrated violence, 178, 184–185
state roles. *See* policy initiatives
statistical social indicators. *See* social indicators and quality-of-life research
statistics
    applied sociology/sociotechnics, 331
    criminal, 363
stereotyping, racial, 22–23. *See also* systemic racism theory
stigma, mental illness, 150, 151, 152
stress process model of mental illness, 151

stress, sociobiology of, 160
strong programme of scientific knowledge, 169–170
structural emotions, 220
structural functionalism
    death and dying sociology, 257–258
    place of leisure in society, 277
    sociobiology, 158
structural perspectives/structuralism
    emotion, 223
    racism, 9
    risk, 130
    social class, 43
    teaching sociology, 352
    violence sociology, 179, 181–182
students of sociology, teaching, 348–354
subjective social indicators, 105–107
suicide, criminology, 360–361
Suicide (Durkheim), 148
Supreme Court cases, critical race theory, 34
surveys, popular culture, 286–287
sustainability, sociology of consumption, 272–273
Sutherland, Edwin, 364
Swedish level of living approach, 106
swine flu example, risk, 132
symbolic interactionism
    animal sociology, 97
    death and dying sociology, 258
    emotion sociology, 392–393
    leisure sociology, 280
    music sociology, 306
    self and identity, 393
symbolic meaning
    goods, 268–270
    popular culture, 288–289
symbolic racism. *See* color-blind racism
symmetry, strong programme of scientific knowledge, 169–170
Systemic Racism (Feagin), 33–34
systemic racism theory (SRT), 12–13, 18–19
    anti-oppression counter-frames, 16
    competing theories, 15–16
    and critical race theory, 33–34
    European examples, 16–17
    and racial formation framework, 10, 17–18
    white racial frame, 14
systems theory
    risk sociology, 136
    social work, 378–379, 381–382

Taft-Hartley Act (1947), 66
taste, sociology of consumption, 270–271
taste publics/taste cultures, 285
teaching
    social work, 382
    sociology, 348–354
Teaching Resources and Innovations Library for Sociology (TRAILS), 348
technology, role of social work, 384–385
technology, social construction of (SCOT), 170, 171. *See also* science and technology; social constructionism

teenagers
  criminal justice, 370
  criminology, 361–362
tenure, academic, 328
terrorist attacks (September 11, 2001). *See* World Trade Center terrorist attack
testing, animal, 100
The Theory of the Leisure Class (Veblen), 265, 279–280
third wave argument, science and technology, 172
third world feminism, 86–87
Thompson, E. P., 43–44
time pressure, sociology of leisure, 277–278
Total Liberation (Pellow), 102
totemic principle, 96
Toward Humanist Sociology (Lee), 324
transgender awareness, feminist methodologies, 88–89
transitional neighborhoods, 361
translation, sociology of, 405
  Bourdieu, 403–405
  community/public service interpreting, 402
  relation to sociology, 400
  social practice of translation, 400–402
  theoretical foundations, 402–403
  translation studies, 399–400
transnational class theory, 48. *See also* globalization
transnational families, risk society, 133–134
trinitrotoluene (TNT) ship explosion, 139–141
twin studies, sociobiology, 160–161

Under Western Eyes: Feminist Scholarship and Colonial Discourses (Mohanty), 75
under-determination of scientific knowledge, 173–174, 174
Unequal Childhoods: Class, Race, and Family Life (Lareau), 242–243
UNESCO database Index Translationum, 404–405
UNICEF "Schools for Africa" posters, 16–17
union movement, class-dominance theory, 64–67
United Kingdom
  applied sociology/sociotechnics, 331–332
  consumption, 266–267
United Nations Convention on the Rights of the Child (UNCRC), 241
United Nations Development Programme (UNDP), 107–113, 114
United States
  applied sociology/sociotechnics, 331–332
  class-dominance theory of power, 61–64
  clinical sociology, 341
  human development index, 108–113, 114
  sociology of consumption, 266–267
university teaching, sociology, 348–354
urban birds, 99–100. *See also* animal sociology
urbanization, criminal justice studies, 372–373
us versus them, music sociology, 306–307
utilitarian Christianity, applied sociology, 331

value-based profession, social work as, 378
value-oriented sociology, 322, 324–325. *See also* humanist sociology
values, criminology, 360–361

values proper, sociotechnics, 332–333
Veblen, Thorsten, 200–202, 265, 279–280
vegetarianism, 101–102, 202
Venus, interplanetary theory of gender, 211
victim precipitated homicide, 363
victimology, 364
violence, sociology of, 185
  civilizing processes, 179
  confrontation-tension fear barrier, 182–183
  gender, 183–184
  nature of violence, 178–179
  state perpetrated violence and war, 184–185
  zones of violence, 181–182
violence graduation hypothesis, abuse of animals, 98
visible voice projects, 123
visual sociology, 119–121, 126–127
  collaborative visual ethnography, 121, 124–125
  ethics, 125–126
  methodology, 121
  participatory/collaborative research, 122
  participatory video, 123–124
  photo elicitation, 121, 123
  photo voice, 123
  public exhibition, 125
  visual tours, 122–123
Voting Rights Act (1965), 13
vulnerability analyses, disasters, 144

Wagner, Senator Robert F., 64–65
Walker, David, 16
war
  applied sociology, 335–336
  networks of power, 60–61. *See also* class-dominance theory of power
  violence sociology, 184–185
Ward, Lester, 331–332
Warde, Alan, 204
warning systems, disasters, 144–145
Weber, Max, 56, 62
  animal sociology, 96
  art sociology, 294
  death and dying, 256–257
  music sociology, 305
WEIRD (Western, educated, industrialized, rich, and democratic), social psychology, 390
welfare policy, color-blind racism, 24–25
well-being. *See* social indicators and quality-of-life research
Western societies, sociology of leisure, 276–277
White, Cynthia and Harrison, 299
white, middle-class perspectives. *See* elite whites
white categorizations, racialization, 6
white racial frames, 14, 16–17
white speaker effect, systemic racism, 14
Wickersham Commission, 371
wildlife, and social problems, 99–100
Will and Grace television show, 286–287, 289–290
Wilson, E. O., 156
Wilson, O. W., 373
Wilson, William Julius, 365

Winant, Howard, 5–10, 17–18, 33
Winternitz, Milton C., 341–342
Wirth, Louis, 342, 361
Wolfgang, Marvin, 362–363
women's centers, 414–415
women's studies, 408, 410
   activism, 409, 410
   birth control and sexual revolution, 410–411
   historical perspectives, 408
   institutionalization, 413–414
   integration with sociology, 415–416
   labor force participation, 410
   private/public spheres of work, 409–410
   programs, 82
   waves of feminism, 410, 411
   women's centers, 414–415
work ethic, and sociology of leisure, 276–277
work/employment
   private vs. public spheres, 409–410
   women's participation, 408
Working Group on the Sociology of Childhood, International Sociological Association, 240
works of art, 300. *See also* art
World Trade Center terrorist attack (September 11, 2001), 141, 142
   criminal justice, 367–368
   teaching sociology, 351–352
World War II
   applied sociology/sociotechnics, 335–336
   social psychology, 388
worried well, 152–153, 379
Wrede, C., 374
Wright, Erik Olin, 315
Wright Mills, C., 53, 323, 349

Year of the Child (1979), 241

zoo animals, animal sociology, 100–101
Zorbaugh, Harvey Warren, 342–343
Zwarte Piet, systemic racism example, 17

Lightning Source UK Ltd.
Milton Keynes UK
UKHW052133280421
382809UK00004B/86